CRIMINAL
Justice

Kenneth Mentor, Editor

Kendall Hunt
publishing company

Brief Contents

Section 1: Overview of the Criminal Justice System   1

Chapter 1, Introduction to Criminal Justice   3
Chapter 2, Criminal Behavior   33
Chapter 3, Criminal Law   75

Section 2: The Policing of Crime   111

Chapter 4, The Policing of Crime   113
Chapter 5, Policing: Roles, Functions, and Challenges   149

Section 3: The American Court System   191

Chapter 6, The Court System   193
Chapter 7, Inside a Courtroom   229
Chapter 8, Sentencing and Judgment   263

Section 4: The Consequences of Crime: Corrections   299

Chapter 9, Prisons and Jails   301
Chapter 10, Prison Life   339
Chapter 11, Special Issues in Corrections   371

Section 5: Special Topics in Criminal Justice   413

Chapter 12, Juvenile Justice   415
Chapter 13, Victimology and Victims' Rights   449
Chapter 14, Criminal Justice in a Changing World   483
Chapter 15, The Future of Criminal Justice   517

Contents

Preface   x

About the Editor   xviii

About the Contributing Authors   xviii

Section 1: Overview of the Criminal Justice System   1

Chapter 1, Introduction to Criminal Justice   3

Key Terms   3

Chapter Objectives   3

Case Study: O.J. Simpson and Cameron Todd Willingham   4

What Is Criminal Justice?   5

Models of the Criminal Justice System   6

History of the Criminal Justice System in America   13

What Is Crime?   16

The Formal Criminal Justice Process   18

The Informal Criminal Justice System   23

The Wedding Cake Model of Justice   24

Continuing Challenges   25

Chapter Summary   27

Critical Thinking   29

Media   29

Endnotes   29

Chapter 2, Criminal Behavior   33

Key Terms   33

Chapter Objectives   34

Case Study: Gang Violence   34

What Is Criminal Behavior?   34

Measuring Crime   35

Crime Statistics   46

Correlates of Crime   49

Theories of Crime   50

Chapter Summary 66
Critical Thinking 68
Media 69
Endnotes 69

Chapter 3, Criminal Law 75

Key Terms 75
Chapter Objectives 75
    Case Study: The Rodney King Beating 76
    Constitutional Law 77
    Purpose of Law 79
    Rule of Law 80
    Types of Laws 82
    Basic Features and Elements of a Crime 90
    Defenses for Crimes 93
    Punishments for Crimes 102
    Policy Choices, Politics, and Ideology 104
Chapter Summary 107
Critical Thinking 108
Media 108
Endnotes 108

Section 2: The Policing of Crime 111

Chapter 4, The Policing of Crime 113

Key Terms 113
Chapter Objectives 113
    Case Study: Wickersham Commission 114
    History and Structure of Police Systems 114
    Structure and Organization of Contemporary Law Enforcement 131
    Becoming a Law Enforcement Officer 138
Chapter Summary 143
Critical Thinking 144
Media 144
Endnotes 145

Chapter 5, Policing: Roles, Functions, and Challenges 149

Key Terms 149
Chapter Objectives 149

Case Study: Less Lethal or Deadly Force?   150
Roles of the Police Officer   150
Operational Styles of Policing   158
Functions of Police   160
Changing Philosophy of Policing   172
Challenges for Police Officers   176

Chapter Summary   184
Critical Thinking   186
Media   186
Endnotes   186

Section 3: The American Court System   191

Chapter 6, The Court System   193

Key Terms   193
Chapter Objectives   193
Case Study: Presumption of Innocence?   194
Background History of the U.S. Court System   194
Court Structure   202
Criminal Procedure and Due Process Overview   210

Chapter Summary   223
Critical Thinking   223
Media   224
Endnotes   224

Chapter 7, Inside a Courtroom   229

Key Terms   229
Chapter Objectives   229
Case Study: Right to Counsel: *Gideon v. Wainwright*   230
The Courtroom Workgroup   230
The Criminal Trial: An Overview   231
The Judge and Courtroom Staff   237
The Prosecution and Defense   243
The Jury   249
The Accused   255

Chapter Summary   258
Critical Thinking   259
Media   259
Endnotes   260

Chapter 8, Sentencing and Judgment   263

Key Terms   263
Chapter Objectives   263
  Case Study: *State of Texas v. Robert Coulson*   264
  Goals of Sentencing   264
  Types of Sentences   270
  Special Issues in Sentencing   284
Chapter Summary   293
Critical Thinking   294
Media   294
Endnotes   295

Section 4: The Consequences of Crime: Corrections   299

Chapter 9, Prisons and Jails   301

Key Terms   301
Chapter Objectives   301
  Case Study: Guantánamo Bay Naval Base   302
  The History of Prisons and Jails   303
  Role and Structure of Prisons and Jails   317
  The Privatization of Prisons   328
  The Hiring and Training of Correctional Officers   330
Chapter Summary   332
Critical Thinking   334
Media   335
Endnotes   335

Chapter 10, Prison Life   339

Key Terms   339
Chapter Objectives   339
  Case Study: Richard Speck   340
  Prison Culture   340
  Growth of Corrections   353
  Alternatives to Prison   359
  Career Connections: Correctional Treatment Specialist   362
Chapter Summary   364
Critical Thinking   365
Media   365
Endnotes   366

Chapter 11, Special Issues in Corrections 371

Key Terms 371
Chapter Objectives 371
  Case Study: Return to Society 372
  Introduction 373
  Rehabilitation and Other Goals of Sentencing 375
  Return to Society 392
  Recidivism 401
Chapter Summary 406
Critical Thinking 406
Media 407
Endnotes 407

Section 5: Special Topics in Criminal Justice 413

Chapter 12, Juvenile Justice 415

Key Terms 415
Chapter Objectives 415
  Case Study: *Kent v. United States* 416
  Delinquency 417
  The Nature and History of Juvenile Justice 419
  Emergence of the Juvenile Courts 424
  Contemporary Juvenile Corrections 430
  Problematic Issues in Juvenile Justice 438
Chapter Summary 444
Critical Thinking 445
Media 445
Endnotes 446

Chapter 13, Victimology and Victims' Rights 449

Key Terms 449
Chapter Objectives 449
  Case Study: Tragedy in Tucson 450
  Victimology 450
  Victims' Rights Movement 459
  Victimization Surveys 468
Chapter Summary 477
Critical Thinking 478
Media 479
Endnotes 479

Chapter 14, Criminal Justice in a Changing World   483

Key Terms   483
Chapter Objectives   483
   Case Study: The BTK Killer   484
   Homeland Security   484
   International Justice   495
   Computer Crime   501
   New Technologies in Crime Fighting   506
   Freedom vs. Security   510
Chapter Summary   511
Critical Thinking   512
Media   513
Endnotes   513

Chapter 15, The Future of Criminal Justice   517

Key Terms   517
Chapter Objectives   517
   Case Study: Harrison Bergeron   518
   Trends in the Criminal Justice System   519
   Privacy and Civil Liberties   527
   Global Partnerships   535
Chapter Summary   545
Critical Thinking   546
Media   547
Endnotes   547

Glossary   555

Index   577

Preface

Crime and justice are ever-present and often debated topics in modern society. The public is often attracted to media coverage of celebrities in court and other high-profile cases in the criminal justice system. In the media, cases that involve violence and drug use remain popular—"if it bleeds, it leads." In addition to an apparent interest in sensationalized media, each of us has also developed personal beliefs and ideologies about crime and justice.

Given that the vast majority of the work completed by the criminal justice system is completed without media attention, we must ask whether these sensationalized cases reflect the true criminal justice system. Even more important—do opinions and beliefs created in response to these outliers parallel those developed through careful research? Even when focusing on more mundane crime stories, does the media accurately describe the justice system, crime, and social control? What are the realities of criminal justice, and what are the myths?

In short, how does the criminal justice system really function on an everyday basis, and how do we as citizens interact with the system? *Criminal Justice* aims to answer these questions while providing a clear understanding of many aspects of the U.S. criminal justice system. Readers will develop a thorough knowledge of the elements involved in the criminal justice system, from the start of the process to the end. We also hope readers will begin to understand the complexity of the criminal justice system and the breadth of the challenges faced by justice professionals.

Readers will recognize controversies faced by the criminal justice system. "Real world" examples are offered throughout the text, in each case highlighting difficult choices faced by our society, the justice system, and those attempting to develop a clear and unbiased policy. Ideally, these examples will help readers gain the critical thinking skills needed to reach logical conclusions regarding these controversies.

Learning about Criminal Justice

How do we learn about criminal justice? From what sources do we get this information? How do we filter the massive amount of information available to us on a given subject—especially one as controversial as criminal justice?

This text has taken a few new directions in regard to these questions. First of all, we acknowledge that much of what we know is socially constructed. We also acknowledge that each of us—whether consciously or unconsciously—tends to place ideological blinders on ourselves as we allow preconceived notions to affect our perceptions.

Criminologists are familiar with Herbert Packer's discussion of "crime control" and "due process." Classroom presentation of Packer's version of these concepts typically involves discussion of the "crime control assembly line" and the "due process obstacle course." While assembly lines have value, efficiency may not be an acceptable goal for the justice system. Similarly, obstacle courses can be a great challenge, but a justice system based on constant indecision is not sustainable.

Again, each of us has developed deeply held views about crime, justice, and the justice system. As a result, each of us occupies a unique point on the crime control/due process continuum. While not perfectly correlated with "liberal" and "conservative," our attitudes toward due process and crime control will impact our interpretation of what we know about the justice system—and what we are willing and able to learn. Some of us are due process people. Others are crime control people. These perspectives cause us to engage our filters, often discounting ideas inconsistent with our beliefs.

Bias reduction is the first step in our efforts to learn about crime and justice. Where do you stand? Like it or not, each of us has a political perspective on the issues raised in this text. Readers should realize they have reached this point through a long process of filtering. We want readers to reflect on what positions they hold and why they hold them. We also encourage readers to adopt alternative points of view and understand criminal justice issues from a variety of perspectives.

Organization of the Text

The authors of each chapter include a range of perspectives. Some perspectives will be easy to agree with. Readers may be tempted to discount other ideas on purely ideological grounds.

Some perspectives will also be questioned due to the source. While we will not cite to Wikipedia, we are not inclined to totally dismiss Internet research, especially when much scholarly research and communication is closed to the general public. In spite of the potential to adopt more open models, most scholarly journals continue to restrict access. As a result, the vast majority of citizens, including our students, use the Internet as their primary research tool.

Professors joke about the student perspective that "if it isn't on Google, it doesn't exist." Since our students will not have lifetime access to the university library, there is some truth to this statement. Rather than discount the obvious value of information available with a web search, we hope we have been selective enough with our resources to help students learn to recognize authoritative information. If readers disagree with facts or positions found here each of us has discovered an opportunity to learn.

Our goal is to provide a balanced, full-scale perspective of the criminal justice system, supplemented by scholarly support from criminal justice experts, researchers, and theorists. The contributing authors of this textbook are criminal justice professors and scholars, each with perspectives developed through years of study and experience. Many of the topics discussed in this book are inherently controversial and political. While the editor and each individual author do not necessarily agree with every sentiment shared in this text, we hope to present and promote a robust, well-rounded discussion.

Above all, we wish to give students the facts they need, the skills to find more, and the ability to critically analyze the bias inherent in policy choices—ideally based on fact, research, reason, and compassion. We hope this text provides a rich and rewarding learning experience for learners and educators.

Most criminal justice students have very little prior knowledge about, or experience with, the criminal justice system. Thus, this textbook is designed to introduce the many facets of the criminal justice system in a logical, readily understandable manner. *Criminal Justice* consists of 15 chapters grouped into five overarching sections. We begin with an overview of the criminal justice system, including a brief examination of theories of crime and social control. We then examine the various players and processes of the system, beginning with police and policing, then moving to the courtroom, then finally the corrections system. Our introduction to criminal justice then moves to special topics in criminal justice, including juvenile justice, victimology, and issues related to terrorism, cybercrime, and a variety of contemporary and future challenges.

Section 1: Overview of the Criminal Justice System

Chapter 1, Introduction to Criminal Justice, helps students become acclimated with the structure, organization, history, and goals of the criminal justice system. This chapter invites students to engage in a scholarly examination of the system and consider how political ideologies play a role in one's perspective. This chapter will compare and contrast criminal justice with other social science disciplines, discuss how the U.S. criminal justice system was created, describe the network of agencies within the system, analyze policy choices and their motivations, and walk through the steps in the criminal justice process.

Chapter 2, Criminal Behavior, reviews the extent to which crime occurs and the theoretical propositions used to explain criminal behavior. This chapter will differentiate between criminal behavior and deviance, report crime trends and statistics in the United States, discuss several methods of acquiring crime data, and review scholarly theories of the causes of crime.

Chapter 3, Criminal Law, provides an introduction to common law and the rule of law and examines their effect on western society. This chapter provides a walkthrough of the different types of laws, categories of crimes, and the elements of a crime. The chapter also assesses the categories and types of criminal defenses.

Section 2: The Policing of Crime

Chapter 4, The Policing of Crime, focuses on the role of policing and police systems in the criminal justice system. This chapter provides background information on the history of policing in the United States, including the constant efforts to reform law enforcement and improve police accountability and professionalism. The chapter also identifies local, state, and federal law enforcement agencies and describes the education and training requirements of police and other law enforcement professionals.

Chapter 5, Policing: Roles, Functions, and Challenges, describes the experience of contemporary law enforcement officers in the United States. The chapter outlines the many roles, duties, and functions of police officers and police departments, and distinguishes among different styles of policing. This chapter also examines the challenges that police officers face regarding discretion, stress, ethics, and corruption.

Section 3: The American Court System

Chapter 6, The Court System, explores the American judiciary as a whole, focusing upon the courts themselves at all levels. This chapter discusses the history and background of the courts, including their colonial origins in English common law, and a detailed discussion of the structure of the court system as it exists today. The chapter additionally examines criminal procedure and due process for criminal defendants.

Chapter 7, Inside a Courtroom, gives an overview of the structure and organization of the American courtroom. This chapter describes the various participants in a courtroom and their respective roles, and examines how these roles are interconnected. The chapter also discusses the importance of the jury in criminal trials.

Chapter 8, Sentencing and Judgment, examines the overall philosophy and goals of sentencing for criminal offenders and analyzes the range of sentencing options available. The chapter discusses determinate and indeterminate sentencing and "truth in sentencing," and explains the role of presentence investigations.

Section 4: The Consequences of Crime: Corrections

Chapter 9, Prisons and Jails, focuses on the role of corrections in the criminal justice system. This chapter examines the history of corrections, discusses why there is a prohibition on cruel and unusual punishment, determines differences between prisons and jails, examines custody levels, and discusses the issues and controversies of prison privatization.

Chapter 10, Prison Life, discusses the concept of correctional facilities as total institutions and the roles and subcultures of both inmates and correctional workers within jails and prisons. This chapter discusses the implications of relying on incarceration, as well as including the economic realities, and reviews various forms of community-based alternatives to incarceration.

Chapter 11, Special Issues in Corrections, covers many of the unique challenges regarding the corrections system. This includes a discussion of the range of rehabilitative needs faced by prison inmates and the advantages and challenges of prison rehabilitation programs. This chapter will evaluate how well inmates are prepared for their return to society, discuss the factors that influence recidivism rates, and examine if and how the corrections system can address the needs of those released from prison.

Section 5: Special Topics in Criminal Justice

Chapter 12, Juvenile Justice, gives an overview of the juvenile justice system, including the history of juvenile justice in the United States and the differences between the juvenile and adult systems. This chapter outlines the different types of juvenile corrections and explains theories and patterns of both juvenile delinquency and juvenile victimization. The chapter also analyzes debates regarding the treatment and punishment of juvenile offenders.

Chapter 13, Victimology and Victims' Rights, explores the study of victimology, including the costs and effects of victimization and how victimization is measured. The chapter also discusses the Victims' Rights Movement and its relation to victimology, and examines the future of victims' rights in terms of legislation and social policy.

Chapter 14, Criminal Justice in a Changing World, focuses on recent developments in criminal justice. The chapter analyzes the increased emphasis on homeland security in the United States and examines its primary goals, and discusses the major threats to homeland security and international collaborative efforts to investigate and prosecute terrorism. In addition, this chapter explores the increasing threat of cybercrime and discusses technological advancements in criminal investigation, including computer forensics.

Chapter 15, The Future of Criminal Justice, focuses on upcoming challenges and considerations that the criminal justice system will face moving forward. Issues of discussion include effective and ineffective models of intervention, perceptions of the death penalty in the United States and internationally, trends in drug laws, and the liberty and security implications of technology and social networking. This chapter also explores the growing reliance on global coordination and information sharing between criminal justice entities.

Special Features

This textbook includes a number of chapter-specific features designed to enhance and extend understanding of the content.

- Each chapter includes one **Career Connections** feature that profiles a specific profession related to the chapter, explaining what the job entails and how it connects to criminal justice. This feature is a valuable resource for students who are planning to pursue a career in criminal justice.
- Each chapter also includes an **Ethics and Professionalism** feature, which highlights a real-life or hypothetical ethical dilemma relevant to the chapter and invites discussion of how to address the dilemma.
- Brief **Critical Thinking** questions are scattered throughout the text and in the end-of-chapter materials. These questions invite students to discuss their thoughts and opinions on relevant criminal justice issues.
- Most chapters include **Exhibits**, which are documents and legislation related to criminal justice topics, such as excerpts from Supreme Court decisions.

- At the end of each chapter is a list of **Media** links, which highlight web sites and other media resources that students are encouraged to explore for further information on the topics discussed in the chapter.
- Both students and instructors have access to **online content** that is integrated chapter by chapter with the text to maximize the principles and enrich student learning. The Web access code is included on the inside front cover of the textbook and provides the purchaser of the book the ability to reference all of the online material, including features such as a descriptive **PowerPoint presentation** for each chapter of the book, **flash cards**, and a **test bank**.

Features of This Text
Criminal Justice presents material in a format that provides a clear understanding of many aspects of the U.S. criminal justice system. Readers will have a thorough knowledge of the elements involved in the criminal justice system, from the start of the process to the end.

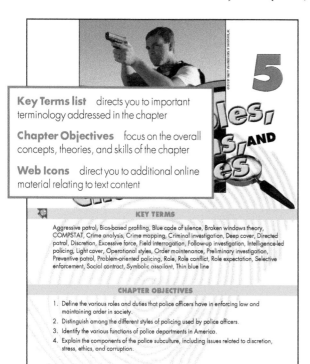

Key Terms list directs you to important terminology addressed in the chapter

Chapter Objectives focus on the overall concepts, theories, and skills of the chapter

Web Icons direct you to additional online material relating to text content

KEY TERMS

Aggressive patrol, Bias-based profiling, Blue code of silence, Broken windows theory, COMPSTAT, Crime analysis, Crime mapping, Criminal investigation, Deep cover, Directed patrol, Discretion, Excessive force, Field interrogation, Follow-up investigation, Intelligence-led policing, Light cover, Operational styles, Order maintenance, Preliminary investigation, Preventive patrol, Problem-oriented policing, Role, Role conflict, Role expectation, Selective enforcement, Social contract, Symbolic assailant, Thin blue line

CHAPTER OBJECTIVES

1. Define the various roles and duties that police officers have in enforcing law and maintaining order in society.
2. Distinguish among the different styles of policing used by police officers.
3. Identify the various functions of police departments in America.
4. Explain the components of the police subculture, including issues related to discretion, stress, ethics, and corruption.

Case Study: Less Lethal or Deadly Force?
Police work can be a dangerous profession, and sometimes the police are required to use physical force to subdue criminals. Historically, the police have carried batons or nightsticks and firearms. In more recent year... developed so the police do not have to r... uses electroshocks into the suspect's bo... trol and contract the muscles in the bo... used by police departments across the c... tional nearly two decades ago. Propone... to be a useful tool that has prevented pol... these proponents view the use of stun gu... pects, an alarming number of suspects ... civil lawsuits have been filed against poli... ers, including TASER International, bu... the plaintiffs and found that the deaths were not a direct result of the electroshock weapon.

On September 22, 2005, the Nashville Police Department was called to the Mercy Lounge, a Nashville nightclub, to remove 21-year-old Patrick Lee. When police arrived, Lee was already outside the club and could be observed undressed and rambling incoherently. Earlier in the evening, Lee had reportedly ingested the hallucinogen LSD. In an attempt to control him, police deployed their TASERS and jolted Lee 19 times. Paramedics were called to the scene when Lee was unresponsive, and he died in police custody 39 hours later. When an autopsy was conducted, the medical examiner ruled that Lee's death was caused by a "drug-induced excited delirium." Lee's parents filed a wrongful death lawsuit against the Nashville Police Department, the police officers involved, and TASER International. Eventually, a federal jury cleared all defendants in the lawsuit.

Do you believe the shocking of Patrick Lee 19 times was an excessive use of police force? With the number of deaths that have occurred following the use of electroshock, even though the courts have yet to find its users responsible, should the police still continue to employ this form of less lethal weapon?

Opening Case Study offers a vivid illustration of content that will be discussed throughout the chapter

Roles of the Police Officer
Seneviratne (2002) described the role of police officers as being the gatekeepers to the criminal justice system.[1] It is their sworn duty to investigate crimes and arrest the offenders. Their arrests lead offenders through the gates into the criminal justice system. In addition to arresting offenders, police officers have a variety of functions and roles they are expected to perform. Performing these functions and roles does not come without a cost. The nature of police work leads to unique challenges as a result of the powers that police have, the dangers they face, and the temptations all around them. This chapter discusses the roles, functions, and challenges for the police officer in American society.

When citizens think of the police, they most likely envision a uniformed officer who is operating a vehicle marked with emblems and striping and emer-

---

saturation patrols, in whic... preventive patrol, directed... Caeti, and Taylor (1999) ... rected toward a particular... researchers found that ag... nificantly reduced gang v... crime reduction effect sim... may inhibit possible offe... quick apprehension of tho...

Career Connections profile a specific profession related to the chapter, offering valuable information for those planning to pursue a career in criminal justice

Career Connections: Uniformed Police Officer
Uniformed police officers from municipal, county, or state law enforcement agencies perform a variety of tasks for the community. In general, the duties of a police officer include enforcing the law, assisting the public, investigating crime, and preventing crime. They also maintain order by directing traffic, issuing traffic citations, making arrests, responding to maintenance of public order incidents, and preparing police reports. Each day can be a new challenge and a new adventure. One day, the police officer may conduct traffic stops at a busy intersection, counsel a distressed mother who is dealing with her adolescent son, and conduct an investigation at a residence that has been burglarized. The next day, this same officer may have completely different duties to perform.

In order to become a police officer, a candidate should be a U.S. citizen, be at least 21 years of age, have at least a high school diploma, and be able to pass a criminal history and background check, physical abilities test, and psychological examination. The specific requirements for employment vary from state to state and within each police department. Candidates must also graduate from a state-approved police academy where they are taught the basic requirements for performing the duties of the police officer position.

The ideal police officer candidate should possess strong interpersonal skills, critical thinking and analytical skills, and problem-solving ability. Because police work can be dangerous and very stressful, a successful police officer should also possess excellent physical conditioning and emotional stability. A career as a police officer can be very rewarding. It takes an individual with a strong commitment and a special mix of knowledge, skills, and abilities to choose to become a police officer. The challenges of police work are extraordinary, but the satisfaction that one receives from serving the public can more than compensate.

Traffic   Vehicular traffic direction is a second function performed by police officers. The police have been given the responsibility for the enforcement of traffic laws, the direction and control of traffic, the investigation of traffic accidents, and the assistance of motorists on the roadways.

Traffic enforcement involves the issuance of citations or warnings for moving and non-moving traffic violations, driver and vehicle licensing violations, and vehicle equipment violations.

The enforcement of traffic laws is usually the responsibility of the patrol officer. When the patrol officer is on routine preventive patrol and not responding

178 Criminal Justice

initially increased sharply and then at a slower rate between years two and six of the police officer's career. After year six, cynicism decreased and leveled off over the remainder of a career.[62]

The unfortunate consequence of police cynicism is that it can cross over into an officer's personal relationships with family and friends. The suspicions that police officers have about people's behaviors and actions may lead them to believe that all people, including those closest to them, should be viewed with suspicion and not be trusted.

Solidarity The third component of the police subculture is solidarity. Police officers develop a strong connection with other members of the profession. Officers must depend upon their partners for backup and protection. Along with their cynicism and mistrust of the public, this solidarity within the ranks causes an "us versus them" mentality. Police officers close their ranks and insulate themselves from others. Just as cynicism can lead to mistrust of family and friends, police solidarity can lead police officers to become isolated from their relationships outside the profession.

One unfortunate result of police solidarity is known as the blue code of silence. This is a code of protection among police officers in which they do not report activities of fellow officers that could violate department policy or the law. The solidarity may be so ingrained within the profession that police officers may be more likely to protect corruption within their ranks—jeopardizing their own careers—than to report corrupt fellow officers.

Critical Thinking How can the blue code of silence be eliminated so honest police officers are willing to report dishonest officers?

Discretion
The autonomy a police officer has to choose from a variety of courses of action in various situations.

officer's autonomy to [...] ons. Alpert, MacDon- [...] to choose a course of [...] icer observes the per- [...] most common exam- [...] e officers use their dis- [...] stopped for a traffic [...] violation should be given a warning or issued a citation.

The patrol officer may exercise the greatest discretionary power in the police department. Officers who are on patrol are usually out of the sight of their supervisors. Walker (1993) wrote that most police-citizen encounters occur without outside supervision, which gives the police officer a great deal of discretion.[64] They have the discretion to stop a vehicle operator for a traffic violation in the first place. They have the discretion to stop a suspicious person on the

---

Critical Thinking questions offer an opportunity to discuss opinions on different criminal justice issues

Running Glossary provides easily accessible definitions to all key terms

---

186 Criminal Justice

Critical Thinking ?

1. Should electronic devices known as "red light cameras" be used to catch traffic violators running red lights at intersections?
2. Should police officers be permitted to accept gratuities such as a free cup of coffee or a half-price meal when on duty?
3. Among the various methods of patrol, which do you believe works the best to prevent crime and apprehend criminals?

[...] f officers killed in [...]

[...] itatus Act? [...] ghts under the [...] nal property [...]

[...] that police [...]

[...] of their duties? [...]

[...] placed in an area [...] ging criminal [...]

Media

Law Enforcement News: www.officer.com
    This website provides information on current events in policing and police officer news around the United States.
Bureau of Justice Statistics: http://bjs.ojp.usdoj.gov/
    The Bureau of Justice Statistics provides comprehensive data on reported criminal activity throughout the country, including frequency of crime and criminal characteristics.
Franklin Zimring Interview: http://www.youtube.com/watch?v=EXZgSnKfN5U
    In this interview, criminologist Franklin Zimring discusses how New York City dramatically reduced its crime rate.

Endnotes

1. Seneviratne, M. (2002). "Ombudsmen and Police Complaints." *The Journal of Social Welfare & Family Law, 24*(2), 195–215.
2. Hunter, A. (1985). "Private, Parochial, and Public Social Order: The Problem of Crime and Incivility in Urban Communities." In G. Suttles & M. Zald (Eds.), *The Challenge of Social Control*. Norwood, NJ: Ablex.
3. Klockars, C. B. (1985). *The Idea of Police*. Beverly Hills, CA: Sage.
4. Dunham, R. G., & Alpert, G. P. (2010). *Critical Issues in Policing*. Prospect Heights, IL: Waveland Press.
5. Reiman, J. (1985). "The Social Contract and the Police Use of Deadly Force." In F. A. Ellison & M. Feldberg (Eds.), *Moral Issues in Police Work*. Savage, MD: Rowman & Littlefield.

Media links offer websites and other resources for exploring further information on the chapter topics

Endnotes comprehensively list all sources and research utilized in each chapter

---

Exhibits illustrate documents and legislation related to criminal justice topics

Exhibit: Law Enforcement Code of Ethics from International Chiefs of Police[81]

Ethics and Professionalism: Blue Code of Silence
On August 9, 1997, a 30-year-old Haitian immigrant by the name of Abner Louima was arrested by New York City Police Department officers following a disturbance outside a Brooklyn nightclub. While being held at the 70th Precinct stationhouse, Louima was brutally assaulted in the precinct's bathroom. He was held down by one officer while the other officer [...] his rectum and then thrust it into his face. The police [...] lieved that he had punched the officer in the head du[...]

It was reported that several NYPD officers either [...] hearing of the incident, then Mayor Rudy Giuliani a[...] the case would prove that the "blue code of silence" [...] perjury and ultimately resulted in convictions of four [...] turned on appeal.

Does the "blue code of silence" still exist in policing, all these years after the Louima case? What would cause a police officer to engage in such violent behavior against a suspect? How could other officers look on and allow this to happen without stepping in to stop it? Why would these officers all choose to lie and cover up the incident?

Ethics and Professionalism feature showcases an ethical dilemma and invites discussion of it

---

actions that will be taken against officers violating established policies. Each police department should require periodic ethics training classes for all officers. A police officers' code of ethics should be prominently placed in the department as a constant reminder to all officers that they have a sworn oath to perform their duties both ethically and professionally.

Police departments should also have an internal affairs unit that investigates [...] activities involving police officers. External investiga-[...] review boards, special investigators or prosecutors, [...] ed to ferret out police misconduct when necessary. [...] y for ending police corruption belongs with each in-[...] way that can be accomplished is for officers to resist [...] e blue code of silence. Instead, honest police officers [...] o rid the law enforcement profession of corrupt offi-[...] ical or illegal behaviors that they observe.

Chapter Summary

- The roles police officers assume are based on the issues and problems that are unique to each community. The police officer's role can be vague and ambiguous because the expectations of police administrators, local political leaders, the public, and police officers themselves can conflict. Role conflict results from what police may prefer to do versus what they are expected to do.

Chapter Summary succinctly summarizes and reinforces chapter content

About the Editor

Kenneth Mentor has been teaching criminology and criminal justice for over 20 years, currently in the Department of Sociology and Criminology at the University of North Carolina Wilmington. Dr. Mentor earned a Masters in Psychology from Central Michigan University, a J.D. from the Syracuse University College of Law, and a Ph.D. in Social Science from the Maxwell School of Citizenship and Public Affairs at Syracuse University. This multi-disciplinary education led to faculty appointments in criminal justice, criminology, sociology, and public administration, with cited publications in the fields of criminal justice, criminology, public policy, organizational development, law, and online learning. An experienced educator and administrator, Dr. Mentor has played key roles in the planning and development of web-based degree programs and learning content for universities and academic publishers. In addition to teaching, Dr. Mentor devotes his time to "EduSane," a consulting practice focused on the development of affordable, effective, and sustainable learning environments.

About the Contributing Authors

Elyshia Aseltine is an Assistant Professor of Criminal Justice and Criminology at Lycoming College in Williamsport, Pennsylvania. She joined the Lycoming faculty after earning her Ph.D. in sociology at the University of Texas at Austin. Her research focuses on juvenile justice, courts, and policing in the United States and Africa.

Scott H. Belshaw is currently an Assistant Professor of Criminal Justice at the University of North Texas in Denton, Texas. Dr. Belshaw holds a Ph.D. in Juvenile Criminal Justice from Prairie View A&M University. He earned his Bachelor of Science in Social Sciences from the University of Houston-Downtown. He also holds both a Master of Arts in Liberal Arts from Houston Baptist University and a Master of Arts in Criminology from the University of Houston-Clear Lake. Dr. Belshaw's criminal justice experience includes working many years with the Harris County Texas Community Supervision and Corrections Department serving as a probation officer, gang intelligence officer, and court liaison probation officer.

Kathryn A. Branch is an Assistant Professor in the Department of Criminology and Criminal Justice at the University of Tampa. Dr. Branch's research focuses on gendered forms of violence (i.e., sexual assault and intimate partner violence). Her current research studies the secondary impact of gendered forms of violence on support providers (i.e., friends and professors) and the role of social support in intimate partner violence victimization and perpetration.

Chris Capsambelis has over 30 years experience in the field of law enforcement. He is a former police sergeant with ten years of police experience. He spent another ten years training police officers in both Pennsylvania and Florida. He holds a Master of Arts degree in Criminology and a Doctor of Philosophy degree in Measurement and Evaluation. Currently, he is an Associate Professor of Criminology at the University of Tampa.

Petter Lovaas has his B.S. in Information Technology Management from the University of Minnesota, and his M.S. and D.Sc. in Information Assurance and Computer Security from Dakota State University. Dr. Lovaas currently teaches in the Computer and Information Sciences Department at Niagara University as an ssistant professor, teaching Computer Forensics and Computer Security courses. Dr. Lovaas also has extensive experience in information security consulting with the banking and financial sector.

David Olson is a Professor of Criminal Justice and Criminology at Loyola University Chicago, and previously served as Department Chair and Director of Loyola's interdisciplinary Forensic Science Program. Dr. Olson is also a Special Assistant to the Cook County Sheriff. For nearly 20 years, Dr. Olson worked at the Illinois Criminal Justice Information Authority, where he was the director of Illinois' Statewide Drug and Violent Crime Control Strategy Impact Evaluation Program. Dr. Olson received his B.S. in Criminal Justice from Loyola University Chicago, his M.A. in Criminal Justice from the University of Illinois at Chicago, and his Ph.D. in Political Science/Public Policy Analysis from the University of Illinois at Chicago. In 2011, Dr. Olson was presented with the Hans W. Mattick Award for outstanding accomplishments in the field of criminology and criminal justice research.

Stephen L. Rayle is an Associate Professor of Criminal Justice at Valencia College in Orlando, Florida. He received his Doctorate in Education at Nova Southeastern University as well as a Master's Degree in Criminal Justice. He has nearly ten years of experience with the Florida Department of Corrections. Dr. Rayle enjoys public service and is currently the Chairman of the Orlando Citizen's Police Review Board.

Mitch D. Sigal is a seasoned investigator with over 20 years of Law Enforcement experience at the city, county, and federal levels. His experience includes patrol, narcotics, and money laundering, and he has significant training and experience in Death Investigation and Disaster Management. Mr. Sigal's writing experience includes over 5 articles on "The Link Between Animal

Abuse, Child Abuse, and Domestic Violence," co-authoring a violence prevention manual that has been sold and employed in several states across the United States, and grants for violence prevention programs as well as new technology in the field of forensics.

Omar Syed is a Lecturer in the Department of Criminal Justice for Texas State University in San Marcos, Texas. In addition, he is an attorney for the University of Texas System's Office of General Counsel, where he advises the 15 University of Texas System institutions on criminal law, employment law, and tort law matters. Before holding these appointments, Mr. Syed served as an Assistant United States Attorney for the District of Minnesota, where he prosecuted defendants charged with federal narcotics, firearms and white-collar offenses.

Megan Houck Timmins is a Senior Law and Policy Analyst at the University of Maryland Center for Health and Homeland Security (CHHS). She graduated from the University of Maryland School of Law and was admitted to the Maryland Bar in 2007. In addition, Megan graduated *magna cum laude* from St. Mary's College of Maryland in 2004, with a B.A. in Economics. Prior to joining CHHS, Megan worked on bankruptcy and white collar crime matters in the private sector and on issues related to higher education institutions with the Maryland Office of the Attorney General. She also studied international and comparative criminal justice in Aberdeen, Scotland.

Michael Richard Vesely is a Senior Law and Policy Analyst at the University of Maryland Center for Health and Homeland Security (CHHS). He graduated with honors from the University of Maryland School of Law and was admitted to the Maryland Bar in 2006. At CHHS, Michael has worked as an instructor for the Department of Homeland Security and has worked with federal, state, local, and private sector partners in numerous areas of national security, including counterterrorism. He has also worked for the State Department's Antiterrorism Assistance Program assisting various international allies of the United States to develop and enhance their own domestic security programs.

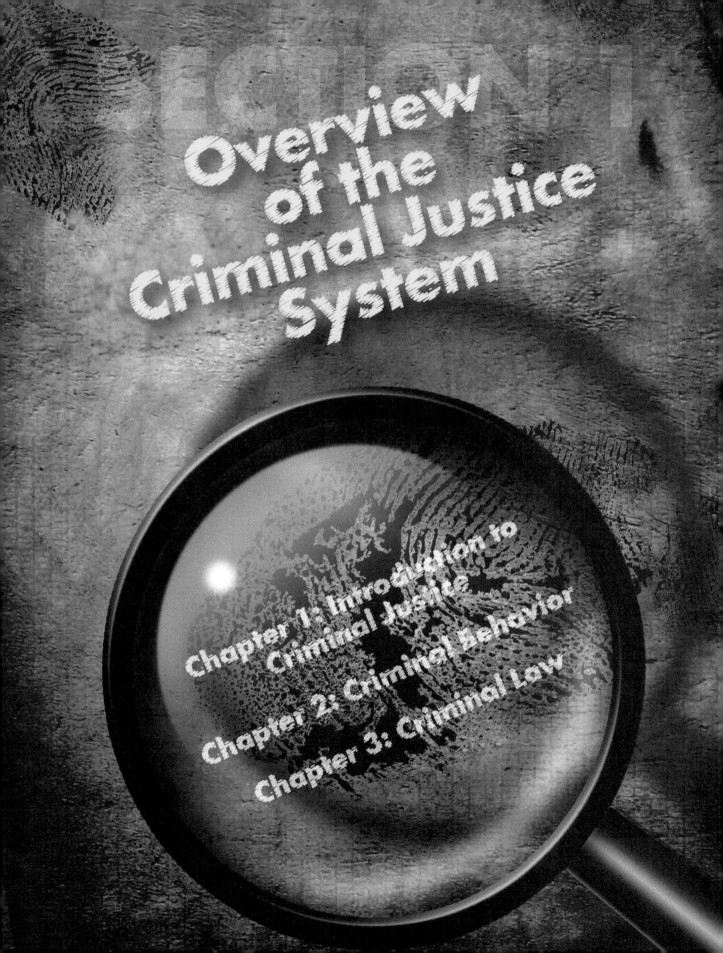

Overview of the Criminal Justice System

Chapter 1: Introduction to Criminal Justice

Chapter 2: Criminal Behavior

Chapter 3: Criminal Law

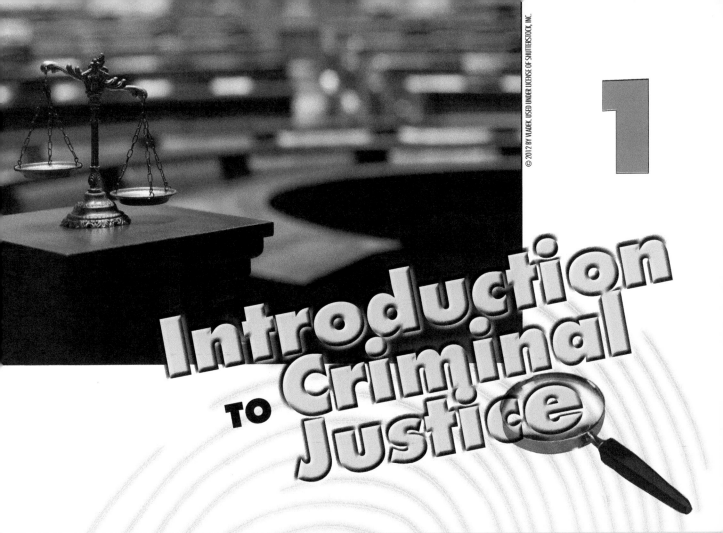

1

Introduction to Criminal Justice

KEY TERMS

Community corrections, Conflict model, Consensus model, Courtroom workgroup, Crime, Crime control model, Criminal justice system, Decriminalize, Department of Justice (DOJ), Due process model, Exclusionary rule, Felony, Misdemeanor, Net-widening, Norms, Plea bargain, Policing, Wedding cake model of justice, White-collar crime

CHAPTER OBJECTIVES

1. Distinguish criminal justice from other social science disciplines.
2. Discuss how the U.S. criminal justice system was created.
3. Understand the justice system as a network of agencies focused on understanding and responding to crime.
4. Analyze a range of policy choices, including the motivations for these choices.
5. Describe the steps involved in the justice process.

Case Study: O.J. Simpson and Cameron Todd Willingham

Can money buy freedom? Most are familiar with the murder trial of O.J. Simpson, a former professional football player and actor. On June 12, 1994, Nicole Brown Simpson, Simpson's former wife and mother of two of his children, and her friend Ronald Goldman were brutally murdered. O.J. Simpson was charged and pleaded not guilty to both murders. After preliminary hearings regarding admissibility of evidence, the trial began; nearly nine months later, the jury found Simpson not guilty of both murders.

Simpson's sizable team of defense attorneys, referred to as the "Dream Team," included high-profile attorneys and DNA experts. The defense questioned the DNA evidence and further raised doubts about the prosecution's case by insinuating that Detective Mark Fuhrman was a racist who had planted evidence to implicate Simpson in the murders.

Simpson's acquittal shocked the nation and caused many who had watched the televised trial to question the inefficiencies and ineffectiveness of the criminal justice system.

Unlike the high-profile Simpson murder trial, which lasted for months, few are familiar with the case of Texas citizen Cameron Todd Willingham. On December 23, 1991, Willingham's home caught fire and Willingham was able to escape with minor burns. His three young daughters were killed and Willingham was charged in their deaths. Prosecutors sought the death penalty and, eight months after the deaths of his daughters, Willingham was convicted of capital murder and sentenced to death.[1]

At trial an expert witness testified that an accelerant had been used to purposely light the house on fire.[2] Further bolstering the prosecution's case, a jailhouse informant testified that Willingham described squirting lighter fluid around the house and lighting it on fire. Willingham's two attorneys, who were appointed to represent him, failed to find a fire expert to counter the prosecution's claims and only presented one witness, a babysitter who did not believe Willingham could have killed his daughters.[3]

Willingham appealed his conviction. The Court of Criminal Appeals of Texas affirmed the judgment and sentence of the trial court. Federal courts granted a temporary stay, but an appeal to the U.S. Supreme Court was denied. The only remaining option was for the Texas governor to grant him clemency.

Willingham's supporters contacted Dr. Gerald Hurst, a scientist and fire investigator, who reviewed the files and was alarmed at the fire marshal's high rate of arson findings. Hurst dismissed the conclusion that the fire's patterns suggested use of an accelerant.[4] He concluded that faulty wiring or a space heater caused the accidental fire. Despite the new evidence that was provided to the governor that indicated the deaths of Willingham's daughters was accidental, Willingham's request for clemency was denied. He was executed on February 17, 2004.

Afterwards, more questions were raised about his innocence and the media took notice of his case. The *Chicago Tribune* wrote an article in December 2004, and *The New Yorker* wrote one in 2009. In 2006, the Innocence Project submitted the case for review to the Texas Forensic Science Commission.[5] In

2008, the commission agreed to review the case, and a final report was issued on April 15, 2011. The report recognized that the science used to convict Willingham was faulty, but it did not exonerate him. The report proposes changes that need to take place in arson cases.[6] Texas has still not admitted that they executed an innocent man, and in the eyes of the law, Willingham remains guilty of the deaths of his daughters.

The cases of Simpson and Willingham displayed two very different sides of the criminal justice system. While the protracted, high-profile Simpson case received overwhelming media and public attention, the reality of the criminal justice system is that most cases—like Willingham's—are decided in quick fashion in courtrooms across the country every day, often at the expense of the defendant's due process rights. Errors can occur on both sides of the spectrum: guilty people will sometimes go free, while innocent people may be unjustly ruled guilty. The strengths and weaknesses of the criminal justice system will be explored in depth in this chapter and this book as a whole. While the media and common opinion often provide easy answers, you are encouraged to look deeper at crime, justice, and the systems used in a justice system charged with protecting both our liberty and security.

What Is Criminal Justice?

The criminal justice system, which comprises the police, courts, and correctional facilities, is how the government enforces social norms, laws, and justice. Criminal justice is also an academic discipline. It is important to understand and study the criminal justice system, in a reasoned and scientifically accurate manner, because this knowledge helps explain why the police, judicial, and correctional systems interact as a part of the larger justice system. Ideally, this knowledge will then lead to intelligent and effective policy choices.

Criminal justice incorporates the study of other social sciences such as sociology, psychology, political sciences, and law. While interdisciplinary, the study of criminal justice is closely related to, and intertwined with, the study of sociology. Sociologists are individuals who study society and apply their findings for the benefit of society. Criminologists use sociological skills to study crime and criminals, often with the goal of advancing theoretical knowledge. Criminal justice scholars have similar goals, often focusing on the benefits and consequences of policy choices.

Criminal justice researchers look at how the decisions of one part of the justice system, widely defined, affect the other parts. These researchers seek to understand how the system adapts to new trends and how the system can handle any problems that arise. Like sociologists and other social scientists, criminal justice researchers pull from many different disciplines to analyze and understand why a problem is occurring. However, while many other disciplines merely look at ideology and the theoretical—trying to postulate how an individual, group, or system would hypothetically react in a given situation based on theory—criminal justice looks at how the system actually *is* reacting. Criminal justice operates within the confines of the real world based on evidence and statistics. Ideally, the criminal justice system, which includes researchers at

By analyzing what programs have worked and failed, lawmakers can design policies and programs where they are really needed.

many levels, examines what is currently happening and analyzes and responds to these behaviors as necessary.

However, we also know that our justice system, as part of our political system, may not always rely on evidence. It is important to look at actual programs and their success—or lack thereof—to better understand what works and what does not. Theory-based research is just that—theory. By looking at actual numbers, what has been successful, and what has failed, better social policy may evolve. With issues as politicized as crime and justice, policy decisions will ideally be rooted in facts, data, and reasoned analysis. Political debate is an important part of the policy process, which leads criminal justice to maintain a multidisciplinary focus. By studying media, politics, education, medicine, and other social institutions, criminal justice scholars integrate other disciplines' findings into their research, ideally leading to a better understanding of crime and the justice system. Simply put, a greater understanding of the justice system can help make the system more effective. By recognizing the needs and problems faced by victims, lawbreakers, and the accused, lawmakers can design policies, programs, and initiatives to address those problems.

Models of the Criminal Justice System

The Constitution of the United States was designed to protect citizens from the power of the government. However, the processes necessary to assure these rights may conflict with the goal of removing dangerous people from the general population. As indicated in the Simpson and Willingham cases, the justice system attempts to strike a balance between liberty and security. Laws protect people's freedoms and do not allow infringements without cause. For example, some liberty is lost due to speed limits, but this loss is determined to be an acceptable cost for assuring security and safety.

Much more freedom or liberty is lost when a person is convicted of a crime. In order for this loss to be considered acceptable, there must be a specific, understandable, and predictable process for determining guilt before an individual's liberty can be taken away by the state. This is the basis for due process protections.

The justice system is also responsible for protecting the freedom and security of a large number of citizens. Due to concerns about time and cost, the system has developed a number of formal and informal processes that are intended to assure efficient operation. Case backloads, cost, and constitutional guarantees of a speedy trial have each contributed to the development of an efficient system for processing criminal cases. Whether the system has become too efficient is the subject of much debate.

In 1968, Herbert Packer, in his book, *The Limits of the Criminal Sanction,*[7] constructed two models of the justice system, each representing competing value systems within the **criminal justice system**. The **crime control model** focuses on controlling crime and protecting citizens in the most efficient way possible. Packer wrote, "The value system that underlies the Crime Control Model is based on the proposition that the repression of criminal conduct is by far the most important function to be performed by the criminal process."[8] The **due process model** focuses on fairness, the rights of all Americans, and the process through which criminal guilt is established.

Both the Simpson and Willingham cases went through the full "obstacle course" that is the American judicial system, although the Willingham case initially moved through the courts at a rapid pace. The due process obstacle course is the result of the court's efforts to make sure a defendant's rights have not been violated. This model, with an emphasis on rights, contrasts with the crime control "assembly line," which strives for efficiency whenever possible, including plea bargaining and other efforts to move cases quickly—including the potential to minimize evidence that is not consistent with the prosecutor's case.

To declare one of these models superior to the other requires a judgment grounded in ideological difference. Conservative values are reflected in the crime control model, while the due process model reflects values more commonly held by liberals. The last 50 years have marked a shift in dominant values, leading to policy choices consistent with Packer's models. During the 1960s, the due process model dominated the justice system. This was a relatively liberal period in the United States, and rulings of the Warren Court greatly expanded the rights of those accused of crime. The Warren Court refers to the U.S. Supreme Court led by Chief Justice Earl Warren from 1953 to 1969. The Warren Court was a liberal-leaning bench and is most noted for expanding civil rights and civil liberties. The political climate began to shift to more conservative values in the mid-1970s. This ideological shift, which continues to this day, resulted in an environment in which conservatives have been able to create criminal justice policies more consistent with Packer's crime control model.

While a logical argument can be made for the benefits of either model, the reality is that an ideological choice has been made. Politicians, supported by much of the public, have embraced a tough-on-crime attitude that includes longer sentences, reduced protections from biased investigations, and fewer opportunities to question police and court practices. However, both models remain active in today's justice system. The O.J. Simpson case can be seen as an example of using due process protections to the benefit of the accused. This was possible, in part, due to the defendant's wealth, power, and prestige. Simpson had the luxury of being able to force his accusers to navigate the due process obstacle course. The final verdict in Simpson's criminal case was rendered almost 16 months after the murders.

In contrast, Willingham's death sentence was issued just eight months after the murders. While some may define the lengthy appeal process that followed the conviction as an obstacle course, the obstacles did not prevent the execution of a man who may have been innocent. The Willingham case is an example of a reduced emphasis on due process typical of the majority of criminal justice cases. While high-profile trials such as Simpson's demonstrate the perils of the obsta-

Criminal justice system
The police, courts, and correctional departments.

Crime control model
A model of the criminal justice system that focuses on controlling crime and protecting the public in the most efficient way.

Due process model
A model of the criminal justice system that focuses on protecting the rights of the accused.

Under the Warren Court, the due process model dominated the criminal justice system.

cle course, often leading to criticism, the vast majority of cases are more similar to the Willingham example. In this example, a very efficient process resulted in an execution, in spite of evidence of innocence.

The differences between the Simpson and Willingham cases demonstrate how equally serious cases can be handled differently by the justice system. Not every case is handled the same way, despite what many people believe. The public's understanding of the justice system comes from many sources: these may include reading a textbook as part of a formal learning experience, but they also include the media and informal discussions with those who have not and will not engage in a structured effort to understand the justice system. As a result, media and popular representations of a high-profile defendant's due process rights may obscure the reality that efficient processes, much more like an assembly line, dominate less publicized trials.

This chapter examines the history and goals of the justice system, the importance of engaging in a scholarly examination of this system, and how the system is organized. Students are encouraged to reflect on their political ideology and the ways they have learned about the justice system as they read this text. In addition to providing a framework for debate about how the justice system should be structured, Packer's models allow for reflection on how individuals' political ideologies may lead to discounting information inconsistent with those values. The examination of the justice system begins with Packer's models, as they will provide a framework for thinking about many of the issues to be introduced in this text. Relying on this model, readers are encouraged to examine their own biases in search of a fact-based review of the criminal justice system.

Crime Control Model

In his examination of the crime control and due process models, Packer offers a clear discussion of the issues raised in the debate about the efficiency of the justice system versus protections for constitutionally guaranteed rights. According to Packer, those who adopt the crime control model argue that punishment and repression of criminal conduct are the most important functions of the justice system. Controlling criminal activity is the most important job of law enforcement, and the system should function quickly and efficiently, much like an assembly line. Proponents of the assembly line model believe that efficiency is key because "the failure of law enforcement to bring criminal conduct under tight control is viewed as leading to the breakdown of public order and thence to the disappearance of an important condition of human freedom."[9]

This model focuses on the efficiency of the criminal justice system to screen suspects, determine guilt, and assign appropriate punishments for those suspects who have been convicted. Efficiency does not require that a suspect be apprehended, tried, and found guilty quickly. Rather, it means that every case should be tried with the proper amount of man-hours devoted to it. The proper amount of man-hours devoted to a case can vary depending upon the severity of the crime, whether it was witnessed or not, and the number of individuals that are involved.

In order for the crime control model to be successful in a country that wants a high conviction rate but does not necessarily want to devote more re-

Proponents of the crime control model believe that the judicial system should move swiftly and efficiently, much like a factory's assembly line.

© 2012 BY REDTC. USED UNDER LICENSE OF SHUTTERSTOCK, INC.

sources and training to the criminal justice system, suspects must be apprehended and convicted at a high rate. As Packer stated in *The Limits of the Criminal Sanction*, "There must then be a premium on speed and finality."[10]

Due Process Model   In contrast to the efficiency of an assembly line, due process protections result in an obstacle course. By viewing the criminal justice system as an assembly line, Packer emphasizes that each stage of the criminal justice process is a decision point. Due to the emphasis on efficiency, each decision has the potential to prevent the quick disposal of cases. In contrast, the due process model focuses on protecting the rights of the accused. These rights are protected through constraints on police, courts, and corrections that make it more difficult to prove guilt. In this model, fairness is the primary goal of the justice process. According to Packer, "Each of its successive stages is designed to present formidable impediments to carrying the accused any further along in the process."[11] This process focuses less on crime control and much more on the defendant's rights as they are protected under the Constitution. There are major differences between the two models that can be seen at its earliest stages. Packer wrote, "The Crime Control Perspective, as we have suggested, places heavy reliance on the ability of investigative and prosecutorial officers, acting in an informal setting in which their distinctive skills are given full sway, to elicit and reconstruct a tolerably accurate account of what actually took place in an alleged criminal event. The Due Process Model rejects this premise and substitutes for it a view of informal, non-adjudicative fact-finding that stresses the possibility of error."[12]

In the due process model, facts are continuously questioned and analyzed, and a case is not considered fully adjudicated until a hearing has been held in the fact-finding context. Proponents of the due process model argue that this is

The due process model sets out to protect the rights of the accused.

the better model because the goal is to eliminate as many mistakes and wrongful convictions as possible. This is the opposite of the crime control model. The crime control model emphasizes finality, even accepting that a certain number of wrongful convictions will occur when dealing with a large volume of cases. Further differences can be emphasized by the deference that the due process model gives to the letter of the law. The due process model requires that certain standards must be met; if they are not, then there are consequences.

The idea that a person is presumed innocent until proven guilty is an essential tenet of the American judicial system and the due process system. The State must prove the defendant is guilty beyond a reasonable doubt. The defendant has no burden in proving his or her case. It is the State's responsibility to convince the judge or jury that the defendant is indeed guilty of the crime of which he or she is accused.

Crime Control vs. Due Process Model in the Courts

The merits and effectiveness of the crime control model and the due process model are in constant debate. The Supreme Court case of *Whren v. United States*, for example, illustrates these contrasting philosophies. On June 23, 1993, plainclothes officers were patrolling a high drug area in Washington, D.C., when they noticed a Pathfinder stopped at a stop sign with two young male African-American occupants. The driver of the car was looking at something in the passenger's hand and remained at the stop sign for over 20 seconds. The car then made a right-hand turn without signaling and sped off. The officers followed and approached the car, identifying themselves as police. An officer noticed that the passenger, Michael Whren, was holding two plastic bags of what appeared to be cocaine.[13] Whren and the driver, James Brown, were arrested and charged with violating various drug laws. The two were eventually convicted of drug-related offenses.

The case was appealed to the Supreme Court. Whren and Brown's defense attorneys argued the legality of the stop and the subsequent seizure of the drugs. The defense argued that the officers had probable cause to believe that traffic laws had been violated but did not have probable cause to search the vehicle for illegal drugs. They believed that the officers used the minor traffic violations as a pretext to search the vehicle and that the officers' behavior deviated from normal police behavior. However, the court declined to overturn the convictions and affirmed the decision of the lower court. In the Supreme Court decision *Whren v. United States*, the court held that "the temporary detention of a motorist upon probable cause to believe that he has violated the traffic laws does not violate the Fourth Amendment's prohibition against unreasonable search and seizures, even if a reasonable officer would not have stopped the motorist absent some additional law enforcement objective."[14]

Proponents of the crime control model would point out that these men were charged and found guilty of drug charges because they had cocaine in plain view. Officers must have probable cause in order to search, but if something is in plain view—as the cocaine was—they may seize it, and that can serve as the probable cause to search the vehicle. The bags could be seized by the police and later could be used by the prosecution. The bags of cocaine would not be subject to the **exclusionary rule**, which states that illegally obtained evidence can be excluded from trial. The crime control model says that the convictions of Whren and Brown were the correct result because they incarcerated drug users and enhanced the security of the public.

Those who identify more strongly with the due process model may claim that this stop was actually an example of profiling. Due process advocates argue that the stop occurred because the police took the defendants' race, vehicle, and location into account. The police did not witness any illegal activity before the stop, which violated the defendants' due process rights. Further, due process advocates argue that the liberty of the public is diminished when police are allowed to initiate an investigation with merely a suspicion that race, location, and vehicle type equate to illegal activity.

The Supreme Court, and the judiciary as a whole, can be a powerful agent of social control and maintaining the public's due process rights. In the near future, as more questions arise regarding the rights of the government to maintain order and an individual's due process rights, the judiciary will play a more prominent role as it sorts through the various legal questions.

Exclusionary rule
A legal mandate applied when a piece of evidence has been obtained in a manner that violates the rights of the defendant under due process.

The Public's Perspective

The public's perception of the criminal justice system can be described as cynical at best, especially when they hear statistics that for every 1,000 crimes, only about 20 people are sent to prison.[15] However, over a 30-year period, crime rates decreased from 51.2 incidences of violent crime per 100,000 people in 1994 to the lowest recorded level of 21 incidences per 100,000 people in 2003.[16] Statistics on homicide rates show further decline, at 5.6 incidences per 100,000 people in 2001 and 2002, a low rate not seen since the 1960s.[17]

Despite the decreasing crime rates, the number of adults in the correctional population has continued to increase. In 1970, there were less than 200,000 inmates in state and federal prisons. By mid-2003, the number had increased to more than 1.2 million inmates. Additionally, nearly 700,000 inmates were held in local jails.[18]

As the judicial system continues to incarcerate people and limit their liberty, it is important to ask why. To limit someone's liberty—or their freedom to make decisions and choices—is not a decision that the judicial system takes lightly. Limiting a person's liberty is done to ensure the security of the public. The public wants to know they will be safe and is often willing to take away an individual's liberty so the collective can feel safer.

The media plays a large role in skewing the public's perception of the criminal justice system by focusing on cases such as that of O.J. Simpson in which offenders escape punishment because of their celebrity status. Constant coverage of crime on television and on the Internet further skews the public's perception of crime. From 1992 to 1996, the number of homicides decreased by 20%, but

Media coverage of high-profile crimes such as homicide influences the public's perception that crime has increased.

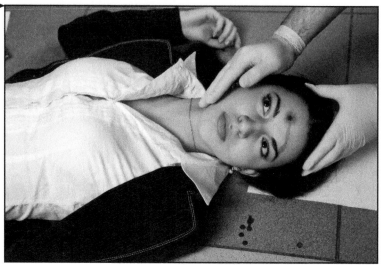

there was a 721% increase in the major news channels' homicide coverage.[19] Media coverage has the greatest impact on how the public perceives crime. Nearly 76% of citizens form their opinions on crime based on what they see in the media.[20] Because of this, from 1992 to 1993 the public believed that crime was the number one problem facing the nation. Media coverage of "sexy" stories that will grab the public's attention is often not proportionate to reality. For instance, nearly 70% of the news stories broadcast or published in California discuss violence that involves youth, when in reality, only 14% of violent crime arrests in the state actually involved youths.[21]

Politicians have sensed the public's dissatisfaction with the criminal justice system and often run campaigns on this platform. Politicians argue that they will be tougher on crime than their predecessors and will implement changes to the system that will result in more convictions. Politicians running for re-election will often tout statistics showing that during their terms crime has dropped and the number of convictions has increased.

Fictionalized law shows on television have brought the courtroom into the public's homes week after week and show an incredibly simplified and fast moving judicial system. This unrealistic portrayal of the criminal justice system can affect the public's understanding and opinions of the process and can even affect public policy.

Critical Thinking   Would you rather live in a society that risks the chance that guilty people will go free in order to protect innocents, or a society that accepts the reality that they will occasionally punish innocent people in order to be sure no guilty people are allowed to go free?

History of the Criminal Justice System in America

America's criminal justice system has its roots in the English common law system. This system did not differentiate between misdemeanors, felonies, and common law crimes like today's judicial system does. It recognized when someone committed a crime—or broke a community standard—and punished them accordingly.

In the United States, as the country became unified and governments were put into place, the criminal justice system evolved because laws became codified and penalties were attached. The criminal justice system began to recognize differences in the seriousness of crimes, and classified them as misdemeanors or felonies. Generally, **misdemeanors** were minor criminal offenses that were punished less severely than felonies, usually with a fine or a prison term of less than one year.[22] **Felonies** were more serious crimes, which typically carried prison sentences of longer than one year.[23]

How, and for what length of time, people should be punished for the crimes they commit has long been debated. In 1764, Italian philosopher Cesare Beccaria wrote *On Crime and Punishments*, a treatise that advocated for publicized laws and consistent punishments for crimes.[24] In 1829, England passed the Metropolitan Police Act and formed the London Metropolitan Police. Fifty years earlier, in 1789, the United States established the U.S. Marshals Service.[25] The first modern police force in the United States was the Boston police department, established in 1838, and followed shortly thereafter by the New York police department.[26]

The **Department of Justice (DOJ)** was founded in 1870. This department within the executive branch of the federal government is designed to enforce the laws of the United States. Within the DOJ is the Office of the Attorney General, which serves as the legal department for all cases that concern the federal government. The attorney general and the deputy attorney general plan and enact department policies and programs and supervise and direct the department's organizational units.[27] There are numerous other offices within the DOJ that often serve specialized functions including appellate work, national security, etc., and employ units of lawyers with specific specialties depending upon the crime being committed.

In 1931, the National Commission on Law Observance and Enforcement, more commonly known as the Wickersham Commission after its chairman George W. Wickersham, published the *Report on Lawlessness in Law Enforcement*.[28] The report was the first major investigation into police misconduct and alleged that the police were misusing their power and using brutality to force confessions and admissions from suspected criminals. Although police departments disagreed with the report's findings, the Wickersham Commission's findings nevertheless spurred dramatic changes, including the formation of internal affairs commissions to investigate police misconduct and Supreme Court decisions that limited police officers' use of physical force. A thorough summary of the Wickersham Commission's report is given in Chapter 4 of this book.

President Lyndon B. Johnson, in 1967, appointed the President's Commission on Law Enforcement and Administration of Justice to provide increased federal law enforcement efforts, to provide assistance to local law enforcement

Misdemeanor
A lesser crime that is punishable by jail time for up to one year and/or a fine.

Felony
A crime that is punishable by imprisonment in excess of a year or by death.

Department of Justice (DOJ)
A department within the executive branch of the federal government designed to enforce the laws of the United States.

President Johnson's Commission on Law Enforcement and Administration of Justice provided increased assistance to local law enforcement.

efforts, and to provide a comprehensive analysis of crime and its origins in the United States.[29]

In 1968, Congress passed the Safe Streets and Crime Control Act, which established the Law Enforcement Assistance Administration (LEAA).[30] The LEAA, which was abolished in 1982, distributed federal funding for educational programs, research, and local crime initiatives to state and local law enforcement agencies.

The Supreme Court's 1966 ruling in *Miranda v. Arizona* was a hugely important legal decision granting criminal defendants a number of rights upon arrest. Defendants must be informed that they have the right to remain silent; anything they say can and will be used against them in court; they have the right for an attorney to be present before and during questioning; and if they cannot afford an attorney, an attorney will be appointed to them to be present before and during questioning.[31] A waiver of these rights is only valid if is the defendant waives them freely, knowingly, and intelligently. Miranda rights are explored further in subsequent chapters of this book.

Another significant decision occurred five years before *Miranda,* in 1961. In *Mapp v. Ohio*, the Supreme Court ruled that a defendant has a right to protection against unreasonable searches and seizures in both federal court and state court.[32] If a government agent (i.e., a police officer or someone working on behalf of the government) obtains evidence in violation of the search and seizure doctrine encased within the Fourth Amendment of the U.S. Constitution, the evidence will not be admissible in a state court.[33]

A defendant's right to an attorney was clarified in the 1963 case *Gideon v. Wainwright*.[34] If the defendant cannot afford an attorney, then the government must appoint one to serve in court on the defendant's behalf. The idea of a public defender's office devoted to providing representation to defendants who cannot afford private counsel is revolutionary and fairly recent. Both the federal and state criminal justice systems employ public defenders whose sole job is to represent defendants. *Gideon v. Wainwright* and the roles of public defenders and defense attorneys are discussed further in Chapter 7.

Career Connections: Defense Attorney

Defense attorneys, like prosecutors, must complete law school and pass the bar exam for the specific state in which they practice law. Criminal defense attorneys can enter into private practice, in which clients pay their fees; alternatively, they can become members of the Office of the Public Defender and be paid a salary. Attorneys for the Office of the Public Defender are required to provide their legal services on any case to which they are assigned. In cases in which the office already represents a co-defendant, the case is given to a private attorney, who is paid by the office and may use all resources available to the office.

Frequently, defense attorneys face difficult challenges when working on a case, both inside and outside of the courtroom. They often do not have the resources that are available to the prosecution. They must rely on the prosecution to have turned over all exculpatory evidence or potentially exculpatory evidence, and they must conduct independent investigations with significantly less funds or manpower than those available to the state.

Defense attorneys have an ethical obligation to provide the most effective defense to each client, devoting a significant amount of time and resources to each case. The defense attorney's legal strategy and approach will, by necessity, vary depending on the circumstances of the case. In cases in which the defendant's guilt is very much in doubt, the attorney will argue motions to suppress witness statements and to exclude potentially damaging evidence, while gathering evidence to support the defendant's innocence such as alibi or character witnesses. In cases in which the defendant's innocence will likely be difficult to ascertain in court, the defense attorney may opt to pursue plea negotiations with the prosecution to limit the amount of time the client will have to spend incarcerated.

The defense attorney's job requires him or her to be realistic about every case and to give a thorough and exhaustive effort regardless of the circumstances of the case or client. Being knowledgeable and creative are essential characteristics for any defense attorney. The attorney must be quick-thinking and prepared for a variety of situations that may arise in the courtroom. The attorney must be intimately familiar with court procedures and provide comprehensive, objective counsel to his or her client about the legal proceedings—even if the advice is not necessarily what the client wants to hear.

Critical Thinking Imagine that you were a defense attorney for the Office of the Public Defender and were assigned to defend an accused child molester. What challenges might you face, and how could you overcome them to represent the defendant fairly?

Scope and Size of Today's Justice System

With the world's population consistently on the rise, it is not surprising that the scope of the criminal justice system has grown steadily larger. In 2007, governments at the federal, state, and local levels in the United States spent an estimated $228 billion on law enforcement, corrections, and court services.[35] As of 2009, there were 7,225,800 people under correctional supervision in the U.S.[36] This number includes adults who were in jail or prison and on probation or parole. Of that number, 841,000 were African-American males who were serving time in state or federal prisons and local jails.[37] Close to 150,000 of those men were between the ages of 25 and 29.[38]

A huge workforce is needed in order to supervise these individuals. A 2001 study indicated that between the local, state, and federal systems, the justice system employed close to 2.3 million persons with a total payroll of $8.1 billion for the month of March 2001 alone. Only 9% were federal employees, roughly a third (31%) were state employees, and more than half (58%) worked at the local level.[39]

But who bears the costs of the criminal justice system? Statistics indicate that nearly half of all justice system expenses are funded by local governments, and another 35% by state governments.[40] Over the years, the amount of money spent per capita has increased. In 1982, the per capita expenditure across fed-

Police departments are primarily funded by local rather than state governments.

© 2012 BY BASSITTART. USED UNDER LICENSE OF SHUTTERSTOCK, INC.

eral, state, and local governments was $158. By 2001, this had increased nearly three times to $586. At the same time, judicial and legal services increased from $34 to $132 per U.S. resident, and police protection from $84 to $254.[41] While it may seem that the local government is bearing a disproportionate burden, most of the money that local government spends is for police protection, which is primarily funded by local governments instead of state governments.

The economy, too, can have a significant influence on how programs are structured within the criminal justice system. During times of economic crisis, policy changes are often rampant as lawmakers search for more cost-effective solutions for the criminal justice system. These cheaper alternatives, however, can lead to less effective treatments for offenders. For example, lawmakers may restructure policies cutting down on court-mandated rehab for drug-addicted defendants in favor of the less expensive alternative of housing them in correctional facilities where they receive little help. As a result, these offenders may be more likely, upon release, to recommit an offense.

Several alternative programs and diversionary classes have been made available to offenders in an effort to decrease the number of offenders going through the criminal court system. However, this system has actually had the opposite effect and has resulted in net-widening—the number of offenders within the court system has increased, because the criminal justice system has expanded the number of offenders it must supervise.

Net-widening

A phenomenon in which the number of offenders within the court system increases as the criminal justice system expands the number of offenders it must supervise.

Crime

A legally prohibited action that injures the public welfare or morals or the interests of the state.

What Is Crime? Crime is considered a social phenomenon that occurs when a person breaks a law or rule of the society in which he or she lives. More specifically, a crime is a legally prohibited action that injures the public welfare or morals or the interests of the state. These definitions reflect the idea that a crime is an action that violates the social norm. While the criminal justice system delineates a formalized way of preventing crimes, social **norms** are the informal process of controlling society's behavior. Societal laws and practices have made it difficult for convicted criminals to find employment, vote, be approved for credit, etc. By stigmatizing bad behavior and increasing the difficulty of achieving success in society when one has been convicted of a crime, the criminal justice system aims to deter people from committing crimes.

It is important to understand the distinction between crime and deviance. Deviance is an action that violates a social norm but does not necessarily violate an established law. Such behaviors may be frowned upon by society but are not criminal.

The concept that committing a crime is something to be avoided is ingrained in people since early childhood. Parents instill in young children the idea that for every action there is a consequence, either positive or negative. Parents teach this by rewarding good behavior and punishing bad behavior. A child who successfully completes his or her chores may be rewarded with an allowance or another privilege, whereas a child who hits a younger sibling will be punished. From an early age, children learn in a very direct way that there is a code of behavior to which they are expected to conform.

The **consensus model** states that members of a society naturally reach a basic agreement regarding shared norms and values.[42] Even a diverse group will have similar norms and values and will endeavor to put into place a structure that emphasizes the norms they value. Laws add structure to a community or group of people, detailing for the society which behaviors are acceptable and expected and which are not.

The consensus model asserts that an action becomes criminal once a society agrees that said behavior is criminal. Durkheim (1893) stated that an act becomes criminal "when it offends strong and defined states of the collective conscience."[43] Stealing a car, for example, is a crime because society has decided that it values an individual's right to his or her property, and that the lawful owner of the property has the right to dictate how and by whom the property is used. When an offender interferes with the owner's right by taking the property without permission (in this case, stealing a car), society has decided that the act violates a value or norm that it finds to be important. To discourage potential offenders from repeating this action, society deems the action criminal and promises punishment for violators.

The opposing **conflict model** assumes that different segments of society—divided by social class, age, race, income, etc.—have different norms and value systems and perpetually struggle against each other for control of society.[44] This model states that there is no stability in what is "the norm," and that criminal activity is determined by whichever group holds the power at that moment.[45] An example of the conflict model in practice is the debate over abortion. The Supreme Court's decision in *Roe v. Wade* marked a dramatic shift on the subject in the United States by allowing women to have an abortion if they so choose.[46] This norm, however, is certainly not unanimously agreed upon in American society, with different factions of the public holding contrasting opinions on abortion, often segmented by political ideology. In a

Norms
Social expectations for appropriate behavior.

Consensus model
The idea that when a group comes together to form a society, they will have mutually shared values and norms and will come to a consensus about what is a crime.

Conflict model
The idea that when a group comes together to form a society there will be differences within the group—i.e., age, race, and socioeconomic differences—that will make it difficult to come to an agreement about what is criminal. The group in power will set the standards.

2011 poll, 68% of Republicans identified themselves as "pro-life," compared to 32% of Democrats.[47] For many years, Republicans have advocated passing legislation that would prohibit any type of abortion with a few very narrow exceptions, but have not been able to do so because they have never had the overwhelming majority they have needed to change policy.

The conflict model holds that diverse societies cannot always reach a general consensus about what is and what is not criminal. In order for a behavior or action to become criminalized, it must go through a lengthy political process that includes considerable debate between the factions. If one group can obtain a majority, the behavior or action will either remain criminalized or will effectively be **decriminalized**. If neither group can obtain a majority, there is no resolution.

Decriminalize
To legalize something that used to be a crime.

Policing
Enforcing the law by monitoring suspected criminal activity and apprehending violators of law.

The Formal Criminal Justice Process

The criminal justice system consists of three major components: law enforcement (or **policing**), the court system, and the correctional system. Each component serves a specific purpose within the criminal justice process, though few cases actually make it through the entire formal process. The following is a brief overview of the process from start to finish, which will be explored in further detail throughout the book.

The formal criminal justice process begins with *initial contact*, during which law enforcement is first notified that an alleged crime has occurred and is first brought into contact with the potential offender. Initial contact should not be confused with custody or arrest.

Once the police have been notified of an alleged crime, they conduct an *investigation* to assure that the alleged crime did in fact occur, that the offender can be correctly identified, and that there is sufficient evidence to support a conviction in the matter.

An investigation may ultimately lead to an *arrest* or multiple arrests. There must be probable cause to legally arrest the suspect. An arrest can be made in a few instances: if the officer has witnessed a crime, if an officer has probable cause to believe an individual committed a crime based upon the statement of another individual, or when an arrest warrant has been issued.

Upon being arrested, a suspect is in police *custody*. At this stage the police may take a photo (mug shot) of the suspect and gather further personal information about them, including taking their fingerprints. Suspects in police custody may also be obligated to stand in a lineup for witness identification and may be subject to interrogation from officers. A suspect has a right to an attorney while being questioned.

A suspect formally becomes a defendant when he or she is *charged* by the state. The state can do this by filing an indictment, which is a formal written statement by the prosecuting attorney charging a person with an offense. Alternatively, in lieu of an indictment, the state can file a statement of probable cause, which is written by a police officer and describes why the defendant is being charged. The type of crime generally dictates how the state will charge the crime. Chapters 4 and 5 provide a thorough description and analysis of the policing and law enforcement process.

FIGURE 1.1 Criminal Justice System Flowchart.

What is the sequence of events in the criminal justice system?

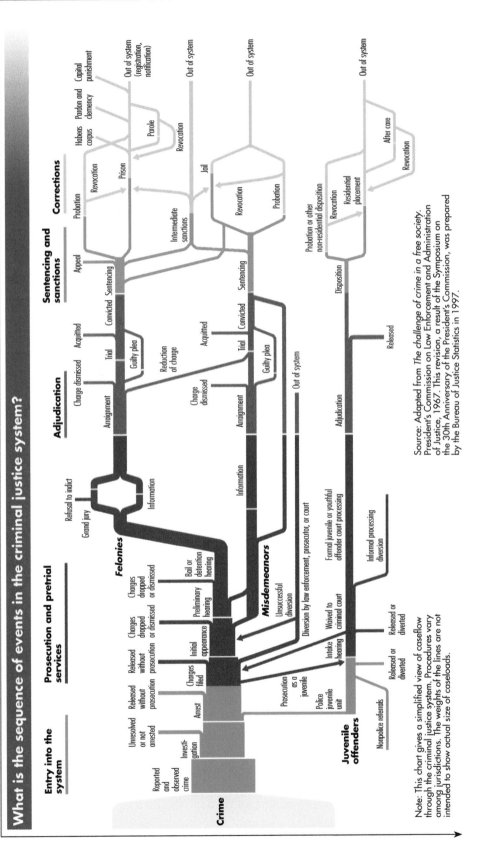

Source: Adapted from *The challenge of crime in a free society.* President's Commission on Law Enforcement and Administration of Justice, 1967. This revision, a result of the Symposium on the 30th Anniversary of the President's Commission, was prepared by the Bureau of Justice Statistics in 1997.

Note: This chart gives a simplified view of caseflow through the criminal justice system. Procedures vary among jurisdictions. The weights of the lines are not intended to show actual size of caseloads.

Policing, including crime scene investigation, is the first component of the criminal justice process.

© 2012 BY BRIAN A JACKSON. USED UNDER LICENSE OF SHUTTERSTOCK, INC.

Once a suspect is arrested and charged, the suspect and the case then interact with the second component of the justice process: the court system. After being charged, the defendant faces a *preliminary hearing* or *grand jury hearing*. This process varies from state to state, but all are based on a similar foundation. A group of citizens, sitting as the grand jury, must determine that there is appropriate probable cause for a suspect to be charged and for a case to move forward to trial.[48] Some states allow the defendant to be present and to testify; other states allow only the prosecution to argue its case. If the grand jury finds there is enough evidence for the case to proceed, they consequently indict the defendant.

An *arraignment* generally marks the defendant's initial appearance in court, as the defendant will appear before the court that will try his or her case. Defendants are informed of the charges against them, including the minimum and maximum punishments and fines they may be facing.[49] Defendants are informed of their constitutional right to have bail set and their constitutional right to a speedy trial. Some courts, though not all, will set a trial date at an arraignment.

A defendant is granted a right to a *bail hearing*, during which the judge can set a monetary bail that will allow for the defendant to be released from jail and to secure his or her presence at all further court dates.[50] Judges are not required to set a monetary bail, and may instead choose to hold the defendant on a no-bail status based upon the severity of the crime. Alternatively, the court can order that a defendant be released on his or her own recognizance or, if a minor, into the custody of a parent or guardian.

Under the Sixth Amendment, the defendant has a right to a trial, but this is not considered an inalienable right. If the defendant or state chooses, he or she can enter into plea negotiations. Almost 90% of all criminal cases end in a plea bargain—an agreement on a sentence without a trial verdict.[51] Plea bargains are considered to be contracts between the defendant and the state.[52]

Prosecutors may have a variety of motivations for entering into plea negotiations based upon the strength of the case, the severity of the case, and the defendant's background. In some cases, the prosecution may be uncertain

Plea bargain
An agreement between the state and defense on a plea and sentence.

whether a trial will result in a conviction; by offering the defendant a deal, the prosecution can guarantee that the defendant receives some manner of punishment. The prosecution may also offer a plea bargain if there are concerns about potential witnesses—for instance, if a witness's credibility with jurors may be troublesome or the witness/victim is a young child whom the prosecution does not want to force to testify in court. Defendants, for their part, will enter into plea negotiations in an effort to protect themselves from harsher punishment.

The ultimate decision rests with the defendant. A defense attorney cannot accept a plea deal without the permission of his or her client. A defendant who has accepted a plea deal may agree to plead to one of the crimes charged and have the rest dismissed, plead guilty to a lesser count, or agree to enter a plea of guilty because he or she wants to limit the amount of time spent in jail. In 2000, guilty pleas accounted for nearly 95% of all felony convictions in state courts.[53]

If the parties do not enter into successful plea negotiations, the next step in the criminal justice process is for the prosecution to bring the defendant to trial. The defendant, and the defendant alone, has the right to choose whether he or she will be tried by a jury or a judge.[54] At trial, the prosecution must prove to a judge or jury that the defendant committed the crime beyond a reasonable doubt.[55] The defendant has the right to confront and cross-examine witnesses and to present witnesses in his or her own defense. The defendant is not required to put on a case. The burden of proof in criminal cases lies with the prosecution, not the defendant, and the trier of fact (the judge or jury) decides whether the state has met its burden.[56]

Some trials may result in a hung jury—a jury that is unable to agree on a unanimous decision regarding the guilt or innocence of a defendant. When a hung jury occurs, the prosecution is faced with the choice of whether or not to retry the defendant. If the prosecution chooses to retry the case, the court will set a new trial date. In cases where the defendant has been incarcerated while awaiting trial, the judge may elect to hold a new bail hearing or release the defendant on his or her own recognizance. If the prosecution chooses not to retry the defendant, the prosecution will dismiss the case or place it on the stet docket, and the defendant will be released.

If a defendant is found guilty, the case then progresses to *sentencing* or *disposition*. In this stage, the defendant is sentenced by the court for the crimes for which he or she was convicted. Disposition can occur immediately after the verdict or can be delayed. A defendant may choose to delay disposition so that a pre-sentence investigation can be done. During the sentencing phase, the defendant can present factors of mitigation, and the victim has the right to give a victim impact statement.

An agent within the correctional system will conduct a pre-sentence investigation report to compile background information on the defendant. This exhaustive report examines the defendant's educational background, family background, past medical history, and past criminal history, information that the agent uses to makes recommendations to the sentencing judges. Those recommendations may include whether or not the defendant is likely to offend again and his or her amenability to treatment and rehabilitation.

The judge can take the pre-sentence recommendation report into advisement when determining the defendant's sentence. The judge can also take into account mitigating factors about the defendant's history to structure a sentence that will both protect the public and help rehabilitate the defendant. Many different sentencing options are available to judges, including a fine, probation, incarceration, or some combination of these options. The judge may sentence the defendant to incarceration in prison for a specific duration, after which the defendant is free to reenter society. The judge might instead deliver a sentence that would incarcerate the defendant and then place him or her on probation upon release. The judge can also place the defendant on straight probation with no prison term.

The defendant still has many rights after sentencing, including the right to appeal. On appeal, an appellate court will review the transcript and evidence to confirm that the defendant received a fair trial. The appellate courts will assure there was sufficient evidence to sustain a verdict and will determine whether evidence was properly admitted and if any reversible error occurred. A defendant may only appeal issues that were preserved at trial when an objection was made.

Defendants also are granted post-conviction rights. The defendant may assert in a post-conviction petition that he or she received ineffective assistance of counsel at trial. At a hearing, both the prosecution and the defense have the ability to call witnesses, and the prosecution will call the defendant's trial attorney. By filing a post-conviction claim for ineffective assistance of counsel, the defendant has waived attorney-client privilege and the attorney may testify about any communications between them. Chapters 6, 7, and 8 of this book provide a comprehensive account of the structure, process, and players of the court system.

A defendant who is found guilty and sentenced falls under the jurisdiction of the department of corrections. The correctional system comprises a multitude of facilities and systems, including jail and prison, parole, and probation systems, which will be discussed at great length in Chapters 9, 10, and 11.

A convicted criminal may be placed in jail or prison, sentenced to probation, or a combination of the two.

Upon the defendant's release from jail or prison, he or she may serve a term of probation. While on probation, the defendant is required to abide by specific rules and conditions, which may include submitting to drug testing and treatment, checking in with probation agents, and avoiding certain locations and people. Defendants, upon their release, may be part of a **community corrections** program and be required to reside at a halfway house. This helps the defendant gradually make the often difficult transition from a secured facility to complete freedom.

Community corrections
A halfway house, rehab facility, or home detention that helps an individual move from a correctional facility to complete freedom.

Critical Thinking
Ninety percent of all criminal cases end in plea negotiations. Do you consider this justice being served or a shortcut to a conviction?

The Informal Criminal Justice System
Many cases are settled in an informal pattern of cooperation between the prosecution, defense, and judge. The informal judicial system relies heavily upon other members of the **courtroom workgroup**, a concept developed by Eisenstein and Jacob (1970)[57] and explored further in Chapter 7. Beyond the judge, the courtroom workgroup consists of the judge's staff—the court clerk, the judge's law clerk, and the court reporter—as well as the prosecution and defense attorneys. The courtroom workgroup collaborates to move cases through the criminal justice system quickly, fairly, and effectively, which in many instances means that a case will not go through the entire extended process of the formal criminal justice system.

Courtroom workgroup
The judge, courtroom staff, prosecutor, and defense attorney.

The informal justice system relies heavily upon the relationships between the prosecution and defense counsel. The legal community is small, and many of the prosecutors and defense counsel have worked alongside each other for years. Longtime members of the defense bar know when and under what circumstances the prosecution will be willing to engage in plea negotiations. This skill is invaluable to defendants who elect to pursue a plea bargain.

A variety of informal systems and functions exist throughout the criminal justice process. Police discretion is one notable example. Discretion, which will be discussed at length in Chapter 5, allows a law enforcement officer to use his or her best judgment when deciding how to proceed with a criminal investigation. An officer's discretion may help determine, for example, whether to make a traffic stop, how to interrogate a suspect or person of interest, how to handle an infraction, and so on. While there are certain limits and guidelines regarding police discretion, in general these situations follow an informal process and are not rigidly structured or formally codified.

Community policing, too, is part of the informal criminal justice system. Community members may work together with law enforcement to identify and solve local problems, such as setting up a neighborhood watch program to provide extra security for a neighborhood that has suffered a number of burglaries. Community involvement is not a specifically delineated process of the formal criminal justice system, but can nevertheless play an essential role in deterring or responding to crime. Chapters 4 and 5 discuss the structure and implications of community policing.

Victims of crime may go through an informal process of restorative justice (explored in Chapter 8) in which they attempt to recover from their victimization. In many cases, this process does not involve any formal systems such as police, courts, or corrections, but may instead consist of communications between the victim and the offender to repair the social damage caused by a criminal act.

Wedding cake model of justice

A four-layer model in which the top layer is celebrated trials, the second layer is major felonies, the third layer is less major felonies, and the fourth layer is misdemeanors.

The Wedding Cake Model of Justice

The wedding cake model of justice examines crime as a four-layer cake in which each layer represents a different type of case. In this model, first developed by Friedman and Percival (1981)[58] and refined by Gottfredson and Gottfredson (1988),[59] the bottommost, largest layer represents the most common type of case that moves through the criminal justice system and the topmost layer the least common type of case.

The top tier of the wedding cake model is populated by the highly publicized cases, such as those of O.J. Simpson, Michael Jackson, Paris Hilton, and Lindsay Lohan, which attract a great deal of media and public attention because of the celebrity status of the defendant or the victim. Such cases, however, do not accurately reflect the everyday criminal justice process.

The second layer includes serious felony cases such as rape or murder in which the defendant would likely not be eligible for bail. These cases are considered relatively high profile and draw some media attention. Cases at this level generally progress further through the criminal justice process than cases leveling the bottom tiers of the model.

The third layer incorporates the less serious felony cases, including some property crimes, drug-related offenses, and other nonviolent crimes. These offenses comprise a significant portion of a court's daily caseload and rarely receive a full formal trial. A majority of these cases are resolved with plea bargains.

The bottommost layer involves misdemeanor offenses, such as disturbing the peace and petty theft, and encompasses the largest number of cases within the criminal justice system. The media generally does not focus on these cases because they do not provide the sensationalized details of a murder trial such as O.J. Simpson's. Misdemeanors are commonly adjudicated swiftly and without any media attention, adhering to a more informal process of criminal justice.

The wedding cake model provides a visual representation of the fact that the majority of cases that appear in courts on an everyday basis are low-profile misdemeanors, while the media-hyped cases that capture the nation's attention are rarities. The media's focus on the "sexy" cases can distort the public's perception of the criminal justice system. These highly publicized, sensationalized celebrity trials do not portray an accurate representation of the criminal justice system as a whole. The media's saturated coverage of the top tier of crimes presents criminal proceedings to the public as a form of entertainment, while ignoring the much more common—and more serious—realities of the criminal justice system. As Walker (2001) notes, these highly publicized but uncommon cases can lead to erroneous public sentiment and misguided policy choices regarding the criminal justice system.[60]

© 2012 BY EMIN KULIYEV. USED UNDER LICENSE OF SHUTTERSTOCK, INC.

In the wedding cake model of justice, the bottom layer represents the most common cases and the top layer represents the least common.

Continuing Challenges This chapter began with a discussion of Packer's two models of criminal justice: crime control and due process. These models illustrate the need to balance freedom and security. In essence, the question that the criminal justice system and members of society ask themselves is how much freedom they are willing to sacrifice in the effort to increase safety and security. For example, establishing a national DNA registry could lead to a nearly 100% conviction rate for sexual predators when DNA is present. An individual who was suspected of a crime—and not yet convicted—would be required to give a DNA sample, which would be entered into the national data bank. Law enforcement could use this national DNA database to identify a perpetrator of any crime for which DNA evidence was present. Ideally, the efficient rate of convictions would most likely deter those responsible for sexual assaults. However, because a DNA registry would include information about people's health, including their predisposition to cancer and other diseases, individuals would be compelled to give up many freedoms in order to increase security. Do the benefits of the DNA database outweigh citizens' losses of certain liberties? These are the kinds of controversies that are subject to perpetual debate among policy makers and the public.

New advancements may also allow society to predict future criminality, perhaps leading to efforts to proactively prevent crimes from occurring. While a predictive model may sound appealing, anticipating crime and taking steps to prevent it from occurring could again lead to a deprivation of individuals' rights. In this scenario, the balance of freedom and security has tilted heavily toward security.

One contemporary example of the preference for security is the presence of street gangs. Street gangs have increasingly moved out of the cities and into the suburbs, expanding their drug distribution areas, increasing their revenue, and recruiting new members. Today, there are approximately 1 million gang members and more than 20,000 criminally active gangs throughout the United States.[61] As a response, the public has demanded more security.

Those worried by gangs are also calling for tougher gun control. Each year, 30,000 people are killed by gunfire in the United States.[62] Close to 95% of all gang-related homicides are carried out with firearms.[63] States have tried to make stricter laws regarding who is allowed to purchase and own guns. Illinois, Pennsylvania, Hawaii, and Rhode Island have some of the strictest gun laws. Each requires a background check, safety locks, and other safety measures.

The criminal justice system faces challenges from more contemporary criminal acts such as **white-collar crime**—crimes against businesses by people in high-profile positions. White-collar crimes are largely hidden, but American corporations lose about 7% of their annual revenue to fraud, amounting to about $1 trillion of the 2008 gross domestic product.[64]

Modern technologies, too, have transformed the scope of crime. The prevalence of the Internet has allowed for cybercrime to develop. Cybercrime involves the targeting of computer systems or networks upon which the public has become increasingly more dependent. These crimes include computer fraud, copyright infringement, distributing illegal sexual material, Internet securities fraud, e-tailing fraud, identity fraud, and cyber vandalism. Cybercrime is

White-collar crime
Crimes against businesses by people in high-profile positions.

uniquely challenging to the criminal justice system because it is difficult to detect through traditional law enforcement channels and is rapidly, continually evolving. Learning to counteract cybercrime demands new technical skills from law enforcement, and new laws and agencies have been created to deal with the constantly changing cyber community. Cybercrime and its effects on the criminal justice system are further explored in Chapters 14 and 15 of this book.

The public's demand for safety has especially escalated since the devastating terrorist attacks on the United States on September 11, 2001. The use of terrorism to promote political agendas is a growing concern. Today's terrorists have diverse motivations and sponsors and view their causes as a global war against the values and traditions of their enemies. The criminal justice system, specifically at the federal level, has strongly responded to terrorism. One of the biggest responses since 9/11 has been the development of the Department of Homeland Security, whose purpose is to reduce the country's vulnerability to terrorism, prevent terrorist attacks, and minimize damage and improve recovery if an attack occurs. Chapter 14 provides a comprehensive analysis of the U.S. and international governments' efforts to protect against terrorism.

As more and more attention is called to these and other contemporary challenges to criminal justice, the public's call for greater safety measures is the rallying point for change. Remember that the ever-present struggle between liberty and security once inspired the country's forefathers to rebel against the British and establish the United States as an independent nation. Today, the government continually attempts to find the right balance between assuring the safety of its citizens and restricting infringements on their civil rights.

As you continue to familiarize yourself with the structure and process of the criminal justice system throughout the book, consider how criminal justice has continued to adapt and evolve based on real-world circumstances. How will the struggle between security and liberty ultimately be resolved? What does the future hold for the criminal justice system and American society as a whole?

The federal government and the criminal justice system have responded strongly to the threat of terrorism.

Ethics and Professionalism: Troy Davis

On September 21, 2011, after nearly 22 years on death row, and three prior execution dates and stays, Troy Davis was executed by the state of Georgia.[65] Davis had been convicted in 1989 for the murder of off-duty police officer Mark McPhail.[66]

Davis, who maintained his innocence throughout his incarceration, was convicted largely on the testimony of nine eyewitnesses who placed him at the scene of the crime. Witnesses testified that they saw Davis beating up a homeless man and that Davis shot McPhail when McPhail tried to break up the fight. Other witnesses testified that they heard Davis confess to killing McPhail. There was no physical evidence connecting Davis to the murder of Officer McPhail.

Since the trial in 1991, seven of the nine eyewitnesses have submitted sworn affidavits recanting their testimony.[67] One witness, Antoine Williams, who eventually recanted his statement, said that he and other witnesses were cajoled by police into testifying against Davis and that they were all illiterate and did not know what they were signing.[68] Two of the State's other key witnesses have not recanted their statements. Evidence has grown that one of them may actually be responsible for the murder of Officer McPhail.

In 2010, the U.S. Supreme Court granted Davis the rare opportunity to prove his innocence to a lower court. Davis, however, was unable to do so, and his death sentence was upheld. As Davis's execution date drew closer, he received support from many high-profile individuals, including Pope Benedict, former President Jimmy Carter, and several musicians, actors, and actresses, all of whom encouraged the state of Georgia to delay the execution because they believed serious questions remained about Davis's guilt. Davis' supporters drew attention to the fact that seven of nine eyewitnesses had recanted their testimony, a gun had never been recovered, and that there was no physical evidence tying Davis to the murder. Georgia's state courts and governor denied requests to delay the execution, and President Obama declined to intervene in the case.

On the evening of Davis's execution, September 21, the Supreme Court reviewed a final petition filed by Davis's defense team. The Supreme Court denied the petition and the execution was carried out.

What would you do if you were Georgia's governor? President Obama? A member of the Supreme Court? Could you allow a man to be executed when there are serious questions about his guilt?

Chapter Summary

- Criminal justice is the study of the interactions between the police, courts, and correctional facilities. Criminal justice looks at how these interactions shape the criminal justice system and looks to see how these interactions play out in the real world based on evidence and statistics.

- Crime control refers to both the formal and informal ways that society looks to control criminal behavior. Formal controls on criminal behavior include incarceration and probation, while informal controls are done through societal norms. Individuals who are subject to formal crime control are guaranteed certain procedures and rights under due process. Due process protects defendants' constitutional rights to a speedy trial, innocent until proven guilty, the right to an attorney, etc.

- The crime control model argues that punishment and repression of criminal conduct is the most important function of the justice system. Controlling criminal activity is the most important job of law enforcement and the system should function quickly and efficiently like an assembly line. At each point in the assembly line, there is an opportunity to end the case. The due process model focuses on protecting the rights of the accused. This results in an obstacle course in which each decision has the potential to prevent the quick disposal of cases.

- The criminal justice system in the United States has a long and ever-changing history that has seen each branch of the system become more centralized and unified. In the past, policing systems varied from one locality to another, but now they all use a very similar structure and process. The judicial system has changed as well, as the elements of crimes and the penalties for crimes have been codified in the law and the consequences for breaking the laws have become more consistent. Correctional facilities, too, have undergone extensive changes to become more centralized as prison populations have grown.

- A crime is a wrong against society as proclaimed by law and, if committed under certain circumstances, punishable by society. The consensus model assumes that when a group gathers to form a society, the society will naturally form shared values and norms. The conflict model assumes that within a society there will be different segments, separated by social class, income, age, and race, that will have different values and norms and will engage in a struggle to define what is criminal. The group in power will decide what behavior is criminal.

- There are many different steps in the judicial process—both formal and informal. The formal steps include initial contact, investigation, arrest, custody, charging, preliminary hearing, arraignment, bail/detention, trial, sentencing/disposition, appeal, correctional treatment, release, and post-release. Informal processes are those that deter from the formal process, such as plea bargains, which are agreed upon by the prosecution and defense to move cases quickly and fairly without going through the full formal process.

- The wedding cake model of justice examines crime as a four-layer cake in which the smallest, top layer represents highly publicized, media-driven cases; the second layer represents serious felony cases; the third layer represents less serious felony cases; and the largest, bottom layer represents misdemeanor cases. Cases on the bottom layers are much more common in the criminal justice system than those in the top layers.

- The criminal justice system faces continuing challenges in addressing modern, technologically advanced crimes, as well as satiating a public that demands greater security at the expense of civil liberties.

Critical Thinking

1. Do you believe that programs designed to give offenders life skills help the recidivism rate? Why or why not?
2. Who or what do you think has the biggest influence on how we as a society view crime? Is it our communities? Television shows? The news?
3. Many states, in an effort to be tougher on crime, have enacted a "three-strikes" rule regarding drugs. On the third conviction, the prosecutor may seek a minimum mandatory sentence that the offender will have to serve. The rule only takes into account how many drug convictions the offender has and not the amount of drugs that the offender had in his or her possession. Do you agree with this policy?
4. What is your opinion of plea bargaining? Is it a necessary evil or does it do a disservice to justice?
5. How do you think the prevalence of technology will continue to change the way that crimes occur and the way we view crimes?
6. Frequently, defendants will ask for a delayed disposition so that a pre-sentencing investigation can be completed. Do you think a judge should take the defendant's background into account when sentencing the defendant for a crime, or should every defendant face the same consequence for the same crime?
7. What are some ways that the United States conducts racial profiling?
8. Compare the cases of Todd Willingham, Troy Davis, and O.J. Simpson. What was the media's role in each case? Does it color your perception of the judicial system?
9. What are the differences between the conflict and consensus models?
10. Do you believe in the crime control model or the due process model? Why? Which model plays a bigger role in our legal system?

Media

Amnesty International: http://www.amnesty.org/
Amnesty International, a global organization that campaigns against abuses of human rights, including the death penalty, provides comprehensive overviews of the Cameron Todd Willingham and Troy Davis cases.

Department of Justice: http://www.justice.gov/criminal/
The United States Department of Justice website gives an overview of the federal criminal justice system, its players, and current news.

National Association of Criminal Defense Attorneys: http://www.nacdl.org/
The NACDL is the largest association of criminal defense attorneys in the United States. This website gives overviews of recent cases and provides defense attorneys with resources and connections with other defense attorneys in their area.

Endnotes

1. *Willingham v. State*, 897 S.W.2d 351, 354 (1995).
2. Ibid.
3. Grann, D. (2009, September 7). "Trial by Fire." *The New Yorker*.
4. Ibid.

5. The Innocence Project. (2011). "Cameron Todd Willingham: Wrongfully Convicted and Executed in Texas." Retrieved from http://www.innocenceproject.org/Content/Cameron_Todd_Willingham_Wrongfully_Convicted_and_Executed_in_Texas.php#summary

6. Texas Forensic Science Commission. (2011, April 15). *Report of the Texas Forensic Science Commission: Willingham/Willis Investigation.*

7. Packer, H. L. (1968). *The Limits of the Criminal Sanction.* Stanford, CA: Stanford University Press.

8. Ibid.

9. Ibid.

10. Ibid.

11. Ibid.

12. Ibid.

13. *Whren v. United States,* 517 U.S. 806, 808-09 (1996).

14. Ibid.

15. Department of Justice, Bureau of Justice Statistics. (2003). "Violent Crime Rates Have Declined since 1994, Reaching the Lowest Level Ever Recorded in 2003."

16. Ibid.

17. Ibid.

18. Department of Justice, Bureau of Justice Statistics. As cited by the Sentencing Project (2004, June 28). Retrieved from http://www.sentencingproject.org/pdfs/1035.pdf

19. *Defending Justice: An Activist Resource Kit: Trends in the Criminal Justice System.*

20. *The Prison Policy Initiative.* Portland, OR: Bridgetown Printing, 12.

21. *Defending Justice: An Activist Resource Kit: Factsheet.*

22. Beyer, G. W., & Redden, K. R. (2001). *Modern Dictionary for the Legal Profession* (3rd ed.). Buffalo, NY: W.S. Hein.

23. Ibid.

24. Beccaria, C. (1764). *On Crime and Punishment.*

25. U.S. Marshals Service. (n.d.). *Historical Timeline.* Retrieved from http://www.usmarshals.gov/history/timeline.html

26. City of Boston. (2011). *A Brief History of the B.P.D.* Retrieved from http://www.cityofboston.gov/police/about/history.asp

27. United States Department of Justice. (n.d.). *Department of Justice Agencies.* Retrieved from http://www.justice.gov/agencies/index-org.html

28. United States, Wickersham Commission, Chafee, Z., Polak, W. H., & Stern, C. S. (1931). *Report on Lawlessness in Law Enforcement.* Washington, DC: U.S. Government Printing Office.

29. Johnson, L. B. (1965, March 8). "102—Special Message to the Congress on Law Enforcement and the Administration of Justice." *The American Presidency Project.* Retrieved from http://www.presidency.ucsb.edu/ws/index.php?pid=26800#axzz1QsIMq0qt

30. The Omnibus Safe Streets and Criminal Control Act of 1968, Pub. L. No. 90-351 (1968).

31. *Miranda v. Arizona,* 384 U.S. 436 (1966).

32. *Mapp v. Ohio,* 367 U.S. 643 (1961).

33. Ibid.

34. *Gideon v. Wainwright,* 372 U.S. 335 (1963).

35. United States Department of Justice, Bureau of Justice Statistics. (2011). *Employment and Expenditure.* Retrieved from http://bjs.ojp.usdoj.gov/index.cfm?ty=tp&tid=5

36. United States Department of Justice, Bureau of Justice Statistics. (2011). *Key Facts at a Glance.* Retrieved from http://bjs.ojp.usdoj.gov/content/glance/tables/corr2tab.cfm

37. West, H. (2010). *Prison Inmates at Midyear 2009—Statistical Tables* (NCJ 230113). Retrieved from http://bjs.ojp.usdoj.gov/index.cfm?ty=pbdetail&iid=2200

38. Ibid.

39. "Justice Expenditure and Employment in the United States." (2001), 1–2.

40. Ibid., 1.

41. Ibid., 1–2.

42. Thomas, C. W., Cage, R. J., & Foster, S. C. (1976). "Public Opinion on Criminal Law and Legal Sanctions—An Examination of Two Conceptual Models." *Journal of Criminal Law and Criminology,* 67(1).

43. Durkheim, E. (1893). *The Division of Labor in Society.* New York, NY: The Free Press.

44. Thomas et al., 1976.

45. Ibid.

46. *Roe v. Wade,* 410 U.S. 113 (1973).

47. "Republicans More Unified Than Democrats on Abortion." (2011, June 6). *Gallup Poll.*

48. United States Courts. (n.d.). *Jury Service.* Retrieved from http://www.uscourts.gov/FederalCourts/JuryService.aspx

49. *Black's Law Dictionary.*

50. Ibid.

51. Sandefur, T. (2003, Fall). "In Defense of Plea Bargaining." *Regulation*, 28–31.

52. Ibid., 28.

53. Durose, M. R., & Langan, P. A. (2003). *Felony Sentences in State Courts 2000* (NCJ 198821). Retrieved from http://bjs.ojp.usdoj.gov/index.cfm?ty=pbdetail&iid=913

54. United States Courts. (n.d.). *Criminal Cases.* Retrieved from http://www.uscourts.gov/FederalCourts/Understanding theFederalCourts/HowCourtsWork/CriminalCases.aspx

55. Ibid.

56. Ibid.

57. Eisenstein, J., & Jacob, H. (1970). *Felony Justice: An Organizational Analysis of Criminal Courts.* Boston, MA: Little, Brown.

58. Friedman, L. M., & Percival, R. V. (1981). *The Roots of Justice.* Chapel Hill, NC: University of North Carolina Press.

59. Gottfredson, M. R., & Gottfredson, D. M. (1988). *Decision Making in Criminal Justice.* New York, NY: Plenum.

60. Walker, S. (2001). *Sense and Nonsense about Crime and Drugs.* Belmont, CA: Wadsworth.

61. United States Department of Justice. (2009). *2009 National Gang Threat Assessment*, 5.

62. Retrieved from http://webappa.cdc.gov/cgi-bin/broker.exe

63. United States Department of Justice, Bureau of Justice Statistics. (n.d.). *Percent of Homicides Involving Guns by Circumstance, 1976–2005.* Retrieved from http://bjs.ojp.usdoj.gov/content/homicide/d_circumgun.cfm

64. Allen, S. (2011, July 9). "The New ROE: Return on Ethics." *Forbes Magazine.* Retrieved from http://www.forbes.com/2009/07/21/business-culture-corporate-citizenship-leadership-ethics.html

65. Amnesty International. *Troy Davis.* Retrieved from http://www.amnestyusa.org/our-work/cases/usa-troy-davis

66. Curry, C., & James, M. S. (2011, September 21). "Troy Davis Executed After Stay Denied by Supreme Court." *ABC News.*

67. Ibid.

68. Pilkington, E. (2011, September 21). "Troy Davis: 10 Reasons Why He Should Not Be Executed." *The Guardian.* Retrieved from http://www.guardian.co.uk/world/2011/sep/21/troy-davis-10-reasons

2

Criminal Behavior

KEY TERMS

Atavistic man, Biological theories, Chicago School, Classical school, Compurgation, Conflict theory, Crime index, Criminal behavior, Dark figure of crime, Deterrence theory, Developmental pathways, Deviance, Differential association theory, Feminist theories, General deterrence, General strain theory, General theory of crime, Integrated theories, Labeling theory, Left realism, Life course theories, National Incident-Based Reporting System (NIBRS), National Crime Victimization Survey (NCVS), Peacemaking criminology, Personality theories, Positivist school, Pre-classical school, Reintegrative shaming, Routine activities theory, Self-report survey, Social control theory, Social disorganization theory, Specific deterrence, Strain theory, Trial by battle, Trial by ordeal, Uniform Crime Reports (UCR)

CHAPTER OBJECTIVES

1. Differentiate between the concepts of criminal behavior and deviance.
2. Report how much crime there is in the United States and crime trends.
3. Define and discuss the various methods of gathering crime data.
4. Demonstrate an understanding of the causes of crime.
5. Analyze the various theoretical perspectives explaining the causes of crime and their application to behaviors.

Case Study: Gang Violence

Luis Sanchez was born in Chelsea, Massachusetts, and exposed to the perils and temptations of a gang lifestyle at an early age. His mother had systematically kicked out his older siblings as teenagers, and Sanchez too was nearly legally disowned by his mother, but at age 13 he was considered too young by the court. After being mugged for the first time, Sanchez decided he needed a different means of protection due to his lack of family support. He soon joined a gang and became involved in a variety of criminal activities, including selling illegal drugs such as cocaine and marijuana. Sanchez, fortunately, was able to escape his criminal lifestyle by joining a youth program in Boston in 2004, breaking his gang connections, and becoming a student at Boston College.[1]

Sanchez's case is not at all uncommon: many other young people are in similar situations. Sadly, in many cases, these individuals are unable to escape a life of crime and deviance as Sanchez did. A perennial concern for the criminal justice system in the United States is gang-related crime and violence. Much of the worry consists of trying to determine precisely what events, factors, environment, and inherited traits combine to produce a gang member inclined to commit crime.

Understanding the causes of crime is instrumental in our ability not only to predict future offending, but also to determine the appropriate responses to the crime and the offender. The example of Luis Sanchez illustrates that the causes of crime may be the product of multiple underlying factors (poverty, gang allegiance, drugs, personal quarrels, alcohol). Why do some people in Sanchez's situation join gangs while others do not? This chapter will review the extent to which crime occurs and the various theoretical propositions used to explain the behavior.

What Is Criminal Behavior?

The concept of crime and its subsequent causes has been debated for centuries. Many theories about the causes and reasons for criminal behavior have been presented. These include the classical perspective, in which offenders are considered to be free will thinkers, and the positivist perspective that looks to the individual or their environment for causes or influences toward crime. Despite these categorical explanations for crime, debate still exists among practitioners, lawmakers, criminologists, and the general public as to what constitutes criminal behavior. More specifically, within this context and framework, one must differentiate between deviance and criminal activity.

The concept of **deviance** is usually defined as behaviors considered outside of or inconsistent with normal behavior for that community or group.[2] Therefore, deviance may differ depending on where you live and the accepted norms, ethics, and morals of the community. Broadly speaking, deviance can be understood from either a positivist or a constructionist point of view. Positivism basically asserts that things have distinct, real "essences," and therefore deviant behavior is wrong because it is inconsistent with what is objectively right. In the context of positivist criminology, deviance is thought to be caused by internal and external factors beyond the criminal's control.[3] Related to positivism is rational choice theory, which posits that criminals make a cost/benefit analysis to determine whether or not to commit crime.[4] Constructionist interpretations of deviance believe that categories of right and wrong, and therefore deviance from them, are social constructs that depend greatly on the perspective of the individual observer.[5] In sociology, deviance refers to actions (or behaviors) that contravene either social norms or written legal codes.

Criminal behavior, appropriately, is defined by legislation, statutes, and codes. There are two classifications of these behaviors. The first classification, *mala in se* crimes, covers acts that are deemed illegal because they so violate the norms and moral code of society that they are wrong in and of themselves. Such offenses—murder, for example—are almost universally prohibited. The other classification is behaviors that are deemed illegal not so much due to inherent immorality, but because they are defined as such by those living within that particular society. Essentially, they are crimes because society has enacted laws and statutes that say they are crimes. These are known as *mala prohibitum* crimes. Such crimes are likely to vary from culture to culture (e.g., sex crimes, gambling restrictions, drug and alcohol laws, and so forth).

These two definitions are both incorporated into a legal system based on an understanding of crime that is, to some extent, socially constructed. To be sure, crime can be understood as a codification of deviance: violating social norms, taboos, and laws is often legally criminal. Crime has been succinctly described by Morrison (2006) as "an act or omission that is defined by the validly passed laws of the nation state in which it occurred so that punishment should follow from the behavior."[6] It is within this framework and context that the criminal justice system operates and functions. Therefore, what constitutes criminal behavior and the appropriate punishments ascribed to those violations of law may change over time.

> **Deviance**
> Behaviors considered outside of or inconsistent with normal behavior for a community or group.

> **Criminal behavior**
> Behavior defined by legislation, statutes, and codes.

Mala in se crimes, such as robbery, are almost universally prohibited.

Measuring Crime
To understand how much crime there is in the United States, it is important to assess not only the different types of measures that

are used but their origins, strengths, and weaknesses. The most frequently used means of data collection are the Uniform Crime Reports (UCR), the National Incident-Based Reporting System (NIBRS), the National Crime Victimization Survey (NCVS), and self-report surveys.

Uniform Crime Reports (UCR)

Prior to 1930, no centralized program for gathering crime statistics existed. Data that were collected were deemed unreliable because of legislative differences in criminal codes and enforcement practices. Because of the diversity of techniques and procedures, it was nearly impossible to compare crime data in any meaningful way between jurisdictions, let alone states. Law enforcement officers and legislators needed a better way to assemble data to assist with allocation of resources and manpower. This desire to improve data collection efforts was best demonstrated in 1927 by the International Association of Chiefs of Police (IACP). The IACP formed the Committee on Uniform Crime Records to assess the possibility of developing a standardized, centrally located mechanism for gathering crime statistics.[7] Most important was the creation of standardized definitions of crime. These efforts resulted in the 1929 publication of the first standardized collection of statistics on crimes reported to the police and crimes cleared by arrest.

Beginning in 1930, this tool, known as the **Uniform Crime Reports (UCR)**, was officially implemented on a large-scale basis, with law enforcement agencies volunteering for participation in data collection and reporting to the FBI. The primary purpose of the UCR was to provide uniform definitions for gathering crime data so that results could be compared by month, year, state, and jurisdiction. Since its inception, the UCR has added information on law enforcement officers killed and assaulted on duty as well as hate crime statistics.[8] Today the UCR, which is still a voluntary program, includes approximately 17,000 reporting law enforcement agencies nationally, representing more than 97% of the entire U.S. population.

UCR data are divided into two categories: Part I index offenses and Part II offenses. The Part I **Crime Index** includes a total of eight offenses divided into a violent crime index and a property crime index. Part II covers the less serious offenses. (See Figure 2.1 for an overview of the included index offenses.)

In order for an offense to be included in the UCR,[9] it must follow the counting rule, which states that only the most serious offense committed in a single incident is included in the UCR data although the offender may be charged with more crimes. Additionally, the UCR follows what is known as the hierarchy rule. Offenses are placed in the specific order in which they are supposed to be recorded, beginning with criminal homicide and ranging through runaways in the Part II Offense category. The UCR further distinguishes between time and place. If a criminal event that occurs is a continuation of another event, then the UCR counts those as one single incident. If the criminal events are related but not a single incident, then law enforcement officers must record those as separate incidents.

Data are reported in one of three ways: (1) crimes reported to the police (reported in raw numbers), which includes any offenses that have been reported

Uniform Crime Reports (UCR)
An official data-reporting tool created in 1930 to provide uniform definitions for crime data so that results could be compared by month, year, state, and jurisdiction.

Crime index
An index reported by the Uniform Crime Reports. Crimes are divided into Part I and Part II index offenses. The Part I index includes a total of eight offenses divided by violent crime index and the property crime index. The Part II index includes a total of 21 categories of crimes.

FIGURE**2.1** UCR Offenses

Part I Offenses

Part I offense classifications include:

Violent Offenses

Murder

The willful (non-negligent) killing of one human being by another.

Forcible Rape

The carnal knowledge of a female forcibly and against her will. Attempts or assaults to commit rape by force or threat of force are also included; however, statutory rape (without force) and other sex offenses are excluded.

Robbery

The taking or attempting to take anything of value from the care, custody, or control of a person or persons by force or threat of force or violence and/or by putting the victim in fear.

Aggravated Assault

Unlawful attack by one person upon another for the purpose of inflicting severe or aggravated bodily injury.

Property Offenses

Burglary

The unlawful entry of a structure to commit a felony or theft.

Larceny-Theft

The unlawful taking, carrying, leading, or riding away of property from the possession or constructive possession of another.

Motor Vehicle Theft

The theft or attempted theft of a motor vehicle. In the UCR Program, a motor vehicle is a self-propelled vehicle that runs on land surfaces and not on rails.

Arson

Any willful or malicious burning or attempting to burn, with or without intent to defraud, a dwelling house, public building, motor vehicle or aircraft, personal property of another, etc.

Information from FBI: http://www2.fbi.gov/ucr/cius2009/index.html

Part II Offenses

Part II offenses encompass all other reportable classifications outside those defined as Part I. Law enforcement agencies report to the FBI only arrest data involving the Part II crimes:

1. Other Assaults
2. Forgery and Counterfeiting
3. Fraud
4. Embezzlement
5. Stolen Property: Buying, Receiving, Possessing
6. Vandalism
7. Weapons: Carrying, Possessing, etc.
8. Prostitution and Commercialized Vice
9. Sex Offenses
10. Drug Abuse Violations
11. Gambling
12. Offenses Against the Family and Children
13. Driving Under the Influence
14. Liquor Laws
15. Drunkenness
16. Disorderly Conduct
17. Vagrancy
18. All Other Offenses
19. Suspicion
20. Curfew and Loitering Laws—(Persons under 18)
21. Runaways—(Persons under 18)

From Uniform Crime Reporting Program Staff. (2004). *Uniform Crime Reporting Handbook*. Clarksburg, WV: Federal Bureau of Investigation, p. 8.

to the police and have been verified as possible crimes by law enforcement; (2) rates per 100,000 residents, calculated as Total Number of Crimes Reported ÷ Total U.S. Population × 100,000 = Rate per 100,000 Residents; and (3) rate of crime over time or trends. Finally, crimes cleared by arrest are included in the final report. These data include the number of reported offenses where either an arrest was made or at least one person was charged in the incident.[10] Data are further aggregated by community type. These divisions include Standard Statistical Metropolitan Areas (SMSAs); other cities, most of which are not incorporated; and rural counties.[11] Although the data do not allow for individual comparisons by the victim or specific characteristics of crimes, they do allow for comparisons by these types of jurisdictions. Despite every effort to account for all criminal offending, there still exist a number of offenses that go unreported to the police. This category of crime is known as the **dark figure of crime**.

Dark figure of crime
Offenses that go unreported to the police.

Although the UCR does provide a mechanism for comparison between jurisdictions and states, there still are some data that are excluded from these efforts. For example, demographic characteristics of the offender are excluded from crimes reported to the police and in most instances with crimes cleared by arrest. The reason for this exclusion is because the witnesses may not be able to accurately account for the offender characteristics or data may not be available in any consistent manner even when crimes are cleared by arrest. Second, law enforcement officers are not required to collect and submit data on crime victims. Third, because data are collected on an aggregate level, individual cases are not followed throughout the system. Therefore, it is impossible to determine whether the offenders were charged in a particular event and/or whether conviction was obtained; UCR data only include whether an arrest has been made or a confirmed suspect has been identified. Finally, the UCR excludes some offense categories, such as the federal offense of kidnapping, that are deemed important. This limits the ability to compare and track data over time.[12]

There are a variety of factors that affect the reporting of crimes from both a law enforcement and an individual perspective. For example, when assessing criminal events, responses to crime by law enforcement are often in reaction to citizen complaints as opposed to the officer witnessing the event themselves. Likewise, many non-serious crimes go unreported. Therefore, inclusion of the most serious criminal offenses makes sense, given the ability to compare across jurisdiction and offense categories. This also includes the difficulty with the type of crime, even if serious. For example, the crime of rape, although serious by nature, often goes unreported because of the sensitive nature of the event, embarrassment, and fear of reprisal.

Because most crime comes to the attention of law enforcement through the efforts of the victims or witnesses, it is important to consider why a victim may not report a criminal event. Research has suggested that many victims report they believe nothing can be done. Lack of faith in the system to either detect or prosecute may preclude many of them from going through the "hassle" of reporting the event. Some victims report they believe their victimization is not important enough to occupy the law enforcement community's time and they do not want to bother the police with such trivial matters. Other victims report that the incident is a personal or private matter that should be handled within the family or between friends, while others fear reprisal. In some cases, the relationship between the victim and offender is such that the victim does not want harm to come to the offender. Crimes that occur between strangers are most likely to be reported. Finally, victims indicate that they report their victimization to others such as family members or social services for assistance with the event.[13]

Law enforcement officials report that there are a variety of factors that affect whether an offense is recorded. Influences such as funding decisions may dictate whether an agency wishes to participate in the UCR at all. Most federal and state funding initiatives require that law enforcement participate in either the UCR or NIBRS (see the next section for a more detailed explanation of NIBRS). While in theory the UCR is a voluntary program, these funding requirements all but force an agency to participate.

Community desires or needs will also influence whether an agency processes a crime officially or unofficially, particularly for less serious offenses. Communities that have seen an increase in certain types of offense categories, i.e., drug usage, may choose to "crack down" on these offenses and formally prosecute violators. Communities may also face political pressures to reduce crime.

Other extralegal factors may play a role, such as the sex, age, and race of the offender and whether the dispatcher names the offense when notifying law enforcement officers.[14]

One of the key benefits of participating in the UCR program is the ability to examine crime trends within a single jurisdiction. These data may be particularly important to a chamber of commerce or tourism bureau that uses the information to market a community.[15] Data may also be used to examine homicide trends across jurisdictions. These trend data can be very beneficial in determining or making staffing decisions or informing legislators to craft new anti-crime policies.[16] Further data may be used to inform the public about crime trends and to encourage appropriate support and response to crime prevention techniques. Finally, researchers use UCR data to test theories and to identify causes of crime.[17]

National Incident-Based Reporting System (NIBRS)

Because of changes in the nature and complexity of crime since the UCR's inception, the law enforcement community during the 1970s began studying the benefits and limitations of the UCR program. The result of this study was the creation of the National Incident-Based Reporting System (NIBRS). The goal of the NIBRS program was to enhance the quantity and quality of the information provided and to enhance the methodology for collecting, analyzing, and publishing crime data.[18] As of 2007, 6,444 law enforcement agencies participated in the NIBRS system.[19] Although participation is more limited than the UCR reporting program, many state and local agencies are in various stages of transitioning from the UCR to NIBRS. One impediment to this transition is the limited resources available for technology upgrades and training. Data for the NIBRS are not currently reported as separate categories. Instead they are incorporated into the UCR reports and included in the annual *Crime in the United States* publication.

National Incident-Based Reporting System (NIBRS)
A national crime data collection program created and implemented during the 1980s in an effort to enhance the methodology for collecting, analyzing, and publishing crime data.

There are a significant number of key differences between the UCR and the NIBRS systems. The NIBRS system includes an expanded offense reporting tool.[20] The program includes a total of 22 offense categories made up of 46 crimes. An additional 11 offenses are included in a group B category (see Figure 2.2 for a list of the offenses in Groups A and B). This expanded list of NIBRS offenses does not follow a hierarchy rule. The NIBRS is an incident-based system.[21] Information is collected on all individual incidents and arrests. Prescribed data allow for the researcher to collect information on each individual offense such as the type, age, sex, race, ethnicity, and residence status of the victim as well as the type of offense and injury sustained. The same type of information is included on the offender, along with the elements of the crime.

The NIBRS uses new and revised definitions from the UCR, such as the definition of rape. The NIBRS also includes new definitions of offense categories that are not represented by the UCR. The NIBRS system provides an opportunity for more specificity in the criminal acts. This includes the ability to compare offenses by individual characteristics as well as business crimes, residency status, weapons used, injuries incurred, etc. The NIBRS system includes a category representing crimes against society, which are *mala prohibitum* categories of crime such as drug offenses, gambling, prostitution, etc. Unlike the UCR, which only records the distinction between attempted and completed crimes in cases of forcible rape and murder, the NIBRS system distinguishes between attempted and completed for each offense category.

In addition, the NIBRS gives the ability to conduct correlations between the offense categories, property, victims, offenders, and arrestees. These linkages are both explicit and implicit. There are implied linkages between the victim and the offender within the offense category and explicit linkages to the crimes committed against the victim. The NIBRS includes the victim-offender relationship. Unlike the UCR, which only records this information for homi-

Both the UCR and NIBRS include circumstantial information on homicides.

cides, the NIBRS reporting system records victim-offender relationships for all crimes against persons and robbery.

Another key difference between the two systems is that the NIBRS reports more of the circumstances surrounding the event. In the UCR, information about the circumstances of the event is only included for homicides. NIBRS has expanded this system to include circumstantial information on assaults as well as homicides.

The NIBRS incorporates the hotel rule in a different way. For the UCR, the general hotel rule relates to the number of dwellings and how burglaries are reported. If there are a number of burglaries in one complex and they are likely to be reported by the manager, then they are counted as one offense. With the NIBRS, these data are expanded to include rental storage units and to include the number of rooms, units, or storage compartments that were victimized.

Lastly, the NIBRS and UCR report data to the FBI in different ways. For the UCR program, local agencies are permitted to use manual forms to submit data. State agencies must record their data on magnetic tapes. For the NIBRS system, all reporting agencies must record their data on magnetic strips.[22]

National Crime Victimization Survey (NCVS)

Victimization surveys give researchers and policymakers the opportunity to delve further into a criminal incident from the perspective of the victim. Although a variety of

FIGURE2.2 National Incident-Based Reporting System (NIBRS) Offense Categories

Group A Offense Categories:	Group B Offense Categories:
1. Arson	1. Bad Checks
2. Assault Offenses	2. Curfew/Loitering/Vagrancy Violations
3. Bribery	3. Disorderly Conduct
4. Burglary/Breaking & Entering	4. Driving Under the Influence
5. Counterfeiting/Forgery	5. Drunkenness
6. Destruction/Damage/Vandalism	6. Family Offenses, Nonviolent
7. Drug/Narcotic Offenses	7. Liquor Law Violations
8. Embezzlement	8. Peeping Tom
9. Extortion/Blackmail	9. Runaway
10. Fraud Offenses	10. Trespass of Real Property
11. Gambling Offenses	11. All Other Offenses
12. Homicide Offenses	
13. Kidnapping/Abduction	
14. Larceny/Theft Offenses	
15. Motor Vehicle Theft	
16. Pornography/Obscene Material	
17. Prostitution Offenses	
18. Robbery	
19. Sex Offenses, Forcible	
20. Sex Offenses, Non Forcible	
21. Stolen Property Offenses	
22. Weapon Law Violations	

For more information on NIBRS see *National Incident Based Reporting System, Volume 1: Data Collection Guidelines* (2000) at http://www.fbi.gov/about-us/cjis/ucr/nibrs/nibrs_dcguide.pdf (p. 11)

National Crime Victimization Survey (NCVS)

A survey conducted on households in the United States that includes detailed descriptions of criminal events, including the victim, potential precipitation, consequences of the event, and the offender.

different victimization surveys have been developed, the most widely used ongoing effort is known as the **National Crime Victimization Survey (NCVS)**. First administered in 1973 and originally known as the National Crime Survey (NCS), the NCVS is conducted on households in the United States by the U.S. Census Bureau on behalf of the Bureau of Justice Statistics. The NCVS may be used to accomplish a variety of different goals from a crime prevention perspective. Most importantly, it is used to tap into the dark figure of crime, enhance the ability to compare victimizations by types of areas and over time, provide uniform definitions of crime, and include detailed descriptions of the criminal event, including the victim, potential precipitation, consequences of the event, and offender.[23] Approximately 76,000 households representing approximately 136,000 individuals are chosen for the study, based on a random probability design. Once addresses are selected, residents living in the household are interviewed every six months for a maximum of three years, at which time a new address is chosen.[24]

The key to the NCVS is that the study population is the household as opposed to the individuals. Should the individuals move, the address/house will remain in the study for a maximum of three years. Each member of the household age 14 and older is interviewed directly and asked to report the frequency and details of individual victimization(s), including characteristics of the victims and crimes both reported and not reported to law enforcement. Children ages 12 and 13, or individuals who are older and physically unable to participate, are interviewed via a proxy. The proxy also reports household victimizations.[25]

There are two types of counts that are collected from the NCVS: incidents of crime and victimizations. Incidents of crime correspond with the UCR categories, while victimizations include the number of victimizations the individual experiences[26]; the relationship between the offender and the victim; the month, date, and location; self-protective actions; losses incurred; the consequences of victimization; whether the offense is reported and why or why not; the presence of weapons, drugs, and alcohol; and the demographic information of both the victim and the offender.[27]

The NCVS records data on property victimizations, such as burglary, as well as personal victimizations.

The advantages of the NCVS include the ability to record data on the individual level for personal crimes and the household level for household crimes.[28] Because the NCVS data are only recorded for a sample of households, not all victimizations are included in the data set or the data collection instrument. Likewise, not all cities are represented in the sample; therefore, you cannot estimate crime rates for most of the United States, nor can you estimate crimes for most cities.

As with any data collection effort, there are various problems associated with the NCVS. First, one of the most common problems associated with any form of interview data collection effort is the interviewer effect. There is always the potential for the interviewee to become bored or resistant to the interview process. There is also a possibility that the interviewer has very little to give the participant in terms of rewards for participating in the study. One of the ways to verify the information provided in the study is to conduct reverse records checks for those offenses that were reported to the police.

A second problem associated with the NCVS is telescoping.[29] Telescoping refers to remembering events as occurring more recently (forward telescoping) or further in the past (backward telescoping) than when they actually occurred. Time bounding the survey instruments is one way to minimize this shortcoming of the data collection effort.

Household movement, also known as mover-stayer, is a third problem with the NCVS. Because the NCVS tracks household crime, if the residents at the current address move away, the study does not follow them. Instead, the new residents will be included in the study. This is of particular concern for time bounding as well as differences in lifestyle. Time bounding is an issue because the survey is ongoing and the first interview with the new residents will not be time bounded, so telescoping is a real concern. Likewise, lifestyle differences may skew data for increases or decreases in reported victimization. For example, should the original study group be elderly, the research demonstrates that these individuals are among the least likely to be victimized, particularly by personal crimes. Should a young college-age couple with no children move into the residence, because of their lifestyle difference (out later, access to entertainment, etc.), they are more likely to be victimized than the previous residents.

A fourth problem is sampling error. Although the sample includes 76,000 households in the United States, these households may not represent all demographics and regions, such as rural areas. To account for differences, researchers must use very high confidence intervals (meaning the range for margin of error is quite large) to obtain significance.

A final problem arises with the proxy interviews themselves or response bias. For example, if there is only one person over the age of 14 in a household, that person is responsible for reporting all crime committed within the household. If the representative for the household is the perpetrator, such as in domestic offenses, these crimes are not likely to be reported, thus resulting in response bias.

Career Connections: Survey Researcher

Survey researchers, along with market researchers, are primarily responsible for finding out what people think. In general, they collect statistical data about people and their opinions; as a result, they spend the balance of their time designing and implementing surveys. This requires precision, diligence, and attention to detail, since data analysis is an important part of their job. Additionally, they must be able to work well as part of a research team, and be able to communicate effectively when reporting their findings.[30]

Survey researchers come from diverse backgrounds; there is no specific academic or professional path they must travel. Typically, researchers will have at minimum a bachelor's degree in order to enter the field. Advancement or a more technical position might necessitate a master's degree or doctorate.[31] A background in the social sciences is common, as well as some exposure to business, psychology, marketing, and sociology. Due to the central role of statistical data gathering and analysis in their work, survey researchers must possess a strong background in quantitative analysis. Math and science courses, with sampling theory and survey design as part of the curriculum, will be helpful in acquiring the necessary analytical and mathematical skills, especially in statistics and data analysis.

Survey researchers use questionnaires and surveys to collect information about people, including their beliefs, behaviors, thoughts, and personal data. They should therefore be adept at interacting with people, interviewing, and writing reports to present and summarize their findings.[32] Students interested in careers as survey researchers should investigate the possibility of an internship with a consulting firm, nonprofit organization, or government agency to gain practical experience with conducting surveys and gathering data.

There are many employment opportunities for survey researchers in both the government and the private sector. Survey researchers can find work as consultants for management, scientific, and technical companies. They work in market research, public opinion polling, and data gathering. Many work in academia, at colleges or universities.[33] Given the pace of globalization and the demographic shift in the U.S. toward a more diverse population, it is vitally important to have accurate information on foreign populations and how they affect the 21st-century economy. According to the Bureau of Labor Statistics, employment in survey (and market) research is likely to grow 28% from 2008 to 2018, making its growth far bigger than most other fields.[34]

↑ Professional survey researcher.

Self-Report Measures   Another method of collecting data is the self-report survey. There is no one standard method for collecting data using the self-report method. However, this technique was developed and began being used more frequently during the 1950s. Probably the most frequently recognized historical study was conducted by Short and Nye (1957, 1958) and the National Youth Survey. More recently, the Office of Juvenile Justice and Delinquency Prevention (OJJDP) has supported a multi-site, multi-year study to follow youth throughout their childhood and into adulthood in three specific locations: Denver, Colorado; Rochester, New York; and Pittsburgh, Pennsylvania.[35] Another study funded by OJJDP in Maricopa County, Arizona, has explored possible ways to stop youth offending.[36] Results from these recent studies have been used to inform policy and establish best practices in the juvenile justice field.

As stated, there is no one standardized technique for collecting or counting self-report data. Typically, convenience samples are drawn from school-aged populations. These populations are either given a survey instrument or are interviewed to determine the prevalence and incidence of delinquent or criminal offending. *Prevalence* refers to one or more persons reporting the same offense or behavior during the reference period, while *incidence* refers to the reporting of one delinquent or criminal behavior during the reference period.[37] Advantages of using a self-report survey include tapping into the dark figure of crime, collecting more detailed information on the participants/delinquents, and collecting information on the causes or motivations behind the offending.

Although self-report studies provide another tool for tapping into offenses that are not known to the police, there are still a number of weaknesses that must be taken into consideration when using self-report studies or measures. First, because the majority of self-report studies include a convenience sample of school-aged youth, it is possible that these data do not reflect the larger community and cannot be generalized to all youth. Second, there exists the possibility for overreporting or underreporting delinquent or criminal activity. One way to validate the responses is to include a random records check; this technique gives researchers an opportunity to verify the accuracy of results, or at least establish confidence intervals to draw conclusions. Third, many self-report studies

Self-report survey
A data collection effort asking participants to report the number of criminal offenses or activities they have committed.

Ethics and Professionalism: Honest Reporting

You are a police chief in a large U.S. city. One of the biggest problems in your city is an increase in the occurrence of hate crimes. Recently, the Attorney General of the United States has called for more comprehensive and accurate reporting of hate crimes. You are especially afraid of sensationalist coverage by the mainstream media; specifically, you worry that this will lead to negative perceptions of your department that will, in effect, penalize you. It may also lead to charges of departmental incompetence or insensitivity. For example, if an individual reports the murder of a black man in an Asian community, your desk officer may not have thought to investigate whether the murder was racially motivated.[38] Should you report your embarrassing statistics in their entirety? Or should you not report the hate-driven motivation of such crimes?

have been criticized for low response rates and usability of returned surveys. Fourth, there is some debate about which type of methodology should be used to collect data (e.g., surveys versus interviews). This is most important when you are asking participants to report their delinquent or criminal behaviors. For participants, this may be a concern when they have actually violated the law and fear that researchers will report their behavior. From a research standpoint, an ethical dilemma may arise between protecting the confidentiality of the participants and having an implied and sometimes stated duty to report criminal behavior. One final weakness of self-report studies is that because there is no one single technique, it is nearly impossible to compare results across studies.

Crime Statistics

Given the various data collection efforts, it is important to understand the various crime trends from both officially reported offense data and victimization data. This section of the chapter reviews the crime data recorded in the Uniform Crime Reports (UCR) and the National Crime Victimization Survey (NCVS).

According to the UCR, in 2009, there were more than 10.6 million Part I index offenses committed. Of those, approximately 88% were property offenses while 12% were violent offenses. Larceny-theft accounted for 67.1% of all property offenses, while aggravated assault accounted for 61.2% of all violent crime.

More than 13.6 million arrests were made in 2009. Drug abuse violations accounted for the largest number of arrests while driving under the influence and larceny-theft followed. The five-year property crime trends (see Figure 2.3)

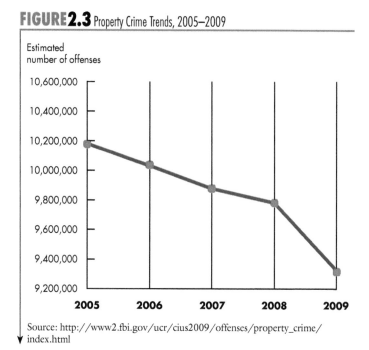

FIGURE 2.3 Property Crime Trends, 2005–2009

Source: http://www2.fbi.gov/ucr/cius2009/offenses/property_crime/index.html

FIGURE2.4 Violent Crime Trends, 2005–2009

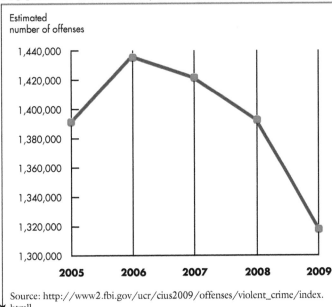

Source: http://www2.fbi.gov/ucr/cius2009/offenses/violent_crime/index.
htmll

revealed an 8.4% decrease, while violent offenses (see Figure 2.4) declined 5.2% during that same time period and 7.5% during a 10-year time period. Males accounted for nearly 75% of all persons arrested, while "69.1 percent of all persons arrested were white, 28.3 percent were black, and the remaining 2.6 percent were of other races."[39]

According to the NCVS, there were approximately 20 million violent and property victimizations in the United States in 2009.[40] The reported victimizations included an estimated total of 4.3 million violent victimizations and 15.6 million property crimes. Similar to the UCR data, the NCVS indicated an 11.2% decrease in violent crimes and a 7.7% decrease in property offenses between 2008 and 2009 (see Figure 2.5 for criminal victimization trends).

Critical Thinking   How might data collected from the UCR and NCVS shape policy?

FIGURE 2.5 Criminal Victimization

Type of crime	Number of victimizations		Rates[a]		Percent change
	2008	2009	2008	2009	2008–2009[b]
All crimes	21,312,400	20,057,180	~	~	
Violent crime[c]	4,856,510	4,343,450	19.3	17.1	–11.2%*
Serious violent crime[d]	1,595,590	1,483,040	6.3	5.8	–7.7%
Rape/sexual assault[e]	203,830	125,910	0.8	0.5	–38.7**
Robbery	551,830	533,790	2.2	2.1	–4.0
Assault	4,100,850	3,683,750	16.3	14.5	–10.8*
Aggravated	839,940	823,340	3.3	3.2	–2.7
Simple	3,260,920	2,860,410	12.9	11.3	–12.9*
Personal theft[f]	136,710	133,210	0.5	0.5	–3.3%
Property crime	16,319,180	15,580,510	134.7	127.4	–5.5%*
Household burglary	3,188,620	3,134,920	26.3	25.6	–2.6
Motor vehicle theft	795,160	735,770	6.6	6.0	–8.4
Theft	12,335,400	11,709,830	101.8	95.7	–6.0*

Note: Detail may not sum to total because of rounding. Total population age 12 or older was 252,242,520 in 2008 and 254,105,610 in 2009. Total number of households was 121,141,060 in 2008 and 122,327,660 in 2009.

~Not applicable.

*Difference is significant at the 95%-confidence level. Differences are described as higher, lower, or different in text.

**Difference is significant at the 90%-confidence level. Differences are described as somewhat, slightly. marginally, or some other indication in text.

[a]Victimization rates are per 1,000 persons age 12 or older per 1,000 households.

[b]Percent change calculated based on unrounded estimates.

[c]Excludes murder because the NCVS is based on interviews with victims and therefore cannot measure murder.

[d]Includes rape/sexual assault, robbery, and aggravated assault.

[e]See *Methodology* for discussion on changes in the rate of rape/sexual assault between 2008 and 2009.

[f]Includes pocket picking, completed purse snatching, and attempted purse snatching.

Source: Truman, J. L. & Rand, M. R. (2010). *Criminal victimization, 2009. National Crime Victimization Survey* (NCJ 231327). Washington, DC: U.S. Department of Justice, Bureau of Justice Statistics.

Drop in Crime Rates The data cited above demonstrate that there has been a general drop in the overall crime rate in recent years. This is unusual at first glance, as logically a poor economy would seem to correlate with an increase in crime, but the recent statistics are consistent with the overall trend toward a decrease in crime since the 1990s.[41] Explaining this drop in crime rates is a challenge, with no clear consensus as to an explanation. Tufts University sociology professor John Conklin, in his book *Why Crime Rates Fell*, asserts that the drop is due to the fact that more Americans are incarcerated than ever before.[42] For Conklin, the simple drop in the number of criminals on the street means fewer of them are able to commit crime. A more controversial theory, espoused by economist Stephen Levitt, is that the legalization of abortion in the early 1970s was one of the main causative factors in the decrease in crime.[43] In short, he argued that fewer unwanted children in the 1970s and 1980s led to fewer criminals from the 1990s until today.

Correlates of Crime
Sociologists, and criminologists in particular, are especially interested in the study of the causes and correlates of crime. Causes are the factors that directly precipitate criminal offense. Correlates are factors that are mutually related, but are not necessarily causal. The important distinction is that correlation does not necessarily imply causation. The most prominent correlates for criminal offending that are of interest to researchers are age, race, socioeconomic status, education, and previous exposure to violence. Each of these correlates/causes has differing levels of empirical support.[44]

Age
Crime is most common in the second and third decades of the life of the offender.[45] This is a long-accepted tenet of criminology. The aggregate number of arrests in a society may change over a period of time, but the basic breakdown of the relative magnitudes of age groups remains fairly consistent. The 15–17 age group continues to have the highest arrest rate.[46] Moreover, according to Hirschi and Gottfredson, the relationship between age and crime is consistent across both race and sex,[47] which would tend to suggest that it is almost a constant (it does not vary across different categories).

Race
Race is one of the most studied correlates of crime in the U.S. There are many theories about the relationship between race and crime, most of which are concerned with environmental and social factors. Relatively few researchers advocate for biological reasons to explain race as a cause of crime.[48] The disproportionately large representation of minorities in both arrest and victimization reports is generally accepted,[49] while the root causes of that disparity are hotly debated. Generally speaking, areas that are racially diverse tend to experience higher crime rates.[50] While the majority of arrests are white offenders, African-Americans are represented at a rate two to three times their presence in the general population.[51]

Socioeconomic/Education Status
Generally speaking, higher socioeconomic status (affluence, education, health, etc.) correlates with lower rates of criminal offense.[52] Criminality correlates highly with unemployment and high frequency of career change. However, it should be borne in mind that so-called "white-collar" crime is a poignant reality, in addition to violent crime and petty theft. The effects of such crime can be equally devastating: doctors cheat on Medicare, lawyers misappropriate funds, business owners run Ponzi schemes, and industrialists dispose of hazardous waste in illegal and unsafe ways.[53] Therefore, explaining criminality solely by reference to the socioeconomic status of the offender is insufficient (although not without merit).

Previous Exposure to Violence
A final potential correlate for deviance is previous exposure to violence. Children who are exposed to violence at a young age are especially vulnerable to offending as adults.[54] The trauma of witnessing violence at a young age may cause mental stress that leads to delinquency or violent behavior.[55]

Theories of Crime

Each of us brings to the world our own unique ideological viewpoints, based upon traditions or what we inherently "know" to be true. How do these ideological foundations affect criminological theory? As Lilly, Cullen, and Ball (2007) note, why is it that crime is higher in some communities?[56] Why is it that some people break the law and others do not? Why is it that people, regardless of economic status, commit crimes? From a criminological viewpoint, it is important that we delve into this behavior to capture answers and offer solutions. Criminological theory should guide efforts to react to deviant and/or criminal behavior and prevent it from occurring. Most importantly, theory should inform policy.

Understanding theory is critical in exploring every facet of the criminal justice system, from prevention to crime detection, enforcement, prosecution, sentencing, punishment, incarceration, and re-entry. Theory should help establish the consequences for criminal offending and deviant behavior. Historically, criminological theory can be categorized into three different schools of thought: the pre-classical school, classical school, and positivist school.

Pre-classical school
A school of thought that held that crime was caused by supernatural forces as opposed to natural forces.

Trial by battle
A mechanism for privately resolving disputes during the pre-classical time period, in which the victim or a chosen member of the victim's family would battle with the offender or a chosen member of the offender's family to determine guilt.

Trial by ordeal
A method of handling conflict privately during the pre-classical time period, in which proving innocence involved the use of extremely painful or life-threatening methods of punishment.

Compurgation
A method of handling offenses during the pre-classical time period, in which individuals who could find a reputable person in their community to speak on their behalf would be found innocent.

Pre-Classical School

Prior to modern-day naturalistic explanations of crime and criminal behavior, crime was understood as a concept of spiritualism and retribution. It was believed that crime was caused by supernatural forces as opposed to natural forces. This was the **pre-classical school** of thought. During the Middle Ages in Europe, the old adage "the devil made me do it" was the guiding philosophy for determining what was considered a crime. Individuals turned to religion and the Bible to determine what constituted violations of law. Crimes that today are not considered illegal—possibly just deviant, or not enforced at all—were worthy of retributive responses, including death or excruciating pain. Likewise, crime and offenses were considered to be private matters, and the responses to these private matters were handled by the individuals and their families.

One response to criminal offenses and punishment was the **trial by battle**. Trials by battle were handled by the victim and the offender. Since it was a private matter, the victim or a chosen member of the victim's family would battle with the offender or a chosen member of the offender's family to determine guilt. The belief was that if offenders were innocent, they would win or not be harmed, therefore proving their innocence.

Another variation of handling the matter privately was the **trial by ordeal**. The trial by ordeal method for proving innocence involved the use of extremely painful or life-threatening methods for punishment. The belief was that if you were innocent, then God would protect you. Examples of punishments included dunking individuals or burying them in heavy stones.

The final example of punishment as a private matter was **compurgation**. In this method of handling offenses, individuals who could find a reputable person in their community to speak on their behalf would be found innocent. This practice led to distinctions by class and in some instances the truly guilty never being held accountable. It should be obvious to a modern observer that the cure did not always logically follow from the cause.

The primary shortcoming of any spiritualistic explanation of crime is that it cannot be scientifically proven. Naturalistic explanations, on the other hand, rely on science to explain the causes of crime. Evidence suggests that as early as 460 B.C., Hippocrates was pointing to the brain as an "independent organ of the mind."[57] Since naturalistic explanations could be used to explain behavior, they could also be used to scientifically study criminal offending. Naturalistic explanations were used to scientifically advance the understanding of behavior during the 16th and 17th centuries in Europe with the development of the classical school of thought.

Archaic methods of punishment and deterrence involved extremely painful or life-threatening acts.

Classical School of Thought

The Enlightenment brought an end to the use of brutal and arbitrary punishments. In his 1764 publication, *On Crimes and Punishments*, Cesare Beccaria, known as the father of classical criminology, proposed the removal of harsh punishments and a focus on deterrence principles, in which the offense was punished rather than the offender. The Enlightenment philosophers argued that individuals were free-will thinkers who had the ability to weigh the costs of the punishment with the benefits of the offense. Known also as the pleasure-pain principle, this placed the responsibility for behavior on the offender. Further, these philosophers believed that the creation and enforcement of laws should be equal and follow the utilitarian principle of the greatest good for the greatest number. Beccaria and his fellow philosophers further contended that each person in a society agreed implicitly to adhere to the social contract, in which they forfeited certain rights to those in charge in exchange for protection. There was the belief that the government had a right to punish, and that failure to do so was a violation of the social contract.

One of the most important tenets put forth by Beccaria was the idea that punishments should be just, and no greater than the harm caused to society. This tenet called for an end to brutal responses to seemingly minor offenses. More specifically, Beccaria was opposed to the use of the death penalty as a punishment. Instead, he advocated for what we now know as deterrence. **Deterrence theory** is based upon the premise that for any punishment to be effective, it must be swift, severe, and certain. If these three conditions are met, the argument goes, then crime will diminish. There are two forms of deterrence: general and specific. The goal of **general deterrence** is to deter the public from committing future criminal acts by ensuring that punishment is focused on potential criminals as opposed to the individual. The goal of **specific deterrence** is to deter a particular individual from committing future criminal acts by focusing the punishment on that individual.[58]

Jeremy Bentham, in his work, *Introduction to the Principles of Morals and Legislation*, extended the work of Beccaria to include the concept of utility or

Deterrence theory

A theory of punishment based upon the premise that in order for any punishment to be effective it must be swift, severe, and certain. There are two forms of deterrence: general and specific.

General deterrence

A form of deterrence used to deter the populace from committing future criminal acts by ensuring that the principles of punishment are focused on potential criminals as opposed to the individual.

Specific deterrence

A form of deterrence used to deter an individual from committing future criminal acts by focusing the punishment on that individual.

Classical school
A philosophy of crime that placed the responsibility for behavior on the offender.

Routine activities theory
A theory of criminal offending positing that crime is a function of opportunity—the convergence of a motivated offender, a suitable target, and a lack of guardianship.

Positivist school
A school of thought on crime arguing that some behavior occurs as a result of factors outside the control of individuals.

Biological theories
Theoretical propositions that look to the body to identify individuals who are predisposed to criminal offending.

utilitarianism. "Bentham further specified the idea of utility, or utilitarianism, which emphasizes maximization of pleasure and minimization of pain. This can be viewed on both the individual and aggregate level. On the individual level, this means that an individual will engage (or not engage) in activity that maximizes pleasure and minimizes pain, as perceived by the individual prior to the act. On the aggregate scale utilitarianism argues that the state or government will implement laws that benefit the 'greatest good for the greatest number.'"[59]

Although the classical school was an advancement from the spiritualistic view of crime and punishment, it still often resulted in harsh punishments. As scientific exploration and knowledge grew, so too did the pursuit of science to explain criminal behavior. Despite losing favor in recognition of what is now known as the positivist school, the views of the classical school have been revitalized in theories such as routine activities theory.

Routine activities theory posits that crime is a function of opportunity. More specifically, as Lawrence Cohen and Marcus Felson (1979) contend, crime occurs when a motivated offender, a suitable target, and a lack of guardianship all converge.[60] Crime as a function of everyday life becomes most prevalent when an individual's routine, either the mundane or the normal, creates a circumstance where the elements converge. Using elements of crime prevention through environmental design allows potential victims to address the issues of routine and mundane behavior.

The theory of rational choice contends that traditional theories fail to recognize the merit of choice in criminal acts. Rational choice theorists believe that acts made by offenders are sequenced and purposeful. Under this theory, the criminal act is the result of a rational choice made in the course of a cost/benefit analysis; if the potential gains exceed the punishment, the perpetrator will commit the crime. This perspective advocates for situational crime prevention to reduce opportunities for crime and victimization.[61]

Positivist School

The classical school, though popular, still came under attack by scientists who argued that not all behavior is reflective of free-will thinking or rational decision-making. Rather, some behavior occurs as a result of factors outside of the control of individuals. This idea led to the formation of the **positivist school** of thought, a philosophy based on biological, psychological, and sociological theories of crime.

Biological Theories of Crime

The first **biological theories** of criminal offending were geared toward the elimination of certain groups or classes of individuals. Most notable was the development of eugenics, which focused on monitoring and controlling the deviant population through sterilization. Many of the techniques used in such monitoring were essentially pseudoscience, such as craniometry and phrenology.

One example of using biological explanations was the development of craniometry as a field of exploration. Scientists studying craniometry believed they could identify superior versus inferior groups by the size of the skull, and applied this belief to racialized propaganda.[62] The belief was that the skull mirrored the shape of the brain and therefore predicted superiority. Most studies by craniometrists found that white western Europeans were most likely to have the largest skulls and therefore to be superior. This proposition held true until one key researcher, K.F. Gauss, died and an autopsy revealed that his skull and brain were smaller than average. Scientists have subsequently tended to emphasize factors other than the size of the skull or brain, such as the complexity of its development.[63]

Eventually the study of craniometry waned and gave way to phrenology, the study of the bumps on an individual's head. Borrowing from craniometry, phrenologists believed that the skull mirrored the shape of the brain; therefore, skulls that did not conform to the norm were deemed inferior and predictive of criminal offending. Although phrenology as a predictor of criminal offending was not supported by scientific research, more recent studies have revealed a connection between trauma to the left temporal lobe above the ear and violent offending.

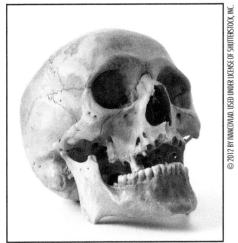

Scientists studying craniometry believed they could identify superior versus inferior groups by the size of the skull.

Another example of early biological propositions was physiognomy, the study of facial and other features that led to the development of problem behaviors such as criminal offending. The study of facial and body features led to the argument that certain races and ethnicities were superior to others. Such arguments were often made implicitly; for example, James Redfield in *Comparative Physiognomy* (1852) compared the features of different races with different animals, in terms of both appearance and character.[64]

The final proposition that set the framework for the study of biology and crime was the work of Charles Darwin in *The Origin of Species*. In this work, Darwin argued that man evolved from earlier primitive species, and that certain individuals within the species would thrive while others would fail to thrive. This led to the conclusion that there were certain ethnic groups that were essentially throwbacks to an earlier time and therefore inferior. Although Darwin did not specifically study criminality, he did lay the groundwork for the study and application of these principles to understanding the causes of crime.

Cesare Lombroso conducted the first major scientific study of crime, incorporating tenets of all the previously mentioned biological theories. Lombroso first presented his ideas in 1876 and argued that criminal behavior could be differentiated from what one considers to be normal behavior. He contended that individuals who participated in criminal offending were throwbacks from a primitive time, also known as the **atavistic man**. He argued that individuals most likely to be criminals could be identified through recognition of at least five stigmata or characteristics, including both physical and extraphysical abnormalities such as "ears of unusual size, sloping foreheads, excessively long arms, receding chins, and twisted noses."[65] He also contended that individuals who displayed tattoos and had a family history of epilepsy and other disorders were more likely to be criminal.[66] Further, Lombroso argued that offenders could be

Atavistic man
An identification of individuals participating in criminal activity as throwbacks from a primitive time.

classified into four major categories: "(a) born criminal or people with atavistic characteristics; (b) insane criminals including idiots, imbeciles, and paranoiacs as well as epileptics and alcoholics; (c) occasional criminals or criminaloids, whose crimes are explained primarily by opportunity, although they too have innate traits that predispose them to criminality; and (d) criminals of passion, who commit crimes because of anger, love, or honor and are characterized by being compelled to crime by an 'irresistible force.'"[67, 68]

Although Lombroso's theory did not withstand the test of time, his ideas continued to guide researchers. For example, the ideas put forth by Lombroso were further expanded by Raffaele Garofalo. Garofalo shared the belief that certain physical characteristics indicated a criminal nature: for instance, he thought criminals had less sensitivity to physical pain, demonstrated by the fact that prisoners frequently received tattoos while in prison. Enrico Ferri continued these ideas but included a sociological and psychological component, stating that a combination of many biological, social, and organic factors caused delinquency.[69]

More recent research explored the connection between criminality and inherited traits. One widely cited study was conducted by Richard Dugdale.[70] Dugdale identified a family of individuals, the Jukes (not their real name), who were known to participate in criminal activity. He studied these individuals to determine whether there were specific traits that were inherited by families. He concluded that the poor environment in which the Jukes lived was responsible for their criminality, and that "environment tends to produce habits which may become hereditary."[71]

Another biological explanation for crime was put forth by William Sheldon.[72] Sheldon argued that criminals could be distinguished from the normal population based upon physical characteristics that made them more prone to criminality. He identified three specific body types, known as *somotypes*, that he used to classify the general population. The first body type classification was the *endomorph*: these individuals were characterized as having heavier builds and moving slower. The second type of body classification was the *ectomorph*, tall and slim. The final body type, *mesomorphs*, were best characterized by their overall athletic appearance and build. These individuals were very strong and tended to be aggressive. Sheldon argued that most criminal offenders would be classified as mesomorphs. Further studies and research revealed little or no empirical support for these propositions. Therefore, this theory lost intellectual credibility (though it remains present in ingrained cultural stereotypes).

Researchers have also explored the influence of genetics on criminal offending, questioning whether crime is a function of nature (genetics) or nurture (environment). One way this phenomenon has been studied has been through twin studies. Early studies of twin behavior revealed a significant relationship between identical twins (monozygotic) and crime, whereas the relationship between criminal associations and fraternal twins (dizygotic) was not significant. A review of relevant studies conducted between 1929 and 1961 found that 60% of MZ twins shared criminal behavior patterns compared to only 30% of DZ twins. Karl Christiansen studied 3,586 male twin pairs and found a 52% concordance for MZ pairs and 22% for DZ twins.[73]

Another way to explore these connections between nature and nurture is through adoption studies. The most frequently cited study on adopted children was conducted by Hutchings and Mednick.[74] They analyzed 1,145 adopted male children born in Copenhagen, Denmark, between 1927 and 1941. They were most interested in looking at the connection between biological or adoptive parents. A total of 143 criminal adoptees (that is, children whose biological fathers had criminal records) were matched with 143 non-criminal adoptees. Results revealed that adopted youth whose biological fathers had criminal records were 24.5% more likely to have a criminal conviction.

Critical Thinking
What policy/policies to prevent crime would a biological theorist most likely support?

Psychological Theories of Crime Psychological theories, in general, deal with individual traits that manifest themselves in criminal behavior. For the purposes of this chapter, psychoanalytical and personality theories will be reviewed. More recent expansions of psychological concepts combine these propositions with biological and sociological theories.

© 2012 BY LIGHTSPRING. USED UNDER LICENSE OF SHUTTERSTOCK, INC.

Sigmund Freud correlated crime to the interplay between the id, ego, and superego.

Psychoanalytical perspectives have their roots in the works of Sigmund Freud. Freud argued that all behavior is motivated by wishes and desires found within our unconscious (or subconscious) minds. It is the interplay between the id, ego, and superego that dictates which unconscious desires will be fulfilled.[75] In Freudian terms, the id includes the unconscious wishes developed in the early stages of life. The superego includes the unconscious wishes developed from watching others around us, such as our parents. The ego serves as the mediator between the id and the superego, translating complex wishes and desires with realistic expectations on a daily basis.[76]

A frequently cited example of Freud's work in practice is August Aichhorn's 1925 book *Wayward Youth* (translated into English in 1935). Aichhorn described how he utilized Freud's work to resolve chronic delinquent behaviors in youth in both conventional and individual settings. He recognized the interplay between the ego and the superego, arguing that an ill-developed superego led to delinquent activity. For Aichhorn, the key to addressing delinquent activity was moral education. His techniques could be used in a training school setting in small groups. Long-term follow-up studies of youth who worked with Aichhorn revealed changes in behavior after only one session.[77]

Personality theory is another way that psychological perspectives have been used in a criminal justice setting. Unlike psychoanalytical theories that explore the involvement of unconscious wishes and desires, **personality theories** look to explain criminal behavior as expressions of impulsiveness, aggression, or sensation-seeking. A variety of tools have been used in criminal justice settings to identify problems and disorders associated with personality. These include the Minnesota Multiphasic Personality Inventory (MMPI), the California Psychological Inventory (CPI), and the Hare Psychopathy Checklist (PCL-R).

Another psychological theory is behavioral and/or learning theory using operant conditioning. This therapeutic approach uses reinforcers (both positive and negative) to encourage individuals to perform desired social behaviors.[78]

Personality theories
Theories of crime that look to explain criminal behavior as an expression of impulsiveness, aggression, or sensation-seeking.

Critical Thinking What policy/policies to prevent crime would a psychological theorist most likely support?

Chicago School
A specialized body of work in urban sociology that made use of the city of Chicago to study alcoholism, homelessness, suicide, psychoses, and poverty.

Sociological Theories of Crime   By the early 1900s the city of Chicago, Illinois, had experienced unprecedented growth that ultimately would change the face of the United States. Immigrants from all over the world were flocking to the city in the hope of a better life. This cultural and structural shift prompted faculty members and students from the University of Chicago to explore and study the impact of growth on the city during the 1920s. The result was a specialized body of work in urban sociology that has come to be known as the **Chicago School**,[79] which made use of the city to study "alcoholism, homelessness, suicide, psychoses and poverty." Robert Park, a journalist and sociologist by training, played a significant role in reviewing and covering how the city developed. He focused specifically on the assimilation of immigrants into the general population of the United

States, seeing Chicago as a crucible for the process of civilization and a way to view it "under a microscope."[80]

Ernest Burgess, a colleague of Robert Park, sought to graphically depict the outward growth of the city of Chicago. Unlike previous researchers, Burgess contended that there was a distinct pattern to the city's growth.[81] According to Burgess's **concentric zone theory**, the development of the city of Chicago could be divided into five distinct zones or rings. Zone I was the Loop, or the business district. This zone was the heart of the industrial complex. There was a great deal of transportation in and out of the city, including rail and waterways. Zone II, known as the zone in transition, was located just adjacent to the business district. This zone was best defined by deteriorated housing, tenement conditions, continual displacement of residents, and a high rate of turnover by the immigrant population, and was the least desirable place to live in the city.[82] Zone III, working men's homes and multiple-family dwellings, was an area where apartment buildings and modest homes were found. Zone IV, known as the residential zone (single-family homes), consisted of nicer apartments and higher-priced homes. Zone V, known as the commuter zone, was a suburban area.[83]

Park and Burgess's descriptions of the development and growth of Chicago led Clifford Shaw and Henry McKay, sociologists employed by the state of Illinois, to explore the effect of the city's growth patterns on juvenile delinquency. Shaw and McKay[84] proposed that communities with higher rates of social ills—including a breakdown in family composition, dilapidated buildings, unsupervised teenagers, high rates of poverty, high rates of residential mobility, and ethnic heterogeneity—were most likely to experience high rates of crime and delinquency. They postulated that the controls or bonds that would keep youth from committing delinquent acts would be diminished because of these social ills, therefore resulting in increases in delinquent and criminal activity. Communities characterized by intact homes and neighborhoods were known to be more socially organized. Known as social disorganization theory, this theory laid the foundation for looking at the causes of crime in the environment, not just at the individual level.

To test their theory, Shaw and McKay[85] reviewed juvenile court records, commitments to correctional schools, alleged delinquency handled by police or probation, and juvenile arrests and commitments. Using census data, juvenile court records, and housing and welfare records, they confirmed that crime flourished in zones I and II of Chicago. The highest rates of delinquency were found in communities with the highest rates of social ills that failed to regulate behavior and had the most unsupervised teens. This theoretical premise became the foundation for many advancements in understanding crime and behavior.

In 1930, Edwin Sutherland joined the faculty of the University of Chicago. Rejecting the individual explanation of crime, Sutherland argued that crime was a product of the social environment in which individuals gained their values

In Burgess's concentric zone theory, Chicago's Zone II was characterized by deteriorated and abandoned buildings.

Social disorganization theory

A theoretical proposition stating that communities with higher rates of social ills, such as breakdown in family composition, dilapidated buildings, unsupervised teenagers, high rates of poverty, high rates of residential mobility, and ethnic heterogeneity, are most likely to experience high rates of crime and delinquency.

Differential association theory

A sociological theory positing that crime is a product of the social environment whereby values are gained from those around individuals.

from those around them.[86] Sutherland proposed that criminal behavior was learned like all other conventional behavior. In his **differential association theory**, Sutherland identified nine different propositions to explain learning:

1. "Criminal behavior is learned.
2. Criminal behavior is learned in interaction with other persons in a process of communication.
3. The principal part of the learning of criminal behavior occurs within intimate personal groups.
4. When criminal behavior is learned, the learning includes (a) techniques of committing the crime, which sometimes are very complicated, sometimes are very simple; [and] (b) the specific direction of motives, drives, rationalizations, and attitudes.
5. The specific direction of motives and drives is learned from definitions of legal codes as favorable and unfavorable.
6. A person becomes delinquent because of an excess of definitions favorable to violation of law over definitions unfavorable to violation of law. This is the principle of differential association.
7. Differential associations may vary in frequency, duration, priority, and intensity.
8. The process of learning criminal behavior by association with criminal and anti-criminal patterns involves all the mechanisms that are involved in any other learning.
9. While criminal behavior is an expression of general needs and values, it is not explained by those general needs and values since noncriminal behavior is an expression of the same needs and values."[87]

During the 1930s, the Chicago School dominated thought and explanations for crime and criminal behavior. Robert K. Merton, however, rejected these ideas. He was influenced by an understanding of the breakdown of norms and values (normlessness) that was termed "anomie" by Emile Durkheim.[88] Merton expanded upon this, and proposed that when individuals failed to conform to cultural values or achieve financial success, they turned to crime and deviance. In other words, society puts pressure on individuals to live up to certain cultural norms, which can frustrate and put strain on those who are unable to meet those norms. Merton's theory was known as **strain theory**.

Strain theory

A theoretical proposition contending that crime rates are produced by an individual's inability to conform to cultural values or achieve monetary success through accepted norms.

General strain theory

An expansion of strain theory stating that the more strain individuals are exposed to, the more likely they are to participate in delinquent or criminal activity. Types of strain include the failure to achieve positive goals, the removal of positive stimuli, and the presentation of negative stimuli.

Strain theory was further expanded in Lloyd Ohlin's study of delinquent boys. As a student of Merton, he contended that delinquent youth banded together by abandoning middle-class values and creating their own separate sets of values.[89] Richard Cloward (also a student of Merton's) later joined with Ohlin to extend this notion, arguing that the social environment generated pressure for deviance. They argued that the high level of strain experienced by lower-class youth permitted them to adopt illegitimate means for obtaining their goals. In organized slums, younger members of the slums modeled older youth and formed a separate subculture. Similarly, some drug-involved youth further separated themselves as a distinct subculture.[90]

During the 1990s, strain theory was further expanded by Robert Agnew in his **general strain theory**.[91] According to Agnew, Merton did not include all of

Social disorganization theory holds that communities with higher rates of social ills — including high rates of poverty — are most likely to experience high rates of crime and delinquency.

the strains that existed in an individual's life. Agnew argued that strain could be categorized into three distinct types: 1) "strain as the failure to achieve positively valued goals (traditional strain)"[92]; 2) "strain as the removal of positive stimuli from the individual"; and 3) "strain as the presentation of negative stimuli."[93] The more strain individuals were exposed to, the more likely they were to participate in delinquent or criminal activity.

Control theories seek to add a component of motivation. Like strain theory, social control theory has its roots in the work of Emile Durkheim. Durkheim contended that crime is a normal function of society that serves to unite individuals against a common threat. He further argued that a society without crime is by definition abnormal. Crime and deviance, therefore, serve to establish the moral boundaries for those living within the community.

There are a number of variations of control theories. One of the most significant is Travis Hirschi's **social control theory**. Unlike other theories that sought to explain why individuals committed crimes, Hirschi's theory sought to understand why individuals chose *not* to participate in delinquent or criminal activity. Hirschi characterized the social bond as having four elements. The first, attachment, involved identification, emotional bond, concern, and respect for peers or parents, as well as engagement in activities with peers, supervision and intimate communications by parents, attitudes toward school, and concern and sensitivity for the opinions of parents, peers, and teachers. The second element, involvement, involved time-consuming activities such as work, sports, recreation, hobbies, and homework, as well as nonactive leisure time, lack of boredom, and time spent interacting with friends. The third element, commitment, involved investment in education, career, family, and society, as well as academic and educational competence, aspirations, and expectations, achievement orientation, expected occupation, and importance of reputation. The fourth element,

Social control theory
A theoretical proposition that contends that the more strongly individuals are bonded to their community, the less likely they are to participate in delinquent activity.

belief, involved respect for authorities and law, and the absence of neutralizations. Many have argued that social control theory may be best for explaining less serious forms of delinquency.[94]

In 1990, Travis Hirschi diverged from his original theory of social control and bonding when he, along with Michael Gottfredson, proposed the **general theory of crime**. Departing from Hirschi's original theoretical premise, they argued that crime was not controlled by bonds to society, but rather by an individual's inability to demonstrate self-control. Crime and other analogous behaviors such as smoking, drinking, driving fast, having multiple sexual partners, etc., provide short-term gratification for those with low self-control. These behaviors begin in early childhood and continue on into later adulthood. Individuals with low self-control are more impulsive, participate in risk-taking behavior, are self-centered, have extreme tempers, and are more physically active.[95] These individuals typically fail at life events that require delayed gratification, such as marriage, education, employment, or other activities that require planning. Crime in general is a not a planned event; rather, offenders act on impulse as a mechanism for gratifying their needs. Gottfredson and Hirschi (1990) contended that there were 10 elements of social control that kept individuals from committing and participating in criminal activity. Those elements of self-control are as follows:[96]

10 Elements of Social Control
1. Criminal acts provide immediate gratification of desires.
2. Criminal acts provide easy or simple gratification of desires.
3. Criminal acts are exciting, risky or thrilling.
4. Crimes provide few or meager long-term benefits.
5. Crimes require little skill or planning.
6. Crimes often result in pain or discomfort for the victim.
7. Crimes require the interaction of an offender with people or their property.
8. The major benefit of many crimes is not pleasure but relief from momentary irritation.
9. Crimes involve the risk of violence and physical injury of pain and suffering on the part of the offender.
10. The risk of criminal penalty for any given criminal act is small but this depends in part on the circumstances of the offense.

Opponents of the general theory of crime have argued that many of the theoretical principles involve circular reasoning. For example, how do we know whether an individual is impulsive or just acting out? This theory further fails to account for personality disorders, racial and gender issues, moral beliefs, and ecological or individual differences. Similarly, this theory purports that behavior does not change over time, and that once an individual demonstrates low self-control, this behavior will continue throughout his or her lifetime. However, other theoretical propositions, such as life course theory, have demonstrated that criminal propensity can change.

Some criminological theories focus on the criminal self as it develops through its relation to others. In 1902, Charles Horton Cooley proposed the idea of the "looking-glass self," which postulated that the self was determined by the perception of others and society's interpersonal interactions.[97] Cooley was a direct influence on George Herbert Mead, a sociologist commonly associated with the Chicago School. Mead saw the self in symbolic terms, specifically as a symbol that can be understood only in its relationship to society as a whole.[98] For Mead, the self is, in some sense, disintegrated by its encounter with society, and then reconstituted as a response to it.[99] Cooley's and Mead's ideas directly influenced labeling theory.

Labeling theory was developed by Edwin Lemert. He argued that when an individual is labeled by society as deviant or criminal, the individual is likely to accept the label as true and begin to self-identify as an offender. These individuals are more likely to continue this form of behavior.

Howard Becker further advanced the concept of labeling, arguing that there are four distinct categories of individuals: conformists, pure deviants, falsely accused, and secret deviants.[100] The *conformist* abides by all of the rules and laws of society. The *pure deviant* commits criminal acts and is caught. The *falsely accused* individual does not commit criminal acts, but instead is falsely accused of crimes, typically as a result of factors such as socioeconomic status, sex, age, race, etc. The *secret deviant* commits acts but is not formally caught and processed; there are a significant number of individuals who fall within this category.[101]

Another variation of labeling theory, known as radical nonintervention, was put forth by Edwin Schur, who argued that juveniles who violated delinquency laws should receive no punishment or intervention. Schur contended that any intervention would label an individual as delinquent and would therefore make him or her more likely to commit delinquent behavior—a sort of self-fulfilling prophecy.

More recently, the concept of labeling has been extended into John Braithwaite's theory of **reintegrative shaming**. In *Crime, Shame and Reintegration* (1989), Braithwaite contends that punishments designed to stigmatize the offender are counterproductive.[102] Instead of reducing crime, these efforts may in fact further encourage delinquent or criminal offending. Publicly shaming offenders may lead them to be alienated from society and make it difficult, if not impossible, for them to reintegrate. With this in mind, Braithwaite argues that societies should use reintegrative shaming, whereby offenders are punished—therefore repaying their debt to society—and then forgiven for their transgressions and reintegrated back into society. This reintegrative shaming technique has been shown to reduce criminal activity in other countries.[103]

Labeling theory
A theoretical tradition in which criminals become set in their roles as criminals as a result of their stigmatized status.

Edwin Lemert's labeling theory contends that when an individual is labeled by society as deviant, the individual is likelier to self-identify as an offender.

Reintegrative shaming
A process whereby offenders are punished, therefore repaying their debt to society, and then forgiven for their transgressions and reintegrated back into society.

Conflict theory

A theory concerned with how power is maintained in a society rather than how individuals function within that continuum. Conflict theory holds that those with the most wealth in society are more likely to create the laws, maintain control, and have power over the lower classes.

Conflict theory emphasizes how power is used to create conflict in society.[104] This theory builds off the works of Karl Marx and Friedrich Engels, who argued that capitalist societies create power structures that produce struggles for more money and wealth. This power struggle results in conflict and crime.[105] Power is typically associated with wealth and resources; therefore, those with the most wealth in society are more likely to create the laws, maintain control, and have power over the lower classes.[106]

As Reiman and Leighton (2010) contend, the "repressive" nature of law helps maintain the current criminal justice system. In the Marxist tradition, those in power establish a system that fills the needs of the "haves" at the expense of the "have-nots."[107] A variety of different forms of conflict theory exist. More recent versions of conflict theory include peacemaking criminology and left realism.

Critical Thinking

What policy/policies to prevent crime would a conflict theorist most likely support?

Peacemaking criminology

A theory proposing the use of mediation, love, respect, and forgiveness to resolve societal conflicts and reduce recidivism and crime.

Peacemaking criminology utilizes the concepts of religion, spiritualism, and forgiveness to resolve the conflict that exists within society. Richard Quinney and Harold Pepinsky[108] argued that the keys to reducing recidivism and crime were mediation, love, respect, and forgiveness. They recognized that conflict would continue to exist in any society, but advocated that responses should come from a place of forgiveness.[109]

Left realism

A philosophical approach advocating for more minimal responses or sanctions for street-level crimes and less serious offenses, and more stringent responses and social control for white-collar crimes and crimes against society.

Another modern-day variation of conflict theory is known as left realism. Developed in Britain in the 1980s, left realism branched off from the traditional focus on understanding crime as a class issue and focused on what it deemed the "real aspects of crime."[110] Left realists sought to understand the etiology of everyday crimes that were being committed by the working classes. They advocated for more minimal responses or sanctions for less serious offenses—such as drug use, prostitution, minor property offenses, and victimless crimes—and more stringent responses and social control for white-collar crimes and crimes against society.[111] According to Akers and Sellers (2009), left realism is a philosophical approach that in essence calls for the dismantling of the entire criminal justice system.[112] This approach has been criticized for a variety of reasons. Most notably, the lack of empirical research classifies this approach as philosophical rather than theoretical. Also, this approach calls for punishment responses to offenses rather than rehabilitation or forgiveness, which does not hold to the values of other types of conflict theory.[113]

Feminist theories

Theoretical explanations of crime, justice, and the entire criminal justice system from an androgynous perspective.

Feminist theories of criminal justice seek to extend the understanding of criminal justice from an androgynous perspective. Many traditional criminological theories fail to take into account that women commit crimes for different reasons than men and they respond to treatment differently as well. No one single feminist perspective exists, but for the purposes of this chapter, a general description of feminist theory will be provided. Feminist theorists argue that the disparities in treatment of men and women in the criminal justice system are as important, if not more important, than the disparities in race and class. Traditional theories of crime have focused on patriarchal explanations.

The chivalry hypothesis states that women and girls are treated more leniently in the criminal justice system. This is dismissed by most feminists, though, who instead argue that there is a paternalistic approach in which women are treated on the opposite ends of the continuum—either very leniently or very harshly as a mechanism of control.

Daly and Chesney-Lind (1988)[114] contended that women's roles in society differ fundamentally from those of men, and that these differences in how men and women are viewed in society greatly impact both our understanding of behavior and responses to it.

Another area of feminist literature that has gained recent attention is the gendering of crime. This is the exploration of how gender and the roles ascribed to both men and women influence the types of offenses committed. As Messerschmidt contends, boys and men are raised to be masculine. A sense of being a "man" is defined by "toughness" or assertion. Women, unlike men, take on socially ascribed roles of being the "nurturer" or homemaker. Therefore, if these roles are fulfilled, men should be committing more violent acts as opposed to women, who would be responsible for more property-related offenses.[115]

Integrated theories stem from the idea that there are many different theories about crime. Many of these theories fall short because they lack empirical support or because they do not thoroughly explain the causes of crime. One way to address these shortcomings is to combine the most powerful components of each theory into a new theoretical proposition, known as an integrated theory.[116] Theory integration seeks to combine elements of two or more theories into one explanation.

Theory integration may combine elements such as control and social learning theories to explain why gangs are formed, or combine strain with social learning theories to explore the impact of the weakening of the social bonds on conventional society.[117]

Wilson and Herrnstein (1985),[118] in their book, *Crime and Human Nature*, proposed an integrated biosocial theory that combined biology with psychology. These authors proposed that biology affects how an individual reacts to their social environment. More specifically, they contended that parents play a crucial role in how children respond to their environment. Individuals seek approval from those closest to them (peers, friends, family) as a mechanism to support acceptable behavior. Wilson and Herrnstein further believed that for punishment to be effective, it must begin with parents and be state-reinforced as a deterrent.

A second variation of integrated theory is the integrated strain-control paradigm developed by Elliott et al. (1985).[119] Elliott and his colleagues proposed that theories of strain, control, and learning could be combined to create a more robust explanation of juvenile offending. For example, they proposed that "(1) strain (in the family and school) weakens (2) social bonds to conventional society, which in turn promotes (3) strong bonds to delinquent peers. It is these strong bonds to delinquent peers, therefore, that are principal factors in (4) the

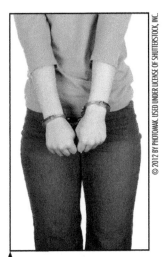

Women commit crimes for different reasons than men and respond to treatment differently.

Integrated theories
Theories that identify the most powerful elements of other theories and combine two or more of them into one explanation.

commission of delinquent behavior."[120] They further contended that strong attachments to conventional activities such as school or church reduced the propensity toward crime and delinquency.

In general, integrated theories have been criticized for a variety of reasons. One of the biggest concerns is that combining two different theories may violate their own assumptions: for instance, control theories seek to explain why individuals do not commit crime, while learning theories seek to explain why they do.[121]

Life course theories
The contention that criminal offending is influenced by an individual's previous experiences as well as traits or characteristics that are not changeable, such as impulsivity, age, etc.

The study of criminal behavior has traditionally focused on the causes of offending among youth or young adults. Theories fail to follow the paths of offending from birth through death. One exception to this rule has arisen in the development of **life course theories**. The life course theorists contend that criminal offending is influenced by two specific patterns of behavior. First, crime is dependent upon the state of the perpetrator: that is, it is malleable based upon previous experiences that influence the individual. Second, crime and behavior are governed by traits that are not changeable, such as impulsivity, age, etc.[122] Individuals establish patterns of behavior in infancy through attachments and reinforcements with parents or caregivers. These attachments or the ability to bond with positive influences continue on into adulthood.

One of the most influential studies of the life course perspective was developed by Robert Sampson and John Laub.[123] They found that criminal or delinquent offending does not occur in a vacuum. Rather, this behavior is influenced by one's environment and structural characteristics such as poverty, residential mobility, family size, and other factors. The family serves as the strongest instrument of control in a child's life through monitoring and attachments. Children reared in unstable homes with few bonds are more likely to grow into adults who have few stable bonds such as employment or marriage. Despite these deficits, research demonstrates that it is not impossible for individuals to overcome these barriers. If individuals are able to establish meaningful bonds in adulthood, these elements may function as "turning points" in their lives to keep them from continuing down a path of crime and delinquency. As noted by Sampson and Laub, it is these informal social controls and bonds that are most important in reducing or preventing crime throughout an individual's lifetime.

Critical Thinking
most likely support?

What policy/policies to prevent crime would a life course theorist

In 1986, the Office of Juvenile Justice and Delinquency Prevention commissioned a study on the causes of delinquency. As part of this study, researchers from the University of Colorado, the University of Pittsburgh, the University of Albany, and the State University of New York interviewed over 4,000 youth at regular intervals, collecting information on their characteristics and behaviors. Information gathered from the study of all-male youth conducted by the team at the University of Pittsburgh helped identify three distinct pathways to crime: the authority conflict pathway, covert pathway, and overt pathway.[124] These

Damaging property is a characteristic of the covert pathway of juvenile crime.

© 2012 BY COREPICS. USED UNDER LICENSE OF SHUTTERSTOCK, INC.

developmental pathways were characterized by differences between these youths and normal offenders. For certain youth, disruptive behavior would manifest itself early in life and continue throughout their lifetime. Research revealed that for stubborn behavior, the median age was nine, with some displaying these characteristics as early as the age of three.

Figure 2.6 illustrates the distinct pathways to crime. The first pathway, the *authority conflict pathway*, begins when a child displays stubborn behavior at an early age. This leads to defiance (such as doing things one's own way and disobedience) and then to an avoidance of authority (such as staying out late or running away). The second pathway, the *covert pathway*, begins with minor dishonest or deceitful behavior (such as lying, shoplifting, or damaging property). This behavior then escalates to more serious crimes, ranging from joyriding, pocket picking, and larceny to using stolen credit cards, breaking and entering, dealing drugs, and stealing cars. The third pathway, the *overt pathway*, includes aggressive acts such as annoying others and bullying, and eventually leads to physical fighting and violent crimes (attacking someone, robbery).[125]

Developmental pathways
A description of the various paths a youth may take into delinquent or criminal offending. These pathways include the authority conflict pathway, covert pathway, and overt pathway.

FIGURE 2.6 Three Pathways to Boys' Disruptive Behavior and Delinquency

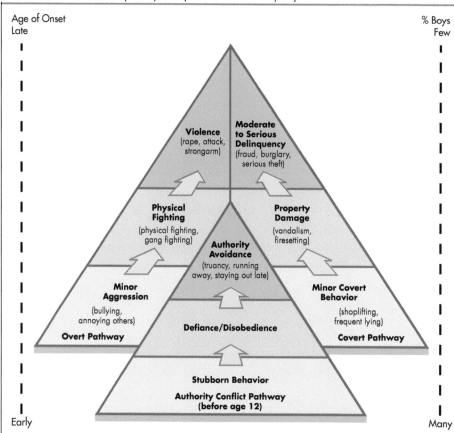

Source: Kelley, B. T., Loeber, R., Keenan, K. & DeLamatre, M. (1997). Developmental pathways in boys' disruptive and delinquent behavior (NCJ 165692). *Juvenile Justice Bulletin.* Washington, DC: Office of Juvenile Justice and Delinquency Prevention, p. 9.

As further noted by the study, of most concern were the issues related to those whose offending persisted over time. Youth who experienced both family dysfunction and neurological problems were most likely to continue down these paths.[126]

Chapter Summary

- Society differentiates between the concepts of deviance and criminal behavior. Deviance is defined as behaviors considered outside of or inconsistent with normal behavior for a community or group, while criminal behavior is defined by legislation, statutes, and codes. It is important to understand these differences in terms of how society and the criminal justice system respond to illicit activities and behaviors.

- In 1930, the Federal Bureau of Investigation began collecting data on crimes reported to the police and crimes cleared by arrest on a voluntary wide-scale basis. This information is collected in the Uniform Crime Reports (UCR), and divided into Part I and Part II offenses. Part I index offenses are the most serious crimes committed in the United States.

- During the 1980s, the FBI sought to rectify some of the problems encountered with the UCR. The result was the creation of the National Incident-Based Reporting System (NIBRS). There are 13 key differences between the UCR and the NIBRS systems. Unlike the UCR, the NIBRS system includes a total of 22 offense categories made up of 46 crimes. This is an incident-based system that allows for the inclusion of both completed and attempted offenses. Although this is an enhanced version of the UCR, to date it has not been implemented widely. All data collected by the NIBRS system are collapsed into the UCR categories for reporting.

- The National Crime Victimization Survey (NCVS), first administered in 1973 and originally known as the National Crime Survey (NCS), is conducted by the U.S. Census Bureau on behalf of the Bureau of Justice Statistics on households in the United States. The most important functions of NCVS are to tap into the dark figure of crime, enhance the ability to compare victimizations by type of area and over time, provide uniform definitions of crime, and include detailed descriptions of the criminal event, including the victim, potential precipitation, consequences of the event, and the offender.

- Another method for collecting data is the self-report survey. There is no one standard method for collecting data using the self-report method. However, this technique was developed and began being used more frequently during the 1950s. Data from self-report surveys are used to identify the number of crimes not reported to the police.

- Understanding theory is critical for exploring every facet of the criminal justice system, ranging from prevention to crime detection, enforcement, prosecution, sentencing, punishment, incarceration, and re-entry. Theory should establish the context in which consequences are developed for criminal offending and deviant behavior.

- Prior to the modern-day naturalistic explanations of crime and criminal behavior, crime was understood as a concept of spiritualism and retribution. This school of thought is known as the pre-classical school. At that time, it was believed that crime was caused by supernatural forces as opposed to natural forces. Therefore, punishments were considered a private matter and handled as such.

- The Enlightenment brought an end to the use of brutal and arbitrary punishments. Cesare Beccaria set forth a series of propositions advocating the removal of harsh punishments and a focus on deterrence principles whereby the offense was punished versus the offender. The Enlightenment philosophers argued that individuals were free-will thinkers who had the ability to weigh the costs of the punishment with the benefits of the offense. This "pleasure-pain principle" placed the responsibility for behavior on the offender.

- With the development and use of scientific principles, a new realm of theoretical understanding developed known as the positivist school of thought. These theories are best understood in terms of the following categories: biological, psychological, sociological, critical, feminist, peacemaking, and left realist. In all of these explanations, theorists contend that criminal behavior can be explained by forces either inherent within the individual or as a response to societal conditions.

Critical Thinking?

1. As noted in the beginning of the chapter, distinct differences exist between behaviors that are considered deviant and those considered criminal. Historically, behaviors such as drug use or prostitution were once legal but considered deviant. What factors do you believe should be taken into consideration when deciding whether behavior is illegal? What are some of the unintended/intended consequences of criminalizing behavior?

2. As noted in the statistics presented from both the UCR and the NCVS, crime rates have declined since 2008. What do these statistics reveal to us about crime reduction strategies? How might these data be used on a local and state level to respond to crime?

3. You have just been elected mayor in your community. You ran on a platform of reducing both spending and crime in your community. Given what you know about crime and its causes, how might you accomplish this task?

4. In the case study example provided at the beginning of the chapter, how might biological theory explain the shooting? Create a policy using biological theory that would prevent this crime from occurring in the future.

5. In the case study example provided at the beginning of the chapter, how might psychoanalytical theory explain the shooting? Create a policy using psychoanalytical theory that would prevent this crime from occurring in the future.

6. In the case study example provided at the beginning of the chapter, how might social disorganization theory explain the shooting? Create a policy using social disorganization theory that would prevent this crime from occurring in the future.

7. In the case study example provided at the beginning of the chapter, how might life course theory explain the shooting? Create a policy using life course theory that would prevent this crime from occurring in the future.

8. In the case study example provided at the beginning of the chapter, how might the general theory of crime explain the shooting? Create a policy using the general theory of crime that would prevent this crime from occurring in the future.

9. In the case study example provided at the beginning of the chapter, how might conflict theory explain the shooting? Create a policy using conflict theory that would prevent this crime from occurring in the future.

Media

Bureau of Justice Statistics: http://www.ojp.usdoj.gov/bjs

The Department of Justice website discusses the methodology of crime statistics and provides archived results from the past.

The National Center for Victims of Crime: http://www.ncvc.org/ncvc/Main.aspx

The NCVC is a resource and advocacy organization for victims. This website has useful information for both researchers and victims.

National Crime Victimization Survey: http://bjs.ojp.usdoj.gov/index.cfm?ty=dcdetail&iid=245

The NCVS is the crime victims' survey favored by victimologists. It allows researchers to track trends in victimization.

National Criminal Justice Reference Service: http://www.ncjrs.gov

The NCJRS is a federally funded, comprehensive website run by the Office of Justice Programs. It contains information relating to the Justice Department for research and public policy.

National Institute of Justice: http://www.ojp.usdoj.gov/nij/

The National Institute of Justice is dedicated to using science to help understand and reduce crime.

Occupational Outlook Handbook, 2010–11 Edition: http://www.bls.gov/oco/

This government-run site, published by the Bureau of Labor Statistics, details careers and their future outlook.

U.S. Department of Justice: http://www.usdoj.gov

The official website of the Department of Justice includes information about the roles of the department and the attorney general.

Uniform Crime Reports: http://www.fbi.gov/ucr/ucr.htm

The UCR, published by the FBI, are the most comprehensive statistical reports on reported crime in the United States.

Endnotes

1. McCaffrey, F. (2011). "Panel Examines Youth Gang Violence." *The Gavel Online.* Retrieved from http://bcgavel.com/2011/03/20/gang-violence-examined-presidential-scholars-program-hosts-panel-of-speakers/

2. Clinard, M. B. (1968). *Sociology of Deviant Behavior* (3rd ed.). New York, NY: Holt, Rinehart, and Winston, 28.

3. Lombroso, C. (1876). *L'Uomo Delinquente.*

4. Cornish, D., & Clarke, R. V. (1986). "Introduction." In D. Cornish & R. Clarke (Eds.), *The Reasoning Criminal* (pp. 1–16). New York, NY: Springer-Verlag.

5. Goode, E. (2001). *Deviant Behavior* (8th ed.). Upper Saddle River, NJ: Prentice Hall.

6. Morrison, W. (2006). *Criminology, Civilisation and the New World Order.* London: Routledge.

7. Uniform Crime Reporting Program Staff. (2004). *Uniform Crime Reporting Handbook.* Clarksburg, WV: Federal Bureau of Investigation, 2.

8. Ibid.

9. See the Uniform Crime Reporting Handbook at http://www.fbi.gov/about-us/cjis/ucr/additional-ucr-publications/ucr_handbook.pdf for more information on how data are collected and reported to the FBI.

10. O'Brien, R. M. (1985). *Crime and Victimization Data.* Thousand Oaks, CA: Sage.

11. Ibid., 22.

12. Federal Bureau of Investigation (FBI). (2011). *Uniform Crime Reporting Statistics: Their Proper Use.* Retrieved from http://www.fbi.gov/about-us/cjis/ucr/ucr-statistics-their-proper-use

13. Ibid.

14. O'Brien, 1985.

15. FBI, 2011.

16. Ibid.

17. Ibid.

18. FBI. (2000). *National Incident-Based Reporting System, Volume 1: Data Collection Guidelines*. Clarksburg, WV: Federal Bureau of Investigation, 1.

19. FBI. (2009). *National Incident-Based Reporting System (NIBRS): Frequently Asked Questions*. Retrieved from http://www.fbi.gov/about-us/cjis/ucr/frequently-asked-questions/nibrs_faqs08.pdf

20. FBI, 2000, 9.

21. FBI, 2000.

22. Ibid., 9.

23. National Archive of Criminal Justice Data (NACJD). (2011). *National Crime Victimization Survey Resource Guide*.

24. O'Brien, 1985.

25. NACJD, 2011, 1.

26. O'Brien, 1985.

27. NACJD, 2011.

28. O'Brien, 1985, 47.

29. NACJD, 2011.

30. U.S. Department of Labor, Bureau of Labor Statistics. (2009a). "Market and Survey Researchers." *Occupational Outlook Handbook, 2010–11 Edition*. Retrieved from http://www.bls.gov/oco/ocos013.htm#addinfo

31. Council of American Survey Research Organizations (CASRO). (n.d.). "What Qualifications/Education Do I Need?" *CASRO Careers*. Retrieved from http://www.casro.org/careers/page1.html

32. U.S. Department of Labor, Bureau of Labor Statistics, 2009a.

33. CASRO. (n.d.). "Employment Outlook." *CASRO Careers*. http://www.casro.org/careers/page4.html

34. U.S. Department of Labor, Bureau of Labor Statistics. (2009b). "Occupational Information Included in the Handbook: Job Outlook." *Occupational Outlook Handbook, 2010–11 Edition*. Retrieved from http://www.bls.gov/oco/oco2001.htm#outlook

35. Thornberry, T. P., Huizinga, D., & Loeber, R. (2004). "The Causes and Correlates Studies: Findings and Policy Implications." *Juvenile Justice Journal, IX*(1), 3–19.

36. Mulvey, E. P. (2011). *Highlights from Pathways to Desistance: A Longitudinal Study of Serious Adolescent Offenders* (NCJ 230971). Washington, DC: Office of Juvenile Justice and Delinquency Prevention.

37. O'Brien, 1985.

38. CNN U.S. (2000, October 5). "Reporting Hate Crimes Presents Dilemma for Many Officials." Retrieved from http://articles.cnn.com/2000-10-05/us/justice.hate.crime_1_crimes-ethnicity-or-national-origin-incidents?_s=PM:US

39. FBI, 2001, 1.

40. Truman, J. L., & Rand, M. R. (2010). *Criminal Victimization, 2009. National Crime Victimization Survey* (NCJ 231327). Washington, DC: U.S. Department of Justice, Bureau of Justice Statistics, 1.

41. FBI. (2006). "Crime in the US, by Volume and Rate per 100,000 Inhabitants, 1986–2005." *Crime in the United States 2005*. Retrieved from http://www2.fbi.gov/ucr/05cius/data/table_01.html

42. Conklin, J. (2003). *Why Crime Rates Fell*. New York, NY: Allyn and Bacon.

43. Levitt, S. D. (2004). "Understanding Why Crime Fell in the 1990s: Four Factors That Explain the Decline and Six That Do Not." *Journal of Economic Perspectives, 18*(1), 163–190.

44. Ellis, L., Beaver, K. M., & Wright, J. (2009). Handbook of Crime Correlates. San Diego, CA: Academic Press.

45. Ibid.

46. Blumstein, A., & Cohen, J. (1979). "Estimation of Individual Crime Rates from Arrest Records." *Journal of Criminal Law and Criminology, 70*(4), 561–585.

47. Gottfredson, M. R., & Hirschi, T. (1990). *A General Theory of Crime*. Stanford, CA: Stanford University Press, 126.

48. For a critical overview of the latter, see Tubman-Carbone, 2009, 50–54.

49. Gabbidon & Greene, 2005a, 31–33; Walsh, 2004, 19–36; Wright, 2009, 143–144.

50. Ellis, Beaver, & Wright, 2009.

51. Gabbidon & Greene, 2005a, 31–33; Walsh, 2004, 22–23, 37–51.

52. Ellis et al., 2009.

53. Gottfredson & Hirschi, 1990, 184.

54. Lauritsen, J. L., Sampson, R. J., & Laub, J. H. (1991). "The Link between Offending and Victimization among Adolescents." *Criminology, 29*, 265–292.

55. Mazerolle, P., Burton, V. S., Cullen, F. T., Evans, T. D., & Payne, G. L. (2000). "Strain, Anger, and Delinquent Adaptations: Specifying General Strain Theory." *Journal of Criminal Justice, 28*(2), 89–102.

56. Lilly, J. R., Cullen, F. T., & Ball, R. A. (2007). *Criminological Theory: Context and Consequences* (4th ed.). Thousand Oaks, CA: Sage.

57. Ibid., 14.

58. Ferris, T. (2005). *Sentencing: Practical Approaches.* Toronto: Lexis-Nexis, 357.

59. Tibbetts, S. G., & Hemmens, C. (2010). *Criminological Theory: A Text/Reader.* Thousand Oaks, CA: Sage, 90.

60. Cohen, L. E., & Felson, M. (1979). "Social Change and Crime Rate Trends: A Routine Activities Approach." *American Sociological Review, 44*, 588–608.

61. Cornish, D. B., & Clarke, R. V. (Eds.). (1986). *The Reasoning Criminal: Rational Choice Perspectives on Offending.* New York, NY: Springer.

62. Thomas, D. H. (2001). *Skull Wars: Kennewick Man, Archaeology, and the Battle for Native American Identity.* New York, NY: Basic Books, 38–41.

63. Cosgrove, K. P., Mazure, C. M., & Staley, J. K. (2007). "Evolving Knowledge of Sex Differences in Brain Structure, Function, and Chemistry." *Biological Psychiatry, 62*(8), 847–855.

64. Redfield, J. W. "Comparative Physiognomy or Resemblances between Men and Animals: Illustrated."

65. Lombroso, 1896.

66. Ibid.

67. Wolfgang, M. E. (1973). "Cesare Lombroso." In H. Mannheim (Ed.), *Pioneers in Criminology* (2nd ed., pp. 232–291). Montclair, NJ: Patterson Smith.

68. Lilly et al., 2007, 19.

69. Ferri, E. (1897/1917). *Criminal Sociology.* Boston, MA: Little, Brown.

70. Dugdale, R. L. (1910). *The Jukes: A Study in Crime, Pauperism, Disease and Heredity.* New York, NY: G.P. Putnam's Sons.

71. Ibid., 66.

72. Sheldon, W. H. (1940). *The Varieties of Human Physique: An Introduction to Constitutional Psychology.* New York, NY: Harper & Brothers.

73. Moffitt, T. E., Ross, S., & Raine, A. (2011). "Crime and Biology." In J. Q. Wilson & J. Petersilia (Eds.), *Crime and Public Policy* (pp. 53–87). New York, NY: Oxford University Press.

74. Mednick, S. A., Gabrielli, W. F., & Hutchings, B. (1984). "Genetic Influences in Criminal Convictions: Evidence from an Adoption Cohort." *Science, 224*, 891–894. doi:10.1126/science.6719119

75. Lester, D., & Van Voorhis, P. (2000). "Psychoanalytic Therapy." In P. Van Voorhis, M. Braswell, & D. Lester (Eds.), *Correctional Counseling & Rehabilitation* (4th ed., pp. 111–128). Cincinnati, OH: Anderson.

76. Ibid.

77. Barton-Bellessa, S. M. (2010). "August Aichhorn: Wayward Youth." In F. Cullen & P. Wilcox (Eds.), *Encyclopedia of Criminological Theory.* Thousand Oaks, CA: Sage.

78. Ibid.

79. Cavan, R. S. (1983). "The Chicago School of Sociology, 1918–1933." *Urban Life, 11*, 415.

80. Park, R. E. (1928). "Human Migration and the Marginal Man." *American Journal of Sociology, 33*(6), 890.

81. McKenzie, R. D., Park, R. E., & Burgess, E. W. (1967). *The City.* Chicago, IL: University of Chicago Press.

82. Ibid.

83. Lilly et al., 2007.

84. Shaw, C. R., & McKay, H. D. (1942). *Juvenile Delinquency in Urban Areas*. Chicago, IL: University of Chicago Press.

85. Ibid.

86. Sutherland, E. (1934). *Principles of Criminology*. Chicago, IL: J.B. Lippincott.

87. Sutherland, E. H., & Cressey, D. R. (1970). *Criminology* (8th ed.). Philadelphia, PA: Lippincott, 75–76.

88. Durkheim, E. (1951). *Suicide: A Study in Sociology*. New York, NY: The Free Press.

89. Ohlin, L. (1956). *Sociology and the Field of Corrections*. New York, NY: Russell Sage Foundation.

90. Cloward, R., & Ohlin, L. (1960). *Delinquency and Opportunity*. New York, NY: The Free Press.

91. Agnew, R. (1992). "Foundation for a General Strain Theory of Crime and Delinquency." *Criminology, 30*(1), 47–87.

92. Ibid., 50.

93. Ibid., 57.

94. Hirschi, T. (1969). *Causes of Delinquency*. Berkeley, CA: University of California Press.

95. Brown, S. E., Esbensen, F., & Geis, G. (2004). *Criminology: Explaining Crime and Its Context* (5th ed.). Cincinnati, OH: Lexis-Nexis.

96. Gottfredson, M. R., & Hirschi, T. (1990). *A General Theory of Crime*. Stanford, CA: Stanford University Press, 89–90.

97. Cooley, C. H. (1902). *Human Nature and the Social Order*. New York, NY: Scribner's.

98. Mead, G. H. (1913). "The Social Self." *Journal of Philosophy, Psychology and Scientific Methods, 10*, 374–380.

99. Ibid., 379.

100. (1963). *Outsiders: Studies in the Sociology of Deviance*. New York, NY: The Free Press.

101. Brown, Esbensen, & Geis, 2004.

102. Braithwaite, J. (1989). *Crime, Shame, and Reintegration*. Melbourne, Australia: Cambridge University Press.

103. Braithwaite, J. (2000). "Shame and Criminal Justice." *Canadian Journal of Criminology, 42*(3), 281–298.

104. Akers, R. L., & Sellers, C. S. (2009). *Criminological Theories: Introduction, Evaluation, and Application* (5th ed.). New York, NY: Oxford University Press.

105. Lilly, J. R., Cullen, F. T., & Ball, R. A. (2011). *Criminological Theory: Context and Consequences* (5th ed.). Thousand Oaks, CA: Sage.

106. Williams, F. P., & McShane, M. D. (2004). *Criminological Theory* (4th ed.) Upper Saddle River, NJ: Prentice Hall.

107. Reiman, J., & Leighton, P. (2010). *The Rich Get Richer and the Poor Get Prison: Ideology, Class, and Criminal Justice* (9th ed.). Boston, MA: Allyn & Bacon.

108. Pepinsky, H., & Quinney, R. (Eds.). (1991). *Criminology as Peacemaking*. Bloomington, IN: Indiana University Press.

109. Pepinsky, H. (1999). "Peacemaking Primer." In B. A. Arrigo (Ed.), *Social Justice: Criminal Justice* (pp. 52–70). Belmont, CA: Wadsworth.

110. Lilly et al., 2011, 208.

111. Ibid.

112. Akers & Sellers, 2009.

113. Lilly et al., 2011.

114. Daly, K., & Chesney-Lind, M. (1988). "Feminism and Criminology." *Justice Quarterly, 5*, 497–538.

115. Lilly et al., 2011.

116. Barak, G. (1998). *Integrating Criminologies*. Boston, MA: Allyn and Bacon.

117. Ibid.

118. Wilson, J. Q., & Herrnstein, R. J. (1985). *Crime and Human Nature*. New York, NY: Simon & Schuster.

119. Elliot, D. S., Ageton, S. S., & Huizinga, D. (1985). *Explaining Delinquency and Drug Use*. Beverly Hills, CA: Sage.

120. Ibid., 94, 146.

121. Akers & Sellers, 2009.

122. Wright, J. P., Tibbetts, S. G., & Daigle, L. E. (2008). *Criminals in the Making: Criminality across the Life-Course*. Thousand Oaks, CA: Sage, 6.

123. Sampson, R. J., & Laub, J. H. (1993). *Crime in the Making: Pathways and Turning Points Through Life*. Cambridge, MA: Harvard University Press.

124. Kelley, B. T., Loeber, R., Keenan, K., & DeLamatre, M. (1997). "Developmental Pathways in Boys' Disruptive and Delinquent Behavior" (NCJ 165692). *Juvenile Justice Bulletin*. Washington, DC: Office of Juvenile Justice and Delinquency Prevention, 8–9.

125. Ibid.

126. Ibid.

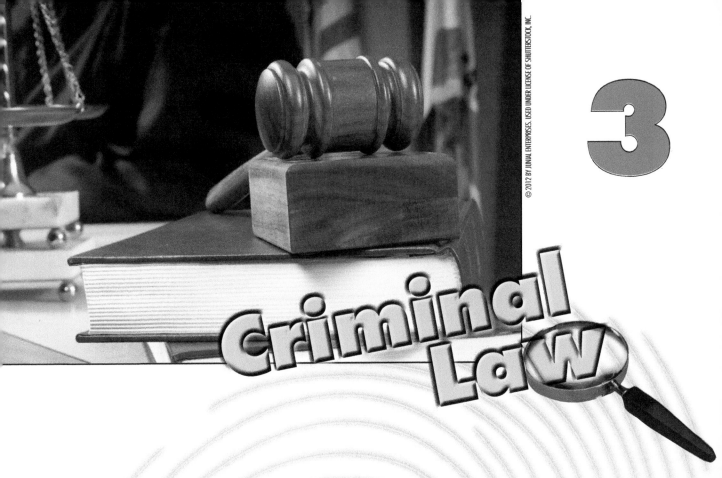

3

Criminal Law

KEY TERMS

Actus reus, Administrative law, Alibi, Alter ego rule, Case law, Causation, Civil law, Common law, Concurrence, Constitutional law, Corpus delicti, Criminal law, Damages, Double jeopardy, Ex post facto, Gross negligence, Infraction, Jurisprudence, Legal cause, Mens rea, Motive, Parole, Penal code, Precedent, Probation, Procedural law, Rule of law, Self-defense, Stare decisis, Statutory law, Tort

CHAPTER OBJECTIVES

1. Discuss and understand how common law affects the criminal justice system.
2. Discuss the rule of law and its place in western society.
3. Discuss the types of laws and the parts they play in the criminal justice system.
4. Identify categories of criminal law violation.
5. Describe the elements of a crime.
6. Identify and discuss the four categories of criminal defenses.

Case Study: The Rodney King Beating

On March 2, 1991, Rodney Glen King had just left the home of a friend, where he had been watching a basketball game and drinking beer. At about 12:30 A.M. on March 3, King and two friends were speeding down Interstate 210 in King's Hyundai. After traveling at speeds in excess of 110 mph, ignoring a marked California Highway Patrol cruiser that was following him, and running a red light and almost causing an accident, King was stopped. As two California Highway Patrol officers ordered King out of his car at gunpoint, four Los Angeles police officers—Sgt. Stacey Koon, Theodore Briseno, Laurence Powell, and Timothy Wind—arrived to render assistance. The four officers proceeded to arrest King, and even though he was handcuffed and on the ground, the officers struck King over 50 times with their metal batons.

George Holliday, a witness to the incident, filmed the beating. Holliday subsequently sent the videotape to a Los Angeles television station, which turned a copy over to the Los Angeles Police Department for review. The FBI launched an investigation against the police officers for the violation of King's civil rights. Days later, the LAPD chief of police and the Los Angeles County district attorney announced they would prosecute the officers for the King beating.

The defense filed a motion to change the venue out of Los Angeles County. Though the motion was initially denied by Judge Bernard Kamins, in July a California court of appeals unanimously granted a change of venue, and the trial was transferred to predominately white and conservative Simi Valley in Ventura County, California. The trial jury was ultimately comprised of 10 whites, one Hispanic, and one Filipino-American, and equally split between men and women.[1] The makeup of this jury was preferable for the defense, which hoped to avoid controversies about race. Some felt the white defendants would get more support or sympathy from a predominantly white, conservative jury. Many in the jury were pro-police and NRA supporters, increasing the chances of an acquittal.

The state trial of the four white police officers for beating Rodney King began on February 3, 1992. The officers held that King had been under the influence of an illegal substance and was not compliant with their orders to surrender. They maintained that they did not demonstrate excessive force, only that which was necessary to subdue King. On April 29, 1992, a state jury acquitted Koon, Briseno, and Wind, and was not able to reach a verdict on a charge against Powell. Much of the public was outraged by the acquittal, and large-scale riots broke out in Los Angeles, resulting in over $1 billion of property damage, 53 deaths, and over 7,000 people arrested.[2]

Although the officers were acquitted by the state court, they were later tried in federal court. On August 4, 1992, after an in-depth investigation by the FBI, a federal grand jury returned an indictment against Sgt. Koon and Officers Briseno, Powell, and Wind for violating the civil rights of Rodney King. The following April, Sgt. Koon and Officer Powell were sentenced to 30 months in a federal corrections camp, while Officers Briseno and Wind were found not guilty of any crimes. The prosecution appealed the decision, stating that the sentences were too lenient. The Ninth Circuit Court of Appeals sided with the prosecution's motion, but in June the U.S. Supreme Court reversed the Ninth Circuit Court's decision and upheld the original sentencing because of procedural errors.[3]

King filed a civil suit against the city of Los Angeles and was awarded $3.8 million in damages because of the actions of the police officers. A similar civil suit filed by King against the police officers themselves ended in no damages awarded. As a result of this incident, several changes were made by the Los Angeles Police Department to ensure that an incident like this would not happen again.[4] While this event had unfortunate consequences for King and the city of Los Angeles, ultimately the outcomes of the criminal and civil trials led to significant and beneficial changes to policing policies.

The U.S. Constitution is the foundation of the criminal justice system.

Constitutional Law   The U.S. Constitution is the foundation of the United States and serves as the backbone of criminal law. It is the Constitution that defines the relationship between states and the federal government and enumerates the basic rights that are afforded to all citizens of the United States. The Constitution also delineates the roles and functions of the three branches of federal government—executive, legislative, and judiciary—and directs law enforcement, the court system, and the legal systems as a whole.

The interpretation and implementation of the Constitution is the basis of **constitutional law.** Throughout the many steps of the criminal justice process, from the inception of a criminal investigation to the disposition of an offender, citizens' constitutional rights cannot be violated. The Fourth Amendment

Constitutional law
A judicial interpretation of the U.S. Constitution for court cases.

states, "The right of the people to be secure in their persons, houses, papers, and effects, against unreasonable searches and seizures, shall not be violated, and no Warrants shall issue, but upon probable cause, supported by oath or affirmation, and particularly describing the place to be searched, and the persons or things to be seized."[5] During a criminal investigation, law enforcement is constitutionally prohibited from conducting unreasonable searches of suspects or their property, a protection that was the crux of the Supreme Court case of *Mapp v. Ohio* (1961).[6]

In this case, the Cleveland Police Department received a tip from an informant that Dolly Mapp and her daughter were hiding a suspected bombing suspect. The police demanded entry and Mapp refused. She contacted her attorney, who advised her to continue to refuse their entry until police obtained a warrant. A few hours later, the police returned and this time forced entry, waving a piece of paper that they implied was a warrant but in fact was not. In the course of their search, the police discovered a trunk in Mapp's basement—left by a previous tenant, of which she had no knowledge—containing obscene materials. Neither the fugitive nor any other evidence was located inside the house during the search, but Mapp was arrested and later convicted for the illegal possession of obscene materials. At her appeal in the Ohio Court of Appeals, her attorney argued that the evidence was obtained from an illegal, warrantless search. The court upheld the conviction, stating that the evidence was not forcibly taken from her, but rather peacefully from an inanimate object, the trunk. Mapp's appeal was later taken to the U.S. Supreme Court, which ruled that Mapp's Fourth Amendment rights were violated and decided the case in Mapp's favor by a vote of 6–3.[7]

Another notable case, *Miranda v. Arizona* (1966), challenged the violation of a defendant's Sixth Amendment rights to a fair and speedy public trial by a jury of one's peers, the right to confront witnesses and the accuser, and the right to counsel.[8] After 23-year-old Ernesto Miranda was identified by the victim that he had kidnapped and raped, the Phoenix Police Department took him into custody for a two-hour interrogation. For the majority of the interrogation, Miranda maintained that he was innocent, but he finally relented and signed a written confession. The typed and signed confession contained the statement "I do hereby swear that I make this statement voluntarily and of my own free will, with no threats, coercion, or promises of immunity, and with full knowledge of my legal rights, understanding any statement I make may be used against me."[9] At trial, Miranda's court-appointed defense attorney argued that at no time during the arrest or interrogation was Miranda afforded legal counsel, and that he did not make the confession voluntarily and without coercion. The defense's objection was overruled, and Miranda was convicted of rape and kidnapping. In an appeal to the Arizona Supreme Court, the conviction was upheld based on the fact that Miranda did not specifically request an attorney.[10] This case did, however, change the practices of law enforcement throughout the United States. From that time forward, all suspects taken into custody have been read their Miranda rights, explicitly expressing that they have the right to remain silent, the right to an attorney, and that anything they say can be used against them in court.[11]

The Eighth Amendment prohibits excessive fines and bails.[12] Courts must ensure that each fine and bail is commensurate to the crime that was committed. This amendment also prohibits cruel and unusual punishments,[13] meaning that all punishments should fit the crime and capital punishment should not be used for non-homicidal crimes. Other constitutional freedoms and safeguards provided to criminal defendants—and all Americans—will be discussed throughout this book.

Several matters of constitutional law were evident in the trial of the officers in the Rodney King case. King's rights under the Constitution were determined by the courts to have been violated. Another matter of constitutional concern was whether the state and federal trials of the Los Angeles police officers constituted double jeopardy. However, an interpretation of the charges in both courts demonstrates that this was not a violation of constitutional law. The officers were tried in both state court and federal court because of the dual sovereignty doctrine, which holds that a person can be tried for similar crimes at the state and federal levels because they are considered to be different states or sovereignties. Furthermore, in this case, the officers were actually tried for two different crimes in the two courts—assault and battery in the state court and civil rights violations in the federal court. Thus, this was not a case of double jeopardy.

Critical Thinking   Should the federal government be able to prosecute someone for a similar crime if they have been acquitted by the state for the charges? Would this be considered double jeopardy and a violation of the U.S. Constitution?

Purpose of Law

Conflicts and crimes, both large and small in nature, occur in society every day. With the presence of laws, conflicts and crimes can be minimized, if not avoided. Durkheim's theory of social class holds that harmony, rather than conflict, defines society,[14] thus supporting the need for law and order. The development of norms set boundaries and helped maintain order in society, and these norms evolved into written laws, both civil and criminal. Some of these laws are created by the federal government, while similar laws are created and adopted at the state level, conforming to the individual state's needs. Norms set expectations of behavior for residents or visitors, defining the acts that are not accepted by society, and laws dictate how people should be punished if they do not conform to these standards of behavior. Norms and laws are essential to maintain order, regulate interactions, enforce moral beliefs, define the economic environment, promote orderly social change, identify wrongness, set punishment or restitution, and set the groundwork for rehabilitation.

Laws are created from customs, morals, and philosophies of acceptance by society, and they directly affect how people relate to one another, businesses, and the government. This principle is described as **jurisprudence** or the philosophy of the law. Jurisprudence consists of analytical, theological, and sociological components.[15] The analytical component defines the terms of law, which allows for consistency in the legal system. The theological component addresses

Jurisprudence
The philosophy of law.

Statutory law

A written law explicitly describing actions that are prohibited.

Case law

The entire collection of published legal documents and decisions of the courts; comprises a large portion of the legal rules that apply to modern society.

Precedent

A prior opinion from a court of appeals establishing the legal rule or authority for future questions on the same legal matter.

Common law

Law that is based on customs and legal precedents developed in Britain over hundreds of years.

Rule of law

A doctrine that no branch of government or public official may act arbitrarily outside the law. The rule of law dictates that any law enforced by the government must be fair, moral, and just.

the ideals behind the law—more of a concept than a concrete fact. Finally, the sociological component looks at how the law affects people in society.[16]

Laws are divided into statutory and case laws. **Statutory laws** are written laws and are comprised of criminal (or penal) codes and civil codes. **Case law** differs from statutory law in that it refers to decisions in legal cases that have previously been ruled upon by the courts. **Precedent** allows the courts to apply a consistent and equitable decision to a charge or defense. Unlike statutory law, case law can change depending on the circumstances of a specific case and the facts about a particular defendant.

Laws can be traced as far back as the Middle Ages in the courts of England. The laws were based upon **common law**, or unwritten and accepted customs, precedents, rules, and practices.[17] There are two forms of common law. The simplest form is the passing down of order, rules, and the concepts of right and wrong from parent to child. At school, teachers continue to develop children, teaching them socially acceptable norms. These unwritten rules have evolved into the official, written, codified laws of today's society. The other form of common law is precedent (or case law), in which prior judicial rulings have been made and the practice of those decisions has been set into place.

Rule of Law

In an effort to help establish a stable society—social, political, and economic—the **rule of law** (also referred to as the supremacy of law) was created by the government and enforced by the courts. Under the rule of law, no individual can be punished or compelled by the government to pay civil damages except in strict accordance to previously set, defined, and established procedures and laws. In addition, no government or government official can ever operate outside of the law. Furthermore, a universal principle of fairness and equality must dictate the enforcement of any law.

The origins of the rule of law date back to ancient Greece. The philosopher Aristotle stated that the government should be governed, as it became apparent that the government had the potential to abuse its power.[18] Aristotle further stated that the government must be "servants" of the people, meaning that laws should be established to help the government serve the people and ensure their freedom, not to turn the government into a dictatorship.

In order for laws to be effective and fair under the rule of law, each law must meet certain criteria. First and foremost, the law must be obeyed by everyone, including the government.[19] All laws must be published so that anyone can access them. Every law should be clearly written so that there is no confusion about its meaning, and it should not be contradictory to any other current law. The laws are published in a variety of

Case law is a decision in a legal case that was previously ruled upon by the courts.

President Nixon was denied the ability to block a subpoena for tapes that linked him to the Watergate conspiracy.

documents such as the government code, administrative code, penal code, and vehicle and labor codes, among many others. Additionally, all laws must be reasonable and allow for formalization of the rules, while allowing room for revision based upon social and political changes. Any official action must be consistent with the stated rule or law. Returning to the Chapter 1 discussion of Packer, societies need to have laws in place that will not only protect society from criminals, but will also punish criminals equally and fairly.[20]

All laws must be current and not **ex post facto**. In other words, the government cannot prosecute someone for an act if it was not illegal at the time it was committed, even if a law has since been passed that makes the act illegal. To use a hypothetical, if smoking cigarettes were made illegal, the government would not be permitted to punish anyone who was caught smoking a cigarette before the law went into effect. Any such punishment of an ex post facto crime is a violation of the U.S. Constitution and an individual's civil rights, and an abuse of the government's authority.[21]

One example of the rule of law in practice occurred when President Richard Nixon attempted to exercise his executive privilege to block a subpoena for a series of tapes that would have linked him to the Watergate conspiracy. Because of the U.S. Constitution's provision that no one governmental body has unlimited power, nor can it interfere with a criminal investigation, President Nixon could not block the subpoena.[22] [23]

The establishment of the rule of law ensures that all laws that are created are fair and unbiased, and are set up as a standard for everyone to understand and follow. This is not to say that laws, codes, and precedents cannot change, however. To the contrary, as the society changes, so can laws, adapting to the changes and values of society.

Ex post facto
A law dictating that a person cannot be charged or punished for a crime that occurred before the rule, law, or procedure was created.

Critical Thinking   Why is the "rule of law" necessary in western society?

Types of Laws
Laws can best be categorized into the following groups: criminal law, civil law, administrative law, and case law. Following is an overview of each group.

Criminal law
A set of rules and statutes that defines conduct prohibited by the government and establishes punishment for committing prohibited acts.

Criminal Law
Because society has established laws to assure the safety of its citizens, there must be a clear definition of what these laws are and what happens if an individual breaks them. Criminal law is the law that defines crimes and punishments. It can be divided into two components: substantive criminal law and procedural law. Substantive criminal law defines the law and establishes penalties. Procedural law describes or defines how the laws are enforced.

Given the number of criminal laws created by the federal government and by individual states, crimes are further classified into felonies, misdemeanors, infractions, and city, municipal, or county ordinances, and are then classified under different codes, such as the U.S. Code, penal codes, municipal codes, etc. The distinction between more serious crimes and lesser crimes is based upon the severity of the crime and the duration of the punishment or imprisonment.

But how do societies decide what is a serious crime and what is not? According to the early works of Sellin and Wolfgang, the seriousness of a crime is based upon the social norms of acceptance.[24] In 1964, Sellin and Wolfgang's study on the measurement of delinquency gave rise to one of the most used methods of weighing the seriousness of criminal offenses, the Crime Seriousness Index. Sellin and Wolfgang believed that "an accurate measure with which society views a broad range of criminal events would be helpful to lawmakers and policymakers. It could provide a measure of the appropriateness of sentencing practices and it could assist in the allocation of scarce justice resources."[25] They surveyed police officers, judges, and students to create a ranking of serious crimes, which was later incorporated into the legal system.

Critical Thinking   How might a change in society's view of crime change the seriousness of a particular crime? How might the advent of technology play a part in determining the seriousness of a crime and how it can potentially affect the victim?

Penal code
A set of codified laws in a legal system that describe a crime and its punishment at the state level.

Penal Codes
Penal codes are local or state codes of laws that set safety standards and dictate the punishments should an individual violate the laws. The penal code typically describes in great detail what entails a crime, the various types of crimes, and the punishments. The penal code also defines the criminal procedure, including the rights that are afforded to the defendant or suspect. It specifies that the defendant has the right to have counsel or representation and to have witnesses testify on his or her behalf. Another section of the penal code discusses state

prisons and county jails and defines the functions of these facilities to provide moral rehabilitation and restoration to good citizenship, and describes specifications regarding inmate rights, employment, and length of imprisonment. Finally, the penal code typically defines the law enforcement bodies established to prevent crime and apprehend criminals.

Felonies   A felony can be characterized as serious misconduct that is punishable by death or by imprisonment for more than one year. Felonies comprise all of the more serious crimes, broken down by degree.

In general, a felony such as murder may have several levels, such as first-degree murder, second-degree murder, and manslaughter. First-degree murder is the commission of the crime with premeditation and malice aforethought. An example of first-degree murder is a man who pursues his intended victim with the full intent of taking the person's life, plans the best time and place to find the victim, and prepares an escape route. Serious crimes such as murder usually involve a **motive** such as rage, jealousy, or revenge. For a charge of second-degree murder, unlike first-degree, the crime may not have been premeditated. Consider a case in which two coworkers get into a heated argument and the attacker fatally stabs the victim with a pair of scissors. This crime includes malice, but is not characterized by the same level of forethought as a first-degree murder.

Motive
In a criminal investigation, a probable reason that a person committed a crime.

A killing that involves no intent, forethought, or malice may lead to a charge of manslaughter. A drunk driver who is involved in a traffic accident and kills someone can be charged with vehicular manslaughter. The driver knew the potential consequences of his or her actions by driving drunk, but did not intend to take a human life.

Another serious and possibly violent felony is robbery. Robbery can be defined as the felonious taking of personal property in someone else's possession, in his or her immediate presence, against his or her will and by means of force or fear. As with murder, a defendant may be charged with different degrees of robbery depending on the circumstances of the crime. First-degree robbery applies if, in committing the robbery, the suspect is armed with a deadly weapon or anything that resembles a gun, or causes great bodily harm. First-degree robbery also applies to cases where the victim is driving a vehicle, using an ATM, or inside his or her home. The lesser version of this crime is second-degree robbery, which encompasses all robberies that are not covered in the first degree. The seriousness of the crime, naturally, determines the severity of punishment. A first-degree robbery conviction may be punishable by incarceration for a sentence of three to nine years; a second-degree robbery sentence may be two to five years.

Misdemeanors and Infractions   A misdemeanor is a less severe crime than a felony and is punishable by a fine and/or imprisonment in a county jail for no more than one year. A misdemeanor does not usually involve an act of violence.

An example of a misdemeanor is simple assault and battery ("simple" meaning that the victim did not suffer great bodily injury). Assault and battery is a crime in which one person physically hits or strikes another person, or acts in a threatening manner that causes fear in the victim. Another example of a misdemeanor is driving under the influence (DUI), which entails operating a motor vehicle while under the influence of alcohol or drugs (illegal or prescription) at a level that has been preset by statutory law.

Some misdemeanors can be reclassified as felonies based upon the crime. If a victim is seriously injured in an assault and battery case, the suspect can be charged with aggravated assault and battery, which is a felony. A drunk driver who seriously injures or kills a victim can be charged with felony drunk driving. Additionally, a misdemeanor can be moved into a felony class for a suspect who has committed the offense previously. Shoplifting is one such crime. Anyone who has been convicted more than three times is usually eligible for this enhancement because there is an obvious habitual trait and failure by the defendant to rehabilitate. The enhancement from a misdemeanor to a felony is written into the penal code to explicitly delineate which act or crime is punishable by either a felony or misdemeanor charge. In one California case, Andrew Pena Valenzuela was convicted of a petty theft in Merced, California. Valenzuela had been convicted twice before, but had served just one day in custody. Because of the repeated nature of his offense, the California courts enhanced his charge from a misdemeanor to a felony.[26]

Infraction
A lesser crime that is usually punishable by a fine.

Crimes that are considered less serious than misdemeanors are infractions, which are the most minor of all crimes and are punishable by a fine with no incarceration. This could include traffic tickets, parking tickets, or violations of city ordinances.

Federal Crimes and Special Crimes   In addition to laws that are specific to each state, there are established federal laws governing crime on a nationwide level. These cover crimes where the offender is in violation of several different laws at once, crimes that involve more than one state, or crimes that occur on or involve federal property. An example of a federal crime is narcotics trafficking. This crime

While driving under the influence is considered a misdemeanor, it can become a felony if a victim is injured or killed.

usually encompasses several federal crimes, such as the transportation of illegal drugs from one state to another, the use of a telephone or the mail to arrange for or transport the drugs, and tax evasion when there is a failure to pay federal taxes for a business transaction.

Crimes such as treason and espionage are considered "special crimes"—special not just because of the relative infrequency of these crimes, but because of their impact on society, the severity of the crime, and the punishment, which can include death.

Treason is the act of betraying one's own country or sovereignty by waging war against the country or purposefully aiding the enemy of one's country. This crime traces its origins as far back as 1327, when King Edward III of England created a statute that prohibited levying war against the king or aiding his enemies. Currently, under Article III, Section 3 of the U.S. Constitution, any person who levies war against the United States or gives aid and comfort to enemies has committed treason. The punishment for treason can be death, but no one has been executed for treason since World War II.[27]

One notable case of treason is the indictment of Adam Gadahn in October 2005. Gadahn, an American citizen living in Orange County, California, was charged with aiding and abetting terrorists. He showed his clear support of Al-Qaeda by appearing in videos as an Al-Qaeda spokesman and making statements such as "The streets of America shall run red with blood." His allegiance to Al-Qaeda was supported by pictures of Gadahn being introduced to the second-in-command for Al Qaeda.[28] Gadahn attempted to recruit soldiers for a jihad and then encouraged them to strike locations other than military installations in efforts to cripple the United States. After the indictment was filed against him, Gadahn fled to the Middle East and served as a captain in the Taliban Army, remaining at large as of October 2011.

Criminal espionage is the act of betraying the U.S. government's secrets to other nations. People that commit espionage are commonly referred to as spies. Most people convicted of espionage serve a life term; however, as with treason, the penalty for espionage can be death. In 1953, husband and wife Julius and Ethel Rosenberg were executed after stealing technical information from an atom research facility and selling the information to the Soviet Union.[29]

A more recent example of espionage is former FBI Agent Robert Hanssen, who was charged and convicted of being a spy against the United States for the Soviet and the Russian intelligence service for over 20 years. Because of his assignment with the FBI in the counterintelligence program, Hanssen not only had the training to avoid detection, but also the access to sensitive programs and information. Over the course of his career, Hanssen received cash and diamonds totaling over $600,000 and clandestinely exchanged valuable government documents, computer disks, and sensitive materials more than 20 times.[30]

Critical Thinking Would the criminal justice system be more effective and more uniform if there were only one set of codes that every state followed with no specific changes for any state?

Civil law

A body of laws that regulate non-criminal disputes, derived from Roman law. In civil law, laws are written and codified.

Legal cause

In tort law, the behavior or action that causes harm or proximate cause.

Tort

A breach of a civil duty or wrongful act that results in an injury to another or damage to their property.

Damages

Monetary compensation awarded by the court when someone has wronged another person or their property.

Civil Law

Civil law addresses non-criminal disputes. In civil law, disputes are generally due to a **legal cause**, an action that creates the genesis of the dispute. In other words, if not for the initial action, the dispute would not have occurred. The legal cause can include contracts, divorce, child custody, ownership of property, or monetary damages for personal property. Civil laws are based on state and federal statutes and on precedents set by cases previously tried. There are many types of civil law, as listed in Figure 3.1.

The basis of all civil law is a **tort**, which is a breach of a civil duty or a wrongful act that results in an injury to another or damage to their property. Depending on the nature of the breach, there is possibility for a criminal action to arise, such as fraud.

A civil lawsuit or trial is different from a criminal trial in that, instead of a defendant being charged with a crime by the state or federal government, an individual party (the plaintiff) files suit against another party who has allegedly wronged him or her. When a plaintiff successfully wins a civil lawsuit, he or she can be awarded compensatory damages or punitive damages. Compensatory **damages** are awarded to the victim for the actual financial or dollar loss. These damages can also include financial compensation for pain and suffering as well as the long-term quality of one's life.

FIGURE3.1 Types of Civil Law

Agricultural law	Includes areas such as crop harvesting, gardening, dairies, poultry farms, soil preparation, seed planting, and apiculture or raising bees.
Business law (or corporate law)	Includes corporate transaction and contracts, personnel issues, and the manufacturing and selling of various business and consumer goods.
Consumer law	Protects consumers against the production of faulty products and provides legal representation to make changes to correct the problems.
Employment law	Protects employees in their jobs, including but not limited to the hours of work, location and use of safety equipment, and overall working conditions.
Entertainment law	Protects actors and actresses, musicians, contracts, electronic game concepts, written manuscripts, and copyright issues.
Family law	Includes divorces, child custody, prenuptial agreements, and adoption issues.
International law	Includes making and enforcing interactions or contracts dealing with personal and business transactions or sales with other countries outside of the United States.
Medical malpractice	Deals with the receipt of bad medical care or treatment that caused temporary or permanent harm or damage.
Negligence law	Protects a consumer against misconduct, treatment, or misrepresentation by doctors, lawyers, or other licensed professionals.
Sports law	Protects athletes and teams in areas including contracts, management, and product production and distribution.
Tax law	Involves the protection of an individual or business when dealing with the Internal Revenue Service or other governmental agencies dealing with or pertaining to monetary transactions.

In addition to compensatory damages, the prevailing civil litigant can receive punitive damages. Punitive damages, or exemplary damages, are a way to punish the defendant for any harm the victim may have incurred as a result of the defendant's negligence or near criminal act. **Gross negligence** is defined as any reckless action or intentional failure to act that negatively affects a person or their personal property.

In cases in which more than one plaintiff brings a suit against a person or business, the civil action is referred to as a class action suit. While the plaintiffs may have varying levels of involvement or complaint, each one has been allegedly wronged for a similar behavior or violation.

Gross negligence
Lack of care or obvious disregard for another that results in damage or injury to another.

FIGURE3.2 Steps of the Criminal Justice Process

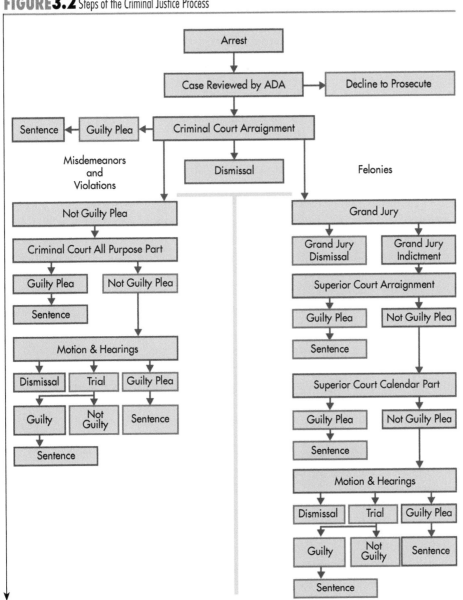

The Rodney King case, which was explored in the opening case study, demonstrates how criminal and civil law can overlap. At a California state trial, Officers Koon and Powell were found not guilty of assault and battery. However, the two defendants were then tried in a federal court for the civil rights violation against King, resulting in the convictions of Powell and Koon.[31] After this victory, King filed a civil suit against the officers for the violation of his civil rights. Because their actions had already been proven in the criminal trials, King was awarded $3.8 million dollars for compensatory damages, but was not awarded punitive damages.

Although the criminal act resulted in a conviction, a conviction is not always necessary for a civil suit to be filed and won. Most notably, in his criminal trial, O.J. Simpson was acquitted of the murder of his former wife, Nicole Brown Simpson, and her friend Ronald Goldman. However, Simpson was later found guilty in a civil suit for the wrongful death and battery of Brown and Goldman and was ordered to pay damages in the amount of $33,500,000.[32]

Procedural law

A set of laws that describe the formal steps to be taken in the legal process to protect the rights of all parties.

Procedural Law
Procedural law defines the process or steps that a criminal case will go through from beginning to end. As explained by Packer's due process model, the defendant's guilt is established in each step of the judicial process from the arrest to the exoneration or conviction.[33] The steps are clearly defined and include the initial arrest of a suspect; the collection, process, and preservation of evidence; the arraignment, preliminary hearing, trial, sentencing, and appeal; and the release of a defendant if found innocent or incarceration if found guilty.

These laws function both to protect society from criminals, as in Packer's crime control model,[34] and to ensure that every person who is accused and convicted of a crime is treated equally as appropriate for the crime they have committed, as in Packer's due process model.[35] One of the primary purposes of procedural law is to protect the defendant and assure the fairness of his or her trial.

Although each state has its own unique code of criminal procedure, they are all very similar, and usually follow a process like the following:

1. A suspect is arrested based upon probable or reasonable cause.
2. The prosecutor, state or federal, files charges against the accused.
3. The accused is arraigned on the charges filed.
4. The accused indicates whether he or she wishes to be represented by private counsel or public defenders.
5. A bail amount is set on the case (or denied depending on the circumstances).
6. A date is set for a court appearance.
7. If a plea agreement is not reached, then a date is set for pre-trial and trial if necessary.
8. If convicted at trial, the defendant has the right to an appeal.[36]

Administrative law

The area of law that controls, creates, and/or governs the administrative and regulatory agencies of the government.

Administrative Law
Administrative law is the area of law that controls, creates, and/or governs the administrative and regulatory agencies of the government. Administrative and regulatory agencies can be seen at the city,

county, state, and federal levels. Based upon the powers bestowed upon these agencies by Congress, they are responsible for creating procedures regarding laws, rules, regulations, applications, licenses, permits, hearings, and appeals for non-criminal cases.

Because the administrative agencies have expertise in their specific areas, they are tasked by Congress to make or recommend laws that are appropriate, applicable, and pertinent to the matters they regulate. They are tasked with ensuring the equality and fairness of each law that is created and guaranteeing due process for all administrative laws.

All government agencies are subject to checks and balances to make sure they do not abuse their power. The Administrative Procedure Act (APA), set into law in 1946, defines how agencies can propose and create regulations. Also contained in this act is a provision that allows the federal courts to review each agency's decisions.[37] Some administrative agencies include:

- The Environmental Protection Agency (EPA), which regulates the environment and its direct relationship to human health. This can include water and air quality.
- The Federal Communications Commission (FCC), which regulates radio and television and protects against inappropriate or vulgar materials in programming.
- The Federal Deposit Insurance Commission (FDIC), which protects the public against failing banks and insures financial deposits up to $100,000 should the bank fail.
- The Federal Trade Commission (FTC), which ensures a competitive marketplace and protects consumers against false advertising and unfair business practices.
- The Securities Exchange Commission (SEC), which protects securities and other investments.

Administrative law can overlap with criminal law. For example, a violation regarding illegal toxic waste disposal involves both a criminal and an administrative component. From an administrative standpoint, the company that illegally dumped the waste into a water source has violated the rules for proper disposal of toxic materials. The criminal component is that the company exhibited gross negligence that directly affected those who became ill from drinking the water. Such a case occurred in 1993 when the Pacific Gas & Electric Company was charged with trying to buy land that it had contaminated with deadly toxic waste because the waste was making the local residents very sick.[38]

Case Law   Case law refers to legal decisions based upon judicial decisions and precedents. When rendering a verdict or sentencing a criminal, a judge may use the precedent set by previous cases to help him or her make a decision. Similarly, the prosecution or defense counsel may reference a previous case that involved a similar situation or circumstance to help argue the defendant's innocence or guilt. Case law also applies to civil actions involving disputes over people or property.

Stare decisis
The doctrine that a trial court must adhere to appellate decisions or precedents raised in a lower court.

Many case laws are derived directly from judges' decisions and reasoning on a particular case in a lower court. In making these decisions, judges will review the verdicts or decisions in previous similar cases and precedents, and make a ruling that incorporates both the facts of the case at hand and previous judgments in similar cases. The act of relying on previously heard and decided cases is based on the principle of **stare decisis**. *Stare decisis* is Latin for "to stand by a decision," an appropriate description of the courts' ability to mirror previous court doctrines.[39]

Case law played a significant role in the Supreme Court case *Mincey v. Arizona*.[40] This case involved a narcotics raid during which an undercover narcotics officer was shot and killed. Police officers initiated a thorough search of suspect Rufus Mincey's residence without a search warrant. The Fourth Amendment prohibits illegal or unwarranted search and seizure, but there are exclusions to this rule if there are exigent circumstances such as a crime in progress; in this case, the exigent circumstances of a police officer getting shot allowed police to enter Mincey's home without a warrant. However, the investigation of the defendant's apartment continued over the course of four days, when there was no longer an urgent need to enter, and thus a warrant was needed. Meanwhile, Mincey was in a hospital being treated for injuries related to this shooting. He was investigated and interrogated, all while in a feeble state. He asked for an attorney, but one was not afforded to him.

Mincey's counsel, in arguing that the evidence and confessions were not admissible, made reference to prior case law and decisions such as *Escobedo v. Illinois*. In *Escobedo v. Illinois*, Danny Escobedo was arrested for the murder of his brother-in-law and subsequently taken to police headquarters for interrogation in connection to the fatal shooting. Throughout the interrogation process, Escobedo was placed in unreasonable conditions such as having to stand for hours and was disregarded every time he requested his attorney. The court's decision in the Escobedo case set the precedent that if a suspect asks for an attorney, police cannot continue to question or interrogate the suspect until he or she has counsel.[41]

This case law helped influence the *Mincey* decision. The courts ultimately ruled that Mincey's Fourth Amendment rights had been violated and, therefore, any evidence collected from his home was not admissible in court. The house search was deemed unreasonable because there was no danger that evidence would be destroyed if the police waited to get a search warrant. Additionally, the statements made by the defendant in the hospital, which were obtained after he had requested and been denied an attorney, were excluded because of the violation of his Sixth Amendment rights. He had no ability to leave the police interrogation because of his condition.[42]

Basic Features and Elements of a Crime

For a person to be found guilty of a crime, he or she must meet certain minimum standards or criteria—the elements of a crime. Once a suspect is in custody, it is the prosecution's responsibility to assure that all supportive evidence exists and meets the specific elements of a particular crime. For someone to be charged with murder, for example, the elements of the crime must include the killing of a person by another individual with malice aforethought.

The four key components that must be present for a criminal act to have been committed are actus reus, mens rea, concurrence, and causation. If the prosecution is missing any one of these elements, a case can be very difficult to prosecute.

Actus reus
The act that is committed in a crime.

Actus Reus: The Criminal Act
Any violation of law is a criminal act or actus reus. *Actus reus* is a Latin term that translates to "the guilty act," which is the first of the key elements of a crime—i.e., the commission of the crime. Every statutory law outlines a list of "elements" or requirements for a criminal act to occur, each one of which must be met. For example, for someone to be convicted of kidnapping, the following must occur: a victim must be (1) taken by fear or force, held, detained, or arrested by another person, **and** (2) taken to another location. If one part or one element is missing—for instance, if a victim is asked to go with the suspect, and is free to leave at any time—then the act does not legally constitute the crime of kidnapping.[43]

This does not, however, prevent a defendant from being charged with a conspiracy to commit a crime, or a lesser charge that will carry a lesser sentence if convicted. Attempted murder, for example, does not require the actual death of someone, just the intent to commit or conspire to commit murder.

To be found guilty of a crime, a person must meet minimum criteria known as the elements of a crime.

Mens Rea: A Guilty Mind
Another critical element in the criminal act is mens rea. *Mens rea*, Latin for "guilty mind," refers to the state of mind to commit a crime.[44] Mens rea is equally as important as actus reus. Without proof of malicious intent by the offender, the crime may be considered an accident or unintentional. Ultimately, the prosecution needs to demonstrate that the act was either committed with the perpetrator's full knowledge that the act was wrong, committed with a purpose, performed as an act of recklessness, or committed as the result of a negligent act. A burglar who breaks into a locked residence intending to steal items has clear and full knowledge that his or her actions are criminal. The burglar is attempting unlawful access to a residence without an invitation and is taking someone else's possessions.

Mens rea
The intent to commit a criminal act.

A drunk driver who knows that he or she should not be driving but does it anyway has shown the "guilty mind" for being intoxicated in public. If the drunk driver then runs a red light, strikes another vehicle, and kills another person, he or she has acted recklessly. The driver did not intend to kill someone, but by knowing that he or she was not in a state of mind or sober to drive, the driver has committed a reckless act.

Critical Thinking What makes it challenging to prove mens rea beyond a reasonable doubt? What are some of the ways that mens rea can be proved?

Concurrence

The combination of actus reus (the commission of the crime) and mens rea (the intent to commit the crime).

Causation

A definitive link between the offender's criminal act and the victim's suffering.

Corpus delicti

The body of evidence; proof that a crime has been committed.

Concurrence

The third required element of a crime is **concurrence**, the combination of actus reus and mens rea. It refers to the simultaneous merging of a person's intent to commit a crime with the actual commission of the crime.

An example of concurrence is a suspect who closely watches a bank for several days and formulates a plan for robbing it. Ultimately he enters the bank, threatens the teller with a gun, steals several thousand dollars in cash, and then exits in a getaway car. In this case, the robber had full knowledge that he was planning to commit a criminal act and then followed through on the crime of robbing the bank, giving full concurrence.

Conversely, if a man is stopped by a police officer for a traffic violation in front of a bank and, in the process of giving him a ticket, the officer sees a mask and a large bag on the front seat, the officer cannot arrest the man for robbery. Although those items are commonly used in robberies, the actus reus has not occurred—the man has not actually committed the act of robbing the bank. This demonstrates a lack of concurrence.

Causation

The final element of a crime is **causation**—a definitive link between the offender's criminal act and the victim's suffering. If the act cannot be proved to have been the source of the victim's pain, the element of causation is not met. In certain cases, causation can lead to charges being brought against a suspect long after the initial criminal act. In Michigan, a man was shot in the heart by two suspects during a robbery attempt. He survived the attack, but his heart was weakened by the shooting. Four years later, he died of a heart attack. The Michigan courts convicted the shooters of murder because their initial act eventually caused the victim's death.[45]

While examining the criminal act, it is important to discuss the **corpus delicti**. *Corpus delicti* is a Latin term meaning "body of evidence."[46] In a violent crime such as murder, the corpus delicti is the dead body. The prosecution has its strongest case when corpus delicti is present, although when it is not, they

A criminal act that includes corpus delicti generally gives the prosecution a stronger case.

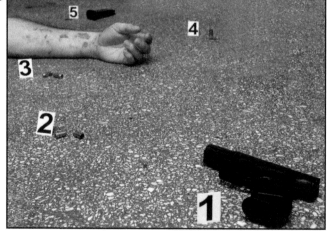

can still move forward with the case and prosecute a suspect based upon strong circumstantial evidence. Circumstantial evidence refers to presumed evidence rather than conclusive evidence. For example, even if a victim's body is not found, the prosecution may focus on circumstantial evidence, noting that a significant amount of blood was found at the crime scene along with bullet cases, and that the victim is missing.

Defenses for Crimes

Just as it is the responsibility of the prosecution to prove that a crime has been committed, the defense attorney's role is to mitigate the punishment of the defendant or argue that the defendant is not criminally accountable.

Alibis

A common defense is for a defendant to claim that he or she is not guilty because he or she was in a different location at the time the crime was committed. This is known as an *alibi*, a Latin word that means "in another place."[47] A defendant's alibi is made stronger if he or she can produce a corroborating witness or physical evidence for support.[48] If a defendant accused of murdering his wife claims he was out of town on a business trip, but cannot produce witnesses or evidence to support his alibi, his defense will carry little weight. If, however, he can provide a plane ticket, hotel reservations, and witnesses to testify that he was at a business meeting at the time of the crime, his alibi would likely support his innocence.

Alibi
A defense to a criminal charge stating that the accused was somewhere other than at the scene of the alleged crime.

Justifications and Excuses

Defendants may use justifications or excuses to defend their actions in a court of law. Justifications usually refer to situations in which the defendant admits to committing the act, but claims that he or she did so for appropriate or necessary reasons. A justification is the offering of a reason for acting in a particular way in a particular situation. Excuses, in a similar vein, refer to situations in which the defendant confirms being the perpetrator but denies responsibility for his or her actions because of extenuating circumstances, such as a lack of free will.

Self-Defense

One justification for a criminal act, based on the Second Amendment of the U.S. Constitution, is the right to **self-defense**.[49] Every person has the right to protect himself or herself from harm from another individual. Self-defense is further supported by the Criminal Law Act of 1967, which states, "A person may use such force as is reasonable in the circumstances in the prevention of crime, or in effecting or assisting in the lawful arrest of offenders or suspected offenders or of persons unlawfully at large."[50] If, in that process, the other person is injured or killed, the action may be excusable because the intent was not to harm the attacker, but rather to protect oneself from harm.

Self-defense
The use of force to protect oneself or one's family from bodily harm from an attacker.

For example, if a person is being attacked by a person with a knife, and in the process the victim disarms and stabs the suspect, then the victim is employing self-defense. Only the necessary force to stop the aggressive act is permissible for justification of defense. In other words, it may be necessary to stab the suspect, but once the victim has stopped the threat, he or she cannot continue to cause damage or harm to the suspect beyond what is necessary to alleviate the threat. This holds true of all other defenses.

Defense of Others   As with self-defense, there may also be a situation in which another person may be in danger of harm, injury, or death, but cannot protect himself or herself due to age, mental state, or medical condition. In such cases, a third party can use necessary force to protect the victim from grave harm or danger. A classic example is a parent defending a child who is in grave danger from an attacker. It is reasonable for the parent to use whatever means possible to free the child and restrain the attacker until the police arrive. As with self-defense, one can only use the necessary force to terminate the threat that is immediate and imminent.

Very similar is the **alter ego rule**, in which a person acts for another who is in the position of needing to be defended but does not have the capability himself or herself. If a woman in a wheelchair were being assaulted, a bystander could step in to defend her with necessary force against the attacker. This is an acceptable defense because if the woman in the wheelchair were not incapacitated, she would have defended herself. Support of these actions is similar to self-defense as described under the Criminal Law Act of 1967[51] and the Second Amendment.[52]

Alter ego rule
A criminal defense where one person defends another person who cannot defend themselves.

Defense of Home and Property   Individuals have the legal right to protect not only themselves, but also their homes and property. A homeowner could incapacitate a burglar who had broken into the house and detain him or her until the police arrive. Defense of home and property operates under the same provisions as self-defense, in that a homeowner has the right to use only the necessary and reasonable amount of force to stop the criminal act. If the homeowner shouts at the burglar to leave and the burglar is fleeing the scene and no longer poses any threat, the homeowner does not have the legal right to shoot him or her.

Necessity   The necessity defense presents the argument that if the defendant had not committed a criminal act, a more serious criminal act would have or could have occurred—in other words, a person engaged in a criminal act only to avoid an even greater harm to themselves or others. This defense applies only if there is reasonable belief that the defendant or someone else was in danger of suffering significant bodily harm, that there was no reasonable alternative other than engaging in the criminal conduct, that the criminal act ceased as soon as the danger had passed, and that the defendant did not create the danger himself or herself. An example could include a customer in a liquor store who shoots a robbery suspect who is attempting to set fire to the store, which would cause harm or death to a large number of people. The taking of one life, barring any alternative, ultimately prevented the potential loss of multiple lives and property.

Many court cases have established the limits of the necessity defense. One of the more historic cases occurred in England in 1884. The case of *The Queen v. Dudley and Stephens* involved four men—Thomas Dudley, Edwin Stephens,

Edmund Brooks, and Richard Parker—who were cast away in a storm while on a yacht. The four were stranded on a life vessel for 20 days, and eventually decided that the only way to survive was to kill and eat one of the survivors. The 17-year-old Parker was chosen against his will because he was the weakest and youngest. Upon being rescued, the three other men were brought to trial, where they claimed the necessity defense. The defendants were found guilty of murder because they had no need to defend themselves against Parker, who was not posing any threat.[53]

Consent The defense of consent argues that no crime was actually committed because the accused had permission to act as he or she did. For example, a suspect accused of stealing a car may claim that she had permission from the owner to use the car. If the suspect did in fact have consent, then not all elements of the crime were met and thus, by legal definition, a crime was not committed. By contrast, if a couple is engaged in sexual intercourse and the woman tells her partner to stop and he does not, the element of consent is not present. The act is against her will and is a crime of sexual assault.

Resisting Unlawful Arrest The defense of resisting unlawful arrest occurs when a suspect, in the process of being arrested, feels that he or she has been wrongfully accused of a crime and therefore should not be taken into custody. Consider the scenario of a suspect who, while being detained through physical force by a store security guard after being falsely accused of theft, attempts to get free and causes physical injury to the guard. The defendant may attempt to use the resisting unlawful arrest defense in this instance.

In the case of *Plummer v. State*, 136 Ind. 306, the defendant was approached by a police officer because he was carrying a gun and threatening violence. Before Plummer was told that he was under arrest, he was struck over the head by the police officer. The officer then shot at Plummer, who shot back, killing the police officer. Plummer was convicted of murder, but upon appeal, the Indiana Supreme Court overturned the verdict, citing that all individuals have a right to defend themselves, even against a police officer. Because the officer had not yet placed Plummer under arrest, he had the right to fight back.[54]

Accident The accident defense states that a criminal act occurred as a result of an accident. The crux of this defense is that the defendant had no forethought to commit a crime—the element of mens rea is not present.

The accident defense may be used, for example, in a situation in which two intoxicated bar patrons begin to fight and one man shoves the other, causing the victim to fall and hit his head on the floor, killing him. The accident defense is presented because the defendant had no intent to kill the victim, but rather the victim accidentally lost his balance during a fight, leading to his death. In this scenario, the defendant could be charged with negligence because of his behavior.

The accident defense was presented in the case of *Wright v. State of Delaware* (2008). The defendant, Jerrin Wright, was in the parking lot of a bar when he took out a handgun and attempted to shoot another person. In the process, he missed his intended target, striking and killing an innocent person. Wright's defense claimed that the crime was an unfortunate accident, but the jury convicted him of second-degree murder. The court found that although the victim was not Wright's intended target, he did use a loaded weapon in a public place with the intent to harm another.[55]

Duress The duress defense states that a criminal act was committed because of an extremely compelling or threatening reason. This defense contends that if the defendant did not commit the crime, his or her life, family, or property would be at risk. In order to prove that the defendant was under duress, the defense must demonstrate that a threat of serious bodily harm or death existed, that the threat of harm outweighed the crime, that the threat was immediate and inescapable, and that the defendant did not cause the threat of harm.

In *Dixon v. United States* (2006), Keshia Dixon was arrested for illegally purchasing firearms. At trial, Dixon stated that she had no choice but to purchase the firearms because her boyfriend had abused her and she feared he would harm or kill her or her children if she did not buy the firearms. The court denied her duress defense, as Dixon was unable to prove that she had not acted willingly. Her conviction was upheld on appeal.[56]

Age The age defense can range from young to old, from a suspect who is a minor (under 18) to an elderly person who cannot understand that what he or she has done is illegal because of decreased mental capability. The prevailing thought by the courts and society is that minors under the age of 18 may know the difference between right and wrong but are not fully aware of the law or what constitutes a crime or violation of the law. On the other end of the spectrum, older people (usually over 60) may have some genetic deficits or medical conditions such as

The age defense can apply to a suspect who is under the age of 18.

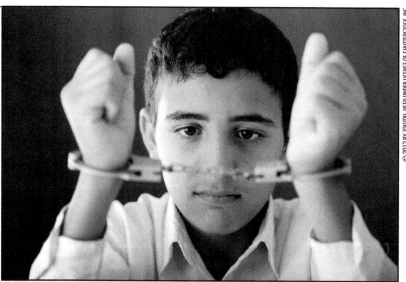

Alzheimer's disease or dementia that leave them unaware of their actions due to a lack of higher brain function.[57]

There are some circumstances, however, in which a minor can be tried as an adult and the excuse of age is not applicable. One notable case involving a youthful offender was *Roper v. Simmons* (2005). Seventeen-year-old Christopher Simmons was convicted of burglary and the murder of Shirley Crook after breaking into her house, tying her up, and throwing her off of a bridge. Simmons confessed to the crime and was sentenced to death. On appeal, however, the U.S. Supreme Court found it unconstitutional to impose capital punishment for an offender under 18 years old.[58]

Mistake   The mistake defense articulates that a defendant was not aware that his or her actions were criminal. This mistake or ignorance of the law is generally not accepted by the courts, even if the defendant attempts to prove that there was no mens rea in the crime. An example is a woman who answers an ad on an Internet site such as Craigslist where items are routinely sold, and ends up buying stolen items. The defendant may use the mistake defense because she had no expectation or awareness that the items were not truly owned by the seller and were actually stolen goods.

Involuntary Intoxication   The defense of involuntary intoxication asserts that a defendant was given alcohol and/or a drug without their consent or knowledge, and committed a crime as a result. Because of the intoxication, the defendant was not fully aware of his or her actions or that what he or she was doing was illegal. An example is a man who is—unbeknownst to him—given a drug in his drink, and as a result strikes and kills a pedestrian while driving home.

Unconsciousness   The defense of unconsciousness asserts that a defendant was sleeping, delirious, or having a seizure when he or she committed a crime, and thus was unaware of his or her actions because of this altered state. This defense may be used by someone who has a medical condition such as seizures or narcolepsy and takes medications to control the condition. The defendant may allege that he or she was taking a medication that made him or her lose consciousness.

In the case of *United States of America v. Walton Dawson* (2006), Dawson was arrested for being a felon in possession of ammunition. During his trial, Dawson tried to use the defense that he had suffered from an "alcoholic blackout," or a loss of memory as a result of his chronic alcoholism, and was not aware of how he obtained the ammunition that was found in his pocket at his arrest. The court convicted Dawson, stating that the unconsciousness defense did not apply to voluntary intoxication. Dawson attempted to appeal the decision, claiming that he suffered from a brain dysfunction as the result of years of drinking. The court upheld the conviction.[59]

Provocation   The provocation defense argues that a suspect acted in the heat of passion or uncontrollable anger caused by another. If not for an act that made the suspect angry or enraged, he or she would not have acted irrationally or committed a crime. Although it does not excuse the crime, the provocation defense can be offered in an effort to receive a reduced sentence or judgment. An example is a jealous husband who, upon finding his wife engaged in sexual conduct with another man, strikes the other man with a lamp, killing him. The defendant may argue that there was no premeditation for the murder; rather, it was a crime of passion.

In *R v. Doughty* (1986), the defendant argued that he killed his 17-day-old baby because it provoked him by constantly crying.[60] Doughty was convicted because he was not able to show that the baby had provoked him into the murder. Furthermore, the Homicide Act of 1957 states, "Where on a charge of murder there is evidence on which the jury can find that the person charged was provoked to lose his self-control, the question whether the provocation was enough to make a reasonable man do as he did shall be left to be determined by the jury."[61] Clearly Doughty could not show any provocation that would justify killing an infant.

Insanity   A more common excuse for committing a crime is that the defendant was not legally sane or of a sound mind when the crime was committed. The defense must definitively prove the defendant's state of mind at the time of the crime. Courts usually conduct a special hearing to determine whether a defendant is of sound mind and can stand trial. The test that many states have accepted for determining if someone is legally sane is the M'Naghten test, which is designed to indicate whether someone knows the difference between right and wrong.[62] It is the responsibility of the defense to prove that the defendant could not distinguish right from wrong at the time of the crime or was unaware that the actions constituted a crime.

The insanity defense took center stage in the case of LaShaun Harris and the drowning of her three kids—a six-year-old, a two-year-old, and a 16-month-old—in the San Francisco Bay on October 19, 2005. Witnesses observed Harris undressing her three kids, whom she knew could not swim, and tossing them into the water. Her reasoning for performing such an act was that God had instructed her to do it so that her kids would go to heaven. Harris was later found to be a schizophrenic and borderline mentally retarded. In lieu of her 25-year sentence for second-degree murder rendered on January 16, 2007, Harris was committed to a psychiatric hospital where she could receive mental health help.[63]

Diminished Capacity   The defense of diminished capacity claims that a defendant is not guilty because his or her mental functions were diminished or impaired. This can include a person with an IQ of less than 60. For example, in a state-run hospital for individuals with severe disabilities such as Down syndrome or mental retardation, a patient with a chronological age of 42 may have a mental age of six. If this patient throws a chair at another resident and causes serious injury, he likely cannot decipher that what he did was wrong.

In September of 1982, Betty Horn drove into a gas station and tried to pay for her gas with an AAA Towing card. When the clerk would not accept the card or allow her to drive home to get money, Horn called a friend to bring her the money. While she was waiting, however, Horn went back to her car and drove away, with the clerk pursuing her. During the chase, Horn ran a red light at an intersection and struck and killed a motorcyclist. Horn was initially charged with and convicted of vehicular manslaughter, but on appeal, she was found to not have been of sound mind at the time of the accident and the charge was overturned. Her attorney demonstrated that she had a history of mental illness, including manic depression and bipolar disorder.[64]

Procedural Defenses

Procedural defenses differ from excuses or justifications in that rather than defending the defendant's actions, they challenge the procedure by which the defendant was arrested or tried. Procedural defenses include collateral estoppel, denial of a speedy trial, entrapment, double jeopardy, selective prosecution, and prosecutorial misconduct.

Double Jeopardy

The Fifth Amendment of the U.S. Constitution states, "No person shall be subject for the same offence to be twice put in jeopardy of life or limb."[65] This defense, known as **double jeopardy**, means that a person cannot be prosecuted a second time for the same crime following an acquittal or receive multiple punishments for the same crime.

In the Supreme Court case of *Ashe v. Swenson* (1970), Bob Ashe was accused with several other men of breaking into a house and robbing six men who were playing poker. In the first trial, Ashe was acquitted of the charges after the prosecution was unable to show that that any of the victims or witnesses could positively identify him. Upon gathering new evidence, the state once again charged Ashe, and this time he was convicted to a sentence of 35 years in prison. On appeal, Ashe's defense team argued that trying Ashe for a crime for which he had already been acquitted was a violation of his Fifth Amendment rights. The court found in his favor and he was released.[66]

Collateral Estoppel

Collateral estoppel is a legal doctrine that prevents a person from re-litigating an issue or crime. Usually, collateral estoppel pertains to civil actions and is done to preclude and prevent legal harassment and abuse of judicial resources by refiling and retrying the same case; however, it can also apply to criminal cases. It is very similar to the protection against double jeopardy in the Fifth Amendment, and in fact, collateral estoppel falls under the double jeopardy clause. Several elements must occur in order to employ a collateral estoppel defense: the defendant must be tried for the same crime or civil matter, the defendant must be charged by the same prosecutor or plaintiffs, and there must not have been a conviction or judgment in the previous trial.

Denial of Speedy Trial

The Sixth Amendment of the U.S. Constitution guarantees the right to a speedy trial by an impartial jury of the defendant's peers, as well as the right to legal counsel.[67] Speedy, in this case, means that there is no unreasonable delay such as weeks or months before the court process is begun. While the trial itself might not occur until several days, weeks, or months after the initial plea is entered before the court, the suspect has the right to be brought in

Double jeopardy
A provision of the U.S. Constitution that prohibits state and federal governments from prosecuting individuals for the same crime more than once, or imposing multiple punishments for a single offense.

front of a judge or magistrate within a reasonable time period (which can be a few days), and he or she must be allowed to have an attorney (or counsel) if requested. This amendment also carries the provision that if the defendant does not have money for an attorney, a public defender will be appointed to his or her case to assure the defendant receives a fair trial.

Entrapment The defense of entrapment contends that police coerced, harassed, or threatened an individual to commit a crime that the defendant would not have normally committed. In order to prove entrapment, defense counsel must prove that one of the parties was an agent of the government, and that the defendant would not have committed the crime if he or she had not been presented with the opportunity. Consider a scenario in which a man goes to a massage parlor with the intent of simply getting a massage. During the massage, the masseuse—who is actually an undercover police officer—offers a sexual favor to the man for money, and he agrees. The man is then arrested for soliciting a prostitute. This could be considered entrapment because the man went into the business for a massage and not intending a sexual encounter until coerced.[68] Entrapment can be construed as a violation of due process under the Sixth Amendment, which dictates that the government has the responsibility to follow the law.

Selective Prosecution The defense of selective prosecution argues that a defendant cannot be charged with a crime solely based on his or her age, race, religion, or gender. In other words, anyone who was engaged in the same illegal action as the defendant must be prosecuted equally. Within the Fourteenth Amendment of the U.S. Constitution is the equal protection clause, which clearly states that "all men are created equal"[69] and they are subject to all of the same laws. Anyone who is treated differently by the police or the courts would be able to use the defense of selective prosecution. A prime example of selective prosecution is a police officer or firefighter who gets pulled over for driving under the influence and does not get arrested because of professional courtesy. There is no law that excludes police officers or firefighters from the statutory laws.[70]

Prosecutorial Misconduct The prosecutorial misconduct defense contends that a defendant should not be held criminally liable for his or her actions because the prosecution acted in an inappropriate or unfair manner. Prosecutorial misconduct may include inappropriate actions such as failing to share all evidence that could convict or exonerate the defendant, or knowingly allowing inaccurate testimony or evidence. The prosecution is mandated to turn over all evidence to the defense when asked, even if the evidence can help the defense with their case to exonerate the defendant.

Police Fraud The police fraud defense alleges that the police acted improperly toward a defendant. This defense holds that the police knowingly and willingly violated a suspect's rights by not allowing them the constitutional rights afforded by law. Examples might include the police continuing to question the

Police fraud can include falsely coercing a confession.

suspect even after he or she asked for a lawyer, depriving a suspect of water, food, or sleep, or promising a lesser charge for a confession.

Police Misconduct   Police misconduct is the defense that police operated in an unethical or illegal manner by planting evidence, lying about the facts of the case, or using unreasonable force for a particular situation. This misconduct can include false arrest or imprisonment, intimidation or false confession, brutality or corruption, racial profiling or discrimination, falsified evidence, political oppression, sexual abuse, surveillance abuse, or even off-duty misconduct.[71] Abuse or misconduct can extend into lying or using the official position, badge, or uniform to receive special privileges or discounts.

Police misconduct generally consists of much more serious offenses than police fraud. A police misconduct defense was presented by O.J. Simpson's attorneys at trial. Simpson's defense team alleged that Detective Mark Fuhrman planted a "bloody glove" at the crime scene in order to implicate Simpson as the killer.[72]

Lawmakers have put several laws in place in an effort to eliminate police misconduct, including Section 1983 in Title 42 of the United States Code, which was originally passed as part of the Civil Rights Act of 1871, stating that everyone shall be entitled to the laws and protections in the U.S. Constitution.[73] Other safeguards include the Fourth Amendment, which protects against false arrest in which there is no legal or valid reason for the search and seizure, and the Fourteenth Amendment, which ensures citizens' right to liberty.

Reviewing Packer's theories of crime, a supporter of Packer's crime control model,[74] which favors getting criminals off the street at any cost, might have a different perspective on police misconduct than would a supporter of Packer's due process model,[75] who would seriously object to police misconduct in any form.

The exclusionary rule dictates that any evidence that was illegally obtained cannot be admitted into court or used for prosecution. Any act of police fraud or misconduct would lead to the use of the exclusionary rule. The genesis of this rule extends back to the Fourth Amendment of the U.S. Constitution, which states that no one shall be subjected to an unwarranted search or seizure.

Qualified Immunity Defense   A qualified immunity defense can be used to defend a police officer accused of a crime. This defense states that a police officer has immunity from breaking the law while in the course of defending the law. Abuse of this immunity, however, can be considered police misconduct.

Lack of Probable Cause   The defense of lack of probable cause means there is belief that the police did not have probable or reasonable cause to seize evidence that led to a defendant's arrest. This lack of probable cause is closely related to the Fourth Amendment of the U.S. Constitution and its protection against unlawful search and seizure. An example could include a police officer who pulls over and searches a car because the driver "looks like a wanted suspect," when in fact there is no wanted suspect and this was just the officer's excuse to justify his actions. In the process of searching the car, the officer finds drugs in the trunk. Because the initial car stop was flawed, all subsequent evidence that was seized is inadmissible under the exclusionary rule.

Mistaken Identity   The mistaken identity defense contends that a defendant was arrested based solely upon a similarity to the actual suspect (looks, clothing, car, etc.). The defense may try to convince the judge or jury that the defendant cannot be positively identified as the perpetrator of the crime, and that the police wrongly identified the defendant because he or she is similar in some way to the actual perpetrator, such as ethnicity, age, hair color and style, and other physical features.

Abuse Defense   The abuse defense claims that a defendant acted as a result of extended or unusual abuse, either physical or psychological. This defense could be used by a victim of domestic abuse who hurts or kills the attacker to end any further abuse or neglect. Because the abuse is an ongoing issue, the psychological damage can be cumulative. As a result, the abuse victim may strike out even at a time when there is no abuse occurring.[76]

Punishments for Crimes

When a defendant is convicted of a crime, a specific punishment is levied based on the nature and circumstances of the crime. Penalties can vary from state to state, but they are usually determined based upon similar criteria such as the type of crime, prior criminal record, age, and other ancillary factors such as cooperation with law enforcement. Punishments can include incarceration, probation or parole, fines, restitution, or even death.

For a crime that is minor in nature, such as speeding, the punishment can include paying a fine in lieu of going to court to defend one's actions. It does, however, mean admitting guilt of that crime.

For a more serious crime such as murder, the jury is tasked with deciding not only whether the prosecution has met all the elements of the crime, but also to what degree the defendant—if found guilty—must be sentenced. As previously discussed, there can be a variation in degree of a crime based upon what elements of that specific crime are met or not met. During the sentencing phase, the judge has the authority to override the jury's decision, but this is rare. In many states, courts conduct a separate sentencing hearing in which various witnesses are allowed to testify before the jury, which then decides on the sentence.

State and federal cases include sentencing guidelines. Federal guidelines usually include the following criteria for sentencing:

"(1) Protecting society;
 (2) Punishing the defendant;
 (3) Encouraging the defendant to lead a law-abiding life in the future and deterring him or her from future offenses;
 (4) Deterring others from criminal conduct by demonstrating its consequences;
 (5) Preventing the defendant from committing new crimes by isolating him or her for the period of incarceration;
 (6) Securing restitution for the victims of crime; and
 (7) Achieving uniformity in sentencing."[77]

Punishments for crimes can include incarceration, as well as probation or parole, fines, restitution, or even death.

Not every case goes through the process of a trial. When the prosecution has a very strong case and the defendant knows that he or she is likely to be found guilty, the defense attorney might try to mitigate the sentence with a plea bargain. A plea bargain is an agreement between the prosecution and the defense in which the defendant pleads guilty to the crime, but for a lesser sentence. The plea bargain can occur anytime before the final sentence has been delivered. Depending on the plea bargain, the defendant may receive a dismissal of charges, a reduction of jail time, a fine, restitution, or even a life sentence in prison instead of death.

In some cases, defendants are required to pay restitution. Restitution is a repayment for the loss that the victim endured as a direct result of the crime. For example, if a chief financial officer is convicted of embezzling funds from a company, the sentence may include paying back the money that was illegally taken.

Other alternatives to incarceration include probation and parole. Those who have been convicted of a misdemeanor and are required to serve jail time can be assigned probation. **Probation** can be a suspension of jail time based upon a promise to not commit any further crimes and abide by formal conditions such as submitting to search and seizure, drug testing, or attending Alcoholics Anonymous meetings. Probation can also be a condition of an early re-

Probation
A supervised release from incarceration in lieu of serving any time or a full term in jail.

Parole
A supervised release from incarceration in lieu of serving a full sentence.

lease from jail. Those who violate probation can be incarcerated to serve their original prison sentence.

Parole is similar to probation in that it shortens the stint of incarceration and allows the defendant to have a supervised release before the full prison sentence has expired. Parole cannot be granted in lieu of serving a prison sentence. Parole includes terms and conditions similar to probation, and a violation can result in the defendant being returned to prison to complete the remainder of the prison sentence. Those on probation may be required to meet with a probation officer, while those on parole would be required to report to a parole agent.

In especially heinous crimes, primarily murder, a convicted criminal can be punished by a life term in prison or by death. Because death is permanent and wrongful executions are to be avoided at all costs, the criminal justice system puts many provisions in place to make sure that those sentenced to death have exhaustive appeal options available to them before the execution is carried out.

Critical Thinking   How should punishments be decided for crimes?

Policy Choices, Politics, and Ideology   Since the beginning of time, laws and policies have been written, evaluated, and changed to keep pace with the current philosophies and developments of society. These changes are the result of various ideologies, including—among many others—personal interest or power, religion, politics, media, or any combination thereof. Many laws have the backing or influence of the church or financial entities with a personal interest. In his book *In the Division of Labor in Society*, Durkheim wrote that primitive society's major goal was to be "cohesive and cooperative."[78] As times changed and society evolved, Durkheim noted, ego and the need for competition began to play more significant roles.

In the 18th century, British monarchs and judges could impose fines and punishments with little or no justification, simply to show that they had power. It was common in Europe for those belonging to higher social classes to receive much more effective treatment in courts based upon their financial means and ability to have fair representation, while lower-class defendants received harsher treatment and unfair penalties.[79]

Even today, there is an obvious, direct connection between money and politics. Those who have financial backing, whether by family money or donors, succeed in getting into political office and having a significant impact on creating laws and policies. Large corporations and businesses sometimes provide financial support with the goal of creating or defeating laws that will benefit their bottom line. In 1998, Morgan Stanley donated over $3.7 million in political contributions in an effort to privatize Social Security benefits.[80] As one of the major companies that would stand to benefit from the deregulation of Social Security benefits, Morgan Stanley had a clear strategy behind its donations.

Religion, too, can be a major influence on laws and policy. The Catholic Church has placed pressure on politicians not to pass laws that would contradict its moral values, especially on issues such as same-sex marriage. In November 2009, the Roman Catholic Archdiocese of Washington, D.C., openly threatened that if lawmakers passed a bill allowing same-sex marriages, the church would cease all social service programs to the city. Because these programs helped about one-third of the homeless population, the church knew this promise would put a substantial amount of pressure on politicians.[81]

Ideology plays a significant role in law and policy. Many substantive laws are developed by legislators who have fully embraced the "get tough on crime" model. Politicians know they can more effectively pass laws if supported by their constituents, so they tell the public that citizens need increased security and that

Career Connections: FBI Special Agent

At every level of government—federal, state, and local—there are specially tasked agencies that investigate specific crimes. One such federal agency is the Federal Bureau of Investigation (FBI), which was created to protect the United States against terrorism, both domestic and foreign; enforce and investigate various crimes that cross state and country lines such as murder, kidnapping, civil rights violations, gang activity, drug trafficking, and crimes involving U.S. citizens on foreign territories; and be a leader and resource for all city, county, and state law enforcement agencies.

A special agent can serve in any number of roles and functions. He or she can be assigned to a variety of specialized groups, such as a bank robbery squad, white-collar crime squad, civil rights violations squad, organized crime squad, or foreign counterintelligence squad, or as a legal attaché (liaison with principal law enforcement and security services) in a foreign country. Much like those of law enforcement officers at all levels, an FBI agent's tasks can vary greatly from day to day, from gathering intelligence, collecting evidence, executing searches, and arresting suspects to testifying in court and completing paperwork.

Because of the types of crimes that FBI agents investigate and the potentially sensitive information that they may be exposed to while working in foreign counterintelligence, applicants for the FBI must adhere to strict requirements. An applicant must be at least 23 years old and no older than 37 years old by the time he or she is appointed to be a special agent. An applicant must be in top physical shape; have a four-year degree specializing in accounting, computer science, foreign languages, or law; have three years of work experience; and be a U.S. citizen free of criminal arrest and financial problems.[82]

Ethics and Professionalism: North Carolina Crime Labs

In 2010, the North Carolina State Bureau of Investigation was placed under scrutiny when crime lab workers testified to having omitted, exaggerated, or falsely reported blood evidence over a period of 16 years.[83] Crime lab agents admitted that complete blood test results were often excluded from reports sent to defense attorneys. As a result of this investigation, over 15,000 lab files from 1986 through 2003 had to be reviewed. The result of the review uncovered 230 instances in which the lab's reports to defense attorneys did not clearly reflect all information from the lab notes.

One case that was dramatically affected by this discovery was that of Greg Taylor, who was convicted of killing a prostitute in 1991 and received a death sentence for this crime. The conviction came after agents of the North Carolina crime lab alleged that his vehicle contained blood belonging to a prostitute who was found dead nearby his car. Taylor claimed that he and a friend had gotten stuck in the mud and left his car, then discovered the prostitute when they returned. Taylor, who had a history of drug use, was convicted primarily on the crime lab's findings. After the investigation revealed that the supposed blood found on Taylor's SUV was not even blood, Taylor was released after serving 17 years in prison.[84]

Another case that was reopened as a result of this investigation was the conviction of 18-year-olds Larry Martin Demery and Daniel Andre Green, both from North Carolina, who allegedly killed James Jordan, the father of NBA basketball player Michael Jordan. On July 23, 1993, Jordan's father was sleeping inside his car, which was parked along a road, when Demery and Green allegedly killed him during a robbery attempt. The defendants were later sentenced to life in prison based upon the evidence that was presented by the North Carolina crime lab. The crime lab reported a finding of blood at the initial crime scene, but failed to disclose that all subsequent tests for blood were negative. In this particular case, the blood evidence was not conclusive, though Demery and Green later confessed to the crime and were convicted.[85] One agent, Duane Deaver, was responsible for this failure to properly report lab findings. Several wrongful convictions were based upon the crime lab's evidence and the testimony of Deaver and others.

The shocking results of the investigation led to changes in the North Carolina crime lab's process and structure. As of 2003, the North Carolina crime lab has lab reports available electronically for the prosecution, which can send them directly to the defense should they be requested.

This poses an important ethical dilemma for the North Carolina crime laboratory. Should every case be reinvestigated that was examined by Deaver and the other agents who admitted to negligence? How far back should these re-examinations go? What protective systems of checks and balances should be put into place so that such a miscarriage of justice does not happen again?

The ethical dilemmas extend beyond this case and are illustrative of the challenges that face the criminal justice system as a whole. Is society's belief in due process so strong that we are willing—and in fact, morally required—to bear the expense of overhauling the criminal justice process to assure fairness for everyone? Or should society simply accept the fact that innocent people may occasionally be caught up in the crime control "assembly line"?

unemployment and crime rates are increasing throughout the country. The media has become a useful crutch for these politicians' ideologies with sensationalized coverage of crime and the criminal justice system. Politicians and the courts have exploited the public's fear of crime, including the "us vs. them" mentality that often overlooks the constitutional rights of criminals. Therefore, it is important to study criminal law in order to encourage rational responses to the problems of crime, rather than the ideological positions that dominate political discourse.

Chapter Summary

- The interpretation and implementation of the U.S. Constitution is the basis of constitutional law. The Constitution establishes specific rights and liberties that are granted to all citizens and criminal defendants. Throughout the many steps of the criminal justice process, from the inception of a criminal investigation to the disposition of an offender, citizens' constitutional rights cannot be violated.

- Laws are created through jurisprudence or philosophy of law, encompassing our customs, morals, and acceptable practices by society. Criminal law can be broken down into two components: substantive criminal law and procedural law. Substantive laws define the laws and explain the punishments for breaking a particular law. Procedural laws outline the process that a criminal case goes through from beginning to end.

- Some laws are the result of case law. Case law refers to precedents or legal decisions in cases that have previously been ruled upon by the courts. Those decisions can be used in subsequent cases that are similar in nature.

- The rule of law helps to maintain a stable society in which everyone is equal. This rule or application of law means that there is little chance for abuse of power by the government and that everyone is equally protected under the law. It maintains that all laws are current and that a person cannot be charged ex post facto or after the fact of a law being created or passed.

- Criminal law can further be broken down into felonies, misdemeanors, and infractions at the state level, federal crimes, and city or municipal laws. Each violation of law has specific elements that must be met, including the actus reus, mens rea, concurrence, and causation of the crime.

- Each violation of law carries a specific punishment. Punishments for felonies can range from imprisonment to death and can include fines or restitution to victims. Misdemeanors can also be punished by incarceration in a jail and may also require fines or restitution to victims. Infractions are the most common crimes and include traffic violations, most of which are punishable by fines.

- Criminal defendants may use a variety of defenses to justify or excuse their actions. These include defense of others, defense of home and property, necessity, consent, resisting unlawful arrest, accident, duress, age, mistake, involuntary intoxication, unconsciousness, provocation, insanity, and diminished capacity.

- Conflicts between people that do not involve criminal actions are governed by civil law. Disputes are generally due to a legal cause, or an action that has a direct effect on something else. Penalties for civil law involve the returning of property or a monetary penalty. Civil law can include agricultural law, business law, family law, and sports law, among others.

- Laws and policies are often passed or revised as the result of various ideologies, and can be influenced by power, religion, politics, media, or any combination thereof. Many laws have the backing or influence of churches or financial entities with a personal interest.

Critical Thinking?

1. What is the purpose of law?
2. Why do we need different types of laws?
3. Why is it necessary to have basic elements of a crime?
4. Can you explain why the law must have mens rea?
5. Distinguish between negligence and recklessness. Which should receive a more severe punishment? Why should it get this punishment?
6. There are specific elements for the crimes of homicide and rape. Should these elements be the same in each state? Why or why not?
7. Should prior cases be changed as a result of current case law?
8. Can someone be insane temporarily? What constitutes "temporary"?
9. Why is it important for all facets of criminal justice to be ethical? What can happen if there is a breakdown in ethics?
10. How does western society affect common laws? Why do you think that common law is so strong in western society?

Media

Charters of Freedom: http://www.archives.gov/exhibits/charters/charters.html
   This government website provides the full text of historic U.S. documents, including the U.S. Constitution, the Bill of Rights, and the Declaration of Independence.
Arrests in the United States, 1980 to 2009: http://bjs.ojp.usdoj.gov/content/pub/pdf/aus8009.pdf
   This report from the U.S. Department of Justice provides a comprehensive description and visual representations of arrests in the United States over a 30-year period, broken down by crime.

Endnotes

1. Cannon, L. (1999). *Official Negligence: How Rodney King and the Riots Changed Los Angeles and the LAPD*. Boulder, CO: Westview Press.
2. Gooding-Williams, R. (1993). *Reading Rodney King, Urban Uprising*. New York, NY: Routledge.
3. Deitz, R. (1996). *Willful Injustice: A Post-O.J. Look at Rodney King, American Jusice, and Trial by Race*. Washington, DC: Regnery.
4. *Allen v. City of Los Angeles*, Nos. 95-55475, 95-55477 (1996).

5. Constitution of the United States.

6. *Mapp v. Ohio*, 367 U.S. 643 (1961).

7. Ibid.

8. *Miranda v. Arizona*, 384 U.S. 436 (1966).

9. Ibid.

10. Ibid.

11. Ibid.

12. *Amendments to the Bail Reform Act of 1966: Hearings, United States Congress, Senate Committee on the Judiciary, Subcommittee on Constitutional Rights.* 91st Cong. (1969).

13. Constitution of the United States.

14. Morrison, K. (1995). *Marx, Durkheim, Weber: Formations of Modern Social Thought.* Thousand Oaks, CA: Sage.

15. D'Amato, A. A. (1984). *In Jurisprudence: A Descriptive and Normative Analysis of Law.* Hingham, MA: Kluwer.

16. Lemert, C. C., & Winter, M. F. (2000). *Crime and Deviance.* Lanham, MD: Rowman & Littlefield.

17. Milsom, S. F. C. (2003). *A Natural History of the Common Law.* New York, NY: Columbia University Press.

18. Dillon, M., & Garland, L. (2000). *Ancient Greece: Social and Historical Documents from Archaic Times to the Death of Socrates (c. 800–399 B.C.).* New York, NY: Routledge.

19. Preiss, B., & Osterlund, D. (1987). *The Constitution of the United States of America.* New York, NY: Bantam Books.

20. Packer, H. L. (1968). *The Limits of the Criminal Sanction.* Stanford, CA: Stanford University Press.

21. Center for Law and Military Operations. (2007). *Rule of Law Handbook: A Practitioner's Guide for Judge Advocates.* Charlottesville, VA: U.S. Government.

22. *United States v. Nixon*, 418 U.S. 683 (1974).

23. Lockard, D., & Murphy, W. F. (1987). *Basic in Consitutional Law.* Washington, DC: CQ Press.

24. Sellin, T., & Wolfgang, M. E. (1964). *The Measurement of Delinquency.* New York, NY: Wiley.

25. Ibid.

26. *People v. Andrew Pena Valenzuela*, 116 Cal. App. 3d 798 (1981).

27. Books LLC. (2010). *American Nazi Collaborators: William Joyce, Constance Drexel, Tyler Kent, Mildred Gillars, Herbert Hans Haupt, Fred W. Kaltenbach.* Memphis, TN: General Books.

28. *United States v. Gadahn*, No. SA CR 05-254(A) (2005).

29. Feklivos, A., & Kostin, S. (2001). *The Man Behind the Rosenbergs.* New York, NY: Enigma Books.

30. Federal Bureau of Investigation (FBI). (n.d.). *Robert Philip Hanssen Espionage Case.* Retrieved from http://www.fbi.gov/about-us/history/famous-cases/robert-hanssen

31. Asch, S. H. (1968). *Civil Rights and Responsibilities under the Constitution.* New York, NY: Arco.

32. *Brown v. Simpson*, No. SC036876 (Cal. Super. Ct., 1995).

33. Packer, 1968.

34. Ibid.

35. Ibid.

36. Advisory Committee on the Federal Rules of Criminal Procedure. (2007).

37. *Hearing on the 60th Anniversary of the Administrative Procedure Act.* 104th Cong. (2006).

38. Schwartz, N. (2011, March 9). "Erin Brockovich Returns to Hinkley Testing Chromium-Polluted Water." *Huffington Post.* Retrieved from http://www.huffingtonpost.com/2011/03/09/erin-brockovich-returns-to-hinkley_n_833423.html

39. Black, H. (1979). *Black's Law Dictionary* (5th ed.). St. Paul, MN: West.

40. Hogrogian, J. G. (1999). *Miranda v. Arizona: The Rights of the Accused.* San Diego, CA: Lucent Books.

41. *Escobedo v. Illinois*, 378 U.S. 478 (1964).

42. *Mincey v. Arizona*, 437 U.S. 385 (1978).

43. "California Law." (n.d.). Retrieved from http://www.leginfo.ca.gov/calaw.html

44. Black, 1979.

45. *People v. Harding*, 443 Mich. 699–703, 506 N.W. 2d 486–487 (1994).

46. Black, 1979.

47. Ibid.

48. Sloan, I. J. (1987). *The Law of Self-Defense: Legal and Ethical Principles.* New York, NY: Oceana Publications.

49. Constitution of the United States.

50. Criminal Law Act 1967 (c. 58). Office of Public Sector Information, Parliament of the United Kingdom, 1967.

51. Ibid.

52. Constitution of the United States.

53. *The Queen v. Dudley and Stephens*, 14 Q.B.D 273 (1884).

54. *Plummer v. State*, 136 Ind. 306.

55. *Wright v. State*, No. 84, 953 A.2d 144 (2008).

56. *Dixon v. United States*, 548 U.S. 1 (2006).

57. "Alzheimer's Disease." (2010). *PubMed Health*. Retrieved from http://www.ncbi.nlm.nih.gov/pubmedhealth/PMH0001767/

58. *Roper v. Simmons*, 543 U.S. 551 (2005).

59. *United States v. Walton Dawson*, 184 Fed. Appx. 14 (2006).

60. *R v. Doughty*, Crim LR 625 (1986).

61. Homicide Act of 1957.

62. *M'Naghten's Case*, 10 Cl. & F. 200, 8 Eng. Rep. 718 (1843).

63. Chiu, J. (2005, October 21). *San Francisco Mom Pleads Innocent to Murder.*

64. *People v. Betty Horn*, 158 Cal. App. 3d 1014; 205 Cal. Rptr. 119 (1984).

65. Constitution of the United States.

66. *Ashe v. Swenson*, 397 U.S. 436; 90 S. Ct. 1189; 25 L. Ed. 2d 469 (1970).

67. Lieberman, J. K. (1987). *The Enduring Constitution: An Exploration of the First Two Hundred Years*. New York, NY: Harper & Row.

68. Ibid.

69. Ferdico, J. N. (2005). *Criminal Procedure for the Criminal Justice Professional* (9th ed.). Belmont, CA: Thomson/Wadsworth.

70. Lieberman, 1987.

71. Dunne, D. (2001). *Justice: Crimes, Trials, and Punishments*. New York, NY: Crown.

72. Associated Press. (1997, January 27). "Key Testimony in O.J. Simpson Civil Case." *USA Today*. Retrieved from http://www.usatoday.com/news/index/nns172.htm

73. Lloyd, G., & Lloyd, M. (1998). *The Essential Bill of Rights: Original Arguments and Fundamental Documents*. Lanham, MD: University Press of America.

74. Packer, 1968.

75. Ibid.

76. Sloan, 1987.

77. United States Sentencing Commission. (2011). *United States Sentencing Guidelines*. Retrieved from http://www.ussc.gov/

78 Durkheim, E. (1997). *The Division of Labor in Society*. New York, NY: The Free Press.

79. Radzinowicz, L. (1966). *Ideology and Crime*. New York, NY: Columbia University Press.

80. Salant, J. D. (2009, October 20). "Morgan Stanley Resumes PAC Giving After TARP Funding Repayment." *Bloomberg*. Retrieved from http://www.bloomberg.com/apps/news?pid=newsarchive&sid=aKaJ8n7MVrBw

81. Urbina, I. (2009, November 12). "New Turn in Debate Over Law on Marriage." *The New York Times*. Retrieved from http://www.nytimes.com/2009/11/13/us/13marriage.html

82. FBI. (n.d.). *Become a FBI Special Agent*. Retrieved from http://www.fbijobs.gov/11.asp

83. Hopper, J. (2010, July 18). "Feds: North Carolina Crime Lab Buried Blood Evidence." *ABC World News with Diane Sawyer*. Retrieved from http://abcnews.go.com/WN/fbi-north-carolina-crime-lab-buried-blood-evidence/story?id=11431980

84. Weiss, D. C. (2010, August 19). "NC Report: State Crime Lab Withheld or Overstated Evidence in 230 Cases." *ABA Journal*. Retrieved from http://www.abajournal.com/news/article/nc_report_state_crime_lab_withheld_or_overstated_evidence_in_230_cases/

85. Johnson, A. (2008, February 25). "Killer of Michael Jordan's Father Might Get Parole With Resentencing." *WRAL.com*. Retrieved from http://www.wral.com/news/local/story/2484423/

SECTION 2

The Policing of Crime

Chapter 4: The Policing of Crime

Chapter 5: Policing: Roles, Functions, and Challenges

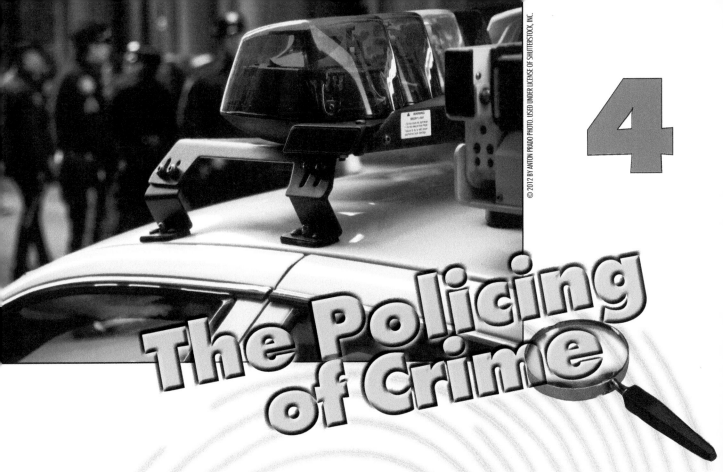

4

The Policing of Crime

KEY TERMS

Black codes, Community policing, Constable, Corruption, Early Warning Systems, Extralegal policing, Grass eaters, Law Enforcement Assistance Administration, *Law Enforcement Bulletin*, Lynch mob, Meat eaters, Miranda rights, Night watches, Pinkertons, Posse, Racial profiling, Sheriff, Slave patrols, SWAT (Special Weapons and Tactics) team, Texas Rangers, Third degree, Vigilantism, Wickersham Commission (National Commission on Law Observance and Enforcement)

CHAPTER OBJECTIVES

1. Describe the history of policing in the United States.
2. Review significant efforts to reform law enforcement and improve police accountability and professionalism.
3. Identify the variety of law enforcement agencies located at the local, state, and federal levels.
4. Describe the education and training requirements of contemporary law enforcement professionals.

Case Study: Wickersham Commission

Contemporary police are generally held in high regard and perceived as trustworthy and honest by the majority of the American public. This has not always been the case. In fact, the professionalism and public support characteristic of most modern-day policing agencies is the result of many years of reform efforts. Efforts to reform the police have been undertaken by law enforcement agencies and officers themselves, as well as by government officials and concerned community groups.

One of the earliest reports outlining the problems with policing in the United States was the "National Commission on Law Observance and Enforcement," or the Wickersham Commission. The Wickersham Commission was established in May of 1929 by President Hoover. Its purpose was to provide a comprehensive examination of crime and criminal justice in the United States. The commission's membership was bipartisan and included a number of notable legal scholars of the time, such as Roscoe Pound, the dean of Harvard Law School, and Ada Comstock, president of Radcliffe College. The findings of the commission were published in 14 reports[1] and covered a range of topics such as the causes and costs of crime, the enforcement of prohibition laws, and the state of policing and law enforcement. The reports were released to the public in January 1931.

The Wickersham Commission's report was significant because it was the first national publication to highlight a number of shortcomings of American law enforcement agencies in the early 20th century. The report authors revealed problems with police officer selection and training, effectiveness of police leadership, and law enforcement agencies' success at controlling crime. They also identified three primary concerns with policing that remain today: inappropriate use of force and treatment of suspects, the need for professional and effective police officers, and the necessity of positive community/police relations.

The inappropriate use of force by police officers received significant attention in the commission reports, and the authors describe in detail some of the abusive practices of police officers in the early 1900s, including cases of suspects being savagely beaten or tortured and denied food, drink, or sleep.[2]

While American policing practices and regulations have made significant strides since the days of the Wickersham Commission, the concerns outlined in the report continue to receive the bulk of scholarly attention and are consistently the focus of contemporary police reform initiatives. Though we are moving toward more professional, accountable, and democratic policing in the United States, these issues still exist in modern policing.

History and Structure of Police Systems

Today, police are generally viewed positively—they are perceived as both honest and effective by the majority of the American public.[3] But the positive light in which contemporary policing is viewed is a relatively recent phenomenon. For much of its history, policing could best be characterized as disorganized, ineffective, and corrupt. Early police officers were poorly paid, ill prepared to address the complexities of crime and disorder, and disrespected by the larger community.[4]

Beginning in the 1900s and continuing today, policing has undergone a series of significant reforms. The objectives of many of these reforms were to transform police officers into unbiased professionals who were capable of upholding the law while enforcing it, and to create well-equipped law enforcement agencies that used their resources effectively to reduce crime. Though there are concerns surrounding American policing that persist today, it has improved significantly since its beginnings.

History of Policing in the United States

In early American history, the responsibility for policing was left to residents and local and state authorities. Local policing developed in unique ways in different parts of the country. In the Northeast United States, immigrant communities often reproduced the forms of law enforcement most commonly used in Europe. Policing in these areas emphasized the informal enforcement of laws and often relied upon local citizens to act as enforcers.[5] Meanwhile, the practice and legacy of slavery significantly influenced the development of policing in the Southern states. Many of the early policing efforts focused on enforcing slave laws and, after the abolition of slavery, special legal codes designed to regulate the activities of the black population. Policing in the "Wild West" was insufficient, unregulated, and often violent. Due to a lack of formal law enforcement agencies, vigilante groups and private security agencies often performed law enforcement functions on the frontier.

Though historically most policing was locally managed, the federal government did create some law enforcement agencies in early American history. These agencies tended to focus on offenses such as counterfeiting, interstate or international crimes, and issues related to war, such as spying and draft dodging.

Policing in the Northeast

Early American colonists typically adopted the English system of shire reeves (now referred to as "sheriffs"), constables, and night watches. These forms of policing emerged in England during the medieval period and remained the most common forms of enforcement well into the mid-1600s. When the first waves of immigrants came to the United States from Europe, they brought these law enforcement practices with them.[6]

Colonial American **constables** and **sheriffs** were appointed to their positions by the local community. Such positions were not desirable, as they were often unpaid and time-consuming. In order to earn money, constables and sheriffs would take a percentage of the fees collected for serving warrants, making arrests, or collecting fines.[7] In addition, early law enforcement officers were not well respected by the larger community.

Constables were often responsible for forming **night watches** in their colonial towns and cities. They were called night watches because they performed their duties during the night. The first recorded night watch was in Boston in the 1630s, though other Northern cities followed soon after. For much of the colonial period, night watches were sporadically utilized. In fact, Boston was the first city to require a permanent night watch, which it did not do until 1801.[8]

The night watch typically consisted of rotating groups of adult, able-bodied male residents. In addition to watching out for criminal activity, night

Constable

A local law enforcement officer who was responsible for collecting taxes and enforcing ordinances in the colonial and post-colonial United States, similar to a sheriff; today, constables are typically law enforcement officers in small towns.

Sheriff

A local law enforcement officer responsible for collecting taxes and enforcing ordinances in the colonial and post-colonial United States, similar to a constable; today, sheriffs serves as law enforcement officers at the county level.

Night watches

Groups of local, unpaid citizens who would patrol the community at night to deter crime and alert residents of the time, weather, and hazards.

watches were also required to watch for fires, and to report on the time and on local weather conditions. Night watch duty was not considered a prestigious activity, and men with the political and economic means would often be able to avoid performing this service. This resulted in night watch crews that were either understaffed or staffed by community members of questionable esteem.[9] The system of constables and night watches continued to be the most common form of policing in the Northeastern United States well into the late 1800s.

The primary law enforcement agent in Northeastern cities was the high constable or, in some places, the marshal. It was this person's job to enforce state laws and local ordinances, execute arrest warrants, suppress riots, and maintain general order. These policing executives were often chosen in various ways—some were popularly elected, while others were appointed by the mayor, by members of the local council, or by state governors. These positions were considered undesirable by the general public and it often proved difficult to find willing and appropriate people to fill them. As in colonial times, constables were not paid, but rather worked on commission. They would earn money by taking a percentage of the revenues they obtained through executing arrest warrants or through the collection of local taxes and fees. Local residents continued to be used to form the ranks of the night watch; however, members of the night watch did not possess police power and were only able to execute an arrest if a crime was committed in their physical presence.

Critical Thinking

How might working on commission have affected early officers' enforcement of the law?

By the beginning of the 19th century, the United States was experiencing significant social and economic change as a result of the Industrial Revolution. The population was growing dramatically, especially in urban areas, and citizens were experiencing significant economic and political changes. Riots triggered by ethnic tensions and economic insecurity were relatively common in the rapidly growing cities. Local enforcement agents were ill equipped to address mass social unrest, and it was not unusual for the state militia to be called out to restore order to the city.[10]

During the Civil War years (1861 to 1865), urban disruption continued. Perhaps the most memorable of such uprisings was the New York draft riot in 1863. During this protest of President Lincoln's efforts to draft citizens into the Union forces, mobs destroyed property, looted establishments, and killed 1,200 people. The state militia and federal troops were sent to the city to quell the uprising. This is the most violent riot in the United States to date.[11]

By the mid-1800s, local governments began to realize that policing in the form of constables and night watches was inadequate. American cities and towns moved to create their own forms of permanent and professional law enforcement. The British influenced early American efforts to develop a permanent police force. In 1829, British Home Secretary Sir Robert Peel persuaded Parliament to establish a professional police department. As a result of Peel's efforts, 1,000 "bobbies" (the name given to London police officers, in honor of Peel) permanently patrolled the streets of London.

New York City became the first city in the United States to adopt a permanent police force. In 1845, the New York City police force consisted of 800 full-time officers. Other cities followed soon after: Chicago in 1851, Philadelphia and Boston in 1854, and Baltimore in 1857.[12]

Corruption within early police forces was rampant.[13] Local government officials had significant control over determining who could be a police officer and over policing activities. Some local officials took advantage of their significant power over law enforcement. Appointments to policing positions were made based on political and ethnic affiliations rather than an individual's skill or commitment to legal principles. Police officers were often uneducated and were rarely screened for suitability for a law enforcement position. It was not uncommon for individuals with criminal records to become police officers and for police officers to engage in illegal activities.

Policing in the South   Early policing efforts in the Southern states focused on upholding the slave system and its legal codes.[14] Beginning in the late 1600s, groups of local citizens formed **slave patrols**, whose primary objectives were to track down runaway slaves and return them to servitude, and to stave off potential slave rebellions. Slave patrols were composed of poor, non-slave-owning whites and individuals who were recruited from the state militias. Initially, slave patrols were organized in similar ways to military groups, with an officer who was in charge of a group of men. After the American Revolution, responsibility for the slave patrols shifted to the citizenry, though the patrols never lost their military overtones.

Slave patrols are frequently discussed in slave narratives.[15] These narratives describe the everyday forms of abuse and harassment that slaves would be subjected to by the slave patrols. When traveling off a plantation, for example, slaves were required to carry documentation indicating their owner's approval for their travel. Members of the slave patrol could stop anyone they suspected of being a slave and ask for ownership information and travel authorization. Even when slaves carried the appropriate documentation, they would be subject to verbal and physical abuse by the slave patrol. The slave patrols had tremendous power and could enter any property they desired to without cause or without warrant.

After the Civil War and the formal end of slavery, slave codes aimed at regulating the activities and opportunities of African-Americans were refashioned into "**black codes**." Common laws incorporated into black codes included prohibiting interracial marriages, disallowing African-Americans from testifying against whites in court, and making it illegal for former slaves to own firearms. After the abolition of slavery, those who had served in the slave patrols or in the Confederate army often assumed posts as police officers.

Regulation of the activities of newly freed slaves was not limited to the formal law enforcement agencies, however, and **vigilantism** was a relatively com-

Sir Robert Peel was credited with convincing the British Parliament to institute a permanent police force in London in 1829.

Corruption
Abuse of police authority for personal gain.

Slave patrols
Regulatory groups in the South in the colonial era focused on regulating the activities of slaves.

Black codes
Laws created after the end of slavery designed to regulate the activities of African American citizens.

Vigilantism
The taking on of law enforcement responsibilities and the dispensing of punishment by private citizens.

Lynch mob
A group of individuals seeking to punish someone suspected of having committed a social transgression.

mon practice in the American South after the end of the Civil War.[16] Vigilantism, or the taking on of law enforcement responsibilities and the dispensing of punishment by private citizens, often took the form of a **lynch mob**, a group of individuals seeking to punish someone suspected of having committed a social transgression. Such transgressions could be as minor as an African-American man looking inappropriately at a white woman, and punishments could include hanging, burning at the stake, or shooting.

Policing in the "Wild West"   For much of the 1800s, the U.S. western frontier was a dangerous and lawless place. Early homesteaders, cattle ranchers, miners, and entrepreneurs who tried to make a living for themselves in the "Wild West" often had to provide for their own protection and enforcement.[17]

In places where there was some law enforcement presence, local law enforcement agents were often as crooked and violent as the individuals they were supposed to control. In fact, it was not uncommon for men who were outlaws themselves to take up the role of local sheriff or marshal, or for men who were once lawmen to return to outlaw activities.

On the frontier, violence by law enforcement was considered a necessity for maintaining social order. Local law enforcement often acted as the investigator, the judge, and, in some cases, the executioner. Punishments were brutal, and law enforcement officers proved their usefulness to the local community through their willingness and ability to dispense these forms of harsh justice.[18] As with police posts in most other parts of the country, law enforcement officers in the West were poorly paid and would often have to find additional means of earning money in order to supplement their meager salaries.

Posse
A group of residents temporarily enlisted by law enforcement agencies to assist in law enforcement functions.

When local sheriffs or marshals were faced with incidents that required additional personnel in order to be effectively addressed, such as tracking a fugitive or quelling large-scale unrest, they would often have to rely on local community members. Local residents were temporarily enlisted by law enforcement agencies to form a **posse**. Posses allowed under-resourced sheriffs to expand their forces in terms of both bodies and weapons. The challenge for the local officer was to manage the activities of these posses to ensure they acted within the constraints of the law. Often, this was not an easy task.

Texas Rangers
One of the earliest law enforcement agencies in the American West.

Perhaps the most infamous law enforcement agency in the American West is the **Texas Rangers**.[19] The Rangers were first formed by Stephen F. Austin in the 1820s, when Texas was a Mexican territory. Like other law enforcement groups in the West, the Rangers were formed as a self-protection group focused on battling local Native American groups and pursuing cattle thieves and other outlaws. They were similar to a military force in that they had a military organizational structure and they participated in military campaigns (e.g., the Indian Wars and the Mexican Wars). By 1835, there were nearly 200 Rangers performing law enforcement and military functions throughout the region. By 1845, when Texas became the 28th state to join the American Union, the Rangers had become a formalized law enforcement agency.

Extralegal policing
Policing that is not regulated or sanctioned by law.

When local law enforcement was available on the frontier, it was often insufficient to meet local needs. **Extralegal policing**—policing that was not regu-

In addition to law enforcement responsibilities, the Texas Rangers participated in military campaigns.

lated or sanctioned by law—was typical in the West. Two types of extralegal policing were common: vigilantism and private policing. Citizens would frequently band together to form vigilance committees that served as the mechanism for law enforcement and punishment in remote areas. One of the most notorious vigilante groups was the Regulators of Shelby County, East Texas.[20] This group was initially formed to prevent cattle and horse theft, but began to use its power to harass local residents. In response, members of the community, including several law enforcement officers, formed another group, called the Moderators. The two groups began to wage a war over power and land that ended only after the president of Texas (then a republic independent from Mexico) sent the militia to the area to arrest leaders from both groups and establish peace in the area.

Wealthy groups often responded to the shortage of formal law enforcement officers in the West by hiring their own protective forces. Merchant groups, banks, and mining companies hired private security agencies to protect valuable goods, such as gold and silver, that were being shipped by stagecoach and train across the United States. These goods were especially vulnerable to robbers as they traveled through the sparsely populated or uninhabited places on the frontier.[21]

Though they were not without problems, private protection agencies had several advantages over formal law enforcement. First, they were not limited to a particular area—they were free to pursue suspects across jurisdictions, even across state lines. Second, as for-profit businesses, they had little interest in politics and complete the jobs for which they are paid. This was not a trivial consideration, as many law enforcement agencies of the time were subject to the whims of political authorities. The downside of private security was that they were not subject to the same forms of legal constraint as formal law enforce-

Pinkertons

A private investigation and security company formed in the 1880s that assisted in protecting goods, tracking down suspects, and breaking strikes.

ment officers. There was little to prevent them from using questionable methods to pursue, apprehend, and even punish suspects.

Perhaps the most legendary of these private protection agencies was the Pinkertons.[22] The Pinkerton National Detective Agency was formed in the mid-1880s by a former presidential security officer, Allan Pinkerton. The motto of the Pinkertons was "The eye that never sleeps." Pinkerton agents were hired by wealthy companies to protect goods, to track down robbers and other criminals, and to break strikes. Though the Pinkerton ranks included skilled detectives, they also included individuals with few reservations about the use of force. For example, when performing a raid in search of the legendary bank robber Jesse James, Pinkerton agents threw a bomb wrapped in fuel-soaked rags into the home where he was believed to be hiding out. James was not in the home at the time, but the bomb ended up killing his younger brother and maiming his mother. This episode serves as a good example of the potential problems associated with using private security as law enforcement.

Critical Thinking   Though policing developed differently in the North, South, and West, there are some commonalities. What are the similarities in early American law enforcement approaches in these regions?

History of Federal Law Enforcement

Most early law enforcement was handled by local or state entities, but there were some federal agencies formed early in American history. Under the first president, George Washington, the U.S. Marshals were created. They were established by the Judiciary Act of 1789, the same act that created the federal court system. One U.S. Marshal was appointed for each of the 13 federal districts. It was the responsibility of each U.S. Marshal to enforce federal laws, to pursue violators of laws enacted by the U.S. Congress or the President, to facilitate federal judicial processing of violators, and to assist in the implementation of punishments meted out by the federal courts within their district. While the number of U.S. Marshals was small, they were granted the authority to deputize others to assist them in the administration of their duties. In addition, U.S. Marshals were given the right to *posse comitatus*, allowing them to summon a posse of men to assist in the pursuit of a fugitive. The activities of U.S. Marshals have varied significantly over time. Prior to the Civil War, U.S. Marshals focused their attention on enforcing the Fugitive Slave Act of 1850. This act required that slaves captured in non-slave states be returned to their owners in slave states. During the Civil War, U.S. Marshals shifted their attention to tracking Confederate spies. Beginning in the 1890s, much of the focus of the U.S. Marshals was on protecting federal judges.[23]

The creation of subsequent federal law enforcement was haphazard, as the U.S. Congress tended to create law enforcement agencies in response to particular crises rather than as part of a strategic plan. The U.S. Secret Service, for example, was created as a part of the Treasury Department in 1865 to deal with growing problems with counterfeit currency and postage stamps. It assumed responsibility for protection of the president after the assassination of President William McKinley at the Pan-American Exposition held in Buffalo, New York, in September 1901.[24]

The Federal Bureau of Investigation (FBI) was created as part of the Department of Justice in 1908 under President Theodore Roosevelt. When the FBI was created, there were a limited number of activities that had been established as federal crimes by the national government. Many of the existing laws focused on issues surrounding banking, immigration, business monopolies, and involuntary servitude. The first substantial federal crime legislation introduced after the formation of the FBI was the Mann Act of 1910, also known as the White Slave Traffic Act. The goal of the Mann Act was to control prostitution and make illegal the transportation of women over state lines for "immoral purposes." Exaggerated concerns about "white slavery" were more likely responses to significant social changes occurring as a result of industrialization, urbanization, and immigration. Women were beginning to move away from their family homes into urban centers where they enjoyed increased autonomy, including sexual autonomy.[25]

It was common for federal law enforcement on the fronteir to enlist the help of local citizens to enforce the law.

During World War I, the FBI became responsible for spy operations and foreign intelligence-gathering efforts. A series of new laws were passed that expanded the list of federal crimes that the FBI could investigate. New laws included the 1917 Espionage Act, which prohibited interference with military recruitment, refusal to perform military duty, or disclosure of information related to national defense, and the 1918 Sedition Act, which prohibited public criticism of the American government. After the end of the war, the FBI returned its attention to non-war-related crimes.

In 1924, the Justice Department appointed J. Edgar Hoover as the director of the FBI. Hoover made several changes to FBI personnel processes and to the agency's responsibilities, including requiring all new agents to pass a background screening and physical agility tests, and to have prior training in the law or in accounting. He also established formal training programs for new agents in modern investigative techniques and changed promotion policies so that agents would be promoted based on regular performance evaluations rather than political patronage or seniority.[26]

By 1935, the training programs available to FBI agents were being offered to local and state police forces. Very few local policing agencies offered formal training to their officers at this time. In addition to developing a national training center, the FBI created an Identification Division and Technical Laboratory. The Identification Division became the national collection center for fingerprint cards. Soon, law enforcement agencies from around the country were submitting fingerprint cards to the FBI. The Technical Laboratory was equipped with specialized microscopes as well as extensive data on guns, watermarks, typefaces, and automobile tire designs. These resources were used for forensic analysis in federal investigations and, in some cases, state and local investigations. In the 1930s, the FBI took over responsibility from the International Association of Chiefs of Police for collecting crime statistics from law enforcement agencies

Infamous bank robber John Dillinger evaded the FBI for years.

Law Enforcement Bulletin
A publication of the Federal Bureau of Investigation that includes articles on law enforcement issues as well as information on wanted federal suspects.

across the nation. This program, the Uniform Crime Reports, continues today.[27] Finally, in 1932, the FBI released the first issue of its *Law Enforcement Bulletin*, which included a list of most wanted fugitives and is still published today.

The types of law enforcement activities in which the FBI engaged continued to expand throughout the first half of the 20th century as new federal laws were passed that expanded the FBI's jurisdiction. Such laws focused on enforcing the nationwide prohibition of alcoholic beverages, protecting banks from the growing number of robbers, and preventing the transportation of stolen goods and the flight of felons over state borders.

Policing from the 20th Century to Today

In the early 1900s, policing agencies across the country suffered from a number of common problems.[28] Police were closely tied to political authorities. Close ties to politicians meant weak boundaries between local politics and policing functions. Policing agencies were often subject to the political whims of local leaders rather than serving the larger needs of their communities. In many places, policing appointments were doled out based on political and ethnic alliances rather than the skill or character of the police officer. When local leadership changed after an election, new leaders would frequently disband the existing police force and replace the officers with individuals from a similar ethnic background or with the same political affiliation.

Local political leadership enjoyed significant power and frequently used this power in inappropriate or illegal ways. Police would assist government officials in rigging elections. They would be used by local politicians to enforce laws against political enemies or be instructed to ignore the criminal activities of political allies. Police officers also engaged in corruption on their own. For example, police officers would solicit payoffs for protecting gambling and prostitution houses. Close ties between police and corrupt political figures and the participation of police in their own illegal endeavors did little to promote trust in, or respect for, police officers.[29]

In addition to corruption, police were often incompetent and ill prepared for the duties of law enforcement.[30] This was due in part to serious problems with the police officer screening and selection processes and, once hired, with their training. Law enforcement agencies and police leadership rarely employed screening processes such as criminal background investigations or physical agility tests to identify strong candidates for police positions. Once hired, officers were given the basic tools for policing, such as a brief handbook and a nightstick, and then sent out into the streets. There was no instruction on criminal law, how to effectively manage physical altercations, or other skills that might be useful for a new officer to possess.

A related problem was that police officers were often responsible for miscellaneous duties that did not fall under the responsibility of other local government groups.[31] In fact, police in the early 1900s were responsible for a broad range of government functions, some of which had little to do with law enforcement, such as cleaning public streets and maintaining street lamps. Some police agencies, such as those in Boston, also had significant social service responsibilities, such as providing food and temporary lodging to homeless people within the city. Early police reformers believed that the primary function of a police officer should be to fight crime and that engagement in tangential or unrelated activities detracted from this function.

One of the most notable early police reformers was August Vollmer.[32] Vollmer began his career in law enforcement in 1905 when he was elected as the town marshal in Berkeley, California. He is best known for advocating the adoption of a "professional" model of policing. A professional police officer, according to Vollmer, was well educated, well trained, and adept at using science and modern technologies to solve crimes and to prevent new ones from occurring. Many of Vollmer's ideas about how the police should function are described in his influential 1936 book, *The Police and Modern Society.*

Vollmer had significant influence over the conclusions drawn about policing in the United States that were included in the Wickersham Commission's reports on law enforcement. Vollmer wrote or directed many of the portions of the reports that focused on policing. The reports highlighted some of the concerns mentioned above, but also included recommendations about improving outdated or ineffective law enforcement technologies, creating a more racially and ethnically diverse police force, and reducing the high levels of abusive policing nationally.[33]

According to the commission's final report, it was a common practice throughout the country for police officers to inflict pain—both physical and mental—on suspects of crime in order to solicit information or confessions. The infliction of pain by police officers in order to solicit evidence about a crime was called the third degree. According to the report, the types of physical pain most commonly inflicted by police officers included beating with fists or objects (e.g., rubber hoses, leather straps, and sticks), sleep deprivation, withholding of food, and unsanitary detention facilities. The most common forms of mental suffering inflicted upon suspects by police officers included verbal threats and foul or violent language; illegal detention; preventing contact with family, friends, and legal counsel; and protracted questioning. The typical victim of the third degree was younger than 25, poor, and African-American.[34]

The commission made several recommendations to improve policing, including insulating police agencies from the corrupting influence of politics, improving training and pay of officers, improving policing equipment and record-keeping, and expanding state-level law enforcement agencies. The Wickersham Commission's reports on policing, however, were overshadowed by the sections of the reports that focused on the enforcement of Prohibition. Prohibition became law in 1919 when the 18th Amendment to the U.S. Constitution banned the sale and manufacture of intoxicating beverages.[35]

Enforcing Prohibition was no easy task.[36] Bootlegging—the illegal manufacture and sale of alcohol—was a lucrative business, and criminal syndicates quickly organized to capitalize on the sale of a commodity that many Americans desired to consume. Federal law enforcement agencies like the Customs Bu-

Wickersham Commission (National Commission on Law Observance and Enforcement)
A commission that published a comprehensive report on the state of the American criminal justice system the 1930s.

Third degree
The infliction of pain by police officers in order to solicit evidence about a crime.

Police often disposed of illegal alcohol during Prohibition.

SOURCE: LIBRARY OF CONGRESS.

reau, the U.S. Coast Guard, and the Federal Bureau of Investigation were largely unsuccessful in curbing the smuggling of alcohol (called rum-running) and the growth of illegal bars (called speakeasies) and in keeping up with the creative ways the public came up with to consume alcohol. Enforcement of Prohibition by local police was spotty at best and, in some cases, exacerbated problems of corruption among police officers, as it introduced a new enterprise from which police could take bribes in exchange for protection against enforcement. In addition, the lack of formal regulation over alcohol production often resulted in beverages of low quality or potentially dangerous potency.

The public was becoming increasingly frustrated with criminal justice interventions into their personal lives and with the growth in organized crime that resulted from Prohibition laws. The lack of public support for Prohibition did little to bolster confidence in and public support of law enforcement. In 1933, lawmakers succumbed to public pressure, and Prohibition was repealed by the 21st Amendment.

The Wickersham Commission's reports were the most comprehensive study of the American criminal justice system to date. They were complete with a broad range of recommendations aimed at improving the approach to criminal justice in the U.S., including its methods of policing. Unfortunately, the reports were issued at an inopportune time—the United States had just entered a period of substantial social and economic turmoil, known as the Great Depression. In the midst of a significant national depression, there was little motivation for a sustained focus on the improvement of the criminal justice system. It was not until the 1960s that the criminal justice system again received significant public and political attention.

In the 1960s, the United States was undergoing dramatic social change and experiencing significant episodes of unrest. Both population and crime rates were increasing, as was public fear of crime and disorder.[37] Public fears were exacerbated by a number of assassinations of prominent political figures in the 1960s, including President John F. Kennedy in 1963 and Reverend Martin Luther King, Jr. and New York Senator Robert F. Kennedy in 1968, and by significant media attention to serial killers and mass murderers, including the Boston Strangler, the Zodiac Killer, Charles Manson, and Charles Whitman.

In addition, large-scale urban unrest occurred in a number of cities across the country.[38] According to President Lyndon Johnson's Commission on Law Enforcement and the Administration of Justice, residents in ghetto communities were frustrated by unemployment, discrimination, substandard housing, and underfunded schools. These deep-seated frustrations over broader social inequalities were inflamed by poor relationships between the police and members of the community.[39]

Unrest was not restricted to poor, urban areas, however. College and university students across the country participated in sit-ins, protests, and revolutionary acts to express frustrations with discrimination, inequality, and the Vietnam War. One of the most famous episodes of student unrest occurred at Kent State in Ohio on May 4, 1970. During the protest, members of the National Guard fired 61 shots into the crowd, killing four students and wounding nine. The events at Kent State led to protests at more than 700 other colleges across the nation.[40]

As a result of numerous urban riots and incidents like the Kent State shootings, police agencies began to experience significant pressure to change the ways they addressed large-scale protests. Two strategies adopted by policing agencies were improving relationships between the community and the police and adopting crowd control technologies, such as riot gear. These strategies can be seen in contemporary practices such as community policing and SWAT teams.

Critical Thinking   Military groups such as local militias and the National Guard have been used relatively frequently in American history to deal with large-scale protests. What are the advantages and disadvantages of using the military to quell domestic disturbances?

Wide-scale unrest and increasing crime rates and fear of crime brought renewed attention to policing in the 1960s. One issue that became the focal point of concern for reformers was police/community relations. In "The Challenges of Crime in a Free Society," a report published by a commission organized by President Johnson, the authors recommended improving police/community relations by increasing community participation in police decision-making, creating policing units specifically devoted to community relations, increasing recruitment of officers from diverse backgrounds and from the college-educated, establishing procedures for handling citizen complaints and an internal investi-

Exhibit: National Advisory Commission on Civil Disorders 1967 (The Kerner Report)

The Kerner Commission was assembled to determine the causes of the riots that spread across the U.S. in the 1960s. In the following excerpts from the summary of the commission's report, the authors highlight the roles of social inequality and poor police/community relations in creating conditions conducive to rioting:

"We have visited the riot cities; we have heard many witnesses; we have sought the counsel of experts across the country. This is our basic conclusion: Our nation is moving toward two societies, one black, one white—separate and unequal . . . Discrimination and segregation have long permeated much of American life; they now threaten the future of every American . . . Segregation and poverty have created in the racial ghetto a destructive environment totally unknown to most white Americans . . . 'Prior' incidents, which increased tensions and ultimately led to violence, were police actions in almost half the cases; police actions were 'final' incidents before the outbreak of violence in 12 of the 24 surveyed disorders . . . What the rioters appeared to be seeking was fuller participation in the social order and the material benefits enjoyed by the majority of American citizens. Rather than rejecting the American system, they were anxious to obtain a place for themselves in it . . . The police are not merely a 'spark' factor. To some Negroes police have come to symbolize white power, white racism and white repression. And the fact is that many police do reflect and express these white attitudes. The atmosphere of hostility and cynicism is reinforced by a widespread belief among Negroes in the existence of police brutality and in a 'double standard' of justice and protection—one for Negroes and one for whites."[41]

© BETTMANN/CORBIS.

↑ Wide-scale unrest, such as the Watts, Los Angeles riot in 1965, brought renewed attention to policing.

gative unit to investigate problematic officers, and establishing policies that limited the use of a firearm to life-or-death situations.[42] Many of these recommendations were reiterated in the 1980s, when policing agencies begin to adopt community policing models.

Exhibit: Excerpt from "The Challenge of Crime in a Free Society" by the 1967 Commission on Law Enforcement and the Administration of Justice

In the following excerpt, the link between social unrest and poor police/community relations is reiterated:

"Since this is a time of increasing crime, increasing social unrest and increasing public sensitivity to both, it is a time when police work is peculiarly important, complicated, conspicuous, and delicate . . . It is hard to overstate the intimacy of the contact between the police and the community . . . Since police action is so often so personal, it is inevitable that the public is of two minds about the police: Most men both welcome official protection and resent official interference . . . Yet policemen, who as a rule have been well trained to perform . . . have received little guidance from legislatures, city administrations, or their own superiors, in handling these intricate, intimate human situations . . . The peacekeeping and service activities, which consume the majority of police time, receive too little consideration."

"Finally, more than public attitudes toward the police and, by extension, toward the law, are influenced by the way any given policeman performs his duties . . . Most of the recent big-city riots were touched off by commonplace street encounters between policemen and citizens . . . In short, the way any policeman exercises the personal discretion that is an inescapable part of his job can, and occasionally does, have an immediate bearing on the peace and safety of an entire community, or a long-range bearing on the work of all policemen everywhere."[43]

The findings from "The Challenges of Crime" report provided a foundation for the Omnibus Crime Control and Safe Streets Act of 1968. This act was the first comprehensive crime legislation to be introduced by the federal government. It designated federal funds to support local law enforcement agencies to engage in research and evaluation, as well as monies to improve cross-jurisdictional cooperation and support. It also created the **Law Enforcement Assistance Administration** (LEAA) within the Department of Justice as the body responsible for implementing its provisions and for improving policing across the country. The LEAA was abolished in 1982, but while it was in existence it provided millions of dollars in funds and program support to law enforcement agencies across the country.

Law Enforcement Assistance Administration
A body created by the 1968 Omnibus Crime Control and Safe Streets Act to serve as a federal resource for local law enforcement agencies.

Grass eaters
Those police officers who engage in relatively passive forms of inappropriate behavior by accepting small favors or money for looking the other way when illegal activities are taking place.

Concerns over police corruption continued through the 1960s, and several commissions and workgroups conducted investigations of police corruption. The Knapp Commission, which was responsible for investigating corruption within the New York City Police Department, described two types of corrupt police officers: "grass eaters" and "meat eaters."[45] **Grass eaters** were those po-

Exhibit: Excerpt from the Omnibus Crime Control and Safe Streets Act of 1968

This act was designed to improve a number of components of the American criminal justice system. The following excerpt focuses on provisions related to policing:

"Congress finds that the high incidence of crime in the United States threatens the peace, security, and general welfare of the Nation and its citizens. To prevent crime and to insure the greater safety of the people, law enforcement efforts must be better coordinated, intensified, and made more effective at all levels of government.

Congress finds further that crime is essentially a local problem that must be dealt with by State and local governments if it is to be controlled effectively.

It is therefore the declared policy of the Congress to assist State and local governments in strengthening and improving law enforcement at every level by national assistance. It is the purpose of this title to (1) encourage States and units of general local government to prepare and adopt comprehensive plans based upon their evaluation of State and local problems of law enforcement; (2) authorize grants to States and units of local government in order to improve and strengthen law enforcement; and (3) encourage research and development directed toward the improvement of law enforcement and the development of new methods for the prevention and reduction of crime and the detection and apprehension of criminals."[44]

Meat eaters
Police officers who are more aggressive in their illegal behavior and actively search for ways to make money illegally while on duty.

lice officers who engaged in relatively passive forms of inappropriate behavior, such as accepting free goods or services from citizens and local businesses—for example, accepting free coffee from a local diner. **Meat eaters** were characterized as more aggressive in their illegal behavior: for example, a meat eater might solicit money from an offender in exchange for ignoring the individual's criminal activities.

Police themselves were also expressing frustration with their work. Officers in cities around the country participated in strikes and other forms of protest over low wages and poor working conditions. Practices they employed to express their discontent included the "blue flu," where officers would call in sick en masse, and ticket blizzards, where officers would overwhelm government offices and courthouses by writing a large number of non-revenue-generating tickets.

Critical Thinking Many states have policies that prohibit crucial personnel, such as police officers and firefighters, from forming unions or participating in strikes. What are the advantages and disadvantages of such policies? Do you agree with the use of these policies? Why or why not?

Ethics and Professionalism: Early Intervention Systems

Police corruption and abuse of power are serious concerns for many police administrators and local government officials. They can be expensive and result in decreased public confidence in the local police. Often police administrators must develop policies that clearly distinguish between police officer behaviors that are acceptable and those that are not. In addition, they must outline how the department will respond when an officer behaves in an inappropriate or illegal manner.

The newest trend in dealing with problematic officers is the use of **early warning systems (EWS)**. Early warning systems are implemented as a means to identify potentially problematic officers before their behavior becomes very serious. Not all jurisdictions use EWS, and the types of information collected by those agencies that do use EWS vary significantly. Some common types of data monitored by EWS include number and frequency of citizen complaints (including lawsuits), resisting-arrest incidents, use of force incidents, firearm-discharge reports, and pursuits and vehicular accidents. In addition, responses to officers who are identified as problematic by EWS vary—some jurisdictions emphasize punishment, while others emphasize more supportive or corrective types of interventions, e.g., counseling or additional training. Some agencies may utilize both punitive and corrective responses.

Critical Thinking   Imagine that you are the chief of your local police department. What kinds of information do you think should be collected on your department's officers? What responses would you recommend for officers who are identified as potential problems? Would you implement corrective or punitive responses?

Changes to Policing   A number of court decisions and professional reports in the latter half of the 20th century attempted to change policing in significant ways. For much of the history of policing, the U.S. Supreme Court maintained a hands-off policy, intervening infrequently in issues involving police practices.[46] This changed in the mid-1900s under the tenure of Chief Justice Earl Warren. The Warren Court decisions fundamentally changed policing practices, such as procedures for search and seizure, suspect access to legal counsel, and officers' responsibilities to inform suspects of their rights.

In the case of *Mapp v. Ohio* (1961), the Supreme Court ruled that evidence seized illegally could not be used in a criminal trial. The case began in 1957, when law enforcement officers believed that Cleveland resident Dollree Mapp was hiding a suspect in a bombing incident in her home. When officers first contacted her at her residence, she refused to let them enter without a search warrant. A few hours later, the officers returned, claiming to have obtained a search warrant, and broke down Mapp's door. The officers refused to let Mapp see the document, and at one point she grabbed the sheet from the officer and put it in her dress. The officer wrestled with Mapp to reclaim the piece of paper. During the search of Mapp's home, they uncovered pornographic material.

Early Warning Systems

A means used by police leadership to identify a potentially problematic officer before his or her behavior becomes very serious; sometimes called Early Intervention Systems.

Mapp claimed the materials belonged to a boarder who had since moved. Mapp was charged with possession of obscene material and found guilty at trial. No evidence of a warrant was presented at her trial. The Supreme Court asserted that the pornographic material should have been excluded as evidence, as it was obtained from an illegal search.[47]

In *Escobedo v. Illinois* (1964), the Supreme Court ruled that officers must allow suspects accused of crime the opportunity to consult with an attorney and inform them of their right to remain silent. In this case, 22-year-old Danny Escobedo was questioned regarding his involvement in the fatal shooting of his brother-in-law. Though Escobedo was not formally arrested, he was not allowed to leave police custody. In addition, though he asked repeatedly to speak with his lawyer, officers refused to let Escobedo access counsel. Officers involved in the questioning informed Escobedo that he would be able to leave if he confessed to the murder. Escobedo confessed and was convicted of murder, but the case was later reversed in the Supreme Court. The Supreme Court asserted that, once questioning shifted from being investigatory to accusatory, the suspect had the right to consult with an attorney.[48]

Miranda rights
The obligation of police officers to inform suspects of their right to remain silent and their right to an attorney.

In 1966, the Supreme Court made its famous ruling on **Miranda rights** in *Miranda v. Arizona*. In this case, Supreme Court justices heard arguments about four cases in which law enforcement officers in California, New York, and Arizona questioned suspects without informing them of their right to counsel. Ernesto Miranda, after whom the famous Supreme Court ruling was named, was a suspect in an Arizona kidnapping and sexual assault. In March 1963, Miranda was arrested by Phoenix police and questioned about the crimes. After a two-hour interrogation, Miranda confessed to the crimes and signed a written confession. The confession included statements from Miranda that he had full knowledge of his legal rights, that he understood that statements he made during the interrogation could be used against him, and that he knowingly waived his rights. Miranda was convicted of kidnapping and rape and sentenced to 20 years in prison. The Supreme Court ruled that the police did not properly inform Miranda of his constitutional rights. As a result of this case, officers are now required to inform suspects of their right to remain silent and that, if they do choose to speak, the information could be used against them. They must also inform them that they have the right to an attorney.[49]

There were two influential advisory boards assembled in the 1970s aimed at reforming policing in the United States. The first, a federal commission organized under the newly created LEAA called the National Advisory Commission on Criminal Justice Standards and Goals, made recommendations on a broad array of criminal justice issues, including policing. The second advisory board was assembled by the American Bar Association. Its recommendations focused more narrowly on establishing a set of organizational and behavioral standards for the police. Similar to earlier commissions already discussed, these groups advocated for, among other things, clear policies on the use of force, insulation of police leadership from inappropriate political pressures, a sustained focus on improving police/community relationships, increased training for officers, and increased diversity of police officers. Though these groups' recommendations were not binding, they have influenced police organization and practices. For

FIGURE4.1 The Use of Force Continuum used by U.S. Customs and Border Patrol. Similar continuums have been adopted by policing agencies nationwide.

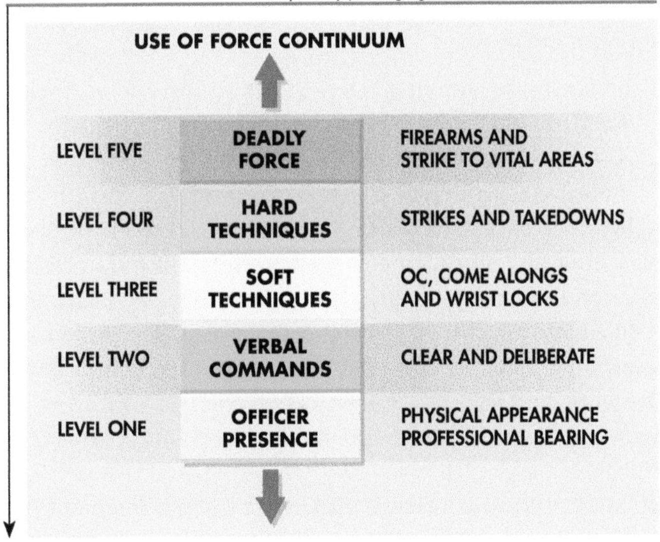

USE OF FORCE CONTINUUM

LEVEL FIVE	**DEADLY FORCE**	FIREARMS AND STRIKE TO VITAL AREAS
LEVEL FOUR	**HARD TECHNIQUES**	STRIKES AND TAKEDOWNS
LEVEL THREE	**SOFT TECHNIQUES**	OC, COME ALONGS AND WRIST LOCKS
LEVEL TWO	**VERBAL COMMANDS**	CLEAR AND DELIBERATE
LEVEL ONE	**OFFICER PRESENCE**	PHYSICAL APPEARANCE PROFESSIONAL BEARING

example, many of the recommendations have been incorporated into the Commission on Accreditation for Law Enforcement's (CALEA) accreditation process.[50] Though accreditation through CALEA is voluntary, nearly every U.S. state has at least two law enforcement agencies that have successfully sought accreditation through CALEA.[51]

Critical Thinking   Should accreditation by a national body be required of all law enforcement agencies? What are the advantages and disadvantages of requiring accreditation?

Structure and Organization of Contemporary Law Enforcement

As discussed earlier in the chapter, British policing practices had a significant influence on policing in the United States. One important difference between the two countries' approaches to policing is the level of government responsible for its oversight and management. In Britain, policing is largely managed at the federal level by Parliament or other national authorities; in the United States, however, the majority of policing agencies are controlled at the local (e.g., city and county) or state level.

Local and State-Level Policing

Many states have a combination of state police forces and local police forces. For example, Pennsylvania, the first of the U.S. states to create a state police force, also has a number of city and county law enforcement agencies. The state police have jurisdiction throughout the commonwealth—this means they can investigate criminal activities and enforce traffic laws in any region of the state. Other states, such as California, however, have created state police forces that focus more narrowly on traffic enforcement, leaving criminal investigations to be handled by local and regional law enforcement agencies.[52]

Most of the law enforcement officers in the country work for a local police department. Based on the most recent data from the Law Enforcement Management and Administrative Statistics (LEMAS) survey, there were an estimated 12,575 local police departments in the United States during 2007.[53] These agencies employed approximately 463,000 full-time, sworn personnel. A brief consideration of the law enforcement agencies in California offers some detail on the number and diversity of local law enforcement agencies in the United States. California has over 200 city or municipal police departments, 110 county sheriff agencies, 35 college or university police departments, 20 school district police departments, and nearly a dozen other types of other law enforcement agencies, such as animal cruelty prevention and enforcement and transit authorities.[54]

The high level of local control in American law enforcement presents both challenges and advantages. Perhaps the most pressing challenges posed by local control are that it makes it difficult to draw conclusions about the state of policing at the state or national level and it limits possibilities for the implementation of needed or desirable systemic changes to policing. Though all law enforcement agencies are accountable to the standards set by the U.S. Constitution, there is significant variance in the policies and practices such agencies choose to adopt. For example, local agencies are free to determine the educational requirements for new recruits, their departmental data collections procedures, their use-of-force policies, etc. These variations may have significant effects on the preparedness of officers, the comprehensiveness (and usefulness) of departmental assessments, and the number and nature of injuries that result from public-police encounters.

The challenges associated with local control may be best illustrated through an example—racial profiling. Racial profiling is a contemporary concern that many states and jurisdictions are attempting to address.[55] Profiling more generally is a relatively common policing strategy. Law enforcement investigators often create "profiles" of individuals who frequently engage in a particular type of criminal activity to aid in their detection. Profiles are developed based on observable characteristics and behaviors. **Racial profiling**, however, entails using race or ethnicity as the primary or only indicator that an individual may be participating in criminal activity. Most of the recent attention to racial profiling has been related to its use in the decision to make a traffic stop.[56]

While studying the problem of racial profiling in traffic stops may seem straightforward, there are a number of challenges associated with such studies. One challenge is that procedures for conducting traffic stops may vary from place to place: for example, speeding laws may be consistently enforced in one jurisdiction but under-enforced in another. Another challenge is that agency policies for collecting data about such stops may vary. Some jurisdictions may require officers to collect data on all stops, regardless of outcome, while others may have no data collection requirements. Finally, different law enforcement

Racial profiling
The use of race or ethnicity as the primary or the only indicator that an individual may be participating in criminal activity.

agencies may have different policies with regard to the appropriateness of considering the race or ethnicity of a motorist when making traffic stop decisions. Some agencies may have strict policies against the use of race and ethnicity as factors, while others may allow it if other factors are also taken into consideration. These different policies make it difficult to discern broad patterns in racial profiling practices in the United States. They also make it difficult to fashion wide-scale solutions to the problem.

In terms of advantages, local control may allow police departments more flexibility to meet local norms and needs. Local law enforcement agencies are able to determine how to focus their resources based on the needs that are present in their community and to establish forms of policing that work well with the types of populations, issues, and concerns police are most likely to encounter. For example, it may be easier for local law enforcement agencies to determine enforcement priorities based on local concerns and crime patterns, rather than based on goals determined at the state or national level. They also may be able to craft recruitment and promotion policies based on local demographics, applicant pools, and skill sets of their current officers.

The flexibility associated with local control may be beneficial when it comes to implementing **community policing**, a method of policing that has its roots in many of the reform efforts of the 1960s and 70s and that has become increasingly popular since the 1990s.[57] Community policing differs from traditional policing in that it is a proactive, rather than a reactive approach to law enforcement and problem solving. In a traditional, or reactive, policing model, the police engage with the public in response, or in reaction, to a crime or to a call for assistance. In contrast, community policing requires that police officers be proactive in addressing problems in the community that may lead to crime. Though there is some debate over what exactly constitutes community policing, it is typically described as the engagement of the community in policing efforts as well as the participation of police officers in community affairs. For example, if a particular park is known to be a consistent source of problems in the community, police officers may work with local residents to determine strategies to reduce problems in the area. One solution might be for community members, the police, and the local government to improve lighting and landscaping in the park to make the area more visibly accessible. Police might also work with local community members to establish a citizens' patrol in the area. Members of the citizens' patrols may observe, record, and report suspicious activities to local police for rapid response.

In addition to increased involvement of police with the public, community policing also entails a conception of police officers as problem-solvers rather than as strict enforcers of the law. Though police do deal with violent and serious crimes, more often they are called upon to address minor crimes and interpersonal conflicts.[58] In these cases,

Community policing
A method of policing that emphasizes community participation in police decision-making and police officer participation in community activities.

Community policing efforts often include patrols on foot or on bicycles. The belief is that getting officers out of patrol cars and onto the streets will increase officer interaction with community members.

the best police response may be something other than issuing a ticket or making an arrest. The problematic individual may be better served by a referral to mental health or drug rehabilitation services or by immediate mediation of the issue.

Community policing has been advanced by its proponents as an effective solution to many of the problems that have plagued policing since its inception. Advocates argue that police involvement in addressing issues of social disorder (rather than a strict focus on crime) will allow the police to better address the underlying causes of crime and, therefore, prevent future crimes from happening. Also, community policing is seen as a means to promote positive public-police relations. If people engage with the police outside of a strict enforcement setting, the community will begin to have more favorable views of police officers.

Despite considerable debate over whether community policing has been effective in reducing crime and fostering positive relationships, it is a popular method of policing. The federal government has devoted significant resources to its implementation in local jurisdictions. In 1994, with the passage of the Violent Crime Control and Law Enforcement Act, $8.8 billion was allotted to hire 100,000 community policing officers throughout the nation.[59] The U.S. Department of Justice continues to fund and sponsor community policing efforts through the Office of Community Oriented Policing Services (COPS).[60] Current data suggest that community policing is unlikely to disappear anytime soon. According to Bureau of Justice Statistics data, in 2006, 90% of law enforcement academies offered training on community policing topics, including identifying community problems, the history of community policing, problem solving, and organizing/mobilizing the community.[61]

Military-style police units are becoming increasingly common across the United States.

In light of the increased focus on community policing, it is surprising that paramilitary or military-style policing is also growing in popularity. In contrast to a community-relations approach, which emphasizes the long-term benefits of positive relationships between the public and law enforcement, military-style police operations emphasize the immediate goal of controlling or suppressing unrest through the use of force. Rather than focusing on increased accountability and engagement with the community, it emphasizes the utilization of sophisticated technologies and strategies similar to those used by the military to root out criminal suspects. The targets of military-style operations are framed as internal security threats or enemy combatants, rather than as problematic or disruptive community members.[62]

The most common manifestation of military-style policing is the special response team, often referred to as **SWAT** (Special Weapons and Tactics Team). The first SWAT team was organized in 1966 by Daryl Gates, who would later become chief of the Los Angeles Police Department. Members of the elite team were selected by Gates and trained in various military tactics by former and current military personnel. In 1969, the newly organized SWAT team engaged in its first substantial conflict with members of the Black Panther Party at their Los Angeles headquarters. Thousands of rounds of ammunition were exchanged in the four-hour conflict, and each side incurred four wounded each. The incident received substantial news coverage, and led to the creation of similar tactical units across the nation. By 1997, three-fourths of the nation's police departments had military-style units.[63]

Though SWAT teams were initially designed to deal with snipers, hostage situations, or other dangerous confrontations between police and the public, they are now frequently used for more day-to-day policing activities, including drug raids, serving warrants, and patrol.[64] There are a number of criticisms of the increased reliance on paramilitary policing, including the increased potential for injury and loss of life. In addition, the confrontational and aggressive nature of SWAT interactions may be counterproductive to fostering positive police-community relations. Ironically, such an approach to policing may counteract gains being made by community policing efforts.

SWAT (Special Weapons and Tactics) team
A paramilitary policing unit originally formed to deal with dangerous confrontations, but increasingly being used in everyday policing.

Critical Thinking Describe how the goals and means of achieving these goals differ between the community policing model and paramilitary policing units.

Federal Law Enforcement There are far fewer law enforcement officers employed by the federal government than by local jurisdictions. According to Bureau of Justice Statistics data, there were approximately 105,000 federal law enforcement officers employed in 2004.[65] Figure 4.2 lists the largest federal law enforcement agencies; border protection and corrections employ the most law enforcement personnel. The list also serves as a good illustration of the diversity of law enforcement positions available in the federal government.

FIGURE 4.2 Federal Law Enforcement Agencies Employing More than 500 Officers, 2004

Agency	Full-time officers
U.S. Customs and Border Protection	27,705
Federal Bureau of Prisons	15,214
Federal Bureau of Investigation	12,242
U.S. Immigration and Customs Enforcement	10,399
U.S. Secret Service	4,769
Drug Enforcement Administration[a]	4,400
Administrative Office of the U.S. Courts[b]	4,126
U.S. Marshalls Service	3,233
U.S. Postal Inspection Service	2,976
Internal Revenue Service, Criminal Investigation	2,777
Veterans Health Administration	2,423
Bureau of Alcohol, Tobacco, Firearms and Explosives	2,373
National Park Service[c]	2,148
U.S. Capitol Police	1,535
Bureau of Diplomatic Security, Diplomatic Security Service[a]	825
U.S. Fish and Wildlife Service, Division of Law Enforcement	708
USDA Forest Service, Law Enforcement & Investigations	600

Note: Table excludes employees based in U.S. territories or foreign countries.

[a]Data are estimates based on information provided by the agency.

[b]Includes all Federal probation officers employed in Federal judicial districts that allow officers to carry firearms.

[c]Includes 1,536 Park Rangers and 612 U.S. Park Police officers.

Though policing remains a largely local and state responsibility, federal law enforcement agencies are diverse and growing. In addition to the agencies discussed earlier in the chapter (FBI, U.S. Marshals), the federal government oversees a number of other law enforcement agencies, including the U.S. Bureau of Alcohol, Tobacco, Firearms, and Explosives, the U.S. Drug Enforcement Administration (DEA), and the Department of Homeland Security. These organizations enforce a range of federal laws pertaining to legal and illegal drugs, weapons, and interstate crime.

The Department of Homeland Security is the most recent creation of the national government. On September 11, 2001, four commercial airline jets were hijacked by 19 members of the terrorist group Al-Qaeda. Two of the jets were crashed into the World Trade Center in New York City, and one was crashed into the Pentagon. The final jet was crashed into a field in Shanksville, Pennsylvania, after its crew and passengers diverted the plane from its intended target in Washington, D.C. Three thousand people were killed as a result of the hijackings. Eleven days later, President George W. Bush announced intentions to create an Office of Homeland Security, whose responsibility would be to coordinate anti-terrorism efforts. By November 2002, legislation to establish a permanent Department of Homeland Security was passed.

FIGURE 4.3 Department of Homeland Security Organizational Chart

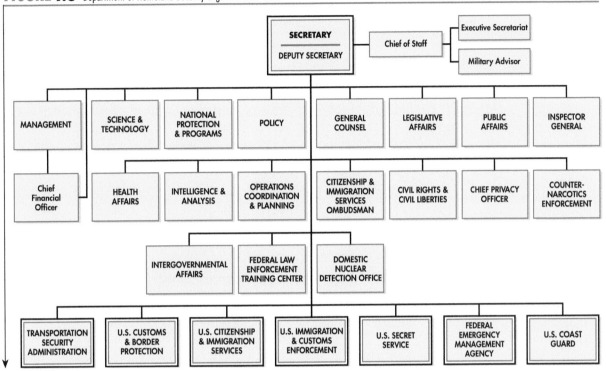

The creation of the Department of Homeland Security (DHS) was the most massive reorganization of federal agencies since the creation of the U.S. Department of Defense during World War II. The Homeland Security Act of 2002 brought 22 different agencies under the umbrella of the DHS, including, among others, the U.S. Coast Guard, U.S. Secret Service, and U.S. Immigration and Customs Enforcement (ICE). The ICE is the principal investigative arm of the DHS. Its responsibilities include preventing terrorist attacks, enforcing immigration laws, and securing borders against illegal trade.

After the attacks of 9/11, terrorism became a major focus of federal law enforcement, and significant funding has been directed to terrorism detection and prevention. The federal focus on terrorism prevention and detection has trickled down to local jurisdictions, as evidenced by the increase in the number of terrorism-related trainings offered by local and state training academies. In 2006, 90% of academies provided at least some basic training on issues surrounding terrorism. Examples of training topics include understanding the nature of terrorism, the role of anti-terrorism task forces, and responding to the use of weapons of mass destruction.[66]

Exhibit: Homeland Security Act of 2002

"The primary mission of the Department is to—

(A) prevent terrorist attacks within the United States;

(B) reduce the vulnerability of the United States to terrorism;

(C) minimize the damage, and assist in the recovery, from terrorist attacks that do occur within the United States;

(D) carry out all functions of entities transferred to the Department, including by acting as a focal point regarding natural and manmade crises and emergency planning;

(E) ensure that the functions of the agencies and subdivisions within the Department that are not related directly to securing the homeland are not diminished or neglected except by a specific explicit Act of Congress;

(F) ensure that the overall economic security of the United States is not diminished by efforts, activities, and programs aimed at securing the homeland; and

(G) monitor connections between illegal drug trafficking and terrorism, coordinate efforts to sever such connections, and otherwise contribute to efforts to interdict illegal drug trafficking."[67]

Becoming a Law Enforcement Officer

The requirements to be a police officer vary from jurisdiction to jurisdiction. Some common requirements of applicants for law enforcement positions include passing written and oral examinations; completion of a minimum level of education; passing background investigations, often including a psychological assessment; and successfully completing physical exams. Some policing agencies also review the credit histories and social networking web pages of applicants. Though the minimum education requirement for most local police departments continues to be a high school diploma, this is changing. Increasingly, police departments are requiring new recruits to have some college credits completed. During 2007, about 30% of local police officers worked for departments where some college education was required.[68]

After passing each of the applicant screening procedures for the appropriate jurisdiction, applicants are typically required to participate in a police training academy. Again, the training requirements for new recruits vary across law enforcement agencies. New recruits may be required to complete trainings in topics such as constitutional or criminal law, self-defense, and diversity/cultural awareness. In 2007, the average local police agency recruit completed 1,370 hours in required training.[70] The number of training hours required for new recruits continues to increase. As mentioned above, the newest addition to mandatory police training programs is terrorism-related trainings. Figure 4.4 describes some of the common types of trainings offered during police academies and the number of hours devoted to the topic.

Exhibit: Requirements for New Recruits in Two Local Police Departments: Reno, Nevada and New York City Police Department[69]

Reno, Nevada
- U.S. citizenship
- At least 21 years old
- High school diploma or equivalent
- Successful completion of a background investigation—considers drug use, domestic violence, previous employment, military history, driving record, financial history
- Pass medical examination and physical tests—includes hand grip strength, sit-ups, push-ups, and running exercises
- No felony convictions or convictions involving moral turpitude or a controlled substance; no history of physical violence
- A personal history that reflects honesty, reliability, and responsible financial management.
- Tattoos and exposed jewelry discouraged

New York City Police Department
- U.S. citizenship
- Between the ages of 21 and 35
- 60 college credits with a 2.0 GPA or two years of military service (no dishonorable discharge)
- Unrestricted driver's license
- Residency in one of the five NYC boroughs
- Pass medical examination
- Pass character assessment and background investigation
- Pass written and oral psychological evaluation
- Successfully complete oral interview
- Pass physical agility tests
- No felony convictions, convictions of a crime that indicates lack of good moral character or disposition toward violence, convictions of a crime punishable by one or more years of imprisonment, or repeated convictions, regardless of nature of crimes

Diversity in Law Enforcement   Government commissions, like the Wickersham Commission and President Johnson's 1967 Crime Commission, have often reiterated the need for a police force that reflects the diversity of the community in which it works. Some policing agencies have implemented special programs to recruit candidates from groups that do not typically pursue law enforcement careers, including minorities, women, and homosexuals; however, in many jurisdictions, police officers continue to be predominantly white males.

The first recorded appointment of a female police officer was in 1893 by the Chicago Police Department. Marie Owens was the widow of a male police officer and was appointed to a patrol position upon his death. In 1910, the Los Angeles Police Department appointed its first female police officer, Alice Wells. By 1915, 25 cities had at least one female police officer.[71]

FIGURE4.4 Topics Covered in State and Local Law Enforcement Training Academies, 2006

Topics	Percent of academies with training	Median number of hours of instruction
Operations		
Report writing	100%	20 hrs.
Patrol	99	40
Investigations	99	40
Basic first aid/CPR	99	24
Emergency vehicle operations	97	40
Computers/information systems	58	8
Weapons/self-defense		
Self-defense	99%	51 hrs.
Firearms skills	98	60
Non-lethal weapons	98	12
Legal		
Criminal law	100%	36 hrs.
Constitutional law	98	12
History of law enforcement	84	4
Self-improvement		
Ethics and integrity	100%	8 hrs.
Health and fitness9646		
Stress prevention/management	87	5
Basic foreign language	36	16
Community policing		
Cultural diversity/human relations	98%	11 hrs.
Basic strategies	92	8
Mediation skills/conflict management	88	8
Special topics		
Domestic violence	99%	14 hrs.
Juveniles	99	8
Domestic preparedness	88	8
Hate crimes/bias crimes	87	4

Historically, female police officers duties differed from their male counterparts. Often female police officers were responsible for issues related to children or enforcement of moral norms. For example, female police officers were responsible for runaway children, young girls who were perceived as behaving immorally, and the suppression of negative influences on children (e.g., dancehalls, liquor sales, etc.). In addition to receiving less desirable assignments, female police officers were paid significantly less than male police officers.[72]

Women continue to be underrepresented in law enforcement. However, they are better represented in federal law enforcement than in local law enforcement as Figure 4.5 indicates, since 2002, women comprise around 15% of all federal law enforcement officers.

As Figure 4.6 demonstrates, women's representation in state and local police departments has shown steady improvement since the 1980s, but their representation in these local departments is lower than their representation in federal law enforcement agencies. In 2007, around 12% of local police officers were women. In the same year, around 6% of state police officers were female. Representation of women in sheriff's departments has been declining since 1997. In 2007, women comprised about 11% of local sheriff forces.

Representation of minorities in federal, state, and local law enforcement varies. As Figure 4.7 reflects, some federal agencies, such as U.S. Customs and Border Protection, have high rates of representation for minority officers. In 2004, U.S. Customs and Border Protection was comprised of nearly 47% minority officers, the majority of which were Hispanic or Latino. The federal agency with the second highest rate of employment for Hispanic or Latino officers is U.S. Immigration and Customs Enforcement. African American officers are best represented in the U.S. Capitol Police, Veterans Health Administration, and Federal Bureau of Prisons. Representation of American Indian officers typically is less than 1%, with the exception of the National Park Service, in which about 2% of park rangers are Native American. Asians and Pacific Islanders compose between 1% and 5% of most federal law enforcement agencies.

With regard to local police departments, larger departments—departments in areas with populations of 100,000 or more—tend to fare better in terms of employing officers from diverse racial and ethnic backgrounds.

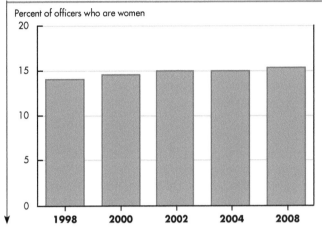

FIGURE4.5 Percentage of Women in Federal Law Enforcement, 1987–2008

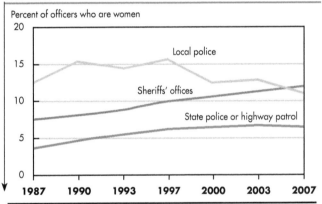

FIGURE4.6 Percentage of Women in State and Local Law Enforcement, 1987–2008

Note: Data on state police and highway patrol agencies were obtained from the Federal Bureau of Investigation's Uniform Crime Reports. Data on local police departments and sheriffs' offices were obtained from the BJS Law Enforcement Management and Administrative Statistics (LEMAS) series.

Critical Thinking Why do you think women and minorities are less likely to pursue careers in law enforcement? What might be some of the barriers to their participation? Should law enforcement agencies implement programs to increase recruitment for underrepresented populations?

FIGURE4.7 Percentage of Racial/Ethnic Minority Federal Law Enforcement Officers by Agency, 2004

Agency	Number of officers	Female	Total minority	American Indian	Black or African American	Asian or Pacific Islander	Hispanic or Latino, any race	Other race
U.S. Customs and Border Protection	28,200	15.3%	46.8%	0.6%	5.0%	4.2%	36.9%	0.0%
Federal Bureau of Prisons	15,361	13.3	39.7	1.3	24.2	1.5	12.7	0.0
Federal Bureau of Investigation	12,414	18.5	17.2	0.4	5.8	3.6	7.4	0.0
U.S. Immigration and Customs Enforcement	10,691	13.7	33.9	0.6	8.6	2.7	22.0	0.0
U.S. Secret Service	4,780	10.5	19.6	0.6	11.2	2.6	5.2	0.0
Drug Enforcement Administration	4,500	8.9	19.4	0.4	7.6	2.5	8.9	0.0
Administrative Office of the U.S. Courts	4,166	44.2	32.2	0.5	15.3	1.6	14.1	0.6
U.S. Marshals Service	3,233	10.2	20.0	0.7	7.3	2.3	9.6	0.1
U.S. Postal Inspection Service	2,999	19.6	36.4	0.5	21.6	4.7	9.6	0.0
Internal Revenue Service, Criminal Investigation	2,791	30.0	24.0	0.8	10.2	4.5	8.1	0.4
Veterans Health Administration	2,474	6.9	40.1	0.9	26.8	2.5	10.0	0.0
Bureau of Alcohol, Tobacco, Firearms & Explosives	2,398	13.3	19.9	1.1	9.3	2.1	7.5	0.0
National Park Service—Ranger Division	1,547	18.2	10.3	2.1	2.5	2.4	3.0	0.3
U.S. Capitol Police	1,535	18.8	34.7	0.3	28.9	1.2	4.2	0.0
Bureau of Diplomatic Security, Diplomatic Security Service	825	11.8	20.0	0.7	9.7	3.4	5.5	0.7
U.S. Fish and Wildlife Service	713	8.7	13.6	3.5	1.7	1.4	7.0	0.0
National Park Service—U.S. Park Police	612	11.4	18.8	0.0	10.9	2.8	5.1	0.0
USDA Forest Service	604	17.5	17.4	6.5	3.3	1.3	6.3	0.0

Note: Table includes employees in U.S. Territories.

FIGURE4.8 Race and Ethnicity of Full Time Personnel in Local Police Departments by Size of Local Population, 2007

Population served	White	Black/African American	Hispanic/Latino	Asian/Pacific Islander	American Indian/Alaska Native	Multi-race
All sizes	74.7%	11.9%	10.3%	2.0%	0.7%	0.3%
1,000,000 or more	56.0	17.6	22.9	3.2	0.3	0.0
500,000–999,999	60.6	24.1	9.3	4.1	0.4	1.6
250,000–499,999	69.5	16.5	11.2	2.0	0.6	0.1
100,000–249,999	73.7	13.4	9.1	2.6	0.9	0.3
50,000–99,999	83.6	7.0	7.5	1.4	0.3	0.3
25,000–49,999	88.2	5.0	5.1	0.9	0.6	0.2
10,000–24,999	87.5	5.6	5.1	0.6	1.0	0.2
2,500–9,999	87.9	5.1	4.4	0.6	1.8	0.1
Under 2,500	88.3	5.8	3.0	0.1	2.3	0.5

Career Connections: Police Dispatcher

There are a growing number of positions available for civilians in the law enforcement field, including crime analysts, information technology specialists, and researchers, among others. One crucial member of the law enforcement team is the police dispatcher. Dispatchers are often the first responders to citizens in need of police or medical assistance. They serve an essential communication role between the public and the local police. They are responsible for providing support for distressed callers, determining the nature and severity of the problem, and dispatching officers to the scene.

At a minimum, police dispatchers must be able to work well under pressure and possess strong communication and computer skills. Often dispatchers will be required to have some knowledge of first aid in the event that a caller needs immediate medical advice while waiting for emergency personnel. As with many other law enforcement professions, proficiency in more than one language is also desirable. Most dispatchers are required to have a high school education and receive the bulk of their position specific training on the job.[73] The Bureau of Labor Statistics estimates that emergency call responder positions will increase by 18% by 2018. The mean annual wage for dispatchers is $36,900, and full-time dispatchers are often provided with health and retirement benefits.[74]

Chapter Summary

- For much of its history, policing could best be characterized as disorganized, ineffective, and corrupt. Early police officers were poorly paid, ill prepared to address the complexities of crime and disorder, and disrespected by the larger community. Early policing efforts often involved local citizens in law enforcement. The United States did not move toward a model of permanent police forces until the mid-1800s.

- Beginning in the 1900s, policing underwent significant reforms. The objectives of many of these reforms were to transform police officers into unbiased professionals who are capable of upholding the law while enforcing it, and to create well equipped law enforcement agencies that used their resources effectively to reduce crime. Police reform efforts reached their peak in the 1960s and 70s.

- Policing is largely a local affair. Local control allows for greater flexibility to meet local needs, but also makes it difficult to implement systemic changes to policing practices and policies.

- Two contradictory trends are occurring in contemporary policing: community policing, which aims at increasing democratic participation in policing processes, and paramilitary policing, which emphasizes aggressive suppression of criminal activity. The effectiveness of these two trends in reducing crime has been heavily debated.

- The process of becoming a police officer varies from jurisdiction to jurisdiction, but often entails passing psychological and physical tests, possessing a clean employment and criminal history, and having a high school diploma or equivalent.

- Women and racial and ethnic minorities are underrepresented in both local and federal law enforcement positions. Since 2002, women have comprised around 15% of all federal law enforcement officers.

Critical Thinking?

1. What role have private citizens played in law enforcement historically? What role do they play in the contemporary community policing model?
2. What role has race/ethnicity played in policing throughout its history?
3. Numerous commissions have recommended increasing the diversity of American police personnel. How might increasing the diversity of police forces be beneficial?
4. What are the advantages and disadvantages of local control of policing? Can you think of other issues surrounding local control that were not addressed in the chapter?
5. What role has federal law enforcement played in law enforcement throughout history? Do you think the federal government should play a greater or lesser role in law enforcement in the future? Explain.
6. Policing is a popular topic in contemporary television shows and movies. What kinds of messages about policing are conveyed in modern media about the police? What effect do you think media depictions have on public support or criticism of police?
7. Consider Figure 4.4, which lists the most common topics covered in police academies. Do you think the number of hours devoted to each topic is sufficient? Are there additional topics you think should be offered to new police officers?
8. Imagine this hypothetical situation: Officer Phillips is responsible for patrolling the downtown area of Sunshine City. There are a number of coffee shops on his route, and it is not unusual for Officer Phillips to receive free coffee and pastries from these shops during his shift. Is Officer Phillips's behavior unethical? Explain.
9. Do you think policing agencies should require police officers to have a college education? What are the advantages and disadvantages of such a policy?
10. Though it does not receive much media or scholarly attention, private policing is becoming increasingly popular. Think of your regular routines—how often do you encounter private security or police officers in your normal activities? What do you think are the advantages and disadvantages associated with private policing/security?

Media

Bureau of Justice Statistics Law Enforcement Agency Surveys and Data Collections http://bjs.ojp. usdoj.gov/index.cfm?ty=tp&tid=7#data_collections

> This website includes results and reports from a number of surveys on law enforcement practices and officer demographics.

Police Assessment Resource Center http://www.parc.info/home.chtml

> PARC is a nonprofit organization that publishes articles related to police oversight and accountability.

Officer.com http://www.officer.com

> This website includes a number of resources related to law enforcement, including job postings, media reports, and listings of upcoming events.

Endnotes

1. Wickersham Commission. (1968). *U.S. National Commission on Law Observance and Enforcement*, Montclair, NJ: Patterson Smith.
2. Chafee, Z., Pollak, W., & Stern, C. (1969). *The Third Degree*. New York: Arno Press & The New York Times, 60–61.
3. Brown, B., & Benedict, W. (2002). "Perceptions of the Police: Past Findings, Methodological Issues, Conceptual Issues and Policy Implications." *Policing, 25*, 543–580.
4. Wadman, R., & Allison, W. (2004). *To Protect and Serve: A History of Police in America*. Upper Saddle River, NJ: Pearson Prentice Hall.
5. Greenberg, M. A. (2005). *Citizens Defending America: From Colonial Times to the Age of Terrorism*. Pittsburgh, PA: University of Pittsburgh Press.
6. Bayley, D. (1998). "The Development of Modern Police." In L. Gaines & G. Cordner (Eds.), *Policing Perspectives: An Anthology* (pp. 59–78). Oxford: Oxford University Press.
7. Stevenson, L. *Policing in America*.
8. Bopp, W., & Schultz, D. (1972). *A Short History of American Law Enforcement*. Springfield, IL: Charles Thomas.
9. Wadman & Allison, 2004.
10. Schneider, J. C. (1980). *Detroit and the Problem of Order, 1830–1880*. Lincoln, NE: University of Nebraska Press.
11. Bernstein, I. (1990). *The New York City Draft Riots of 1863: Their Significance for American Society and Politics in the Age of the Civil War*. Oxford: Oxford University Press.
12. Monkkonen, E. H. (1981). *Police in Urban America*. Cambridge: Cambridge University Press.
13. Walker, S. (1998). *Police in America*. New York, NY: McGraw-Hill.
14. Hadden, S. (2001). *Slave Patrols: Law and Violence in Virginia and the Carolinas*. Cambridge, MA: Harvard University Press.
15. Ibid., 94.
16. Tolnay, S., & Beck, E. M. (1995). *A Festival of Violence: An Analysis of Southern Lynchings, 1882–1930*. Champaign, IL: University of Illinois Press.
17. Prassel, F. (1972). *The Western Peace Officer: A Legacy of Law and Order*. Norman, OK: University of Oklahoma Press.
18. McNab, C. (2009). *Deadly Force: Firearms and American Law Enforcement, From the Wild West to the Streets of Today*. Westminster, MD: Osprey.
19. Prassel, 1972.
20. Utley, R. (2002). *Lone Star Justice: The First Century of the Texas Rangers*. Oxford: Oxford University Press.
21. Cox, M. (2008). *The Texas Rangers*. New York, NY: Forge.
22. O'Neal, B. (2006). *War in East Texas: Regulators vs. Moderators*. Lufkin, TX: Best of East Texas.
23. Mackay, J. (1996). *Allan Pinkerton: The First Private Eye*. New York, NY: John Wiley & Sons.
24. Ibid.
25. Calhoun, F. (1989). *The Lawmen: United States Marshals and their Deputies, 1789–1989*. Washington, DC: Smithsonian Institution Press.
26. Melanson, P., & Stevens, P. (2002). *The Secret Service: The Hidden History of an Enigmatic Agency*. New York, NY: Carroll & Graf.
27. Jeffreys-Jones, R. (2007). *The FBI: A History*. Binghamton, NY: Vail-Ballou Press.
28. Gentry, C. (1991). *J. Edgar Hoover: The Man and the Secrets*. New York, NY: W.W. Norton and Company.
29. Jeffreys-Jones, 2007.
30. Walker, S. (1977). *A Critical History of Police Reform: The Emergence of Professionalism*. Lexington, MA: Lexington Books.
31. Sherman, L. (1974). *Police Corruption: A Sociological Perspective*. New York, NY: Anchor Press.
32. Kappeler, V., Sluder, R., & Alpert, G. (1994). *Forces of Deviance: Understanding the Dark Side of Policing*. Prospect Heights, IL: Waveland Press. Goldstein, H. (1975). *Police Corruption: A Perspective on its Nature and Control*. Washington, DC: Police Foundation.
33. Uchida, C. (1993). "The Development of the American Police: An Historical Overview." In R. Dunham & G. Alpert (Eds.), *Critical Issues in Policing: Contemporary Readings* (2nd ed.). Prospect Heights, IL: Waveland Press.

34. Ibid.

35. Carte, G., & Carte, E. (1975). *Police Reform in the United States: The Era of August Vollmer.* Berkeley, CA: University of California Press.

36. Vollmer, A. (1936). *The Police and Modern Society.* Berkeley, CA: University of California Press.

37. National Commission on Law Observance and Enforcement. (1931a). *Report on Lawlessness in Law Enforcement.* Washington, DC: United States Government Printing Office.

38. National Commission on Law Observance and Enforcement. (1931b). *Report on Police.* Washington, DC: United States Government Printing Office.

39. National Commission on Law Observance and Enforcement. (1931c). *Report on the Enforcement of the Prohibition Laws of the United States.* Washington, DC: United States Government Printing Office.

40. Ibid.

41. Ibid.

42. Beckett, K. (1999). *Making Crime Pay: Law and Order in Contemporary American Politics.* Oxford: Oxford University Press.

43. McPhail, C., Schweingruber, D., & McCarthy, J. (1998). "Policing Protest in the United States: 1960–1995." In D. Della Porta & H. Reiter (Eds.), *Policing Protest: The Control of Mass Demonstrations in Western Democracies.* Minneapolis, MN: University of Minnesota Press.

44. Commission on Law Enforcement and Administration of Justice. (1967). *The Challenge of Crime in a Free Society.* Washington, DC: United States Government Printing Office.

45. Hensley, T. R., & Lewis, J. M. (Eds.). (2003). *Kent State and May 4th: A Social Science Perspective* (3rd ed.). Kent, OH: Kent State University Press.

46. *Report of the National Advisory Commission on Civil Disorders.* New York, NY: Bantam Books, 1–29.

47. Commission on Law Enforcement and Administration of Justice, 1967.

48. Ibid.

49. Federal Communications Commission. (n.d.). Retrieved from http://transition.fcc.gov/Bureaus/OSEC/library/legislative_histories/1615.pdf

50. Chin, G. J. (Ed.). (1997). *New York City Police Corruption Investigation Commissions, 1894–1994.* Buffalo, NY: William S. Hein.

51. Avery, M., Blum, K., & Rudovsky, D. (2010). *Police Misconduct: Law and Litigation* (3rd ed.). Eagan, MN: Westlaw.

52. *Mapp v. Ohio*, 367 U.S. 643 (1961).

53. *Escobedo v. Illinois*, 378 U.S. 478 (1964).

54. Stuart, G. (2004). *Miranda: The Story of America's Right to Remain Silent.* Tucson, AZ: University of Arizona Press.

55. Walker, S. (1985). "Setting the Standards: The Efforts and Impact of Blue-Ribbon Commissions on the Police." In W. Geller (Ed.), *Police Leadership in America* (pp. 354–370). Westport, CT: Praeger.

56. Commission on Accreditation for Law Enforcement. (2009). *CALEA 2009 Annual Report.* Retrieved from http://www.calea.org/sites/default/files/2009%20Annual%20Report.pdf

57. *Pennsylvania State Police.* (n.d.). Retrieved from http://www.psp.state.pa.us/portal/server.pt/community/psp/4451

58. Reaves, B. A. (2010). *Local Police Departments, 2007.* Retrieved from http://bjs.ojp.usdoj.gov

59. USACOPS. (n.d.). *California.* Retrieved from http://www.usacops.com/ca/

60. Pampel, F. (2004). *Racial Profiling.* New York, NY: Infobase.

61. Smith, M., & Petrocelli, M. (2001). "Racial Profiling? A Multivariate Analysis of Police Traffic Stop Data." *Policing Quarterly, 4*, 4–27.

62. Skogan, W. (Ed.). (2004). *Community Policing: Can It Work?* Belmont, CA: Wadsworth.

63. Moore, M. H., Trojanowicz, R., & Kelling, G. (1988). *Crime and Policing.* Washington, DC: National Institute of Justice. Retrieved from https://www.ncjrs.gov/pdffiles1/nij/111460.pdf

64. Goldstein, H. (1990). *Problem Oriented Policing.* Columbus, OH: McGraw-Hill.

65. Violent Crime Control and Law Enforcement Act, Pub. L. No. 103–322, 108 Stat. 1902 (1994).

66. Community Oriented Policing Services. (n.d.). *COPS Office: Grants and Resources for Community Policing.* Retrieved from http://www.cops.usdoj.gov/

67. Reaves, B. A. (2009). *State and Local Law Enforcement Training Academies, 2006.* Retrieved from http://bjs.ojp.usdoj.gov

68. Fry, L., & Berkes, L. (1983). "The Paramilitary Police Model: An Organizational Misfit." *Human Organization, 42,* 225–234.

69. Auten, J. H. (1981). "The Paramilitary Model of Police and Police Professionalism." *Police Studies, 4,* 67–78.

70. Kraska, P., & Kappeler, V. (1997). "Militarizing American Police: The Rise and Normalization of Paramilitary Units." *Social Problems, 44,* 1–18.

71. Kraska, P. (Ed.). (2001). *Militarizing the American Criminal Justice System: The Changing Roles of the Armed Forces and the Police.* Boston, MA: Northeastern University Press.

72. Reaves, B. A. (2006). *Federal Law Enforcement Officers, 2004* (NCJ 212750). Retrieved from http://bjs.ojp.usdoj.gov/content/pub/pdf/fleo04.pdf

73. Reaves, 2009.

74. Homeland Security Act of 2002, Pub. L. No. 107-296, 116 Stat. 2135 (2002). Retrieved from http://www.dhs.gov/xlibrary/assets/hr_5005_enr.pdf

75. Reaves, 2010.

76. City of Reno. (n.d.). *Police Recruiting.* Retrieved from http://www.reno.gov/Index.aspx?page=1094 NYPD. (n.d.). *Application Process.* Retrieved from http://www.nyc.gov/html/nypd/html/careers/application_overview.shtml

77. Reaves, 2009.

78. Schulz, D. M. (1995). *From Social Worker to Crimefighter: Women in United States Municipal Policing.* Westport, CT: Praeger.

79. Ibid.

80. U.S. Department of Labor, Bureau of Labor Statistics. (2009). "Police, Fire, and Ambulance Dispatchers." *Occupational Outlook Handbook, 2010–11 Edition.* Retrieved from http://www.bls.gov/oco/ocos343.htm

81. U.S. Department of Labor, Bureau of Labor Statistics. (2011). "Occupational Employment and Wages, May 2010: 43–5031 Police, Fire, and Ambulance Dispatchers." *Occupational Employment Statistics.* Retrieved from http://www.bls.gov/oes/current/oes435031.htm

Policing: Roles, Functions, AND Challenges

5

KEY TERMS

Aggressive patrol, Bias-based profiling, Blue code of silence, Broken windows theory, COMPSTAT, Crime analysis, Crime mapping, Criminal investigation, Deep cover, Directed patrol, Discretion, Excessive force, Field interrogation, Follow-up investigation, Intelligence-led policing, Light cover, Operational styles, Order maintenance, Preliminary investigation, Preventive patrol, Problem-oriented policing, Role, Role conflict, Role expectation, Selective enforcement, Social contract, Symbolic assailant, Thin blue line

CHAPTER OBJECTIVES

1. Define the various roles and duties that police officers have in enforcing law and maintaining order in society.

2. Distinguish among the different styles of policing used by police officers.

3. Identify the various functions of police departments in America.

4. Explain the components of the police subculture, including issues related to discretion, stress, ethics, and corruption.

Case Study: Less Lethal or Deadly Force?

Police work can be a dangerous profession, and sometimes the police are required to use physical force to subdue criminals. Historically, the police have carried batons or nightsticks and firearms. In more recent years, new, less lethal technologies have been developed so the police do not have to resort to deadly force. Stun gun technology uses electroshocks into the suspect's body that cause a loss of neuromuscular control and contract the muscles in the body. The most commonly known stun gun used by police departments across the country was developed by TASER International nearly two decades ago. Proponents of the use of the TASER have found it to be a useful tool that has prevented police from having to use deadly force. While these proponents view the use of stun gun technology as preventing deaths of suspects, an alarming number of suspects have died after being "tased." Numerous civil lawsuits have been filed against police departments and stun gun manufacturers, including TASER International, but at present, the courts have ruled against the plaintiffs and found that the deaths were not a direct result of the electroshock weapon.

On September 22, 2005, the Nashville Police Department was called to the Mercy Lounge, a Nashville nightclub, to remove 21-year-old Patrick Lee. When police arrived, Lee was already outside the club and could be observed undressed and rambling incoherently. Earlier in the evening, Lee had reportedly ingested the hallucinogen LSD. In an attempt to control him, police deployed their TASERs and jolted Lee 19 times. Paramedics were called to the scene when Lee was unresponsive, and he died in police custody 39 hours later. When an autopsy was conducted, the medical examiner ruled that Lee's death was caused by a "drug-induced excited delirium." Lee's parents filed a wrongful death lawsuit against the Nashville Police Department, the police officers involved, and TASER International. Eventually, a federal jury cleared all defendants in the lawsuit.

Do you believe the shocking of Patrick Lee 19 times was an excessive use of police force? With the number of deaths that have occurred following the use of electroshock, even though the courts have yet to find its users responsible, should the police still continue to employ this form of less lethal weapon?

Roles of the Police Officer

Seneviratne (2002) described the role of police officers as being the gatekeepers to the criminal justice system.[1] It is their sworn duty to investigate crimes and arrest the offenders. Their arrests lead offenders through the gates into the criminal justice system. In addition to arresting offenders, police officers have a variety of functions and roles they are expected to perform. Performing these functions and roles does not come without a cost. The nature of police work leads to unique challenges as a result of the powers that police have, the dangers they face, and the temptations all around them. This chapter discusses the roles, functions, and challenges for the police officer in American society.

When citizens think of the police, they most likely envision a uniformed officer who is operating a vehicle marked with emblems and striping and emergency lights mounted on the roof. This description is of the officer who is patrolling a beat and responding to calls for service in the community. Although there are many different law enforcement agencies on the federal, state, and local levels of government, each with its own geographic or criminal responsibility, the patrol officer is the face of law enforcement in America.

The relationship between the public and the government is commonly referred to as the social contract. This contract is the agreement into which the public enters with its government allowing it to provide for public safety and security. One form of protection that the public seeks is that of the law enforcement agencies that police America. The police represent a formal state control that is necessary and embodies what Hunter (1985) referred to as public social control.[2] Without the police, the public would be left to its own devices, and crime and victimization would undoubtedly result. The police are said to be a thin blue line, named for the color of most police uniforms, between the lawful and the lawless on our streets. Klockars (1985) defined police as "institutions or individuals given the general right to use coercive force by the state within the state's domestic territory."[3]

A role is defined as the position one holds within a social structure. The role police officers assume when policing a community can be vague and ambiguous. Take, for example, a community that has an ordinance against doing vehicle repairs on the street. Community residents in an upper-class neighborhood who do not want to see cars sitting on cement blocks and motor oil spills on their streets may call the police department demanding action against a violator. In contrast, residents in a poorer neighborhood may overlook this violation because they know the neighbor doing his own repair work cannot afford to take the car to an automobile repair shop. This example refers to what is termed as role expectation. While the residents of the upper-class neighborhood expect the police to issue a citation for the ordinance violation, the residents in the poorer neighborhood do not. Role expectation is the behavior that is expected of someone in a particular role.

Dunham and Alpert (2010) saw the role of the police officer becoming increasingly more complex and citizens' expectations of the police continually expanding.[4] The expectations of the police officer's role do not only reflect the wishes of community residents: the officer must also deal with the expectations of police administrators, political leaders in the community, and sometimes the state legislature. In our example involving vehicle repairs on the street, although residents in the poorer neighborhood do not want violators cited, the police chief may expect officers to cite any violator of the ordinance regardless of where they reside in the community. The mayor of the community may insist that the police department escort funeral processions to the local cemetery as a service to the public, while the officers may not see this role as one that law enforcement should assume. State legislatures have enacted laws restricting police officers' use of discretion when dealing with domestic violence cases: police officers may prefer to mediate a domestic dispute, but they may be required by law to make an arrest in the case.

Role conflict can result from the opposing expectations that police officers receive from different sources. Role conflict is the conflict between what police

Social contract
An agreement between the public and government in which the public allows the government to provide safety and security.

Thin blue line
The line between the lawful and the lawless and between social order and chaos on the streets.

Role
The position one holds within a social structure.

Role expectation
The behaviors and activities that people expect from a person in a particular role.

Role conflict
The conflict between what a person may prefer to do and what the person is expected to do.

Role conflict is the conflict between what police officers may prefer to do and what they are expected to do.

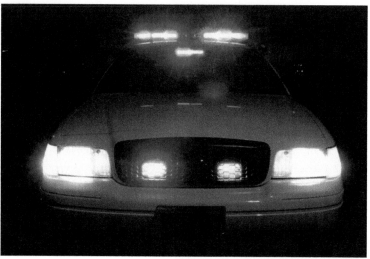

© 2012 BY CAROLINA K. SMITH, M.D. USED UNDER LICENSE OF SHUTTERSTOCK, INC.

officers may prefer to do and what they are expected to do. While police officers may view themselves as crime fighters, the public may see them as peacekeepers or even "social workers" whose role is to control social problems. They may be expected to serve as social workers and intervene in a domestic dispute, but then have to arrest one of the parties involved because they are legally bound to do so even if they believe arrest may be unwarranted. The police may want to pursue a traffic violator who did not stop after they activated their emergency lights and siren, but not be able to because agency policy prohibits vehicle pursuits of vehicle operators wanted only for a traffic violation. The community and the police department largely base the police officer's role on the social contract that has been agreed upon.

Controversial Police Roles
The police are expected to ensure that the rights of citizens are not violated and they are afforded their due process. If police engage in unethical or coercive practices, they are only serving to endanger the public and subject citizens to the very risks the police were given power to prevent. Reiman (1985) argued that the police must be accountable to the public they serve for their use of public power.[5]

Police searches, use of force, vehicle pursuits, and citizen encounters can cause controversy among the public if not performed ethically and within the legal boundaries of the law. For example, in the case of *Mapp v. Ohio* (1961), the United States Supreme Court ruled that evidence obtained illegally by the police must be excluded in state prosecutions.[6] Stuntz (1997) found this exclusionary rule, as it is known, to be useful in that it allows the courts to serve as watchdogs for police misconduct regarding the collection of evidence against a suspect. Stuntz called the exclusionary rule the best legal tool available for regulating the police. While critics of the exclusionary rule might focus on a suspect walking out of a court as a result of a legal technicality due to police misconduct, Stuntz stated that the rule is important because the courts see the consequences of the constitutional rules they create for the police.[7]

In contrast, Keenan (1998) noted that another Supreme Court decision of the 1960s involving police searches was widely criticized for being too pro-police.[8] In *Terry v. Ohio* (1968), the court ruled that police have the authority to detain or "stop" a person briefly for questioning and "frisk" the person for weapons if the officer has a reasonable suspicion the person may be armed and dangerous. The court found the "*Terry* Rule" to be necessary for the safety of police officers when dealing with suspicious persons. However, police must have a legitimate reason for conducting a "stop and frisk" so as not to violate an individual's rights against unreasonable search and seizure.[9]

The authority to use force in the line of duty is a second controversial aspect of police work. The videotaped beating of Rodney King in 1991 by several police officers from the Los Angeles Police Department provided the nation with an example of the possible consequences of police use of force. More controversial is the use of deadly force by police. In the landmark *Tennessee v. Garner* (1985) case, the Supreme Court ruled that a police officer may not use deadly force to prevent the escape of a suspect unless probable cause exists that the suspect poses a threat of serious physical injury or death to the officer or other persons present.[10] As a result of the *Garner* decision, police departments began to make changes in agency policies regarding the use of deadly force.[11]

Deadly force must be the last resort for the police officer. Unfortunately, police are usually unable to choose the time, place, or circumstances of a potential deadly encounter. Fyfe (1986) described the split-second syndrome police officers face when they encounter violence, during which time they must diagnose a problem, perform under stress and time constraints, and make an assessment of the justifiability of their actions.[12]

Another controversial role of the police officer involves vehicle pursuits. Alpert (1993) observed that pursuit driving on public streets at excessive speeds is a dangerous police tactic that presents risks to all involved, including the officer, the suspect, and any innocent motorists or pedestrians who may be nearby. Alpert stated that police must balance the need to immediately apprehend a suspect with the likelihood that an accident or injury may occur.[13]

Hicks (2006) warned that police officers are charged with protecting the public, and exposing these members of the public to unnecessary risk is counter to this primary police responsibility. As a result of the danger posed by high-speed police chases, Hicks recommended that police officers be provided with written guidelines regarding the procedures that should be followed when considering the initiation of a vehicle pursuit.[14] The police may argue that policy restrictions imposed on pursuits inhibit their ability to apprehend serious offenders. Many police pursuits initiated for simple traffic violations lead to the apprehension of suspects wanted on felony charges. In a study of police pursuits in the state of Michigan, one-third of pursuits—most of which were initiated for traffic offenses—were found to lead to a felony arrest.[15]

A fourth issue of controversy involves police-citizen encounters and particularly the issue of **bias-based profiling**. Bias-based profiling, previously referred to as racial profiling, is defined as the selection of individuals based solely on a common trait of a group such as race, ethnicity, gender, sexual orientation, or economic status. Race is a significant factor influencing individual attitudes

Bias-based profiling
Selection of individuals based solely on a common trait of a group such as race, ethnicity, gender, sexual orientation, or economic status.

African-Americans are more likely than whites to view police traffic stops as unjustified.

about police, with African-Americans having the most negative attitudes toward police while whites hold the most positive attitudes toward police.[16]

The most common site for a police-citizen encounter is the traffic stop,[17] and the most controversial aspect of those is the phenomenon known as "driving while black."[18] Research has indicated that blacks stopped by the police are more likely than whites to view the stop as unjustified.[19] Brown (2005) wrote that many public surveys have shown that a great number of American citizens believe the police treat African-Americans more harshly than white Americans. In Brown's study of police-suspect encounters in Cincinnati, Ohio, the findings suggest that police base arrest decisions on strict legal criteria when encountering white suspects, but are influenced by demeanor, age, and gender when encountering black suspects.[20]

Critical Thinking Should police officers be permitted to engage in vehicle pursuits for traffic violators who are not suspected of having committed a more serious offense?

Duties of the Police Officer In the broadest sense, the role of the police officer is multidimensional. The influence that the community has on the role of police officers requires them to perform a variety of duties. The police are expected to be crime fighters, security guards, peacemakers, lawyers, judges, investigators, social workers, clergymen, psychologists, and medical first responders.

Generally, the role of the police officer falls into four categories of duties:

- Law Enforcement
- Order Maintenance
- Crime Prevention
- Service Provider

These duties that police officers are required to perform are based in large part on the size of the police department and the expectations of the community. Police officers may view themselves as law enforcers, but actually spend most of their time maintaining order in the community. For example, in a large urban police department, the police may deal with a major crime problem that would preclude them from responding to scenes of minor traffic accidents. On the other hand, in a small rural police department, the crime problem may be minimal, so officers are expected to investigate every traffic accident, regardless of how minor it may be. The large urban police department might be exerting most of its efforts maintaining order and enforcing the law, while the smaller rural department is providing services to the community and preventing crime from occurring.

Additionally, the duties police officers perform often overlap. For example, a police officer might be dispatched to the scene of a dispute between two neighbors over the boundary line between their properties. The officer may expect to reach a peaceful resolution to the dispute to maintain order in the neighborhood, but when one neighbor decides to punch the other, the officer may now have to perform a law enforcement duty and arrest the aggressive neighbor. While each category of duties is discussed below, the reality is that the police officer's role includes many overlapping and sometimes conflicting responsibilities.

Law Enforcement Enforcing the law is traditionally considered to be the primary responsibility of police officers. Police officers have the power to investigate crimes and arrest offenders. Within these two broad powers are numerous duties, including enforcing traffic laws, interviewing victims of and witnesses to crimes, interrogating persons suspected of committing crimes, collecting physical evidence at crime scenes, conducting undercover and covert operations, and assisting in the prosecution of individuals charged with crimes. When performing these duties, police officers must always be mindful of the legal rights of any accused persons under the United States Constitution to ensure that they have been safeguarded against violations such as unreasonable searches and seizures and notified of their right against self-incrimination and right to counsel.

Police officers are sworn to uphold and enforce *all* laws, but this can be unrealistic or unwanted. Most police departments practice selective enforcement of the law, in which they decide which laws they wish to enforce and when they choose to enforce them. Police departments must allocate manpower and budgetary resources where they can do the most good and deal with the more serious offenses and offenders. Police officer discretion also plays a role in law enforcement. Traffic enforcement efforts usually permit police officers to decide whether to issue a warning or a citation to traffic violators. But at times, the police department may choose to set up a "speed trap" and selectively enforce excessive speed violations, issuing citations to all violators on a particular roadway in the community where they have observed an increase in fatal traffic accidents.

Selective enforcement
The decision made by police as to which laws they wish to enforce and when they choose to enforce them.

The fact that the public often refers to police officers as "law enforcement officers" suggests that they see this duty as the primary function of the police. In reality, law enforcement takes up a small percentage of time spent by police officers when they are on duty.

Order Maintenance

A method of policing whereby officers interpret the law and decide a course of action based on each individual situation when assigning blame and choosing whether or not to arrest.

Order Maintenance

The duty of the police officer to act as a peacekeeper and maintain order in the community dates back to the early English watchman with his lantern and baton. Police officers may engage in **order maintenance** more than any other duty that they perform.

Order maintenance situations may or may not involve criminal activity. For example, crowd control may be necessary at a public event such as the state fair. In this case, it is unlikely that criminal activity will occur, because these events are typically family-oriented. The police presence is usually meant to ensure that the flow of pedestrian and vehicular traffic remains orderly, though of course unruly persons at the fair would be dealt with and arrested when necessary. In contrast, order maintenance at the site of a political rally involving a hotly de-bated issue will most likely involve citizens who have a different agenda than those seeking a fun day at the state fair. Arresting drunk or unruly people at the fair is a very different use of state power than arresting protestors engaging in the political process.

Police officers are often dispatched to domestic disputes between individuals such as family members, neighbors, or landlords and tenants. In domestic disputes, police officers intervene and attempt to resolve the situation to the satisfaction of all parties involved. If the problem is unresolved, or one of the parties involved has violated criminal law, then the police may choose to make an arrest. Even loud music complaints or dog barking calls can be resolved by simply issuing warnings to the responsible parties. If the music is turned down and the dog is kept from barking by its owner, then order is maintained. If not, then it might be necessary for police to make an arrest.

Police officers prefer to deal with order maintenance issues without having to arrest a citizen. Generally, the public favors this approach. But there are times

One of the duties of police is maintaining order, such as at a protest, concert, or other gathering.

when what began for police as an order maintenance duty becomes a law enforcement duty.

Crime Prevention

Crime prevention is another duty that the community expects the police to perform. When police officers are on routine patrol in marked patrol vehicles, they are looking for criminal activity that may be in progress. Their mere presence may also deter crime. The public views the high visibility of police as one of the most important ways to prevent crime. It is also common for the police department to increase its visibility in high-crime areas or areas of the community where the public congregates. This is done by use of a variety of patrol techniques. For example, the police may utilize foot patrols and mounted horse patrols on a Saturday night in the nightclub section of the community. These increased patrols can have the effect of inhibiting bar patrons from engaging in criminal activity they may otherwise have attempted if police had not made their presence so evident.

In addition to the use of routine patrols and increased visibility, the police department may engage in activities specifically designed for crime prevention. For example, police units will often conduct speed traps using radar devices to apprehend speeding violators. These traps also serve as a deterrent by discouraging motorists from exceeding the speed limit on roadways known to be locations that police frequently monitor. DUI checkpoints, which are often previously announced in the local newspaper, are meant to prevent vehicle operators from driving while drunk. Even visible foot and vehicle patrols in areas of the community known to be frequented by prostitutes and their potential customers have been useful in dealing with this crime problem.

Finally, many police departments implement organized crime prevention programs. Neighborhood watch programs are designed to encourage neighborhood residents to collaborate with the police department and maintain security in the community. A program for juveniles such as the Police Athletic League (PAL) is another example of crime prevention that targets at-risk youths.

Visher and Weisburd (1998) argued that for decades there was very little positive evidence that police crime prevention strategies worked. These authors reported that in more recent years, there has been reason for optimism, as police departments have begun to focus more on high rate offenders and "hot spots" of crime.[21] Still, even with these newer strategies that target specific offenders and crime areas, the sight of a patrol car passing by a resident's home can provide a sense of security for community residents.

Service Provider

The services provided by the police department typically depend on the size of the department and the amount of time officers can devote to providing service. Kennedy (2002) stated that as 24/7 agencies, police departments are always available. As such, agencies must prioritize calls and make decisions regarding which calls will be answered and which ones will not. It is expected that the public will seek the assistance of the police when they have been a victim of or witness to a crime, or have been in some other emergency situation. In some communities, it is also expected that the police will perform services for their residents and respond to non-emergency situations. Large police departments may

The mere presence of a police car may help prevent crime from occurring in a particular area.

Police officers act as service providers, performing such tasks as giving directions.

Operational styles
The approaches police officers use to perform their duties.

not be able to provide the community with the more personal attention that small departments can.[22] While busier police departments that must respond to numerous emergency calls might offer no assistance to non-emergency callers, a small local police department may respond to both emergency and non-emergency calls.

Quite often, the non-emergency service calls to which a police department responds reflect the wishes and expectations of the community. For example, the police department may be expected to assist stranded motorists, provide directions to lost motorists, escort funeral processions, and unlock car doors. A large police department may not have the time to remove cats from trees or provide parenting advice to a distraught parent with a troubled teenager, but the public may expect these types of services from a small-town police department.

Operational Styles of Policing

Several researchers have studied the police officer position in an attempt to determine how officers approach their jobs. These approaches to performing police duties are referred to as **operational styles**. These operational styles can reflect community expectations for police officers, the expectations of police administrators for their departments, and individual police officers' own philosophies on how they should perform their duties. In police departments that do not have a formal agreement on how the community should be policed, individual officers may adopt their own styles.

For example, the community may expect its police officers to adopt a watchman style. This style may be adopted in a very small community where the officers in the police department are familiar with members of the community. The community and the police may agree on informal controls instead of strict enforcement of laws. Informal social control refers to a willingness of local residents to actively participate in crime prevention in their neighborhoods.[23] Reisig and Parks (2004) believed the movement toward community policing, which is discussed in further detail later in this chapter, emphasized the positive contribution of police-citizen partnerships that could control crime and build informal social control.[24] Silver and Miller (2004) found that when residents believe police are successful in addressing their crime problems and represent a legitimate institution of public social control, they feel more empowered to partner with police and to engage in their own informal social control.[25] The community and the police department may agree that it is preferable to warn traffic code violators for minor violations instead of issuing citations. The community may prefer that juveniles who are caught in the act of underage drinking should be escorted home to their parents instead of charged with a violation. The community and the police will most likely agree that in serious cases, criminal law must be enforced and offenders charged.

It should be noted that the public's perception of the police department or an individual officer is often determined by the style of policing officers are practicing as a result of the police-citizen contact. The traffic violator who receives a citation may believe that the officer's style is that of an enforcer. This may or may not be valid. Often, the officer is acting in the role of enforcer because strict enforcement of traffic violators at a particular intersection has been ordered due to the high volume of traffic accidents at the location. While an officer would typically practice a watchman style, orders from the police chief have required the use of an enforcer style.

Wilson's Styles of Policing

Wilson (1968) developed one of the earliest studies of the operational styles of police officers. Wilson found three distinct styles that he termed the watchman style, legalistic style, and service style.

In the *watchman* style, the police officer emphasizes a more informal way of handling disputes within the community. The watchman is most interested in keeping the peace and chooses to arrest only as a last resort to resolve a dispute. This style of policing would be best suited for poorer, economically deprived communities and small towns where informal control is practiced.

Wilson's second style of policing is the *legalistic* style. As the name implies, this style of policing emphasizes strict enforcement of the law and the use of arrests to resolve disputes in the community. Communities with higher crime rates, which are more common within our larger metropolitan areas, would more likely practice the legalistic style of policing, believing that the community will become safer if more offenders are removed from the streets.

The third operational style is Wilson's *service* style. Affluent communities may be more likely to emphasize this style of policing where the police are asked to serve the public's needs. The emphasis of the service style is to assist the community rather than arrest offenders. The use of social service agencies, diversionary programs, and community treatment programs is preferable to the use of the criminal justice system.[26]

Broderick's Styles of Policing

A second approach to the operational styles of police officers was developed by Broderick (1987). Broderick labeled his officer styles as enforcers, idealists, realists, and optimists.

The *enforcer* has more concern for maintaining the social order and puts little emphasis on the individual rights of citizens or due process. The *idealist* emphasizes social order as well, but unlike the enforcer, places a high value on individual rights and due process. The *realist* places little value on social order or due process and seems to accept society as it is. Finally, the *optimist* values individual rights and due process and is mainly concerned with acting as a public servant, giving a lower value to social control.[27]

Muir's Styles of Policing

A third classification by Muir (1977) studied the methods by which police officers used their authority on the streets. Muir saw police officers as using *passion*, which was defined as the ability to use force to resolve conflict, or *perspective*, which was described as using force ethically and dealing empathetically with those who are less fortunate. Muir's styles of police officers included the enforcer, reciprocator, avoider, and professional.

The *enforcer* is the police officer who possesses the passion for enforcing laws and has a comfort level with using force to deal with problems. The *reciprocator* lacks any passion for the job, takes little action enforcing law or making arrests, and has a difficult time using force when it is warranted. The *avoider* is the officer who has neither passion nor perspective and takes little action to deal with problems. Unlike the avoider, the *professional* police officer has both the passion and the perspective necessary to successfully perform the job.[28]

Critical Thinking   Among the various styles of policing discussed in the chapter, which type of police officer would you like policing your community?

Functions of Police

The functions that are carried out by the police are determined based on the size of the police department, the makeup of the community, and the crime problems that the community faces. The following are some of the major functions of a police department.

Patrol

Patrol is considered to be the backbone of policing. The uniformed police officer in the marked police vehicle patrols the streets of the community and serves as the first responder to calls for service and citizen complaints. In a small police department, it would not be uncommon for all officers, including the police chief, to engage in patrol. In larger police departments that have a variety of specialized functions, patrol officers comprise the largest unit in the department.

The patrol officer is the first police officer dispatched to calls for service. Patrol officers respond to family disputes, neighborhood disputes, traffic accidents, burglar alarms, and any other kind of call that is made to the police department by the residents of the community. In addition to responding to calls for service, the patrol officer is expected to look for criminal activity that might be occurring in the community. The patrol officer's duties can involve investigating crimes such as traffic law violations, driving under the influence, disorderly conduct, domestic violence, burglary, and theft.

Preventive Patrol

Adams (2006) identified a number of methods that the police employ to patrol the community. The most common method is preventive patrol, which is sometimes referred to as routine or random patrol. **Preventive patrol** involves patrolling the police officer's sector or district in the community on an unpredictable, random basis. The amount of time spent by police officers on preventive patrol is often dependent on the number of calls for service to which they respond. The more time the patrol officer spends answering calls, the less time he or she can spend patrolling the community to prevent crime or look for crimes that may be in progress.[29]

Preventive patrol
Patrolling the community on an unpredictable and routine or random basis.

Patrol officers are dispatched to calls for service, including traffic accidents.

Although preventive patrol has been used for centuries, its effectiveness was not studied until 1972 in the well-known Kansas City Preventive Patrol Experiment.[30] This study is still considered to be the most comprehensive look at preventive patrol. The experiment divided the patrol districts in Kansas City, Missouri, into 15 beats, with five beats in each of three different groups. Each of the three groups was similar in demographics and calls for service. The first group of five beats were "proactive beats," in which two to three times the normal level of preventive patrol was conducted. The second group of five beats were "reactive beats," in which no preventive patrol was used, and officers only entered the beats when responding to a call. Finally, the third group of five beats were the "control beats." Control beats maintained the usual level of preventive patrol that had historically been conducted.

Following the year-long study, the surprising results indicated that neither increasing nor decreasing patrols impacted crime rates in the community. Furthermore, the citizens of Kansas City were unaware that any changes to the way the community was being patrolled had occurred. Citizens' fear of crime, attitudes toward the police, and even their review of police response time to their calls for service remained unchanged. In more recent studies involving police patrol, researchers have found that instead of using a generalized preventive patrol, the focus should be on specific places or "hot spots" where crime is most concentrated.[31,32,33]

The results of the Kansas City Preventive Patrol Experiment caused many police administrators to rethink their positions on the effectiveness of routine patrol. Yet, years after the study, preventive patrol remains the most widely used method for patrolling our communities. As a result of the study, however, alternatives to preventive patrol are being practiced when particular problems in the community warrant their use.

Directed Patrol   A directed patrol requires that patrol officers spend an amount of their patrol time in a specified area of the community.[34] These may be known high-crime areas or areas where there has been a noticeable increase in one type of criminal activity. For example, the police department may be aware as a result of crime analysis information that during the three weeks prior to Christmas, the parking lot at the local mall has had an increase in vehicle burglaries and muggings of shoppers. As time permits during the shift, police officers may be ordered to direct frequent patrols through the mall parking lot in order to prevent these crimes from occurring or possibly catch suspects in the act of committing these crimes.

Foot Patrol   Prior to the use of motorized patrol vehicles, police officers patrolled on foot. Adams (2006) stated that although foot patrol confines police to small areas, it is among the most effective types of patrol.[35] The motorized patrol vehicle has permitted patrol officers to cover more ground and respond more quickly to calls for service. Unfortunately, a negative effect of the use of the patrol vehicle was that police officers began to become more distant and aloof from the community. Foot patrols allow police officers to have more personal contact with the community and move more quietly into areas of the community where the sound of an approaching vehicle may alarm a suspect.

FIGURE5.1   Schematic of 15 Beats in Kansas City Patrol Experiment

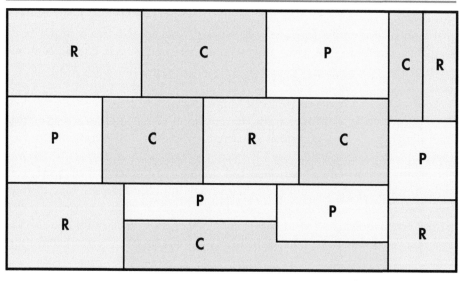

P = Proactive   C = Control   R = Reactive

Two important studies were conducted in an attempt to determine the possible benefits of the use of foot patrol. The Newark, New Jersey Foot Patrol Experiment found that foot patrols did not affect crime rates, but had a positive impact on citizen satisfaction with foot patrol officers.[36] In a similar study conducted by Trojanowicz (1982) in Flint, Michigan, it was found that citizens also showed an increase in satisfaction with police services and a decrease in fear of crime.[37] Whether or not foot patrol reduces crime is uncertain, but it has led to a more positive relationship between the police and the public.

Aggressive Patrol   Aggressive patrol strategies require patrol officers to maintain a more active or "aggressive" style of policing. Gaines (1996) recommended the use of aggressive patrol because it maximizes police effectiveness in crime reduction.[38] When conducting aggressive patrols, officers are expected to make frequent traffic stops and inquiries of suspicious persons on the streets of the community. The intent of an aggressive patrol is to potentially uncover criminal activity that might otherwise have been missed had officers not stopped the motorist or the pedestrian. For example, stopping a motorist who has not made a complete stop at a stop sign may seem to be an unnecessary and inconvenient action to some residents of the community, but if the stop results in a drunk driving arrest, the residents may feel otherwise. A stop by a patrol officer who conducts a **field interrogation**, which is a temporary detention in order to question a suspicious person, may lead to the arrest of a person who is wanted by the police. Gaines called field interrogation an indispensable part of police efforts to control street crime and disorder.[39]

Aggressive patrol
Patrolling the community by making frequent and numerous traffic stops and field interrogations of suspicious persons.

Field interrogation
A temporary detention of an individual in order to question the individual about a suspicious circumstance.

One concern about the use of aggressive patrols is that police will often stop and question citizens who have not engaged in any criminal activity. These inconvenient stops may anger law-abiding citizens. On the other hand, aggressive patrols that lead to arrests for offenses that might not have been discovered had the police not acted aggressively are often applauded by law-abiding citizens in the community.

Saturation Patrol   It is sometimes necessary for the police department to increase patrol activity in a particular area of the community. Crime analysis information may indicate an unusual increase in a certain type of crime in that area. It might also be evident that on Friday and Saturday nights, the increased population of patrons in the bar and club areas of the community requires increased police presence. In these instances, the police department may employ

Aggressive patrol can lead to arrests of lawbreakers, such as drunk drivers, who otherwise might not have been caught.

saturation patrols, in which they utilize a variety of patrol methods such as routine preventive patrol, directed patrol, and foot patrols to "saturate" the area. Fritsch, Caeti, and Taylor (1999) found that saturation patrols work provided they are directed toward a particular offender, place, victim, or offense. In their study, these researchers found that aggressive curfew and truancy enforcement resulted in significantly reduced gang violence in Dallas, Texas.[40] Saturation patrols can have a crime reduction effect similar to that of aggressive patrols because police visibility may inhibit possible offenders, while the additional police presence may lead to quick apprehension of those persons choosing to commit crime.

Career Connections: Uniformed Police Officer

Uniformed police officers from municipal, county, or state law enforcement agencies perform a variety of tasks for the community. In general, the duties of a police officer include enforcing the law, assisting the public, investigating crime, and preventing crime. They also maintain order by directing traffic, issuing traffic citations, making arrests, responding to maintenance of public order incidents, and preparing police reports. Each day can be a new challenge and a new adventure. One day, the police officer may conduct traffic stops at a busy intersection, counsel a distressed mother who is dealing with her adolescent son, and conduct an investigation at a residence that has been burglarized. The next day, this same officer may have completely different duties to perform.

In order to become a police officer, a candidate should be a U.S. citizen, be at least 21 years of age, have at least a high school diploma, and be able to pass a criminal history and background check, physical abilities test, and psychological examination. The specific requirements for employment vary from state to state and within each police department. Candidates must also graduate from a state-approved police academy where they are taught the basic requirements for performing the duties of the police officer position.

The ideal police officer candidate should possess strong interpersonal skills, critical thinking and analytical skills, and problem-solving ability. Because police work can be dangerous and very stressful, a successful police officer should also possess excellent physical conditioning and emotional stability. A career as a police officer can be very rewarding. It takes an individual with a strong commitment and a special mix of knowledge, skills, and abilities to choose to become a police officer. The challenges of police work are extraordinary, but the satisfaction that one receives from serving the public can more than compensate.

Traffic   Vehicular traffic direction is a second function performed by police officers. The police have been given the responsibility for the enforcement of traffic laws, the direction and control of traffic, the investigation of traffic accidents, and the assistance of motorists on the roadways.

Traffic enforcement involves the issuance of citations or warnings for moving and non-moving traffic violations, driver and vehicle licensing violations, and vehicle equipment violations.

The enforcement of traffic laws is usually the responsibility of the patrol officer. When the patrol officer is on routine preventive patrol and not responding

Traffic direction is a function of the patrol officer.

to a call for service, observing motorists obeying traffic laws should be of high priority. Many police departments also create organized traffic units with the specific responsibility of traffic law enforcement.

Police officers are responsible for the direction and control of the flow of traffic at busy intersections, at scenes of emergencies such as traffic accidents, or during special community events when an increased number of vehicles can be expected. Parking enforcement is also a responsibility of many police departments that do not have a designated civilian parking enforcement unit.

The responsibility for the investigation of traffic accidents also belongs with the police officer. The police officer's role in accident investigation and reconstruction can affect both criminal and civil liability. A traffic accident may be due to negligence on the part of a motor vehicle operator, which can result in violations of traffic laws or more serious criminal charges such as drunk driving or even vehicular homicide. A police investigation of a traffic accident can also be used by automobile insurance companies to determine the operator who may have been at fault for the accident and affect the civil settlement for any losses as a result of the accident.

Police officers are sometimes called upon to assist motorists when they are on traffic patrol. This assistance may include providing directions to lost motorists, assisting stranded motorists whose vehicles have broken down on the roadway, or changing a flat tire for a motorist.

Investigations   A third function of the police is to investigate criminal activity. The term *criminal investigation* usually conjures up a vision of a plainclothes detective. In reality, all police officers conduct investigations. Uniformed

Criminal investigation

A lawful investigation to reconstruct the circumstances of an illegal act, determine or apprehend the guilty party, and assist with the state's prosecution.

Preliminary investigation

Evidence-gathering activities performed at the scene of a crime immediately after the crime was reported to or discovered by the police.

Follow-up investigation

Continuation of the preliminary investigation in an attempt to reconstruct the circumstances of a crime.

police officers who are called to domestic disputes investigate to determine if an arrest is warranted. At scenes of traffic accidents, these same officers investigate to determine if any traffic citations should be issued or other more serious charges filed.

Criminal Investigation Defined   Criminal investigation is defined as a lawful investigation to reconstruct the circumstances of an illegal act, determine or apprehend the guilty party, and assist the state's prosecution.

Generally, a criminal investigation process is divided into two separate parts. The **preliminary investigation** consists of evidence-gathering activities that are performed at the scene of a crime immediately after the crime was reported to or discovered by the police. The patrol officer is usually the first responder to a crime scene. This officer is responsible for assessing the situation; determining if a crime has, in fact, been committed; securing the scene; interviewing complainants, witnesses, and victims; making an arrest, if appropriate; arranging for crime scene assistance; and documenting the incident in a report.

If the police department in which the responding officer works does not have a detective unit, the officer will also be responsible for the second part of the criminal investigation. This is referred to as the **follow-up investigation**. The follow-up investigation is the continuation of the preliminary investigation in an attempt to reconstruct the circumstances of the crime. The results of the preliminary investigation are reviewed; crime scene evidence is analyzed; complainants, witnesses, or victims are re-interviewed; suspects are apprehended; and the prosecutor is assisted with the court case. In a police department that has a detective unit, the follow-up investigation is assigned to one of its detectives.

As part of the criminal investigation process, a police officer may take and analyze fingerprints from suspects.

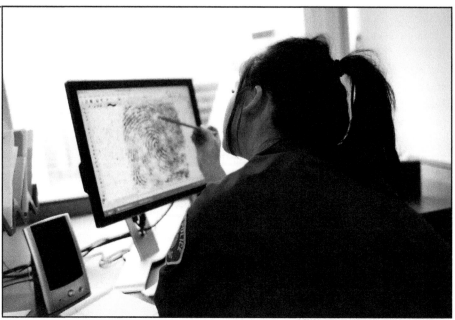

Major Case Investigations

Undercover Investigations   One of the most common forms of criminal investigation conducted by police departments is the undercover or covert investigation. Undercover operations involve the police while a criminal activity is in progress or prior to the crime actually being committed. These operations typically involve crimes such as drug trafficking, gambling, prostitution, and the buying and selling of stolen property.

Police investigators may operate undercover for short periods of time referred to as **light cover**. A light cover investigation might involve using a male undercover officer to act as a "john" in an attempt to solicit prostitutes in the red light district of the community. In contrast, a **deep cover** operation may involve undercover investigators who infiltrate a criminal organization, gain their confidence, and spend a lengthy period of time gathering intelligence while preparing for major arrests within the organization.

Undercover operations can be extremely dangerous for police officers. Undercover investigators are often without any communication with fellow police officers, and if their true identity is discovered, it may lead to safety concerns for the officer. Miller (1987) found undercover police work to be extremely emotionally draining for officers and the risks to be greater as the undercover officer penetrates more deeply into an illicit activity. Miller also indicated a concern that undercover officers could be tempted to engage in entrapment, in which an otherwise innocent citizen is coaxed by police to commit a crime they had no intention of committing.[41]

Terrorism Investigations   Following the September 11, 2001 attacks on the World Trade Center and the Pentagon, the prevention of terrorism has become an important focus of law enforcement in America. The primary responsibility for the war on terrorism has been given to federal law enforcement agencies. The creation of the Department of Homeland Security brought together several federal enforcement agencies to collaborate and share information and intelligence necessary to keep America safe.

The role of most state and local police departments is to assist in this effort by being better trained and equipped to respond to suspicious activity that might uncover a possible terrorist plot. Lyons (2002) wrote that the war on terrorism would place powerful pressure on local police to expand collaborative efforts with state and federal law enforcement agencies. Lyons stated that these efforts require increased information sharing, use of crime analysis, and the development of paramilitary task forces.[42] In addition, community-police partnerships should be encouraged in order to build trust within the community and gain their cooperation. O'Connell (2008) stated that the military and intelligence communities would not be able to succeed in our defense without active cooperation from local police departments that are well informed and well prepared, which requires training and financial support.[43]

Tools of the Investigator   There have been a number of advances over recent decades that have assisted criminal investigators in bringing criminals to justice. The following are a few of these newer tools of the investigator.

Light cover
Undercover police operations for a short period of time.

Deep cover
Undercover police operations for a lengthy period of time.

FIGURE5.2 Advances in Police Technology in the 20th Century

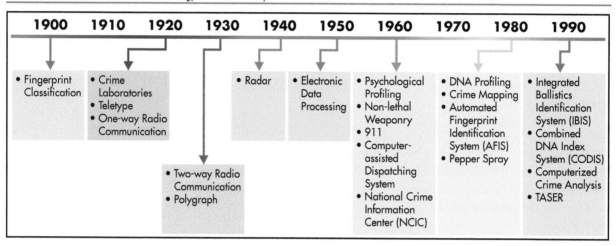

DNA Profiling The use of DNA profiling has revolutionized crime fighting and has led to both the conviction and exoneration of criminal defendants. The genetic profile that can be derived from blood, semen, hair, or other bodily substances collected at a crime scene can be matched with DNA samples taken from suspects, giving a high probability of guilt or innocence. DNA profiles can be used at murder scenes where a suspect's blood or tissue may have been left, or at rape scenes where a suspect's semen has been found.

The Combined DNA Index System (CODIS) is a DNA database maintained by the Federal Bureau of Investigation (FBI) that has a collection of samples from biological evidence found at crime scenes and samples from individuals who have been convicted of crimes in states throughout the country. DNA samples have typically been collected from convicted murderers and rapists, but more recently samples have also been taken from convicted burglars. In time, it is believed that DNA samples may be collected from all persons convicted of crimes. Some proponents of the use of the CODIS database would like samples to be taken from all individuals who have been charged with crimes. Just as "mug shots" and fingerprints are taken of arrestees during the booking process, proponents believe that DNA samples should also be collected. Berson (2009) reported that about 20 states and the federal government have already passed legislation requiring DNA collection upon arrest.[44]

Critical Thinking Should DNA samples be collected from all arrestees, regardless of the criminal charges, for submission to the CODIS database during the booking process just as fingerprints and photographs are taken today?

Crime Analysis and Mapping   Crime analysis involves a systematic collection and analysis of crime data used to support a police department's efforts in crime and disorder reduction and crime prevention. The study of police activities can provide data to analyze current crime trends, patterns, and series.

A related technological advancement to crime analysis is **crime mapping**. Crime mapping involves using geographic information systems to conduct spatial analysis and investigation of crime. Prior to the use of computers, police investigators identified a crime pattern by putting push pins on a map to indicate where crime was occurring. Crime mapping acts as a computerized "push pin" method of tracking crime. Geographic information system (GIS) software tools allow crime analysts to map crime in various ways, such as a simple point map or a three-dimensional visualization.

The more sophisticated computerized crime analysis and mapping systems can identify crime patterns much more rapidly. Many police departments have computerized report writing systems that give the crime analyst instantaneous access to the reports. If a crime pattern is occurring, it becomes apparent much sooner, allowing investigators to compare the evidence that they have gathered in each individual case to look for similarities that may tie the crimes to one offender or group of offenders.

Investigative and patrol units can both benefit from the use of crime analysis and mapping. For example, if it has been determined that a series of convenience store robberies are occurring and it is apparent that they are being committed by the same offender, both units can be positioned at a certain time of day or day of the week as well as a location where the offender is most likely to strike next.

Crime analysis also has other applications. It is being used as a tool to evaluate police department efficiency and effectiveness, crime clearance rates, and tracking of registered sexual offenders.

Crime analysis
A systematic collection and analysis of crime data used to support police efforts in crime and disorder reduction and crime prevention.

Crime mapping
A process of using geographic information systems to conduct spatial analysis and investigation of crime.

Electronic Surveillance   Newer advances in electronic surveillance have greatly enhanced the abilities of police investigators to gather intelligence related to criminal activity. Law enforcement agencies are increasingly using surveillance technologies such as thermal imaging technology, closed circuit television, miniature voice transmitters and video cameras, voice and retinal scanning devices, and more. Still, the wiretap that is used to listen to conversations between persons suspected of crime is the most common electronic surveillance technique for the investigator.

With all of the sophisticated surveillance devices that are available, it is important that procedural safeguards are in place to ensure that citizens' rights against unreasonable searches and seizures are not violated and that a reasonable expectation of privacy is ensured. In *Kyllo v. United States* (2001), the United States Supreme Court addressed the issue of the use of thermal imaging devices by law enforcement. In this case, a federal agent used a thermal imaging device to scan the home of Danny Lee Kyllo, whom they suspected of harvest-

The use of thermal imaging can help build evidence in a case.

ing marijuana, to determine whether heat emanating from the residence indicated the use of heat intensity lamps. When several relatively high levels of heat were found in areas of the home, agents secured a search warrant and found over 100 marijuana plants. Kyllo was arrested as a result of the use of the thermal imaging device as well as other evidence, and was subsequently convicted. His conviction was appealed based on the evidence gathered by use of the device. The Supreme Court sided with Kyllo, ruling that the warrantless use of thermal imaging technology aimed at a private home to detect the amount of heat within the home constituted an unlawful search and a violation of a citizen's expectation of privacy.[45]

Psychological Profiling   Psychological profiling has become a tool used by criminal investigators when they suspect that a series of similar crimes are occurring and the pattern seems to indicate the same offender is committing the crimes. Profiling uses major personality and behavioral characteristics of an individual determined by analyzing the series of crimes that have been committed.[46] Psychological profiling is most often used in unsolved cases involving serial murderers or serial rapists, and aids in the investigation by providing investigators with a profile of the characteristics of the probable offender that may be matched to a suspect in the case.

Automated Fingerprint Identification System   The Automated Fingerprint Identification System (AFIS) is a computerized database system that stores thousands of sets of fingerprints and is used to match and identify latent prints found at crime scenes. This automated system has replaced the older method that required fingerprint examiners to sort through fingerprint cards by hand, which could take several months to review. The FBI has the largest AFIS database, with over 60 million prints on file. Many states have their own AFIS-like systems as well.

Integrated Ballistics Identification System   The Integrated Ballistics Identification System (IBIS) is a computerized method to digitally compare images of ballistic evidence stored in a large database. When bullets are fired, unique marks can remain on the projectile and on the shell casing. Forensic firearms examiners can then link the projectile and the shell casing with a particular firearm and crime. The IBIS technology allows police investigators to match over 30,000 pieces of firearms evidence currently stored in the database.

Special Police Functions   All police departments, regardless of size, employ patrol, traffic, and investigations functions. In a small department where it is necessary for all police officers to patrol the community, officers will be required to perform each function.

Other special police functions may include a canine unit, marine unit, aircraft unit, mounted unit, or SWAT team. Canine units are used for search and rescue efforts, drug enforcement, and building searches. Police officers may be assigned a canine that is trained to sniff out drugs, follow the trail of a missing or wanted person, or go into buildings or other structures in search of suspects. Marine units are employed by police departments that border lakes, rivers, and other waterways. Marine unit officers will enforce vessel safety regulations and investigate cases of drunk operation of vessels. Police departments deploy aircraft units for traffic enforcement and searches for missing and wanted persons. Aircraft units are very expensive to maintain, but can prove invaluable as air support for police officers on the ground. Mounted units can be used for crowd control at community events and patrols in areas that may be more difficult for

Mounted patrol units are often used for crowd control at community events.

© 2012 BY L. KRAGT BAKKER. USED UNDER LICENSE OF SHUTTERSTOCK, INC.

the patrol vehicle to navigate. Mounted patrols are also useful for conducting search and rescue missions in undeveloped areas and natural terrain.

The SWAT team is specially trained to perform in high-risk situations such as barricaded suspect incidents, hostage rescues, and counterterrorism operations. As a result of the Posse Comitatus Act of 1878, the four branches of the military—with the exception of the United States Coast Guard and National Guard units—are not permitted to participate in domestic law enforcement. The military services have served as an auxiliary to law enforcement in drug interdiction and illegal immigration activities and, more recently, to combat domestic terrorism, but the responsibility for dealing with police issues that require a paramilitary presence has been left to SWAT teams.

Changing Philosophy of Policing

During most of the 20th century, in a period known as the Reform Era, policing in America adopted a professional model that closely resembled the philosophy popular in business and the military. In a historical study of the evolution of policing, Kelling and Moore (1988) viewed it through the framework of a corporate strategy. The authors wrote that the organizational form adopted by police reformers reflected the scientific theory of administration developed by Frederick W. Taylor.[47] This professional model of policing encouraged efficiency, task specialization, chain of command, and written orders and directives. Police officers were expected to respond to calls for service in a timely manner, handle their calls for service as quickly as possible, and return to patrolling the community. Any interaction between the police and the public beyond addressing the reason for the call to police was discouraged because it was assumed that any relationship that might develop could lead to favoritism and corruption.

The turmoil in the 1960s as a result of the civil rights movement and opposition to the Vietnam War led to increased disorder in America. The public viewed nightly news reports depicting the police attempting to quell protests and riots by use of shields and batons. As the crime rate rose steadily over the next two decades, the relationship between the police and the public continued to decline. The public lost trust in the police to solve the crime problem and were angered by what they perceived as an increased use of physical force. Ponsaers (2002) stated the public no longer felt confident that the police could solve their problems. This led many, particularly minority groups, to feel alienated from the police.[48]

Police departments began to implement police-community relations programs in an attempt to heal the strained relationship. Unfortunately, these programs were viewed as little more than "window dressing" and failed to satisfy the community. Kreps and Weller (1973) wrote that the most important factor that led to the expansion of existing community relations programs and the rapid adoption of new programs was the series of urban civil disturbances in the late 1960s. The authors cited a study conducted at Michigan State University in 1967 that found community relations objectives were both ambitious and ambiguous and program goals were too abstract to put into concrete practice. The study also found the public to be suspicious of the conveniently timed adoption of those programs and questioned police motives and sincerity.[49] It began to become apparent that the professional model of policing might have outlived its usefulness. A newer philosophy of policing the community that would foster a partnership between the police and the public was needed to create a safe and secure environment in order to achieve a higher quality of life.[50] The time was right for the implementation of community policing.

Community Policing

Community policing encourages a partnership between the public and the police for the purpose of working together to identify, prioritize, and solve problems within the community.[51] It is the intent of community policing to deal with the problems of crime and disorder, community decay, and the fear of crime in order to improve the quality of life for community residents.

The foundation for the implementation of the community policing philosophy was influenced by the **broken windows theory** introduced by James Q. Wilson and George Kelling (1982). Wilson and Kelling argued that when a window is broken in a building and it is not quickly repaired, more windows will likely be broken. The authors theorized that if the community is apathetic toward the destruction occurring within their neighborhoods, they are sending a message to criminals that they can assume control over the neighborhood. In time, as one broken window leads to another, the neighborhood will succumb to physical decay and disorder. Wilson and Kelling believed that police should consider dealing with both minor and major crimes instead of just the more serious crime problem. Concentrated efforts on minor crimes such as vandalism, public drunkenness, and panhandling will help the public begin to feel safer in

Broken windows theory
A theory involving crime and disorder that states that if a community is allowed to physically deteriorate, an impression will be given that no one cares, causing crime to occur.

The broken windows theory holds that when a community is apathetic toward destruction in their neighborhoods, they are sending a message to criminals that they can assume control over the neighborhood.

their neighborhoods. With a reduced fear of crime, citizens begin to develop a feeling of pride and eventually retake ownership of their neighborhoods.[52]

Gaines and Kappeler (2009) suggested that one of the two major components of community policing was to develop a relationship with the residents of the community.[53] The police understood that for community policing to truly succeed, cooperation with community residents was imperative. In order to achieve this success, community policing officers were assigned to each neighborhood to forge these partnerships and then work together with residents to address their concerns.

One important result of a partnership between the police and the public is the trust that can develop. The police cannot succeed without the assistance of the public, especially when it comes to solving crime. The public can be the eyes and ears of the police in the community. Police need the public to come forward when they are aware of crimes occurring and who may be committing them. Unfortunately, some community residents pressure other residents not to inform or "snitch" on lawbreakers. This "stop snitching" movement has even found its way into pop culture. Masten (2009) wrote that as a result of a cultural campaign spawned rap music and clothing, many teens and young adults were refusing to speak to the police even when they had witnessed violent crimes. Masten saw this "stop snitching" phenomenon as part of a deeply rooted distrust toward the police, posing a potential hindrance to America's criminal justice system. The author suggested that police must repair the decades of mistrust built up between the public and the police in order to make the "stop snitching" code less attractive to follow.[54]

The second major component of community policing, as defined by Gaines and Kappeler (2009), is problem solving.[55] Traditionally, when police have responded to calls for service, they have dealt with the incident, but not necessarily with the underlying problem that led to the call. Herman Goldstein (1979) first proposed **problem-oriented policing** to address the concerns of the public. A problem-oriented or problem-solving approach emphasizes identifying a problem, exploring alternatives to deal with the problem, weighing the merits of each alternative, and finally, implementing the best alternative to solve the problem.[56]

A problem-solving approach to dealing with community concerns requires both creativity and commitment on the part of the police department. The police and the public must be in agreement regarding the problems in the neighborhood that should be addressed. Cooperation may also be required from other stakeholders in the community, such as business leaders, elected officials, and other public and private agencies that serve the community.

Although some police administrators may claim otherwise, the practice of community policing seems to be waning. Federal funding for community policing efforts, which was once in abundance, has all but dried up. In 2010, the Office of Community Oriented Policing Services (COPS) allocated approximately $600 million to assist law enforcement agencies in their community policing initiatives. That amount of funding is a far cry from the $11 billion that had been allocated just 15 years earlier. The apparent demise of community policing

Problem-oriented policing
An approach to policing in which the underlying causes of crime are identified and addressed.

may be due more to the funding drying up than to the failure of the philosophy. A study by Zhao, Scheider, and Thurman (2002) found that funding community policing had a positive effect. The authors examined COPS Office grants awarded between 1994 and 1998 and their effects on crime rates in 6,100 cities in the United States, and their results indicated that funding to medium and large cities had been effective at reducing violent and property crime. Additionally, innovative programs that targeted special crime problems or locations were found to be a most effective contributor to crime reduction.[57]

Still, because federal funding has decreased, many police departments that once displayed an agency-wide commitment to community policing have now resorted to smaller units that operate on an as-needed basis, while some departments have totally abandoned the philosophy, returning to the more traditional incident-based policing.

Intelligence-Led Policing
The latest movement in policing is the use of crime data analysis to influence decision making. **Intelligence-led policing** uses a business model in which data analysis and criminal intelligence are used to facilitate crime reduction, crime prevention, and enforcement strategies that target the most serious offenders.[58]

The move toward an intelligence-led policing model may be a natural progression in policing from the community policing and problem-oriented models. Both community policing and problem-oriented policing require data collection and crime analysis in order to solve crime problems, although not nearly to the extent that intelligence-led policing utilizes data.

One of the first examples of the use of a data-driven method for determining crime problems took place in the 1990s in New York City.[59] The New York City Police Department became known for the implementation of the COMPSTAT program. **COMPSTAT** is a managerial system that uses criminal intelligence that identifies crime problems and then determines a crime reduction strategy. The system provided timely and accurate intelligence that indicated "hot spots" of crime that police officers were expected to eliminate. Police administrators were then held accountable for the implementation of the reduction strategy and a subsequent reduction in crime. Crime was reduced dramatically in the city, although arguments persist over whether the COMPSTAT program was the primary reason for the reduction. Zimring (2011) credited the COMPSTAT program in New York City with being instrumental in the compilation of data on serious crime that led to police emphasis on "hot spots," drug interdiction, and an aggressive program of street stops and misdemeanor arrests. Zimring also praised the city of New York for choosing not to implement a "broken windows" strategy, which he believed would have concentrated precious resources in marginal neighborhoods rather than neighborhoods with the highest crime rates.[60]

The intelligence-led policing model and its use of crime analysis can provide the foundation for crime prevention and reduction and decisions for directing police resources.

Intelligence-led policing
A business model in which data analysis and criminal intelligence are used to facilitate crime reduction, crime prevention, and enforcement strategies that target the most serious offenders.

COMPSTAT
A managerial system that uses criminal intelligence to identify crime problems and determine a crime reduction strategy.

Critical Thinking Should police departments adopt a zero tolerance policy for all crimes, regardless of how minor, or should police concentrate their efforts on the most serious offenses and offenders?

Challenges for Police Officers

The nature of police work can place great demands on the police officer. Police officers are often called upon to make split-second decisions that sometimes involve use of physical force or even deadly force. The ever present dangers that police officers face can come from many different sources. Every day, police officers risk being killed in the line of duty while serving warrants, conducting traffic stops, responding to domestic violence calls, or interviewing suspicious persons.

Besides the dangers that the job brings, police officers are required to witness the worst that society can offer. The police must investigate the most gruesome suicide or homicide scenes, respond to abuse cases where children may have been physically or sexually assaulted, and reconstruct traffic accidents in which several members of a family may have been killed.

The challenges that police officers face play a part in how they come to view themselves, the public, and their jobs. This can lead to a unique subculture within the police profession, a stress level that is often greater than what is found in other professions, and a temptation toward corruption if they stray from expected ethical and professional boundaries.

The Police Subculture

Every profession has its own set of values and behavioral patterns that are unique to members of the profession. The police subculture is a product of the responsibilities of the job along with the effects that can result from having carried out these responsibilities. Common attitudes in the police subculture include authoritarianism, cynicism, and solidarity.

Authoritarianism

Police officers possess a unique power that is not afforded to most professions. The police have the right to arrest individuals, search persons or their belongings, and seize evidence from people. In order to perform these authoritarian duties, police officers are guided by both legal guidelines and their departmental policies. For example, under case law, a police officer who stops a suspicious person may not conduct a warrantless search of the suspect without probable cause to do so.

Additionally, police have the right to use physical force, including deadly force. The police are permitted to utilize physical force when necessary to effect an arrest, although a police officer may be held criminally or civilly liable if the amount of force used is considered to be excessive. Probably the most awesome power that the police officer has is to use deadly force. Of course, this power to use deadly force also comes with responsibility. Deadly force must be the last resort for the police officer.

In the past, police officers only had the baton and the handgun to subdue suspects. In more recent years, new weapons technology has led to the development of nonlethal weapons. Weapons such as rubber bullets and beanbag projectiles have allowed officers to neutralize potentially deadly situations without having to resort to deadly force. The most common type of nonlethal weapon used today by police officers is the TASER technology that sends an incapacitating electric shock to the individual that it strikes.

An important concern regarding police authoritarianism is the abuse of this power. The police must ensure that the rights of citizens are not violated when they engage in arrests, searches, or seizures. They must not use **excessive force**, but only a level of force necessary to effect an arrest or to protect themselves or others from bodily harm. Bohrer and Chaney (2010) wrote that the public's perceptions of police officers involved in shootings are wide and diverse. They point out that while some members of the public believe that if the police shoot someone, the individual probably gave police no choice, many members of the public are quick to assume the police acted inappropriately.[61] Police officers who exceed the authority they have been granted can jeopardize the community's perception of their police department as well as the entire police profession.

Excessive force
An amount of physical force beyond that which is necessary to control a suspect.

Cynicism   Cynicism is a mistrust of human nature and motives. The nature of police work requires that officers view citizens with suspicion. The police interview individuals who will often lie to them. They approach individuals who may be dangerous. Police officers are trained on how to cautiously approach the public on the streets, during traffic stops, or when entering a residence. They are trained to uncover a suspect's lies in order to reach the truth. Through their experience, they can often sense that a suspicious person fits a particular type of individual who may be dangerous. This **symbolic assailant** is an individual whose dress and gestures indicate to the experienced police officer that this person is up to no good.

Neiderhoffer (1969) conducted a classic study of police cynicism in the New York City Police Department. The study found that cynicism among police officers developed as early as the police academy, when recruits were taught about the ignorance of the public and the superiority of the police. Cynicism

Symbolic assailant
An individual whose dress, behavior, and gestures indicate suspicion and possible danger to a police officer.

Police officers may have to use physical force to arrest uncooperative suspects or to protect themselves or others from bodily harm.

© 2012 BY JUSTASC. USED UNDER LICENSE OF SHUTTERSTOCK, INC.

initially increased sharply and then at a slower rate between years two and six of the police officer's career. After year six, cynicism decreased and leveled off over the remainder of a career.[62]

The unfortunate consequence of police cynicism is that it can cross over into an officer's personal relationships with family and friends. The suspicions that police officers have about people's behaviors and actions may lead them to believe that all people, including those closest to them, should be viewed with suspicion and not be trusted.

Solidarity   The third component of the police subculture is solidarity. Police officers develop a strong connection with other members of the profession. Officers must depend upon their partners for backup and protection. Along with their cynicism and mistrust of the public, this solidarity within the ranks causes an "us versus them" mentality. Police officers close their ranks and insulate themselves from others. Just as cynicism can lead to mistrust of family and friends, police solidarity can lead police officers to become isolated from their relationships outside of the profession.

One unfortunate result of police solidarity is known as the **blue code of silence**. This is a code of protection among police officers in which they do not report activities of fellow officers that could violate department policy or the law. Police solidarity may be so ingrained within the profession that police officers may be more likely to protect corruption within their ranks—jeopardizing their own careers—than to report corrupt fellow officers.

Blue code of silence
The unwritten code of protection among police officers.

Critical Thinking   How can the blue code of silence be eliminated so honest police officers are willing to report dishonest officers?

Discretion
The autonomy a police officer has to choose from a variety of courses of action in various situations.

Police Discretion   Discretion is defined as a police officer's autonomy to choose from a variety of courses of action in various situations. Alpert, MacDonald, and Dunham (2005) stated that an officer's discretion to choose a course of action such as stopping a citizen usually begins when the officer observes the person appearing suspicious or violating the law.[63] Probably the most common example of the use of police discretion involves traffic stops. Police officers use their discretionary power to determine if a motorist who has been stopped for a traffic violation should be given a warning or issued a citation.

The patrol officer may exercise the greatest discretionary power in the police department. Officers who are on patrol are usually out of the sight of their supervisors. Walker (1993) wrote that most police-citizen encounters occur without outside supervision, which gives the police officer a great deal of discretion.[64] They have the discretion to stop a vehicle operator for a traffic violation in the first place. They have the discretion to stop a suspicious person on the street to conduct a field interrogation. When dispatched to a loud music call, the patrol officer may have the discretion to charge the resident with the appropriate offense or simply order them to turn the music down.

In some instances, police discretion can be controlled and limited. The National Research Council (2003) found that the most important factors associated with police officers' decisions to use their legal authority included the influence of the police organization, legal factors related to the severity of the crime, and the strength of the evidence.[65] The police department may influence the level of discretion that officers have. For example, as discussed earlier in this chapter, the department may have developed a written policy that limits vehicle pursuits. Department-written policies and procedures are often used to control police officers' behavior. At times, special orders may also temporarily limit police discretion. The police chief may have learned that the number of traffic accidents at a particular intersection has increased, and may order all patrol officers to issue citations to any vehicle operator who is observed committing any traffic violation at the intersection, no matter how minor. Even peer pressure among officers within the department may affect police discretion: veteran officers may chastise the newest officer in the department who is giving too many traffic citations to community residents. Alpert, MacDonald, and Dunham (2005) found that officers employed in a police department that emphasized a service approach were less likely to arrest offenders for low-level crimes than officers from a department practicing a legalistic style of policing.[66]

Legislatures can also limit police discretion. State legislatures and local municipalities enact statutes or ordinances. A local community may pass an ordinance that makes it illegal to panhandle on the roadways. The police department may have previously turned a blind eye to the panhandlers, even though they were well aware that many of them were homeless and could be charged with a vagrancy statute violation, but now their discretion will be influenced by this new ordinance.

An example of legislation influencing police discretion occurred as a result of the Minneapolis Domestic Violence Experiment.[67] Historically, the police have used three methods to resolve domestic violence calls: mediate the dispute and leave the partners together, separate the partners by asking one of them to leave the residence for a "cooling off" period, or arrest one of the partners. In the experiment, police were told to either arrest, separate, or mediate incidents on the basis of a random selection. The results of the experiment indicated that those persons who were arrested in the incident were half as likely to reoffend against the victim. These results led many state legislatures across the country to enact mandatory arrest policies for domestic violence perpetrators when an injury to the victim was observed by the police. These new domestic violence laws greatly inhibited police officers' discretion in responding to domestic violence calls. An interesting side note to the results of this landmark experiment was that when similar studies were later conducted, the results did not confirm that arrest was the most effective way to handle domestic violence interventions.

Finally, our courts can also limit police discretion. Decisions made by courts can take away options that police officers may have to deal with criminals on the streets. For example, patrol officers have a limited number of options when they want to conduct warrantless searches of persons, property, and vehicles because the courts have restricted their actions in order to protect the constitutional rights of citizens.

Additional Factors Affecting Police Discretion There are a number of factors that can affect a police officer's use of discretion. The seriousness of the crime determines if the police will pursue a case more or less vigorously. Homicide cases are usually investigated with vigor, while a minor neighborhood dispute may not be. The strength of evidence in a case may also affect the extent to which police investigate a crime. Initially, the homicide case will receive strict attention, but once the trail of the killer goes cold, police may have no choice but to move on to other cases.

The nature of the individuals involved in a police encounter may factor into police discretion. The relationship between an offender and the victim may affect the decisions that the police officer makes. For example, in a reported theft case involving two ex-lovers who had lived together, in which the accused was removing some items from the residence that he believed were his property, police officers might choose not to make an arrest. Conversely, a victim who is intent on the offender being arrested may exert influence on police to make the arrest against their better judgment. Police may use the demeanor of an individual as a factor to determine the course of action. A polite and respectful traffic violator may be less likely to receive a citation than an angry and verbally abusive motorist. Sometimes, race, gender, or the income of an individual can play a role in a police officer's decision making. This behavior may be inappropriate, but it unfortunately does sometimes occur. A young male motorist might be more likely to be cited than a young female. An African-American male walking on the streets of a community at 3:00 in the morning may be more likely to be stopped and questioned than a white male, and an affluent resident who complains about juveniles running through his upscale neighborhood may receive more appropriate police action than a long-haired and tattooed trailer park resident making a similar complaint. The National Research Council (2003) found that individual variables such as age, race, social class, or demeanor of a suspect play a minor role in a police officer's decision making.[68] In contrast, Sun and Payne (2004) reported that race is the most important individual factor in police-citizen interactions.[69] Although the research may be mixed, it is important to consider the possible influence of individual variables on the police officer's use of discretion.

Police Job Stress Stress can be found to some extent within every vocation and in people's everyday lives. However, Dantzer (1987) stated that law enforcement ranks among the top five most stressful occupations in the world.[70] Police stress is somewhat unique as a result of the nature of the police officer's job. The danger that officers can face, along with the horrors of society that they often witness, can take a great toll on their emotional and physical well-being.

Sources of Police Stress

For the police officer, there are a number of different sources of stress. One is the physical danger that officers face as an inherent part of the job.[71] It is understandable that one major stressful event can affect a police officer. For example, a use of deadly force situation involving police officers can cause great stress. Shootings in which police officers may see a fellow officer killed or be wounded themselves are very stressful events that can leave lasting emotional scars. When a police officer must use deadly force against a suspect, the officer may find it difficult to deal with afterwards.

However, most police officers will not be involved in events like those just described during their careers. Most stress for the typical officer comes from the continued response to daily calls for service. Responding to calls where they see physical injuries as a result of domestic or child abuse or to calls of deadly motor vehicle crashes can leave lasting impressions on a police officer. Even the most routine calls can produce low-grade stressors that, over time, can cause stress for the police officer.

Police stress is sometimes caused by grisly or horrible crime scenes that officers must investigate.

The police organization is a second source of stress for police officers. Anderson, Litzenberger, and Plecas (2002) found that within the organizational structure, issues such as lack of group cohesiveness, lack of support from supervisors, and lack of opportunities for promotion make law enforcement an especially stressful job.[72] Police officers usually work in a quasi-military bureaucracy where they have little input into the decision making. They sometimes observe a lack of administrative support and petty department politics. Police officers often view their job as one with inadequate pay and benefits, work schedules that include shift work, weekends, and most holidays, and sometimes periods of monotony and boredom.

A third source of stress for police officers can result from their own personal behaviors. Police officers often develop poor eating habits while on duty as a result of the emergency nature of their job. It can be easy to stop by a fast-food drive-through for a quick lunch between calls for service. Shift work can also affect proper eating habits and lead to fatigue. If the police officer does not eat properly and exercise regularly, poor health can result.

Effects of Police Stress

The effects of police stress can be both psychological and physical.[73, 74] Stress has been linked to physical disorders such as high blood pressure, ulcers, and heart disease. More common for some police officers is the emotional toll of police stress. The police profession has a high rate of alcoholism, drug abuse, marital problems, and suicide. More police officers commit suicide each year than are killed in the line of duty.

Stress can also affect a police officer's productivity on the job. An officer who has withdrawn from his or her work can become complacent, have lower morale, and feel indifferent toward the job and fellow officers. Posttraumatic stress disorder (PTSD), which is most associated with military personnel, also affects some police officers who have witnessed combat-like situations such as shootings. PTSD can manifest itself in memory loss, loss of concentration, bouts of depression, impulsivity, or anxiety, and can cause recurring nightmares and flashbacks.

Management of Police Stress   Police organizations and each individual police officer within the profession can find ways to manage and reduce stress. Atkinson (2004) stated that stress can be managed by identifying specific strategies in the areas of nutrition, exercise, sleep, and relaxation.[75] Every police officer should be aware of the sources of stress and the effects stress can have. By maintaining a healthy diet and engaging in regular exercise, police officers can do their part to reduce their stress. Family and spiritual support has also been found to be helpful.

Each police department must address police stress by emphasizing stress awareness. Frequent stress reduction training courses should be offered. Support systems such as mental health programs and critical incident stress debriefing teams should also be implemented to assist officers in need of professional assistance.

Police Ethics   Ethics involves the moral choices that individuals must make regarding good and bad conduct. The social contract that the public has with its government to provide for its safety and security comes with the expectation that

FIGURE 5.3 Officers Killed in the Line of Duty, 2000–2010

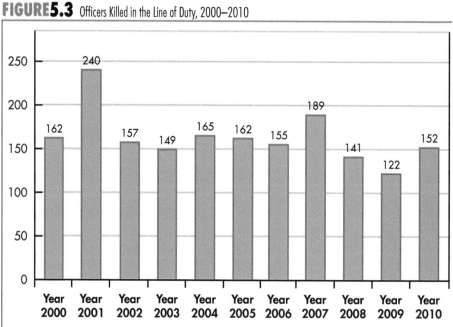

Source: National Law Enforcement Officers Memorial Fund www.nleomf.org

those who are asked to provide that protection maintain high standards of ethics, professionalism, and integrity. Generally, the public expects police officers to exhibit even higher standards of behavior than the general population. A lack of ethical behavior on the part of a police officer can lead to corruption. Whenever officers misuse the authority they have been given, they are engaging in some form of corruption.

Forms of Police Corruption   Police corruption may involve unethical acts that violate department policy or illegal acts that violate the law. Corruption within policing may be department-wide, where all members are engaged in corrupt acts or at least aware that it is occurring and turning a blind eye to it. On the other hand, it is more common that individual officers may be engaged in corrupt acts unbeknownst to others in the police department except the corrupt officers' closest confidants. The more common examples of police corruption include the following.

- **Bribery or Extortion**—Accepting offers of cash or gifts from citizens in the form of a bribe for not enforcing laws against them, or demanding remuneration in the form of cash or gifts as a form of extortion for not enforcing the law against citizens.
- **Theft**—Planning burglaries and thefts on or off duty, or taking items of value from scenes of crimes that officers are called to investigate.
- **Alcohol or Drug Abuse**—Consuming alcoholic beverages or taking illegal drugs while on duty or off duty in violation of department policy or the law.
- **Goldbricking**—Avoiding work when on duty by not responding to calls for service, engaging in private business, or sleeping on duty.
- **Gratuities**—Accepting or demanding free or discounted items such as coffee, meals, or entertainment tickets, which may or may not be in return for favorable treatment for the giver at a future time.
- **Sexual Misconduct**—Engaging in sexual acts while on duty, exchanging favors for sex, or sexually harassing coworkers.

Control of Police Corruption   There is nothing that shakes the public's confidence in police more than learning that the police have engaged in acts of corruption. Weitzer (2002) found that incidents of police misconduct have a pronounced effect on public opinion, particularly when they involve highly publicized events.[76] Walker (1992) stated that corruption can be controlled with effort from law enforcement, but this requires each police department to take a proactive approach to reducing and controlling it.[77]

Several researchers have suggested ways in which corruption can be controlled.[78,79,80] First, it is important that during the recruitment and selection process, police departments set high standards for police officer candidates and have methods in place to determine the ethical and professional values of the individuals they choose to hire.

Additionally, each police department should have written policies that define what constitutes corrupt acts and a disciplinary apparatus that spells out the

Exhibit: Law Enforcement Code of Ethics from International Chiefs of Police[81]

Ethics and Professionalism: Blue Code of Silence

On August 9, 1997, a 30-year-old Haitian immigrant by the name of Abner Louima was arrested by New York City Police Department officers following a disturbance outside a Brooklyn nightclub. While being held at the 70th Precinct stationhouse, Louima was brutalized in the precinct bathroom. He was held down by one officer while the other officer shoved a wooden toilet plunger handle into his rectum and then thrust it into his face. The police officer who assaulted Louima mistakenly believed that he had punched the officer in the head during a street brawl outside the club.

It was reported that several NYPD officers either participated in the assault or witnessed it. After hearing of the incident, then Mayor Rudy Giuliani and Police Commissioner Howard Safir insisted the case would prove that the "blue code of silence" did not exist. The case included allegations of perjury and ultimately resulted in convictions of four police officers—three of which were later overturned on appeal.

Does the "blue code of silence" still exist in policing, all these years after the Louima case? What would cause a police officer to engage in such violent behavior against a suspect? How could other officers look on and allow this to happen without stepping in to stop it? Why would these officers all choose to lie and cover up the incident?

actions that will be taken against officers violating established policies. Each police department should require periodic ethics training classes for all officers. A police officers' code of ethics should be prominently placed in the department as a constant reminder to all officers that they have a sworn oath to perform their duties both ethically and professionally.

Police departments should also have an internal affairs unit that investigates alleged unethical or illegal activities involving police officers. External investigations or reviews by citizen review boards, special investigators or prosecutors, and the courts should be used to ferret out police misconduct when necessary.

Finally, the responsibility for ending police corruption belongs with each individual police officer. One way that can be accomplished is for officers to resist the pressure to adhere to the blue code of silence. Instead, honest police officers should see it as their duty to rid the law enforcement profession of corrupt officers by reporting any unethical or illegal behaviors that they observe.

Chapter Summary

- The roles police officers assume are based on the issues and problems that are unique to each community. The police officer's role can be vague and ambiguous because the expectations of police administrators, local political leaders, the public, and police officers themselves can conflict. Role conflict results from what police may prefer to do versus what they are expected to do.

- The duties performed by police officers are multidimensional and dependent on community needs. Generally, these duties include law enforcement, order maintenance, crime prevention, and providing service. Enforcing the law is considered to be the primary responsibility of police. Police often act as peacekeepers and maintain order in the community, which may or may not involve dealing with criminal activity. The mere presence of police in the community serves as an important way to prevent crime from occurring in the first place.

- The most common functions performed by police departments include patrol, traffic, and investigations. Routine preventive patrol is the most common form of patrol, but police departments will also use special patrol methods such as directed patrols, foot patrols, aggressive patrols, and saturation patrols. The traffic function includes traffic enforcement, control and direction, accident investigation, and assistance to motorists. Types of police investigations include preliminary investigations, follow-up investigations, and undercover investigations. Advances in technology have provided criminal investigators with a variety of new tools to fight crime. Larger police departments may employ more specialized functions such as canine, marine, aircraft, mounted, and SWAT units.

- The community policing philosophy attempted to encourage a partnership between the public and the police for the purpose of working together to identify, prioritize, and solve community problems. As community policing began to fall out of favor, it was replaced by movement toward an intelligence-led policing philosophy, which emphasizes the use of data analysis and criminal intelligence to facilitate crime reduction, crime prevention, and enforcement strategies that target the most serious offenders.

- The nature of police work puts great demands on the police officer. While every profession has its own set of values and behavioral patterns among its members, the police subculture is quite unique with a composition that includes authoritarianism, cynicism, and solidarity.

- Police officers can suffer from job stress that can come from a variety of sources. Many police officers experience stress resulting from continued responses to daily calls for service. Police stress can also result from the police organization and from an officer's own personal behaviors. Police stress can lead to both psychological and physical problems. Police departments can assist officers in dealing with the problem of stress by offering programs that help to manage stress.

- Police ethics involves the moral choices that police officers make regarding good and bad conduct. Corruption within the police profession occurs when police officers misuse their authority for personal gain. Police corruption can be controlled by use of high selection standards, written policies regarding corruption, internal and external investigation of alleged corruption, ethics training classes, and a code of ethics, as well as dismantling the blue code of silence.

Critical Thinking?

1. Should electronic devices known as "red light cameras" be used to catch traffic violators running red lights at intersections?
2. Should police officers be permitted to accept gratuities such as a free cup of coffee or a half-price meal when on duty?
3. Among the various methods of patrol, which do you believe works the best to prevent crime and apprehend criminals?
4. What can be done to keep police officers safe on the streets and reduce the number of officers killed in the line of duty?
5. How might police departments eliminate corruption within the ranks of the police?
6. Can you imagine a situation in which it would be acceptable to repeal the Posse Comitatus Act?
7. Explain why you would be in favor of or against giving up some of your individual rights under the Constitution to allow law enforcement to conduct searches and seizures of your personal property without probable cause.
8. Based on the results of the Kansas City Preventive Patrol Experiment, do you believe that police should still conduct routine random patrols throughout the community?
9. Is it a good idea for police officers to be allowed to use discretion in the performance of their duties? Why or why not?
10. When the police conduct an undercover operation in which female police officers are placed in an area known to be frequented by prostitutes and their customers, are they actually encouraging criminal behavior?

Media

Law Enforcement News: www.officer.com

This website provides information on current events in policing and police officer news around the United States.

Bureau of Justice Statistics: http://bjs.ojp.usdoj.gov/

The Bureau of Justice Statistics provides comprehensive data on reported criminal activity throughout the country, including frequency of crime and criminal characteristics.

Franklin Zimring Interview: http://www.youtube.com/watch?v=EXZgSnKfN5U

In this interview, criminologist Franklin Zimring discusses how New York City dramatically reduced its crime rate.

Endnotes

1. Seneviratne, M. (2002). "Ombudsmen and Police Complaints." *The Journal of Social Welfare & Family Law, 24*(2), 195–215.
2. Hunter, A. (1985). "Private, Parochial, and Public Social Orders: The Problem of Crime and Incivility in Urban Communities." In G. Suttles & M. Zald (Eds.), *The Challenge of Social Control*. Norwood, NJ: Ablex.
3. Klockars, C. B. (1985). *The Idea of Police*. Beverly Hills, CA: Sage.
4. Dunham, R. G., & Alpert, G. P. (2010). *Critical Issues in Policing*. Prospect Heights, IL: Waveland Press.
5. Reiman, J. (1985). "The Social Contract and the Police Use of Deadly Force." In F. A. Ellison & M. Feldberg (Eds.), *Moral Issues in Police Work*. Savage, MD: Rowman & Littlefield.

6. *Mapp v. Ohio*, 367 U.S. 643, 655 (1961).

7. Stuntz, W. J. (1997). "The Virtues and Vices of the Exclusionary Rule." *Harvard Journal of Law and Public Policy, 20*(2), 443–455.

8. Keenan, J. F. (1998). "The Proper Balance: Exclusion of Evidence or Expulsion of Police Officers." *St. John's Law Review, 72*(3/4), 1376–1384.

9. *Terry v. Ohio*, 392 U.S. 1 (1968).

10. *Tennessee v. Garner*, 471 U.S. 1 (1985).

11. Walker, S., & Fridell, L. (1992). "Forces of Change in Police Policy: The Impact of *Tennessee v. Garner*." *American Journal of Police, 11*(3), 97–112.

12. Fyfe, J. J. (1986). "The Split-Second Syndrome and Other Determinants of Police Violence." In A. Campbell & J. Gibbs (Eds.), *Violent Transactions*. New York, NY: Blackwell.

13. Alpert, G. P. (1993). "The Management of Police Pursuit Driving." In W. G. Bailey (Ed.), *The Encyclopedia of Police Science*. New York, NY: Garland.

14. Hicks, W. L. (2006). "Police Vehicular Pursuits: A Descriptive Analysis of the State Agencies' Written Policy." *Policing, 29*(1), 106–124.

15. Payne, D. M. (1997). "Michigan Emergency Response Study—Phase III. Implications of the Failure to Report Pursuits and Inaccurate Accident Reporting: A Research Note." *Policing, 20*(2), 256–269.

16. Weitzer, R., & Tuch, S. A. (2005). "Racially Biased Policing: Determinants of Citizen Perceptions." *Social Forces, 83*(3), 1009–1030.

17. Bureau of Justice Statistics. (2001). *Contacts Between Police and the Public: Findings From the 1999 National Survey*. Washington, DC: U.S. Department of Justice.

18. Harris, D. (1997). "Driving While Black and Other Traffic Offenses: The Supreme Court and Pretextual Traffic Stops." *Journal of Criminal Law and Criminology, 87*, 544–582.

19. Bureau of Justice Statistics, 2001.

20. Brown, R. A. (2005). "Black, White and Unequal: Examining Situational Determinants of Arrest Decisions from Police-Suspect Encounters." *Criminal Justice Studies, 18*(1), 151–168.

21. Visher, C. A., & Weisburd, D. (1998). "Identifying What Works: Recent Trends in Crime Prevention Strategies." *Crime, Law & Social Change, 28*, 223–242.

22. Kennedy, L. W. (2002). "Issues in Managing Citizens' Calls to the Police." *Criminology & Public Policy, 2*(1), 125–128.

23. Silver, E. E., & Miller, L. L. (2004). "Sources of Informal Social Control in Chicago Neighborhoods." *Criminology, 42*(3), 551–583.

24. Reisig, M. D., & Parks, R. B. (2004). "Can Community Policing Help the Truly Disadvantaged?" *Crime & Delinquency, 50*(2), 139–167.

25. Silver & Miller, 2004.

26. Wilson, J. (1968). *Varieties of Police Behavior*. Cambridge, MA: Harvard University Press.

27. Broderick, J. J. (1987). *Police in a Time of Change*. Prospect Heights, IL: Waveland Press.

28. Muir, W. K. (1977). *Police: Street Corner Politicians*. Chicago, IL: University of Chicago Press.

29. Adams, T. F. (2006). *Police Field Operations*. Upper Saddle River, NJ: Prentice Hall.

30. Kelling, G. L. (1974). *The Kansas City Preventive Patrol Experiment: A Summary Report*. Washington, DC: Police Foundation.

31. Weisburd, D., Maher, L., & Sherman, L. (1992). "Contrasting Crime General and Crime Specific Theory: The Case of Hot-Spots of Crime." *Advances in Criminological Theory, 4*, 45–70.

32. Sherman, L., & Weisburd, D. (1995). "General Deterrent Effects of Police Patrol in Crime 'Hot-Spots': A Randomized Controlled Trial." *Justice Quarterly, 12*, 626–648.

33. Weisburd, D., & Green, L. (1995). "Policing Drug Hot-Spots: The Jersey City Drug Market Analysis Experiment." *Justice Quarterly, 12*, 711–735.

34. Gaines, L. K. (1996). "Specialized Patrol." In G. W. Cordner, L. K. Gaines, & V. E. Kappeler (Eds.), *Police Operations: Analysis and Evaluation*. Cincinnati, OH: Anderson.

35. Adams, 2006.

36. Pate, A. M., & Skogan, W. G. (1985). *Reducing the Signs of Crime: The Newark Experiment*. Washington, DC: Police Foundation.

37. Trojanowicz, R. (1982). *An Evaluation of the Neighborhood Foot Patrol Study in Flint, Michigan*. East Lansing, MI: Michigan State University.

38. Gaines, 1996.

39. Ibid.

40. Fritsch, E. J., Caeti, T. J., & Taylor, R. W. (1999). "Gang Suppression Through Saturation Patrol, Aggressive Curfew, and Truancy Enforcement: A Quasi-Experimental Test of the Dallas Anti-gang Initiative." *Crime & Delinquency, 45*(1), 122–139.

41. Miller, G. I. (1987). "Observations on Police Undercover Work." *Criminology, 25*(1), 27–46.

42. Lyons, W. "Partnerships, Information and Public Safety: Community Policing in a Time of Terror." *Policing, 25*(3), 530–542.

43. O'Connell, P. E. (2008). "The Chess Master's Game: A Model for Incorporating Local Police Agencies in the Fight Against Global Terrorism." *Policing, 31*(3), 456–465.

44. Berson, S. B. (2009). "Debating DNA Collection." *National Institute of Justice Journal, 264*, 9–13.

45. *Kyllo v. United States,* 533 U.S. 27, 150 L. Ed. 2nd 94, 121 S. Ct. 2038.

46. Douglas, J., Ressler, R. K., Burgess, A. W., & Hartman, C. R. (1986). "Criminal Profiling from Crime Scene Analysis." *Behavioral Sciences and the Law, 4*, 401–421.

47. Kelling, G. L., & Moore, M. H. (1988). "The Evolving Strategy of Policing." *Perspectives on Policing* (NCJ 114213). Washington, DC: National Institute of Justice.

48. Ponsaers, P. (2002). "Reading about 'Community (Oriented) Policing' and Police Models." *Policing, 24*(4), 470–496.

49. Kreps, G. A., & Weller, J. M. (1973). "The Police-Community Relations Movement: Conciliatory Responses to Violence." *The American Behavioral Scientist, 16*(3), 402–412.

50. Ibid.

51. Gaines, L. K., & Kappeler, V. E. (2009). *Community Policing: A Contemporary Perspective*. Cincinnati, OH: Anderson.

52. Wilson, J. Q., & Kelling, G. L. (1982, March). "Broken Windows." *Atlantic Monthly*.

53. Gaines & Kappeler, 2009.

54. Masten, J. (2009). "'Ain't No Snitches Ridin' Wit' Us': How Deception in the Fourth Amendment Triggered the Stop Snitching Movement." *Ohio State Law Journal, 70*(3), 701–753.

55. Ibid.

56. Goldstein, H. (1979). "Improving Policing: A Problem-Oriented Approach." *Crime and Delinquency, 25*, 236–258.

57. Zhao, J., Scheider, M. C., & Thurman, Q. (2002). "Funding Community Policing to Reduce Crime: Have COPS Grants Made a Difference?" *Criminology & Public Policy, 2*(1), 7–32.

58. Ratcliffe, J. H. (2008). *Intelligence-Led Policing*. Cullompton, UK: Willan.

59. Henry, V. E. (2003). *The COMPSTAT Paradigm: Management Accountability in Policing, Business and the Public Sector*. New York, NY: Looseleaf Law Publications.

60. Zimring, F. E. (2011). "How New York Beat Crime." *Scientific American Magazine, 305*(2), 74–75, 79.

61. Bohrer, S., & Chaney, R. (2010). "Police Investigations of the Use of Deadly Force Can Influence Perceptions and Outcomes." *FBI Law Enforcement Bulletin, 79*(1), 1–7.

62. Neiderhoffer, A. (1969). *Behind the Shield*. Garden City, NJ: Doubleday.

63. Alpert, G. P., MacDonald, J. M., & Dunham, R. G. (2005). "Police Suspicion and Discretionary Decision Making During Traffic Stops." *Criminology, 43*(2), 407–434.

64. Walker, S. (1993). *Taming the System: The Control of Discretion in Criminal Justice, 1950–1990*. Oxford: Oxford University Press.

65. National Research Council. (2003). *Fairness and Effectiveness in Policing: The Evidence*. Washington, DC: The National Academies Press.

66. Alpert et al., 2005.

67. Sherman, L. W., & Berk, R. A. (1984). *The Minneapolis Domestic Violence Experiment*. Washington, DC: Police Foundation.

68. National Research Council, 2003.

69. Sun, I., & Payne, B. (2004). "Racial Differences in Resolving Conflicts: A Comparison Between Black and White Police Officers." *Crime & Delinquency, 50*, 516–541.

70. Dantzer, M. L. (1987). "Police-related Stress: A Critique for Future Research." *Journal of Police Criminal Psychology, 3*, 43–48.

71. Anderson, W., Swenson, D., & Clay, D. (1995). *Stress Management for Law Enforcement Officers*. Upper Saddle River, NJ: Prentice Hall.

72. Anderson, G. S., Litzenberger, R., & Plecas, D. (2002). "Physical Evidence of Police Officer Stress." *Policing, 25*(2), 399–420.

73. Rizzolo, D., & Sedrak, M. (2010). "Stress Management: Helping Patients to Find Effective Coping Strategies." *Journal of American Academy of Physician Assistants, 23*(9), 20–24.

74. Atkinson, W. (2004). "Stress: Risk Management's Most Serious Challenge?" *Risk Management, 51*(6), 20–24.

75. Ibid.

76. Weitzer, R. (2002). "Incidents of Police Misconduct and Public Opinion." *Journal of Criminal Justice, 30*(5), 397–408.

77. Walker, S. (1992). *Police in America*. New York, NY: McGraw-Hill.

78. Ivkovic, S. K. (2005). *Fallen Blue Knights: Controlling Police Corruption*. New York, NY: Oxford University Press.

79. Arrigo, B. A., & Claussen, N. (2003). "Police Corruption and Psychological Testing: A Strategy for Preemployment Screening." *International Journal of Offender Therapy and Comparative Criminology, 47*(3), 272–290.

80. Jones, T. R., Owens, C., & Smith, M. (1995). "Police Ethics Training: A Three-Tiered Approach." *FBI Law Enforcement Bulletin, 64*(6), 22–26.

81. http://www.theiacp.org/PoliceServices/ExecutiveServices/ProfessionalAssistance/Ethics/FocusOnEthics TheLawEnforcementOathofHonor/tabid/167/Default.aspx

SECTION 3

The American Court System

Chapter 6: The Court System

Chapter 7: Inside a Courtroom

Chapter 8: Sentencing and Judgment

The Court System

6

KEY TERMS

Appellate brief, Bail, Complaint, Court of last resort, Custodial interrogation, Discovery, Due process, *En banc*, Fruit of the poisonous tree, Grand jury, Indictment, Initial appearance, Intermediate appellate court, Judicial review, Jurisdiction, *Nolo contendere*, Plain view, Plea, Probable cause, Reasonable doubt, Recusal, Remand, Speedy Trial Act, Suppression hearing, Trial court, Verdict, Warrant, Writ of certiorari

CHAPTER OBJECTIVES

1. Identify the critical steps in the historical development of state and federal court systems in the United States.
2. Distinguish between the structures of the modern-day state and federal court systems in the United States.
3. Identify the procedural protections the modern U.S. court system provides to criminal defendants.
4. Evaluate the adequacy of court procedures provided to criminal defendants.

Case Study: Presumption of Innocence?

The credibility of North Carolina's criminal justice system was called into question recently by a disturbing revelation. After conducting an audit, the attorney general of the state concluded that the state's Bureau of Investigation had distorted or withheld evidence in the cases of more than 200 potentially innocent men and women.[1] The attorney general's audit uncovered memos indicating that crime lab analysts were trained to help prosecutors; it also indicated that the wrongfully suppressed evidence might have helped absolve certain defendants.[2] Many criminal defendants may have been wrongfully convicted because of the lab's failure to overturn potentially exculpatory evidence.

For a variety of reasons, courts sometimes fail to fulfill one of their primary responsibilities: to safeguard accused individuals from the abuses of overzealous policing and prosecution. Unfortunately, these unprofessional tactics are unlikely to stop unless the courts penalize them—even if it means, in extreme cases, occasionally letting an apparently guilty defendant go free due to these abuses. When courts take these measures, of course, the media and public are unlikely to understand the rationale that can possibly justify them.

Is our court system more error-prone than we can imagine? Perhaps so, and this underscores the continuing need for the procedural and constitutional safeguards that are the hallmark of due process under law. This propensity for error also suggests a much more unsettling problem: that there may be many more innocent people in American prisons than we have long thought. Most people are familiar in some way with the use of DNA evidence to clear persons convicted before the technology existed to identify DNA from crime scenes. Several common causes of wrongful conviction include eyewitness misidentification, improper forensics, false or coerced confessions, or informants who provide false testimony.[3]

In the North Carolina cases, the court system failed, for several reasons, to detect professional misconduct by prosecutors and crime labs that led to ill-gotten convictions. Now, the courts will have to fix this, and to revisit many prosecutions that should have concluded long ago. In North Carolina, these errors span many years and include more than 15,000 cases. Why did the court system not detect these problems sooner? At what point does the desire to rapidly convict and punish defendants overwhelm legal safeguards and yield tragic results, falsely incarcerating (or, worse, executing) an innocent person?

Background History of the U.S. Court System

First and foremost, a court is an official venue for resolving disputes. Every day, courts resolve countless conflicts in criminal and civil matters. Under the principle of government known as *federalism*, created in the United States Constitution, the federal government and individual state governments share power. Similarly, the American judicial system exists in two separate but related systems: state and federal, each with its own courts, structure and functions.[4]

As we discuss the American court system, we must first understand that there is no single, unified apparatus that controls the judiciary at every level. To many people, this is a surprising fact. In fact, there are more than 15,000 courts in the United States, covering a broad spectrum of functions and geographic jurisdictions. Rather than a uniform system, the American judiciary is better understood as 50 individual state court systems and one separate, national system that is part of the federal government.[5]

There are four principal sources of law in the United States: constitutions, statutes, administrative regulations, and common law, also known as case law.[6] Constitutional law is based on a formally adopted document, or constitution, that defines the broad powers of the government. In the United States, the supreme law of the land is the U.S. Constitution, which defines the powers held by the federal government, establishes the branches of government, and reserves individual rights to all people who are under the jurisdiction of the United States. Each state also has its own constitution, from which its constitutional law is derived. Statutes are ordinances passed by Congress, state legislatures, and governing bodies at the federal, state, or local level. Administrative regulations, in turn, are rules issued by administrative bodies to exercise and interpret the powers given to them by statutes.[7]

Common law is the oldest source of law in the American legal system. The term *common law* refers to the legal rules formed by the accumulated decisions issued by judges in court cases. The American judicial system traces its roots to its colonial heritage and the legacy of English common law. In England, these decisions were made by judges who traveled across the country and rendered decisions based on rules and social norms common to each area. Common law is unique because it is largely shaped by judges, and not simply by applying statutes passed by a legislature.[8] Colonists carried English common law to the New World and incorporated it into the legal structures of colonial governments.

Significantly, common law also forms precedent, which means it can bind future judges to issue similar rulings in future disputes involving similar facts.[9]

Colonists carried English common law to the New World and incorporated it into the legal structures of colonial governments.

This essentially establishes a set of procedures designed to ensure fairness. These procedures are known as *due process*, which essentially means "fair play" in legal contexts.[10] The operating principle of due process is that it is unjust to treat similar facts and actions in a different way on different occasions.[11]

State Courts

For the most part, colonial courts adhered to the model they inherited from England, though there were some regional differences.[12] Influences such as religion and geography also led to variations in the structure of colonial courts. No attempt was made to unify the colonial courts until after the American Revolution.[13] Most colonies (and, subsequently, the U.S. states they became), of course, were directly influenced by the common law tradition. A notable exception is Louisiana, which today retains an integrated civil law system based on its French and Spanish traditions.[14]

The common law also led to other hallmarks of the American judicial system. In the minds of British subjects, common law came to represent an unassailable natural law that was higher than the laws of men. This view was reinforced by the English Parliament's use of common law to limit the unchecked power of the monarch. Eventually, this use resulted in the passage of significant provisions in English law, including the Bill of Rights, the right of habeas corpus, and the Petition of Right.[15] Each device would find its way into the American judicial system.

The English Bill of Rights in particular would influence American perceptions of justice and democracy. The 1689 Act of Parliament, which established the Bill of Rights in England, contained specific guarantees that later appeared in the U.S. Constitution. The Bill of Rights protected British subjects against excessive bails and fines and cruel and unusual punishment. It also provided jury trials for the accused, and later yielded protections for free speech and parliamentary debate.[16] These protections were incorporated into American state courts, and subsequently, into the U.S. Constitution.

Colonial Judiciary

Before the U.S. Constitution formally established a separation of powers among the three branches of government, judicial power in each colony was vested primarily in the hands of a royal governor. Before the Constitution was ratified, the various state courts existed as colonial judiciaries. By the time of the American Revolution, the colonial judicial system had existed in the same form since the 1720s.[17]

Typically, a justice of the peace, appointed by the royal governor, formed the lowest level of the judiciary. Above him were county courts that adjudicated low-level civil cases and non-capital criminal offenses. The highest-level cases were heard under the jurisdiction of the governor; in some states, the governor appointed a council of judges, while in others, he presided over such a council as a court of appeals.[18] These courts of appeals served as central courts for major offenses, but often traveled only once or twice a year on circuits around the colony.[19] Colonial judiciaries were far more informal than their counterparts in England. Justices of the peace kept few, if any, records. In addition, wealthy members of the community often posted a surety (financial guarantee by one party to assume the debt of another), which would be forfeited if the accused committed another crime.[20]

Colonial courts did not exercise a great deal of power in the colonies. The appeal process from their decisions went to authorities in England, not to the colonial government. Of course, colonial authorities required any laws passed by assemblies or legislatures to accord with English common law. If they did not, they could be overturned by the Privy Council in England, which also could reverse the decisions of colonial judges.[21] Royal governors, the representatives of English control, had the authority to remove judges at their leisure. Additionally, colonial judiciaries were typically less professional and experienced than those in England. Indeed, there were fewer legal experts in the colonies, and judges were often merchants, planters, or wealthy landowners.[22]

Tension between the Judiciary and Legislatures

Tension began to grow between colonial legislatures and the judicial system controlled by a royal governor—and, by extension, the British Crown. During the colonial period, legislative assemblies in the colonies increasingly asserted themselves as law-making bodies. At the same time, the British government in London began to take a much more active and invasive role in colonial affairs.[23] This was because Britain believed the colonies existed only to provide the home country with resources and wealth, and that the colonists did not enjoy the same rights as British subjects at home.

Royal governors, as proxies of the British crown, performed the functions of the executive, legislative, and judicial branches of government.[24] With every ruling that was handed down by courts, colonists believed the British government was infringing on their rights. Not surprisingly, this untenable arrangement led to the relatively weak functioning of the executive and judicial branches under the first national colonial government. Because the executive and judicial branches were so weak, the legislative branch gained increasing power.

Before and immediately after the American Revolution, legislatures were the strongest branch of American government, dominating both the judicial and executive branches. Legislatures had the power to elect and pay judges, and to overrule their decisions or even impeach them. Legislatures could even amend state constitutions without interference from the courts.[25] Adding to the tension was the fact that legislatures and courts had different economic interests in early America. Members of local legislatures, on one hand, were usually interested in protecting the interests of debtors, especially small farmers. Courts, on the other hand, tended to side with the creditors who filed suit against debtors.[26]

Formalization of State Court Systems

Conflict existed not only between the legislature and the judiciary, but also between different levels of the court system. As formalized state court systems developed after the American Revolution, a primary source of tension was the division of power between local and national judicial bodies.

Initially, the federal court system was structured to correspond to state lines. This structure was intended to ensure that federal judges would represent the federal court in their home states, with minimal interference from the federal government.[27] This design was a direct response to the inherent distrust of judicial authority that early American leaders retained from their experiences under British rule. They still saw the judiciary as an arbitrary, coercive, powerful system that interfered with their inalienable rights. Federalists created a basic framework for federal courts that would enforce national law.[28]

Overlap of Civil and Criminal Courts   A second influence on the formalization of the court system was the development of a civil court structure. In the early phases of the American judiciary, the court system was informal enough to allow a great deal of overlap between civil and criminal cases. Justices of the peace met at county courts to hear civil disputes—disputes over contracts, personal injuries, or property—while still holding hearings on petty criminal acts.[29] This overlap of civil and criminal courts continued until the ratification of the U.S. Constitution.

Federal Courts   Initially, the framers of the U.S. Constitution were ambivalent about the need for federal courts and the amount of power they should grant to the courts. This ambivalence is reflected in Article III of the Constitution, which provides for a single supreme court and gives Congress broad powers to establish lower courts at its discretion.[30] Notably, it provides no further detail on the structure of the courts. However, the experience of the relatively weak judiciary underscored the need for a strong, independent federal judiciary, and the founders became concerned with the rights of individual citizens in relation to the government.

Articles of Confederation   In the immediate aftermath of the Revolutionary War, the leaders of the new nation were highly suspicious of strong, centralized executive power as a result of their experiences with the British government. In their writings and actions, they demonstrated an obvious preference for legislative power over executive power.[31]

The first federal courts were created, at least in one sense, by the Articles of Confederation, which were adopted in 1778 and ratified in 1781, as the first constitution of the United States of America. The articles did not create a national judiciary. Congress held almost all power, and there was no true executive or judicial branch. Congress did have the authority to create *ad hoc* courts that would settle disputes between states, as well as cases involving events on international waters.[32] However, the seeds of stronger judicial power were present. During the 1780s, state judiciaries were able to declare several state statutes unconstitutional, presaging a later debate over the extent of judicial authority in American government.[33] This debate would reach a climax with the Supreme Court case of *Marbury v. Madison* (1803), which established the doctrine of judicial review.

U.S. Constitution   For a variety of reasons, the weak and ineffective national government created by the Articles of Confederation lasted only a few years before being replaced. The U.S. Constitution (1787) formally established the federal ju-

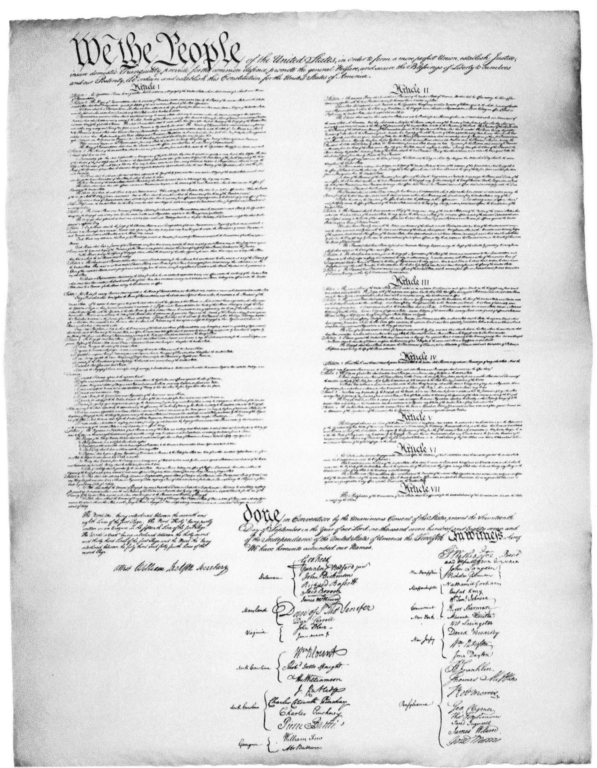

The U.S. Constitution instituted the federal judicial system that is in practice today.

diciary as it exists today. Many founders agreed that an independent judiciary was needed to counterbalance potential abuses by the legislative and executive branches. Additionally, they saw a strong judiciary as the best way to effectively defend the individual rights guaranteed by the Constitution. The Anti-Federalists (later known as the Jeffersonian-Republicans), who still opposed strong national government, favored a network of self-governing state and local courts instead of a strong, federal "supreme" court that would interpret the Constitution.[34] The Federalists, who advocated strong national government, were successful in arguing that the legislature was the branch most dangerous to the personal freedoms secured by the Constitution. They believed that Congress had been granted a disproportionate amount of power.

The Constitution gave courts the power to prevent the legislature, at both the state and federal levels, from passing bills of attainder (acts of the legislature declaring a person guilty of a crime without a trial) and *ex post facto* laws. In addition, it guaranteed citizens the right to trial by jury, and prohibited the suspension of the right of habeas corpus (the right not to be illegally detained), except in wartime.[35] These basic civil rights and others, collectively known as the "Bill of Rights," compose the first 10 amendments to the Constitution.

The U.S. Constitution also underscored the importance of judicial independence by articulating a clear doctrine of separation of powers. In the English system of government, even today, the legislature retains ultimate authority. American colonists, even before the revolution, began to sharply define the difference between what is considered "legal" and what is considered "constitutional." The British system, by contrast, sees the two concepts as inextricably linked. Americans asserted that the rights and principles outlined by the Constitution take priority over any hasty decisions made by the legislature or the executive.[36]

A crucially important feature of the U.S. Constitution, as compared to the Articles of the Confederation, is the establishment of an independent judiciary. The Constitution is, first and foremost, a "contract" between the people and the government. In the American system, the judiciary is granted the authority and responsibility to guard the freedoms guaranteed by that contract. This authority and responsibility leads directly to the doctrine of judicial review.

The U.S. Constitution authorized two types of federal courts: legislative and constitutional. Legislative courts were established by Congress under Article I of the Constitution, and serve functions that are both legislative and judicial. They typically have a narrowly defined role and administer a specific statute, such as bankruptcy law. Legislative courts include the Tax Court, the U.S. Court of Appeals for Veterans Claims, the U.S. Court of Appeals for the Armed Forces, and the U.S. Court of Federal Claims. Constitutional courts include the U.S. Supreme Court, circuit courts of appeals, and district courts.

The Road to Judicial Review The doctrine of judicial review has become the most powerful tool for the judiciary to take an active role in government. The U.S. Constitution tasked federal courts with upholding and supporting the Constitution.[37] Article III provides that "the judicial power of the United States, shall be vested in one supreme Court, and in such inferior Courts as the Congress may from time to time ordain and establish."[38] The scope of those powers was not clearly or comprehensively described in the Constitution itself, but judicial review has become an established—if somewhat controversial—power of the judiciary.

In the words of David O'Brien, **judicial review** is "the power of the Supreme Court and the federal judiciary to consider and overturn any congressional and state legislation or other official governmental action deemed inconsistent with the Constitution, Bill of Rights, or federal law."[39] This idea was not without controversy. The Jeffersonian-Republicans, the party of Thomas Jefferson, felt the court's power should be limited in regard to the legislature, while the Federalists, the party of John Adams, favored a stronger judiciary.

Since the Constitution did not describe a specific structure for the federal judiciary other than the U.S. Supreme Court, Congress used its authority to establish lower courts by enacting the Judiciary Act of 1789. One clause of that act gave the Supreme Court the power to issue writs of mandamus, which are orders from a higher court compelling a lower court or government officer to perform a specified duty.[40] The act also enabled citizens sued by citizens of another state to transfer the lawsuit to federal circuit court and granted the Supreme Court authority to review the decisions of state courts on appeal.[41]

Nonetheless, there was significant debate about what the U.S. Constitution actually allowed the Supreme Court to do. The Constitution did not explicitly provide the Supreme Court or any of the judiciary the power of judicial review. Article III states that the "judicial Power shall extend to" cases and controversies "arising under this Constitution," implying that the judiciary is empowered to resolve constitutional questions. In addition, Article VI asserts that the Constitution is the "Supreme Law of the Land."[42] But a definitive answer on judicial review would not come until the 1803 U.S. Supreme Court case of *Marbury v. Madison*.

Marbury v. Madison   The pivotal Supreme Court case that established the doctrine of judicial review is *Marbury v. Madison*.[43] In this case, the Supreme Court first asserted its authority to declare an act of Congress unconstitutional.

Judicial review
The power of the federal judiciary to overturn any legislation or other governmental action ruled inconsistent with the Constitution, Bill of Rights, or federal law.

Exhibit: Excerpt from *Marbury v. Madison*

"It is emphatically the province and duty of the Judicial Department [the judicial branch] to say what the law is. Those who apply the rule to particular cases must, of necessity, expound and interpret that rule. If two laws conflict with each other, the Courts must decide on the operation of each.

"So, if a law [e.g., a statute or treaty] be in opposition to the Constitution, if both the law and the Constitution apply to a particular case, so that the Court must either decide that case conformably to the law, disregarding the Constitution, or conformably to the Constitution, disregarding the law, the Court must determine which of these conflicting rules governs the case. This is of the very essence of judicial duty. If, then, the Courts are to regard the Constitution, and the Constitution is superior to any ordinary act of the Legislature, the Constitution, and not such ordinary act, must govern the case to which they both apply.

"Those, then, who controvert the principle that the Constitution is to be considered in court as a paramount law are reduced to the necessity of maintaining that courts must close their eyes on the Constitution, and see only the law" [e.g., the statute or treaty].

"This doctrine would subvert the very foundation of all written constitutions."[44]

The dispute arose during the transition between the presidency of John Adams and that of Thomas Jefferson. At the close of Adams' presidency, it became clear that Adams' Federalist party was going to lose power. In a political move designed to frustrate the incoming Jefferson administration, Adams spent his last night as president appointing many fellow Federalists—later called "midnight judges"—to judicial positions in and around Washington, D.C. The next day, the Jefferson administration ordered James Madison, the new secretary of state, not to deliver the commissions to the judges, though they had been approved by the Senate. This order prompted one of the newly appointed justices, William Marbury, to file suit for a writ of mandamus in the Supreme Court that would force Madison to deliver the commissions. Marbury based his claim on the Judiciary Act of 1789, which granted the Supreme Court jurisdiction to issue such writs.

The case reached the Supreme Court, and Chief Justice John Marshall determined that it presented three legal issues: did Marbury have a right to the commission, was there a legal remedy, and was a writ of mandamus from the Supreme Court the correct remedy? Marshall answered the first two in the affirmative, but he determined that the third question involved the jurisdiction of the Supreme Court and was, therefore, a constitutional question.[45] Though he agreed that Marbury was entitled to the commission, he ruled that the Judiciary Act of 1789 conflicted with the Constitution, which did not give the Supreme Court original jurisdiction over writs of mandamus. Essentially, Marshall ruled that Congress did not have the authority to add to the original jurisdiction of the Supreme Court.[46]

The result of Marshall's ruling was that a Supreme Court decision partially invalidated an act of Congress by determining that it conflicted with the U.S. Constitution. The ruling strengthened the power of the judiciary by establishing that the legislature could not add to the jurisdiction of the Supreme Court. This precedent also entrenched the checks and balances system in American government.

In the end, as Justice Marshall put it, "it is emphatically the province and the duty of the judicial department to say what the law is."[47] Judicial review, while controversial at first, has in the past two centuries become a fixture of American constitutionalism. The now-accepted doctrine of judicial review allows the judiciary to adjudicate between two contradictory sources of law.[48]

Court Structure   The American judiciary can best be described as a dual system, including one federal court and 50 state courts. Under this system, federal courts have authority over cases involving an issue of federal law, and state courts have authority over issues of state law.

The separation between the two tiers is not absolute, however some cases can be heard in either state or federal court. For example, civil suits in which the parties reside in two different states can be heard in either state or federal court.

Narcotics cases and interstate kidnapping charges violate both federal and state statutes. The appeals process can also involve both levels of the judiciary. Those convicted in a state court may appeal to their respective states' appellate courts, to the U.S. Supreme Court, or by petition for a writ of habeas corpus to a federal district court. Detained individuals may petition for a writ of habeas corpus to request their release.

To understand the structure of U.S. courts, both state and federal, it is necessary to understand the concept of **jurisdiction**. There are several different kinds of jurisdiction, but— loosely defined—jurisdiction is the power of a court to adjudicate a case, issue orders, and render a decision. The term also refers to the geographic territory over which a court may exercise its power.

Original jurisdiction, as the name implies, is the prerogative of a court— typically, a **trial court**—to be the first to hear a case. Appellate jurisdiction refers to the authority of a higher court to consider an appeal from a decision issued by a trial court. Appellate courts do not hear witness testimony in criminal cases or civil cases. Rather, they consider written and oral appeals about the conduct, procedure, and results of a trial, and then determine if the trial court (or trial court jury) committed errors of fact or law.[49]

Jurisdiction can be further broken down into geographic and subject matter jurisdiction. Subject matter jurisdiction applies in cases where a specific legal issue is in controversy, such as the right of contracts or civil rights. Geographic jurisdiction is the authority of a court to try cases that arise within certain geographical areas, such as a county, city, or state. The state of Maryland, for instance, has no jurisdiction to try a person accused of committing a crime in Pennsylvania.

Geographic jurisdiction can become an issue if a defendant flees a state to avoid prosecution, because the state's prosecutor must request extradition to have the defendant brought to the state in which the crime was committed.[50] In addition, issues of geographic jurisdiction become political when a defendant who commits a capital crime in a state with the death penalty flees to a state that does not impose the death penalty.

Structure of State Courts

State courts handle the vast majority of cases that occur in the United States. They derive their authority from state constitutions and statutes, which are far more exhaustive than the U.S. Constitution. The 10th Amendment to the Bill of Rights states that the powers not specifically granted to the federal government by the Constitution are reserved to the states or the people.[51] As such, state courts resolve most disputes between private citizens, prosecute most criminal defendants, handle most family disputes, and adjudicate most disputes between citizens and the government.[52]

State court systems, like their federal counterparts, are divided into trial courts and appellate courts. In criminal cases, trial courts arraign defendants, set bail, consider guilty pleas, conduct trials, and impose criminal sentences. In civil cases, trial courts inform plaintiffs and defendants of the complaint filed, perform pretrial procedures, conduct trials, and award damages. To carry out these steps, trial courts often handle factual disputes and hear testimony from witnesses.

Jurisdiction
The power of a court to adjudicate a case, issue orders, and render a decision.

Trial court
A court of original jurisdiction that tries a case and renders a judgment.

Appellate courts correct erroneous decisions of lower courts.

Appellate courts correct erroneous decisions of lower courts. Their role is not to determine factual errors or hear witnesses, but rather to determine if the trial court incorrectly interpreted or applied the relevant statute or law. Most rulings of appellate courts become precedent for trial courts. In addition, appellate courts often reassess the application of legal rules, derive new rules for original situations, and interpret ambiguous language in statutes or court opinions.[53]

In general, the lowest level of a state court system consists of county courts, municipal courts, traffic courts, and magistrates, or judicial officers who perform some administrative tasks of a judge without the same level of authority. These are trial courts of limited jurisdiction. Limited jurisdiction refers to the authority of courts over a particular subset of cases.

The next highest level consists of specialized courts that consider juvenile, divorce, family, and housing issues. Superior courts handle serious criminal matters; most trials occur at this level. The highest level is the state supreme court, which has the power to hear appeals from lower courts.

Municipal Courts, District Courts, and County Courts

Municipal courts, district courts, and county courts are typically trial courts of limited jurisdiction, and often are referred to as *inferior* or *lower* courts. They constitute almost 77% of all courts in the United States.[54] Courts in this category frequently use abbreviated procedures due to the commonplace nature of the cases they handle. They sometimes exclude attorneys and do not use juries due to the huge volume of civil and criminal matters they arbitrate, many of which are neither complex nor serious (traffic offenses, moving violations, etc.).[55]

Lower courts of this sort nearly always handle misdemeanor crimes, or crimes for which the penalty does not exceed one year of incarceration, and hear civil suits whose amounts do not exceed $15,000. These courts may also handle the preliminary stages of felony cases, which include preliminary hearings, arraignment, bail, and appointment of counsel. As these courts do not handle serious matters, their proceedings are often not officially recorded. Appeals from trial courts of limited jurisdiction usually go to trial courts of general jurisdiction, instead of directly to an appellate court.

The trial court of general jurisdiction for a state is usually called a district or superior court. Most trial courts have unlimited jurisdiction and are therefore the venue for the majority of serious criminal offenses. Still, there is overlap in some states. Usually, courts are divided into judicial districts or circuits, sometimes along political boundaries, such as counties or boroughs. They are much more formal than lower courts, usually featuring a jury trial and attorneys. Major trial courts often have felony jurisdiction, which gives them the power to issue judgments on cases in which preliminary proceedings have occurred in a lower court of limited jurisdiction. These courts also have incidental appellate jurisdiction, so they can hear appeals from lower-level courts and administrative agencies in certain civil or criminal matters.[56]

Intermediate Appellate Courts

All states have at least one appellate court, but some feature more. In states with large caseloads, there are two levels of appellate courts. The highest is a court of last resort, typically a state supreme court. The lower level consists of **intermediate appellate courts**, which alleviate the burden placed on higher courts in the most populous states. These courts relieve the state's highest court (typically a state supreme court) from having to hear every case that generates an appeal.[57] In 1998, 35 states had at least one intermediate court of appeal.[58] These appeals typically are decided by a three-judge panel, although judges occasionally sit *en banc*, a French term that translates to the phrase "on a bench" and implies that all the judges of the court together will decide a case.

The losing side in a criminal or civil case has the right of appeal, and the appeal takes place either in a **court of last resort** or an intermediate appellate court. Intermediate appellate courts generally must hear cases that are appealed to them.

Courts of Last Resort

State supreme courts are the highest level of appellate court and also are referred to as courts of last resort. These courts generally reserve the right to choose which cases they will hear, and they frequently choose cases that carry broad policy and legal implications.[59] Courts of last resort in states without an intermediate level, however, do not get to choose their cases.

All of these courts are composed of five to nine members (most commonly seven) and generally sit *en banc*. Texas and Oklahoma are notable for being the two states to have separate courts of last resort for civil and criminal matters.[60]

State supreme courts are similar to the U.S. Supreme Court in that they interpret state law and have the power to determine whether it violates the state constitution. These courts follow a model similar to the federal model: they require a notice of appeal, require written legal briefs, consider oral arguments by each party's attorneys, and issue a written decision. State supreme courts, like other courts of last resort, do not retry the facts of the case or hear witnesses, but correct errors of law or procedure.[61]

When it is relevant to do so, state supreme courts exercise the authority to interpret the Constitution and, in some instances, federal law. However, if a state court issues an opinion on federal law, its decision is reviewable by the U.S. Supreme Court, whose authority supersedes that of a state court. The U.S. Supreme Court can review and overrule the state's interpretation of a federal statute or the Constitution.[62]

Specialized State Courts

The state court system also includes specialized courts that handle specific types of cases. These courts have limited jurisdiction that covers their specialty, and generally have a single judge hear cases without a

Intermediate appellate court
The lower level of state appellate courts.

En banc
A French term indicating that all the judges of an appellate court will together consider an appeal.

Court of last resort
The highest court of appeal in a state court system: typically, a state supreme court.

Juvenile courts determine cases involving young offenders, generally those less than 18 years old.

© 2012 BY SASCHA BURKARD. USED UNDER LICENSE OF SHUTTERSTOCK, INC.

jury. Probate courts, for instance, consider the administrative concerns of a deceased person's estate. This usually involves making sure the person's will is executed properly or applying relevant state law if there is no will. Family courts consider divorces, custody disputes, annulments, and alimony. Traffic courts adjudicate speeding tickets and other moving violations.[63]

Juvenile courts determine cases involving young offenders, generally those less than 18 years old. Because these offenders are underage, they are not tried in conventional criminal courts. Juvenile courts operate on the premise that sentences should be rehabilitative, rather than punitive, since minors are not as culpable for most criminal acts an adult would be and can more readily see the error of their ways and remediate their behavior.[64]

Structure of Federal Courts

In their current form, federal courts have three levels. The lowest level is occupied by federal district courts, which function as trial courts. The middle level includes the U.S. Circuit Courts of Appeals, which consider appeals. The top court is the U.S. Supreme Court, which defines and interprets the U.S. Constitution and statutes passed by the legislative branch.[65]

Federal courts have exclusive jurisdiction over "federal questions." These legal issues arise in suits between citizens of different states, or in suits involving foreign ambassadors or public officials, bankruptcy, patent or trademark law, or crimes specifically punishable by federal statutes. Indeed, any crime mentioned in the Constitution (treason, piracy, counterfeiting) or a federal statute qualifies as a federal question, but most statutory crimes are tried in state courts.[66]

Career Connections: Federal Judge

Federal judges sit at the top of the judicial system in the American criminal justice system. They are selected by executive appointment of the president and must be confirmed by at least two-thirds of the U.S. Senate.

This obviously makes the selection process an inherently political one. When a position becomes available, the deputy attorney general of the U.S. Department of Justice conducts a search for qualified lawyers in the state in which the vacancy is located. The initial screening phase involves consulting with local party leaders to ensure that the nominee's political views do not conflict with those of the president.[67]

Federal judges are appointed under Article III of the U.S. Constitution. Judges serve a lifelong term, but can be removed by impeachment. There are no explicit qualifications for a judgeship, but candidates are almost always accomplished attorneys, often working for the government.[68] In addition, it is preferred that judges have a dispassionate demeanor. As arbiters of fairness in the court, judges are expected to be, according to Jackson (1974), "honest, patient, wise, tolerant, compassionate, strong, decisive, articulate, courageous—a list of virtues similar to those in the Boy Scout handbooks."[69]

Some see federal judges as autocratic, but they frequently defer to the advice and opinions of prosecutors and probation officers when it comes to accepting a plea agreement or determining sentencing.[70] In a federal criminal trial, the judge advises the defendant of his or her rights, decides if the defendant should be held in custody until trial, and determines if **probable cause** exists to believe the defendant committed the crime with which he or she is charged. Most defendants (90%) take a plea bargain instead of going to trial, at which point the judge either imposes sentence or waits for a presentence report prepared by a probation officer. If the defendant pleads not guilty, the judge schedules a trial.[71]

Probable cause
Reasonable belief that the accused committed the crime with which he or she is charged.

During the trial, the judge runs the courtroom, acting as a judicial umpire and responding to the actions and requests of defense attorneys and prosecutors. Judges have discretion to determine how the law applies to the facts of a specific case. They determine which evidence is admissible and which survey questions may be used to select potential jurors, and issue instructions of law to guide the jury in its deliberations.

For many Americans, judges are the most identifiable symbol of justice and fairness in the legal system. As such, judges are invested with a high degree of prestige and respect, as well as a high level of power and responsibility. The Judicial Conference of the United States sets the code of conduct for judges, requiring them to maintain integrity, impartiality, and independence and to avoid the appearance of impropriety. To meet these standards, judges must **recuse** themselves from cases in which they have a personal interest or connection. Additionally, federal judges must file regular reports of compensation they receive from extrajudicial activities.[72]

Recusal
The decision by a judge to remove himself or herself from a case if there is a conflict of interest.

Critical Thinking Many outcomes in the judicial system (warrants, grand jury indictments, searches, etc.) depend on the definition of probable cause. Is "probable cause" a strong enough basis on which to grant law enforcement and prosecutors such invasive powers? Why or why not?

U.S. District Courts   U.S. district courts are the federal trial courts. They are courts of limited jurisdiction, as the individual state courts have jurisdiction over the majority of cases. District courts have authority over issues of federal law (a "federal question") and issues between citizens of different states ("diversity jurisdiction"). There are 94 U.S. district courts, with each state having at least one. Districts frequently cover large geographic areas and are subdivided into divisions.

District courts employ anywhere between two and 28 judges per court. The judge determines the issue of law, while the jury (if present) determines issues of fact.[73] In addition, district courts employ magistrates, or federal judges who have the authority to hear lesser charges, conduct trials, accept guilty pleas, and impose sentences. Magistrates are appointed by district judges, but serve a fixed term rather than a lifetime one.[74]

FIGURE6.1 Defendants in Cases Concluded in U.S. District Court. As of 2002, public order offenses exceed drug cases as the most common offense among cases concluded in federal district court.

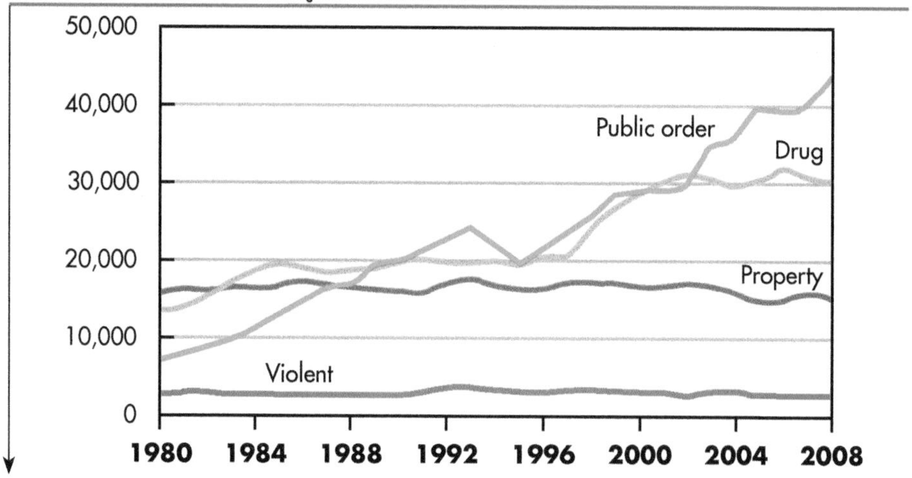

Circuit Courts of Appeals   The U.S. Circuit Courts of Appeals, created in 1891, are the federal counterparts to the states' intermediate appellate courts; they hear appeals on many cases to ease the burden on the U.S. Supreme Court. The 94 federal districts are subdivided into 12 circuits, with one court of appeals per circuit. Each court hears appeals from district courts and federal administrative agencies. Federal appellate courts also hear appeals involving patent laws, which arise from decisions rendered by the U.S. Court of Federal Claims and the U.S. Court of International Trade.[75]

Federal appellate courts first screen cases to decide whether to dispose of a case or hear it. Cases are heard by panels of three judges, unless the panel is unable to reach a conclusion. In that instance, the court may hear the case *en banc*. After an appellate court decides to hear a case, the attorneys submit written briefs, present their case orally, and answer questions from the judges. The judges then either announce their decision or confer at greater length before rendering a written decision.[76]

Circuit judges are appointed in the same way as district court judges. If a party is dissatisfied with a circuit court of appeals' decision, it may appeal further to the U.S. Supreme Court. However, these requests are rarely granted. Appellate courts also may remand cases to a lower court for further proceedings.

Remand
An appellate court's process of returning a case to a lower court for further proceedings.

U.S. Supreme Court   The United States Supreme Court is the highest court in the land. It is composed of nine justices who are nominated by the president and confirmed by the U.S. Senate. Like other judges, most U.S. Supreme Court justices are former attorneys (though this is not a prerequisite), and the majority are elevated to the Court from a judgeship in a lower court. The U.S. Supreme Court is a court of discretionary appeal, so it has discretion to decide which cases it will hear. Typically, it selects cases that carry the most profound legal and political ramifications.[77] Also, as an appellate court, it does not hear witness testimony, but instead reviews legal briefs, hears oral arguments by attorneys, and issues written decisions.

FIGURE6.2 Geographic Boundaries of United States Courts of Appeals and United States District Courts

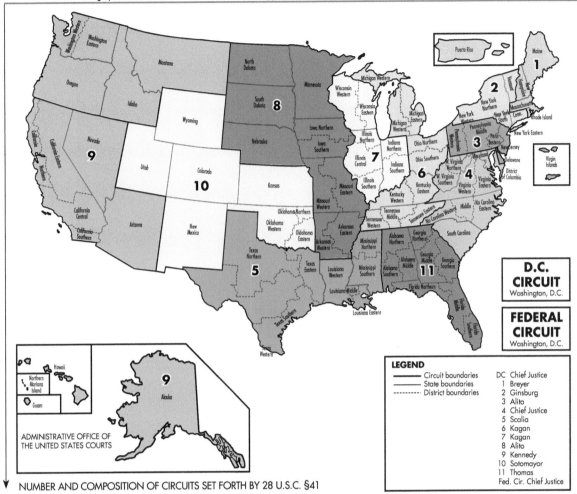

NUMBER AND COMPOSITION OF CIRCUITS SET FORTH BY 28 U.S.C. §41

LEGEND

—— Circuit boundaries	DC Chief Justice
—— State boundaries	1 Breyer
------ District boundaries	2 Ginsburg
	3 Alito
	4 Chief Justice
	5 Scalia
	6 Kagan
	7 Kagan
	8 Alito
	9 Kennedy
	10 Sotomayor
	11 Thomas
	Fed. Cir. Chief Justice

Advancing an appeal to the Supreme Court is not easy; the vast majority of appellants never make it there. The main route to the highest court is through a petition for a **writ of certiorari**, which is a petition filed by a losing party with the Supreme Court, asking it to review the decision of a federal circuit court of appeals or a state supreme court.[78]

The U.S. Supreme Court follows the rule of four: four of the nine justices must vote to hear an appeal, or it will not be heard. Customarily, several criteria must be met in order for an appeal to be heard. First, the plaintiff must have exhausted all other avenues of appeal. Second, the issue must involve a "substantial federal question," as the Supreme Court's jurisdiction is grounded in the U.S. Constitution. Third, the appealed decision must involve an alleged violation of either the Constitution or federal law (the U.S. Code). Finally, the court will not hear cases that ask it to interpret a state's law unless that law violates the U.S. Constitution. This practice rules out most appeals, as they involve either state criminal statutes or personal civil suits. After applying these criteria and others, the Supreme Court hears oral arguments for 75–80 cases per year, out of 10,000 petitions for writs of certiorari.[79]

Writ of certiorari

A document issued by the U.S. Supreme Court to confirm that it will review the decision of a federal circuit court of appeals or a state supreme court.

The U.S. Supreme Court hears between 100 and 200 cases per year.

© 2012 BY GARY BLAKELEY. USED UNDER LICENSE OF SHUTTERSTOCK, INC.

Judicial review, the power to invalidate acts of Congress, is perhaps the Supreme Court's most significant privilege. It gives the court the authority to interpret authoritatively the supreme law of the land, often to profound social, cultural, and legal effect. The Supreme Court has used this authority about 150 times over acts of Congress, and has invalidated 956 congressional statutes and struck down 1,068 state laws.[80]

Specialized Federal Courts   The federal court system has fewer specialized courts of limited jurisdiction than do the individual states. Article III courts, such as district and circuit courts of appeals, derive their authority from the U.S. Constitution. These courts include the U.S. Court of Federal Claims, which adjudicates suits against the government, and the U.S. Court of International Trade, which entertains cases involving international trade and tariffs.

A second type of specialized federal court is created by Congress. These include magistrate courts, which handle certain civil and criminal cases at the behest of the parties involved; the U.S. Court of Appeals for the Armed Forces, which handles appeals under the Uniform Code of Military Justice; the U.S. Tax Court; and the U.S. Court of Appeals for Veterans Claims. Additionally, bankruptcy courts have sole jurisdiction over cases that fall under the U.S. Bankruptcy Code.[81]

Due process
The requirement that an accused person receive notice of the charges made against him or her and the right to respond to those charges before being deprived of life, liberty, or property.

Criminal Procedure and Due Process Overview

Criminal procedure and due process are concepts that describe the rights of individuals accused of crimes. **Due process** is a legal doctrine that requires equitable treatment of accused individuals. Its purpose is to prevent uncertainty in the justice system, and to ensure that the process does not conflict with the provisions of the Constitution.[82] The term *criminal procedure* refers to the rules of procedure that the government and courts must follow when enforcing substantive criminal law.

The constitutional basis for criminal procedure and due process is the Bill of Rights in the U.S. Constitution. The amendments that compose the Bill of Rights were designed to alleviate fears that the strong federal government would threaten the freedoms of everyday Americans. There are two different but related types of due process. The first is procedural due process. *Procedural due process* refers to the judicial procedures that prosecutors, police, and the courts must adhere to when charging an individual with a criminal offense.[83]

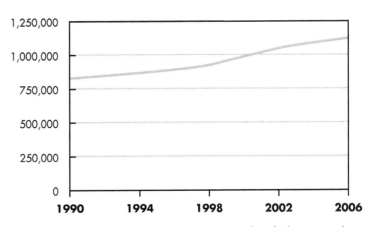

The second is substantive due process, a concept more far-reaching than the first. Substantive due process entails the right to protection against policies and laws that exceed the government's authority, as it is limited by the Constitution.[84] In the context of criminal procedure, this means rights of due process that are not explicitly listed in the Constitution, but are still fundamental liberties. Congress, therefore, cannot pass statutes that violate those rights.[85] Substantive rights are the affirmative rights of citizens to do or say certain things despite the objections of government. These include, in addition to the rights listed above, freedoms of speech and religion.

▲ Number of Felons Convicted in State Courts. In 2006, nearly one million individuals were convicted of felonies in state courts.

The Bill of Rights was designed to alleviate fears that the strong federal government would threaten the freedoms of everyday Americans.

These rights are often not enumerated in the Constitution itself. This makes them basic or, in the words of the Supreme Court itself, "fundamental rights implicit in the concept of ordered liberty."[86] Thus, citizens are protected if the legislature enacts a law that violates substantive due process. For the purposes of criminal procedure, substantive due process requires law enforcement officials to inform defendants, at the time of their arrest, of their right to remain silent and to have an attorney present. This right ensures that defendants do not feel compelled to incriminate themselves.

Constitutional Guarantees   Other rights embodied in the Bill of Rights are of critical importance. The Fourth Amendment, for example, protects citizens against unreasonable searches and seizures. These protections extend to searches of persons, homes, and documents. According to the common law decisions derived from the Fourth Amendment, a search warrant may be issued by a judge only if the judge decides there is probable cause to do so. Specifically, the judge must believe an individual has committed an offense or possesses evidence of an offense.

Exhibit: The Bill of Rights

Amendment I
Congress shall make no law respecting an establishment of religion, or prohibiting the free exercise thereof; or abridging the freedom of speech, or of the press; or the right of the people peaceably to assemble, and to petition the Government for a redress of grievances.

Amendment II
A well regulated Militia, being necessary to the security of a free State, the right of the people to keep and bear Arms, shall not be infringed.

Amendment III
No Soldier shall, in time of peace be quartered in any house, without the consent of the Owner, nor in time of war, but in a manner to be prescribed by law.

Amendment IV
The right of the people to be secure in their persons, houses, papers, and effects, against unreasonable searches and seizures, shall not be violated, and no Warrants shall issue, but upon probable cause, supported by Oath or affirmation, and particularly describing the place to be searched, and the persons or things to be seized.

Amendment V
No person shall be held to answer for a capital, or otherwise infamous crime, unless on a presentment or indictment of a Grand Jury, except in cases arising in the land or naval forces, or in the Militia, when in actual service in time of War or public danger; nor shall any person be subject for the same offence to be twice put in jeopardy of life or limb; nor shall be compelled in any criminal case to be a witness against himself, nor be deprived of life, liberty, or property, without due process of law; nor shall private property be taken for public use, without just compensation.

Amendment VI

In all criminal prosecutions, the accused shall enjoy the right to a speedy and public trial, by an impartial jury of the State and district wherein the crime shall have been committed, which district shall have been previously ascertained by law, and to be informed of the nature and cause of the accusation; to be confronted with the witnesses against him; to have compulsory process for obtaining witnesses in his favor, and to have the Assistance of Counsel for his defence.

Amendment VII

In Suits at common law, where the value in controversy shall exceed twenty dollars, the right of trial by jury shall be preserved, and no fact tried by a jury, shall be otherwise re-examined in any Court of the United States, than according to the rules of the common law.

Amendment VIII

Excessive bail shall not be required, nor excessive fines imposed, nor cruel and unusual punishments inflicted.

Amendment IX

The enumeration in the Constitution, of certain rights, shall not be construed to deny or disparage others retained by the people.

Amendment X

The powers not delegated to the United States by the Constitution, nor prohibited by it to the States, are reserved to the States respectively, or to the people.[87]

The Fifth Amendment, in turn, protects citizens from being put on trial twice for the same crime, a practice known as double jeopardy. It also protects individuals against self-incrimination. A defendant who "takes the Fifth" during testimony is using this constitutional right. The Fifth Amendment also guarantees due process. Specifically, the Fifth Amendment requires an individual to be notified of the charges against him or her, and affords him or her the right to answer those charges before being deprived of life, liberty, or property.

The Sixth Amendment guarantees the right to a speedy trial and the right to a trial by jury. Additionally, it allows a defendant to confront his or her accuser in court, to force witnesses to provide testimony, and to be represented by an attorney. The Seventh Amendment provides the right to trial by jury in certain types of civil cases. The Eighth Amendment protects defendants against excessive bail and cruel and unusual punishment.

Critical Thinking Does the Constitution favor the accused at the expense of the victim? If so, what do you think the justifications are for doing so? Explain.

Constitutional Basis for Due Process   The 14th Amendment guarantees due process to every criminal defendant in the United States. Passed in the aftermath of the Civil War, this amendment initially helped protect the civil rights of African Americans. It contains a due process clause that prevents states from depriving citizens of life, liberty, and property without the due process of law. This clause is similar to the due process clause found in the Fifth Amendment, but the Fifth Amendment version is understood to apply only to the federal government, while the 14th Amendment version also applies to state and local governments.

The judiciary has repeatedly affirmed that the procedural guarantees in the Bill of Rights—specifically the Fifth, Sixth, and Eighth Amendments—limit what the state can do when it charges and prosecutes an individual. If any of these guarantees or rights are violated or denied, then the individual has been denied due process of law, a violation of his or her constitutional rights. The Supreme Court is the ultimate arbiter of remedies for such violations, as it interprets the Constitution. It ruled in *Chapman v. California* (1967) that "we cannot leave to the States the formulation of . . . remedies designed to protect people from infractions by the States of federally guaranteed rights."[88]

The passage of the 14th Amendment allowed the U.S. Supreme Court to enforce the Bill of Rights against state governments. The 14th Amendment contained what has come to be called the "equal protection clause," which prevents a governmental authority from denying an individual equal protection of the laws, such as laws that guarantee civil rights. It was used to force states to provide the same protection under law to individuals of all races.

Amount of Process Due   An accused person is afforded rights even beyond those enumerated in the Constitution and state and federal law. For example, the 14th Amendment's due process clause also prohibits practices that fail to meet a standard of fundamental fairness, even if they do not violate a specific provision.[89] Furthermore, the rights of due process, along with the others enumerated in the U.S. Constitution, can never be repealed by the states. Individual states may add additional rights by amending their own constitutions, but they cannot take away or restrict those guaranteed by the Constitution. Additionally, substantive due process significantly strengthens the power of judicial review. The Supreme Court has retained more extensive discretion in deciding which rights are "substantive" and deserve protection.

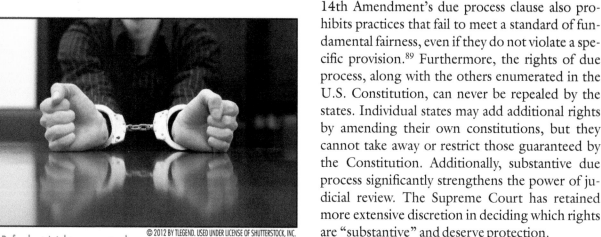

Defendants' rights, guaranteed by the U.S. Constitution, are the subject of controversy.

© 2012 BY TLEGEND. USED UNDER LICENSE OF SHUTTERSTOCK, INC.

Defendants' Rights   In the American criminal justice system, a defendant is presumed innocent unless and until proven guilty. The burden of proof rests on the prosecution (the state); the prosecution must prove that the defendant is guilty rather than the accused proving they are innocent. In practice, this makes it much more difficult to convict a defendant, as he or she must be proved guilty beyond a **reasonable doubt**. If a judge or jury concludes there is a reasonable doubt the defendant committed the crime, the defendant must be acquitted.

These defendants' rights, and the guarantees enshrined in the U.S. Constitution, were influenced by the fear of tyrannical government. Under the Constitution, everyone is equal in the eyes of the law. The accused must not be painted as the enemy of the state and must be judged by the rule of law (e.g., due process and criminal procedure). The rule of law is crucial because, according to J.H. Skolnick, "its essential element is the reduction of arbitrariness by officials."[90]

Defendants' rights are the subject of controversy. Critics believe that too many guilty people go free because of these rights, while proponents claim that these rights are necessary to spare the innocent from unjust prosecution. Both sides, of course, are correct, as experience has shown that these rights generally protect innocent persons, and on occasion let an apparently guilty person go free. In the words of Judge Henry Friendly, this is not an unjust result, for most Americans "would allow a considerable number of guilty persons to go free than to convict an appreciable number of innocent men."[91]

Remedies for Violations   While the law provides remedies for violations of judicial procedure or due process, the hope is that these violations never occur. Accordingly, the law provides procedural safeguards to ensure these violations do not occur. For instance, after a suspect is arrested, his or her case must be reviewed by a prosecutor or magistrate. This process ensures that the police follow the rules of due process and have probable cause to believe the arrested person committed the crime with which he or she is being charged.

Another legal tool is the right to petition for a writ of habeas corpus, which allows criminal defendants to compel the government to explain why it has detained them. This writ is a procedural device that protects persons against unjust imprisonment. It does not, however, protect persons against false arrest, so the scope of this power is more limited than commonly imagined.[92]

Another remedy for violations of criminal procedure or due process is the exclusionary rule. This rule holds that evidence is inadmissible in court if it was improperly obtained. The rule rests on the notion that evidence obtained through an unreasonable search and seizure was obtained by violating the civil rights of the suspect. This evidence is called the **fruit of the poisonous tree**, since it is evidence that was tainted from its source.[93]

As mentioned in the sections dealing with appellate courts, convicted persons may appeal their convictions to a higher court. All states provide appellate review of some sort, and that right cannot be constrained by the appellant's financial limitations. Accordingly, the state must provide an attorney for the defendant, as well as a trial transcript he or she can use during the appeals process. On appeal, an appellant must demonstrate that the trial court made a legal, not factual, error. His or her arguments also must be presented in an **appellate brief**, which is a written legal argument presented to the panel of judges to persuade them that a legal error was made in the trial court, and the trial court's or trial jury's decision should be reversed.[94]

Reasonable doubt
The standard of guilt that the state must meet to convict a criminal defendant; if reasonable doubt exists, the defendant must be acquitted.

Fruit of the poisonous tree
Evidence obtained by law enforcement as a result of an illegal search or seizure.

Appellate brief
A written memorandum filed by the prosecution or defense attorney to explain why the decision of a lower court was erroneous.

Ethics and Professionalism: The Disgraced Duke Prosecutor

Law enforcement officers and prosecuting attorneys are held to a high ethical standard. The 2006 rape allegations filed against the Duke University lacrosse team provide a contemporary example of the dangers wrought by the abuse of prosecutorial power. For his actions during that prosecution, former Durham County, North Carolina District Attorney Mike Nifong was removed from his post and disbarred. As prosecutor, Nifong prosecuted several white Duke lacrosse players who were accused of raping an African-American stripper at an off-campus team party. Although initially praised for his willingness to pursue such a case, Nifong ultimately came under fire for his ethical conduct during the investigation and trial.

Nifong first was criticized for making inflammatory and prejudicial statements, including unfounded accusations about the accused, as well as for omitting exculpatory evidence (evidence tending to exonerate the accused) from the DNA report of the victim's rape. In fact, the full report detected the presence of body fluids from several men who were not charged, and it was later revealed that no DNA evidence implicated the men charged. Nifong claimed this omission was an accident, but his claim was later revealed to be inaccurate, showing his serious breach of the rules of ethics and discovery.

Nifong's misconduct, coupled with the witness's continued changing of her story, ultimately resulted in the charges being dropped.[95] But the damage was done. Nifong was hit with ethics charges by the North Carolina State Bar. He was charged with making prejudicial statements and perpetrating a "systematic abuse of prosecutorial discretion" by withholding the DNA evidence.[96] Nifong was subsequently suspended and disbarred. He was later jailed for one day for contempt of court, and recently filed for bankruptcy after being sued by the accused lacrosse players.

Law Enforcement Investigations Before setting the machinery of the judicial system in motion, the relevant law enforcement agency (usually local or state police) must conduct its investigation. These investigations, like their later prosecutions, must abide by the rules of due process and criminal procedure.

Criminal procedures vary from state to state, but their grounding principles are found in the U.S. Constitution and Bill of Rights. Although the Constitution regulates searches and seizures, as well as interrogations and the right to counsel, law enforcement agencies may conduct investigations free from the interference of the courts. For example, the Constitution does not require police to articulate a reason for focusing their efforts on a certain suspect before investigating him or her.[97]

Law enforcement officials must follow specific guidelines when arresting a suspect, including the reading of Miranda rights, to properly protect the suspect's rights.

The Warrant Requirement and Exceptions

Police use two types of warrants to investigate and apprehend suspected criminals: an arrest warrant and a search warrant. An arrest warrant is issued by a judge or magistrate and authorizes the arrest of a specific person for a specific crime. The majority of arrests occur "in the field," and these arrests do not require an arrest warrant as long as the officer has probable cause to believe the person being arrested has committed a specific crime for which the arrest is authorized. Common law countries allow police officers to take a person into custody if they believe he or she has committed a felony.

Warrant

Legal authorization from a judge to make an arrest, conduct a search or seize evidence.

The second type of warrant, a search warrant, authorizes police to search and seize premises for items or information listed specifically in the warrant. With few exceptions, police must have a search warrant before conducting a search and seizure. One exception is that police may search for and seize evidence if the evidence is likely to be destroyed before they can obtain a warrant. They also may search for and seize evidence if a crime is currently being committed, or if the owner of the evidence explicitly consents to the search.[98] Officers can enter only the address listed on the warrant, and search only in the areas and for the items listed.[99]

Identification

Before entering a residence, police generally are required to announce their entry and intent to search. However, if the police have reason to believe the evidence will be destroyed or they will be injured, they may enter unannounced. If police identify themselves and request the right to search the premises and the suspect or property owner agrees, they generally do not need to obtain a warrant to search the premises.[100]

Arrest, Search, and Seizure

A person cannot be arrested unless the police have probable cause to believe he or she has committed a crime. Probable cause is determined by the judge who signs the arrest warrant, or by a magistrate after the arrest. In a longer-term investigation in which a grand jury has been convened, the grand jury determines if there is probable cause.[101]

When a police officer makes an arrest and holds the suspect in custody, he or she must read a suspect his or her Miranda rights before asking the suspect any questions relating to the crime. This procedure derives its name from the case of *Miranda v. Arizona* (1966) and safeguards a suspect's rights against self-incrimination under the Fifth Amendment when he or she is subjected to police interrogation.[102] In brief, the Miranda requirements are satisfied if officers read suspects a warning, which often is written on a "Miranda card," that they have the right to remain silent, as their words may be used against them, and have the right to an attorney, even if they are unable to afford one.[103]

© 2012 BY LISA F. YOUNG. USED UNDER LICENSE OF SHUTTERSTOCK, INC.

Officers have the right to stop and question individuals if they see or suspect that a crime or violation has been committed.

Exhibit: Miranda Rights

"In the absence of other effective measures, the following procedures to safeguard the Fifth Amendment privilege must be observed: the person in custody must, prior to interrogation, be clearly informed that he has the right to remain silent, and that anything he says will be used against him in court; he must be clearly informed that he has the right to consult with a lawyer and to have the lawyer with him during interrogation, and that, if he is indigent, a lawyer will be appointed to represent him" (*Miranda v. Arizona*, 1966).

Before questioning a suspect who is in custody, law enforcement officers must issue a Miranda warning (the exact wording of the text varies slightly from state to state, but essentially conforms to the example shown below adapted from the Kansas City Police Department.[104]).

1. You have the right to remain silent.
2. Anything you say can and will be used against you in a court of law.
3. You have the right to talk to a lawyer and have him present with you while you are being questioned.
4. If you cannot afford to hire a lawyer, one will be appointed to represent you before any questioning, if you wish.
5. You can decide at any time to exercise these rights and not answer any questions or make any statements.

The following questions should be asked after the specific warning has been made, and an affirmative reply is returned to each question. This secures a waiver to legally question the suspect, such that their responses will be admissible in court.

1. Do you understand each of these rights I have explained to you?
2. Having these rights in mind, do you wish to talk to us now?

Custodial interrogation

The questioning of a witness by law enforcement while he or she is under arrest.

Custodial Interrogations   The Miranda rights of suspects have expanded over time, reflecting a growing concern during the 1960s with **custodial interrogations**, or the questioning of a suspect in custody. Specifically, several of the U.S. Supreme Court's decisions underscore its desire to control custodial interrogations, such as those that occur in a police station, to ensure the police do not harass or intimidate minority defendants and the impoverished, or others who cannot easily pursue traditional avenues of recourse.[105] Miranda rights now apply to people being questioned by the police as part of a criminal investigation, as well as to those arrested. People may waive these rights before speaking to an officer, but all investigations that occur when a person is in custody require the police to notify him or her of the Miranda rights.[106]

Similarly, the validity of confessions obtained by law enforcement is interpreted through the lens of the Fifth Amendment to the Constitution, which states that "no person shall be compelled in any criminal case to be a witness against himself."[107] This means that confessions must be voluntary and uncoerced (the suspect must not be under threat of torture, for instance). For the purposes of custodial interrogation, the interrogated person must acknowledge his or her Miranda rights for such a statement to be admissible in court.[108]

Pretrial Proceedings

Before trial, a defendant appears in the initial, or bail, appearance, as well in as a preliminary hearing.

In a preliminary hearing held before a judge, the defense often presents witness testimony to argue there is insufficient evidence to justify the arrest of the accused. Preliminary hearings are used when a grand jury has not returned an indictment, although a grand jury can also be used after a preliminary hearing to approve the prosecutor's case.

The purpose of a grand jury and a preliminary hearing is to ensure there is probable cause to charge a person with a crime.[109] Preliminary hearings are important because they represent the first time someone other than a law enforcement officer or prosecutor has reviewed the case, thus providing a layer of protection against a baseless charge, as well as the unnecessary humiliation of trial. During these hearings, the burden of proof on the prosecution is far less than it is at trial; it merely must prove it has a *prima facie* (at first sight) case, which requires it to show only that there is probable cause to believe a crime was committed by the accused.[110] This standard of proof, probable cause, is the same used by judges to decide whether to issue an arrest or search warrant. Not all states require preliminary hearings, and such hearings are normally reserved for serious felonies.

The Initial Appearance

The initial appearance in court is the time when a criminal defendant stands in court and hears the formal charges levied against him or her. The defendant enters a plea at this point, most often by declaring himself or herself guilty or not guilty. If the defendant does not yet have an attorney and cannot afford one, the court will appoint one at the public's expense. At this hearing, the official complaint, or list of charges brought by the police, is assessed by a magistrate. These first appearances also are known as bail hearings, at which magistrates determine the legality of the arrest and set bail.[111]

Grand Jury and Indictment

Grand juries are different from trial juries. Grand juries consist of 16–23 people who hear evidence about the crime committed. Usually, the evidence is presented to the grand jury in a secret session by a prosecutor. The grand jury's task is to determine if probable cause exists to believe that the suspect committed a criminal offense.[112] In felony cases, a grand jury returns a formal charge called an indictment, which represents its judgment that there is probable cause to believe the defendant committed a crime.[113]

Grand juries do not, however, decide a defendant's ultimate guilt or innocence; that task is left to the trial judge or trial jury. Additionally, grand jury witnesses are not entitled to have their attorneys present, and the suspect's attorney also has no right to be present, since a grand jury is not a criminal court. Historically, grand juries overwhelmingly return the indictment requested by prosecutors.[114]

Initial appearance
The court hearing at which a defendant hears the formal charges levied against him or her.

Complaint
A document listing the criminal charges brought against a defendant.

Grand jury
A group of 16–23 people that hears evidence and decides if probable cause exists to believe a person has committed a crime.

Indictment
A written document issued by a grand jury to indicate that there is probable cause to believe a person has committed a crime.

Critical Thinking

Do you think grand juries are necessary in pretrial proceedings, especially if they generally side with prosecutors? Should they be replaced by preliminary hearings? Why or why not?

.— SUPERIOR COURT OF THE STATE OF CALIFORNIA
FOR THE COUNTY OF LOS ANGELES

THE PEOPLE OF THE STATE OF CALIFORNIA,

                                  Plaintiff,

             v.

01 ROBERT BLAKE (9/18/1933),
     aka MICHAEL GUBITOSI, and
02 EARLE S. CALDWELL (3/18/1956)

                             Defendant(s).

CASE NO. LA040377

FELONY COMPLAINT

The undersigned is informed and believes that:

COUNT 1

On or about May 4, 2001, in the County of Los Angeles, the crime of MURDER, in violation of PENAL CODE SECTION 187(a), a Felony, was committed by ROBERT BLAKE, who did unlawfully, and with malice aforethought murder BONNY LEE BAKLEY, a human being. "NOTICE: The above offense is a serious felony within the meaning of Penal Code section 1192.7(c)."

"NOTICE: Conviction of this offense will require you to provide specimens and samples pursuant to Penal Code section 296. Willful refusal to provide the specimens and samples is a crime."

It is further alleged that said defendant(s), ROBERT BLAKE personally and intentionally discharged a firearm, a handgun, which proximately caused great bodily injury and death to BONNY LEE BAKLEY within the meaning of Penal Code section 12022.53(d).

It is further alleged that the murder of Bonny Lee Bakley was by defendant(s), ROBERT BLAKE and that the defendant(s) intentionally killed the victim by means of lying in wait, within the meaning of Penal Code Section 190.2(a)(15).

* * * * *

At the defendant's initial appearance, the official complaint is assessed by a magistrate.

Bail   Bail is normally set at the initial appearance or bail hearing stage of the trial. Bail is determined by a judge or magistrate, who considers the seriousness of the crime, the risk the defendant poses to society, and the likelihood that the defendant will flee the court's jurisdiction before trial. If the judge believes the defendant deserves bail, he or she then assigns an amount sufficient to ensure the defendant will appear in court. Bail is usually paid either in cash from the defendant or by bond from a bail bondsman. **Bail** bonds are essentially insurance policies, and the court is the beneficiary if the defendant flees. Excessive bail is prohibited by the Eighth Amendment.

Discovery   **Discovery** is the court-ordered process by which attorneys learn about their opponents' cases before trial. The discovery process commonly includes depositions (testimony under oath), exchanges of interrogatories (written questions), requests for admissions (requests to admit the truth or falsity of statements), and requests for production of documents.[115]

Discovery is very limited in criminal cases because information procured by the defense conceivably can be used to harass or intimidate prosecution witnesses.[116] Nonetheless, the prosecution is obligated by law to, at a minimum, provide the defense any materials that appear to show the defendant is not guilty. In addition, the prosecution must provide the defense any materials that tend to impeach, or diminish, the credibility of any witnesses who will testify for the prosecution at trial. Police reports, laboratory results, forensic evidence, medical tests, ballistics reports, and witness statements are other categories of information that prosecutors provide to defense attorneys during discovery.

Prosecutors usually are required to disclose more information in discovery than defense attorneys must disclose. Still, prosecutors often seek to limit the materials they disclose, for fear that disclosing certain categories of evidence (such as witness statements) will lead witnesses to be intimidated and deterred from testifying at trial. Broadly speaking, discovery of physical evidence and confessions made by the defendant is considered a right of the defense, but written and recorded witness statements are more problematic.[117]

Suppression Hearing   A **suppression hearing** is a hearing held if the defense asks the judge to suppress, or disallow, a piece of evidence that it believes the state obtained illegally during the criminal investigation. Usually, motions (requests) to suppress evidence contend that the evidence was obtained only by violating the defendant's Fourth Amendment or Fifth Amendment rights. Defense attorneys may, for example, ask the judge to suppress a confession if the accused was not informed of his or her Miranda rights or was coerced to confess. They also may ask the judge to suppress the evidence gained from a search if the search was conducted without a warrant or otherwise illegally (i.e., fruit of the poisonous tree). If the search was not conducted during an arrest with a warrant or if the evidence was not in **plain view**, then the results of the search may be inadmissible in court.[118]

Other motions may challenge the accuracy of the indictment, charge the prosecution with entrapment or delay, or contend that the accused already has

Bail
A sum of money that the court receives if a defendant flees from court proceedings.

Discovery
The court-ordered process by which attorneys learn about their opponents' cases to prepare for trial.

During discovery, both testimonial evidence, such as an eyewitness account, and physical evidence, such as fingerprints, are presented.

Suppression hearing
A pretrial hearing where a defendant asks the court to suppress, or disallow, evidence that the police obtained illegally.

Plain view
A method by which police observe physical evidence that is plainly visible to the human eye, without the need for an intrusive search.

been acquitted or convicted of the crime charged (double jeopardy). In addition, the defense may lodge motions about the defendant's physical or mental competency to stand trial.[119] A defendant may also claim that his or her right to a speedy trial has been violated, requiring the judge to dismiss the charge.

Critical Thinking
If evidence obtained through improper procedure turns out to be factually true and is critical to the case, should it be used anyway? Explain.

Speedy Trial Act
A federal law requiring district courts to ensure that a criminal defendant is brought to trial no later than 100 days after his or her arrest, with some exceptions.

Speedy Trials   Under the Sixth Amendment, accused individuals have the right to a fair and speedy trial. The goal of this provision is to prevent undue incarceration before trial, reduce anxiety, and ensure that a delay does not hinder the defense. In 1974, Congress passed the **Speedy Trial Act**. With certain exceptions, the act requires district courts to ensure that criminal cases are heard no later than 100 days after the defendant is arrested. Most states have enacted similar statutes, but they have proven difficult to enforce. It is sometimes difficult to prove that a delay is intentional rather than inherent in the system.[120]

Defendants also have the right to a trial by a jury of their peers. The Sixth Amendment enjoins that a speedy trial shall be conducted by an impartial jury in the state where the crime was committed. The phrase "impartial jury" is problematic for due process. Peremptory challenges to a juror's eligibility based on race have been banned,[121] but attorneys still have a great deal of power over who serves on a jury during *voir dire*, when the jury pool is questioned to determine if potential jurors have any specific biases.[122] The jury selection process has been shown by research to be inherently prejudiced against racial minorities, the poor, women, and those of lower educational achievement.[123] This raises a question of fairness in relation to due process: does the makeup of the jury become a right of due process in its own right? Also, whose right is preeminent, that of the victim who has been wronged or the accused on trial?

Plea
A defendant's in-court statement that he or she is guilty, is not guilty, or will not contest criminal charges.

Nolo contendere
A plea in which the defendant does not admit the charges, but will not contest them.

Verdict
Finding of guilt or innocence by a judge or jury.

Pleas   A **plea** is a defendant's formal, in-court assertion that he or she is guilty or not guilty of the criminal charges.[124] At the arraignment or initial appearance, the accused is advised of his or her rights and invited to enter a plea. Aside from pleading guilty or not guilty, a defendant may plead *nolo contendere*, which means that the defendant does not admit the charges, but will not contest them.[125] A defendant may plead guilty to the charges at any point during the judicial process, as well as negotiate with prosecutors to reach a **plea bargain** agreement, in which the defendant agrees to plead guilty to a lesser charge in exchange for more lenient treatment at the time of sentencing.[126] After a judge accepts a guilty plea, the defendant is sentenced by a judge or jury. Most criminal cases do not result in a finding of guilt or innocence by a judge or jury (**verdict**), but instead are settled by plea bargains.

Chapter Summary

- The American court system was derived from the common law system inherited from England. From this system, the founding fathers derived their basic understanding of fundamental rights, including habeas corpus, the right to trial by jury, the authority of judicial precedent, and due process. Though there were administrative and procedural differences across the colonies, this common legal heritage was the foundation of the American legal system.

- The U.S. court system consists of two parallel judicial structures: state and federal courts. These structures largely mirror each other; both have lower (trial) courts, which hear evidence, try cases, and reach verdicts, in addition to appeals courts, which review the decisions of lower courts. Federal courts handle "federal questions," which deal with explicitly federal law, and legal issues arising between states.

- The United States Supreme Court is the ultimate legal arbiter in the United States on questions of federal law. It has the prerogative of interpreting the Constitution, the highest law in the land. Legislatures, at any level, are bound to abide by the Constitution. If a law or statute contravenes the Constitution, the Supreme Court may declare it unconstitutional. Cases appealed to the Supreme Court from lower courts may be overturned, thus generating case law that becomes binding precedent for the entire American legal system.

- Due process and criminal process provide extensive procedures to safeguard criminal defendants against oppression by the state. The guiding principle is that it is better to let many guilty persons go free than to convict one innocent person. Fundamental, or "natural," rights not explicitly enumerated in the Constitution have been incorporated as substantive due process, largely through the 14th Amendment.

- The Bill of Rights determines the boundaries of "fair play," or due process. The rights enumerated, such as the protections against self-incrimination and unreasonable search and seizure, have been updated to keep pace with the electronic and digital age (ex., wiretaps).

Critical Thinking?

1. Do the procedural protections afforded to criminal defendants lessen the rights available to other participants in the court system? Explain.
2. Under what circumstances may a law enforcement officer lawfully take the confession of a criminal suspect?
3. Does the requirement of a speedy trial benefit a criminal defendant and the prosecution equally? Discuss.
4. How, if at all, are due process protections affected by the racial, ethnic, and socioeconomic makeup of a trial jury pool?

5. When may a police officer search a person's home without a warrant? Do you think that all searches should require a warrant? Explain.

6. May a person refuse to allow a police officer to enter his or her home if the officer does not have a warrant? Explain.

7. Should victims have a Bill of Rights in the same way that the accused do? Why or why not?

8. Is it fair to allow attorneys to share information during the discovery phase? Explain.

9. Is the right to a speedy trial necessary? Is speed or reaching the truth deliberately more important? Why?

10. Why is the Fifth Amendment important to the accused? How might a person incriminate himself or herself even if he or she did not commit a crime?

Media

United States Courts http://www.uscourts.gov/Home.aspx

The website for the federal court system in the United States provides information on federal courts in local areas, as well as educational resources for students and teachers wishing to learn more about the federal judiciary.

Supreme Court of the United States http://www.supremecourt.gov/

The website for the U.S. Supreme Court includes resources related to recent decisions, current justices, court history, and the court's docket.

Code of Conduct for U.S. Judges http://www.uscourts.gov/guide/vol2/ch1.html

This website details the ethical and professional conduct expected of federal judges, and includes information on circumstances in which judges must recuse themselves and relevant disciplinary action.

Rules of Conduct for Lawyers http://www.abanet.org

The website for the American Bar Association, the regulating body for licensed attorneys in the United States, includes information on the ethical standards to which lawyers must adhere, as well as infractions that could lead to disbarment.

Endnotes

1. Locke, M., Neff, J., & Curliss, A. (2010, August 7). *Scathing SBI Audit Says 230 Cases Tainted by Shoddy Investigations*. Retrieved May 13, 2011 from http://www.newsobserver.com/2010/08/19/635632/scathing-sbi-audit-says-230-cases.html

2. Waggoner, M. (2010, September 15). "N.C. Lab Scandal Effects Continue in Court System." *The Herald-Sun*.

3. Innocence Project. (n.d.). *The Causes of Wrongful Conviction*. Retrieved May 15, 2011 from http://www.innocence project.org/understand/

4. Mecham, L. R. (2011). *Understanding Federal and State Courts*. Retrieved May 2, 2011 from http://www.uscourts.gov/EducationalResources/FederalCourtBasics/CourtStructure/UnderstandingFederalAndStateCourts.aspx

5. Neubauer, D. W. (1979). *America's Courts and the Criminal Justice System*. Belmont, CA: Wadsworth, 23.

6. Bergman, P., & Berman-Barrett, S. J. (2008). *Represent Yourself In Court: How to Prepare & Try a Winning Case* (6th ed.). Berkeley: Nolo, 481.

7. Breyer, S., et al. (2001). *Administrative Law & Regulatory Policy* (5th ed.). New York, NY: Aspen.

8. Garner, B. A. (2001). *A Dictionary of Modern Legal Usage* (revised ed.). New York, NY: Oxford University Press, 177–178.

9. Arnold-Baker, C. (2008). *The Companion to British History*. London, UK: Loncross Denholm Press, 484.

10. Orth, J. V. (2002). "Common Law." In K. L. Hall (Ed.), *The Oxford Companion to American Law*. New York, NY: Oxford University Press.

11. Arnold-Baker, 2008.

12. Curry, J. A., Riley, R. B., & Battistoni, R. M. (2003). *Constitutional Government: The American Experience* (5th ed.). Dubuque, IA: Kendall Hunt, 35.

13. Hoffer, P. (2002). "History of American Law: Colonial Period." In K. L. Hall (Ed.), *The Oxford Companion to American Law*. New York, NY: Oxford University Press, 365.

14. Orth, 2002, 126.

15. Curry et al., 2003, 31.

16. Ibid., 36.

17. Middleton, R. (2002). *Colonial America: A History, 1565–1776* (3rd ed.). Padstow, UK: Blackwell.

18. Elson, H. W. (1904). *History of the United States of America*. New York, NY: MacMillan, 210–216.

19. Hoffer, 2002, 366–367.

20. Ibid., 367.

21. U.S. Department of Justice (1976). *Two Hundred Years of American Criminal Justice*. Washington, DC: Government Printing Office.

22. Glick, H., & Vines, K. (1973). *State Court Systems*. Englewood Cliffs, NJ: Prentice-Hall.

23. Curry et al., 2003.

24. Glick & Vines, 1973.

25. Curry et al., 2003, 53.

26. Neubauer, 1979, 46.

27. Richardson, R., & Vines, K. (1970). *The Politics of the Federal Courts*. Boston, MA: Little, Brown, 20–21.

28. Curry et al., 2003, 81.

29. Hoffer, 2002, 367.

30. U.S. Constitution, Article III.

31. Curry et al., 2003, 36.

32. Ibid., 53.

33. Graber, M. A. (2002). "Court Systems." In K. L. Hall (Ed.), *The Oxford Companion to American Law*. New York, NY: Oxford University Press, 182–183.

34. O'Brien, D. M. (2000). *Constitutional Law and Politics: Struggles for Power and Governmental Accountability* (4th ed., vol. 1). New York, NY: W.W. Norton and Company, 46–47.

35. Curry et al., 2003, 62.

36. Ibid., 46.

37. Pittman, R. C. (1953). "Judicial Supremacy in America: Its Colonial and Constitutional History." *Georgia Bar Journal, 16*, 148.

38. U.S. Constitution, Article III.

39. O'Brien, 2000, 23.

40. Garner, B. A. (2004). *Black's Law Dictionary* (8th ed.). St. Paul, MN: Thomson/West, 980.

41. Adamany, D. (2002). "Judicial Review." In K. L. Hall (Ed.), *The Oxford Companion to American Law*. New York: Oxford University Press, 441.

42. O'Brien, 2000, 31.

43. *Marbury v. Madison*, 5 U.S. (1 Cranch) 137 (1803).

44. 5 U.S. (1 Cranch) at 177–178.

45. Ritchie, D. A. (2002). "Government, United States." In K. L. Hall (Ed.), *The Oxford Companion to American Law*. New York, NY: Oxford University Press.

46. O'Brien, 2000.

47. Adamany, 2002, 441.

48. Ibid., 444.

49. Rottman, D. B., Flango, C. R., Cantrell, M. T., & Hansen, R. L. (2000, June). *State Court Organization 1998*. Retrieved May 17, 2011 from http://bjs.ojp.usdoj.gov/content/pub/pdf/sco98.pdf

50. Black, H. C. (1990). *Black's Law Dictionary* (6th ed.). St. Paul, MN: West, 1557.
51. U.S. Constitution, Amendment 10.
52. Hall, M. G. (2002). "Courts, United States: State and Local Courts." In K. L. Hall (Ed.), *The Oxford Companion to American Law.* New York, NY: Oxford University Press, 177.
53. Wheeler, R., & Whitcomb, H. (1974). "The Literature of Court Administration: A Bibliographical Essay." *Arizona State Law Journal,* 689–722.
54. *Advanced Report, State Court Caseload Statistics: Annual Report, 1975.* (1978). Williamsburg, VA: National Center for State Courts.
55. Hall, 2002, 178.
56. Rottman et al., 2000, 315.
57. Hall, 2002, 178.
58. Rottman et al., 2000, viii.
59. Ibid., 75.
60. Hall, 2002, 178.
61. Mecham, 2011.
62. Carp, R. (2002). Courts, United States: Federal Courts. In K. L. Hall (Ed.), *The Oxford Companion to American Law.* New York: Oxford University Press, 176–177.
63. Ibid.
64. Gluck, Susan Mezey, D. (2002). United States Courts: Juvenile Courts. In K. L. Hall (Ed.), *The Oxford Companion to American Law.* New York: Oxford University Press, 180–182.
65. Carp, 2002, 174.
66. 28 U.S.C. § 1331.
67. Grossman, J. (1965). *Lawyers and Judges: The ABA and the Politics of Judicial Selection.* New York, NY: John Wiley.
68. Ibid, 14.
69. Jackson, D. D. (1974). *Judges.* New York, NY: Atheneum, 7.
70. Office of the Federal Defender, Eastern District of California. (n.d.). *Sentencing.* Retrieved from http://www.cae-fpd.org/Client_Sentencing.pdf
71. Mecham, 2011, 19–20.
72. Ibid., 13–14.
73. Ibid.
74. 28 U.S.C. § 631.
75. Mecham, 2011, 9.
76. Carp, 2002, 117.
77. O'Brien, 2002, 771–776.
78. Ibid., 26.
79. Supreme Court of the United States. (2011). *Frequently Asked Questions.* Retrieved from http://www.supremecourt.gov/faq.aspx#faqgi9
80. O'Brien, 2002, 771.
81. Administrative Office of the U.S. Courts. (2003). *Understanding the Federal Courts.* Retrieved May 8, 2011 from http://www.uscourts.gov/EducationalResources/FederalCourtBasics/UnderstandingTheFederalCourts.aspx
82. *Murray v. Hoboken Land,* 59 U.S. 272 (1855).
83. Brown, R. L. (2002). "Due Process: Procedural." In K. L. Hall (Ed.), *The Oxford Companion to American Law.* New York, NY: Oxford University Press, 232.
84. Sandefur, T. (2010). *The Right to Earn a Living: Economic Freedom and the Law.* Washington, DC: Cato Institute, 90–100.
85. White, G. E. (2000). *The Constitution and the New Deal.* Cambridge, MA: Harvard University Press, 244–246.
86. *Palko v. Connecticut,* 302 U.S. 319 (1937).
87. U.S. Constitution, Amendments 1–10.
88. *Chapman v. California,* 386 U.S. 18, 22 (1967).
89. *In re Winship,* 397 U.S. 358 (1970).

90. Skolnick, J. H. (1966). *Justice Without Trial: Law Enforcement in Democratic Society*. New York, NY: John Wiley, 8.

91. Friendly, H. J. (1968). *The Fifth Amendment Tomorrow: The Case for Constitutional Change*. 37 U. Cin. L. Rev. 671, 694.

92. Krislov, D. R. (2002). "Habeas Corpus." In K. L. Hall (Ed.), *The Oxford Companion to American Law*. New York, NY: Oxford University Press, 349.

93. Dressler, J. (2002). *Understanding Criminal Procedure* (3rd ed.). Newark, NJ: LexisNexis.

94. Mecham, 2011, 26.

95. Washington Post. (2006, December 31). *Prosecutorial Indiscretion*. Retrieved from http://www.washingtonpost.com/wp-dyn/content/article/2006/12/30/AR2006123000886.html?referrer=emailarticle

96. North Carolina State Bar. (2007, June 16). *State Bar Verdict on Nifong*. Retrieved May 19, 2011 from http://www.ncbar.com/Nifong%20Findings.pdf

97. Meyer, L. R. (2002). "Criminal Procedure." In K. L. Hall (Ed.), *The Oxford Companion to American Law*. New York, NY: Oxford University Press, 651–652.

98. *Groh v. Ramirez*, 540 U.S. 551, 564–65 (2004).

99. American Civil Liberties Union. (2010). *Know Your Rights: What to Do If You're Stopped by Police, Immigration Agents or the FBI*. Retrieved from http://www.aclu.org/drug-law-reform-immigrants-rights-racial-justice/know-your-rights-what-do-if-you

100. Ibid.

101. Ibid.

102. *Miranda v. Arizona*, 384 U.S. 436 (1966).

103. Meyer, 2002.

104. Kansas City, MO Police Department. (2006). *Miranda Warning and Miranda Waiver*, pp. 384 U.S. 467–473. Retrieved from http://www.kcpd.org/masterindex/files/PI/PI0605.pdf

105. Meyer, 2002, 652.

106. Curry et al., 2003, ch. X.

107. *Bram v. United States*, 168 U.S. 532, 542 (1897).

108. *Miranda v. Arizona*, 384 U.S. 436 (1966); *California v. Hodari D.*, 499 U.S. 621, 626 (1991).

109. Meyer, 652.

110. *United States v. Sokolow*, 490 U.S. 1 (1989).

111. Meyer, 2002, 652.

112. Mecham, 2011, 39.

113. Ibid, 40.

114. Spain, J. (1961). "The Grand Jury, Past and Present: A Survey." *American Criminal Law Quarterly, 2*, 126–142.

115. Mecham, 2011, 38.

116. Bishop, J. (1978). *Studies in Comparative Civil and Criminal Procedure* (vol. 2). Sydney: Law Reform Commission.

117. Ibid.

118. *Arizona v. Hicks*, 480 U.S. 321 (1987).

119. Meyer, 653.

120. Downs, D. A., & Ruggiero, C. (2002). "Fair Trial, Criminal." In K. L. Hall (Ed.), *The Oxford Companion to American Law*. New York, NY: Oxford University Press, 292.

121. *Batson v. Kentucky*, 476 U.S. 79 (1986).

122. Duhaime, L. (n.d.). "Voir Dire Definition." *Duhaime's Legal Dictionary*. Retrieved from http://www.duhaime.org/LegalDictionary/V/VoirDire.aspx

123. Alker, H. R. Jr., Hosticka, C., & Mitchell, M. (1976). "Jury Selection as a Biased Social Process." *Law & Society Review, 11*(1), 9–41.

124. Mecham, 2011, 43.

125. Bibas, S. (2003, July). "Harmonizing Substantive Criminal Law Values and Criminal Procedure: The Case of Alford and Nolo contendere Pleas." *Cornell Law Review, 88*(6).

126. Ibid.

© 2012 BY JUNIAL ENTERPRISES. USED UNDER LICENSE OF SHUTTERSTOCK, INC.

7

Inside a Courtroom

KEY TERMS

Approach the witness, Attorney-client privilege, Bailiff, Bifurcated trial, Case-in-chief, Challenge for cause, Closing argument, Counsel, Court-appointed attorney, Court record, Court reporter, Cross-examination, Defendant, Defense attorney, Degradation ceremony, Direct examination, Expert witness, Judge, Jury nullification, Lay witness, Limited admissibility, Opening statement, Peremptory challenge, Probative value, Prosecutor, Public defender, Sequester, Sidebar, Subpoena, Testimony, Transport officer, Witness

CHAPTER OBJECTIVES

1. Examine the importance of the jury in history of trials.
2. Describe the actual structure of a standard courtroom.
3. Identify the various participants in a courtroom.
4. Discuss the roles of each of the participants.
5. Evaluate how each role is connected and vital to the others.

Case Study: Right to Counsel: *Gideon v. Wainwright*

In 1961, Florida resident Clarence Earl Gideon was accused of breaking and entering into a pool hall with the intention to commit burglary—a combination of offenses that lead to felony charges. At his initial court appearance, Gideon requested that the court appoint an attorney to represent him, as he could not afford to hire one. The judge denied the request, saying that the law in Florida at the time provided appointed attorneys only in capital cases. Gideon was forced to represent himself and conduct his own defense. The jury found him guilty, and he was sentenced to five years in prison.

Gideon made effective use of his time in prison. Using the resources available to him in the prison library, he handwrote an appeal to the U.S. Supreme Court and filed a lawsuit against Louie Wainwright, the Secretary of the Florida Department of Corrections. Gideon argued that as provided by the Sixth Amendment (as applied to the states in the 14th Amendment), the U.S. Supreme Court guaranteed him the right to be represented by counsel, and, therefore, his rights had been violated by the judge's rule to deny him an attorney. Abe Fortas, a well-known attorney from Washington, D.C., was appointed by the U.S. Supreme Court to represent Gideon on the appeal.

The court handed down its unanimous ruling on March 18, 1963: the denial of Gideon's request for appointed counsel did indeed violate his Sixth Amendment right to counsel. The court specified that by requiring Gideon, who was not an attorney, to defend himself, the judicial system had deprived of his right to due process, as provided for in the Eighth Amendment. Further, the court ruled that the U.S. Constitution does not specify whether a criminal case must be capital or non-capital for the accused to have the right to be represented by counsel; therefore, qualified legal representation must be provided in all cases.[1]

Gideon's appeal was affirmed, and the case was returned to the Florida Supreme Court, who, in turn, returned the case to the trial court. Gideon was retried on the original charges with a court-appointed attorney and found not guilty.

The impact of *Gideon v. Wainwright* was far-reaching. In Florida alone, several thousand inmates who had been convicted in a like manner were set free after the ruling. The decision also led to the creation and continued development of the public defender system in the United States. The ruling ensured that not only must indigent defendants be afforded legal counsel, but those court-appointed attorneys must be effectively trained in defense to provide their clients with as fair a trial as possible. The case also inspired a book, *Gideon's Trumpet*, published in 1965, which detailed Clarence Earl Gideon's fight for fair representation. The *Gideon* decision was an important ruling that clarified the rights of criminal defendants as outlined in the U.S. Constitution.[2]

The Courtroom Workgroup

The *courtroom workgroup* plays a hugely important role in criminal justice. This term encompasses the many different players in a courtroom—from the judge to the courtroom staff to the defense

Members of the courtroom workgroup collaborate to move cases through the criminal justice system quickly and fairly.

© 2012 BY TREKANDSHOOT. USED UNDER LICENSE OF SHUTTERSTOCK, INC.

and prosecuting attorneys—and the functions of each. The members of the courtroom workgroup perform particular duties to achieve collaborative goals, such as moving cases through the criminal justice system in a timely fashion and ensuring that justice is pursued fairly. Court operation is based not only on the law but also on the judge's decisions as the highest official in the courtroom.[3]

Workgroups form in all professions, but the courtroom workgroup is unique in that the person at the center—the **defendant**—has very little power. While the system is designed to protect the rights of the accused, the defendant is not involved in most of the proceedings involving the courtroom workgroup. The other participants work together frequently—usually every day—and include the regular courtroom staff, the judge, and any attorneys. These individuals tend to develop a shared set of norms and values from their contact and work. Eisenstein and Jacob (1970) defined the characteristics of the courtroom workgroup as speed, guilt, cohesion, and secrecy.[4] *Speed* indicates the group's desire to dispose of cases quickly rather than administering and dispensing truly fair justice; *guilt* implies the group's belief that the defendant is indeed guilty, despite the idea from the U.S. Constitution that a defendant is considered innocent until proven guilty; *cohesion* is the unity of the individuals as a group, working together toward the common purpose of punishing the defendant; and *secrecy* describes the group's tendency to keep any discussions or negotiations that do not occur in open court private—sometimes even from the defendant. The dynamic of the courtroom workgroup can strongly affect the outcome of a criminal case, sometimes without the defendant knowing what happened.

Defendant
A person charged with a crime.

The Criminal Trial: An Overview
There are two types of criminal trials: a bench trial and a jury trial. A bench trial is a trial argued directly in front of a judge without a jury, with the judge making the sole decision as to the

defendant's guilt or innocence and possible punishment. A jury trial is conducted in front of a jury; the jury listens to all evidence presented and makes the decision as to the guilt or innocence, and later any applicable punishment, of the defendant. The defendant has the right to request either a jury trial or a bench trial, and the choice is generally suggested by the defense attorney as a part of trial strategy.[5] While the U.S. Constitution identifies the right to a jury trial, this was not clarified in all states until the 1968 Supreme Court ruling in *Duncan v. Louisiana*. In *Duncan*, the defendant was charged with a misdemeanor offense that could have resulted in a maximum sentence of two years' imprisonment and a fine of $300. The trial court rejected the defendant's request for a jury trial based on the Louisiana constitution, which allowed jury trials only in cases that could result in a death sentence or hard labor imprisonment. The Supreme Court ruled in favor of Duncan, saying that his right to a jury trial was guaranteed by the Sixth and 14th Amendments.[6]

When the trial begins, the attorneys for each side make opening statements. The **opening statement** is an opportunity for each attorney to provide the jury with a brief summary of what each side intends to show the jury during the trial. The prosecution, which has the burden of proof—the task of demonstrating the guilt of the defendant—makes the first opening statement. The prosecution endeavors to show the jury that it will prove beyond a reasonable doubt that the defendant committed the crime of which he or she is accused.[7] The defense attorney, on the other hand, will focus the opening statement on the weaknesses of the state's case, arguing that the defendant's guilt cannot be proved beyond a reasonable doubt. The manner in which the defense attorney makes the opening statement may vary according to trial strategy. Sometimes attorneys may withhold details during opening statements, preferring to allow particular information to be revealed during the course of the trial. Another tactic is to use a very detailed opening statement, which may be delivered forcefully or passionately in an attempt to predispose the jury to accept the defense's argument.[8]

Opening statement
The initial statement of a trial that an attorney makes to the jury, which outlines the argument that will be made during the trial.

Witnesses help describe the series of events that occurred before, during, and after a crime.

Opening statements are broad, and are not intended—or permitted—to be used as a means for the attorneys to testify or offer evidence. The attorneys from both sides are also bound by "good faith" ethical requirements during opening statements. Each lawyer can mention only the evidence that he or she believes will be presented, and that he or she will be allowed to present during the trial. If either attorney gives the idea that he or she will present evidence that in fact he or she has no intention of presenting, this is not only unprofessional, but has been defined by the U.S. Supreme Court as *professional misconduct*.[9]

The **case-in-chief** is the argument the state's attorney, who is on the side of the prosecution in criminal proceedings, makes against the defendant. It is the job of the state's attorney to show the jury that the defendant committed, or could have committed, the crime of which he or she has been accused. The case-in-chief is different than the case-as-a-whole, as "the case" includes the entire court case and the arguments for guilt or innocence from both sides, the witnesses, and any experts involved.

Witness Testimony

An important part of any criminal trial is the examination of witnesses. This is the primary means by which evidence is introduced in a trial. **Witnesses** have information that helps put together the series of events that occurred before, during, and after the commission of a crime. The **testimony**, or formal statement, from each witness effectively helps paint a picture of what happened, where it happened, how it happened, who caused it to happen, and why it happened. Since the defendant (who may or may not testify), the victim (who may not be able to testify), and the witnesses are the only individuals involved in the trial process who can answer some of these questions definitively, it is important that the judge and jury learn as much information as possible in order to make fair decisions about the defendant's guilt or innocence and any resultant sentence.

Before a witness will be allowed to testify, the attorney questioning the witness must establish that the person is competent to testify. Competency requires that the witness has personal knowledge of the information that he or she will offer and that the witness understands the duty to tell the truth.[10] The trial process relies on the ability of the witness to give accurate and truthful testimony, so it is important to ensure that the witness is capable of telling the truth. This is a practice that developed primarily in the United Kingdom in the 1600s as the adversarial trial process evolved.[11] A **lay witness** is an everyday citizen, who may or may not personally know the defendant or victims involved in the case, who has some personal knowledge about the facts of the case. A spectator at a sporting event who sees an assault occur several seats away would be considered a lay witness if asked to testify in court. It is important to establish that a lay witness is competent and credible to testify because the witness is relaying what occurred that he or she personally witnessed. Incorrect testimony may harm case procedure or the outcome of the case.

Witness competency is also important when an expert witness testifies. An **expert witness** is considered an expert in his or her field of study or work: for example, a physician would be considered an expert in the medical field, while

Case-in-chief
The portion of a criminal case presented by the prosecution.

Witness
An individual who gives testimony in court because he or she has information that is pertinent to the case.

Testimony
The statement of a witness, given under oath, typically in court.

Lay witness
An everyday citizen who has some personal knowledge about the facts of a case.

Expert witness
A person considered to be an expert in his or her profession or field of study who applies that expertise to the facts or circumstances of a case.

an auto mechanic would be considered an expert in the internal working of automobiles. One accepted legal definition of *expert witnesses* is the following: "Persons who through education or experience have developed skill or knowledge in a particular subject so that he or she may form an opinion that will assist the fact finder."[12] The expert witness must be knowledgeable in his or her field, as the information explained by the expert witness has potential bearing on the guilt or innocence of the defendant. A forensic pathologist who testifies in a murder trial about the manner in which a victim died must be as factual and accurate as possible; the judge or jury needs to understand the facts presented in the case so that a decision of guilt or innocence can be made. Because juries may not be qualified to evaluate the validity of presented scientific evidence, the U.S. Supreme Court ruled in *Daubert v. Merrill Dow Pharmaceuticals* (1993) that judges have the duty to perform preliminary evaluations of the scientific basis of any expert testimony prior to allowing the expert to testify in the presence of the jury.[13]

When a witness is first called to the stand to testify, this is called **direct examination**. If the witness is called to testify by the state's attorney, the witness is referred to as a witness for the prosecution. If the witness is called to the stand and questioned by the defendant's legal counsel, or **defense attorney**, the witness is referred to as a witness for the defense. When the witness is being questioned directly, he or she may be asked questions that may be answered with a simple "yes" or "no," or the witness may be asked "narrative" questions, which allow the witness to tell a version of events in his or her own words. During direct examination, the judge will not allow the attorneys to ask "leading questions," which are questions that suggest the answer within the question. A basic example of such a question would be, "You called the police immediately after hearing the shots, correct?"

Any witness who offers testimony in a criminal trial is subject to being cross-examined. **Cross-examination** is the questioning of a witness by someone other than the direct examiner. After a witness for the defense is questioned directly by the defense attorney, the witness is then available to be cross-examined by the **prosecutor**, or the attorney who represents the state and argues the criminal case against the defendant. Cross-examination tests a witness's credibility and memory by challenging facts that have been entered into evidence by the witness's testimony.[14] The cross-examiner may attempt to discredit the witness by questioning the witness's physical or mental status, criminal record, or prior inconsistencies in the witness's statements. Cross-examination may be followed by redirect examination by the state's attorney, which would attempt to clarify anything to which the witness testified under cross-examination. This procedure continues cycling until all the side's witnesses have been called and all evidence presented.[15]

Several Supreme Court rulings have addressed cross-examination of witnesses. In *Ohio v. Roberts* (1980), the court ruled that a statement made by a witness outside of the courtroom could be introduced during trial as long as there were sufficient "indicia of reliability," even if the witness was not available to testify at trial.[16] In the *Roberts* case, the defendant was accused of forging a check and possession of stolen credit cards, both of which belonged to his

Direct examination
The act of a witness being first called to the stand to testify.

Defense attorney
The attorney who represents the defendant in a criminal case.

Cross-examination
The act of challenging a witness's testimony by asking more questions. Cross-examination is conducted by the other side of the case; the prosecution will cross-examine a defense witness, and the defense will cross-examine a witness for the state.

Prosecutor
The attorney, representing the state, who argues the criminal case against the defendant.

Rebuttal evidence is introduced during trial to oppose or contradict evidence already submitted by the opposing side.

© 2012 BY EVERETT COLLECTION. USED UNDER LICENSE OF SHUTTERSTOCK, INC.

daughter. While the daughter was subpoenaed five times to testify at trial, she never appeared. The prosecution offered the transcript of the daughter's testimony to the police at trial, and the defendant was convicted, based partly upon the perceived reliability of his daughter's previous statements.[17] In a later ruling, however, the Supreme Court effectively reversed its position in *Roberts* with the 2004 ruling in *Crawford v. Washington*. In *Crawford*, the prosecution introduced during trial a statement previously made to the police by the defendant's wife. The prosecution used the statement of the wife during trial, particularly during closing arguments, and the defendant was convicted. On appeal, the Supreme Court ruled that the defendant's Sixth Amendment right to confront his accuser had been violated because Mrs. Crawford did not actually testify during the trial, preventing the defense attorney from cross-examining her.[18] The *Crawford* decision effectively means that, when a witness is unavailable to testify at trial, previous testimonial statements made by that witness cannot be admitted into evidence unless the defense had the prior opportunity to cross-examine the witness.

Another way in which an attorney tests the accuracy of the opposing side's case is during the introduction of rebuttal evidence. Rebuttal evidence is evidence that is introduced during trial to oppose or contradict evidence already submitted by the opposing side. Rebuttal evidence is submitted during the side's response to the opposing side's presented case. For example, a witness may testify that he witnessed a robbery at a convenience store on a particular date and time, and then an attorney may introduce into evidence a credit card receipt with the witness's signature proving that he was at another location on the same date and time he claimed to witness the robbery. The receipt would be considered rebuttal evidence.

Critical Thinking   If a witness can verify testimony given by a previous witness, is it critical that his or her competency to testify can be demonstrated? Why or why not?

Closing argument
The final legal argument of a case presented separately by the prosecution and the defense before the case is given to the jury for deliberation.

Closing Arguments and Jury Instructions The closing arguments of a trial are the final legal arguments presented by the prosecution and the defense before the case is given to the jury for deliberation. The closing argument can be considered a review and summary of what was argued during the case and whether the arguments demonstrate the defendant's guilt or innocence. Because the burden of proof is on the state, meaning that it is up to the state to demonstrate the guilt of the defendant, the prosecutor is allowed to make a reply to the defense's closing argument. The closing argument does not necessarily have a time limit, although one may be imposed by the judge. The attorneys may avoid lengthy closing arguments for fear of confusing the jurors or losing their attention. In bench trials, it is not uncommon for the sides to waive making closing arguments in the presumption that the judge has already arrived at a decision.[19]

After all the evidence has been presented and closing arguments have ended, the judge gives the charge and instructions to the jury. Typically, the judge and attorneys for both sides will discuss the jury instructions outside the presence of the jury so that changes may be discussed, argued, agreed upon, or ruled upon. While the words may vary between jurisdictions, every judge will remind the jury of the duty to objectively consider only evidence that has been presented during trial when deciding the defendant's guilt or innocence; the importance of impartiality will also be stressed.[20] Most judges will remind the jury that the burden of proof rests on the prosecution and the defense is not obligated to show proof of innocence. The judge will also explain the concept of reasonable doubt by stressing that if jury members are to determine that a defendant is guilty, they must hold no reasonable doubts regarding the person's guilt. Additionally, judges may remind the jury of the legal requirements of the alleged charge: that is, if the defendant is accused of murder, the judge may remind the jury members of what, according to the law, constitutes "murder."

Issues have arisen from time to time concerning whether juries actually understood the instructions given to them by the judge. One study by Wiener, Pritchard, and Weston (1995) demonstrated that juror impartiality can be affected by misunderstanding jury instructions; when jurors were given several versions of instructions in a sample capital case, a strong correlation was found between misunderstanding the jury instructions and the willingness of the jurors to impose the death penalty.[21] It is also typical for jurors to confuse the burden of proof in criminal court—"beyond a reasonable doubt"—with the burden of proof in civil court—"preponderance of the evidence."[22] The American Bar Association has addressed this, stating, "All instructions to the jury should be in plain and understandable language."[23] States are making changes to jury instructions to increase juror understanding of the instructions. States such as Florida and Illinois are now creating standard jury instructions that can be altered according to the specific criteria of each case.[24]

Jury instructions have also been clarified by Supreme Court rulings. In *Pope v. Illinois* (1987), the defendant appealed a guilty verdict based on the assertion that the jury was given erroneous instructions. The defendant, who was a clerk at an adult bookstore, was arrested after selling certain magazines to police. The jury was instructed to determine whether the magazines would be considered obscene by determining how the material would be viewed by ordinary adults in the state of Illinois. The Supreme Court ruled that, although the jury was erroneously instructed to use a particular community standard—the state of Illinois—when considering the social value of the magazines, if no rational juror who had been properly instructed could find social value in the magazines, the guilty conviction should stand.[25]

The Verdict   When the jury is done deliberating, the foreman will write the verdict on the court's official verdict form. The bailiff will then be notified that a verdict has been reached, and the court will inform all parties to return to the courtroom to hear the verdict. When the parties, audience, and staff return to the courtroom, the jury will be ushered back into the jury box. The foreman hands the jury form to the bailiff, who then gives the form to the judge. The judge makes sure the verdict is properly written and the paperwork is in proper legal order. In some jurisdictions such as California, the clerk of the court reads the verdict aloud in court. In other jurisdictions such as North Dakota, the jury foreperson, referred to as the presiding juror, announces the verdict in court.[26] In cases where unanimous verdicts are required of juries, it is easy to know how each juror voted. However, the prosecuting and defense attorneys do have the right to request of the judge that the jury be polled. If this occurs, each juror must announce individually how he or she voted at the conclusion of deliberations.

Critical Thinking   What possible issues do you believe could arise from polling a jury after they have found a defendant guilty?

The Judge and Courtroom Staff   The concept of the courtroom workgroup was introduced earlier in the chapter. Each member of the courtroom workgroup has particular duties in the criminal trial process, all of which combine to dispose of cases as smoothly and efficiently as possible. Following is an overview of the members of the courtroom workgroup.

The Judge   Many people view the judge as the most important person in the courtroom. While there is an expectation of respect that is bestowed on the person holding a judgeship, the judge makes up only one part of the courtroom workgroup.

Judge
A public officer elected or appointed to administer justice and hear cases in a court of law.

There are different levels of judges: lower court judges, such as justices of the peace; major trial court judges, such as those in district courts; intermediate appellate court judges, who serve in state appellate and superior courts; and judges in the courts of last resort, such as the justices in the U.S. Supreme Court. At each level, judges will hear different types of cases. For example, a justice of the peace may preside over charges of traffic violations or school truancy, while the U.S. Supreme Court serves as the final, highest court in the country, hearing appeals that may originate in those local justice of the peace courts. The Supreme Court generally may decide which cases it will review, utilizing the

The judge has the responsibility of overseeing fairness in the courtroom.

Rule of Four: if four or more justices believe that a case warrants the consideration of the entire court, then the court will review the case.[27]

Selection of Judges   While most judges obtain their positions by election, federal judges hold their offices for life. Judges are selected in different ways. Federal judges are nominated by the president and then confirmed by the U.S. Senate.

FIGURE7.1 The Road to the Supreme Court.

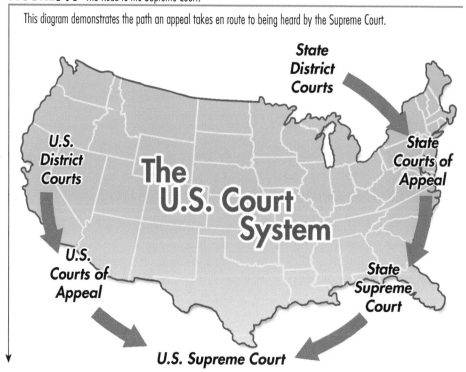

This diagram demonstrates the path an appeal takes en route to being heard by the Supreme Court.

State District Courts

U.S. District Courts

The U.S. Court System

State Courts of Appeal

U.S. Courts of Appeal

State Supreme Court

U.S. Supreme Court

This process is outlined in the U.S. Constitution for the Supreme Court justices; the Judiciary Act of 1789 adopted the process for all other federal judicial positions.[28] State, county, and municipal or lower court judges are elected to their positions. This means that candidates must gain the nomination from a political party and then campaign with that party.

Due to its political nature, the judge selection process can produce controversy. In Texas, for example, elected judges are allowed to preside over cases in which the involved parties and their lawyers have contributed to the judges' election campaigns. In 2000, a public interest group brought this practice to light, claiming it to be unconstitutional.[29] The trial court ruled against the public interest group, saying that the practice should be solved mutually between the citizens and lawmakers of Texas; the Court of Appeals later affirmed this decision.[30] The lawsuit did result in the implementation of the Judicial Campaign Fairness Act, signed into law in 1995 by then-Texas governor George W. Bush, which redefined election campaign donations, imposed limits on the donation amounts, and restricted campaign donations from parties involved with judicial candidates and officeholders.[31]

Critical Thinking
Is it a conflict of interest to permit a judge to preside over a case in which one of the opposing parties is someone who contributed money to the judge's election campaign? Why or why not?

Some state-level judges are appointed by the governor of the state. These positions include the judges for the courts of appeals and sometimes in major district trial courts under certain circumstances. For example, if an elected judge of a district court retires or dies during his or her term, the governor would appoint a replacement. Politics can be involved in this instance as well, as a governor will typically appoint judges who share the same political affiliation.

Qualifications of Judges   Until the 1960s, many states did not require judges to have education, special training, or other qualifications.[32] This meant that anyone who won an election or was appointed to the position—even someone who did not have a law degree—could become a judge. The New York City Criminal Court Act, implemented in 1962, required judges to reside in the city; to have at least 10 years' experience practicing law in the state of New York; and to pass the state bar exam, although it was possible to do so without obtaining a law degree.[33] Now, almost all states require that a judge in general and appellate court have a juris doctor (or Doctor of Law) degree, be a licensed attorney, and be a member of their state's bar association.

It is important that judges receive ongoing legal training to stay current on changes to laws and the application of the laws. Some entities, such as the Texas Justice Court Training Center at Texas State University, hold state-sponsored training sessions for newly elected judges. This training may address such subjects that are foreign to brand-new judges, such as courtroom and evidentiary procedures, dispute resolution, ethics, and other topics.[34] There are also organizations that provide ongoing training for judges, such as the National Judicial College at the University of Nevada, Reno.[35]

Duties of Judges The judge's primary duty is to oversee the standard procedures of the court system to ensure that justice is fairly served. The American Bar Association has laid out a specific description of the duties of the office: "The trial judge has the responsibility for safeguarding both the rights of the accused and the interests of the public in the administration of criminal justice . . . The purpose of a criminal trial is to determine whether the prosecution has established the guilt of the accused as required by law, and the trial judge should not allow the proceedings to be used for any other purpose."[36]

In the courtroom, the judge must make sure that both the prosecution and the defense are given the chance to state their cases, make their arguments, and question the opposing side's witnesses. In each case, the appointed judge decides whether certain pieces of evidence are admissible or inadmissible and gives support for his or her decisions. While the judge has established laws to follow, the judge does have discretion to decide how to apply the laws in his or her courtroom.[37] In this respect, the judge can wield great power over the progression of a criminal case.

During the trial, the judge typically refers to the attorneys of each opposing side as "counsel" or "counselor." A counselor is a legal advisor and advocate for one of the sides in a court case. The judge might use this term when addressing the attorneys directly, such as by saying, "Counsel, approach the bench." This is an instruction for each of the attorneys to come to the judge's bench to discuss something with the judge, perhaps out of earshot of the jury and audience. The attorneys may also request to approach the bench by asking the judge for a sidebar, which is a discussion held between the judge and the lawyers out of the hearing of the jury.

Deciding whether a piece of evidence is admissible in court depends on several criteria and is one of the more important decisions a trial judge will make. The judge will examine whether the evidence is relevant to the case: that is, whether it is important to the argument being presented by either the prosecution or the defense. The judge also has to consider whether the probative value of the evidence outweighs any prejudicial or inflammatory qualities it may have.[38] Evidence has probative value when it is useful and relevant to the case.[39] No matter how useful a piece of evidence may be, it can, however, unfairly sway a jury if it is presented in a way that particularly causes anger, sadness, or disgust. For example, a graphic photo of a murder victim's body may be considered inadmissible if it serves no purpose other than to produce an emotional reaction from the jury. Sometimes evidence is admitted in only a limited way. Limited admissibility means that the evidence may be used for one specific purpose but cannot be applied in other ways.[40] Continuing the previous example, photos of the murder victim's body may only be admissible if they are shown during the questioning of the medical examiner.

Counsel
A title for an attorney presenting a case in court.

Sidebar
A discussion conducted during a court hearing between the judge and attorneys outside the hearing of the jury.

Probative value
Value that is useful in a case.

Limited admissibility
Evidence that may be used for one specific purpose but cannot be applied in other ways.

In some state jurisdictions, there is a chief judge who serves as a trial judge and also manages the court system in the local jurisdiction. A chief judge will typically assume the position by tenure or seniority.

While the criminal court judge has the duty to follow and enforce the law in his or her courtroom, how those laws are followed and enforced is partly up to the judge. This is known as judicial discretion. A judge may disallow certain testimony in a trial because he or she believes it is not relevant to the case; another judge presiding over the same trial may make a different decision. Judges have the discretion to accept or not accept evidence, pleas, and sentencing agreements made between the prosecution and the defense. This discretion can influence the entire courtroom workgroup. As the prosecutor learns the discretionary tendencies of the judge, the prosecutor learns what preliminary evidence to emphasize during the charging process. As the probation officer learns what types of cases the judge may feel most strongly about, the probation officer may suggest additional or alternative conditions of probation for a particular defendant that may coincide with the judge's beliefs.

The Court Clerk

The court clerk has many duties that take place both inside and outside the courtroom, performing many different and important jobs. At minimum, the court clerk calls up cases to be heard before the judge and regularly updates the case files for defendants. Before a trial begins, a court clerk may prepare a jury pool for selection and issue jury summonses. During a trial, the clerk will swear in witnesses who are going to testify and can issue subpoenas for witnesses for the defense and the prosecution. The court clerk, or an assistant clerk, also marks exhibits into evidence and maintains proper custody of that evidence while the case is in court. Additionally, the court clerk performs other duties as requested by the judge. In larger jurisdictions, there may be a court clerk in each courtroom, while in smaller jurisdictions, there may be one or two court clerks for the whole courthouse. Some districts have a chief court clerk, often called a court coordinator, who is in charge of making sure the court clerk staff fulfills these duties properly.[41]

Some jurisdictions assign more power to their court clerks, such as the authority to issue warrants for arrest, prepare formal writs and process court-issued documents, and assist with probate matters (i.e., wills and estates). Sometimes young attorneys will serve as court clerks; this level of responsibility can help them gain valuable hands-on experience with various judicial matters. The court clerk can be a powerful position in the courtroom and may sometimes serve as the gateway to discuss case matters with the judge or prosecutor. In addition, a court clerk may have records or know information about a case, or about the judge's tendencies to rule in certain matters, which would be helpful for defense attorneys to know. This, in turn, may affect how the defense attorney formulates the defense.

The Court Reporter

A court reporter keeps the official record of everything that happens during a trial. This includes accurately recording everything

Court reporter
A person who uses a shorthand typewriter to record everything that occurs or is said during a court hearing.

The court reporter takes notes of all testimony during trial.

Court record

The official written record of everything that occurs in a court case.

that is said, whether by the witnesses, the attorneys, or the judge. Some verbal interactions may include objections, instructions the judge gives to the jury, and expert testimony. It is common for a court reporter to read back a portion of the record if instructed by the judge; such instructions may be prompted by a request from the prosecution, the defense, or the jury. The reading of **court records** can help remind courtroom officials of statements made in the courtroom or verify that certain information is included in the official record.

In years past, court reporters were stenographers who used manual shorthand to take detailed notes quickly. Manual shorthand is now largely a thing of the past, and court reporters usually use machine writers to take the transcript of the proceedings. A machine writer looks similar to a small typewriter but has fewer keys, and it is used to type coded letters and combinations of letters rather than entire words and phrases. After the trial has concluded, the court reporter will translate the notes into the official transcript. The notes may be translated visually by the court reporter or scanned by special equipment. In some courts, the court reporter may use computer-aided transcription (CAT) software, which both takes notes and translates those notes into the transcript. Electronic recording equipment, such as audio or video recorders, is used in place of court reporters in some courtrooms, but there are risks to using these machines. Extraneous noises and comments can be recorded and are not easily erased, and the mechanical recorder cannot interrupt proceedings if any testimony is not audible and cannot be recorded properly.

The Probation Officer

A court probation officer serves as the initial liaison from the local probation department to the defendant who has just been sentenced to probation. Part of a probation officer's duty is to explain the conditions of probation to the defendant for a second time—the judge and defense attorney give the initial explanation—to make sure that the defendant understands. A probation officer will also instruct the defendant on when and where to report for the first probation visit and what to bring to the visit. If there are other procedures, such as reporting for a drug screen or attending a workshop, a probation officer will explain to the defendant how those events will be scheduled as well as handle any associated or monitory paperwork.[42]

Additionally, a probation officer usually serves as an intermediary between the probation department and the judge when dealing with special issues with defendants already on probation. For example, a probation officer from a field office will contact the court probation officer when a probationer tests positive for drugs. The court probation officer will advise the court of the violation and make appropriate recommendations to the field probation officer regarding the handling of the defendant. The court probation officer may also work with the district attorney's office when a defendant returns to court for a probation revocation hearing. A probation officer and the district attorney's office will review the file and determine the best course of action to argue for or against the revocation of a person's probation. A court probation officer is also the court's official custodian of records for the probationer's file while any court hearings are pending. The probation officer becomes familiar with the judge and his or her position on certain types of offenses, as well as the judge's typical rulings on certain criminal matters. In this respect, the probation officer can be a valuable person for a defense attorney to know, especially if the defendant violates probation and must appear before the judge.

The Bailiff

A bailiff is usually an armed law enforcement officer, typically based in the jurisdiction in which the court is located. For example, a state district court based in a particular county usually has a county sheriff's deputy assigned to that court to serve as the bailiff. A bailiff ensures that order is maintained in the courtroom by instructing spectators and participants to keep discussion at a low volume as well as enforcing any orders or instructions given by the judge.[43] When the judge enters the courtroom, the bailiff announces the judge's arrival as he or she takes the seat at the bench. A bailiff sometimes calls witnesses to testify and may even have to prevent the accused from escaping from custody. A bailiff also controls access to the jury while court is in session and during jury deliberations. When a jury is sequestered, or kept from contact with anyone while a trial is in progress, the bailiff supervises contact between the jury and any non-jury members in an attempt to prevent any outside bias from interfering with the case information given to the jury.

Bailiff
A law enforcement officer, such as a sheriff's deputy, assigned to a particular courtroom to assist the judge and courtroom staff and keep the peace.

The Court Process Server

A court process server is responsible for serving subpoenas to witnesses and other persons who are to appear in court. A subpoena is a written document that officially notifies someone that he or she must appear in court. A court process server is typically a sheriff's deputy or local law enforcement officer. While a court process server is able to perform law enforcement duties as the court sees necessary, his or her primary function is to serve process.

Subpoena
A written document that officially notifies someone that he or she must appear in court.

The Prosecution and Defense

The attorneys for the prosecution and the defense have several things in common. Each attorney will have a certain level of college education, usually having graduated from law school. Attorneys must also comply with the licensing requirements of the state where they want to practice law; this is typically done by taking and passing a bar examination. The bar is the governing body that licenses and regulates attorneys within a particular jurisdiction.

The attorneys for each side play critical roles in the legal process.

The Prosecution

The prosecution side of judicial proceedings is led by a prosecutor, whose primary job is to present a state's case against a defendant. The prosecutor is known by several different names depending on the jurisdiction that he or she represents. The prosecutor may be a district attorney (DA), a county at-

The state seal is prominently displayed in most state courtrooms.

torney, a state's attorney, or a U.S. attorney. In most states, district attorneys are elected and typically serve four-year terms, although chief federal prosecutors are appointed. In any case, the prosecutor is the lawyer for the government and is the highest law enforcement authority in a particular jurisdiction. When law enforcement officials bring cases to a prosecutor, it is the prosecutor who decides how those cases will be addressed: whether they will be disposed of or dismissed, whether they will be pursued in court, and whether the charges against an accused person may be reduced to a lesser offense or increased to a more serious charge. In some jurisdictions, prosecutors prepare search and arrest warrants before they are approved and signed by judges.

The role of a prosecutor encompasses many different jobs in one, and each job varies depending on the different stages of the criminal justice process. Prosecutors are involved in various aspects of casework, from investigation, arrest, and trial to sentencing, appeal, and parole, as well as several other additional steps of the judicial process that occur between arrest and trial. Those additional steps may include, but are not limited to, the initial appearance; the preliminary hearing; indictment; arraignment; and pretrial motions. Many prosecutors' offices in the United States have different divisions that handle different types of cases. Each of these divisions may be headed by a chief assistant attorney, who in turn reports to the elected prosecuting attorney. In Franklin County, Ohio, the Criminal Division of the Prosecuting Attorney's Office has 11 different departments, such as the Gang Unit and the Gun Unit, to handle different classifications of criminal offenses.[44]

An initial appearance occurs after a suspect is arrested and becomes a defendant. He or she does not come into contact with a court officer until this appearance. In the initial appearance, the defendant is brought before a magistrate or judge and formally (1) given notice of the charges being brought against him or her, (2) advised of his or her rights, (3) given the opportunity to hire an attorney or request an appointed lawyer, and (4) given the opportunity to request bail. As the agent for the state, a prosecutor is involved in all of these steps, notifying the judge of the charges against the defendant and arguing for a particular bail amount or against bail altogether.

An initial appearance is typically followed by a preliminary hearing, at which the prosecutor for the case must establish probable cause to try the defendant for the crime which he or she is accused of committing. In some instances, a prosecutor will formally notify the court that the case against the defendant will no longer be prosecuted—in other words, charges are dropped. The prosecutor has discretion to decide whether to pursue a case against a defendant. Prosecutorial discretion takes several forms besides the pursuit of charges against a defendant: the prosecutor may offer or accept a plea bargain, may stipulate that the defendant seek counseling or some other treatment before the decision is made to pursue the case, or may dismiss the case entirely.

When judges' discretion, such as on lengths or types of sentences applicable to certain offenses, is limited, discretion often falls by default to the prosecutor. Since the prosecutor is typically voted into office, this can create an ethical conflict. While prosecutors are not supposed to be influenced by political gain or loss that may result from prosecution or non-prosecution of cases, it would be unrealistic to think that this does not occur anywhere in this country. Decisions made by prosecutors are effectively not subject to review by the judicial or administrative processes; this gives prosecutors a great deal of power when deciding whether to proceed with charges against a defendant or in discussion of plea negotiations.[45] Critics argue that the power of the prosecutor's discretion directly contrasts with the ideas of fairness, equity, and accountability upon which the criminal justice system in this country has been based. Still, while plenty of legislation has limited judicial discretion, not much legislation has restrained the discretional power of the American prosecutor.[46]

If a prosecutor decides to proceed with a case, he or she will prepare an information report that demonstrates probable cause to bind over the accused for trial, often called an indictment.[47] In some jurisdictions, such as the state of Texas, the grand jury system is used. In these instances, a prosecutor makes an argument in front of a grand jury to establish probable cause in the hope that the grand jury will return an indictment of the accused. An arraignment may follow.

An arraignment has two purposes: to re-inform the defendant of the charges filed against him or her and to give the defendant the chance to enter a plea.[48] According to the Federal Rules of Criminal Procedure, there are three types of pleas allowed: guilty, not guilty, and "no contest," or *nolo contendere*. The phrase *nolo contendere* is Latin and means, "I do not wish to contest." A plea of *nolo contendere* allows for the judge's decision on the defendant's guilt or innocence, while allowing the defendant to refrain from pleading guilty. Defendants in felony charges are arraigned by prosecutors, who bring the accused forward to answer to the indictment or charging instrument. At this stage, a prosecutor may also engage in negotiating a plea with the defendant. This means that the defendant may be allowed to plead guilty to a lesser charge in exchange for a different or reduced sentence.

Before the trial begins, attorneys from both sides may initiate or participate in the arguments of pretrial motions. Pretrial motions may deal with many different issues, such as a request for a trial to be held in a different venue or a motion *in limine*, in which the prosecution seeks to limit the information made available to the defense. A common pretrial motion is a *motion for continuance*, which simply requests that the court postpone the trial to a future date. This motion is generally filed because the requesting side believes there has not been sufficient time to prepare the case for trial.

During a trial, the prosecutor performs his or her primary duty of attempting to prove the defendant's guilt beyond a reasonable doubt. If a defendant is found guilty, sentencing occurs and the prosecutor may recommend a harsher or more lenient sentence, depending on the circumstances of the crime. If a conviction is appealed by the defendant, a prosecutor will typically argue that a conviction was properly obtained and should be upheld. Sometimes, prosecutors may recommend for or against parole for convicted inmates from their jurisdictions when parole reviews arrive. Typically, prosecutors will oppose parole for serious offenders.

Career Connections: Prosecutor

Working as a prosecutor can be a challenging task. Choosing this field as a career can mean committing to a life of short budgets, large caseloads, and long hours. Prosecutors' salaries may lag well behind those of their peers, and the work can be emotionally taxing. Still, life as a prosecutor can be very fulfilling and rewarding.

Prosecution requires a college degree and three years of law school. Most states require an exam at the conclusion of law school that tests students' overall competency in all of the practice areas they might face. Most prospective prosecutors are required to demonstrate a broad knowledge of legal matters in order to be admitted to the legal bar. They can then be sworn in as lawyers and begin to practice law.

Depending on the size of the jurisdiction, a prosecutor may handle all facets of prosecution or may be able to specialize. Prosecution includes two broad phases: the trial phase and the appellate phase. In large jurisdictions, each phase is handled by separate groups of attorneys working as a team. In smaller jurisdictions, one attorney may handle a particular case throughout both phases. The life cycle of a particular case may vary based on the speed of the jurisdiction and the complexities of the litigation, but the typical life cycle of a case is more than a year.

A prosecutor's job consists of being part social worker, part police officer, and part judge. Prosecutors must be able to handle difficult situations. It is not uncommon for prosecutors to be called out to major crime scenes involving violence and death. Attending autopsies and reviewing crime scene photos may be regular parts of a prosecutor's job. Prosecutors need to have good interpersonal skills, as they deal with law enforcement and victims who may or may not be cooperative. They must be able to make sound decisions quickly. Public speaking is a regular part of the job and a critical skill for effective courtroom litigation.

Prosecution is a career that allows an individual to dramatically impact not only individual lives, but also the community at large. Effectively targeting high-crime areas or violent repeat offenders can make dramatic differences in the day-to-day lives of a prosecutor's constituents. Combining aggressive prosecution techniques with effective public relations campaigns can have a significant deterrent effect within a jurisdiction. Partnering with law enforcement, parent-teacher organizations, and local service organizations can foster educational programs for youth that discourage delinquent behavior that leads to adult criminality.

Students who desire a career in law or prosecution should begin their research and participation in the criminal justice community early. They may seek out internships and service programs with local law enforcement agencies or prosecutor offices. Some police agencies have citizen academies that train local citizens to be ambassadors of law enforcement in the general population and respond to emergencies. Because prosecutorial jobs are becoming harder to acquire, a demonstrated interest in criminal law from an early age can be a tremendous asset when pursuing a prosecutorial job.

Prosecution often leads to other careers. Many prosecutors move on to elected offices such as elected district or county attorneys, judges, legislative positions, or local government officials. Many go on to hold advisory or managerial positions in state and federal government. Many take the extensive trial experience they receive and go on to lucrative private practice careers. Often, prosecutors commit to a lifetime of public service in the prosecutorial field. Prosecutors are in demand in both the private and public sectors.

The Defense

A defense attorney is a lawyer who represents the accused during the criminal trial process. A defense attorney is typically a trained and educated attorney who may specialize in criminal law. It is the job of the defense to ensure that the rights of the accused are maintained and upheld during the criminal trial process. Prior to trial, a defense attorney will prepare an appropriate and adequate defense to be presented at trial. To prepare for his or her defense, he or she may use the services of outside parties such as experts, witnesses to the crime, character witnesses, and even private investigators.

Another pretrial job of the defense attorney is negotiating a plea agreement with the state's attorney. A defense attorney will interact frequently, and often intensely, with the defendant before and during trial. These discussions are called privileged communications and are subject to **attorney-client privilege**, meaning that any information shared between a defense attorney and his or her client (the defendant) is kept confidential and does not need to be shared with other members of the court or the public.

During the trial, the defense attorney has the chance to place witnesses on the stand—including the defendant, if that is part of the legal strategy—and ask questions of them. The defense attorney will also have the opportunity to clarify previously testified statements by the state's witnesses by cross-examining them. When an attorney from either side wants to interact directly with a witness, the attorney must ask permission from the judge to **approach the witness**. This allows the attorney to interact more closely with the witness on the stand, including showing evidence to the witness and asking the witness to identify the evidence.

If the accused is found guilty, the defense attorney will argue matters at the sentencing trial and will almost assuredly advise the defendant on any civil issues that may arise as a result of the guilty verdict. A defense attorney may be asked to file an appeal on the conviction, although whether the attorney continues to represent the defendant during the appeal process is typically up to the defendant, in the case of a hired attorney, or the judge, in the case of an appointed attorney or public defender.

There are several types of defense attorneys. A retained attorney is one that has been hired to represent a defendant: the defendant, or someone on his or her behalf, will pay money to the attorney in exchange for counsel during the criminal process. Retained attorneys may have a world of resources available to them, including investigators, experts, and support staff, which generally correspond with the defendant's ability to pay for such resources.

Sometimes, a court will appoint a local attorney to represent an indigent defendant during the criminal trial, or appeal, process—a process that was af-

The Harper Lee novel *To Kill a Mockingbird*, adapted into a movie starring Gregory Peck, featured the classic defense attorney character of Atticus Finch.

Attorney-client privilege

The privilege that any information shared between a defense attorney and his or her client is kept confidential and does not need to be shared with other members of the court or the public.

Approach the witness

An action that occurs when an attorney moves closer to a witness, who is currently on the witness stand, in order to question the witness further or show him or her an exhibit or document. In most jurisdictions, the attorney must request permission from the judge to approach the witness.

Ethics and Professionalism: Defense Attorneys

As officers of the court, judges and prosecutors are held to ethical standards. Judges must remain impartial and not treat either the defense or the prosecution with hostility, nor must they show favoritism toward either side. Prosecutors must disclose all evidence they will use during trial to the defense, and they are not permitted to allow witnesses or complainants to give false testimony. Judges and prosecutors who do not adhere to the ethical standards imposed upon them by their state bar associations or boards of judicial conduct are subject to sanctions. What, however, about defense attorneys? They are also considered officers of the court, but they are not employed by the government as the judges and prosecutors are. Do defense attorneys have ethical standards that they must follow? Are those ethical standards different than those to which the judges and prosecutors are subjected?

Think about a defense attorney who is representing a man for rape. Not only does the prosecution have enough evidence to show that the defendant committed the rape, but the defendant has also admitted to his attorney that he did commit the rape. How is it ethical for an attorney to defend someone who admittedly committed a terrible crime?

Remember that all persons are afforded certain rights in the U.S. Constitution. Each person is presumed innocent until proven guilty. It is the defense attorney's job to make sure that the defendant receives a fair and impartial trial no matter what the circumstances of the crime may be. The defense attorney will do his or her best to ensure that the prosecution conducts the state's case while following the laws set forth by the state and the federal government. The defense attorney is not present to try to help a guilty criminal go free; the defense attorney helps ensure that the state fulfills its burden of demonstrating the defendant's guilt, as well as ensuring that the defendant's civil rights have not been violated. Think about what would happen if we lived in a country where defendants were not allowed to be represented by counsel and the defendant had the burden to show that he or she did not commit the crime. How would our justice system be different?

Court-appointed attorney
An attorney typically selected from a list of all criminal attorneys in private practice near the jurisdiction who are willing to accept appointed cases.

firmed for all criminal causes following *Gideon* v. *Wainwright*. A **court-appointed attorney** is typically selected from a list of all criminal attorneys in private practice near the jurisdiction who are willing to accept appointed cases. An appointed attorney performs all the services for the defendant that a retained attorney would, but instead of being paid by the defendant or a representative, the appointed attorney is paid by the jurisdiction of the local court. The attorney may submit a voucher detailing his or her work on the case to the local jurisdiction and may be paid by the hour, by the duty performed, or by the court appearance. Fees for appointed attorney work are normally much lower than the fees earned when retained. For example, in Oakland County, Michigan, a court-appointed attorney is paid between $350 and $460 per day for trial appearances.[49] Retained attorneys around the country routinely charge their clients hundreds of dollars per hour for work performed on their cases.

Public defender
An attorney elected in a local jurisdiction to represent indigent defendants in criminal trials.

The ruling in *Gideon* v. *Wainwright* also helped create the public defender system in the courts, as many defendants cannot afford to hire attorneys to represent them. A **public defender** works much like an appointed attorney, with the exception that a public defender's office is a permanently established office dedicated to represent any indigent defendants in the jurisdiction. A public defender's office typically employs paralegals, investigators, and other assistants as well as attorneys to conduct the business of defense for the courts. Approximately 64% of counties nationwide now fund public defender programs.[50] Critics of the current public defender system like to demonstrate the inadequate funding the system receives at the state level. The federal public defender system, however, is not experiencing the same problem. The trial defense of Timothy McVeigh, who bombed the Murrah Federal Building in Oklahoma City, cost taxpayers more than $13.8 million. This includes only trial expenses and not appeals.[51]

There are instances in which the court may decide not to appoint an attorney to represent the defendant or refer the case to the local public defender's office. If a defendant claims to be indigent, but is proven to have money or own assets of some amount, such as a car or a home, that can be used to retain an attorney, the judge may deny the request for appointed counsel.

A jury is empaneled to hear evidence presented by the prosecution and defense attorneys.

The Jury

The jury is an important part of the criminal trial process; some may say that, besides the judge, the jury is the most important entity in the courtroom. In a jury trial, the jury listens to the evidence presented by both sides and decides whether the defendant is guilty or innocent. In essence, the defendant's life is held in the jury's hands.

Article III of the U.S. Constitution stipulates that "the trial of all crimes . . . shall be by jury." The defendant may choose to waive trial by jury in favor of trial by the judge, as has already been mentioned. In any case where a jury trial is involved, the defendant has been guaranteed by the Supreme Court the right to be judged by a jury of his or her peers.[52]

Supreme Court Justification for Jury Trials

The U.S. Constitution guarantees the right to a speedy trial to anyone who is tried in an American courtroom; it is provided in the Sixth Amendment of the Bill of Rights, but it took several rulings from the U.S. Supreme Court to clarify this right. The first ruling to apply the right to speedy trial to the state trial courts was *Klopfer v. North Carolina* in 1967. In this case, the defendant was tried on charges of criminal trespass, but the jury failed to agree on a verdict, resulting in a mistrial. A second trial was supposed to occur, but after one year passed and the second trial did not begin, Klopfer demanded that the trial begin immediately or his case be dismissed. The judge denied Klopfer's request, but granted the state's request to make the case inactive without bringing the defendant to trial, which meant that the case could be made active again at any time the state so chose. Klopfer appealed to the North Carolina Supreme Court, which, in turn, ruled that the right to a speedy trial did not mean the state could be forced to prosecute a defendant. Klopfer's case remained inactive, and Klopfer then appealed to the U.S. Supreme Court. The U.S. Supreme Court ruled in Klopfer's favor, simultaneously striking down the North Carolina law that had allowed the indefinite postponement of Klopfer's trial. This judgment extended the speedy trial provision to the states.[53]

The U.S. Supreme Court has clarified the right to a speedy trial in *Klopfer v. North Carolina* and *Barker v. Wingo*.

The U.S. Supreme Court heard the case of *Barker v. Wingo* in 1972. Prior to this case, courts assumed a defendant that did not demand a speedy trial was not opposed to waiting. The U.S. Supreme Court held in *Barker* that passively allowing a case to plod slowly through the system does not equate to the defendant's waiver of his or her Sixth Amendment rights. While this ruling did not specify time frames, it did list a number of factors that trial courts need to take into consideration when determining whether the right to a speedy trial has been denied: how long the delay has lasted, why the delay has taken place, the demand of the defendant to have a speedy trial, and any bias against the defendant.[54]

The next year, 1973, yielded the U.S. Supreme Court's ruling in *Strunk v. United States*. This case determined that if a defendant is denied a speedy trial, the appropriate and "only possible remedy" is dismissal of the charges.[55] Several years later, the U.S. Supreme Court clarified in *United States v. Lovasco* that the Sixth Amendment right applies to delays that occur between a defendant's arrest and the trial—not any delays prior to the initial charges and arrest of a defendant.[56]

Another right provided under the Sixth Amendment is the right to a public trial. This right stemmed from the practice of secret trials in Europe, such as the Spanish Inquisition and the Star Chamber in England. In 1948, the U.S. Supreme Court ruled in *In re Oliver* that the failure to allow a defendant a reasonable opportunity to defend himself against a charge of contempt of court violated due process of law. In this case, a man was subpoenaed to testify as a witness to a crime that was being secretly investigated by a one-man grand jury, i.e., a single judge. The judge believed that the man's testimony was false and evasive and promptly charged him with contempt, found him guilty, and sentenced him to 60 days in jail. This process occurred without the witness's knowledge and did not allow him the opportunity to defend himself. The U.S. Supreme Court ruled that the 14th Amendment prevents an accused from being deprived of his or her rights without due process of law; therefore, an accused person cannot be sentenced to prison in secrecy.[57]

Jury Selection   A defendant has the right to be judged by a jury of his or her peers. The jury must therefore be comprised of individuals who, in general, reflect the values, rational abilities, and common sense of the average, everyday citizen. A jury of one's peers is supposed to consist of people who are impartial to the case and live in the jurisdiction—typically the county—where the defendant lives. Peer juries are made up of people who represent the community where the alleged crime occurred and where the trial will be held. In 1945, the Supreme Court clarified the meaning of a "jury of one's peers" by stating that while it is unnecessary for each jury to be comprised of representatives of every possible economic, racial, religious, gender, and ethnic variable from the community, potential jurors may not be excluded intentionally or systematically due to their social characteristics.[58] The concept of peer juries has origins in the Magna Carta, which guaranteed jury trials for "freemen."[59] This principle was incorporated directly into the U.S. Constitution in Article III, which states: "The trial of all crimes, except in cases of impeachment, shall be by jury."[60] The Sixth Amendment reaffirms Article III by stating, "In all criminal prosecutions, the accused shall enjoy the right to a speedy and public trial by an impartial jury."[61] While federal criminal cases followed suit, some states, such as Louisiana, applied the right to a jury trial selectively. Until 1968, Louisiana granted jury trials only when capital punishment or imprisonment with hard labor were options for sentencing. The Supreme Court ruling in *Duncan v. Louisiana* further applied the jury trial provisions to state-level criminal trials.[62]

Jury members are selected from a master list of all eligible persons in the local jurisdiction of a trial's location. Typically, juries have 12 members, although this is not always the case. State courts are allowed to use as few as six persons in a jury in noncapital cases; federal courts always use 12-member juries. The Supreme Court ruled in *Williams v. Florida* (1970) that states may use juries comprised of at least six people in noncapital cases.[39]

There are eligibility requirements for jury service in the United States. In general, jurors must be citizens of the United States and be able to read and write. Jurors must also be older than age 18 and, in most jurisdictions, registered to vote. There are several criteria, which may vary between jurisdictions, that will disqualify someone from being eligible. A serious felony conviction will typically preclude someone from being a juror, for example. Persons such as parents who care for young children during the day, the elderly, or the disabled, who would otherwise be eligible for jury duty, may declare themselves exempt due to physical limitations or personal obligations. This is done on a case-by-case basis and does not permanently exempt the potential juror from service; he or she may be selected again in the future. In the interest of keeping jury panels impartial, as the U.S. Constitution instructs, exemptions are limited at least when preparing the master list.

A *venire*, or *venire facias*, is a writ that summons jurors for service. The potential jurors will report to a designated office or building at a particular date and time. They are interviewed to confirm whether they are eligible and available to serve on a jury. Some are dismissed and sent home, thus fulfilling their jury service. Those who are kept in the jury pool are paid a nominal amount for their service. From the jury pool, several jury panels may be selected and sent to various courtrooms that require juries. A jury panel for a misdemeanor trial will typically be smaller than a jury panel for a felony trial. A felony jury panel could be as many as 36 or more persons. The jury panels are selected at random by the county official, usually a clerk of the court.

A *voir dire* examination is an oath sworn by a potential juror concerning his or her qualifications to serve on a jury. The term *voir dire* means "to speak the truth." During *voir dire*, both the prosecution and the defense will ask potential jurors questions about their personal and professional backgrounds, any prior experience with courts or the legal system, and even personal opinions on current events—which may have relevance for the charge against the defendant. Sometimes the judge will ask jurors questions as well. Any juror who is seen by either side as unacceptable for the jury is typically eliminated by either the challenge for cause or the peremptory challenge. A **challenge for cause** is a specific legal reason to exclude a potential juror. The side that makes the challenge must defend the challenge to the judge, as the challenge typically argues that the juror will be unable to fairly judge the accused for a particular reason. The decision to remove the juror is up to the judge, but there are statutes that specify rules for removing jurors. A **peremptory challenge** is an objection to a potential juror without specifying a reason for the objection. The attorney making the peremptory challenge can make the challenge for any reason, or no reason, and whether a peremptory challenge is made is usually an important part of an attorney's trial strategy. There are limits to the number of jurors who may be eliminated due to peremptory challenges. New York allows three peremptory challenges, except in particularly serious cases, while Texas allows six.[63]

There are also limitations to peremptory challenges. Using challenges to purposely exclude persons of a particular race, particularly African-Americans, was a common occurrence until the late 20th century, and the Supreme Court upheld the practice in its 1965 ruling, *Swain v. Alabama*.[64] However, in 1986, the Court partially overruled *Swain*, proclaiming in *Batson v. Kentucky* that blacks may not be excluded from juries due to concern that they will decide in favor of a black defendant.[65] The *Batson* ruling was later expanded to include challenges that purposely excluded jurors based on gender; however, the ruling was delivered via a paternity case, *J.E.B. v. Alabama ex rel. T.B.*, not a criminal case.[66] The number of challenges allowed varies from state to state and is controlled by statute.

Voir dire continues until the entire jury has been filled, no matter how many challenges occur. Sometimes, alternates are selected. These alternates will sit through the trial with the jury and will take the place of a juror who is forced to leave the trial while it is in progress. Reasons that a juror may leave include illness, family emergency, or disqualification.

Challenge for cause
A specific legal reason to exclude a potential juror.

Peremptory challenge
An attorney's objection to the jury service of a potential juror without a particular argument against the juror.

As soon as the jury is sworn in, the criminal trial officially begins. The judge must decide whether to **sequester** the jury for the duration of the trial. Sequestering a jury theoretically removes the jury, and any alternate jurors, from all possible influences that may affect their abilities to fairly judge the accused. The sequestered jury is housed in a hotel and not allowed visitors. Any magazines or newspapers they read or television shows they watch are censored. Typically, a judge will sequester a jury only in a high-profile case, when inflammatory news stories or tabloid articles may potentially unduly influence the jury. Sequestering a jury puts a strain on the jury members, as they must remain away from their homes, jobs, and families until the trial is over—regardless of whether the trial lasts three days or three months.

With innovations in technology over the last few decades, including the Internet and mobile phones, it has become increasingly difficult to separate the jury from all outside influences that might affect their ultimate decision-making process. Jurors who are sequestered must be monitored more closely now than in years past, due to the wide availability of cell phones and Internet access.

After the state presents its case, the defense may enter a motion for a directed verdict. This motion asserts that the state failed to present a case proving the defendant's guilt beyond a reasonable doubt and asks the judge to acquit the defendant. If the judge approves this motion, he or she typically will direct the jury to acquit the defendant. Even when this motion is not filed by the defense, a trial judge may still order a directed verdict of not guilty. The judge may also order a directed verdict because the prosecutor behaved improperly in some way, or the testimony from the witnesses for the prosecution was not credible.

Once closing arguments have been made, the judge issues orders directly to the jury. These orders include that the jury retire to the jury room; consider the facts, evidence, and testimony presented in court; and decide on a fair verdict. The judge's order will include instructions about the possible verdicts the jury may decide on and the legal definition of reasonable doubt. In some jurisdictions, judges are allowed to review all of the evidence that has been presented to the jury, such as the testimony of each witness. This can be helpful if the trial has been lengthy, but it may inadvertently influence a jury as well if the judge has suggested an opinion about the defendant's innocence or guilt. It can take some time to deliver the instructions to the jury due to the complexities of the laws that must be followed. It is important that judges deliver the jury instructions in a way that all the jurors can understand them and fulfill their duties. Generally, the final instruction given to the jurors is that they may not discuss the facts of the case with anyone other than their fellow jurors during official deliberations.

Deliberations and Beyond

After the judge's charge has concluded, the jury is removed so that it may begin deliberations. Once the jury retires to the jury room, a foreperson is selected to be the jury's leader. In some courts of law, the first juror selected during *voir dire* is the foreperson. A foreperson typically sits at the head of the table and calls for a vote. Unanimous jury verdicts are required

Sequester
To remove the jury, and any alternate jurors, from all possible influences that may affect their abilities to fairly judge the accused.

by law in each state except for Oregon and Louisiana. The Oregon Constitution and the Louisiana Codes of Criminal Procedure both allow for non-unanimous jury verdicts in certain non-capital criminal cases. The Supreme Court upheld these state requirements in two 1972 decisions, *Johnson v. Louisiana* and *Apodaca v. Oregon*.[67] There is strength in numbers, however, when it comes to jury deliberation. Twelve unique points of view can expose jury members to different interpretations and opinions about the evidence presented and, thus, discourage them from using only their personal beliefs to select a verdict. Additionally, jurors can work together to refresh improperly or incorrectly recalled memories from the trial.[68]

Jury members are drawn from many different circumstances and situations. They may be schoolteachers, long-haul truck drivers, firefighters, business executives, retired persons, or even students. Because jurors are not always familiar with the legal system, some may not understand legal procedures and complications that arise during the trial process. Even intelligent and well-meaning jurors may not fully understand the judge's charge or some of the jury instructions. Jurors are allowed to ask questions of the court, usually written on paper and delivered to the judge by the bailiff. Communication from the jury is typically read aloud in open court so that it may be entered into the record of the case.

When a jury is unable to generate the required number of votes for a decision, and deliberations have been conducted for some time, the result is a hung jury, which is fairly uncommon. The jury is called into open court and dismissed, and the judge declares a mistrial, allowing the prosecution the choice to drop the case or refile it and attempt to retry the defendant. Juries may be hung due to varying opinions of the significance of a piece of evidence, the meaning of "reasonable doubt," or differing opinions about innocence or guilt.

When a verdict is reached, the jury returns to the courtroom to announce the decision in a formal statement to the court. The jury is then thanked for its service and released by the judge. A prosecutor may request that the court poll the jury members: that is, the judge or bailiff asks each juror whether he or she individually voted for the whole jury's verdict. Polling a jury is typically done to determine whether a juror has been pressured to vote with the remainder of the jurors.

Jury nullification

A process that occurs when a jury uses information not provided during a court case to determine the guilt or innocence of a defendant.

One phenomenon in the criminal trial process is **jury nullification**. This occurs when a jury nullifies, or contradicts, the fair and impartial procedure of the trial process in some way. Jury nullification may also occur when a jury does not follow the court's interpretation of the law. A jury may disregard the court's instructions and consider information not presented in court during the trial as evidence in the case. For example, if a defendant claims to have a medical disability that prevented him from being able to commit a murder, and one of the jurors is a medical expert on that disability and subsequently uses personal knowledge to influence the verdict, that is considered jury nullification. A jury may also exercise nullification by refusing to convict the accused because the members believe the penalty is too severe. An example of this would be a case of a young man who shoots his father to prevent the father from committing another incident of spousal abuse on his wife. The jury, feeling that the young man attempted to protect his mother from harm because he knew the beatings would occur again, may find the defendant not guilty.

Judges clearly state in the charge to the jury that jurors are to consider only evidence presented in court, but this does not always occur in a room full of human beings, each with different knowledge and opinions. Attorneys are considered officers of the court with the duty to promote and uphold the law, and many bar associations consider it a breach of ethics for an attorney to make an argument in court that may cause jury nullification. Judges also have the ability to prohibit statements or arguments that request jury nullification. In the *U.S. v. Moylan* (4th Cir. 1969) decision, the right of jury nullification was affirmed, but the Circuit Court also upheld the court's power to disallow statements that informed the jurors of their right of nullification.[69] In a Sixth Circuit Court of Appeals ruling in 1980, the entire panel of judges agreed unanimously that "in criminal cases, a jury is entitled to acquit the defendant because it has no sympathy for the government's position."[70] In contrast, however, the Second Circuit ruled that a juror may be removed, according to Federal Rules of Criminal Procedure 23(b), if there is evidence that he or she intends to nullify the law.[71]

Sometimes, the criminal trial is **bifurcated**, or split into two parts. In the first part, the defendant's guilt or innocence is decided; in the second part, the defendant's punishment is argued. Juries do deliberate on a defendant's punishment, and their "verdict" comes in the form of a recommendation to the judge. A jury may sentence a defendant to a particular punishment, only to be overruled by the judge, who sentences the defendant to a different punishment. This does not happen often, however.

Bifurcated trial
A criminal trial that has two separate phases: the first phase determines the defendant's guilt or innocence, and the second phase determines the defendant's potential punishment.

Critical Thinking   A jury believes there is evidence beyond a reasonable doubt to show that a defendant, who is an anti-abortion activist, murdered a doctor who performed abortions in an attempt to prevent further abortions from occurring. The jury assesses a verdict of "not guilty" for the defendant. Do you believe this example of jury nullification is a fair result of the criminal trial system? Why or why not?

The Accused   While the accused person is at the heart of the criminal trial process, the defendant can be largely unaware of many of the legal aspects of his or her criminal case that occur behind the scenes. There are discussions between the attorneys about evidence that may be presented and witnesses that may be called, as well as negotiations for plea bargains. There may be discussions between the state's attorney, the defense attorney, and the judge about procedural matters that can affect the outcome of the defendant's case but have nothing to do with the offense the accused reportedly committed. The defendant's guilt or innocence lies in the public and private aspects of the trial process and will likely affect the rest of his or her life.

Some defendants are allowed to bond out of jail after arrest. This means that they guarantee, with money, that they will appear at all court hearings during the trial process, including any hearings prior to the beginning of the trial. Defendants may post bond by providing the required amount of cash to the jurisdiction or using the services of a bail bondsman. The defendant will pay a small portion of the bond, usually around 10%, to the bondsman, who will in turn provide proof to the jurisdiction that the defendant has paid bond. The bondsman guarantees the jurisdiction that the defendant will appear for all court hearings. If the defendant fails to appear in court, or "jumps" bond, the bond is revoked by the court, and the bail bondsman is responsible for paying the court the amount of the defendant's bond. If the defendant is subsequently found and brought into custody, he or she will appear in court, and the bondsman will receive a refund of the monies paid to the jurisdiction.

Some defendants are unable to post bond due to financial constraints. Bond amounts can range from $500 for some misdemeanors to $1,000,000 for high-profile cases. Some defendants are not approved for bond by the judge because the judge feels that the defendant will run away or because the judge feels it is safer to society if the defendant remains in jail. Bail is not guaranteed by the U.S. Constitution; however, the Eighth Amendment does state that "excessive bail shall not be required." This means that a judge may not prescribe an outrageous bail amount when compared to the alleged crime. In other words, the Eighth Amendment prevents judges from assigning a bail amount of $250,000 to a defendant accused of writing a bad check in the amount of $500. Defendants who cannot post bond or do not have an approved bond will remain in jail until trial. **Transport officers** will bring the defendant to court for all court appearances including trial.

Transport officer
A law enforcement officer who transports inmates to and from court and jail.

Actress and celebrity defendant Lindsay Lohan faced felony charges for allegedly taking a necklace from a jewelry store.

During a trial, a defendant will sit next to his or her defense attorney at a table near the front of the courtroom. The U.S. Constitution guarantees an accused person the right to confront his or her accuser, meaning a defendant has the right to be present for all witness testimony. During trial, a defendant will frequently confer with the defense attorney to clarify questions or strategy. Whether or not a defendant testifies is also part of the defense's trial strategy. A defendant has the constitutional right to refrain from testifying in court; this is called the right not to incriminate oneself. If a defendant does testify, he or she is subject to the same process of cross-examination by which any other witness must participate.

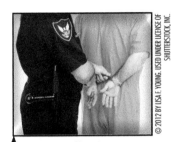

A transport officer brings defendants to and from their court appearances.

If a defendant is in custody during the trial process, he or she will return to a supervised room or area when court is not in session. A defendant is allowed to confer with his or her attorney in private but will not have free access to the building. If a defendant needs to use the restroom, for example, someone will accompany him or her to ensure that there is no escape attempt or harm done to anyone—including the harm of a defendant by another party.

After jury deliberations are over and a verdict is delivered in court, a defendant will be released in the case of a not guilty verdict or remanded to the custody of the local jurisdiction in the case of a guilty verdict. Some judges may, depending on circumstances and arguments from the prosecution and defense, release a defendant who has been found guilty for a temporary time so that he or she can manage personal affairs before punishment is assessed. The defendant may be ordered to turn himself or herself in to the authorities on a particular date and time or may be ordered to return to court for sentencing.

A defendant in a criminal trial is arguably in a precarious situation. On the one hand, a defendant is technically innocent until proven guilty. Due to human tendencies and public opinion, a defendant may be perceived as guilty even if the jury returns a verdict of not guilty. Such perception of a defendant can affect the defendant's reputation and everyday activities for the rest of his or her life. The prosecuting attorney has the task of proving the defendant's guilt; often, the prosecutor publicly makes the defendant look like a bad person in addition to showing guilt. This process is sometimes known as a **degradation ceremony**.[72] For example, the prosecutor may take on a very negative attitude when speaking to the jury, using body language such as a curled lip or deep frown to demonstrate his or her distaste for the defendant. Presenting the defendant in the worst light possible is part of the prosecutor's job. The defense attorney will attempt to salvage the defendant's appearance during counterargument.

Degradation ceremony
The tactic of presenting someone in a negative light so that others may look unfavorably upon that individual. A prosecutor may do this to a defendant, or a defense attorney may do this to a witness for the prosecution.

Critical Thinking   Do you believe it is fair for a prosecutor to embellish negative statements about the defendant in an attempt to win the sympathy of the jury? Why or why not?

Chapter Summary

- The criminal trial process is an important function of the criminal justice system. Criminal trials determine the guilt or innocence of an accused person. Criminal trials may be conducted in front of a judge—a "bench trial"—or a jury—a "jury trial." The typical criminal trial consists of opening statements from the defense and prosecution, witness testimony (including direct examination and cross-examination), closing arguments, jury instructions, and the verdict.

- *Gideon v. Wainwright* (1963) was an integral Supreme Court decision that not only affirmed that all defendants, even poor ones, are entitled to be represented by counsel, but also spurred the creation of the public defender system.

- The courtroom workgroup includes many important people who are part of the criminal justice process: the judge, the court clerk, the bailiff, the probation officer, the court reporter, and the process server. These individuals ensure that the business of the court runs smoothly.

- The judge, though just one part of the court team, is considered by many the most important person in the courtroom. A judge's primary duty is to oversee the standard procedures of the court system to ensure that justice is fairly served. A judge's responsibilities include making sure that the defense and prosecution both have the opportunity to present their cases, determining the admissibility of evidence, giving instructions to the jury, and using judicial discretion to follow and enforce the law in his or her courtroom.

- The prosecutor is the attorney for the state. The prosecutor makes a criminal case against a defendant and argues that the defendant is guilty of the charges. A prosecutor has many different duties to fulfill in the criminal trial process. Prosecutors are involved in various aspects of casework, from investigation, arrest, and trial to sentencing, appeal, and parole.

- The defense attorney is the attorney who represents the accused. The defense attorney may be hired by the defendant or appointed by a judge. Some counties have a public defender's office. A public defender is an attorney who represents indigent defendants who cannot afford to hire attorneys.

- In a jury trial, the decision of the defendant's guilt or innocence lies in the hands of a jury of the defendant's peers. The jury listens to arguments made during the trial and then deliberates and renders a verdict. Sometimes after a defendant is found guilty, a sentencing trial will be held in front of a jury. The jury will determine the punishment that they recommend to the court for the defendant.

Critical Thinking

1. How do you think trials would be different if our system did not have the presumption of innocence? How might this affect the way trials would work?
2. Is it possible for a witness to be competent but not credible? What would be an example of this?
3. Is it important that a judge have experience as an attorney for both the prosecution and the defense? Why or why not?
4. What should be done if a juror lies? What does a "mistrial" really mean for everyone?
5. When might it be in the defendant's best interest to agree, or refuse to agree, to a plea bargain prior to trial? Are the risks in these instances worth it?
6. What is the difference between "not guilty" and "innocent" of a crime? Is there a difference?
7. Do you agree with the concept of limited admissibility of evidence? Why or why not?
8. Legislative efforts to limit judicial discretion shift power from the judge to the prosecutor. How does this affect the intended neutrality of the courtroom process?
9. Is jury nullification an acceptable practice in the criminal trial system? Do you believe it should be allowed? Why or why not?
10. What is the role of the accused in the trial process? Does it matter whether the accused testifies or remains silent?

Media

12 Angry Men (1957): This movie demonstrates the type of interaction and discussion possible during jury deliberation. There is also an example of jury nullification. For a synopsis of the film and detailed descriptions of the different jurors, visit http://www.filmsite.org/twelve.html.

To Kill a Mockingbird (1962): In this movie, based on the book written by Harper Lee, a defense attorney in the Depression-era American South defends a black man against undeserved rape charges. While his choice is unpopular with his friends and neighbors, he shows commitment to the integrity of the judicial process and defends his client to the best of his ability. A full description of the story, its characters, and commentary on the racial tensions outlined in the book and movie may be found at http://www.filmsite.org/toki.html.

Lewis, A. (1966). *Gideon's Trumpet.* New York, NY: Vintage Books/Random House This book chronicles the story behind the *Gideon v. Wainwright* (1963) case, which yielded the U.S. Supreme Court's ruling that criminal case defendants have the right to be represented by an attorney, even if they cannot afford to pay. Commentary on the book is available at http://www.nacdl.org/public.nsf/championarticles/A0301p61?OpenDocument.

Texas Justice Court Training Center: http://www.tjctc.org/ The official website for the Texas Justice Court Training Center provides legal news and updates for judges, bailiffs, constables, and other courtroom personnel.

The National Judicial College: http://www.judges.org/ The agency's official website provides information on continuing education courses, including online offerings, for judges around the country.

Endnotes

1. *Gideon v. Wainwright*, 372 U.S. 335 (1963).
2. McBride, A. (2006). *Supreme Court History: Expanding Civil Rights; Landmark Cases Gideon v. Wainwright.* Retrieved from http://www.pbs.org/wnet/supremecourt/rights/landmark_gideon.html
3. Ulmer, J. (1994). "Trial Judges in a Rural Court Community." *Journal of Contemporary Ethnography, 23*, 79–108.
4. Eisenstein, J., & Jacob, H. (1970). *Felony Justice: An Organizational Analysis of Criminal Courts.* Boston, MA: Little, Brown.
5. Stuckey, G. B. (1976). *Procedures in the Criminal Justice System.* Columbus, OH: Merrill.
6. *Duncan v. Louisiana* 391 U.S. 145 (1968).
7. *West's Encyclopedia of American Law* (2nd ed.). (2004). Farmington Hills, MI: Gale.
8. Katz, B. S. (1997). *Justice Overruled: Unmasking the Criminal Justice System.* New York, NY: Warner.
9. *U.S. v. Dinitz*, 424 U.S. 600, 612 (1976).
10. Federal Rules of Evidence, Rule 601.
11. Schum, D., & Morris, J. (2007, March). "Assessing the Competence and Credibility of Human Sources of Intelligence Evidence: Contributions from Law and Probability." *Law, Probability, & Risk, 6*(1–4), 247–274.
12. Garner, B. (2004). *Black's Law Dictionary* (8th ed.). St. Paul, MN: Thomson West.
13. *Daubert v. Merrill Dow Pharmaceuticals*, 509 U.S. 579 (1993).
14. Jones, D. (1981). *The Law of Criminal Procedure.* Boston, MA: Little, Brown.
15. Jones, 1981.
16. *Ohio v. Roberts*, 488 U.S. 56 (1980).
17. Ibid.
18. *Crawford v. Washington*, 544 U.S. 36 (2004).
19. Jones, 1981.
20. Inciardi, J. (2010). *Criminal Justice* (9th ed.). Boston, MA: McGraw-Hill.
21. Wiener, R., Pritchard, C., & Weston, M. (1995). "Comprehensibility of Approved Jury Instructions in Capital Murder Cases." *Journal of Applied Psychology, 80*(4).
22. Cronan, J. P. (2002). "Is Any of This Making Sense? Reflecting on Guilty Pleas to Aid Criminal Juror Comprehension." *American Criminal Law Review, 39.*
23. American Jury Project. (2005). *Principles for Juries and Jury Trials.* Chicago, IL: American Bar Association.
24. Florida Supreme Court. (n.d.). *Standard Jury Instructions: Criminal Cases.* Retrieved from http://www.floridasupremecourt.org/jury_instructions/index.shtml
    Illinois Courts. (2011). *Recent Criminal Jury Instructions.* Retrieved from http://www.state.il.us/court/circuit-court/CriminalJuryInstructions/default.asp
25. *Pope v. Illinois*, 481 U.S. 497 (1987).
26. North Dakota Supreme Court. (n.d.). *North Dakota Juror's Handbook.* Retrieved from http://www.ndcourts.gov/court/juror.htm
27. Judiciary Act of 1925, 43 Stat. 936.
28. Richardson, R. J., & Vines, K. N. (1970). *The Politics of Federal Courts.* Boston, MA: Little, Brown.
29. *Public Citizen, Inc., v. Bomer*, 115 F. Supp. 2d 743 (W.D. Tex 2000).
30. Becker, D., & Reddick, M. (2005). *Judicial Selection Reform: Examples from Six States.* Des Moines, IA: American Judicature Society.
31. Tex El. Code Ann. 253.151.
32. Inciardi, 2010.
33. New York City Criminal Court Act, Laws of 1962, chap. 697, sec. 22 (1).
34. Texas Justice Court Training Center. (2011). *New Judges Seminar.* Retrieved from http://www.tjctc.org/New-Justices-of-the-Peace/NewJudges.html
35. National Judicial College. (2011). *About the NJC.* Retrieved from http://www.judges.org/about/index.html
36. American Bar Association. (2000). *ABA Standards for Criminal Justice: Special Functions of the Trial Judge* (3rd ed.). Chicago, IL: Author.
37. *Osborn v. Bank* of the United States, 22 U.S. 738 (1824).
38. Friedman, R. (1986). *A Close Look at Probative Value.* 66 B.U.L. Rev. 733.

39. Hill & Hill, 2009.

40. McLaughlin, J. (1989). *Federal Evidence Practice Guide.* Matthew Bender.

41. Holton, N., & Lamar, L. (1991). *The Criminal Courts: Structures, Personnel, and Processes.* New York, NY: McGraw-Hill.

42. Rabe, G., & Champion, D. (2002). *Criminal Courts: Structures, Process, and Issues.* Upper Saddle River, NJ: Prentice Hall.

43. Holton & Lamar, 1991.

44. Franklin County, Ohio. (n.d.) *Franklin County Prosecutor's Office.* Retrieved from http://www.franklincountyohio. gov/Prosecuting_Attorney/

45. Misner, R. L. (1996). "Recasting Prosecutorial Discretion." *The Journal of Law & Criminology, 86*(3).

46. Ma, Y. (2002). "Prosecutorial Discretion and Plea Bargaining in the United States, France, Germany, and Italy: A Comparative Perspective." *International Criminal Justice Review, 12.*

47. LaFave, W. (1965). *Arrest: The Decision to Take a Suspect Into Custody.* Boston, MA: Little, Brown.

48. Inciardi, 2010.

49. Oakland County, Michigan Circuit Court. (2009). *Appointed Attorney Fee Schedule.* Retrieved from http://www.oak-gov.com/circuit/assets/docs/division/atty-fee-sched.pdf

50. Smith, S., & DeFrances, C. (1996). *Indigent Defense.* Washington, DC: Bureau of Justice Statistics.

51. "Nationline: McVeigh's Defense Cost Taxpayers $13.8 Million." *USA Today,* July 3, 2001, p. 3A.

52. *Smith v. Texas,* 311 U.S. 128 (1940).

53. *Klopfer v. North Carolina,* 386 U.S. 213 (1967).

54. *Barker v. Wingo,* 406 U.S. 514 (1972).

55. *Strunk v. United States,* 412 U.S. 434 (1973).

56. *United States v. Lovasco,* 421 U.S. 783 (1977).

57. *In re Oliver,* 333 U.S. 257 (1948).

58. *Thiel v. Southern PacificCo.,* 328 U.S. 217 (1946).

59. Magna Carta of 1215.

60. U.S. Constitution, Article III, Sect. 2, Cl. 2.

61. U.S. Constitution, Amendment 14, Sect. 1.

62. *Duncan v. Louisiana,* 391 U.S. 145 (1968).

63. Federal Rules of Criminal Procedure, Rule 24(6).

64. *Swain v. Alabama,* 380 U.S. 202 (1965).

65. *Batson v. Kentucky,* 476 U.S. 79 (1986).

66. *J.E.B. v. Alabama ex rel. T.B.,* 511 U.S. 127 (1994).

67. Glasser, M. (1997). "Letting the Supermajority Rule: Nonunanimous Jury Verdicts in Criminal Trials." *Florida State University Law Review.* Tallahassee, FL: Florida State University Press.

68. Ellsworth, P. (1989). "Are Twelve Heads Better Than One?" *Law and Contemporary Problems, 52,* 205–224.

69. *U.S. v. Moylan,* 417 F2d 1002 (4th Cir. 1969).

70. *U.S. v. Wilson,* 629 F2d 439 (6th Cir. 1980).

71. *U.S. v. Thomas,* 116 F3d 606 (2nd Cir. 1997).

72. Garfinkel, H. (1956). "Conditions of Successful Degradation Ceremonies." *American Journal of Sociology, 61*(5).

8

Sentencing AND Judgment

KEY TERMS

Aggravating circumstances, Community service, Deferred adjudication, Determinate sentence, Electronic monitoring, Good time credit, House arrest, Incapacitation, Incarceration, Indeterminate sentence, Intensive supervision probation, Just deserts, Law violation, Mandatory minimum, Mitigating circumstances, Mitigation specialist, Parole board, Pre-sentence investigation, Pretrial diversion, Rehabilitation, Restitution, Retribution, Sentence, Shock probation, Technical violation, Three-strikes law, Vengeance

CHAPTER OBJECTIVES

1. Understand the philosophy and goals of criminal sentencing.
2. Describe determinate and indeterminate sentencing.
3. Identify the range of sentencing options.
4. Describe "truth in sentencing" and the motivation for truth-in-sentencing laws.
5. Discuss the role of presentence investigations.

Case Study: *State of Texas v. Robert Coulson*   On
November 13, 1992, the Houston Fire Department discovered five bodies while
extinguishing a house fire. The bodies were those of the adoptive parents, two sisters, and brother-in-law (a county sheriff's deputy) of Robert Coulson. Coulson,
in an attempt to collect an inheritance from his parents, had subdued each victim
with a stun gun, tied their hands and feet, and placed plastic bags over their heads,
which caused all the victims to suffocate. Coulson then poured gasoline on the
bodies in an attempt to set the house on fire. While the home did catch on fire, the
blaze did not entirely engulf the house as planned. It is speculated that while Coulson poured gasoline around the house to destroy evidence, the pilot light from the
water heater ignited the gas fumes earlier than Coulson had expected.

An accomplice, Jared Althaus, later confessed to the Harris County District
Attorney that he had helped Coulson plan the murders. Althaus described in
great detail how he and Coulson left the murder scene and drove to Althaus's
family lake house, discarding various pieces of evidence along the way by throwing them out of the car's windows. Coulson maintained that he was at a shopping mall when his family was murdered. Althaus took investigators to the locations along the highway where the tools from the murder scene had been
discarded, and each piece of evidence was recovered in the corresponding areas.
During the trial, eight witnesses testified against Coulson, who denied their allegations and accused them of lying under oath, but he was subsequently convicted of the murders of his family. At his sentencing, Coulson maintained that
he was innocent of the murders. The State argued that Coulson was a manipula-
tive sociopath and only wanted his inheritance. In jail, Coulson reportedly admitted that he did not harbor any resentment toward his family, but felt that the
murders were the only way out of his dire financial situation.[1]

Robert Coulson was sentenced to death for the slayings of two of his family
members. To avoid a lengthy prison sentence or possibly a sentence of death,
Althaus testified against Coulson and received 10 years in prison, a relatively minor sentence considering his alleged involvement with a series of pre-planned
murders, in exchange for his cooperation with the district attorney's office. On
June 25, 2002, Coulson was executed for the murders of his family members.

Althaus repeatedly denied to investigators that he was inside the Coulson
home while the murders were being committed, and said he was sitting in a car
outside. Like Coulson, Althaus denied committing the murders. Is it probable,
however, that Robert Coulson could have singlehandedly subdued, bound, and
killed five adults, one of whom was a trained law enforcement officer?

In this case, two men accused of the same crime received very different sentences. This chapter will explain and discuss sentencing theories and guidelines,
disparity in sentencing, plea bargaining, and other issues in sentencing.

Goals of Sentencing   In the early days of the criminal justice system
in the United States, punishments generally followed the philosophy that a person
must suffer for committing a crime against society. Historically, the goal of punishing criminals was to cause them to suffer and therefore learn never to commit the

offense again. Punishments were generally imposed by taking offenders out of society and placing them in jail cells for the purpose of having them repent to God for their sins. In fact, the word "penitentiary" is based upon this ideal. This is a practice that was introduced to the United States by the Puritans and Quakers, but this philosophy still influences our modern-day criminal justice system. The goals of punishment in the modern criminal justice system in America are to protect society and to rehabilitate the offender. These goals will be covered in detail in the next few pages.

In a criminal proceeding, a defendant who has either pleaded guilty or been found guilty by a judge or jury must have a punishment imposed. These punishments can range from a simple fine to death. For example, in the Robert Coulson case, Coulson was found guilty of murdering his family and sentenced to death, while Coulson's accomplice testified against him and received 10 years in prison. Sentencing is one of the biggest responsibilities of a judge or jury. A sentence is a punishment given to an offender by a judge or jury for the crime committed by the offender. Sentencing is the process by which this punishment is determined. All sentences are governed by statutory provisions and vary from state to state and even among local jurisdictions. The states are given the authority to punish criminal defendants; however, the federal government can also punish individuals who are convicted of federal crimes.

Sentence
A punishment imposed by a judicial body on an offender who has committed a crime.

Deterrence   Early philosophers such as Cesare Beccaria believed that the only purpose for punishment was the deterrence of crime.[2] Deterrence is a philosophy of punishment that presumes that the punishment inflicted will have the effect of causing criminals to refrain from committing crimes.[3] Deterrence works by influencing the perceptions of potential offenders and, by consequence, their behavior. Punishment can only deter criminals from committing crimes if it is made public. There are two forms of deterrence: general deterrence and special or specific deterrence. General deterrence means that by punishing one defendant for a crime, the legal system makes an example of the individual so that other persons will be deterred from committing crimes. Special or specific deterrence means that after a defendant is punished for committing a particular crime, that individual will refrain from committing further crimes. Gibbs (1975) further established a difference between absolute and restrictive deterrence. When an individual refrains from committing a crime out of fear of being punished for the crime, that individual has been deterred absolutely. When a person limits his or her involvement in committing a crime to reduce the risk of punishment—such as a drug dealer selling smaller amounts of drugs, rather than refraining from the sale of drugs—that person has been deterred restrictively. The individual is still committing the crime, but perhaps on a more limited scale.[4]

Beccaria also asserted that, to be effective, punishment must be swift, certain, and appropriately severe. He believed that punishment for a crime committed must be enacted within a reasonable amount of time after the crime has occurred; if the punishment is delayed for too long, the criminal may not make the connection between the punishment and the crime.[5] For example, if a woman who is arrested on a charge of Driving While Intoxicated (DWI) does not make her first court appearance for six months, will she truly make the connection that her involvement in the justice system is due to her actions? Certainty of punishment means that punishment will be applied, and the potential scope of the punishment is clear to all involved in the process, including the defendant.[6] In the example of the woman arrested for the DWI charge, she should be made to understand the possible range of punishments that she may be subjected to as a result of her crime. Beccaria suggested limitations on the severity of punishments applied: he asserted that the punishment should be proportionate to its corresponding crime, and it should not go beyond the point of severity where it deters others from committing the same crime or prevents the defendant from further harming others.[7] In other words, while the woman charged with DWI did put other individuals at risk by driving drunk, is it appropriate to sentence her, and other persons charged with DWI, to life in prison for the offense?

A complication of general deterrence as a punishment philosophy is that, while it may make sense in theory, its effects cannot be measured by social scientists. This means that whether deterrence works cannot be accurately determined, especially in the cases of people who have been tempted to commit crimes but have refrained from doing so. One cannot easily measure the number of people who have not committed crimes. Only persons who have not been deterred from committing further crimes can be measured, as their repeated crimes are documented by the criminal justice system.[8] For example, a burglar who commits one burglary and then commits no further crimes was successfully deterred from committing further crimes, while an auto thief who repeatedly commits auto thefts keeps re-entering the criminal justice system.

Specific deterrence, however, does seem to have some impact on the behavior of first-time misdemeanor and white-collar offenders whose arrests and entrances into the criminal justice system cause them embarrassment. The threats of public disgrace and negative effects upon professional and family matters appear to have positive effects on these "small-time" criminals, leading to reductions in further crimes committed by these offenders.[9]

Critical Thinking Think about Beccaria's points that punishment should be swift, certain, and appropriately severe. What would sentencing be like if only two of those three ideas were applied, such as swift and appropriately severe punishment without certainty? Would criminals know what punishments they faced for their crimes? What if punishment was swift but not certain or appropriately severe? Could that lead, for example, to murderers being executed by police shortly after their arrests?

Retribution

Retribution
The idea that a criminal should be punished in a manner that is commensurate, or as equal as possible, to the crime committed.

Retribution Societies from the ancient Middle East to the American Quakers primarily justified punishment of criminals based on the principle of retribution. Some of the oldest examples of retributive punishment are in the Code of Hammurabi, a series of nearly 300 laws and punishments detailed thoroughly un-

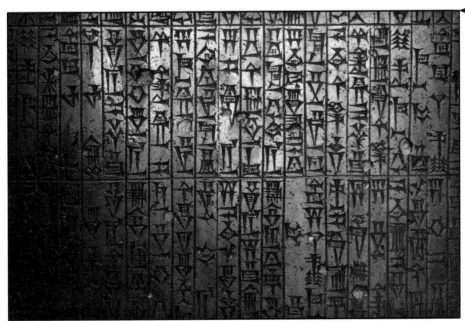

© 2012 BY JOHN SAID. USED UNDER LICENSE OF SHUTTERSTOCK, INC.

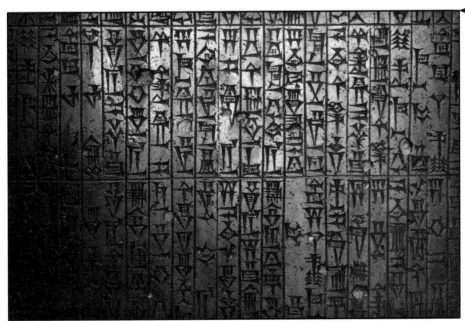

The Code of Hammurabi was one of the oldest known examples to incorporate retribution.

der the order of the sixth Babylonian king, Hammurabi, around 1700 BC. The Code of Hammurabi relies heavily on the concept of "an eye for an eye," as shown by a few examples:

> If a man puts out the eye of a patrician, his eye shall be put out.
> If a man knocks the teeth out of another man, his own teeth will be knocked out.
> If a son strikes his father, his hands shall be hewn off.[10]

Retribution suggests that a person who commits a crime should suffer punishment for that crime, and the punishment must be commensurate with the crime. In other words, offenders who commit more heinous crimes receive the harshest punishments, while lesser criminals receive more lenient punishments. Someone who commits murder would be put to death under the practice of retribution, and someone who steals money from a store may pay back the money and perhaps any legal costs incurred by the store. **Vengeance** is the justification for punishment that draws on the biblical idea of "an eye for an eye." Proponents of vengeance want offenders to pay for what they have done by suffering punishment; a measure of satisfaction is gained from knowing that the criminal has been punished. "**Just deserts**" is a concept that further suggests that the criminal's punishment should be comparable to the crime that was committed. In other words, if a man burns down his neighbor's home, the concept of "just deserts" may force him to lose his home and possessions as well. This justification is based partly on ideas suggested by the German philosopher Immanuel Kant (1724–1804), who stated that offenders should be automatically punished; they have committed crimes, so they "deserve" the punishment.[11] Retri-

Vengeance

The idea, based on the biblical philosophy of "an eye for an eye," of seeing that a criminal is punished, and that some satisfaction is taken from the fact that the criminal is punished.

Just deserts

A philosophy of punishment that states that a person who commits a crime should suffer for that crime; the amount of time or type of punishment for a particular offender is generally proportionate to the type of offense that was committed.

bution is the only justification for criminal punishment that focuses on what has happened in the past. All other rationales for punishment hope to influence the future by preventing an offender from committing future crimes.

Rehabilitation

Rehabilitation

A philosophy of punishment that is based on the idea that the offender's behavior can and will change through treatment programs by professionals. Rehabilitation can involve treating offenders for drug and alcohol issues, anger problems, mental health counseling, and other services.

Rehabilitation Rehabilitation is a corrections philosophy stating that the offender's behavior and personality can be changed by participation in treatment programs provided by qualified professionals. Offenders are typically put through assessments to determine what issues may be challenging for them, but may also participate in particular types of treatment depending on the nature of the offense and the length of the offender's sentence.[12] Treatment may address more than one issue depending on the offender's identified needs. Examples of rehabilitative treatment may include inpatient substance abuse treatment, participation in 12-step groups, individual psychotherapy, anger management classes, educational or vocational training, and other services.[13] Educational services could include preparation to take a high school equivalency examination, but many prison systems offer inmates the opportunity to complete high school diplomas and even college degrees. Vocational training could include on-the-job training in the prison unit, such as working as a cook in the kitchen or as a mechanic in the garage.

Rehabilitation was the primary rationale for punishing criminals from the 1870s to the 1970s. The goal of rehabilitation was to return offenders to society after incarceration as productive, law-abiding citizens. Rehabilitation was de-emphasized in the 1970s in favor of the goals of retribution and incapacitation because the appropriate methods to correct the behavior of offenders are unclear and we do not fully understand what causes crime. This country also experienced a shift away from rehabilitation due to more emphasis on "get tough" policies on crime. While critics suggest that rehabilitation and punishment are not mutually compatible ways to control crime, and that prisons are inappropriate settings to achieve rehabilitation, judges still send offenders to prison for rehabilitation.[14]

Incarceration

The act of confining a person in a jail or prison facility.

Incapacitation

A theory of punishment that imprisons offenders to prevent them from committing other crimes while incarcerated.

Incapacitation The removal from society or restriction of the freedom of criminal offenders is called incapacitation. In some historical societies, banishment or exile was used to achieve incapacitation. Banishment was utilized in ancient Greece and Rome. When banished, offenders were forced out of a civilized area, leaving them to wander the wilderness, significantly reducing their chances of survival and removing any potential future harm they might cause from their home society. In modern times, foreign nationals may be deported out of the United States if they are convicted of particular crimes. For example, a foreign national who has repeated convictions for drug possession may be deported from the United States to his home country and prevented from returning. The purpose of incapacitation is to make conditions all but impossible for offenders to commit crimes during the period of incapacitation. Prisons are used to incapacitate criminals; incarcerated offenders cannot commit crimes in society outside the prison.

At this time, life imprisonment without parole and execution are the only forms of incapacitation guaranteeing that the offender will no longer commit crimes against the community. The foremost issue concerning incapacitation is that incapacitation by perpetual imprisonment is costly. Additional prisons would need to be built and more employees would need to be hired. Temporary incapacitation—that is, imprisonment until the offender will no longer commit crimes—is unreasonable, as criminality cannot always be predicted. Another issue to consider is the humanity, as well as the practicality, of permanent incapacitation. A criminal permanently ensconced in a prison cell would cause no further harm to society, but permanently imprisoning an offender can be considered cruel and unusual punishment, especially in comparison to the crime. Taking Cesare Beccaria's idea of swift, certain, and appropriately severe punishment into account, is it reasonable to incapacitate all criminals by permanently removing them from society, whether their crimes are small thefts or murders? Permanent incapacitation of offenders also violates their civil rights, which are afforded to all citizens in the U.S. Constitution and its amendments.

Restorative Justice

Some jurisdictions are making efforts to restore victims of crime as much as possible to their states before the crimes occurred, making them "whole." John Braithwaite, an Australian criminologist, has encouraged the enabling of both the offender and the victim to repair the social damage caused by the crime. This is the concept of restorative justice. Braithwaite stresses that the focus of the mainstream criminal justice system on punishment irreversibly shames the offender and thereby perpetuates criminal association and activity: "When individuals are shamed so remorselessly and unforgivingly that they become outcasts, or even begin to think of themselves as outcasts it becomes more rewarding to associate with others who are perceived in some limited or total way as also at odds with mainstream standards."[15] Sullivan and Tifft (2005) have written that in situations where people have experienced harm, they as victims hope that the one who has caused the harm will accept responsibility for his or her actions, and perhaps offer an apology; acknowledgement of victims' worsened state and subsequent repair of that state—to the extent that it can be repaired—allows the victims to move on.[16] Restorative justice is, essentially, a means for the offender to "make things right" with society by addressing the needs and rights of the victims of the crime.

In the early 1980s, only four states had laws protecting the basic rights of victims in the criminal justice system. Today, every state has some laws protecting victims' rights, thanks largely to the victims' rights movement and increased research in the area. Over 30,000 statutes related to crime victims have been enacted, and federal legislation has been passed to provide basic rights and services to crime victims within the last 25 years.[17]

Critical Thinking

What are some of the laws in your state to protect victims' rights? Do you believe those laws serve their purpose?

Career Connections: Pre-Sentence Investigator

A pre-sentence investigator compiles a report for the court prior to the sentencing of a defendant. The report, also known as a pre-sentence investigation, details the defendant's background and any extenuating circumstances that may have contributed to the criminal behavior, then recommends an appropriate sentence. Some information that may be included in the pre-sentence investigation report includes family history, educational history, economic data, military record, health history, and prior criminal history.

A pre-sentence investigator will interview the defendant, the victim, and any other persons who may contribute relevant information, such as employers, mental health professionals, or even neighbors. Review and compilation of the defendant's records are common to ensure a thorough report. Effective interview skills, critical analysis, and attention to detail are highly desirable qualities for a pre-sentence investigator. A pre-sentence investigator typically has a bachelor's degree in criminal justice or a social or human science, and almost all pre-sentence investigators work for probation departments or the courts. There are, however, persons who conduct pre-sentence investigations for the defense. These individuals are usually known as mitigation specialists.

Pre-sentence investigation

A report to the court which outlines the defendant's prior alcohol and drug history, medical history, criminal history, education, and other factors that is given to the judge to assist with determination of sentence. Pre-sentence investigations are generally written by local probation departments.

Mitigation specialist

A person educated in the social sciences who assists the defendant in obtaining evidence to minimize the impact of punishment. Mitigation specialists are generally social workers or criminologists who compile past history of the defendant's life to assist with the defense.

Types of Sentences

A sentence is the sanction or sanctions imposed upon a convicted criminal by a judicial body such as a jury or a judge. Once the conviction occurs, the court's purpose shifts from impartial case litigation to imposition of sanctions. Different goals of sentencing exist but can intertwine and overlap depending on multiple considerations. The primary goal is to protect the public from the offender; other goals may be to make an example of the offender to hopefully prevent others from committing the crime, to rehabilitate the offender, or the most obvious and well-known purpose, to punish the offender. In light of the different goals in sentencing, there are also different types of sentences. Some of these sentences may include fines, probation (of which there are different types), and community service, among others.

Fines

Offenders may be forced to pay fines in place of or in tandem with probation or incarceration. Most traffic offenses and many misdemeanors are traditionally addressed by assessing fines on the offenders. Felony offenders may also be assigned fines, although felony fines are much higher amounts than misdemeanor fines. Sometimes fines are twice the amount of what the offender gained from committing the crime. In New York State, for example, a typical fine imposed for a felony drug conviction is $10,000, even if the offender was in possession of drugs with a street value of far less than $10,000.[18] The imposition of fines has declined somewhat due to two Supreme Court rulings: *Williams v. Illinois* (1970) and *Bearden v. Georgia* (1983). The ruling in *Williams* pronounced that a person cannot be incarcerated longer than the length of the maximum sentence needed to work off a fine the individual was unable to pay. At the time of the ruling, 47 states frequently held defendants beyond the maximum sentence.[19] The *Bearden* decision stated that a sentencing court could not revoke a defendant's probation if a defendant had completed every condition of probation but the payment of fines due to the defendant's inability to pay.[20] This keeps offenders who are on probation from having their probation revoked and going to jail, possibly losing their jobs in the process.

Probation   Probation, or community supervision, returns an offender to the community under the supervision of an agent of the court or a probation agency. The word "probation" comes from the Latin word *probare*, which means "to test or prove." Probation offers the offender a chance to prove that if given a second chance, he or she can engage in socially acceptable behavior.

Jail time is one type of sentence a guilty defendant may receive.

Probationers have been found guilty by the court or have pleaded guilty. The offender who has been placed on probation is not confined in jail or prison and must fulfill conditions of a sentence imposed by the court. When a court sentences a criminal to probation, the judge will set the conditions of probation. The conditions are, in effect, a contract between the court and the probationer. The probation agreement usually comes in the form of general and specific conditions. General conditions are those stipulations that are set by law and conduct the behavior and rules that must be followed by all probationers under the court's jurisdiction. Specific conditions are those additional stipulations that a judge may impose in an effort to customize the probation sentence to fit the individual and crime. General and specific conditions of probation for all states and the federal government may be found online in state and federal government statutes. Probation can include a multitude of conditions, such as community service, participation in therapeutic intervention, and fines.

The concept of probation in the United States was first discussed by John Augustus, a Boston shoemaker, in the early 1840s. The "father of probation" volunteered to pay bail and assume responsibility for certain less serious offenders in exchange for the judge deferring their sentences. Augustus provided the offenders with friendship, support with family and personal issues, and even employment assistance for the period of their release. The offenders later returned to court for sentencing. Augustus would report on their progress toward rehabilitation and request that they be required to pay a fine and court costs rather than being imprisoned. If the judge was satisfied with an offender's performance in the community, the charges were dropped; otherwise, the judge proceeded with the sentence.[21] Augustus worked with the Boston courts for 18 years, never receiving any salary for his efforts. He used his own money and donations from others to support his work.[22] The state of Massachusetts used his basic ideas to pass the country's first official probation law in 1878. Most states allowed probation by 1920, but not until 1957 did all states have probation laws.[23]

Probation is not typically given for dangerous or more serious offenders. In the best situations, probation provides a therapeutic alternative to incarceration, where the offender would be surrounded by more hardcore criminals and hostile situations, making prison a more unlikely place for rehabilitation to take

Law violation

A new criminal charge against an offender on probation.

Technical violation

A parole violation that is less serious than a law violation and could include failure to report to the probation officer, failure to make child support payments, or failure to complete other stipulations of probation such as community service hours.

Deferred adjudication

A type of probation in which the court's decision of the case disposition is delayed while the defendant completes certain requirements of probation.

place than the everyday free community. Offenders who are placed on probation and do not successfully complete the court-ordered requirements are violating their probation and are in danger of having their probation revoked. Having probation revoked means the offender typically has to go to jail to complete his or her sentence.

There are generally two types of probation violations: law and technical. A **law violation** occurs when an offender on probation receives a new criminal charge. For most jurisdictions, the probation officer will be notified when this occurs and will then contact the court to notify the judge of the violation, possibly resulting in the offender being brought in front of the judge to address the violation. A **technical violation** is usually noticed only by the supervising probation officer. Technical violations are less serious than law violations and could include failure to report to the probation officer, failure to make child support payments, or failure to complete other stipulations of probation such as community service hours.[24] The probation officer typically then has the discretion to cite the probationer for the violation, involve the probationer in more intensive supervision and counseling, or overlook the violation. Technical violation proceedings are started by the supervising officer and typically begin only when the officer has made the decision to approach the court to request that the offender's probation be revoked. Only the court has the final authority to revoke probation, no matter what violations have been committed by the offender.

Probationers are not incarcerated but are also not free citizens. Probationers do not enjoy the full range of protections under the U.S. Constitution that the rest of society enjoys. As part of the probation agreement, probationers agree that the probation officer may enter their homes or places of business unannounced and conduct contraband and weapons searches. They must also submit to drug and alcohol tests. If a probationer is found to be in violation of the probation agreement, he or she may be ordered to jail or prison by the court.

A probationer has not given up all constitutional protections, though. Probationers have a constitutional right to have an attorney represent them during the revocation process.[25] In *Morrissey v. Brewer* (1972) and in *Gagnon v. Scapelli* (1973),[26] the United States Supreme Court recognized limited due process rights of probationers. As part of the rulings, the court established a three-stage procedure that must be followed during revocation proceedings. These stages include a preliminary hearing, the revocation hearing, and sentencing. Often, in lieu of incarceration, the judge will reimpose probation but with stricter terms.

Deferred Adjudication Probation   Deferred adjudication is a special type of probation. Adjudication is the court's process of decision making; when something is deferred, it is delayed for a period of time. Deferred adjudication, then, is a type of probation in which the court's decision of the case disposition is delayed while the defendant completes certain requirements of probation. Typically, the defendant pleads "guilty" or "no contest" at the disposition hearing, but no final disposition is recorded with the court until the defendant successfully completes the requirements of probation, or fails to do so and has the probation revoked. If the defendant successfully completes the probation requirements, there may be no formal conviction documented on the defendant's record, as the case is typically dismissed altogether.

Critical Thinking Are there advantages to deferred adjudication probation for the defendant and the prosecution? Are there disadvantages for each? What are they?

Community Service

Community service Unpaid labor or service to the community as an intermediate sanction ordered by the court.

Community service is typically not used as a correctional sentence by itself, but may be a condition of probation for offenders found guilty of lesser offenses, such as shoplifting, first or second drunk driving charges, or minor drug possession. Community service is unpaid work performed for public tax-supported or nonprofit agencies. This form of punishment is consistent with the idea that while each crime has a specific victim, communities as a whole are also victimized by crime. Since crime is an offense against the person as well as the community, service is a good way to offer restitution to the community while reminding the offender of the importance of following rules agreed on by residents of the community. As such, community service is a more restorative process than other forms of punishment. Examples of community service jobs could include picking up trash on state highways, shelving books for the local library, or collecting and organizing canned goods for a food pantry. Community service may be integrated into a probation sentence with the purpose of teaching offenders a specific lesson or exposing them to the possible harm their actions may have caused. For example, a person convicted of cruelty to animals may be sentenced to clean stalls at an animal shelter, or an offender convicted of selling drugs may be ordered to perform community service at a drug abuse treatment program.

© 2012 BY DRAGON_FANG. USED UNDER LICENSE OF SHUTTERSTOCK, INC.

Picking up trash in the community is an example of community service.

Ethics and Professionalism: Innocent of the Crime

As a probation officer for your county, you are ordered by a court to complete a pre-sentence investigative report for the court. The defendant pleads guilty to the charge. After interviewing the defendant to get his side of the story, he informs you that he is innocent of the charge and he suspects his brother actually committed the crime. The defendant's brother is a parolee who will probably return to prison if implicated in another crime. The district attorney's office in your county has enough circumstantial evidence to successfully argue that your defendant committed the crime, and if he is found guilty, there is a good chance that he will go to jail, subsequently losing his job and his home. The defendant has elected to plead guilty to the charge in the hope that he will be placed on probation, allowing him to keep his job and his apartment and potentially preventing his brother from returning to prison.

What do you do? Can the defendant plea to a PSI report while stating he is innocent of the charges? Do you include the defendant's disclosure in your report?

Offenders who have community service as a condition of probation will receive a sentence of a particular amount of hours of community service to complete, such as 50 or 100. The maximum number of community service hours an offender can be ordered to complete varies from state to state; in Texas, for example, an offender can be sentenced to a maximum of 1500 hours of community service for a felony charge.[27] In Illinois, an offender convicted of his first charge of Driving Under the Influence (DUI) without proof of driver's license or insurance is automatically sentenced to 480 hours of community service.[28]

Community service is not currently viewed as an alternative to imprisonment. While community service itself is generally looked upon as positive, the general public does not consider the substitution of a community service sentence for a prison sentence to be punitive enough for most offenders,[29] even though one of the benefits of community service is its value to the public. The state of Georgia reported that in 2007, offenders provided $4.5 million worth of work to the state in the form of community service hours.[30] Another benefit of community service is that it is not costly to implement and monitor. Some proponents, such as Petersilia (2002), argue that community service is beneficial to all parties, as the probation department develops and maintains positive relationships with local agencies by sending them workers, the local agencies benefit from the unpaid work, and the offenders are personally inconvenienced, paying back some of their debts to society.[31]

Shock probation

A type of probation in which the court sends offenders to prison for a short period of time to "shock" them by exposing them to the limits of prison life, then returns them to the original jurisdiction to be placed on probation.

Shock Probation
Shock probation—technically a misnomer, since probation is designed to be used as an alternative to incarceration—is allowed by some statutes and involves the court sending offenders to prison for a short period of time, usually less than 180 days.[32] This is designed to "shock" offenders by exposing them to the limits of prison life before returning them to the original jurisdiction to be placed on probation. Incarcerating the offenders for a shorter period of time prevents them from absorbing too much of the "hardcore" inmate culture while allowing them to experience the harsh realities of daily prison existence. The first shock probation law in the United States was passed in the state of Ohio in 1965.[33]

There are several pros and cons to shock probation. Offenders who are sentenced to shock probation are made to understand the seriousness of their offenses without being subjected to the effects—as well as the taxpayers' cost—of a lengthy prison sentence. Shock probation also allows offenders who have positive rehabilitation potential to participate in community-based treatment and services, while the court still acknowledges the responsibility for imposing harsher, deterrent sentences in certain circumstances. Economically speaking, the short prison sentences of shock probation are less costly to society than lengthy sentences. On the negative side, shock probation has cost many offenders their jobs and interfered with their family and community support systems. There is also the possibility that even when offenders spend short periods of time in prison, they are exposed to serious offenders and hardened criminals, who generally have deteriorated social skills and hatred of prison life and other prisoners. Offenders may also be stigmatized by being incarcerated, causing confusion of their self-esteem and self-concepts. Whatever the arguments for or against shock probation, as yet, there is no evidence that shock probation reduces recidivism; the research findings on the subject remain inconclusive.

Intensive Supervision Probation   Some offenders who require additional supervision but may not need outright incarceration may be placed on intensive supervision probation (ISP), which includes a higher level of offender supervision, plus a stricter regimen of other services, including such stipulations as treatment programs and community service. Usually the offender is placed on intensive supervision because the probation department has determined that the offender's level of risk and needs require it; however, the court may order the offender directly to an intensive supervision program if the offense warrants, or if the offender was on a less intensive probation regimen but failed to successfully complete its requirements.

Probation officers who supervise intensive offenders typically have much smaller caseloads than other officers, and they may be trained in additional therapeutic interventions. Some of the stricter requirements of ISP may include:

- Multiple office, home, or work visits each week with an officer.
- Mandatory curfews.
- Participation in treatment programs.
- Employment or education requirements.
- Frequent testing for drug and alcohol use.[34]

While intensive supervision probation can help relieve overcrowding in prisons, it is not utilized frequently due to budget constraints and resource limitations. Every additional active intensive supervision officer occupies a spot that could be held by a routine probation officer with a much higher number of clients. Studies of the effectiveness of ISP show mixed results. A study by social scientists Billie Erwin and Lawrence Bennett (1987) examined the intensive supervision probation program in Georgia and found that recidivism rates for probationers on intensive supervision were better than for those on regular probation. The state also saved nearly $7,000 for each defendant assigned to intensive supervision probation rather than prison.[35] Petersilia and Turner (1993) found no clear relationship between more intensive supervision and recidivism. In other words, probationers on intensive supervision were as likely as offenders on regular probation to commit further crimes. Additionally, probationers on ISP had a substantially higher rate of technical violations than those on regular probation. Those offenders in intensive programs, however, came to believe that their chances of getting caught for committing additional crimes while on ISP were high, and they believed that if caught, they would be treated more severely than those on regular probation.[36] Perhaps this secondary effect of ISP led some offenders to refrain from further criminal activity, but this is not known.

Intensive supervision probation

A type of probation with a higher level of offender supervision, plus a stricter regimen of other services, including such stipulations as treatment programs and community service.

© 2012 BY NIULNIUKAS, USED UNDER LICENSE OF SHUTTERSTOCK, INC.

Frequent alcohol and drug testing may be a requirement of intensive supervision probation.

Restitution

Punishment that requires the offender to repay the victim for the harm that was caused, generally through monetary remuneration or community service.

Restitution   Restitution is an aspect of probation or punishment that requires the offender to repay the victim, or the victim's family, for the harm that was caused. The idea of restitution is to attempt to make the victim or the family of the victim whole again, theoretically restoring things to their original state. Restitution is generally provided by monetary remuneration (paying money to the family) or performing community work service, such as working in nursing homes, alcohol and drug treatment centers, or juvenile counseling or mentoring programs. Restitution not only compensates the crime victims for injuries and other losses, but also forces the offender to take responsibility for the crime committed. Restitution also allows the victim to be included in the process of administering justice.

Critics of restitution programs believe that these programs are punitive rather than rehabilitative because offenders may be subjected to additional sanctions that they cannot fulfill. Some feel that restitution negates any deterrent effects of the offender's sentence because it allows the offender to "pay off" the offense like a traffic ticket or late fee. White-collar criminals are usually sentenced to restitution payments with high dollar amounts to compensate for the large amount of monetary damage their crimes cause victims. The media attention given to white-collar crime also suggests that white-collar restitution amounts compensate for the shorter prison sentences given to these criminals. In other words, the general public seems to feel that white-collar restitution amounts "hit them where it hurts"—in the criminals' wallets.

Critical Thinking   Do you believe restitution as it is practiced today serves the purpose of making the victim, or the victim's family, whole again? Why or why not?

House arrest

A method of punishment in which the defendant is kept under close supervision in his or her own home rather than in prison.

Electronic monitoring

A form of technology used with house arrests to track and limit an offender's movement outside the home with telephone or radio signals.

House Arrest and Electronic Monitoring   House arrest—also known as home detention, home confinement, and several other names—is a program in which the offender is required to remain in the home except at prearranged and preapproved times, such as to attend work, school, or treatment services. **House arrest** is stricter and seemingly more punitive than ISP, but they may be used in combination. House arrest may also be used as an alternative to pretrial incarceration in jail. While house arrest of some form has probably been implemented by parents since ancient times, it was not used in the United States as an official sanction for criminal activity until the mid-1980s.[37] It became a popular punishment idea due to prison overcrowding. House arrest was not readily considered a reasonable alternative to incarceration because without 24-hour surveillance by law enforcement or court officers, there was no perceived way to ensure that a defendant would comply with the stipulations of home confinement.

House arrest became more common with the advent of widely available **electronic monitoring** equipment, which enabled the needed 24-hour surveillance. Electronic monitoring is not a form of detention, but rather a form of technology that tracks and limits an offender's movement outside the home using telephone or radio signals. There are two primary types of electronic monitoring systems used today: continuous monitoring and programmed contact. With the continuous monitoring system, the offender wears a device—typically a type of anklet—programmed to emit continuous signals to a nearby receiver at certain intervals. The receiver communicates with the monitoring agency's computer and cross-checks the offender's location with his or her schedule, which is programmed into the computer, to determine if the offender is in the right place at the required time. With the programmed contact system, the agency's computer makes telephone calls to the offender's approved locations at either random or preprogrammed times, and the offender must respond promptly to those calls to verify his or her location.[38] The type of device utilized governs the offender's response. Some devices require the offender to speak, using voice verification to complete the response. Others require the offender to insert a wrist-worn monitor into a verifier device attached to the telephone. Whatever type of monitoring system is used, each device worn by the offender is usually programmed to detect if it has been tampered with. If an offender tries to remove the device, a signal is sent to the monitoring computer reporting the attempted removal. Offenders who try to remove their monitoring devices may be subjected to more restrictions or incarcerated, as removing the device constitutes failure to comply with the monitoring stipulations.

Supporters state that house arrest and electronic monitoring are more cost-effective than incarceration while allowing the offenders to have more individual supervision than traditional probation. Offenders on electronic monitoring, by not being sent to prison, are spared from the potentially harmful effects of exposure to hardened criminals, some of which were discussed in the section on shock probation. Participants in combined house arrest and electronic monitoring programs are five times more likely to successfully complete their programs and are 50% less likely to abscond from their sentences.[39]

Critics of house arrest and monitoring think that these methods interfere with the offenders' rights to privacy and protection from unreasonable search and seizure as afforded by the U.S. Constitution. This interference, critics say, is also thrust upon those who live in the residence with the offender. Criminologists Rolando del Carmen and Joseph Vaughn (1992) commented, "A review of decided cases in probation and parole indicates that while the use of electronic devices raises constitutional issues, its constitutionality will most likely be upheld by the courts, primarily based on the concept of diminished rights [for offenders]."[40] An offender who is on electronic monitoring experiences a decrease in freedoms, namely the freedom to come and go as one pleases, because he or she is potentially being "watched" at all hours of the day. Other opponents believe that house arrest and electronic monitoring are unfair to economically disadvantaged offenders, who are not as apt to have homes and telephones where the monitoring devices must be installed. Offenders being monitored must also pay costly fees for the monitoring devices and services, which is more difficult for disadvantaged offenders. Another problem with house arrest and electronic monitoring is that while offenders are not allowed to abscond from the program, many still do and may commit more crimes. An examination of Florida's house arrest program revealed that between 1983 and 2008, offenders in the program killed approximately 462 people and committed over 720 sex crimes; approximately 32% of the murderers and 17% of the sex offenders had absconded from their monitoring programs at the time their crimes were committed.[41]

Pretrial diversion

An informal arrangement that involves referring the defendant to rehabilitative programs prior to arraignment in an attempt to address the offense reasonably while offering the defendant the opportunity to keep the offense off his or her criminal record.

Pretrial Diversion   Some jurisdictions offer judges the option to sentence offenders to a **pretrial diversion**, which operates much like a probation sentence. The defendant makes at least one court appearance and, depending on the defendant's personal situation and the crime itself, could be recommended by the district attorney to participate in a pretrial diversion. There is no trial and no plea by the defendant. The defendant sees a pretrial officer—who is a probation officer—and performs whatever tasks are assigned by the court. If the offender completes the tasks satisfactorily, the case is typically dismissed without ever going to trial. Pretrial diversions can last for various periods of time depending on judicial preference and local or state laws.

One example of how a pretrial diversion works might be in the instance of an 18-year-old who has been charged with possession of marijuana but has never previously been in trouble. The offender might be sentenced to complete a substance abuse evaluation, urine drug screens, monthly visits with a pretrial officer, and community service hours, all to be done within six months. If the offender completes all of these tasks within the allotted amount of time and does not test positive for substances, the district attorney would then drop the charges.

Capital Punishment: The Death Penalty   Perhaps the most controversial, hotly debated topic in sentencing for several decades has been capital punishment, also known as the death penalty. A capital crime is a crime that is punishable, according to legislation, by putting the guilty offender to death. Capital crimes, such as the murders committed by Robert Coulson described at the beginning of this chapter, are the most heinous of crimes. Capital punishment is different from any other criminal sanctions not just in its nature but also in its legal process.

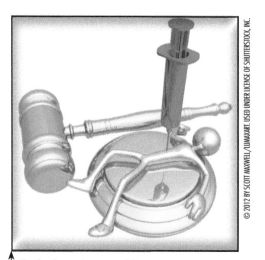

The death penalty is one of the most controversial topics in sentencing.

History of Capital Punishment in the United States   When Europeans settled America, they brought the legal systems and processes from their homelands. The English Penal Code was adopted by the British colonies on America's Atlantic coast and included over 50 capital offenses. The adaptation of the rules varied between colonies, so not every colony executed offenders for the same crimes. As an example, the Massachusetts Bay colony observed 12 crimes that were punishable by death. One of these 12 crimes, murder, is still punishable by death in many states today, but several other current-day lesser crimes were capital offenses in colonial days, including witchcraft, rebellion, and sodomy. In the Massachusetts Bay statute, capital punishment was justified for each crime by a supporting quote from the Bible, and the colony later added arson and grand larceny to the approved list of capital offenses. On the less deadly side of the spectrum, the Great Act of 1682 in Pennsylvania listed only treason and murder as crimes punishable by death.[42]

In colonial America, capital punishment was neither rare nor considered cruel and unusual. It was widely accepted as an effective and efficient way to handle criminals; an executed criminal does not live to commit further crimes. The earliest documented lawful execution in the American colonies happened in Virginia in 1608. Captain George Kendall, a prominent citizen in the colony, was found guilty of spying for Spain and executed. Even execution of juveniles was permitted in colonial days.[43]

When the Eighth Amendment of the Constitution was created to ban cruel and unusual punishment, banning the death penalty was apparently not an issue under consideration. The creators of the Constitution were probably thinking of the more ghastly forms of execution such as boiling in hot oil or impaling with spikes as cruel and unusual.

As time progressed, capital punishment changed. After approximately 1890, the death penalty became an increasingly popular sentence. The 1930s was the peak period for the death penalty: over 1,500 executions occurred in the United States during that decade. After that, use of the death penalty steadily declined, with less than 200 executions carried out in the 1960s.[44] In the southern states, African-Americans were far more likely to be sentenced to death than whites. In mid-1830s Virginia, there were five legislated capital crimes for whites and over 70 for African-Americans. The number of death sentences can be partially explained by the sheer number of states with capital statutes in their penal codes and the offenses listed by state that are punishable by death. In 1961, 48 states had capital offense statutes. Of those 48, 47 considered homicide to be a capital offense; 16 considered rape to be capital; four considered train robbery to be capital; and two considered espionage to be capital.[45]

Critical Thinking Do you believe the death penalty in the Coulson case was cruel and unusual punishment, just deserts, wholly justified, or something else?

The Supreme Court Weighs In The first argument before the Supreme Court which presented the idea that punishment of offenders could be cruel and unusual was in the case of *O'Neil v. Vermont* (1892). The petitioner faced a sentence of a total of 19,915 days—nearly 55 years—in jail for over 300 separate illegal sales of liquor. The sentence imposed by the court in Vermont was upheld because the Supreme Court found that there was no federal dilemma involved in the case, as the Eighth Amendment did not limit state sentences. Three justices strongly dissented with the opinion, and one, Justice Stephen J. Field, stated that punishment more severe than the crime it was intended to punish was cruel and unusual.[46] The Supreme Court did not hear another cruel and unusual punish-

Justices of the U.S. Supreme Court have made important case decisions affecting the death penalty.

ment case until 1910, when *Weems v. United States* was decided. The court reversed a sentence imposed upon an offender who made false entries into official government records: 15 years of hard labor, ankle chains, the permanent loss of certain civil rights, and other stipulations. The court determined that the sentence was severely disproportionate to the offense, and *Weems* became the first case in which the court negated a criminal sentence on Eighth Amendment grounds.[47]

A barrage of court battles over certain parts of capital punishment, as well as the capital sentence itself, occurred between 1968 and 1972. The initial case decision indicating that the death penalty might be in jeopardy was *Witherspoon v. Illinois* (1968). In this case, a court in Illinois had allowed a guilty verdict and subsequent death sentence to be handed down by a jury after the state's attorney had methodically excluded all members from the jury pool who were against, or possibly against, capital punishment. The Supreme Court agreed with Witherspoon, ruling that the "death-qualified jury"—meaning that every single jury member was ready, willing, and able to sentence the defendant to die—was not a proper representation of the community as a whole, and therefore violated the Eighth Amendment.[48]

More death penalty challenges made their way to the Supreme Court. States observed an informal moratorium on executions while awaiting the court rulings: in other words, no executions were carried out during this time. The landmark decision finally came on June 29, 1972, when for the first time in history, the Supreme Court set aside death sentences. Three cases, *Furman v. Georgia, Jackson v. Georgia,* and *Branch v. Texas,* led the court to decide that the capital punishment statutes in those cases were indeed unconstitutional. In those cases, the juries had been given full discretion to decide between imposing the death penalty or a lesser punishment in those capital cases. The majority ruling was five justices to four, and every single justice wrote an opinion—an extremely rare occurrence. The majority justices ruled that those statutes constituted "cruel and unusual punishment" under the Eighth and 14th Amendments because the death penalty was arbitrarily and unfairly imposed against non-whites. This ruling did not declare the death penalty unconstitutional, but rather the methods by which it was administered.[49] The decision in these cases (known collectively as the *Furman* decision) negated the death penalty laws of approximately 35 states, and over 600 inmates had their death sentences set aside and commuted to prison terms. By late 1974, however, 30 states had enacted new death penalty laws that conformed to the *Furman* ruling. Some states mandated capital punishment upon conviction for certain crimes, while others listed specific rules that judges and juries had to follow when deciding whether execution was the appropriate sentence for a specific case.

Another Supreme Court ruling affecting the death penalty was, like the *Furman* decision, a collection of court cases. In *Gregg v. Georgia*, the court addressed the new bifurcated trial structure in the state of Georgia: after defendants were convicted in first-degree murder cases, the punishment was determined in a separate court process. The law at the time in Georgia mandated the judge or jury to take into account any additional **aggravating circumstances** or **mitigating circumstances**, such as a murder occurring while the defendant was attempting to avoid being arrested; a murder of a corrections officer, an on-duty law enforcement officer, or a firefighter; a murder committed in exchange for money; or a murder committed while a rape, armed robbery, burglary, kidnapping, or act of arson occurred. The Supreme Court upheld the Georgia law, saying that because juries had to consider another circumstance in addition to the guilty finding, they were prevented from assessing death sentences with their previous wild abandon. In two companion cases, *Proffitt v. Florida* and *Jurek v. Texas*, the court upheld procedures in those states similar to Georgia's. By handing down these three rulings, the Supreme Court restated that capital punishment laws were indeed constitutional as long as those state laws provided clear and unbiased criteria for judges and juries to follow when determining whether to sentence the guilty party to death.[50]

After the collective *Furman* and *Gregg* decisions, state-sponsored executions resumed. The first state to complete an execution was Utah, on January 17, 1977. Gary Gilmore, convicted of the robbery and murder of a hotel manager, was executed by firing squad. At the time of his sentencing, Utah had two methods of execution—firing squad or hanging—and the judge allowed Gilmore his choice.[51] Since Gilmore's execution, more than half of the executions completed in the United States have occurred in only three states: Texas, Virginia, and Oklahoma.[52]

Methods of Execution
In 1977, several states legally retired hanging, electrocution, and lethal gas as methods of execution and replaced them with death by

Aggravating circumstances
Circumstances that go above and beyond the basic requirements for a crime to be considered serious; the facts or situations that increase the seriousness of a criminal act.

Mitigating circumstances
Circumstances that do not justify a criminal act, but make the crime less reprehensible and may be used to reduce the sentence in a criminal trial.

lethal injection. Supporters of this method argued that it would be a far more humane mode of execution, as the prisoner would fall asleep, and death would be virtually instantaneous. The American Medical Association argued against lethal injection and issued instructions to its member doctors to refrain from taking part in the act, pointing out that the role of a doctor is to protect and save life, not end it.[53] The first inmate to die in the United States by state-supported lethal injection was Charles Brooks, Jr. He was put to death in Huntsville, Texas, on December 7, 1982, for committing capital murder in 1976.[54]

In 1994, a federal court ruled that execution by lethal gas was in violation of the Eighth Amendment clause on cruel and unusual punishment. The presiding judge cited as evidence doctor reports and eyewitness accounts of many past executions, all of which stated that the dying inmates were still conscious for a minute or more once the gas was administered. Consequently, the inmates could be suffering intense physical pain, including the deprivation of air akin to the experience of being strangled or drowning. This ruling stipulated that all future executions in California would be done by lethal injection.[55] The Supreme Court has declared death by electrocution to be constitutional, but due to the gruesomeness of the act, most states do not allow it. At the present time, only Delaware, Washington, and New Hampshire still offer hanging for executions; 10 states offer electrocution; five states allow lethal gas; and one allows death by firing squad. Twelve states and the District of Columbia have no death penalty.[56]

Limits to the Death Penalty   Subsequent Supreme Court rulings have imposed limits on which crimes may appropriately generate death sentences and have further clarified capital punishment as a whole. Following is a list of many of these rulings:

The Debate: To Execute or Not to Execute?   Proponents of the death penalty argue that it is, practically speaking, cheaper to execute offenders than to house them in prison for life, which could be many years. Due to state and federal laws, however, all defendants sentenced to death enter a mandatory appeal process, which has several steps and can take quite a few years. There are multiple sets of documents filed in multiple levels of courts, which must be reviewed by judges and attorneys in those courts, and verbal arguments are taken in some of those courts. The appellate courts are usually in wholly different cities or states than the attorneys' offices and the defendant's prison unit. The entire process is costly, from filing court documents, to traveling to and appearing in the courts, to corresponding with the defendant and his or her legal team. Since a judge appoints the defendant's legal team, the costs fall to the taxpayers. The average amount of time a prisoner spends on death row before being executed is long: 10.6 years in Texas (TDCJ) and at least 12 years in Florida (Florida Dept. of Corrections) and Arizona (Arizona Dept. of Corrections).[66] Most quantitative studies of the economic argument for the death penalty have shown that the death penalty exerts a much higher cost to taxpayers than life imprisonment, due to the costs of the appeals process. The state can spend up to $5 million per appeal.[67]

FIGURE 8.1 Supreme Court Rulings on the Death Penalty

Coker v. Georgia (1977)	Rape without murder does not warrant a death sentence.[57]
Eberheart v. Georgia (1977)	Kidnapping when the victim does not die does not warrant a death sentence.[58]
Ford v. Wainwright (1986)	States are prevented from executing death row inmates who have developed diagnosed mental illnesses while they are on death row.[59]
McCleskey v. Kemp (1987)	State death penalty laws are constitutional even when research shows that they may have been applied in a racially biased or prejudicial manner. While racial discrimination exists, it must be demonstrated in individual and separate cases.[60]
Thompson v. Oklahoma (1988)	States may not execute persons who were under the age of 16 when they committed their offenses unless the states in which the offenses occurred had established a clear, set minimum age for the death penalty.[61]
Stanford v. Kentucky (1989)	It is not a violation of the Eighth Amendment to impose the death penalty upon a defendant who committed his or her crime at the age of 16 or 17 years.[62]
Atkins v. Virginia (2002)	It is considered cruel and unusual punishment to execute the mentally retarded, since it cannot be determined that they understood their crimes, much less their sentences.[63]
Roper v. Simmons (2005)	The *Stanford* ruling was overturned. It is now unconstitutional to sentence a juvenile (person under the age of 18 years) to death.[64]
Kennedy v. Louisiana (2008)	Child rape in which the child victim does not die does not warrant a death sentence.[65]

Probably the most hotly argued reason to discontinue the death penalty is the justifiability of punishing someone who has killed by killing that individual. Murder is against the law, yet many opponents of the death penalty consider capital punishment to be state-sanctioned murder. Cesare Beccaria advocated against capital punishment, writing, "The death penalty cannot be useful because of the example of barbarity it gives to men . . . it seems absurd to me that the laws . . . which punish homicide should themselves commit it."[68] Supporters of capital punishment might argue that by killing another individual, the offender has stolen the victim's right to live, and has thereby forfeited his or her own right to live.[69]

There is also the argument that since the death penalty is irreversible, innocent persons may be executed. Research by Radelet and Bedau determined that between 1972 and 1996, 86 death row inmates were released prior to their executions due to doubts about their guilt.[70] These inmates were tried, found guilty, sentenced to death, and later released due to their erroneous convictions. The number of convicted death row inmates receiving exonerations has increased as well, from three per year from 1973 to 1999, to five per year from 2000 through 2007.[71] Opponents of the death penalty argue that one innocent person executed is too many.

Another issue regarding the death penalty is whether it is applied fairly to all races in this country. Since 1976, approximately 35% of executed offenders have

While a jury may recommend a sentence, the judge may overrule the recommendation and pronounce a different sentence.

been black, despite the black population in the United States being approximately 15% of the total population. Of the current death row offenders in this country, nearly four times as many offenders were convicted in cases involving white victims as were convicted in cases involving non-white victims.[72] Research published in 1989 by Radelet revealed the startling statistic that less than 0.2% of known, sanctioned executions in the United States were of a white individual for committing a crime against a black individual.[73] Updated statistics show that compared to 16 white offenders in the United States who were executed for killing black victims, there have been 253 black offenders executed for killing white victims.[74]

Public support in the U.S. for the death penalty reached its lowest point in 1966, during the height of the Vietnam War and American political activism; the highest was in 1984.[75] Several issues have arisen over time that have led an increasing number of people to question the validity and appropriateness of the death penalty. The fact that putting an offender to death is absolutely irreversible raises huge concerns for many death penalty abolitionists. Some offenders who were on death row have been released after new DNA testing technology proved their innocence of the crimes for which they were convicted. One study showed that out of over 4,500 death penalty cases examined, more than two-thirds contained serious legal discrepancies, such as incompetent defense counsel or corrupt prosecution.[76] Many death penalty states now offer sentences of "life without parole" for offenders who are convicted of capital offenses but are not sentenced to death. Life without parole effectively imparts the benefits of the death penalty—deterrence from committing future murders and no re-release into society—without taking the life of the accused.[77] Since 1998, the number of death sentences pronounced per year has dropped by more than half: 294 offenders were sentenced to death in 1998, while 112 were sentenced to death in 2009.[78]

Indeterminate sentence

A sentence of incarceration without a specific term or ending date. Parole boards or other professionals generally determine when the offender will be released.

Parole board

The governmental board that will determine if an offender receives parole and under what conditions.

Special Issues in Sentencing

The indeterminate sentence is the most common type of sentence. It has fixed minimum and maximum terms for imprisonment. The paroling authority determines the amount of time the inmate serves. When a defendant is sentenced to, for example, one to five years' imprisonment or 20 years to life, those are indeterminate sentences.

The indeterminate sentence is based on the idea of treating offenders to learn to refrain from criminal behavior so they can be returned to society as productive, law-abiding citizens. Theoretically, the indeterminate sentence should meet each defendant's rehabilitative needs. After the inmate is incarcerated, the rehabilitation begins, and the inmate is imprisoned until he or she can demonstrate signs of rehabilitation. The paroling authority, or **parole board**, has the duty to assess the extent to which the offender has been rehabilitated or not rehabilitated and orders the offender's release or return to prison. The readiness of the offender for his or her release theoretically lies with the individual and varies according to the individual's participation in rehabilitation and improvement while incarcerated.[79]

While indeterminate sentencing became popular in the 1950s and 1960s, it lost steam in the 1970s and 1980s. Many offenders who had been deemed to be rehabilitated recidivated, causing politicians and the general public to lose faith in the justice system.[80] Many inmates learned how to "play the game" and behave like they were rehabilitated in order to convince parole officials that they could be released into society. They participated in available treatment programs and learned how to use the appropriate verbiage to obtain their release.[81] As justice system reforms occurred, the decision-making authority regarding the length of an inmate's sentence moved from the parole board and prison staff to the prosecutors and lawmakers when the determinate sentence was introduced.

Offenders sanctioned with **determinate sentences** have fixed spans of incarceration and know precisely when they will be released, which eliminates the need for parole boards. The federal government and some states have established guidelines for determinate sentencing, while other states have sentencing commissions. The purpose of determinate sentencing is not so much rehabilitation as it is incapacitation: its main purpose is to keep criminals out of society. Stories about lenient judges and liberal parole boards releasing offenders back into society when they were not successfully rehabilitated caused legislators to create sentencing laws that controlled criminal justice professionals' discretion in any particular case. Many of these laws stated that the length of an inmate's sentence would not be determined by any person, such as the judge or the parole board, but by the actual crime committed.[82]

While it appears that determinate sentencing is advantageous because it creates uniformity in sentencing, removing any focus from factors such as race, gender, and social class, unintended consequences have been created. With the removal of discretion and decision-making power from those professionals closely involved with the case, the potential to apply the most appropriate sentence for an offender with extenuating or mitigating circumstances is also removed. This means the welfare of society and the offender's punishment cannot be balanced effectively, as in the case of a young man who kills his father to prevent him from repeatedly beating his wife. Legislators also presumably did not take into account the effect that determinate sentencing would have on correctional resources. Prison overcrowding has grown rampant in this country, with limits to even the number of beds in prisons. While many legislators assume a "get tough on crime" agenda in order to get elected or remain in office, the same legislators are loath to increase resource allocation in order to appropriately address overcrowding in jails and prisons. As a result, the civil and human rights of prisoners are violated.[83]

Another effect of determinate sentencing is that it has caused a power shift from the judge to the prosecutor. With determinate sentencing laws limiting the judge's discretion in sentence imposition, the power of the prosecutor to decide what charges can be filed against the defendant has increased. This has unintentionally caused a ripple effect, as defendants who are unwilling to accept longer determinate sentences for some crimes may be pressured into accepting

Determinate sentence
A sentence for a specific criminal act that is determined by the state legislature; a sentence that requires a specific amount of time, as ordered by the trial judge, for a person to serve in prison.

plea bargains for lesser crimes. This gives the prosecutor a huge amount of leverage in coercing defendants and their attorneys to accept plea bargains, particularly in cases involving sex or drug offenses.[84]

Mandatory minimum

A sentence that is imposed by the state legislature with no discretion given by the trial judge. The defendant is required by law to serve a certain amount of time in the state penitentiary.

Mandatory Minimums

The concept of the mandatory minimum sentence came about during the "war on drugs," which took hold particularly during the 1980s. A **mandatory minimum** sentence is governed by the lawmakers in each state and prescribes a set span of imprisonment for drug offenses such as possession or distribution. Other crimes can have punishments dictated by mandatory minimums, such as armed robbery with a gun. All 50 states and the federal government now have at least one mandatory minimum sentencing law. Mandatory minimums do not always work, however, because judges and other officials have the authority to alter those sentences. Mandatory minimum sentencing also does not take into account any special circumstances particular to one crime, forcing defendants who may be small-time or first-time offenders into the hardened culture of prison life with hardcore, repeat offenders.

Three-strikes law

A specific legislative mandate that requires offenders, after their third conviction for any offense, to serve a minimum amount of time in incarceration.

Three-Strikes Law

In the legal systems of some states, if an offender commits three felonies, he or she earns a sentence of life in prison. These "three-strikes" laws earn their collective name from the game of baseball, in which the at-bat is over if the batter earns three strikes. Washington was the first state to pass a **three-strikes law**, in 1993. Washington's Persistent Offender Accountability Act allows for offenders who have committed three felonies to be sent to prison for life without parole. California followed suit in 1994 with what has been deemed one of the most encompassing three-strikes laws. Under California law, some of the felonies considered "strikes" are sexual abuse of a child, kidnapping, murder, or rape. The first two felonies must be in the serious felony category; any third felony committed dooms the offender to a mandatory life sentence.[85] Over half of the

In the legal systems of some states, if an offender commits three felonies, he or she earns a sentence of life in prison.

states, as well as the federal government, have three-strikes provisions in their laws. Opponents of three-strikes laws believe they constitute cruel and unusual punishment. One example is the Supreme Court ruling in *Ewing v. California*, in which Gary Ewing's third felony was the theft of three golf clubs. While it was argued that the life sentence was severely disproportionate to the crime, the court upheld the law, and Ewing is currently serving a sentence of 25 years to life.[86]

Truth in Sentencing   Truth-in-sentencing laws mandate that offenders serve a substantial, or even a majority, of their sentences. These laws were enacted because prisoners typically serve less time in prison than their original sentences stipulated due to time off for good behavior or parole. Inmates are also released early due to prison overcrowding, and in some states, inmates who learn a trade or complete school could get time taken off their sentences. The truth-in-sentencing laws restrict **good time credits**, which in turn increases the percentage of a sentence an inmate serves. Most states have adopted truth-in-sentencing laws, and three states require that 100% of a minimum sentence must be served prior to an inmate becoming eligible to be released.[87]

Good time credit
The amount of time that a state penitentiary gives the offender for maintaining good behavior while incarcerated; time that is taken off the sentence.

Federal Sentencing Guidelines   Sentencing guidelines may be developed by sentencing commissions made up of criminal justice professionals and private citizens. Sentencing guidelines are a way to restrict judges' discretion. Both state and federal jurisdictions have guidelines in place that serve as general rules on which judges may base sentences. While the guidelines used to be considered mandatory, after the Supreme Court ruling in *United States v. Booker*, the guidelines are considered advisory only.[88] This means that judges may use the sentencing guidelines when determining a defendant's sentence, but this is no longer required.

The United States Congress created the U.S. Sentencing Commission in 1985. This commission creates, maintains, and changes federal sentencing guidelines to prevent sentencing disparities at the federal level. The guidelines are suggestions based on the defendant's conduct during the commission of the offense and the defendant's criminal history. There are 43 offense levels, six criminal history categories based on points, and four sentencing zones: A, B, C, and D. The offense levels rank different types of offenses by severity. Sentencing zones group the lengths of sentences into types and lengths of sentences, from least severe to most severe. Zone A includes sentences ranging from zero to six months; Zone B includes sentences ranging from one to seven months up to six to 12 months, with the possibility of using alternate methods of confinement, split sentences, or incarceration only; Zone C sentences range from eight to 14 months up to 10 to 16 months, with the possibility of a split sentence only if at least one half of the minimum sentence is served while incarcerated; and Zone D includes all sentences ranging from 12 to 18 months up to life in prison, with all time required to be served in prison.[89] New sentencing guidelines implemented resulted in increased similarity of sentences between offenders and sent more federal defendants to prison for shorter periods of time. Following is a table of sentencing guidelines:

FIGURE8.2 2010 Federal Sentencing Guidelines (in months of imprisonment). [90]

	Offense Level	Criminal History Category (Criminal History Points)					
		I (0 or 1)	II (2 or 3)	III (4, 5, 6)	IV (7, 8, 9)	V (10, 11, 12)	VI (13 or more)
Zone A	1	0–6	0–6	0–6	0–6	0–6	0–6
	2	0–6	0–6	0–6	0–6	0–6	1–7
	3	0–6	0–6	0–6	0–6	2–8	3–9
	4	0–6	0–6	0–6	2–8	4–10	6–12
	5	0–6	0–6	1–7	4–10	6–12	9–15
	6	0–6	1–7	2–8	6–12	9–15	12–18
	7	0–6	2–8	4–10	8–14	12–18	15–21
	8	0–6	4–10	6–12	10–16	15–21	18–24
Zone B	9	4–10	6–12	8–14	12–18	18–24	21–27
	10	6–12	8–14	10–16	15–21	21–27	24–30
	11	8–14	10–16	12–18	18–24	24–30	27–33
Zone C	12	10–16	12–18	15–21	21–27	27–33	30–37
Zone D	13	12–18	15–21	18–24	24–30	30–37	33–41
	14	15–21	18–24	21–27	27–33	33–41	37–46
	15	18–24	21–27	24–30	30–37	37–46	41–51
	16	21–27	24–30	27–33	33–41	41–51	46–57
	17	24–30	27–33	30–37	37–46	46–57	51–63
	18	27–33	30–37	33–41	41–51	51–63	57–71
	19	30–37	33–41	37–46	46–57	57–71	63–78
	20	33–41	37–46	41–51	51–63	63–78	70–87
	21	37–46	41–51	46–57	57–71	70–87	77–96
	22	41–51	46–57	51–63	63–78	77–96	84–105
	23	46–57	51–63	57–71	70–87	84–105	92–115
	24	51–63	57–71	63–78	77–96	92–115	100–125
	25	57–71	63–78	70–87	84–105	100–125	110–137
	26	63–78	70–87	78–97	92–115	110–137	120–150
	27	70–87	78–97	87–108	100–125	120–150	130–162
	28	78–97	87–108	97–121	110–137	130–162	140–175
	29	87–108	97–121	108–135	121–151	140–175	151–188
	30	97–121	108–135	121–151	135–168	151–188	168–210
	31	108–135	121–151	135–168	151–188	168–210	188–235
	32	121–151	135–168	151–188	168–210	188–235	210–262
	33	135–168	151–188	168–210	188–235	210–262	235–293
	34	151–188	168–210	188–235	210–262	235–293	262–327
	35	168–210	188–235	210–262	235–293	262–327	292–365
	36	188–235	210–262	235–293	262–327	292–365	324–405
	37	210–262	235–293	262–327	292–365	324–405	360–life
	38	235–293	262–327	292–365	324–405	360–life	360–life
	39	262–327	292–365	324–405	360–life	360–life	360–life
	40	292–365	324–405	360–life	360–life	360–life	360–life
	41	324–405	360–life	360–life	360–life	360–life	360–life
	42	360–life	360–life	360–life	360–life	360–life	360–life
	43	life	life	life	life	life	life

Commentary to Sentencing Table
Application Notes:
1. The Offense Level (1–43) forms the vertical axis of the Sentencing Table. The Criminal History Category (I–VI) forms the horizontal axis of the Table. The intersection of the Offense Level and Criminal History Category displays the Guideline Range in months of imprisonment. "Life" means life imprisonment. For example, the guideline range applicable to a defendant with an Offense Level of 15 and a Criminal History Category of III is 24–30 months of imprisonment.
2. In rare cases, a total offense level of less than 1 or more than 43 may result from application of the guidelines. A total offense level of less than 1 is to be treated as an offense level of 1. An offense level of more than 43 is to be treated as an offense level of 43.
3. The Criminal History Category is determined by the total criminal history points from Chapter Four, Part A, except as provided in §§4B1.1 (Career Offender) and 4B1.4 (Armed Career Criminal). The total criminal history points associated with each Criminal History Category are shown under each Criminal History Category in the Sentencing Table.

Victim Characteristics That Affect Punishment Some crimes are determined to be more heinous than others depending on the circumstances of the crime or even the characteristics of the victims. For example, the difference between murder and capital murder in some states can be the age or mental capacity of the victim. In Texas, the murder of a peace officer is considered a capital offense, as is a murder committed during the commission of abuse of a minor under the age of 16 years in Wyoming.

Critical Thinking Is there a difference between the murder of a six-month-old infant girl and the murder of her 60-year-old grandmother? What about the murder of 11-year-old twin boys, one of whom has been diagnosed with Down Syndrome? Should some conditions be taken into consideration when pronouncing sentence on the defendants who committed those crimes, or should the defendants be sentenced equally?

Plea Bargaining Plea bargaining is a process involving the prosecutor and the accused or the defense counsel. During this process, the parties discuss the stipulations under which the defendant will plead guilty to a charge in exchange for some kind of concession, or trade-off, from the prosecutor or the judge.[91] One or more of several things may happen as the result of plea bargaining. The charges the defendant is facing may be reduced, which leads to a reduction in the defendant's sentence. If the defendant is charged with multiple crimes, the number of crimes may be reduced, also leading by default to a reduction in the defendant's sentence. The prosecutor can choose to recommend that the judge be lenient on the defendant, which could reduce the defendant's sentence from jail or prison time to probation. And finally, in cases involving crimes with negative or inflammatory labels—such as sex crimes—the charge may be reduced to a less incendiary one, thus sparing the defendant from several hardships that may arise due to the label.

Plea bargaining has advantages for both the state and the accused. The financial costs of prosecuting the defendant are reduced. Cases that are taken to plea bargain do not go to trial, which not only saves the government money but also increases the efficiency of the courts.[92] The prosecution is also able to dedi-

"Let's take some of the pleading out of your plea bargain."

cate its time and resources to more involved and serious cases. For the defendant, the possibility of jail time during the pretrial and trial periods is reduced, as are the costs of legal representation. The defendant also increases his or her chances of receiving a reduced sentence.

There are issues with plea bargaining, the foremost being the possibility that an innocent person who faces a harsh sentence if found guilty agrees to plead guilty and accept a lighter punishment rather than risk going to prison or worse. When a defendant accepts a plea bargain, he or she also waives the constitutional rights to trial and appeal. Opponents of plea bargaining argue that by accepting a less severe charge or punishment, the defendant has defeated the system.[93]

The Supreme Court formally upheld the practice of plea bargaining, saying that it served the interests of both the court and the defendant, in *Brady v. United States* in 1970.[94] The Supreme Court has also supported the position of the prosecution in the plea bargaining process with its ruling in *North Carolina v. Alford*. In this ruling, the court announced that a judge can accept a guilty plea from a defendant who declares his or her innocence if the defendant makes the plea both voluntarily and with understanding of the plea, and if there is enough factual evidence to demonstrate that the defendant is guilty.[95]

Race and Gender
Race and gender are examples of extralegal factors that can affect sentencing. Extralegal factors are aspects concerning the defendant, the victim, or the crime that may not be clearly defined by law and, thus, are not supposed to be taken into consideration when assessing a sentence; however, this is sometimes not the case. Examples of extralegal factors include race, gender, socioeconomic status, and class status. The two perhaps most controversial of these factors, race and gender, will be addressed in this section.

In the United States, there is a disproportionate percentage of non-whites in prison. In 2007, although non-whites made up only 20% of the country's population, they made up over 60% of inmates.[96] The Sentencing Project, an organization that promotes reforms in sentencing laws, conducted research on state rates of incarceration. Their research showed that Hispanics are incarcerated at almost twice the rates of whites. The disparity is even more interesting to consider when one learns that blacks are incarcerated over five times as frequently as whites. The chance that a white male will spend some time in prison during his lifetime is less than 10%, while there is a nearly 20% chance that a Hispanic male will be in prison and an over 30% chance that a black male will go to prison.[97] Some argue that the higher number of blacks in prison is a result of racial profiling and unfair criminal justice practices. Federal statistics show that although blacks and whites sell and use drugs at comparable rates, blacks are 10 times likelier to be imprisoned for drug offenses than whites.[98] Some of these numbers are attributed to the higher number of drug arrests in metropolitan areas than in rural areas. Non-whites, particularly African-Americans, are more likely to live in metropolitan areas than whites, who are more likely to live in rural areas. The majority of drug arrests occur in metropolitan areas. Inner cities typically suffer from more social problems than urban or suburban areas: unemployment, social isolation, lack of resources, community violence, etc. Other factors include prosecutorial discretion as to which cases go to court and which ones can end in plea bargains.

Gender is another important consideration in sentencing, especially since the fastest-growing population in prisons is women. There has been a tremendous increase in female prisoners since 1995. Two-thirds of women in prison are non-white, only one-third of women sentenced to prison have graduated from high school or gotten a GED prior to entering prison, and many of them suffer from major depression or other serious psychological disorders. Being sentenced to prison does not seem to act as a deterrent: 65% of women in prison have been found guilty of prior criminal charges. One of the reasons for the increase of women in prisons may be the changes in sentencing laws relating especially to drug offenses. Nearly one-third of female inmates in state prison facilities and over one-half of women sentenced to federal prisons are incarcerated for drug-related and nonviolent crimes.[99] Figures 8.3 and 8.4 show numbers from the Bureau of Justice Statistics demonstrating the overall growth of the female prison population for the years 2000 to 2009.

FIGURE8.3 Female Prisoners Under the Jurisdiction of State or Federal Correctional Authorities, by Jurisdiction, December 31, 2000, 2008, and 2009.

Region and jurisdiction	Number of female prisoners			Average annual change, 2000–2008	Percent change, 2008–2009
	12/31/00	12/31/08	12/31/09		
U.S. total	93,234	114,649	113,462	2.6%	−1%
Federal	10,245	13,273	13,625	3.3	2.7
State	82,989	101,376	99,837	2.5	−1.5
Northeast	9,082	9,601	9,287	0.7%	−3.3%
Connecticut/a	1,406	1,502	1,335	0.8	−11.1
Maine	66	156	158	11.4	1.3
Massachusetts	663	751	719	1.6	−4.3
New Hampshire/b	120	181	167	5.3	−7.7
New Jersey	1,650	1,299	1,206	−2.9	−7.2
New York	3,280	2,587	2,489	−2.9	−3.8
Pennsylvania	1,579	2,764	2,828	7.2	2.3
Rhode Island/a	238	243	230	0.3	−5.3
Vermont/a	80	118	155	5	31.4
Midwest	14,598	17,783	17,454	2.5%	−1.9%
Illinois	2,849	2,721	2,590	−0.6	−4.8
Indiana	1,452	2,493	2,506	7	0.5
Iowa	592	749	723	3	−3.5
Kansas	504	569	565	1.5	−0.7
Michigan	2,131	1,957	1,755	−1.1	−10.3
Minnesota	368	670	674	7.8	0.6
Missouri	1,993	2,449	2,427	2.6	−0.9
Nebraska	266	390	366	4.9	−6.2
North Dakota	68	160	174	11.3	8.8
Ohio	2,808	3,913	3,989	4.2	1.9
South Dakota	200	355	380	7.4	7
Wisconsin	1,367	1,357	1,305	−0.1	−3.8
South	39,652	49,050	48,878	2.7%	−0.4%
Alabama	1,826	2,231	2,455	2.5	10
Arkansas	772	1,060	1,061	4	0.1
Delaware/a	597	557	493	−0.9	−11.5
District of Columbia	356	~	~	:	:
Florida	4,105	7,151	7,283	7.2	1.8
Georgia/c	2,758	3,692	3,774	3.7	2.2
Kentucky	1,061	2,270	2,295	10	1.1
Louisiana	2,219	2,516	2,616	1.6	4
Maryland	1,219	1,060	1,049	−1.7	−1
Mississippi	1,669	1,981	1,735	2.2	−12.4
North Carolina	1,903	2,778	2,808	4.8	1.1
Oklahoma	2,394	2,524	2,625	0.7	4
South Carolina	1,420	1,633	1,517	1.8	−7.1
Tennessee	1,369	2,129	2,009	5.7	−5.6
Texas	13,622	13,853	13,570	0.2	−2
Virginia	2,059	2,967	2,904	4.7	−2.1
West Virginia	303	648	684	10	5.6
West	19,657	24,942	24,218	3%	−2.9%
Alaska/a	284	503	589	7.4	17.1
Arizona/c	1,964	3,766	3,777	8.5	0.3
California	11,161	11,620	10,989	0.5	−5.4
Colorado	1,333	2,294	2,101	7	−8.4
Hawaii/a	561	728	701	3.3	−3.7
Idaho	493	758	744	5.5	−1.8
Montana	306	361	391	2.1	8.3
Nevada	846	982	949	1.9	−3.4
New Mexico	511	569	660	1.4	16
Oregon	596	1,109	1,125	8.1	1.4
Utah	381	640	581	6.7	−9.2
Washington	1,065	1,404	1,397	3.5%	−0.5%
Wyoming	156	208	214	3.7	2.9

~Not applicable. As of December 31, 2001, responsibility for sentenced felons from the District of Columbia was transferred to the Federal Bureau of Prisons.

:Not calculated.

a/Prisons and jails form one integrated system. Data include total jail and prison populations.

b/Jurisdiction counts for yearend 2008 are as of January 2, 2009.

c/Prison population based on custody counts.

FIGURE8.4 Prisoners Under the Jurisdiction of State or Federal Correctional Authorities, December 31, 2000–2009.

Year	Total	Federal	State	Male	Female	Sentenced to more than 1 year/a	Imprison-ment rate/b
2000	1,391,261	145,416	1,245,845	1,298,027	93,234	1,331,278	478
2001	1,404,032	156,993	1,247,039	1,311,053	92,979	1,345,217	470
2002	1,440,144	163,528	1,276,616	1,342,513	97,631	1,380,516	476
2003	1,468,601	173,059	1,295,542	1,367,755	100,846	1,408,361	482
2004	1,497,100	180,328	1,316,772	1,392,278	104,822	1,433,728	486
2005	1,527,929	187,618	1,340,311	1,420,303	107,626	1,462,866	491
2006	1,569,945	193,046	1,376,899	1,457,486	112,459	1,504,660	501
2007	1,598,245	199,618	1,398,627	1,483,740	114,505	1,532,850	506
2008	1,609,759	201,280	1,408,479	1,495,110	114,649	1,547,742	504
2009	1,613,740	208,118	1,405,622	1,500,278	113,462	1,548,721	502
Average annual change, 2000–2008	1.8%	4.1%	1.5%	1.8%	2.6%	1.9%	0.7%
Percent change, 2008–2009	0.2	3.4	−0.2	0.3	−1	0.1	−0.4

Note: Jurisdiction refers to the legal authority over a prisoner, regardless of where the prisoner is held.
a/Includes prisoners under the legal authority of state or federal correctional officials with sentences of more than 1 year, regardless of where they are held.
b/Imprisonment rate is the number of prisoners sentenced to more than 1 year under state or federal jurisdiction per 100,000 U.S. residents. Resident population estimates are from the U.S. Census Bureau for January 1 of the following year for the yearend estimates.

Chapter Summary

- There is no single primary guiding principle for sentencing, so most practices tend to blend multiple schools of thought. Common theories behind sentencing in the United States are deterrence, incapacitation, rehabilitation, and retribution. Alternatives or partners to sentencing include fines, probation, rehabilitative programs, and community service. Additional options for sentencing, depending on the circumstances of the offense, include imprisonment and the death penalty.

- Deterrence attempts to prevent crime by making examples of offenders in the hope of deterring others from committing crime, or by inflicting punishment on a person with the intent to impart the lesson that crime is not worth committing. Rehabilitation attempts to change the behavior and thinking of offenders by providing them with services that will help change their behavior. Restorative justice seeks to return the crime victims as closely as possible to their original states before the crime was committed. Incapacitation attempts to control crime by removing the offender from the community.

- Retribution refers to the idea that individuals who commit crimes should be punished to a degree commensurate with the seriousness of the crime. Vengeance and "just deserts" fall under retribution: vengeance suggests that satisfaction will be gained simply by punishing the criminal, while "just deserts" intends for the punishment to be comparably equal to the crime.

- The death penalty has been under review for many years to determine whether aspects of it constitute cruel and unusual punishment. The Supreme Court has further clarified stipulations of the death penalty with numerous rulings, but the two most groundbreaking rulings were *Furman v. Georgia* (1972) and *Gregg v. Georgia* (1976). *Furman* negated the enforcement of state death penalty laws on Eighth Amendment grounds, causing a halt to executions and the commutations of many death sentences to life in prison. *Gregg* upheld the revised laws, which required a multiple-step process in order for judges or juries to assess a death sentence on an inmate.

- Other issues to consider in sentencing are truth in sentencing, mandatory minimum sentences, characteristics of the victim, three-strikes laws, race, and gender. Whether each aspect has measurable effects on sentencing is being studied on a regular basis. Available data is typically a minimum of two to three years old due to reporting and measurement limitations.

Critical Thinking ?

1. Does offense type influence a probation officer's recommendation in the pre-sentence investigation report? Explain why or why not.
2. If deterrence does not work on capital offenders, why do states still utilize the death penalty?
3. How does the law apply rehabilitation and retribution at the same time?
4. Compare and contrast the various sentencing theories. Would the same theory that applies to a large metropolitan city also apply to a rural village in Alaska?
5. What is the purpose of a jury that is death penalty qualified?
6. Who should sentence, the judge or the jury?
7. The concept of jury nullification was introduced in a previous chapter. How might jury nullification affect the sentencing process?
8. In many cases, offenders are offered plea bargains by the prosecuting attorneys. Do you feel that the plea bargain process is fair to all parties involved in the case? The accused? The victim(s)? Why or why not?
9. Do gender and race play a role in sentencing procedures and, if so, how much?
10. Why do you think sentencing disparities still exist?

Media

Free Sentencing Guidelines Calculator: http://www.sentencing.us/
   Based on 2010 guidelines, this website allows users to get an idea of the length of a federal prison sentence based on the crime committed and special circumstances that may apply.
The Death Penalty Information Center: http://www.deathpenaltyinfo.org/
   The Death Penalty Information Center is a nonprofit organization that provides the media and the general public with facts and information relating to capital punishment.
Texas Department of Criminal Justice: http://www.tdcj.state.tx.us/ and Florida Department of Corrections: http://www.dc.state.fl.us/
   The official websites for some state correctional systems offer a wealth of information, including statistics, about their prison systems.

Death Penalty Blog: http://www.deathpenaltyblog.com
    Written by attorneys from Florida and Texas, the Death Penalty Blog shares news articles about legislation and other current events relating to capital punishment.
Death Row Information Sheet on Robert Coulson: http://www.tdcj.state.tx.us/statistics/deathrow/drowlist/coulson.jpg
    The Texas Department of Criminal Justice provides death row information on Robert Coulson.

Endnotes

1. Riddle, L. (1997). *Ashes to Ashes*. New York, NY: Pinnacle Books.
2. Beccaria, C. (1764). *Dei Delitti e delle Pene*. (Of Crimes and Punishment)
3. Ibid., 32–24.
4. Gibbs, J. (1975). *Crime, Punishment, and Deterrence*. New York, NY: Elsevier.
5. Beccaria, 1764.
6. Ibid.
7. Ibid.
8. Zimring, F., & Hawkins, G. (1973). *Deterrence*. Chicago, IL: University of Chicago Press.
9. Pontell, H. (1994). *A Capacity to Punish: The Ecology of Crime and Punishment*. Bloomington, IN: Indiana University Press.
10. King, L. W. (2005). *The Code of Hammurabi: Translated by L.W. King*. New Haven, CT: Yale University Press.
11. Kant, I. (1790). *The Science of Right*.
12. Texas Department of Corrections. (2004). *Offender Orientation Handbook*. Mississippi Department of Corrections. (2009). *Inmate Handbook*, State of Washington Department of Corrections. (2008). *Reception, Initial Classification, and Custody Facility Plan*.
13. Inciardi, 2010.
14. Bohm & Haley, 2010.
15. Braithwaite, J. (1989). *Crime, Shame, and Reintegration*. New York, NY: Cambridge University Press.
16. Sullivan, D., & Tifft, L. (2005). *Restorative Justice: Healing the Foundations of Our Everyday Lives* (2nd ed.). Boulder, CO: Lynne Reiner Publishing.
17. U.S. Department of Justice, Office for Victims of Crime. (2004, December). "New Directions from the Field: Victims' Rights and Services for the 21st Century." *OVC Bulletin*. Washington, D.C.
18. New York State Unified Court System. (2010). *Statistics*.
19. *Williams v. Illinois*, 399 U.S. 235 (1970).
20. *Bearden v. Georgia*, 33 CrL 3103 (1983).
21. Petersilia, J. (1998). "Probation and Parole." In M. Tonry (Ed.), *The Handbook of Crime and Punishment*. New York, NY: Oxford University Press. New York City Department of Probation. (n.d.). *History of Probation*. Retrieved from http://www.nyc.gov/html/prob/html/about/history.shtml
    Center on Juvenile and Criminal Justice. (n.d.). *The History of the Presentence Report*. Retrieved from http://www.cjcj.org/files/the_history.pdf
22. National Probation Association. (1939). *John Augustus, First Probation Officer*. New York.
23. Rothman, D. (1980). *Conscience and Convenience: The Asylum and Its Alternatives in Progressive America*. Boston, MA: Little, Brown.
24. Inciardi, 2010.
25. *Mempa v. Rhay*, 389 U.S. 128 (1967).
26. *Morrissey v. Brewer*, 389 U.S. 128 (1972).
    Gagnon v. Scarpelli, 411 U.S. 778 (1973).
27. *Texas Code of Criminal Procedure*, Art. 42.12.
28. Illinois General Assembly. (2011). 625 ILCS 5/11–501.
29. Inciardi, 2010.
30. Georgia Department of Corrections, Probation Division. *FY 2007 Annual Report*. Atlanta, GA.

31. Petersilia, J. (2002). *Reforming Probation & Parole in the 21st Century.* Lanham, MD: American Correctional Association.

32. Waldron, J., & Angelino, H. (1977). "Shock Probation: A Natural Experiment on the Effect of a Short Period of Incarceration." *Prison Journal, 57.*

33. Ohio Department of Rehabilitation and Correction. (2005). *Ohio Adult Parole Authority: 1965–2005.*

34. The Judicial Branch of Arizona. (2011). *Intensive Probation Supervision.*

35. Erwin, B., & Bennett, L. (1987). *New Dimensions in Probation: Georgia's Experience with Intensive Probation Supervision.* National Institute of Justice Research in Brief.

36. Petersilia, J., & Turner, S. (1993). *Evaluating Intensive Supervision Probation/Parole: Results of a Nationwide Experiment.* National Institute of Justice Research in Brief.

37. Ball, R., & Lilly, J. (1986). "A Theoretical Examination of Home Incarceration." *Federal Probation, 50,* 17–24.

38. Gowen, D. (2001). "Remote Location Monitoring—A Supervision Strategy to Enhance Risk Control." *Federal Probation, 65*(2).

39. Florida Department of Corrections. (2007). *Annual Statistics for Fiscal Year 2005–2006.*

40. Del Carmen, R., & Vaughn, J. (1992). "Legal Issues in the Use of Electronic Surveillance in Probation." In T. Ellsworth (Ed.), *Contemporary Community Corrections.* Prospect Heights, IL: Waveland Press.

41. Bureau of Probation & Parole Field Services, Florida Department of Corrections. (2008).

42. Bohm, R. (2007). *Deathquest III: An Introduction to the Theory and Practice of Capital Punishment in the United States* (3rd ed.). Cincinnati, OH: Anderson.

43. The Death Penalty Information Center.

44. Teeters, N., & Zibulka, C. (1974). "Executions Under State Authority: 1864–1967." In W. Bowers (Ed.), *Executions in America.* Lexington, MA: Heath.

45. Bedau, H. (1964). *The Death Penalty in America.* Chicago, IL: Aldine.

46. *O'Neil v. Vermont,* 144 U.S. 323 (1892).

47. *Weems v. United States,* 217 U.S. 349 (1910).

48. *Witherspoon v. Illinois,* 391 U.S. 510 (1960).

49. *Furman v. Georgia, Jackson v. Georgia, Branch v. Texas,* 408 U.S. 238 (1972).

50. *Gregg v. Georgia,* Proffitt v. Florida, Jurek v. Texas, 428 U.S. 153.

51. Katz, L. (1980). *The Justice Imperative.* Cincinnati, OH: Anderson.

52. The Death Penalty Information Center.

53. Ibid.

54. Reinhold, R. (1982, December 7). "Technician Executes Murderer in Texas by Lethal Injection." *The New York Times.*

55. *Fierro v. Gomez,* 56 CrL 1085 (1994)

56. The Death Penalty Information Center.

57. *Coker v. Georgia,* 433 U.S. 584 (1977).

58. *Eberheart v. Georgia,* 433 U.S. 917 (1977).

59. *Ford v. Wainwright,* 477 U.S. 399 (1986).

60. *McCleskey v. Kemp,* 481 U.S. 279 (1987).

61. *Thompson v. Oklahoma,* 487 U.S. 815 (1987-1988).

62. *Stanford v. Kentucky,* 492 U.S. 361 (1989).

63. *Atkins v. Virginia,* 536 U.S. 304 (2002).

64. *Roper v. Simmons,* 543 U.S. 551 (2005).

65. *Kennedy v. Louisiana,* 554 U.S. 407 (2008).

66. The Death Penalty Information Center.

67. Ibid.

68. Beccaria, 1764.

69. Pojman, L., & Reiman, J. (1998). *The Death Penalty: For and Against.* Lanham, MD: Rowman & Littlefield.

70. Radelet, M., Lofquist, W., & Bedau, H. (1996). "Prisoners Released from Death Rows Since 1970 Because of Doubts About Their Guilt." *T.M. Cooley Law Review, 13* (907).

71. The Death Penalty Information Center.

72. Stull, B. (2009). *Race and Death Penalty Links Run Deep and Wide*. New York, NY: American Civil Liberties Union.

73. Radelet, M. (1989). "Executions of Whites for Crimes Against Blacks." *Sociological Quarterly, 30*, 529–44.

74. The Death Penalty Information Center.

75. Ibid.

76. Liebmann, J., Fagan, J., & West, V. (n.d.). "A Broken System: Error Rates in Capital Cases, 1973–1995." *The Justice Project*. Retrieved April 12, 2011, from http://www.thejusticeproject.org

77. Bedau, H., Radelet, M., & Putnam, C. (2004). "Convicting the Innocent in Capital Cases: Criteria, Evidence, and Interference." *Drake Law Review, 52*, 587–603.

78. Bureau of Justice Statistics. (2010). *Capital Punishment 2009*. Washington, D.C.

79. Tonry, M. (1999). "Fragmentation of Sentencing and Corrections in the United States." *Research in Brief—Sentencing & Corrections: Issues for the 21st Century*. Washington, D.C.: National Institute of Justice.

80. Lab, S., & Whitehead, J. (1990). "From 'Nothing Works' to 'The Appropriate Works': The Latest Stop in the Search for the Secular Grail." *Criminology, 28*, 405–418.

81. Jacobs, J. (1977). *Statesville: The Penitentiary in Mass Society*. Chicago, IL: University of Chicago Press.

82. Ulner, J. (1997). *Social Worlds of Sentencing: Court Communities Under Sentencing Guidelines*. Albany, NY: State University of New York Press.

83. Austin, J., & Irwin, J. (1997). *It's About Time: America's Imprisonment Binge* (3rd ed.). Belmont, CA: Wadsworth.

84. Harris, J., & Jesilow, P. (2000). "It's Not the Old Ball Game: Three Strikes and the Courtroom Workgroup." *Justice Quarterly, 17*, 185–204.

85. Fischer, C. (2003). "Supreme Court Allows Penalties Under California 3-Strikes Law." *Corrections Journal, 1*(3).

86. *Ewing v. California*, 538 U.S. 11 (2003).

87. Durose, M., & Langan, P. (2004). "Felony Sentences in State Courts, 2002." *Bureau of Justice Statistics Bulletin*. Washington, D.C.

88. *United States v. Booker*, 543 U.S. 200 (2005).

89. Kitchens, C. (2010, August). "Federal Sentencing Data and Analysis Issues." *United States Sentencing Commission Research Notes*.

90. United States Sentencing Commission. (2010). *2010 Federal Sentencing Guidelines Manual*.

91. Bibas, S. (2004). "Plea Bargaining Outside the Shadow of Trial." *Harvard Law Review, 117*(8), 2463–2547.

92. Ibid.

93. Nagel, I., & Schulhofer, S. (1992). "A Tale of Three Cities: An Empirical Study of Charging and Bargaining Practices Under the Federal Sentencing Guidelines." *Southern California Law Review, 66*, 501–530.

94. *Brady v. United States*, 397 U.S. 742 (1970).

95. *North Carolina v. Alford*, 40 U.S. 25 (1970).

96. Mauer, M., & King, R. (2007). *Uneven Justice: State Rates of Incarceration by Race and Ethnicity*. Washington, D.C.: The Sentencing Project.

97. Bonczar, T. (2003). *Prevalence of Imprisonment in the U.S. Population, 1974–2001*. Washington, D.C.: U.S. Department of Justice, Bureau of Justice Statistics.

98. King, R. (2008). *Disparity by Geography: The War on Drugs in America's Cities*. Washington, D.C.: The Sentencing Project.

99. Schmalleger & Smykla, 2011.

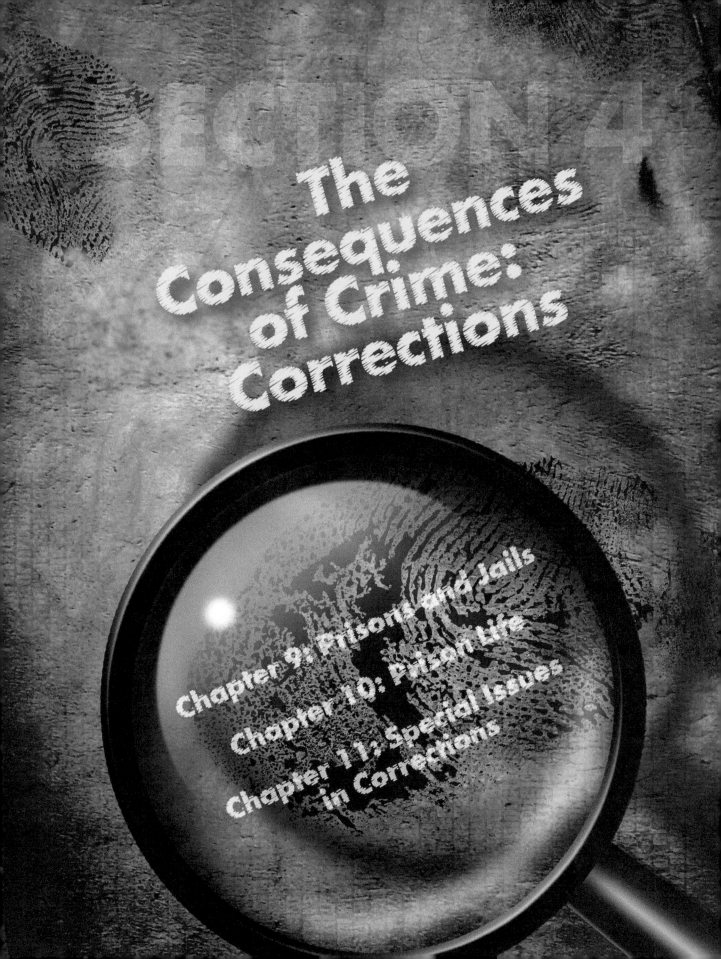

SECTION 4

The
Consequences
of Crime:
Corrections

Chapter 9: Prisons and Jails

Chapter 10: Prison Life

Chapter 11: Special Issues
in Corrections

9

Prisons and Jails

KEY TERMS

Absconder, Auburn System, Bridewells, Classification officer, Conditional release, Correctional officer, Correctional institution, Deterrence, Disciplinary report, Early release, Escape, Inmate, Institutional capacity, Jail, Juvenile, Offender, Panopticon, Pardon, Pennsylvania System, Prison, Recidivism, Sanctuary, Special Housing Unit (SHU), Supervised release, Youthful offender

CHAPTER OBJECTIVES

1. Understand the historical events preceding the modern prison system.
2. Identify the Eighth Amendment and its prohibition on cruel and unusual punishment.
3. Differentiate between prisons and jails.
4. Differentiate between minimum, medium, maximum, and supermax prisons.
5. Discuss the privatization of correctional facilities.

Case Study: Guantánamo Bay Naval Base

The terrorist attacks of September 11, 2001 and the wars in Afghanistan and Iraq have populated arguably the most notorious prison of modern times. The detention center at Guantánamo Bay Naval Base, presumably outside of U.S. legal jurisdiction, has been accused of violating the human rights of its detainees. This special-purpose prison does not hold criminals. It holds terrorists and others who have waged war against the United States. In 2009, President Barack Obama signed an order to close the Guantánamo Bay detention facility within one year. Three years later, the facility remains in operation.

In a 2002 Department of Defense news briefing, Vice Admiral John Stufflebeem stated in reference to those imprisoned at Guantánamo Bay, "These are the worst of the worst, and if let out on the street, they will go back to the proclivity of trying to kill Americans and others." The detainees were captured fighting for Al-Qaeda or the Taliban, and were not recognized as lawful warriors under international law.[1] By February 10, 2009, 581 tribunals had been held, and it was determined that the 539 current detainees were properly classified as enemy combatants.[2]

Unlike criminals, prisoners of war are not detained as punishment. They are held for security and for strategic and tactical necessity. Though their purposes may be different, the role of detention remains comparable for both criminal prisons and prisoner of war facilities. Most countries recognize that the detention of enemy forces is a legitimate wartime function that serves to prevent detainees from returning to the battlefield.

The Department of Defense is committed to a safe, secure, and humane detention experience for its detainees. Detainees receive three meals per day, comfortable sleeping implements, running water, full uniform and hygiene products, mail privileges, a library, recreation, and religious supplies and opportunity.[3] These amenities are similar to those afforded inmates in U.S. jails and prisons.

The Guantánamo Bay detention center has gained notoriety in part because some Americans and their congressional representatives believe that the detainees are not receiving full constitutional protections.[4] Some have proposed that the detainees be transferred to federal prisons and tried in criminal courts. Here, the detainees would receive the full protection of the U.S. Constitution. These protections are so important to Americans that many feel these rights should be extended even to those considered enemies of the United States. Others, though, do not believe that constitutional protections should apply to these prisoners or other terrorist suspects.

The top-security detention facility at Guantánamo Bay has been compared to America's supermax prisons. Many of the security measures are similar, especially those that subject some inmates to long-term restrictions on social interaction and meaningful activity. Experts studying the supermax and Guantánamo inmates assert that even inmates with no prior mental health issues may become considerably ill from long-term isolation. Comparisons of inmates in isolation with inmates who are allowed regular social interaction demonstrate higher rates of psychiatric and psychological health problems among those in isolation.[5]

Experts note that Guantánamo Bay and the nation's supermax prisons share many of the same practices and procedures, and therefore, cause similar injuries to the inmates' mental health.[6] The wisdom of inflicting psychological trauma on the Guantánamo Bay detainees and in America's supermax prisons is in question, especially since most of those supermax inmates are expected to one day return to open society in America.

The detention center at Guantánamo Bay is introduced here as an extreme example of an American top-security detention facility. While it serves a different purpose than criminal prisons, and its detainees are classified as terrorists and not as prisoners, it demonstrates how difficult and harsh the living conditions may be for extreme and difficult populations.

The History of Prisons and Jails

Throughout history, societies have found ways to punish individuals who break laws and commit crimes. Individuals and governments both have employed a variety of methods to prevent and to punish the transgressions of these offenders. Within the last few hundred years, detention has been an acceptable method of punishment.

Incarceration is now one of the most widespread criminal punishments throughout the world. Though the details differ widely among countries of the world, most use incarceration for punishment or pretrial detention. As detention methods have advanced, the types of facilities used to detain individuals have evolved as well. The most common of these detention facilities are known as prisons and jails.

In early American history, jails were used primarily to hold for trial those who could not make bail or those who were unable to pay debts.[7] The living conditions in these primitive houses of detention bred most every form of immorality one can imagine. Men, women, and children of all ages were thrown together in undisciplined and poorly supervised micro-communities where the strong overpowered the weak. There was little medical treatment and most were poorly fed. More often than not, those who did manage to eat did so because family or other benefactors delivered food to the jail. Those lacking outside support often suffered significantly.[8]

At trial, those convicted were regularly sentenced to public humiliation such as the stocks and pillories. Other punishments included whippings, transportation, banishment, branding, amputation, or even death. The offenders would rarely see the jail again after conviction. The jail was used as detention for trial; then the real punishment would be imposed.

Eventually, society began to recognize the cruelty they were inflicting on others in the name of justice. The public began to demand punishments that were more sophisticated and more effective in reducing recidivism, or repeat crime by offenders. Forcing offenders to repent or to offer penitence eventually became the new method of punishment. Thus, the inspiration for the penitentiary was born.

Offender
One who breaks a rule or commits a crime.

Prison
A correctional facility that confines those convicted of felonies; may hold both misdemeanants and felons convicted of federal crimes.

Jail
A correctional facility that holds people accused of or convicted of crimes.

Recidivism
The rate of repeat crime by offenders; the rate of relapse back into criminal activity or behavior.

A pillory device, which secured the head and hands in an uncomfortable position, was used to inflict physical punishment and public humiliation.

© 2012 BY WERNER MUENZKER. USED UNDER LICENSE OF SHUTTERSTOCK, INC.

This fresh and novel plan for a house of penitence spread throughout the early American colonies. The Constitution of Pennsylvania in 1776 decreed that "houses ought to be provided for punishing by hard labour, those who shall be convicted of crimes."[9] The "House of Hard Labour" requirement led to the development of the Walnut Street Jail, which is widely recognized as the first jail or prison where one would be incarcerated as punishment for crimes.

Early Punishments

History is rife with imaginative techniques to punish criminals. Codified punishment of criminals goes back to ancient Sumerian (1860 B.C.) and Babylonian (1750 B.C.) codes. Both codes contained descriptions of crimes and the punishment meted out to those who committed them. These penalties included whipping, servitude, mutilation, and death.[10]

The Codex Justinianus, or Code of Justinian, in sixth-century Rome was an attempt to codify all possible crimes with an appropriate balance of punishment. The "scales of justice" metaphor is assumed to have developed in this period, as they are depicted in art of the time. The Code of Justinian vanished with the fall of the Roman Empire.

Several decades after the Codex Justinianus, Greece enacted the Code of Draco. This harsh form of criminal law provided the same criminal penalties for citizens and slaves alike. It also allowed any citizen to prosecute an offender. Equal enforcement among citizens was an important advancement in the treatment of criminals. Public interest and public order were now recognized as superior to individual revenge and harm.[11] The Code of Draco has found its way into the modern lexicon through the eponymous term *draconian*, meaning markedly harsh or cruel.

The Inquisition, an invention of the Catholic Church in the Middle Ages, established a tribunal to seek out offenders and heretics and then to determine their innocence or guilt. The Inquisition, which lasted about 500 years, expected those charged to demonstrate their innocence rather than to have guilt proven by evidence at trial. The Inquisition also officially recognized the concept of free will. The concept of free will means that individuals choose their actions and are responsible for them; this concept can be found in our modern system of justice.

At least since the Code of Hammurabi (18th century B.C.) and the Sumerians a thousand years earlier, forms of criminal punishment included death, torture, mutilation, branding, fines, and the loss of property.[12] Ancient Mediterranean societies in the first century B.C. practiced banishment and slavery.[13] These criminal punishments existed in many forms throughout much of human history. In the 17th and 18th centuries in America, creative punishments such as the stocks and pillories were used. Often, the public was invited to watch and even to participate in the punishment of an offender.

The death penalty has long been imposed as a punishment against offenders. Trials, sometimes nothing more than a summary judgment from a group of interested citizens, would merely take offenders straight to their punishment. Punishment of death was accomplished by both crude and sophisticated methods. Impaling, beating, drowning, hanging, crucifixion, and burning at the stake have all been used as methods of execution.[14]

As technology advanced, instruments of death such as the guillotine were invented. Many of these executions were performed in public. Often, there would be a festival of sorts with public executions as the main attraction, especially if there were several condemned prisoners. In some cases, the public would be invited to participate in the execution process. Stoning is one of those participatory punishments and is still used in some parts of the world. Though the details may vary among eras and cultures, the condemned would be prepared for stoning by tightly binding their limbs and then burying them halfway or more in the ground. The public would then hurl rocks at the fated individuals until they died.[15]

Lesser punishments also involved the public. In colonial America, the pillory and the stocks were used for minor offenses, and they were often staged as community entertainment. Stocks, which held the offender's wrists and ankles while he or she sat on a stool, and the pillory, which locked around a standing offender's neck and wrists, were forms of public humiliation. After an offender was placed in the device, a flogging was often administered. The public would take part by yelling, spitting, and throwing garbage at the offender. At times, the offender might even have his or her ears nailed to the wooden pillory.[17] Those in the crowd were encouraged to get creative in their efforts at destroying the dignity of the offender. Young boys were especially creative with this form of amusement.

The guillotine is an instrument of capital punishment by beheading. French physician Joseph-Ignace Guillotine introduced the mechanism in 1792 during the French Revolution.[16]

Critical Thinking

Historical punishments for minor crimes involved state-sponsored humiliation. Though practices such as stocks and pillories are now prohibited, some argue that state-sponsored humiliation remains through online arrest records, prisoners working on roadsides, DUI offenders placing stickers on their cars to alert others, and even some offenders being sentenced to carry placards or post signs in public areas identifying them by their crime. Do you think that these public notices and actions should be allowed? Are these just "modern" forms of the pillory?

Mutilation was another method of criminal punishment. Often, the type of mutilation was determined by the crime. A thief's hand might be cut off; liars or people who talked too much might have their tongues cut out; a rapist might also receive a targeted amputation. Branding, a form of mutilation, would burn a word or a letter onto the offender's body so that she or he could always be recognized. A burglar might have a "B" branded on one hand and possibly another letter on the opposite hand for a subsequent offense. Adulterers, gossips, debtors, and others might all have received similar fates, as creative and even unusual punishments were typical for all levels of crime. Many of these punishments were used in early colonial America, and some, such as the removal of a thief's hand, are still used in a few parts of the world.

Critical Thinking Could mutilation and branding be considered a form of life punishment? In some states, convicted felons often never regain all of their civil rights. Is this a modern form of life punishment even after the sentence has been served?

Such early punishments seem barbaric by today's standards. It is important to note that many of the punishments were not designed to kill, yet nonetheless, they often resulted in death. The ducking stool is a good example of unintended execution. The ducking stool was a contraption whereby the offender, strapped to a seat, would be submerged in a pond or lake. Every so often, a person would be held underwater beyond their capacity to hold their breath and would drown. In some early societies, offenders would even be put to a test of death to prove or disprove guilt. For instance, if someone were deliberately held underwater beyond what was thought survivable and lived, that person would be determined to be innocent.

Not all criminals were mutilated or tortured: some were simply forced to leave their homes. In some ancient societies, when an individual was determined to have committed an egregious offense against the group, the group would force the offender from the tribe. This was a simple yet effective way to keep order within small societies.

Later civilizations, most notably the British Empire, continued this practice and banished criminals in bulk to lands far away. From 1718 to 1775, the British criminal system transported nearly 50,000 convicts to colonial America. With the exception of African slaves, this group of convicted criminals was the largest immigration population to America during the period.[18] The practice was halted when the American colonies asserted their independence from English rule in 1776. However, Captain Cook had discovered the Australian continent in 1770, and it became the new destination for criminal transportation. It is estimated that more than 135,000 people were transported to Australia before this system was abandoned in 1875.[19]

Those early methods were part of the evolution of how criminals are treated in modern society. The U.S. founding fathers who framed the Constitution had a different vision for how people should be treated. They established the Bill of Rights so that those living under the new Constitution would be protected from governmental abuses. One of these rights, a prohibition against cruel and unusual punishment, was formed from the desire to treat convicted criminals humanely and professionalize the criminal justice system. The founding fathers were well aware of the past abuses of offenders, and they therefore sought to prohibit the government from inflicting cruel and unusual treatment on the criminally accused and those convicted of crimes.

In spite of our efforts to treat criminals humanely, we still struggle to define *cruel and unusual*. The death penalty is a good example. Many consider the death penalty to be cruel, and others do not. There is also controversy over the methods used to deliver the death penalty. Some even consider the death penalty to be a practice that should be prohibited.

The Eighth Amendment states, "Excessive bail shall not be required, nor excessive fines imposed, nor cruel and unusual punishments inflicted."

Major Figures The practice of punishing criminals has evolved over the course of human civilization. The evolution of the modern prison and jail system is a result of the collective thoughts and efforts of many, but there have been a few key individuals who have revolutionized or made a lasting impact on the global detainment framework.

Montesquieu (1689–1755) Charles-Louis de Secondat, Baron de Montesquieu, or simply Montesquieu, a French nobleman, wrote on the political thought of the day and published it in his work *The Spirit of Laws* in 1748. Montesquieu believed in liberty for every man; however, he also believed in classes and a hierarchy of people, which classified people into three descending categories: monarchy, aristocracy, and commoner. Still, he asserted that no man of any class should be in fear of another.[20]

Montesquieu wrote about the separation of powers in government affairs. His philosophy, taken for granted today, maintained that the legislative, executive, and judicial branches of a government should not unduly be influenced by one another. If any of these were to combine, there could be no liberty.[21]

Much of Montesquieu's writing concerned the structure of governments and the protection of liberty. This was the age of the Enlightenment, which took place during the 17th and 18th centuries, and man's yearning to be free

Critical Thinking The U.S. Constitution's Eighth Amendment prohibits cruel and unusual punishment. This means a punishment must be declared both unusual *and* cruel in order for it to be prohibited. Some states have tightened this requirement in their own constitutions and state that cruel *or* unusual punishment is prohibited. Examine your own state's constitution. Does it prohibit cruel and unusual punishment, or does it prohibit cruel *or* unusual punishment? If the issue is not addressed, what do you suppose the default prohibition would be?

was a changing force for governments around the world. These philosophies were especially influential on the British colonies as they moved closer and closer to a revolution. James Madison, considered the father of the U.S. Constitution, was heavily influenced by Montesquieu, and much of the Constitution reflects the philosophy of this French nobleman.

John Howard (1726–1790)

John Howard was an early English prison reformer. Having inherited wealth, Howard traveled throughout Europe. He was captured by French privateers during a voyage to Portugal and was imprisoned. Eventually, he was freed in a prisoner exchange, and it is assumed that this experience was the catalyst for Howard's interest in prison reform.[22]

Appointed as High Sherriff of Bedfordshire, Howard witnessed the appalling conditions of prisons throughout England. He published his findings in his work *The State of Prisons of England and Wales* in 1777, which described, in detail, the conditions he had witnessed. He particularly abhorred the practice of the jailer's fee, which demanded payment for one's detention before release.[23]

Howard proposed many improvements in the prison system. His plans included physical reforms such as improved locations, construction, and furnishings of the prisons. He also insisted on proper diets, fresh water and air, exercise, hygiene, and general health. Moreover, he believed that prison personnel should be of a high quality and prisons should be subjected to independent inspections.[24]

Howard contracted typhus on a prison visit and died in 1790. His legacy remains today in the John Howard Society, a Canadian group that seeks effective solutions to the causes of crime, as well as other groups around the world that invoke his philosophies and remember him as one of the original reformers of modern systems of criminal justice.

Cesare Beccaria (1738–1794)

Like his contemporaries, Cesare Beccaria was a social reformer who believed in criminal justice transformation. Born to a wealthy family in Milan, Italy, Beccaria anonymously published his work *On Crimes and Punishment* in 1764. Only after this work was widely approved did he claim authorship. Many influential people approved of his treatise: Catherine the Great of Russia, Voltaire, Thomas Jefferson, and Adam Smith all praised his work.

Beccaria believed that a government is right to have laws and punishments so that all obey the social contract, and that those laws should be created by dispassionate, educated, and enlightened males who would create such rational laws to benefit the greatest number in the community. Furthermore, the government has the right and the duty to punish those who violate the law, but punishments should have limits and should fit the degree of the offense. His thoughts on improvements in government, crime, punishment, and human rights influenced methods of punishment and the design of **correctional institutions** around the world.

Beccaria wrote on criminal theory and on how the system should work. He stated that laws should be simply written so that the people and judges do not need to interpret their meaning. He also championed that judges be impartial,

Correctional institution
A jail or a prison where offenders are confined.

suspects be judged by their peers, questions and proceedings at trial be fair, punishment be swift and certain, torture not be used to gain confessions, harsh crimes be punished with longer periods in prison than less harsh crimes, attempting crime be punished, accomplices to crime be punished, and lesser crimes be punished by fines. Moreover, Beccaria was against the death penalty. He asserted that a public murder does nothing to deter a private one.[25]

Much of Beccaria's influence is found in the U.S. Bill of Rights. In the document one will find conventions such as the right to a trial by a jury of one's peers, the right to be informed of accusations, the right to bail, the right to have representation, the right to a speedy trial, the right to confront witnesses, the prohibition on cruel and unusual punishment, and even the right to bear arms, all of which parallel many of Beccaria's reform recommendations. America's forefathers supported the thoughts of the classical criminologists and insisted these principles be codified into the law of the land.

After Beccaria's death, his work lived on and his reputation expanded. He is called the father of classical criminal theory, and many criminologists and other criminal justice experts consider Beccaria's work *On Crimes and Punishment* to be the foundation on which all modern criminology theory is based.[26]

Panopticon
A circular prison designed with a central observation area so that officers can view all parts of the facility, originally designed by Jeremy Bentham. Variations of this concept are still used in modern correctional facilities so that correctional officers have an unobstructed view of most inmate areas.

Jeremy Bentham (1748–1832)   Jeremy Bentham is considered one of the first and most significant reformers of criminal punishment and social thought. Schooled as a lawyer, Bentham never practiced law but instead chose to influence social and legal reform. He was a strong supporter of utilitarianism, a form of social thought that—while stated many different ways—essentially means the greatest good for the greatest number.[27] Here, the term *utility* means usefulness or satisfaction.

Bentham also was a reformer in prison design. In order to maximize observation of inmates, he conceived the idea of the **Panopticon**, or all-seeing prison. Designed as a circular building with a watchtower in the middle, the Panopticon afforded the prison guards the ability to see every cell and to observe the inmates within. Many contemporary prisons utilize this concept in various forms to maximize the observation of inmates.

Modern prisons with a rotunda structure and central guard post are reminiscent of Jeremy Bentham's Panopticon.

Alexis de Tocqueville (1805–1859)   Alexis de Tocqueville was a French aristocrat, historian, and philosopher in the early nineteenth century. In 1831, de Tocqueville was granted a commission by King Louis Philippe of France to travel to America and study penitentiaries. The French and other European governments were interested in the new approach in America called rehabilitation, which was the restoration of offenders to a lawful and useful place in society. He traveled with his friend Gustave de Beaumont. Together, they toured the American landscape and wrote about American politics, social systems, and prisons. Though de Beaumont was instrumental in this project and wrote his own books on prison systems, he did not achieve the acclaim of de Tocqueville. The results of their observations were published as *On the Penitentiary System in the United States and its*

Inmate
An offender or an arrestee in a correctional institution.

Application in France and *Democracy in America*. The work *Democracy in America* continues to be printed and is still studied widely, often as assigned reading for those majoring in the political and social sciences, including the study of criminal justice.[28]

Tocqueville and Beaumont focused their work on the Auburn State Prison in New York and the Eastern State Prison in Pennsylvania. In Pennsylvania, inmates were isolated 24 hours a day. The idea was that they would have ample time to read their Bibles and reflect on their lives. At Auburn, the inmates were isolated only at night, and they performed simple labor and ate with other inmates during the day. Though strict silence was enforced at Auburn, there was human contact, unlike at Eastern State. By the middle of the 19th century, the Auburn system was the model for U.S. prisons and the Pennsylvania system became the standard for other countries.[29]

Not content only to observe, de Tocqueville offered his philosophies on most issues. He believed that prisons should rehabilitate and not simply punish. He opposed the death penalty and corporal punishment. He connected poverty with crime, suggesting that those with fewer opportunities would resort to criminal acts. He opposed the constant solitude found at Eastern State and approved of the partial isolation at Auburn. He observed that constant isolation destroyed inmates' spirit and that the interludes of social contact were productive. Additionally, de Tocqueville lamented that though the criminals might be rehabilitated, they would likely return to the conditions that encouraged their criminal activity in the first place.[30]

Early Forms of Imprisonment

Thanks to advancements in criminal thought, led by de Tocqueville and other reformers, the value of human dignity and life has greatly increased. In most of the industrialized world, prisoners are treated immensely better than in the past. Though prisons are oppressive places and provide for an onerous existence, most countries at least provide prisoners a survivable diet, some medical care, human contact, and some form of classification that separates **juveniles** from adults and men from women.

Incarceration as punishment is a recent development in human history and its treatment of criminals. Early jails were used primarily for the temporary detention of a prisoner before trial. In the early 18th century, England had the gaol (pronounced *jail,* and the source of the modern word *jail*). Upon trial, if an offender were found guilty, he or she would not be returned to the gaol, but instead be subjected to demeaning or abusive forms of punishment as discussed earlier. The concept of "locking up" criminals did not exist until the late 18th century in early America.

Though there may be anecdotal events during which detention was used as a form of punishment, it was most often a byproduct of the intended punishment. In some societies, people of high standing, such as the English nobility, were sentenced to house arrest. In other punishments, detention was only incidental. Consider those sentenced to servitude or to the galleys. These offenders had to be detained somewhere during their sentence or they would simply be able to escape. Some early prison administrators used abandoned mines and quarries to hold inmates, or prisoners.

Juvenile
A young person, usually a minor.

The Mamertine Prison

The Mamertine prison, one of the oldest known prisons, was constructed in Rome around 640–618 B.C. Mamertine, also known as the "Prison of Kings," still exists beneath the church of S. Giuseppe dei Falegnami in Rome. It is said to have held St. Peter, who baptized his jailers while imprisoned there.[31]

Mamertine was originally a cistern for water from a nearby spring. Later, it was used for the temporary detention of prisoners of some importance. These higher-level prisoners would eventually be paraded through the streets of Rome and then publicly executed. Others would simply be put to death inside the prison.[32]

Sanctuaries, Fortresses, Hulks, and Bridewells

Throughout human history, many other forms of detention have been used. Sanctuaries were mentioned in the Old Testament, and this form of safe haven was common through the 12th century. A person accused of a crime could seek sanctuary at a church, and he or she would often be protected from the authorities. Early Christians formalized a policy that if any part of a criminal's body touched the church, then he or she would be given protection from prosecution.[33]

Sanctuary
A sacred place of worship where one can take refuge.

Another historical place of detention and imprisonment is the fortress. Fortresses were simply fortified structures for defense. Though designed to keep enemies out, they were often used to keep criminals in. The criminals would be held until their punishment was decided. Often, they were publicly executed. The Tower of London is an example of a fortress being used as a prison, though that was not its primary purpose.[34]

A *hulk* is a non-functional ship. Ships that were no longer seaworthy were ready-made facilities that were easily used for criminal detention purposes. These opportune facilities have long been used by governments to hold prisoners. As recently as 1997, England used the *Weare*, a decommissioned ship, to re-

The Tower of London imprisoned infamous historical figures such as William Hastings, Anne Boleyn, and Lady Jane Grey before their ultimate death by beheading.[35]

Bridewells
Jails and police stations in England and Ireland in the 16th century that typically housed petty criminals.

lieve prison overcrowding. The ship was never intended to be a permanent facility, and it closed as a prison in 2005.[36]

Bridewells were jails in England and Ireland in the 16th century that typically housed petty criminals. The name came from Bridewell Palace, which was originally a home to King Henry VIII; it ultimately became a poorhouse and a correctional facility for prostitutes with the intent of rehabilitation. Soon, *Bridewell* became a common term for any jail or police station in England or Ireland. These poorhouses were at first considered successful, but eventually their conditions and the treatment of prisoners became deplorable. There was no classification of prisoners based on crime, sex, age, or other criteria. Corruption became rampant among staff and inmates alike, and disease and death were common. After public outcry over the conditions, Bridewells were no longer used.

The Walnut Street Jail   The Walnut Street Jail was named after the Philadelphia street on which it was located. It was originally constructed in the 18th century to alleviate the overcrowding of another Philadelphia jail, the Old Stone Jail, where men, women, and boys were all housed together. The Walnut Street Jail instituted reforms that are still in use today.

The reforms at the Walnut Street Jail included the classification of inmates according to gender, type of crime, and violent tendencies. It also separated juveniles from adults. In addition, they began attempts at rehabilitation by providing work and trade skills to the inmates. Even with these reforms, the Walnut Street Jail, too, eventually became overcrowded. The Walnut Street Jail continued its service for a number of years as a confinement facility for the more difficult prisoners at the newer Eastern State Prison.

Walnut Street in Philadelphia was home to an overcrowded prison. By 1795, each of the Walnut Street Jail's 18-square-foot cells held 30 to 40 inmates at one time.[38]

The Walnut Street Jail was still being used as a prison during the Constitutional Convention in Philadelphia after the Revolutionary War. Benjamin Franklin, now an old and frail man in poor health, could barely walk, and prisoners from the Walnut Street Jail would carry Franklin on a sedan chair to the convention meetings.[37]

The Pennsylvania System The Walnut Street Jail had actually originated before the American Revolution. After the United States gained its independence, this jail on Walnut Street in Philadelphia was expanded to abide by the new Pennsylvania Constitution requiring that "houses ought to be provided for punishing by hard labour."[39] This expansion of the Walnut Street Jail included a cellular construction for housing prisoners, with some cells reserved for the isolation of some of the inmates.

The Philadelphia legislature, having heard the protests of Quakers who rejected the shedding of blood, had created a substitution for corporal punishment. Here, prisoners were classified based on their crimes. Solitary cells were used for those sentenced to absolute isolation by the courts and for those who refused to work. Those inmates in isolation did not perform any labor.

This new method of dealing with criminals was a great leap from past methods used to punish offenders. Offenders who previously would have been sentenced to death were now sentenced to isolation in one of the individual cells at the Walnut Street Jail. Since belligerent inmates and those who refused to work were also forced into isolation, the jail grew quite large by period standards. This became quite expensive.

This system of cellular isolation was soon copied by other states. Maryland, Massachusetts, Maine, New York, New Jersey, and Virginia adopted the Philadelphia form of isolation for certain classes of criminal.[40] These reforms, though well intentioned, did not have the desired results. The prisons found that many of the same individuals kept returning after their release and the expense of housing all of the criminals was "ruinous to the public treasury."[41] It was believed that the solution was simply to add more cells. This however, involved an even greater expense to the states that chose this method.

Roughly two decades after the advent of the Walnut Street Jail, the Western Penitentiary in Pittsburgh opened. This penitentiary, somewhat modeled after Jeremy Bentham's Panopticon, at first was designed only for the isolation of inmates. Later, inmates were forced to perform some labor within their isolation. Exercise areas were also constructed. Western Penitentiary was considered superior to previous systems, and soon yet another Pennsylvania prison, the Eastern State Penitentiary in Philadelphia, was built not far from the Walnut Street Jail.

The Eastern State Penitentiary was the model for what became known as the Pennsylvania System. Here, the Quaker belief that man is inherently good and can be reformed was a foundation for rehabilitation. Proponents of the Pennsylvania System believed that solitary confinement and penitence could reform people into productive and honest citizens.[42]

The Eastern State Penitentiary was constructed similar to Jeremy Bentham's Panopticon, but it was square. Additionally, individual cells had an adjoining

Pennsylvania System
A penal system advocated by Quakers that used solitary confinement and penitence to reform offenders. Eventually, work such as shoemaking and weaving was allowed to be done in the cells.

Auburn System

A prison system, also known as the New York System, in which silence is enforced at all times. Inmates work during the day and spend nights in solitary confinement.

Both the Pennsylvania and Auburn Systems focused on inmate isolation, a practice that philosophers believed could devastate the human mind.

outside cell that was used as an exercise yard. This system advocated individual isolation combined with labor. The labor consisted of making crafts in one's cell that were sold to help support the institution. It was assumed that this isolation would prevent corruption through association with other inmates and that prisoners would concentrate more on redemption. Thus, in theory, isolation should require shorter sentences, and it would be less expensive per inmate to run the prison.

The Auburn System In 1816, some time after the Eastern State Penitentiary opened, a new prison was constructed in Auburn, New York. With this new prison came a new prison system. The Auburn System was different in many respects from the Pennsylvania System. The cells at Auburn Prison were smaller than those at Eastern State Penitentiary, and they were all enclosed with no individual exercise yard. These cells were for sleeping only, and the inmates worked in a large room with one another. Though silence was strictly enforced, it was thought that the human contact would be good for the inmates and for their rehabilitation.

The discipline at Auburn was harsh by today's standards. Silence was enforced by the whip and with isolation cells. Inmates marched in step when being moved, and they sat facing away from one another during meals. Though this was considered an improvement over Eastern State Penitentiary, the forced silence even when seated next to another took its toll on the inmates, and by some accounts, on the jailers as well.

These two new prison systems competed somewhat for recognition of superiority.[43] The Pennsylvania System boasted a solitary existence and solitary work, while the Auburn System boasted group work in silence. Nineteenth-century philosophers debated the two systems. Though they disagreed on much, they did agree that isolation without work would devastate the human mind. Total isolation was attempted at various institutions of the time. Inmates often went mad and suicide rates went up. The jailers, it was found, often developed psychological issues as well.[44]

Notorious Contemporary Prisons

Nothing today can compare with the prisons of the past. The squalid living conditions and the brutality imposed cannot be matched. This does not mean that the modern world is without prisons and jails that have achieved notoriety for their conditions and their contents. Alcatraz Prison, though closed since 1963, is famous for its legendary inmates, and the Maricopa County Jail, still in operation, is known for its tough sheriff, Joe Arpaio.

Alcatraz In the early 20th century, the federal prison system included specialized institutions. Some were less restrictive, "easy" prisons that housed the less dangerous inmates, and some were very grim, dungeon-type, supermaximum prisons. These supermaximum prisons held the most notorious and hated criminals of the country. One such prison was built on Alcatraz Island in San Francisco Bay. Alcatraz, also known as "The Rock," was surrounded by swift currents of cold water that, presumably, would kill any prisoner trying to traverse the path to freedom. Thus, the location alone provided its greatest resource; that of being able to contain all of its prisoners and prevent escape.

With one guard to every three prisoners, the inmates at Alcatraz were strictly monitored. At 6:30 A.M., the wake-up call was sounded, and by 7:00 A.M., the prisoners, having dressed, cleaned their cells, and been counted, would march off to the mess hall for the morning meal. Then, it was off to their individual jobs.

The routine at Alcatraz was sternly enforced and rarely varied. The most brutal aspect, at least in Alcatraz' early years, was the forced silence. Many inmates considered this the most unbearable punishment. The silence policy was relaxed in the prison's later years, but it was one of the few rule changes to occur.

Most know Alcatraz Island only for its infamous federal prison. However, Alcatraz was also a civil war fortress, a bird sanctuary, the home of the first lighthouse on the West Coast, and the site of an American Indian occupation in the 1960s.[45] The 1979 movie *Escape from Alcatraz*, which was loosely based on the only known successful escape from the maximum-security prison, further sealed the prison's notoriety. Alcatraz is now a tourist attraction that is visited by hundreds every day.

Maricopa County's Tent City

Joseph "Joe" Arpaio, the popular yet widely criticized sheriff of Maricopa County, Arizona, has become known as America's toughest sheriff. Sheriff Arpaio runs a jail that has gained notoriety because of his unconventional methods. From forcing inmates to wear pink underwear to housing some of them in tents to endure sweltering heat, the sheriff has earned an extreme reputation among both critics and supporters.

The Maricopa County Jail in Phoenix, Arizona, includes a modern, state-of-the-art facility with more than 2,000 beds and seven smaller facilities, including the infamous tent city. According to the Maricopa County Sheriff's Office website, in 1993 Sheriff Arpaio began housing inmates in surplus army tents, due in

Sheriff Joseph Arpaio brands himself as "America's toughest sheriff."

Early release

Release from a correctional institution prior to the expiration of an offender's sentence.

Institutional capacity

The maximum number of inmates an institution can hold.

Deterrence

The threat of punishment that will result from criminal activity. Deterrence is further categorized into general deterrence, which threatens everyone with criminal sanctions, and specific deterrence, which is a threat to a specific individual who may offend or reoffend.

part to his promises that there would be no **early releases** because of overcrowding.[46] He houses less dangerous inmates in the tents because of the lower level of security. He was able to create this tent city jail with minimal expense. Currently, it can hold up to 2,000 prisoners. Other jail administrators have considered using Arpaio's methods when their own facilities begin to exceed **institutional capacity**, resulting in overcrowding.

The sheriff made a number of other changes to the prison system, such as eliminating coffee to save money, and even bragged that it cost him less per day to feed an inmate than a police dog. He brought back several long-abandoned features from decades past, such as chain gangs and the iconic, stigmatized black-and-white striped jumpsuits. In an attempt to humiliate inmates, Sheriff Arpaio requires them to wear pink underwear and other pink clothing. Additionally, cigarettes, adult magazines, regular television programming, and many other comfort items have been forbidden. The conditions of tent living in the hot and arid Arizona elements can be brutal, and the sheriff considers this a consequence of going to jail. These harsh conditions of detention are expected to have a **deterrence** effect on offenders so they will not commit additional crimes and return to the jail. Though the sheriff has saved the taxpayers much money, critics claim that the high legal costs from lawsuits that he incurs because of his methods negate any savings.[47]

Sheriffs are publicly elected officials, and thus, Sheriff Arpaio must gain support from sufficient numbers of voters to win elections. Arpaio's methods have won him some eager supporters, but also vociferous opponents. Some claim that Arpaio's main objective is publicity. Organizations have developed with the objective of getting rid of Joe Arpaio at the ballot box. These organizations present evidence that the sheriff wastes public funds in his "publicity stunts." They also claim that deputies on county time are assigned as his personal bodyguards, that Arpaio will not debate political opponents, that he is vindictive and abuses his authority, and that he has lied to the public about his biographical information, the costs of lawsuits, and the money he claims to save taxpayers. As evidence, critics tell of Arpaio's claim that an $8.25 million settlement over a dead inmate cost the county nothing because of the jail's liability insurance. What he neglected to say, though, was that the jail had a $1 million deductible.[48]

In 2010, the U.S. Department of Justice sued Arpaio for civil rights violations.[49] There have been other lawsuits as well. The *New York Times* states that according to Maricopa County Risk Management, the sheriff has had over 6,000 claims and lawsuits filed against him since he was first elected, at a cost to taxpayers of over $50 million.[50]

The case study at the beginning of this chapter noted that the detention center at Guantánamo Bay and supermax facilities can be considered extreme examples of prisons. The human suffering at these prisons has generated and maintained their notorious reputations. The Maricopa County Jail is similar in that it may be considered an extreme example of an American jail. The jail receives incredible publicity because of the atypical methods used on the inmates and the unreserved behavior of the sheriff.

Role and Structure of Prisons and Jails

The history of jails and prisons, discussed in the previous section, has brought us to the modern system of corrections. Modern correctional facilities have evolved from past successes and mistakes. Currently, in the United States, there are more than 7 million people incarcerated or under correctional supervision.[51] This is larger than the populations of many states. Since there are so many American citizens incarcerated, the issue of corrections has become a significant issue for all levels of government and the public as well.

Modern correctional facilities exist at the local, state, and federal levels. All have their own missions and roles in criminal justice. Some are old and outdated, and others are modern and very secure. Many have inmate amenities for recreation, education, and training. All have access to medical care. There are also different levels of security, ranging from minimum security to supermaximum prisons. None of the facilities and systems exists without controversy.

Prisoners in America have gained many constitutional rights in the past 50 or so years. Of course, some may argue that these rights were already present, but simply not recognized until the U.S. Supreme Court asserted their existence. Among these rights is access to reasonable medical care. In 1976, the U.S. Supreme Court presented the "deliberate indifference" standard pertaining to correctional facilities and the medical care afforded inmates. The court held that deliberate indifference of correctional staff to an inmate's serious medical illness or injury constitutes cruel and unusual punishment.[52]

In the late 1970s, the American Medical Association addressed this issue by creating a program to assist correctional facilities in establishing proper levels of inmate medical care. This program evolved into what is now known as the National Commission on Correctional Health Care (NCCHC). The not-for-profit NCCHC sets standards and offers education, accreditation, and assistance to correctional facilities. Participation is voluntary, but the program is well established, recognized, and respected; many correctional facilities have adopted the standards of the NCCHC and sought their accreditation.[53]

The U.S. Supreme Court has also ordered that correctional facilities must provide law libraries. An inmate's right to access to a law library and to those skilled in providing legal assistance was established in *Bounds v. Smith*[54] (1977) and in *Younger v. Gilmore*[55] (1971). The decisions were based on an inmate's widely accepted constitutional right to court access.[56] Subsequent U.S. Supreme Court cases have ruled on this issue even further. *Lewis v. Casey*[57] (1996), for example, may have relaxed some of the privileges gained from the 1971 and 1977 cases. *Lewis* limits access to the types of legal proceedings an inmate may pursue and tightens the rules for an inmate's legal standing in order to file a lawsuit.[58]

Critical Thinking   Correctional administrators tell us that television is a good way for inmates to pass the time and to keep them occupied. Is television for inmates a good idea in prisons and/or jails? What about cable television? Expand some on this concept. What about Internet access, weightlifting, gyms, pool tables, and basketball courts? What about entertainment venues such as comedians and musicians? Are any or all of these a good idea or not? Why?

The Historical Role of Incarceration

Throughout human history, prisoners have been confined for a variety of reasons. Mostly, confinement was used for the temporary detention of individuals until they could be brought to judgment by the governing authority and either released or punished accordingly. If the offender was found guilty, he or she would receive a punishment. As discussed earlier in the chapter, these punishments often included methods that by contemporary standards would be considered cruel and unusual, such as stoning or boiling.

When the American colonies declared themselves independent from English rule, the colonists also insisted that this independence included rules concerning criminal justice. Whereas the British legal system recognized that the monarch was the ultimate source of law, many colonists felt that the ultimate source of law should originate in the people and that leaders should also be bound to laws. British law was, at the time, so merciless that even a petty thief could be put to death. Some higher-class criminals, however, were able to escape justice through a system of patronage. This system allowed offenders to appeal to the crown or others in local authority who would either issue a **pardon**—an exemption from penalty—or otherwise suspend or delay the offender's sentence. The colonists demanded a justice system that treated suspects the same without consideration of their social status.

Having won independence in the Revolutionary War, the United States created its own system of laws. Issues of criminal justice are addressed in several sections of the U.S. Constitution. Some of these sections include laws against counterfeiting, treason, and piracy. In addition, there are laws that prohibit federal and state governments from enacting bills of attainder, which are edicts that proclaim a person or group guilty without the benefit of a trial, and ex post facto laws, which are laws retroactively applied to previous events.

Criminal law was addressed more specifically in the Bill of Rights. The Bill of Rights recognizes the right of people to be free from governmental abuse and codifies this natural human rights acknowledgment into law. Among other things, the Bill of Rights prohibits the government from unreasonably searching or seizing persons or property, from trying someone repeatedly for the same crime, from holding someone "for a capital [death penalty eligible], or otherwise infamous [felony] crime," and from demanding confessions in that a person is not compelled to "be a witness against himself." It also prohibits the government from bringing charges except upon indictment or presentment. Additionally, the Bill of Rights states that an individual has a right to a speedy trial by an impartial jury and punishments deemed cruel and unusual are prohibited.

The provisions in the Bill of Rights were not based on hypothetical situations: they were responses to known abuses from tyrannical governments that the framers of this document intended to prohibit. The text of the Declaration of Independence includes a long list of these "abuses and usurpations." The Bill of Rights was created to protect all citizens from unchecked power and to prevent the government from tyrannical abuses. The Eighth Amendment outlawed cruel and unusual forms of punishment and permitted the modern philosophies

Pardon
To forgive, release, or exempt a person from a penalty.

With the goal of establishing a system based on fair adjudication and punishment, the U.S. founding fathers created the Eighth Amendment to protect the basic human rights of the innocent and the guilty.

of penitence to replace them. Thus, penitentiaries became the new method of punishment.

At first, the Bill of Rights applied only to federal laws. The states had their own bills of rights, but most were fashioned from those in the U.S. Constitution. It was not until the mid-19th century with the enactment of the 14th Amendment that many of the U.S. Constitutional rights were applied to the states.

The Role of Incarceration in Contemporary Society

It is a commonly held tenet of criminal justice that people are sent to prison *as* punishment, not *for* punishment. This is a fine distinction, but an important one. In other words, the loss of freedom and many rights is the punishment. Inmates are not to receive punishment in excess of what was ordered by the court.

There have been many correctional ideologies proposed and tried over the centuries. Most of them fall into the categories of punishment, rehabilitation, or prevention. Of course, there is no defined position where one ideology ends before another one begins. They often overlap. For instance, one could easily make a reasonable argument that the goal of both punishment and rehabilitation is prevention.

Punishment of criminals falls into three general categories. The first of these categories is retribution. Retribution has come in many forms through the ages, and is viewed by some as the basest of human qualities. It means getting even, such as in the maxim "an eye for an eye." Banishment, death, and humiliation are all forms of retribution.[59]

The next form of punishment is deterrence. This simple term means a person is deterred from doing wrong because he or she fears the punishment. Deterrence is further broken down into the categories of general and specific deterrence. General deterrence is what all members of society feel that prevents them from doing wrong. This feeling can come from a moral or a religious view, or it can come simply from a fear of being caught. Specific deterrence is a sanction imposed upon a specific person in hopes that the punishment will deter that specific individual from reoffending, or recidivating.[60]

A third reason for punishment is incapacitation. To incapacitate an offender means to remove him or her from the opportunity and availability to commit further criminal acts. This usually means that an offender is locked up, preventing further criminal opportunity and actions.[61]

Rehabilitation, discussed earlier in the chapter, means to restore an offender to a lawful and useful place in society. This, in theory, is accomplished through treatment and education. The treatment model is often referred to as the medical model. In the medical model, an offender is viewed as "ill" and in need of treatment. The educational model recognizes the offender as disadvantaged and in need of education, training, and discipline. Rehabilitation seems easier in theory than in practice. High rates of recidivism tend to challenge the success of rehabilitation efforts.[62]

The prevention ideology is often recognized as something that must begin in early life. Prevention programs attempt to identify early signs of behavior that are statistically tied to criminal behavior. Truancy, dropping out of school, and poor school performance are often viewed as precursors to criminal behavior later in life. Prevention programs attempt to break the path to crime by developing specialized classes, counseling, vocational training, and even alternate schools.[63]

Critical Thinking Incarcerated individuals lose many of their civil rights, such as the right of liberty, the right to assemble, and in most states, the right to vote. What rights do you believe inmates should be allowed to keep?

Countless state, federal, appeals, and U.S. Supreme Court cases address issues of prisoner rights. In *Wolff v. McDonnell,* a 1974 case involving prison inmate rights, Supreme Court Justice Byron White asserted in the majority opinion, "But though [the prisoner's] rights may be diminished by the needs and exigencies of the institutional environment, a prisoner is not wholly stripped of constitutional protections when he is imprisoned for crime. There is no iron curtain drawn between the Constitution and the prisons of this country."[64]

Exhibit: *Wolff v. McDonnell*

"Petitioners assert that the procedure for disciplining prison inmates for serious misconduct is a matter of policy raising no constitutional issue. If the position implies that prisoners in state institutions are wholly without the protections of the Constitution and the Due Process Clause, it is plainly untenable. Lawful imprisonment necessarily makes unavailable many rights and privileges of the ordinary citizen . . . But though his rights may be diminished by the needs and exigencies of the institutional environment, a prisoner is not wholly stripped of constitutional protections when he is imprisoned for crime. There is no iron curtain drawn between the Constitution and the prisons of this country. Prisoners have been held to enjoy substantial religious freedom under the First and Fourteenth Amendments. They retain right of access to the courts. Prisoners are protected under the Equal Protection Clause of the Fourteenth Amendment from invidious discrimination based on race. Prisoners may also claim the protections of the Due Process Clause. They may not be deprived of life, liberty, or property without due process of law."

FIGURE9.1 U.S. Adult Correctional Population Trends 1980–2009 This figure demonstrates that the total number of adults under correctional supervision as of 2009 was more than 7 million. That is more than one out of every 40 adults.

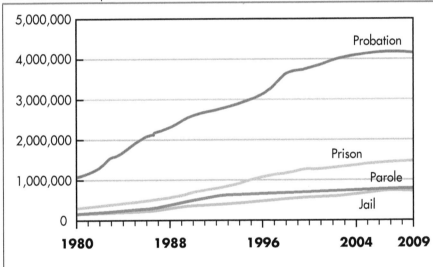

Source: Bureau of Justice Statistics. (2011). *Total Correctional Population*. Washington, D.C.: Author.

Is It a Prison or a Jail?

In the United States and in many other countries, there are distinct differences between prisons and jails. Jails and prisons are both **correctional institutions**, but have different missions and therefore serve different purposes. Jails are usually run by local governments or a county sheriff's office. This is most often determined by the local government or individual state laws. Prisons are run by the states and the federal government and are often sprawling complexes with varying degrees of security. Some prisons are run by pri-

Youthful offender

Typically, an offender under 18 years old, though the age requirements may be different among the several states.

Escape

The illegal departure of an offender from legal custody.

Absconder

One who leaves without authorization. This term is usually used in reference to walk-offs from work crews, work release centers, halfway houses, and other inmate areas not inside the main secure facility.

Conditional release

The release of a defendant under specific conditions such as an order to enter a treatment program.

Supervised release

Court-ordered supervision of someone who is awaiting trial or serving probation or parole.

vate organizations, but they are usually under contract with the state. The status of the offender and his or her crime are normally what determines whether the person is in a jail or a prison. In addition, youthful offenders—typically offenders under the age of 18—may be tried and sentenced as adults to jail or prison, but most often, juveniles are adjudicated as delinquent and not as criminals. They may then be sent to a juvenile detention facility.

Jails and prisons have evolved significantly over the centuries. In early human history, confinement areas were built from whatever could be used. This often was a natural formation such as a cave. As humankind progressed, cages, special rooms in castles, and even specially built structures would hold prisoners. While some jails today may still be old and poorly built, most jails and prisons are technological wonders with modern security built into the structure. They are designed for maximum observation of inmates by correctional staff. Escapes from inside the secure area are very rare. Many of the escapes mentioned in the media are inmates who have simply absconded. Absconders are walk-offs from work crews, work release centers, halfway houses, and other inmate areas not inside the main secure facility itself. Typically, the inmates in these other areas are considered less dangerous to society or are nearing the ends of their sentences.[65]

Jails and prisons are now often designed in sections called pods. The goal of the pod system is to maximize observation while sectioning off areas for security reasons. These pods may be used to separate inmates based on gender, classification of their crimes, medical reasons, etc. Additionally, should a disturbance erupt, the officers can secure the area and prevent the spread of violence and therefore maintain control of the facility while addressing the disorder.

Jails   Jails are multipurpose facilities operated by local governments or sheriffs. Almost all offenders begin their experience with the correctional system in a local jail. Many minor offenders will go no further. For major offenders, jail may be only the first stop in their progression through the correctional system. Most of a jail's population includes those recently arrested, those awaiting trial, and those serving sentences of one year or less. Others found in jail include mentally ill inmates for whom no other facility is available, parolees and probationers awaiting violation hearings, federal prisoners awaiting pickup by marshals, and bail jumpers held overnight by traveling bounty hunters.

Jails are usually the first contact an offender has with the correctional system. When an individual is first arrested, he or she is taken to a jail and is "booked," or has personal information placed in the facility's books. Here, an inmate may be held until trial, known as pretrial detention, or may be given a conditional release, which allows the inmate to be released under specific conditions such as an order to enter a treatment program. Others may be released on bail, also known as a bond. Sometimes, charges may be dropped very quickly. Those who are convicted of their offense may be sentenced to jail or prison. Often, sentencing involves probation, which is a form of supervised release. Offenders convicted of misdemeanors and sentenced to one year or less of detention usually serve their time in jail. Those convicted of felonies and sentenced to more than one year (at least 366 days) of detention usually go to prison.[66] These situations do have exceptions, as there are few absolutes in criminal justice. Moreover, these procedures are determined by state law, and not all states follow the same practice. For instance, in some states, a misdemeanor sentence can carry a punishment of up to two years of imprisonment, which may be served in a jail. Moreover, some states have indeterminate sentencing laws that mandate a penalty, such as six months to a year or five to 10 years, instead of a determinate amount of time. An inmate may gain an earlier release date based on his or her behavior and efforts to rehabilitate.

Staffing at the jail includes correctional officers, classification officers, medical professionals, and administrative workers. **Correctional officers** are usually academy-trained individuals who meet strict criteria for physical condition, mental condition, and a noncriminal history. **Classification officers** are those who determine the inmate's placement and level of dangerousness. They also calculate sentences as mandated by the courts.

Depending on the size of the jail, there may be a staff of administrative professionals. These individuals perform the back-office functions such as managing funds or ordering supplies. All jails have access to medical care, and jails of significant size often have their own staff for routine medical needs and emergencies. The Eighth Amendment's prohibition on cruel and unusual punishment provides that inmates receive a minimum standard of living, which includes access to medical services.

Prisons

Prisons are run by the states and the federal government. In some cases, the government oversees a private facility contracted to perform correctional services. Usually, state prisons hold those convicted of felonies who are sentenced to more than one year of imprisonment. States enact their own laws concerning sentencing and correctional facilities, so there is some variation throughout the country. Federal prisons house those convicted of federal crimes, both misdemeanants and felons. Whether the inmate was convicted of a state or a federal crime determines whether he or she goes to a state or a federal prison.

Sometimes, a person is accused of a crime that is prohibited by both state and federal law. Weapons and drug offenses commonly involve both jurisdictions. Since there are state and federal laws against illegal drugs and weapons, offenders may find themselves prosecuted in both state and federal courts. The offender may even be convicted and sentenced in both jurisdictions. If that occurs, the offender may serve a segmented sentence in both state and federal prison. In practice, however, the jurisdictions often work together to bring a resolution to the case. Sometimes, jurisdictions may defer to the prosecution with the strongest case or the longest sentence. In other cases, one jurisdiction may delay completion of the investigation to see what happens in the other jurisdiction's court before deciding whether to proceed. There may even be a cross-jurisdictional agreement in exchange for a guilty plea.

Correctional officer
An officer, also called a prison guard, jail guard, or corrections officer, who oversees and supervises all inmate activity.

Classification officer
The officer assigned to determine individual inmate needs and assign them to appropriate custody levels, institutions, and programs.

Critical Thinking Higher-custody prisons not only keep inmates from escaping, but also prevent inmates from committing crimes while in prison. What kinds of crimes are committed inside of prison? How does prison design help deter or prevent crime from occurring?

It is important to note that the Fifth Amendment's prohibition on double jeopardy allows an individual to be convicted in two jurisdictions for the same crime. This is because there are two separate jurisdictions that prohibit the offense. The Fifth Amendment states that no person can be tried twice for "the same offense," but if there are separate offense statutes for a crime on the state and federal levels, then they are not considered the same offense. Thus, an offender may be tried and convicted under both jurisdictions. This is known as the dual sovereignty exception. In *United States v. Lanza*, Chief Justice Howard Taft in delivering the opinion of the court stated, "It follows that an act denounced as a crime by both national and state sovereignties is an offense against the peace and dignity of both, and may be punished by each."[67]

When an inmate is received into most state prison systems, he or she is processed through a classification system. The classification of inmates simply is a means to fit an inmate into a specific category of custody level, medical needs, predisposition to violence or escape, training and educational needs, and other categories as determined by state statute. This classification procedure will determine primarily which security level the inmate requires. Then, after considering the other criteria, the inmate will be assigned to a state prison facility that fits his or her characteristics. The classification procedure usually continues at the receiving facility, and decisions will be made concerning the inmate's abilities, training, counseling, and efforts regarding the inmate's reentry to open society.

Accurate classification of inmates is an admirable goal, and the objectives are achieved to a significant degree. However, institutional needs are the primary forces that determine classification efforts. Often, classification decisions are made based on availability of programs and space at the institution where the inmate's needs would best be served.

Custody Levels

Inmates are classified to a custody level in jails and in prisons. In jail, the inmate may bond out for pretrial release or may be serving a relatively short sentence of one year or less. In prison, proper classification becomes a continuous process that involves constant reclassification for many inmates based on their behavior and history. These levels of custody usually include minimum, medium, and maximum security. There are others such as community custody, typically for those on parole or probation; death row custody; and supermax custody. The various states determine their own categories and criteria for custody levels. For instance, in Florida prisons, most inmates are classified as minimum, medium, or close custody. Maximum custody refers to death row inmates and a few other categories of especially dangerous individuals.

FIGURE9.2 U.S. Imprisonment Rates, 1980–2009. This chart represents that over 500 of every 100,000 people are incarcerated in correctional institutions.

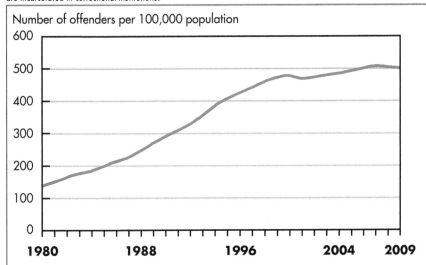

Number of offenders per 100,000 population

Source: Bureau of Justice Statistics. (2011). *Total Correctional Population*. Washington, D.C.: Author.

Minimum and medium custody levels are usually assigned to the least dangerous inmates. Inmates at higher levels may also be reclassified to a lower level if they are nearing the end of their sentence. The theory is that they are less of a trouble and escape risk because they want to complete their time easily and get out. Unfortunately, this theory does not always prove true because many criminals are unable to process this kind of logic. They may be impulsive and unable to understand the consequences of current actions and the result on their future. However, most do finish the end of a sentence quietly. The Bureau of Justice Statistics once estimated that 25% of inmates lost good time credits for good behavior, which means that a full sentence was served without an early release.[68]

Lower-custody institutions are less expensive to operate. Not only is the architecture designed with fewer security barriers, there is usually a lower staff-to-inmate ratio. Since fewer escape attempts and disturbances are expected, fewer security staff are required to supervise the population. When a prison is deemed a close- or maximum-custody institution, there will be more security staff per inmate and the prison design is such that disturbances can be contained in a small area. Escape is nearly impossible. The secure perimeter will often have more than one high fence with razor wire coiled at the bottom and up the side of the fence and topped off as well. The fences are frequently electrified and will contain detection devices to alert control room staff of any movement. In addition, the outside perimeter is patrolled by armed security staff that is in constant contact with the control room, and they will respond to all detected perimeter alerts.

Inmates at most levels of security have jobs that keep them busy on the prison grounds. Most labor in a prison is performed by inmates. Simple jobs such as mowing the grass, picking up trash, cleaning tables at the dining hall, or washing dishes are part of prisoners' daily routines. Skilled inmates may also paint, maintain plumbing and air conditioning, repair structural issues, and maintain prison vehicles. All jobs are supervised by security staff.

The Supermax   Most prisons have special housing units for disruptive inmates who pose disciplinary problems. Inmates will be placed in one of these units usually after an officer writes a **disciplinary report** describing the offense committed by the inmate. Often, these segregated areas are referred to as the **Special Housing Unit**, or the **SHU**, which is pronounced *shoe*. Inmates needing special housing due to assaultive behavior, escapes, escape attempts, inciting others, gang activity, and other categories of prohibited behavior may be reclassified to a higher custody level. In some states, such inmates will be reclassified to a supermaximum status. This is a management decision in response to an inmate's dangerous and disruptive behavior. The supermax facility may be special housing on the institutional grounds. The supermax that most have heard of is a separate facility designed and staffed exclusively for supermax inmates.

The first supermax prison in this country was Alcatraz. Currently, the only freestanding federal supermax facility is the Administrative Maximum facility in Florence, Colorado, called by some "the Alcatraz of the Rockies." Better known as ADMAX, the prison opened in 1994 and has never incurred a successful escape. Here, the most dangerous and escape-prone long-term inmates live a strict lifestyle that is controlled by officers who operate the prison remotely so that staff/inmate contact is kept to a minimum. As of early 2011, ADMAX houses notorious prisoners such as terrorist Zacarias Moussaoui, Unabomber Theodore Kaczynski, Oklahoma bombing accomplice Terry Nichols, shoe bomber Richard Reid, and FBI agent turned Soviet spy Robert Hanssen.[69]

Many states have supermax facilities constructed on the grounds of existing facilities. There, those deemed the worst of the worst reside. These special housing units are closely monitored and movement is restricted. Inmates in these units are often kept in isolation and are escorted in chains whenever they leave their cells. The supermax inmate is often granted a few hours a week out of the cell for fresh air and exercise in a monitored cage. Even this privilege may be revoked based on the inmate's behavior. Because of the extreme restrictions, the supermax prison is considered by some to be a violation of the Eighth Amendment's prohibition on cruel and unusual punishment. Numerous lawsuits have been filed by inmates and human rights groups. The United Nations has even weighed in on the controversy surrounding supermax prisons, calling for guidelines concerning torture and cruel, inhuman, and degrading treatment and punishment. Specifically, practices such as solitary confinement, excessive use of restraints, and forced psychiatric interventions are viewed as violations by the United Nations.[70]

Disciplinary report
A written report describing the inappropriate behavior or the breaking of institutional rules by an inmate.

Special Housing Unit (SHU)
Usually an area of confinement within a correctional facility designed to hold the more dangerous or violent inmates, those who are discipline problems, or those who need supervised protection from others.

Current Notorious Prisons

Many prisons throughout history have achieved notoriety for one reason or another. Some have become famous for alleged human rights violations. The ADMAX prison in Colorado and its extreme conditions is an example of such infamy. Across the nation, other prisons have their own unique characteristics.

In California's Marin County, on 275 acres of valuable waterfront property, sits San Quentin Prison. Home to California's only gas chamber and death row, San Quentin is one of the nation's best-known prisons. It was constructed in 1852 by inmate labor, and inmates slept on a ship while the prison was built. With more than 5,000 inmates, San Quentin is one of the largest prisons in the nation. San Quentin's notoriety comes mostly from its legendary depictions in movies and in song. San Quentin has been home to many infamous criminals, such as Richard Ramirez, known as the Night Stalker; Charles Bolles, known as Black Bart; Eldridge Cleaver of the Black Panthers; Charles Manson; and Sirhan Sirhan, who assassinated Robert Kennedy.[71]

Sing Sing Prison in Ossining, New York, is where the phrases "the big house" and "up the river" originated in the American lexicon.[72] Over Sing Sing's nearly two-century existence, it gained notoriety for its historic brutal discipline such as beatings, extended solitary confinement, and withholding of food for even minor violations. Though it is now a fully modern and accredited facility, Sing Sing is legendary in American criminal lore. Famous inmates include Ethel and Julius Rosenberg and bank robber Willie Sutton.

New York is also home to Attica Correctional Facility. Attica gained notoriety in 1971 when a riot erupted in which 29 inmates and 10 correctional officers were killed.[73] By many accounts, among the many grievances that inmates suffered, racial issues seemed to be the touch point that sparked the riots. New York eventually settled with the families of those killed. Nearly $12 million went to the families of the inmates killed, and another $12 million went to the families of those officers who died.[74]

France is home to an especially notorious prison. In 2000, the *New York Times* published an expose about the La Santé prison in Paris. Dr. Veronique Vasseur began working at La Santé in the 1990s and was so shocked by the conditions that she began recording her experiences. Among the atrocities, she found high suicide rates, brutal guards, rapes, bug and rodent infestations, regular beatings, poor medical care, disease, and even the intentional placement of younger inmates in cells knowing they would be raped by men with AIDS.[75] Though conditions may have improved, La Santé can still be found on lists of the most brutal and deadly prisons of the world.

Tibet's Drapchi Prison easily ranks as one of the most notorious prisons on earth. At Drapchi, there are special units for male prisoners, female prisoners, criminals, and political prisoners. The official methods of controlling inmates include torture and other inhumane treatment. Some punishments include standing in the sun for extended periods without moving, running for lengthy times without stopping, and beatings. There are few medical services, especially for the political prisoners. The inmates' diet is poor and barely sustainable, and suicide rates are high. Human rights groups, protest groups, and even international organizations have tried to influence the conditions at Drapchi. However, the Communist regime in China prevents any serious outside investigation or interference. Most information about the prison is gained from former inmates and guards. Conditions are so atrocious that the United Nations Commission on Human Rights has tried, without success, to intervene.[76]

The Privatization of Prisons

Prisons are very expensive and labor-intensive operations. State governments dedicate tremendous amounts of taxpayer money to correctional systems, both publicly and privately owned. The costs of staffing and running a prison are unlikely to come down anytime soon, if ever. With constant court challenges and demands from the citizenry to improve conditions for prisoners, costs will only increase.[77]

A current movement to reduce costs is to contract out correctional responsibilities to private organizations. Private correctional organizations have contracted with governments at the federal, state, and local levels to assume responsibility for criminal custody and detention functions. There are many successful private correctional organizations operating profitably in the United States. Often, the private facility is paid on a per-inmate basis.

The incentive for governments to turn over correctional functions to private organizations usually involves cost savings for taxpayers. In 2001, the cost for operating state prisons, excluding the cost of the land and the infrastructure, was $100 per U.S. resident.[78] This was up more than 10% from only five years earlier. This trend for increasing expenditures on prisons, operating costs, and inmate expenses will likely continue.

These private companies often promise to deliver reduced costs per inmate and better conditions through cost-efficient construction, cost-efficient operations, and competitive incentives to provide high-quality services while keeping expenses low. This efficiency and competitiveness is expected to leave room for the organization to make a profit. The state governments also expect that the funds paid to the private organizations will be less than the costs to state-run correctional facilities. Some local governments hire private correctional organizations to operate jails as well.[79]

Opponents of privatization point to the many indirect costs for the taxpayer. These costs include contract administration, contract monitoring, and the additional government regulation required. The government also retains legal liability for contractor actions. This alone has the potential for tremendous amounts of taxpayer money to be paid out in legal expenses and for lost or settled lawsuits. Research indicates that these tangential expenses negate any savings expected from the privatization of correctional systems.[80]

The criminal justice system consists of the police, the courts, and corrections. This system is an established government obligation, and some believe that that no part of it can be severed from its foundation. Correctional systems traditionally are a government responsibility. The duty of the government to punish lawbreakers is confused when private organizations fulfill the correctional functions. Harvard political scientist John Dilulio is vocal with this view.

He says, "It is precisely because corrections involves the deprivation of liberty, precisely because it involves the legally sanctioned exercise of coercion by some citizens over others, that it must remain wholly within public hands."[81]

A Brief History of Private Correctional Facilities

Modern private prisons appear to have originated from the convergence of two separate events. In the 1970s, the U.S. prison population began to expand somewhat rapidly. A decade later, under the leadership of President Ronald Reagan, the government began to look to the private sector for government solutions. These private-sector solutions were applied to the problem of rising prison populations.

The first known private prison in the United States was San Quentin Prison in California in the 1850s.[82] Even then, the basis for privatization was reduced costs. It was also assumed that there would be less corruption.[83] The first government award for local correctional services occurred in Hamilton County, Tennessee.[84] As of 2009, there were more than 25,000 federal prisoners in private facilities and more than 95,000 in privately operated state facilities.[85]

Correctional Corporations

Some of the largest private correctional corporations build, manage, and operate prisons with strict government oversight. The CCA claims the title of "America's Leader in Partnership Corrections." The corporation, established in the early 1980s, operates federal, state, and local correctional facilities around the nation. The CCA is a publicly traded corporation that operates about 50% of the private correctional facilities in the nation. This makes CCA the largest private correctional provider, with more than 17,000 employees. The organization also owns and operates TransCor America. TransCor provides inmate transportation services to correctional facilities that need to move inmates from one location to another.[86]

Private prisons have become a very profitable part of the prison-industrial complex. However, saving money for states and the federal government is still in question. A study by Vanderbilt University claims that states can save $13 million to $15 million by contracting out correctional services,[87] while a study by Cornell University demonstrates that the savings are accounting shifts.[88] Many states have taken notice, and those who do not yet use private correctional services are examining the possibility.

Privatization is often criticized because these private organizations may assume custody of healthy populations of inmates and lower-custody inmates. This reduces the costs to the private companies because there are fewer medical expenses and they need less secure facilities and fewer security staff to supervise the inmates. This leaves the more expensive populations, such as the violent, dangerous, elderly, and those with special medical needs, for the government facilities.

Major criticisms of prison privatization often come from criminologists who are convinced that privatization does not result in the promised savings. Comparing the actual costs of private prisons with those of state and federally operated institutions is complex and is often illusory. Cost analysis studies frequently return different results depending on what organization is conducting the study.

In addition, the accounting methods and populations can be very different. Since there is no private prison that is exactly like a corresponding government prison, precise cost comparisons are nearly impossible.

To study this issue, in 2007, the National Institute of Justice brought together researchers, private service providers, government prison officials, and proponents and opponents of prison privatization. The study focused on two separate analyses of the same four prisons that produced different results.[89] The privatization study concluded that overhead costs and inmate population sizes were being measured differently between private and government prisons. It found that private prisons were only measuring direct costs—such as staffing, food, medical care, and other services—while government prisons were measuring both direct costs and indirect costs associated with planning, automation, computer services, and budget development. It was assumed that the government would continue to absorb the indirect costs even for those prisons operated by private organizations, thereby eliminating promised savings. The study concluded that, in order to obtain a more accurate measurement of the costs of privatization, these indirect costs should be included in the estimates for private prisons.[90]

The Hiring and Training of Correctional Officers

Correctional officers provide security and maintain accountability of inmates for detention centers, jails, and prisons. In detention centers, they may be known as detention officers, though *correctional officer* is the generally accepted universal term. The officer must always diligently work to prevent disturbances, assaults, and escapes.

In order to become a correctional officer, one must meet stringent standards. Federal and state requirements mandate that officers have a high school diploma or GED, and some governments require at least a bachelor's degree. Certain states and local governments will also accept military service in lieu of college credit. Others will also accept combinations of college, military, counseling, and supervisory experience.[91]

Recruit officers receive academy training that varies by state. The Federal Bureau of Prisons has its own recruit and training requirements.[92] The American Correctional Association and the American Jail Association provide accrediting and certification services as well as guidelines for correctional officer training.[93] Officers also receive ongoing education and inservice training provided by their own organizations. Advanced training is also made available to those officers performing specialized functions such as K-9, emergency response teams, special weapons and munitions, and others.

The occupational outlook for correctional officers is expected to increase by 48,000 between 2008 and 2018.[94] This means that the growth of this field is favorable to those seeking such careers. Mandatory sentencing in many states has increased the correctional inmate populations and, in turn, has increased the need for additional correctional officers. Should the trend for mandatory sentencing reverse, as is being considered in some states for budgetary reasons, the need for correctional officers may decline.

In 2008, correctional officers and jailors accounted for approximately 454,500 jobs in the United States. Employment in this career is expected to increase 9% by 2018. However, cash-strapped prisons are also using technology to eliminate the staffed towers so prominent at many prisons.

Career Connections: Correctional Officer

Correctional officers provide security, maintain order, and prevent escapes in detention facilities, jails, and prisons. Employers are state and local governments and private correctional services providers. All officers must be certified by their respective federal and state governments, and recruits must be trained by government-approved training facilities. Most require applicants to have at least a high school diploma, be at least 18 years old and of good character, and have a stable job history. In addition, the correctional officer candidate must not have an extensive or significant criminal history. Some agencies will accept minor violations such as a childhood minor theft incident or misdemeanor drug charges. However, they generally will not tolerate recent charges or allow current officers who commit crimes to remain employed.

The working conditions are sometimes harsh. A correctional officer must be able to perform all job functions in all weather conditions and in sometimes dirty or cramped environments. This occupation can be hazardous and stressful. Correctional officers have one of the highest non-fatal on-the-job occupational injury rates and face the risk of assault daily. Because correctional facilities operate around the clock, officers work at all times, including holidays and weekends. Correctional officers are often required to work overtime. Typically, because of the diverse populations, jails tend to be more dangerous facilities than are prisons. Prisons generally have populations that have been segregated based upon violent tendencies of inmates and have higher staff-to-inmate ratios. Therefore, in general, prisons are safer places to work than are jails.[95]

According to the Bureau of Labor Statistics (BLS), the outlook for correctional officers is favorable and is expected to increase by about 9% of current numbers by 2018. This means that an additional 48,000 officers will be needed based on 2008 figures. In 2010, the median salary of correctional officers was $39,040. Supervisors and managers can earn significantly more. The turnover for correctional officers appears to be about average for all occupations.

FIGURE 9.3 National Estimates for Correctional Officers

Percentile wage estimates for this occupation:

Percentile	10%	25%	50% (Median)	75%	90%
Hourly Wage	$12.52	$14.97	$18.77	$25.25	$32.33
Annual Wage	$26,040	$31,140	$39,040	$52,530	$67,250

Source: Bureau of Labor Statistics. (2011). *Correctional Officers and Jailers.* Washington, D.C.: Author.

All officers in the United States are required to have at least a high school diploma. Some states may require some college or military experience. Local governments may have requirements in addition to what is required for an officer to be certified by the state. Federal prison officers are required to have at least a bachelor's degree or other acceptable work experience in lieu of the degree.

New officers receive academy training in subjects ranging from basic report writing to defensive tactics and weapons training. Federal officers receive training at the Federal Law Enforcement Training Center (FLETC) in Glynco, Georgia. Officers also receive ongoing inservice training and specialized training for those on special teams such as K-9 and emergency response. Both female and male officers receive the same training and must meet the same standards. It has been found that female correctional officers may be especially well suited to defuse potentially violent situations in the early stages.[96]

FIGURE9.4 National Estimates for Correctional Officers

States with the highest employment level in this occupation:

State	Employment	Employment per thousand jobs	Hourly mean wage	Annual mean wage
Texas	49,250	4.88	$15.96	$33,190
California	44,120	3.15	$31.49	$65,500
New York	34,310	4.11	$27.15	$56,480
Florida	33,960	4.78	$19.09	$39,710
Pennsylvania	17,940	3.27	$21.90	$45,560

Source: Bureau of Labor Statistics. (2011). *Correctional Officers and Jailers*. Washington, D.C.: Author.

Most states have public service unions, and correctional officers are often represented by collective bargaining organizations. There are arguments both for and against correctional officer unions. However, unions have a very strong presence, and they negotiate with governments and private correctional organizations for higher wages and increased benefits for members. Contracts also define working conditions and promotional guidelines. In states that do not require union membership as a condition of employment, officers who are not members will still be recipients of most negotiated benefits, just like those officers who are members and who pay union dues.[97]

Critical Thinking skilled workers?

Should correctional officers be considered professionals or simply

Chapter Summary

- Detention has been an acceptable method of punishment for criminal offenders for only a few hundred years. In early American history, jails were used primarily to hold for trial those who could not make bail or those who were unable to pay debts. The living conditions in these early jails were cruel and immoral. Men, women, and children of all ages were thrown together in undisciplined and poorly supervised micro-communities where the strong overpowered the weak. There was little medical treatment and most were poorly fed. Early prisons around the world included the Mamertine Prison as well as fortresses, hulks, workhouses, and Bridewells.

Ethics and Professionalism

The warden at a major corrections institution has several correctional officer positions he needs to fill. He has more than enough applications because the poor economy has left many people looking for work. As he peruses the applications, he ponders what kind of applicant would best serve the mission of the department.

He has many tools at his disposal, including the usual background checks, psychological exams, and truth detection technologies. However, the warden wants to upgrade the professionalism in his ranks. He contemplates tests such as career aptitude inventories, aggressiveness profiles, and ethical assessments. He also wishes to narrow his selection to those with at least some college experience.

Do you believe that he would get a better-quality officer using these recruitment tools? If the warden uses these new tests, how might the hiring decisions he makes differ from his hiring decisions of the past? Why are ethics important for new officers? Are college-educated officers necessarily better officers?

- Early techniques to punish criminals date back to the ancient Sumerians and Babylonians and included whipping, servitude, mutilation, and death. Over the centuries, thanks to reformers such as Montesquieu, John Howard, Cesare Beccaria, Jeremy Bentham, Alexis de Tocqueville, and Gustave de Beaumont, human dignity and life became increasingly valued. In most of the industrialized world, prisoners are treated immensely better than in the past. Though prisons are oppressive places and provide for an onerous existence, most countries at least provide prisoners a survivable diet, some medical care, human contact, and some form of classification that separates juveniles from adults and men from women. The Walnut Street Jail in Philadelphia was one of the first to institute reforms.

- Modern correctional facilities exist at the local, state, and federal levels. Jails are multipurpose facilities operated by local governments or sheriffs and are usually the offender's first contact with the criminal justice system. Prisons are operated by the states and the federal government and usually house offenders who are serving a sentence of more than one year. All correctional facilities have their own missions and roles in criminal justice. Some are old and outdated, and others are modern and very secure. Many have inmate amenities for recreation, education, and training. All have access to medical care. There are also different levels of security, ranging from minimum security to the supermaximum prisons.

- When an inmate is received into most state prison systems, he or she will be processed through a classification system. Classification of inmates simply is a means to fit an inmate into a specific category of custody level, medical needs, predisposition to violence or escape, training and educational needs, and other categories as determined by state statute. This classification procedure will determine primarily which security level the inmate requires. The inmate will be assigned to a state prison facility that fits his or her characteristics.

- Most prisons have special housing units for disruptive inmates who pose disciplinary problems. Inmates needing special housing for assaultive behavior, escapes, escape attempts, inciting others, gang activity, and other categories of prohibited behavior may be reclassified to a higher custody level. In some states, such inmates will be reclassified to a supermaximum status. The supermax facility may be special housing on the institutional grounds or a separate facility for particularly dangerous offenders.

- A current movement to reduce costs is to contract out correctional responsibilities to private organizations. These private companies often promise and deliver reduced costs per inmate and better conditions through cost-efficient construction, cost-efficient operations, and competitive incentives to provide high-quality services while keeping expenses low. This efficiency and competitiveness is expected to leave room for the organization to make a profit. Privatization is a topic of controversy; while some studies indicate that private prisons save money for states and the federal government, critics believes privatization has not led to the anticipated savings. Studies have noted irregularities in measurements of costs between private prisons and government prisons.

- In order to become a correctional officer, one must meet stringent standards. Federal and state requirements mandate that one have a high school diploma or GED, and some require at least a bachelor's degree. Some state and local governments will also accept military service in lieu of college credit. Others will also accept combinations of college, military, counseling, and supervisory experience.

Critical Thinking?

1. Why was the Eighth Amendment's prohibition on cruel and unusual punishment incorporated into the Bill of Rights?
2. Is there a difference between the U.S. Constitution's prohibition on cruel *and* unusual punishment and several state constitutional prohibitions on cruel *or* unusual punishment?
3. Could supermax prisons be considered cruel and unusual? Could they be considered cruel but not unusual? Or unusual but not cruel?
4. Some people are sent to prison for very long periods, even for life. Do you feel this is a good public expenditure of taxes, or is there a better way to deal with those who violate laws?
5. In 1986, Congress enacted legislation that sentenced offenders differently for possessing different forms of cocaine. Possession of five grams of crack cocaine results in a minimum sentence of five years in federal prison. It takes nearly 100 times that amount in powdered cocaine to receive a comparable sentence. Crack cocaine is found heavily in African American communities, while powdered cocaine is found primarily in white areas. Is there an issue with disparity in sentencing or is this fair?
6. Civil rights restoration for inmates returning to open society is becoming increasingly popular. What civil rights should be restored and which, if any, should not?
7. With all of the security measures in place, how is it possible that drugs, weapons, and other contraband manage to get into prisons and into prisoners' possession?

8. Since many inmates are able to function well in work release centers and halfway houses, is it a good idea to simply release these inmates to cut down on costs?
9. Do privately owned correctional facilities provide the same services as government-run facilities? Is there any difference as far as criminal justice is concerned?
10. Is the money spent on jails and prisons justified? Is there a better way to punish criminals than by imprisoning them?

Media

Federal Bureau of Prisons: http://www.bop.gov/
> This website contains much information about the correctional system, its history, and references for further reading.

Bureau of Justice Statistics: http://bjs.ojp.usdoj.gov/
> This government website contains official statistics for all areas of law enforcement.

Search and Seizure Video: http://www.intelecomonline.net/VideoPlayer.aspx?Code=03FE46882E7BD E8D817DE78A8CC080CB45C925322BCDE599E9353C25E8127110885EB21F1DB8D6A 712FA88B990A5C1CD
> This short video covers search and seizure issues.

National Institute of Justice Multimedia: http://www.ojp.usdoj.gov/nij/journals/media.htm
> This website contains multimedia from the National Institute of Justice.

Occupational Employment Statistics, Correctional Officer: http://www.bls.gov/oes/current/ oes333012.htm
> This is the official government website for statistics that may be of interest to those wishing to become correctional officers.

Endnotes

1. JTF-GTMO. (2011). *Overview: Joint Task Force Guantanamo.* Retrieved from http://www.jtfgtmo.southcom.mil/ index/Fact%20Sheets/GTMO%20Overview.pdf
2. U.S. Department of Defense (DOD). (2011). *Combatant Status Review Tribunal Summary.* Retrieved from http:// www.defense.gov/news/csrtsummary.pdf
3. JTF-GTMO, 2011.
4. Congressional Research Service. (2009). *Closing the Guantanamo Detention Center: Legal Issues.* Retrieved from http://www.henrywaxman.house.gov/UploadedFiles/R40139.pdf
5. Human Rights Watch. (2008). *Locked Up Alone: Detention Conditions and Mental Health at Guantanamo.* Retrieved from http://www.defense.gov/pubs/pdfs/App7.pdf
6. Ibid.
7. Friedman, L. (1993). *Crime and Punishment in American History.* New York, NY: Basic Books.
8. Ibid., 50.
9. American Archives. (1776). *Constitution of Pennsylvania.* Retrieved from http://lincoln.lib.niu.edu/cgi-bin/ amarch/getdoc.pl?/var/lib/philologic/databases/amarch/.22309
10. King, L. W. (1997). *Hammurabi's Code.* Retrieved from http://eawc.evansville.edu/index.htm
11. International World History Project. (n.d.). *A History of Ancient Greece: Draco and Solon Laws.* Retrieved from http://history-world.org/draco_and_solon_laws.htm
12. Halsall, P. (1998). "Ancient History Sourcebook: Code of Hammurabi, c. 1780 BCE." *Fordham University.* Retrieved from http://www.fordham.edu/halsall/ancient/hamcode.html
13. Roman Colosseum. (2008). *Roman Punishment.* Retrieved from http://www.roman-colosseum.info/roman-life/ roman-punishment.htm

14. *Capital Punishment.* (2000). Retrieved from http://autocww.colorado.edu/~toldy2/E64ContentFiles/Law AndCourts/CapitalPunishment.html

15. Alasti, S. (2007). *Comparative Study of Stoning Punishment in the Religions of Islam and Judaism.* Retrieved from http://ggu.academia.edu/SanazAlasti/Papers/195679/Comparative_Study_of_Stoning_Punishments_In_the_Religions_of_Islam_and_Judaism

16. "Guillotine." (2011). *Britannica Online Encyclopedia.* Retrieved from http://www.britannica.com/EBchecked/topic/248765/guillotine

17. Friedman, 1993, 42.

18. Ekirch, R. (1987). *Bound for America: The Transportation of British Convicts to the Colonies.* New York, NY: Oxford University Press.

19. Montgomery, R. (1998). *A History of Correctional Violence.* American Correctional Association.

20. Halsall, P. (1997). "Modern History Sourcebook: Montesquieu: The Spirit of the Laws, 1748." *Fordham University.* Retrieved from http://www.fordham.edu/halsall/mod/montesquieu-spirit.html

21. Ibid.

22. Hay, G. (2011). "Biography of John Howard." *The John Howard Society of Canada.* Retrieved from http://www.johnhoward.ca/about/biography

23. Ibid.

24. Ibid.

25. Beccaria, C. (1764). *Of Crimes and Punishments.* Retrieved from http://www.constitution.org/cb/crim_pun.htm

26. Ibid.

27. Bentham, J. (1789). "An Introduction to the Principles of Morals and Legislation." *Library of Economics and Liberty.* Retrieved from http://www.econlib.org/library/Bentham/bnthPML1.html#Chapter%20I,%20Of%20the%20Principle%20of%20Utility

28. De Tocqueville, A. (n.d.). *Democracy in America.* Retrieved from http://xroads.virginia.edu/~HYPER/DETOC/home.html

29. Ibid.

30. Ibid.

31. Hassett, M. (1910). "Mamertine Prison." *The Catholic Encyclopedia.* Retrieved from http://www.newadvent.org/cathen/09579a.htm

32. *The Carcer—Mamertine Prison.* (n.d.). Retrieved from http://www.mmdtkw.org/VCarcer.html

33. Salvi, S. (2011). *The Original List of Sanctuary Cities, USA.* Retrieved from http://www.ojjpac.org/sanctuary.asp

34. Historic Royal Palaces. (2011). *Tower of London.* Retrieved from http://www.hrp.org.uk/TowerOfLondon/stories.aspx

35. Ibid.

36. Morris, S. (2005). "Britain's Only Prison Ship Ends Up on the Beach." *The Guardian.* Retrieved from http://www.guardian.co.uk/uk/2005/aug/12/ukcrime.prisonsandprobation

37. Independence National Historical Park. (2007). *Following in Franklin's Footsteps.* Retrieved from http://www.independenceparkinstitute.com/FranklinDropInPacket6-26-07.pdf

38. Johnston, N. (2000). "Prison Reform in Pennsylvania." *The Pennsylvania Prison Society.* Retrieved from http://www.prisonsociety.org/about/history.shtml

39. Ibid.

40. Stohr, M., Walsh, A., & Hemmens, C. (2009). *Corrections, a Text Reader.* Thousand Oaks, CA: Sage.

41. Ibid.

42. Northstar Gallery. (n.d.). *Eastern State Penitentiary.* http://northstargallery.com/esp/easternstatehistory01.htm

43. Friedman, 1993, 79.

44. Ibid., 79–80.

45. National Park Service. (2011). "Alcatraz Island: History & Culture." *NPS.gov.* Retrieved from http://www.nps.gov/alca/historyculture/index.htm

46. Ibid.

47. Overthrow Arpaio. (2009). *Top Ten Reasons to Recall Joe.* Retrieved from http://www.arpaio.com/top-ten/index.php#9 *Maricopa County Sheriff's Office.* (2011). Retrieved from http://www.mcso.org

48. *Overthrow Arpaio.* (2009). Retrieved from http://www.arpaio.com

49. Lacy, M. (2010, September 2). "Justice Dept. Sues Sheriff Over Bias Investigation." *New York Times.* http://www.nytimes.com/2010/09/03/us/03sheriff.html
Wingett, Y., Hensley, J. J., & Kiefer, M. (2010, September 3). "Sheriff Joe Arpaio Sued by Justice Department in Civil-Rights Probe." *AZCentral.com.* Retrieved from http://www.azcentral.com/news/election/azelections/articles/2010/09/02/20100902joe-arpaio-sued-by-justice-department-brk-02-ON.html

50. Rangel, C. (2011, May 13). "YOUR Tax Dollars: How Much Does It Cost to Defend the Maricopa County Sheriff's Office?" *ABC15.com.* Retrieved from http://www.abc15.com/dpp/news/local_news/investigations/your-tax-dollars-being-spent-to-fight-sheriff-joe-arpaio%E2%80%99s-lawsuits

51. Bureau of Justice Statistics. (2011). *Key Facts at a Glance: Correctional Populations.* Retrieved from http://bjs.ojp.usdoj.gov/content/glance/tables/corr2tab.cfm

52. *Estelle v. Gamble,* 429 U.S. 97 (1976).

53. National Commission on Correctional Health Care. http://www.ncchc.org/index.html

54. *Bounds v. Smith,* 430 U.S. 817 (1977).

55. *Younger v. Gilmore,* 404 U.S. 15 (1971).

56. *Bounds v. Smith,* 1977.

57. *Lewis v. Casey,* 518 U.S. 343 (1996).

58. Ibid.

59. Stanford Encyclopedia of Philosophy. (2008). *Legal Punishment.* Retrieved from http://plato.stanford.edu/entries/legal-punishment/

60. Ibid.

61. Ibid.

62. Ibid.

63. Ibid.

64. *Wolff v. McDonnell,* 418 U.S. 539 (1974).

65. Council of State Governments Justice Center. (2011). *Reentry Policy Council.* Retrieved from http://reentrypolicy.org

66. United States Attorney's Office, District of Minnesota. (2009). *Federal Criminal Prosecution.* Retrieved from http://www.justice.gov/usao/mn/downloads/federal%20criminal%20brochure.2009.final.pdf

67. *U.S. v. Lanza,* 260 U.S. 377 (1922).

68. Tibbs, D. (2006). "Peeking Behind the Iron Curtain: How Law 'Works' Behind Prison Walls." *Southern California Interdisciplinary Law Journal, 16,* 137-182. Retrieved from http://www-bcf.usc.edu/~idjlaw/PDF/16-1/16-1%20Tibbs.pdf
Bureau of Justice Statistics. (n.d.). *Prison Rule Violators.* Retrieved from http://bjs.ojp.usdoj.gov/index.cfm?ty=gsearch

69. Federal Bureau of Prisons. (2011). *Inmate Locator.* Retrieved from http://www.bop.gov/iloc2/LocateInmate.jsp

70. U.S. Department of Justice, National Institute of Corrections. (1999). *Supermax Prisons: Overview and General Considerations.* Retrieved from http://static.nicic.gov/Library/014937.pdf
United Nations. (2008). *Torture and other Cruel, Inhuman or Degrading Treatment or Punishment.* Retrieved from http://www.un.org/disabilities/images/A.63.175.doc
For a cost analysis, see Lawrence, S., & Mears, D. (2004). *Benefit-Cost Analysis of Supermax Prisons.* Retrieved from http://www.hawaii.edu/hivandaids/Benefit-Cost_Analysis_of_Supermax_Prisons.pdf

71. California Department of Corrections and Rehabilitation. (2011). *Adult Facilities Locator: San Quentin State Prison.* Retrieved from http://www.cdcr.ca.gov/Facilities_Locator/SQ-Institution_Stats.html

72. Investigation Discovery. (2011). *Notorious Prisons: Sing Sing Correctional Facility.* Retrieved from http://investigation.discovery.com/investigation/notorious-prisons/sing-sing/sing-sing.html
New York Correction History Society. (n.d.). *Images of America: Sing Sing Prison.* Retrieved from http://www.correctionhistory.org/html/chronicl/state/singsing/cheliindex.html
For further reading and a firsthand account by a Sing Sing correctional officer, see Conover, T. (2000). *Newjack: Guarding Sing Sing.* New York, NY: Random House.

73. Jackson, B. (1999). "Attica: An Anniversary of Death." *Artvoice*. Retrieved from http://www.acsu.buffalo. edu/~bjackson/attica.htm

Libcom.org. (2006). *1971: The Attica Prison Uprising*. Retrieved from http://libcom.org/ history/1971-the-attica-prison-uprising

National Geographic. (n.d.). *The Final Report: Attica* [Video]. Retrieved from http://channel.nationalgeographic. com/series/final-report/3418/Videos#tab-Videos/05524_00

74. Ibid.

75. Daley, S. (2000, January 28). "Expose of Brutal Prison Jolts France's Self-Image." *New York Times*. Retrieved from http://www.nytimes.com/2000/01/28/world/expose-of-brutal-prison-jolts-france-s-self-image.html

76. Tibetan Center for Human Rights and Democracy. (n.d.). *Drapchi Prison: Tibet's Most Dreaded Prison*. Retrieved from http://www.tchrd.org/publications/topical_reports/drapchi_prison-2001/

News Blaze. (2011, January 5). *Tibetan Political Prisoner Tortured After Speaking To UN*. Retrieved from http:// newsblaze.com/story/20110105080436zzzz.nb/topstory.html

77. Bureau of Justice Statistics. (2004). *State Prison Expenditures, 2001* (NCJ 2020949). Retrieved from http://bjs.ojp. usdoj.gov/content/pub/ascii/spe01.txt

78. Ibid.

79. Austin, J., & Coventry, G. (2001). *Emerging Issues on Privatized Prisons* (NCJ 181249). Retrieved from https:// www.ncjrs.gov/pdffiles1/bja/181249.pdf

80. Ibid.

81. Dilulio, J. J. (1986). "Prisons, Profits, and the Public Good: The Privatization of Corrections." *Research Bulletin No. 1*. Huntsville, TX: Sam Houston State University Criminal Justice Center.

82. Austin & Coventry, 2001.

83. Ibid.

84. *Privatization of Prisons*. (2008). Retrieved from http://privatizationofprisons.com

85. Bureau of Justice Statistics. (2009). *Correctional Populations in the United States, 2009*. Retrieved from http://bjs. ojp.usdoj.gov/content/pub/pdf/cpus09.pdf

86. Corrections Corporation of America. (2011). *CCA*. Retrieved from http://www.cca.com/

87. Blumstein, J., Cohen, M. A., & Seth, S. (2007). "Do Government Agencies Respond to Market Pressures? Evidence from Private Prisons." *Social Science Research Network*. Retrieved from http://papers.ssrn.com/sol3/papers. cfm?abstract_id=441007

88. McFarland, S., McGowan, C., & O'Toole, T. (2002). *Prisons, Privatization, and Public Values*. Retrieved from http://government.cce.cornell.edu/doc/html/PrisonsPrivatization.htm#_Opponents_of_Privatization:

89. Gaes, G. (2008). "Cost, Performance Studies Look at Prison Privatization." *NJJ Journal, 259*. Retrieved from http://www.nij.gov/journals/259/prison-privatization.htm

90. Ibid.

91. Bureau of Labor Statistics. (2010). *Occupational Outlook Handbook, 2010–2011 Edition: Correctional Officers*. Retrieved from http://www.bls.gov/oco/ocos156.htm

92. Ibid.

93. Ibid.

94. Ibid.

95. Cheeseman, K. A., & Worley, R. (2006). "Women on the Wing: Inmate Perceptions about Female Correctional Officer Job Competency in a Southern Prison System." *Southwest Journal of Criminal Justice, 3*(2), 86–102. Retrieved from http://www.utsa.edu/swjcj/archives/3.2/CheesemanWorley.pdf

96. Ibid.

97. Greenhouse, S. (2011, January 3). "Strained States Turning to Laws to Curb Labor Unions." *New York Times*. Retrieved from http://www.nytimes.com/2011/01/04/business/04labor.html

© 2012 BY DAN BANNISTER. USED UNDER LICENSE OF SHUTTERSTOCK, INC.

10

Prison Life

KEY TERMS

Day fine, Day reporting center, Deprivation, Doing time, Halfway house, Importation, Indigenous model, Inmate code, Outlaw motorcycle gangs, Pains of imprisonment, Principle of least eligibility, Prison gangs, Prisonization, Street gangs, Total institution

CHAPTER OBJECTIVES

1. Discuss correctional facilities as total institutions.
2. Understand the roles of both inmate and officer subcultures behind institutional walls.
3. Discuss the implications of relying on incarceration and other corrections-based responses to crime.
4. Discuss the economic realities of incarcerating persons in the United States.
5. Define the various forms of community-based alternatives available.

Case Study: Richard Speck

On July 13, 1966, the city of Chicago was shaken by the methodical torture, rape, and murder of eight nurses from the South Chicago Community Hospital. One victim survived the attack, and she was later able to provide a detailed description of her assailant. A few days later, 24-year-old Richard Speck saw his likeness and description in a local newspaper. Speck then attempted suicide by slashing his wrists.[1] Apparently, his desire to die was overcome by his will to live, because he called authorities for help.

The police did not realize whom they were assisting as Speck was taken to the hospital. It was not until a doctor noticed the identifying tattoos and compared him to photographs in the newspaper that his identity was known. He was then arrested. Speck was eventually tried and convicted of all eight murders and was sentenced to death.[2] Fortunately for Speck, the United States Supreme Court abolished the death penalty in 1972.[3] His death sentence was subsequently set at consecutive life sentences.

Speck had a lurid history of abuse toward women along with accusations of murder. His abhorrent behavior continued behind the institutional walls at Statesville (Illinois) Correctional Center; his escapades in prison were infamous. While incarcerated, he was included in a study by the Federal Bureau of Investigation Behavioral Science Unit (BSU), which was collecting information to develop a profile of mass murderers.[4]

A homemade video Speck made while in prison that leaked following his death in 1991 from a heart attack showed him having sex with another inmate, waving around $100 bills, and ingesting cocaine. He further bragged about the "good" time he was having while incarcerated. The leaking of this video launched an investigation into the Illinois Department of Corrections.[5] Because the tape had been made years earlier, it was too late to bring any criminal charges; however, the Illinois prison system was prompted to make changes in their operations as a result.

The Richard Speck case is an extraordinary example of life inside prison. Though certainly not a typical representation, it is not particularly shocking to those who have studied and worked in high-security facilities. The appalling aspects of the Speck video are the lack of security and the apparent cooperation of the security staff that allowed the taping session to take place. This experience and countless others worldwide have contributed to the development of modern correctional principles. This chapter examines the prison existence and the way of life for those who reside in prison.

Prison Culture

Charles Dickens, in *A Walk in a Workhouse*, wrote, "We have come to this absurd, this dangerous, this monstrous pass, that the dishonest felon is, in respect of cleanliness, order, diet, and accommodation, better provided for, and taken care of, than the honest pauper."[6] This is understood to mean that the living conditions of the criminal in the workhouse should be no better than that of the poorest laborer outside of the workhouse.

Early English law attempted to uphold this rule. An early English statute, the Poor Law Amendment Act of 1834 (PLAA)[7], first codified the **principle of** least eligibility. The principle simply means that the conditions provided (in this case, for the poor) by the government should not be better than the existence of the poorest member of society. Only the truly destitute would qualify for aid under the PLAA. This limitation was meant to discourage those who would simply take advantage of the public generosity.

The principle of least eligibility has long been society's attitude for those who have been duly incarcerated. Edward Sieh suggests that if imprisonment is to act as a deterrent, then those in the lowest socioeconomic class should lead a better existence than those imprisoned.[8] The attitude that prison should present a harsh existence clashes with many who feel that the imprisoned are treated inhumanely at worst and indifferently at best. Some further believe that the treatment of America's prison and jail populations is unconstitutional.

Indeed, the federal government, along with most state and countless local authorities, has been under court order to improve conditions in prisons and jails.[9] Numerous cases brought before the Supreme Court have challenged the conditions of incarceration, arguing that deprivation of certain liberties constitutes cruel and unusual punishment. One notable case, *Pell v. Procunier* (1974), outlined a benchmark for prisoners' rights, establishing that each inmate "retains those First Amendment rights that are not inconsistent with his status as a prisoner."[10] Two years later, *Estelle v. Gamble* (1976) clarified that prison officials have a responsibility to provide medical care to prisoners because "deliberate indifference" to prisoners' medical needs was a violation of constitutional rights.[11] The concept of "deliberate indifference" has become something of a baseline in determining which prison conditions are deemed unconstitutional and which are legal forms of punishment.

The Supreme Court has ruled on countless issues related to prison policies and prisoners' rights, further delineating which practices are considered acceptable. Some of these rulings have sided with prison policies, such as *Procunier v. Martinez* (1974), which affirmed that prison staff can monitor inmates' mail for security purposes,[12] and *Block v. Rutherford* (1984), which upheld a Los Angeles prison's policy of denying prisoners any outside visitors.[13] Additionally, cases such as *Hudson v. Palmer* (1984) ruled that prisoners do not have a right to privacy and can be subjected to searches.[14] By contrast, other Supreme Court rulings have established prisoners' freedoms, such as *Cruz v. Beto* (1972), which gave inmates the opportunity to pursue their religious faith,[15] and *Wolf v. McDonnell* (1974), which stated that appropriate due process must be followed before sanctions can be levied on a prisoner.[16]

Principle of least eligibility

The view that those who commit crimes, particularly those in prison, are the least deserving members of society to benefit from government-provided assistance and support, such as education, vocational training, and other forms of support.

Critical Thinking

Should prisoners have a living standard while incarcerated that exceeds that of the poorest in our society? Should they have better medical care? Should they have better recreation? Should they have better food? Stated differently, should the poorest of the honest citizens have better living conditions than convicted felons in prison?

Exhibit: *Estelle v. Gamble*

"An inmate must rely on prison authorities to treat his medical needs; if the authorities fail to do so, those needs will not be met. In the worst cases, such a failure may actually produce physical 'torture or a lingering death,' ... In less serious cases, denial of medical care may result in pain and suffering which no one suggests would serve any penological purpose. . . .

"We therefore conclude that deliberate indifference to serious medical needs of prisoners constitutes the 'unnecessary and wanton infliction of pain,' . . . This is true whether the indifference is manifested by prison doctors in their response to the prisoner's needs or by prison guards in intentionally denying or delaying access to medical care or intentionally interfering with the treatment once prescribed."

Pains of imprisonment
Described by Gresham Sykes as the pains that develop from the deprivations and frustrations of those who are incarcerated.

Deprivation
Described in Sykes's "pains of imprisonment" as loss of freedom, a scarcity of goods and services, and the loss of domestic relationships for inmates.

Total institution
An institution that provides everything a person needs for survival, usually at a lower level than what is enjoyed in an open society.

Adjusting to Prison Life When a convicted criminal is first incarcerated, he or she often undergoes a painful adjustment to prison. These experiences were dubbed the "pains of imprisonment" by sociologist Gresham Sykes, who in 1958 published *The Society of Captives*, his study of prison life at the New Jersey State Prison. His work is still considered one of the most important criminological studies conducted, and it laid the foundation for subsequent studies on the effects that prisons have on both inmates and staff.

Sykes explains that the **pains of imprisonment** on a person's personality, though less obvious than physical injuries, are "no less fearful."[17] These pains develop from those deprivations and frustrations that are felt by those who must suffer this threat to self-esteem and personal security. Sykes further notes that this loss of freedom, a scarcity of goods and services, the loss of domestic relationships, and so on, may be acceptable and unavoidable for those imprisoned, but the effects on the inmate must be recognized as serious, just as are physical punishments.[18]

The **deprivation** of liberty, or loss of freedom, is the most obvious of the painful conditions of imprisonment.[19] In a prison, inmates are restricted to their assigned living space, most likely a cell. Sociologist Erving Goffman described prisons as **total institutions**.[20] The prison as a total institution defines the inmate and his or her entire life. Interaction with the world outside of the institution is tightly controlled, and perhaps nonexistent. For the incarcerated, other people have arranged life and the inmate must follow the same general routine that the other inmates are required to follow. The inmate's freedom to make choices is limited to what the institution allows.[21] Here, a new cultural and social world develops. Discipline is tightly controlled and rules are abundant. Punishment for infractions is usually swift and more severe than it is for similar violations in open society. Every aspect of the inmate's life is closely monitored, and privacy is minimal. Movement throughout the institution is tightly regulated by a system of permissions, passes, and standardized orderliness. In a total institution, human needs for the entire group are controlled by a bureaucracy.[22]

The total institution is a fully self-contained community that provides all required needs and services to its residents.

Additionally, the act of imprisonment represents the rejection of the individual from the free society. The inmate (and eventually, the former inmate) has sacrificed his or her status as a trusted member of society. There are certain rights that the inmate will find it difficult or impossible to regain, such as the rights to vote, to hold political office, and to obtain certain employment. Sykes suggests that in order for convicts to endure psychologically, they must find some method of "rejecting [their] rejectors."[23]

The deprivation of goods and services, too, is outlined by Sykes as a pain of imprisonment.[24] Attempts to compare the free world with prison are difficult. In prison, the inmate exists in a threadbare environment. Even the floor is usually only bare concrete. The inmate has very few possessions; Bruce Hood, director of the Bristol Cognitive Development Center in Bristol, England, maintains that prisons remove all belongings deliberately in order to eradicate inmates' sense of self.[25] Goffman describes what happens to an inmate when first introduced to the total institution as a stripping process. This process is one that mortifies, humiliates, degrades, and crushes the self-identity of the new inhabitant. The inmate is stripped of personal physical property that is placed in an area of inaccessible storage. The new inmate will then receive replacement property, such as a prison uniform, that defines his or her new self as an inmate. The effects of this experience are further compounded as the inmate witnesses the mortification process of fellow inmates.[26]

Though basic needs such as food, medical care, and dry living areas are provided, all these resources are strictly supervised and scheduled. An established square footage of living space, defined amounts of calories per day, and scheduled opportunities for exercise and recreation must be considered deprivations from what one is accustomed in the free world. Though some may claim that the inmate is provided all that is necessary, inmates will define their "material impoverishment" as a painful loss.[27]

Another of Sykes's pains of imprisonment is the deprivation of autonomy. Autonomy, which means one's self-government or self-directing freedom and moral independence,[28] is effectively removed from the inmate through rules and orders that control the inmate's every movement.[29] Every aspect of an inmate's life is regulated. Even the inmate's personal mail may be read by prison staff looking for statements of which the organization does not approve. Moreover, sleeping hours, eating times, and the exact routes taken to different areas of the institution are strictly controlled.

Inmates often express frustration with certain rules, viewing them as nonsensical authoritarian acts on the part of the prison. Inmates may be prohibited from removing anything from the dining hall, even an item such as a packet of sugar that may simply have gone in the trash. Many prisons require that inmates walk down a small painted-off section of the sidewalk while the larger part is reserved for officers and staff. Inmates may also be required to maintain uniform short haircuts and to shave every day. Rules are often enforced without explanation. An inmate may be denied parole one day and told that mail has been delayed another, but rarely given reasons. Moreover, an inmate who demands justification is viewed as a troublemaker and will be treated as such.

This indifference and lack of concern are often institutional policy. The worry is that if prison staff explains the enforcement of the rules to inmates, the inmates may find the explanations unsatisfactory and will begin challenging the situation and arguing with captors. This could then disrupt the power relationship that prison staff must maintain over inmates.[30] This denial of their ability to make choices and the denial of rule and order explanations have profound effects on inmates' psyches. They are rendered helpless, weak, and dependent. The normal self-determining individual has lost his or her autonomy and must somehow develop a method to cope.[31]

Indeed, under Goffman's total institution concept, facilities such as prisons and jails, which protect society from those who are deliberate dangers, present a major division between those who live there and those who work there. This partitioning between staff and inmate is of necessary intent, as they share common sociological worlds with one another. The two sides must spend considerable time together, and each views the other with a great deal of disdain and distrust.[32]

John Irwin, a noted criminologist who himself was incarcerated for an armed robbery in the 1950s, states, "The human density and total lack of privacy expose them to one another in ways that can occur only in total institutions."[33] Everyone witnesses each other's most private activities and habits because the prisoner in a total institution no longer has the privacy once taken for granted.[34]

Irwin notes that the "functionaries" of the criminal justice system, officers and others, contribute to the degradation felt by prisoners because they openly express contempt and hostility toward them.[35] Inmates may view staff as mean and condescending. Staff often views inmates as untrustworthy and secretive. This divide is usually quite wide by design, and even the tones of voice used for communication between the groups are different. Security staff tends to speak to inmates in a firm and commanding tone, while inmates speak to staff in a tone of deference and respect, even if not genuine. Staff members tend to feel superior and inmates, in some ways, feel inferior.[36]

In the total institution, sociological roles are somewhat different from such roles in open society. In an open society, and in the case of the prison staff, people usually work for a particular reward, most often to be paid for their contributions. In a prison, inmates will work not for reward, but from threat of severe punishment if they do not. Another confusion of roles is that of family. The inmate cannot sustain a family existence in the customary sense. Of course, a staff member leaves at the end of a shift and returns to his or her family.[37] This widens the divide even further between the actors in this total institution.

The last of Sykes's pains of imprisonment is the deprivation of security that an inmate must endure. Sykes believes it is strange that society chooses to reduce criminal behavior in offenders by placing them in the company of so many other offenders.[38] Though an individual inmate may not prey on other inmates, it is reasonable for one to believe that others will take advantage of weaker and less resourceful inmates. Therefore, there are those within the criminal population who are considered criminal even to the average inmate. Since the inmate is living with and associating with outlaws of all sorts, it is rational for the inmate to experience, on some level, a lack of personal security.[39]

In prison, the inmate is aware that he or she will likely be faced with another aggressive inmate. The inmate believes that he or she must be prepared to defend person and property. If he or she loses this battle for dominance, the inmate will be considered weak and defenseless. Conversely, should the inmate win this battle, other inmates may seek to gain greater standing by defeating the one who has already earned a reputation for toughness. Since both success and

Gresham Sykes describes the pains of imprisonment as those deprivations and frustrations felt by inmates.

Prisonization
The taking on in greater or lesser degree of the customs and general culture of the penitentiary.

Inmate code
Rules and roles that inmates adopt while incarcerated.

Doing time
Jargon used by inmates to describe their good behavior.

failure in personal battles may bring additional attacks, the inmate never fully gains a sense of security.[40]

Despite these many deprivations, over time, many inmates begin to acclimate themselves to prison life. The term **prisonization** was coined in 1940 by Donald Clemmer, who defined it as "The taking on in greater or lesser degree of the folkways, mores, customs, and general culture of the penitentiary."[41] This refers to the socialization process into the culture and life of a prison inmate. Prisonization also describes those whose prison socialization has become so psychologically ingrained into their personalities that they would have difficulty readjusting to life outside of the prison. Prisonization may be thought of as a subcategory of institutionalization, which describes an excessive dependency on the institution.[42]

Prisonization is a process that does not happen to all incarcerated individuals at the same rate. However, most prisoners do learn a few simple rules, roles, and **inmate codes** very quickly. Inmates learn to behave as good cons **doing time**, meaning they are on their best behavior and are not causing trouble. They learn many informal codes of conduct for being an inmate, such as not getting involved in other inmates' personal affairs, refusing to report another inmate who is breaking rules, never crying or backing down from a fight, never associating with officers, and warning other inmates when an officer is approaching. These informal rules blend into the inmate subculture and allow them to coexist in very cramped and close living arrangements. These learned behaviors aid the progression of the prisonization process.

Prisonization has been identified as one of the variables that frustrate a former inmate's reintegration back into open society. Many ex-inmates can never completely regain the social position they held before entering the institution. The stigmatization of being an ex-prisoner creates an individual who is secretive about his or her past and who wishes to conceal particular characteristics of his or her identity.[43] The effects of prisonization often lead inmates to internalize their emotions, which later interferes with their ability to form intimate interpersonal relationships, to find employment, or to gain a sufficient economic level. These frustrations of reintegration have been identified as one possible factor of recidivism.[44]

Inmate Subcultures   The inmate culture and subcultures are defining factors in the prisonization of inmates. There are many subcultures to be found in correctional institutions. These sociological divisions may be positive or negative in nature. It appears that each institution has its own dominant culture and subcultures. The cultures deemed positive are those where inmates offer encouragement and support to other inmates for engaging in programs that reinforce successful reentry and institutional behavior. Other cultures and subcultures are negative and create barriers to successful rehabilitative and reentry efforts. High-security institutions tend to have more negative cultures than do those of lesser security, though this is partly because these high-security institutions tend to have more inmates with strong criminal and anti-authority personalities. The negative cultures create a paradox of sorts. The more difficult the inmates become, the more staff

The indigenous model evolves from the isolation and loss of freedom an inmate will suffer while incarcerated.

© 2012 BY ROOK76. USED UNDER LICENSE OF SHUTTERSTOCK, INC.

will assert their control. This, in turn, will create a cycle of conflict with little chance of resolution.[45]

According to Kelly Cheeseman of Sam Houston State University, there are two predominant theories regarding inmate subcultures. One is the importation model, which simply means that the criminal culture one participates in outside of prison is often how the person will continue to behave inside the prison. Those inmates who were violent on the outside are likely to be violent on the inside. The inmate subcultures are therefore influenced by characteristics and experiences obtained before and outside of prison.[46]

The second of Cheeseman's major subculture theories is the indigenous model, also known as the deprivation model.[47] This model holds that those pre-existing conditions of deprivation in a prison have a great effect on how the inmate will adjust to prison life. The indigenous model evolves from the isolation, constant monitoring, loss of possessions, and the loss of freedom an inmate will experience.[48] This is consistent with Sykes's pains of imprisonment and the other models discussed in this section. This model refers to the scarcity of all that was known socially and materially to the inmate. The deprivation of human wants and desires and the pains of imprisonment will be the primary factors in the individual's response to incarceration.[49]

According to Dr. Mandeep Dhami, et al., indigenous and importation models both explain how inmates adapt to prison. It has been found that each model may have a greater effect than the other on certain behaviors. Even different characteristics within each model may elicit certain manners of conduct. For instance, when trying to predict which inmates are more likely to violate institutional rules, the importation model—considering age, gender, and marital status—is a better predictor than the indigenous model. However, the importation model characteristics of education, mental illness, and substance abuse are not significant predictors of rule violations. Conversely, some researchers have found that indigenous characteristics, such as security, explain fewer breaches of violence against staff and other inmates.[50]

Importation

The tendency for inmates to bring into the prison the criminal culture they participated in outside of prison.

Indigenous model

A model that refers to the scarcity of all that was previously known socially and materially to the inmate. This model evolves from the isolation, constant monitoring, loss of possessions, and loss of freedom an inmate will experience.

Gangs   One ever-present subculture in America's jails, prisons, and juvenile facilities, both public and private, is that of gangs. The importation model helps explain this culture. Inmates who belonged to a gang before coming to prison often continue their gang involvement behind bars. In fact, in early 2011, U.S. District Attorney Paul J. Fishman remarked in reference to a gang in New Jersey, "The presence of this gang is unacceptable, whether its leaders are on the streets or behind bars. Prison sentences must mean more than a change of a gang's base of operations."[51] This is a typical challenge that correctional authorities must address when setting gang policy in their institutions.

Inmates typically come from a wide geographic area and they represent all races and socioeconomic groups. Therefore, competing gangs are often imported into prison simply by chance. In addition, it should be noted that not all gangs are first formed on the street. Some gangs originate in prison; they are frequently referred to as "prison gangs." Gangs such as the Black Guerrilla Family and the Aryan Brotherhood are examples of pure prison gangs.[52]

The designation of a gang belongs to the greater category of "Security Threat Group." A Security Threat Group, or STG, is defined by the National Gang Crime Research Center as "any group of three or more persons with recurring threatening or disruptive behavior." Some definitions of an STG or a gang require that there be only two participants.[53] On the other hand, federal law defines a gang as numbering at least five participants.[54] However, in the sociological sense, a true social group must have three or more members,[55] so that will be the working definition in this chapter. Regardless of size, the overarching characteristic of an STG is that it poses a threat to the security of the institution.

Defining a gang is even more problematic than agreeing on the minimum number of its members. According to the United States Department of Justice, there is no nationally accepted standard definition of a gang. Therefore, different jurisdictions may have diverse definitions that may even disagree with one another. One measure that is standard in most gang definitions is that the group is involved in ongoing criminal activity.[56]

Gangs are comprised of all races and ethnicities, and include groups representing immigrants, youths, neighborhoods, motorcycles, drugs, and prisons.[57] Again, the importation theory of prison subcultures explains that many gang members bring their gang activity with them when they are admitted into prison. Therefore, gangs are found at almost all prisons, though statistics show there is more gang activity in state prisons than at their federal counterparts.[58]

Critical Thinking   How might correctional officers protect weaker inmates? What alternatives for protection exist in a correctional institution?

Gang membership in the U.S. as of September 2008 was estimated at around 1 million. This is an increase of about 20% over 2005. It was estimated that about 90% of those gang members resided in local communities, with the rest being incarcerated in local, state, and federal correctional facilities. The FBI believes that some of the increase in gang membership is attributable to better reporting and identification methods by law enforcement. However, most of the increase is due to gang recruitment efforts and the release of incarcerated gang members. The three basic types of gangs identified by law enforcement are street gangs, prison gangs, and outlaw motorcycle gangs.[59]

Street Gangs   Street gangs are those gangs that originate at the street level. These gangs are a significant threat group because of the large geographic areas where they proliferate. National and regional-level street gangs have expanded their membership outside the United States to Mexico, Central America, and Canada. Currently, 11 national street gangs have been identified in one or more of these three countries.[60] Street gangs are imported into correctional facilities and are often found in jails and prisons; they will often continue running outside business from inside the prisons.

The Bloods street gang consists of large structured and smaller unstructured gangs that have joined together, forming a single culture. Most Blood members are African-American males, and membership may be as high as 20,000.[61] The Bloods were formed in the 1970s for protection against the Crips.[62]

The Crips street gang is estimated to have up to 35,000 members, mostly African-American males. Their main source of income is drug distribution. Secondary sources come from all manner of felony crime.[63]

Another significant street gang is the Latin Kings, a Chicago-based gang with an estimated membership of 20,000 to 35,000 nationwide. Most of the members are Mexican-American or Puerto Rican males. Again, the gang's main source of income is drug distribution, though the Latin Kings are also known for money laundering activities.[64]

Prison Gangs   Prison gangs are organized criminal networks within the federal and state prison systems. These gangs also operate in communities, where they usually consist of members who belonged to the gang while incarcerated. Prison gangs frequently maintain alliances with other gangs both inside and outside prison, and remain highly influential even while behind bars. When a prison gang member is released from prison, he will often become a representative in his home community and will recruit members to perform criminal activity on behalf of the gang.[65]

One infamous prison gang, the Aryan Brotherhood, is comprised mostly of Caucasian males. It is strongest in the Southwest and Pacific regions of the United States. The Aryan Brotherhood is extremely violent and is known to commit murder-for-hire. Some of the Aryan Brotherhood membership is aligned with Mexican gangs to smuggle drugs into the Southwest from Mexico.[66]

The Black Guerrilla Family prison gang was founded at California's San Quentin State Prison. Its organization is similar to that of a paramilitary organization. It is highly structured with a national charter, code of ethics, and oath of allegiance. The BGF operates mainly in California, Maryland, Missouri, and

Street gangs
Organized criminal networks that originate at the street level.

Prison gangs
Organized criminal networks within the federal and state prison systems.

Many gangs use drug distribution and violence as sources of income.

© 2012 BY EMIN KULIYEV. USED UNDER LICENSE OF SHUTTERSTOCK, INC.

Georgia. The membership is relatively small, with around 300 members, all African-American males. Their main source of income is drug distribution.[67]

One of the largest and most violent prison gangs is Neta, which began in Puerto Rico and spread to the mainland United States. Neta members in Puerto Rico exist only in prison rather than on the streets. Once a member is released from prison, he is no longer considered a member. Mainland Neta members, however, usually maintain membership after prison release. The main source of income for Neta is drug distribution.[68]

Outlaw motorcycle gangs
Organized criminal networks with a motorcycle lifestyle.

Outlaw Motorcycle Gangs   Outlaw motorcycle gangs are a serious threat to local public safety because of their extensive criminal activities. They are characteristically quick to use violence. Members engage in drug trafficking, weapons trafficking, and violent crime. They usually have a strong centralized leadership that implements rules, regulates membership, and coordinates criminal activity. It is estimated that there are between 280 and 520 outlaw motorcycle gangs in the United States that have a cumulative membership of around 20,000.

The Hells Angels Motorcycle Club is one of the most well-known of the outlaw motorcycle gangs. This gang comprises about 2,500 members and has chapters in 26 foreign countries. The HAMC indulges in drug distribution, money laundering, extortion, homicide, assault, and motorcycle theft.[69]

Another outlaw motorcycle gang is the Mongols Motorcycle Club. The MMC is established mostly in the Southwest and Pacific regions. The gang numbers about 300 and consists mostly of Hispanics residing in the Los Angeles area. Many members of the Mongols formerly belonged to street gangs and have a long history of violence. The MMC is allied with several other gangs in opposition to the Hells Angels.[70]

The Outlaws Motorcycle Club consists of more than 1,700 members. Their main source of revenue is drug distribution. They are also involved in such crimes as assault, robbery, kidnapping, money laundering, extortion, fraud, arson, explosives, prostitution, and theft.[71]

Critical Thinking   Most gangs earn income primarily from the distribution of drugs. The United States expends tremendous resources on the "war on drugs." Do you think that the current methods authorities use in this "war" are effective? How would you do things differently?

Correctional Officer Subcultures   Within any organization or group of people, cultures and subcultures will ultimately develop. All cultures and subcultures share certain values, beliefs, and norms of behavior, influenced by their leaders, their followers, the national culture, the geographical environment, and the industry.[72] The industry of corrections has developed its own unique culture.

Just as prison inmates have developed their own subcultures, prison staff—particularly correctional officers—have done the same. Correctional officers have an occupation that offers danger every time they go to work. They are surrounded by hostile individuals who have already demonstrated their propensity for breaking laws and not conforming to society's prevailing culture. Officers also face long hours, shift work, and overtime that may or may not be desired.[73] Because prisons and jails never close, this 24-hour industry can make family life challenging. The working schedules are especially challenging for families with young children and even more challenging for single parents.[74]

There are norms of correctional officer behavior that are a part of the officers' code. Correctional officers expect each other to adhere to certain guidelines—some of which are "unwritten" rules. Among these rules: Officers are expected to show positive concern for fellow officers and always come to the aid of another officer in dangerous situations. Officers should always support each other in disputes with inmates and in punishments of inmates, and should never make another officer look bad in front of inmates. Officers are expected to maintain solidarity with each other against outside groups.[75]

Exhibit: Florida State Correctional Officers' Code of Conduct.

I.   I will never forget that I am a public official sworn to uphold the Constitutions of the United States and the State of Florida.

II.   I am a professional committed to the public safety, the support and protection of my fellow officers, and co-workers, and the supervision and care of those in my charge. I am prepared to go in harm's way in fulfillment of these missions.

III. As a professional, I am skilled in the performance of my duties and governed by a code of ethics that demands integrity in word and deed, fidelity to the lawful orders of those appointed over me, and, above all, allegiance to my oath of office and the laws that govern our nation.

IV.   I will seek neither personal favor nor advantage in the performance of my duties. I will treat all with whom I come in contact with civility and respect. I will lead by example and conduct myself in a disciplined manner at all times.

V.   I am proud to selflessly serve my fellow citizens as a member of the Florida Department of Corrections.

Source: Florida Department of Corrections Website. http://www.dc.state.fl.us/vision.html

Correctional officers are trained to look for and address any signs of trouble.

The officers' code becomes a part of the correctional officers' subculture. This subculture is distinct from the larger culture of the organization that includes civilian staff and the administration. The behaviors of officers are observed and imitated by new recruits, and the culture of the correctional officer passes to newer generations. The new officers develop beliefs and thoughts that are similar to those of officers before them. Sometimes, this can lead to further conflict between officers and inmates. Officers develop a perception that inmates view them as the enemy. Officers typically strongly dislike inmates, and some may look for opportunities to make an inmate's life especially difficult. Moreover, they believe that inmates cannot be trusted.

Still, the subculture also develops positive traits in officers. Officers learn to anticipate trouble at any time. They learn what signs to look for to identify trouble, such as unusual quietness or loudness. An officer who does not develop the proper skills for detecting what is unusual or usual may be excluded from the subculture. Officers will also learn inmate management, though the officer subculture encourages as little interaction with inmates as possible.[76] The correctional officer subculture, like subcultures in other industries, can help the officers handle stress in an occupation that constantly puts them at risk.

There are many studies demonstrating that correctional officers experience higher levels of stress than most other occupations. Often, the correctional officer is required to perform the role of treatment counselor and custody officer at the same time. These seemingly opposite functions can lead to stress and eventually burnout among officers.[77]

Correctional officer role conflict occurs when an officer has conflicting orders. Role conflict also occurs when there is disagreement about how a task should be handled. An additional stressor on correctional officers is role ambiguity, which occurs when an officer does not have enough information about how to perform a particular job function, especially when responsibilities are vague and poorly defined. In some cases, policies are contradictory. These issues seem to afflict correctional officers more than many other occupations and are a significant cause of officer burnout.[78]

Ethics and Professionalism

Smuggling in prisons is an ongoing concern. Heroin, marijuana, tobacco, other drugs, and weapons can all make their way into prisons throughout the country. Over a five-year stretch, the Bureau of Prisons recorded more than 2,800 positive drug tests for each of those years in federal prisons.[79] The same report recognizes that weapons smuggling is also a serious threat to the security of the institutions. Though there are several mechanisms in place to prevent the entry of contraband into prisons, the found weapons, drugs, and overdoses demonstrate a serious problem.

When officers are caught smuggling drugs, weapons, or other contraband into a jail or a prison, they are usually prosecuted. This general form of deterrence, however, has not stopped the problem. Why would an officer risk his or her occupation, reputation, and personal way of life by trying to introduce contraband into a correctional institution?

Correctional officers face many ethical dilemmas, and they generally receive training on how to handle such situations. The temptation, though, must be too great for some officers to resist.

Consider the following situation. A young officer, already struggling to meet monthly expenses, is soon expecting his first child. Correctional officer pay is not enough to support a growing family and to service the debts already accumulated. A friend of a friend offers him a few thousand dollars a month to take cell phones and drugs to a contact in the prison. Because he knows how the prison security system works, he knows he would likely be able to do so without being caught. It would be easy and profitable. What would you do?

Consider another situation. You are an experienced correctional officer approaching your 20th year. You have known some of your coworkers for most of that time, and many are considered good friends. One day, you see a fellow correctional officer and close friend drop what appears to be a small bag of marijuana while he is adjusting his clothing. What do you do? Do you ignore it? Do you demand to see it? Do you report it? What circumstances would you need to take into account?

Growth of Corrections

When 2009 ended, the United States held roughly 2.3 million people in jails and in prisons throughout the country. In addition, more than 5 million were on probation or parole.[80] Both the prison population and the imprisonment rate in the United States are the highest in the world.[81] One will find differences in statistical numbers depending upon the source. The figures above are the official United States government statistics and are more conservative than many others are. Therefore, depending on the source, one may find a much higher prison population and rate than what has been quoted here.

In 1980, the United States had a rate of 139 per 100,000 of population that were incarcerated at some level. In 2009, that rate was 502 per 100,000. That is almost a fourfold increase in only 29 years. To demonstrate the significance of a 502 per 100,000 rate of incarceration, it may help to think of other countries where, by American standards, people are oppressed and imprisoned without the cherished rights that we enjoy under our laws and customs. Rwanda, Cuba, Russia, and countries known for human rights violations have lower incarceration rates than does the United States.[82] Overall, including probation and parole, one in every 31 adults in this country is under some sort of correctional supervision.[83] Some feel this is a shameful indictment of our system of justice.

FIGURE10.1 Comparison of imprisonment rates (selected countries).

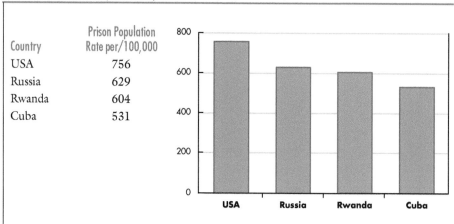

Country	Prison Population Rate per/100,000
USA	756
Russia	629
Rwanda	604
Cuba	531

Source: http://www.kcl.ac.uk/depsta/law/research/icps/downloads/wppl-8th_41.pdf

The dramatic increase in the prison population has affected the economy. As the rate of incarceration increases, the demand for correctional workers increases as well. Nearly 800,000 people in the United States were employed in corrections in 2008. Some rural areas have entire communities with local economies tied to correctional facilities.[84] The U.S. Labor Department projects about a 9% growth for the field of corrections through 2018.[85]

The growth of corrections is tied to several factors. One factor is mandatory sentencing laws, which put criminals behind bars for longer periods than in recent history. Another significant factor is the proliferation of "tough on crime" laws. Current laws that take a hard-line stance on crime have been legislated throughout the country in an effort to reduce crime. Whereas previously an individual might have served a fraction of an imposed sentence, the get-tough laws have created mandatory minimums that are closer to the imposed sentence. Some states now require an inmate to serve at least 85% of a sentence in prison before becoming eligible for probation or parole. Moreover, life sentences, true to their meaning, may mean that the person will never be allowed to go free.[86]

Critical Thinking The crime rate has been decreasing and the prison population has been increasing. Many argue that it does not make sense to lock up so many people when the crime rate is down. Others argue that the reason crime rates are down is because those who would normally be committing crimes are now in prison for longer periods. Are both or either of these arguments credible? Discuss.

Some criminologists suggest that the trend to incarcerate more people for longer periods has reached a position where it is no longer effective. One prominent criminologist, James Q. Wilson, states that we have reached a point of diminishing returns on our correctional efforts and investment.[87] Wilson says that judges have always sentenced violent offenders to long sentences, but that we now are "dipping deeper into the bucket of person's eligibility for prison, dredging up offenders with shorter and shorter criminal records."[88] He explains that if we continue to lengthen prison sentences and increase the numbers of people sent to prison, a diminishing marginal return on crime rate reductions will occur. In other words, at some point, imposing longer sentences will have no more effect on the crime rate. Some would argue that this point has already passed.

Special Populations

All manner of people are represented within the prison population—men, women, the young, the elderly, those with mental illnesses, those with physical illnesses, and those with physical disabilities. Every one of these subsets is represented by all races as well. Many of these special populations are segregated from other populations for security reasons as well as for medical and program functions.

Female Inmates

Female inmates have special needs that are not typically required by the male population. They require the same generalists and specialists for health needs that any woman outside of prison requires. Moreover, as many as 10% of women are pregnant when they are incarcerated.[89]

The typical female prisoner has been sentenced for a nonviolent crime and is a recidivist, which means she has previously been incarcerated or on probation. Of all female inmates, one-third report that they were under the influence of drugs or alcohol when they were arrested. More than 80% had been drug users at some time in their lives, which is slightly higher than the rate for men, and about 40% had been in drug treatment at some point in their lives. Further, many have a history of sexual abuse.[90]

Youthful Inmates

While there is a separate system for juvenile justice, some juveniles are tried and convicted in adult courts and sentenced as adults. Many states have special facilities for youthful offenders. Where this is not practical, the young and weak are typically segregated from the adult population. For example, in Florida, the Youthful Offender Act was passed in 1978. It was designed to improve youth corrections with the goal of successful reentry to open society. Since the act was first passed, it has expanded to provide vocational education and training, counseling, and public service opportunities to young inmates, and requires that the youthful offender attend substance abuse programs.[91]

The Florida Youthful Offender Act applies to those offenders who are under the age of 21 when sentenced. The act also includes those juveniles who have been tried and sentenced as an adult. Moreover, even if a court does not sentence an offender as youthful, the correctional authorities may designate those less than 25 years old as youthful offenders if they are deemed vulnerable in the adult prison population.[92]

Many facilities have special facilities for youthful offenders to separate them from adult inmates.

© 2012 BY GLENN R. MCGLOUGHLIN. USED UNDER LICENSE OF SHUTTERSTOCK, INC.

Elderly Inmates   Some researchers, such as Rikard and Rosenberg (2007), estimate that by the year 2020, 21% to 33% of prison residents will be elderly.[93] This increase is partially attributable to medical advances that extend life. However, substance abuse, lack of adequate diet, and poor medical care are found disproportionately in elderly criminals when compared to law-abiding seniors. This lifestyle places elderly offenders' physiological health at about 11.5 years older physically and mentally than their non-incarcerated peers.[94]

An inmate typically is designated elderly at 50 years old. This reflects the physiological age averages discussed in the previous paragraph. Moreover, their elderly status is a reflection of poorer health, including chronic conditions, substance abuse issues, and the fact that they suffer psychological problems more than younger inmates do. An elderly inmate costs roughly three times as much to incarcerate as a younger inmate. They are also more likely to have committed violent acts. Seventy-five percent of elderly inmates are still serving time for their first offense.[95]

Mentally Ill Inmates   The rate of mental illness among prison inmates is considerable. It is estimated that between 200,000 and 300,000 inmates suffer from mental illnesses, including bipolar disorder, schizophrenia, and major depression.[96] This makes the mentally ill percentage of the prison population two to four times higher than that of the general population.[97]

Mentally ill inmates often find it difficult to comply with the many rules and regulations that control prison populations. Mentally ill inmates tend to break rules at a higher rate than do other inmates. Often, rule breaking is the illness showing itself through aggression and disruptive behavior. These rule violators are regularly punished as discipline problems and without a diagnosis of mental health issues.[98]

Prison authorities have responsibility for the safety and security of staff and inmates. This often does not help the mentally ill inmate who is "acting out" and may be viewed as a discipline problem. Some prison systems have taken measures to diagnose and treat more discipline problems as psychological problems; however, some experts, such as Abramsky and Fellner (2003), maintain that there is an urgent need to reassess the disciplinary procedures as possible mental health issues.[99]

Chronically Ill Inmates   Another important category of special needs inmates is those with chronic illnesses such as hepatitis, HIV, and AIDS. Much chronic illness is imported into prisons and jails, but other illnesses arise from the sexual activity and drug use that take place in correctional facilities. Therefore, the spread of disease is of significant concern to correctional administrators.[100]

Since many diseases are spread through sexual and drug activity, some researchers have suggested that needle exchanges and condoms should be provided in prisons. Though there are no needle exchange efforts in the United States, some European countries have reported success in these programs. Those countries that have adopted needle exchanges have reported no increase of security issues.[101]

Only a few correctional facilities in the United States provide condoms, but the practice is standard in many other countries, including Canada. There is one such condom exchange program in Washington, D.C. A survey of 100 correctional officers and 300 inmates there showed that condom distribution was largely supported and caused no additional security problems. Such prevention measures provide significant protection not only to the inmate population but to the general population as well, because most inmates will return to a life outside of prison.[102]

Economic Realities   Government at all levels spent about $228 billion on police, courts, and corrections in 2007. Of this, $104 billion went for police protection, $50 billion went for the courts, and $74 billion went for corrections. Breaking it down further reveals that over half of all criminal justice spending came

FIGURE 10.2 Criminal Justice Expenditures by Level of Government.

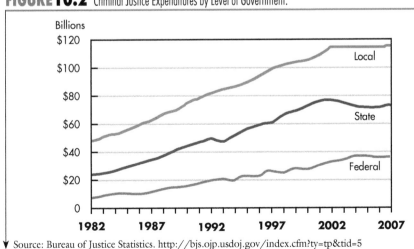

Source: Bureau of Justice Statistics. http://bjs.ojp.usdoj.gov/index.cfm?ty=tp&tid=5

FIGURE 10.3 Expenditures by Criminal Justice Function.

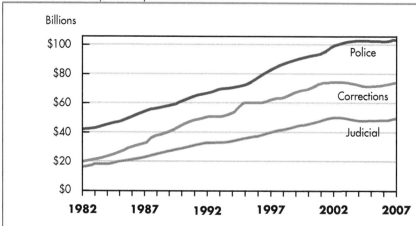

Source: Bureau of Justice Statistics. http://bjs.ojp.usdoj.gov/index.cfm?ty=tp&tid=5

from local governments.[103] These expenses are quite heavy considering that government budgets at all levels are facing difficult decisions regarding spending and resource allocation in the corrections system.

In 1982, $20 billion was spent on corrections at all levels of government. In 2007, this expense had increased 3.7 times to $74 billion. Over the same period, inflation increased by 115.20%.[104] This means that one dollar in 1982 bought what now takes $2.15, an increase of a little over two. Meanwhile, the amount of money spent on corrections in 25 years increased by 3.7 times. The difference, again, is quite significant.

The realities of correctional expenses have caused the nation's elected leaders at all levels of government to reconsider how money is spent. Americans want prisons that will hold people accountable for their crimes and keep communities safe. However, citizens also deserve to have their tax money used in appropriate and intelligent ways.

One major reason for the escalating expenditures in corrections is the high rate of recidivism in the United States, which ultimately requires incarcerating the same individuals for multiple stints. A 2009 Pew study demonstrated that more than 40% of inmates will ultimately return to prison for new crimes.[105] For prison systems, reducing these high rates of recidivism is essential in order to help the incarcerated, protect the safety of American communities, and reduce state spending on corrections.

Many prison systems have established programs designed to aid inmates' rehabilitation and produce a positive prison culture that can demonstrably reduce recidivism. These programs include faith-based prisons, GED and college credit opportunities, vocational training, and substance abuse training. These reentry programs implemented at the state and federal levels show great promise for changing offenders' lives.

Many states are already demonstrating success with lowering recidivism through these prison programs. A study for the Florida Department of Corrections recidivism efforts found that inmates who complete the programs designed to reduce recidivism are more successful than those who do not. Specifically, the study found that inmates who earned a GED are 8.7% less likely to recidivate, inmates who earn a vocational certificate are 14.6% less likely to recidivate, and inmates who complete substance abuse programs are 6.2% less likely to recidivate.[106]

The federal government, recognizing this pressing need for correctional transformation, has enacted legislation to aid the successful return to society for adults and juveniles leaving prison. In 2008, the Second Chance Act was enacted. The act allows for government agencies and nonprofits to receive grants that will aid in reducing recidivism. Programs such as substance abuse treatment, assistance in finding employment and housing, mentoring, and victim support are made available through these grants.[107] In 2009, $28 million was awarded to grant recipients. The following year saw an even larger allocation of grant money. In October 2010, more than $82 million was awarded to 187 grant recipients to reduce adult and juvenile recidivism, for reentry courts to monitor and provide treatment services, to establish and enhance existing substance abuse treatment programs, to improve education and vocational training at adult and juvenile facilities, to train inmates for technology jobs, and to provide mentors to adult and juvenile offenders.[108]

Alternatives to Prison

As prison populations continue to expand, governments at all levels look for more ways to control costs. While doing this, they must also attempt to live up to the implied promise of returning repentant former criminals back to the streets as law-abiding citizens. The unfortunate

FIGURE 10.4 FY2010 Second Chance Act Grant Program Application Results

FY10 Grant Program	FY2010 SCA Grant Program Application Results		
	Total applications received	Total grants awarded	Total amount awarded
Adult Demonstration (101)	145	52	$27,324,543
Juvenile Demonstration (101)	39	14	$7,955,996
Reentry Courts (111)	9	9	$2,651,703
Family-Based Substance Abuse Treatment (113)	36	23	$6,645,611
Evaluate and Improve Education in Prisons, Jails, and Juvenile Facilities (114)	12	1	$2,463,635
Technology Career Training Demonstration (115)	44	7	$4,679,466
Substance Abuse & Criminal Justice Collaboration (201)	77	22	$11,705,855
Adult Mentoring (211)	613	50	$13,968,672
Juvenile Mentoring (211)	214	9	$5,018,909
Total	1189	187	$82,414,390

Source: National Reentry Resource Center.http://www.nationalreentryresourcecenter.org/about/second-chance-act

truth, though, evidenced by alarming recidivism rates, is that many former prisoners return to criminal activity.

There are a number of objectives for imprisonment. One is that the convicted criminal is punished through deprivation of liberty. Another is that the criminal is incapacitated from committing further crimes while incarcerated. Presumably, rehabilitation efforts are attempted with the expectation that the individual will leave prison better able to live and work in a law-abiding manner.

Many of those sentenced to jail or prison come from disadvantaged socio-economic backgrounds. Many are in prison for violent crimes, while others are in prison for nonviolent offenses. Some are incarcerated for traffic offenses or simple possession of illicit substances. Their crimes range from the most horrible imaginable to the relatively mundane and victimless, yet are still eligible for sentences that may involve incarceration. This can easily compound already difficult issues in many lives. Incarceration interferes with an inmate's employment and family life. It also decreases the inmate's employment prospects after release and limits his or her access to other opportunities, such as an education financed with federal student loans.

Overcrowding of prisons is associated with the spread of infectious diseases such as tuberculosis and HIV. In addition, violence is always a possibility. These fears alone can create health problems associated with stress. Moreover, overcrowding generates the demand for more prison space, meaning more money must again be allocated to build, operate, and maintain these human warehouses.

For these and many other reasons, the criminal justice system utilizes a number of alternatives to prison. The goal of these alternatives, in addition to relieving overcrowding in prisons and giving less severe punishments to offenders who commit less severe crimes, is to move from a punishment model to one of restorative justice and to help reintegrate former criminals back into society.

Probation and Parole: Effectiveness and Statistics

Probation is the most common form of modern court-imposed punishment. Probation is still a sentence, but unlike jail or prison, a sentence of probation is court-ordered supervision that is served while living in the community.[109] Probation may also be a part of a combined sentence in which the community supervision follows incarceration. Probation has three primary goals: rehabilitation, protection of society, and protection of victim rights.[110]

At the end of 2009, there were more than 4 million people on probation in the United States.[111] This is actually the first decrease in the number of probationers since 1980.[112] Of those on probation, 72% were on active probation, 51% were felons, and 27% of probationers were convicted of violent crimes.[113]

In 2009, 65% of probationers completed their terms of probation either by completing their sentences or through early discharge.[114] Those who have had probation revoked are usually sent to jail or to prison because of technical violations or law violations.

Unlike probation, which is an actual sentence but is served in the community, parole is the early supervised release of someone already incarcerated. Often, probationers and parolees are supervised by the same state agencies. Many states and the federal government, however, have abolished parole.[115]

The federal government and many states have shifted away from indeterminate sentences, which establish a range rather than an exact length of a prison term, and now use determinate sentencing, which places mandatory, specifically set sentences on offenders and no longer offers parole. However, some states have defined mandatory sentencing as a percentage of time served. For instance, by statute, some states require that an offender serve at least 85% of a sentence in prison. The other 15% may be served on probation or parole depending on the offender's behavior while in prison. These statutes are known as truth-in-sentencing laws. In 1994, the federal government passed a law that provided funding to states that enacted truth-in-sentencing laws. As of 2008, 35 states qualified to receive the federal funding for truth-in sentencing.[116]

Economically speaking, the probation system is cheaper than incarceration. For example, for the fiscal year of 2009–2010 in the state of Florida, it cost an average of $53.34 per day to house an offender in prison, while monitoring an offender on pretrial release cost approximately $7 per day.[117]

Critical Thinking
Should states continue to use indeterminate sentencing structures and parole boards to release offenders early? Explain.

Other Community-Based Alternatives Community-based alternatives are used effectively for less serious crimes, so-called victimless crimes, and public order crimes. This is also cost-effective in that it does not cost as much to supervise someone in the community as it does to house them in a prison or in a jail. In 2010, at least 26 states have cut the budgets of their corrections departments.[118]

Many of the states that have cut corrections budgets have already increased efficiencies and are now looking to cut costs in other areas.[119] States have reduced inmate healthcare expenses, frozen officer hiring, reduced staff salaries, reduced staff benefits, and eliminated pay increases. Some are considering the consolidation of facilities and forgoing planned expansions.[120]

The largest savings in correctional budgets come from reducing the number of people who come to prison and the length of stay for those who do. Staffing accounts for up to 80% of a prison's budget. In order to reduce staffing, the number of inmates must be reduced. Therefore, states look for ways to close prisons, or at least parts of them, in order to achieve savings. In 2010, states found that they could identify offender populations that could be safely released from prison after serving reduced sentences. Much of these savings can be realized through community-based alternatives to incarceration.[121]

House arrest allows an offender to live at his or her residence, but he or she is restricted from activity outside of the home.

Halfway house

A group home often used by newly released offenders who have nowhere else to go. Many halfway houses are specifically designed for sex offenders, providing a supervised residence and resources specifically designed for this population.

Day reporting center

A location for offenders to receive services such as counseling, life skills education, drug abuse treatment, and substance abuse testing. The offender only reports according to a specified schedule and does not live there.

Day fine

A fine based on a person's daily income; the amount of the fine is progressive in relation to the money the offender earns.

A variety of community-based alternatives are currently in use throughout the United States. House arrest allows an offender to live at his or her residence. The offender is restricted from activity outside the home. Usually, the individual is only allowed to leave for work, school, church, or court-approved activities. The offender is under close scrutiny and there is often electronic monitoring equipment in use to ensure compliance.

Electronic monitoring is often an active system whereby an ankle bracelet transmits a continuous signal to a landline telephone to verify the offender's location. Any deviation or attempts to tamper with the equipment will send a signal to the monitoring station to be reported to the proper authorities.[122] Many agencies are now using more advanced GPS devices, especially for high-risk sex offenders.[123]

Halfway houses are group homes that often house newly released offenders with nowhere else to go. They may not have family, friends, or anyone willing to give them a place to live, at least temporarily. Many halfway houses, however, are specifically for sex offenders; they provide a supervised residence and resources specifically designed for this population.

Day reporting centers are locations for offenders to receive services such as counseling, life skills education, drug abuse treatment, and substance abuse testing. The offender only reports according to a specified schedule and does not live there. These centers also offer access to community services for employment, housing, health services, proper identification, legal support, and wellness.

Community service is often an intermediate sanction imposed by a court. Community service is an unpaid service to the community, often at a nonprofit organization that provides a service to society. Sometimes a judge will impose community service that is related to an offender's skill. For instance, a person skilled with animals may work at a pet adoption center or a person with legal skills may work at a community legal aid center.

Day fines are popular in some European countries. A day fine is a fine that is based on a person's daily income. The amount of the fine is progressive in relation to the money the offender earns. The more income one has, the higher the fine.

Critical Thinking What factors do you think would or should influence a judge's decision to sentence an offender to confinement or to community supervision?

Career Connections: Correctional Treatment Specialist

The United States Department of Labor publishes statistics and general information for a large number of occupations. Within these pages, the occupation outlook sections offer current and projected future needs. The highest rating outlook for employment in any given occupation is excellent. One of those occupations expected to have excellent growth and opportunity is that of correctional treatment specialist.[124]

Correctional treatment specialists plan educational and occupational programs to improve inmates' likelihood of a successful transition to open society.

Correctional treatment specialists may work from probation offices, jails, or prisons. They evaluate inmate progress, administer psychological tests, and work with probation and parole offices to coordinate inmate releases to community supervision. They also plan educational and occupational programs to improve inmates' likelihood of a successful transition to open society. In addition, they may provide anger management skills, drug and alcohol abuse education, and counseling related to crimes such as sexual offenses.[125]

Daily duties of the correctional treatment specialist may include referring offenders to social services agencies, determining specific needs for rehabilitation, consulting with attorneys and judges, and following up on offender progress. Further, the correctional treatment specialist will confer with the offender's family members to help tend to family business that may impede the inmate's transition or help the offender's family group. The correctional treatment specialist may also be required to testify in court.[126]

The correctional treatment specialist must have specific knowledge and skills. Some of the most important knowledge is that of counseling. The person in this occupation must understand how to use rehabilitative techniques for a population that may not be receptive to treatment and may have other mental ailments. They must also be able to evaluate the effects of treatment. Knowledge of psychology, law, public safety, sociology, computers, and other subjects is considered important.[127]

A bachelor's degree is often a requirement, as is a clean criminal record. Entry into this field may require extensive testing for psychological fitness, physical fitness, and drug use, as well as written exams. One must have good interpersonal skills and good report writing skills. Advancement in this field is often dependent upon experience, performance, and education. A graduate degree may be helpful or required for advancement into the senior ranks.[128]

Chapter Summary

- Early English law first applied the "principle of least eligibility," meant to discourage anyone from intentionally having themselves completely cared for by the government by making such care no better than the most destitute of society. The principle of least eligibility has long been society's attitude for those who have been duly incarcerated.

- In 1958, sociologist Gresham Sykes presented a study on the effects that prisons have on both inmates and staff. Sykes explains that the pains of imprisonment on a person's personality, though less obvious than are physical injuries, are "no less fearful." Sykes explains that this loss of freedom, a scarcity of goods and services, the loss of domestic relationships, and so on, may be acceptable and unavoidable for those imprisoned, but the effects on the inmate must be recognized as serious, just as are physical punishments.

- Erving Goffman described prisons as total institutions. In the total institution, everything is provided for those who reside there. All aspects of life are conducted within the total institution. Rules are abundant and punishment is swift.

- The term *prisonization* was first used in 1940 by Donald Clemmer, who defined it as "the taking on in greater or lesser degree of the folkways, mores, customs, and general culture of the penitentiary." This refers to the socialization process into the culture and life of a prison inmate. Prisonization also describes those whose prison socialization has become so psychologically ingrained into their personalities that they would have difficulty readjusting to life outside of the prison.

- There are many subcultures in correctional institutions. The importation model means that the criminal culture one participates in outside of prison is often how the person will continue to behave inside the prison. The indigenous model holds that the preexisting conditions of deprivation in a prison have a great effect on how the inmate will adjust to prison life.

- Gangs present an ongoing problem for correctional facilities. Gangs originate from the street and in prison. The designation of a gang belongs to the greater category of "Security Threat Group," defined by the National Gang Crime Research Center as "any group of three or more persons with recurring threatening or disruptive behavior." The three basic types of gangs identified by law enforcement are street gangs, prison gangs, and outlaw motorcycle gangs.

- The industry of corrections has developed its own unique cultures and subcultures among both inmates and correctional officers. Inmates and officers each adhere to certain unwritten rules to help them adapt to the daily routines of the prison culture.

- When 2009 ended, roughly 2.3 million people were incarcerated in the United States and more than 5 million were on probation or parole. Both the prison population and the imprisonment rate in the United States are the highest in the world. Government at all levels spent about $228 billion on police, courts, and corrections in 2007.

- Because of the high cost of incarcerating inmates, states look for alternative methods to punish offenders in order to achieve savings. Such alternatives include probation, parole, and community-based alternatives such as house arrest, halfway houses, day reporting centers, community service, and day fines.

Critical Thinking?

1. Why is it less expensive to supervise offenders using methods other than incarceration? Should these alternatives be expanded? Why? Is money the only concern?
2. Are those who are incarcerated entitled to free medical care? If so, to what level? Should there be a limit on medical procedures that inmates are allowed to receive?
3. What categories of offender should be subjected to electronic monitoring? What categories of offender should not be candidates for electronic monitoring?
4. How might inmates lessen the pains of imprisonment? How would you attempt to lessen these pains should you be imprisoned?
5. How would you explain the rising prison population?
6. What effects might prison overcrowding have on treatment programs?
7. Do you believe the failure rate of recidivism is too high? What can be done to correct the problem?
8. Gang members in prisons are sometimes separated. What might be an undesirable result of gang member separation?
9. Should a correctional treatment specialist have correctional officer training as well? Should they receive training in defensive tactics?
10. What types of rights should inmates lose? Should there be any loss of rights for those who have completed their sentences? Why or why not?

Media

Community Corrections Act: http://centerforcommunitycorrections.org/?page_id=78
   Here, you can find the relevant state statutes and codes that relate to the Community Corrections Act. The site also includes much information concerning community corrections.

National Institute of Corrections: http://nicic.gov/
   The National Institute of Corrections helps to shape and advance effective correctional practice and public policy.

National Institute of Justice Electronic Monitoring Resource Center: https://emresourcecenter.nlectc.du.edu/
   This site provides law enforcement and correctional agencies with assistance in the development and maintenance of electronic monitoring programs.

American Probation and Parole Association: http://www.appa-net.org/eweb/
   The American Probation and Parole Association is actively involved with probation, parole, and community-based corrections, in both adult and juvenile sectors.

Bureau of Justice Statistics: http://www.ojp.usdoj.gov/bjs
   This is a premier website for law enforcement and correctional statistics.

Endnotes

1. Secter, B. (1966, July 13). "The Richard Speck Case." *Chicago Tribune*. Retrieved from http://www.chicagotribune.com/news/politics/chi-chicagodays-richardspeck-story,0,4911196.story
2. Ibid.
3. *Furman v. Georgia*, 408 U.S. 238 (1972). The death penalty was reinstated in *Gregg v. Georgia*, 428 U.S. 153 (1976).
4. Olson, J. *Historical Dictionary of the 1960s.*
5. Ibid.
6. Dickens, C. (1850). *A Walk in a Workhouse*. Retrieved from http://www2.hn.psu.edu/faculty/jmanis/dickens/pieces.pdf
7. "The Poor Law Amendment Act of 1834." (1834). *The Workhouse*. Retrieved from http://www.workhouses.org.uk/poorlaws/1834act.shtml
8. Sieh, E. W. (1989). "Less Eligibility: The Upper Limits of Penal Policy." *Criminal Justice Policy Review, 3*(2), 159–183.
9. Rubin, E. L., & Feeley, M. M. (2003, April). "Judicial Policy Making and Litigation against the Government." *University of Pennsylvania Journal of Constitutional Law,* 617.
10. *Pell v. Procunier*, 417 U.S. 817, 822 (1974).
11. *Estelle v. Gamble*, 429 U.S. 97 (1976).
12. *Procunier v. Martinez*, 416 U.S. 396 (1974).
13. *Block v. Rutherford*, 486 U.S. 576 (1984).
14. *Hudson v. Palmer*, 468 U.S. 517 (1984).
15. *Cruz v. Beto*, 405 U.S. 319 (1972).
16. *Wolff v. McDonnell*, 94 S.Ct. 2963 (1974).
17. Sykes, G. (1958). *The Society of Captives: A Study of a Maximum Security Prison*. Princeton, NJ: Princeton University Press.
18. Ibid.
19. Ibid.
20. Goffman, E. (1961). *Total Institutions*. Retrieved from http://www.markfoster.net/neurelitism/totalinstitutions.pdf
21. Ibid.
22. Ibid.
23. Sykes, 1958.
24. Ibid.
25. "Mine!" *Scientific American Mind, 22*(4), 59.
26. Goffman, 1961.
27. Sykes, 1958.
28. "Autonomy." (2011). *Merriam-Webster Dictionary*. Retrieved from http://www.merriam-webster.com/dictionary/autonomy
29. Sykes, 1958.
30. Ibid.
31. Ibid.
32. Goffman, 1961.
33. Irwin, J. (1992). *The Jail*. Berkeley, CA: University of California Press, 73.
34. Ibid.
35. Ibid., 74.
36. Goffman, 1961.
37. Ibid.
38. Sykes, 1958.
39. Ibid.
40. Ibid.

41. Clemmer, D. (1940). *The Prison Community*. Boston, MA: Christopher Publishing House, 279.

42. O'Toole, M. (Ed.). (2003). "Institutionalization." In *Miller-Keane Encyclopedia and Dictionary of Medicine, Nursing, and Allied Health* (7th ed.). Philadelphia, PA: W.B. Saunders.

43. Goffman, 1961.

44. Harrison, B., & Schehr, R. C. (2004). "Offenders and Post-Release Jobs: Variables Influencing Success and Failure." *Journal of Offender Rehabilitation, 39*(3), 35–68.

45. *Report of the Task Force on Security, Respect*. (2008). Correctional Service Canada.

46. Cheeseman, K. (2003). "Importing Aggression: An Examination and Application of Subculture Theories to Prison Violence." *The Southwest Journal of Criminal Justice*, 1(1), 24–38. Retrieved from http://www.utsa.edu/swjcj/archives/1.1/Cheeseman.pdf

47. Goffman, 1961; Sykes, 1958; Sykes & Messinger, 1960.

48. National Council on Crime and Delinquency. (1994). *Understanding why Inmates are Misclassified*. Retrieved from http://static.nicic.gov/Library/011994.pdf

49. Dhami, M. K., Ayton, P., & Loewenstein, G. (2007). "Adaptation to Imprisonment: Indigenous or Imported?" *Criminal Justice and Behavior*. Retrieved from http://sds.hss.cmu.edu/media/pdfs/loewenstein/AdaptPrisonment-Indigenous.pdf

50. Ibid.

51. United States Attorney District of New Jersey. (2011, January). *Sweeping Racketeering Indictment Charges 15 Members of the Fruit Town and Brick City Brims Bloods Set*. Retrieved from http://www.atf.gov/press/releases/2011/01/012411-new-sweeping-racketeering-indictment-charges-15-members-of-the-fruittown-and-brick-city-brims-bloods-set.pdf

52. Knox, G. W. (2005). *The Problem of Gangs and Security Threat Groups (STG's) in American Prisons Today: Recent Research Findings from the 2004 Prison Gang Survey*. Retrieved from http://www.ngcrc.com/corr2006.html

53. Ibid.

54. 18 U.S.C. § 521.

55. Knox, 2005.

56. "Gangs." (2006). *United States Department of Justice Attorney's Bulletin, 54*(3).

57. Ibid.

58. Ibid.

59. FBI National Gang Intelligence Center. (2009). *National Gang Threat Assessment 2009*. Retrieved from http://www.fbi.gov/stats-services/publications/national-gang-threat-assessment-2009-pdf

60. Ibid.

61. United States Department of Justice. (2008). *National Drug Intelligence Center, Attorney General's Report to Congress on the Growth of Violent Street Gangs in Suburban Areas*. Retrieved from http://www.justice.gov/ndic/pubs27/27612/appendb.htm

62. Ibid.

63. Ibid.

64. Ibid.

65. FBI National Gang Intelligence Center, 2009.

66. Ibid.

67. United States Department of Justice. (2008). "Appendix B. National-Level Street, Prison, and Outlaw Motorcycle Gang Profiles." *Attorney General's Report to Congress on the Growth of Violent Street Gangs in Suburban Areas*. Retrieved from http://www.justice.gov/ndic/pubs27/27612/appendb.htm

68. Ibid.

69. Ibid.

70. Ibid.

71. Ibid.

72. Smircich, L. (1983). "Concepts of Culture and Organizational Analysis." *Administrative Science Quarterly*, 342.

73. Bureau of Labor Statistics. (2011). "Correctional Officers." *Occupational Outlook Handbook, 2010–11 Edition*. Retrieved from http://www.bls.gov/oco/ocos156.htm

74. Dial, K. C., & Johnson, W. W. (2008). "Working Within the Walls: The Effect of Care From Coworkers on Correctional Employees." *Professional Issues in Criminal Justice*, 3(2), 17–31. Retrieved from https://kucampus.kaplan.edu/documentstore/docs09/pdf/picj/vol3/issue2/PICJ_Volume3_2_dial.pdf

75. Kauffman, K. (1988). *Prison Officers and Their World*. Cambridge, MA: Harvard University Press, 86.

76. Marquart, J. W., & Crouch, B. M. (1984). "Coopting the Kept: Using Inmates for Social Control in a Southern Prison." *Justice Quarterly, 1*, 491–509.

77. Lambert, E. G., Cluse-Tolar, T., & Hogan, N. L. (2007). "This Job is Killing Me: The Impact of Job Characteristics on Correctional Staff Job Stress." *Applied Psychology in Criminal Justice, 3*(2). Retrieved from http://www.apcj.org/documents/3_2_correctionalstaff.pdf

78. Ibid.

79. Federal Bureau of Prisons. (2003). *The Federal Bureau of Prisons' Drug Interdiction Activities*. Retrieved from http://www.justice.gov/oig/reports/BOP/e0302/final.pdf

80. Bureau of Justice Statistics. (2011). *Key Facts at a Glance: Correctional Populations*. Retrieved from http://bjs.ojp.usdoj.gov/content/glance/tables/corr2tab.cfm

81. Walmsley, R. (2008). *World Prison Population List* (8th ed.). Retrieved from http://www.kcl.ac.uk/depsta/law/research/icps/downloads/wppl-8th_41.pdf

82. Ibid.

83. Kirchhoff, S. M. (2010). "Economic Impacts of Prison Growth." *Congressional Research Service*. Retrieved from http://www.fas.org/sgp/crs/misc/R41177.pdf

84. Ibid.

85. Bureau of Labor Statistics, 2011.

86. Ditton, P. M., & Wilson, D. J. (1999). *Truth in Sentencing in State Prisons* (NCJ 170032). Retrieved from http://bjs.ojp.usdoj.gov/content/pub/pdf/tssp.pdf
Mauer, M., King, R. S., & Young, M. C. (2004). "The Meaning of 'Life': Long Prison Sentences in Context." *The Sentencing Project*. Retrieved from http://www.hawaii.edu/hivandaids/The_Meaning_Life__Long_Prison_Sentences_in_Context.pdf

87. Wilson, J. Q. (1995). "Crime and Public Policy." In J. Q. Wilson & J. Petersilia (Eds.), *Crime* (pp. 489–507). San Francisco, CA: Institute for Contemporary Studies Press.

88. Ibid., 501.

89. Maruschak, L. M. (2011). "Medical Problems of Prisoners." *Bureau of Justice Statistics*. Retrieved from http://www.bjs.gov/content/pub/html/mpp/mpp.cfm
Law Students for Reproductive Justice. (2008). *Women in Prison*. Retrieved from http://lsrj.org/documents/factsheets/08-09_Women_in_Prison.pdf

90. U. S. Department of Justice. (1999). *Substance Abuse and Treatment, State and Federal Prisoners*.

91. Florida Senate. (2010, October). *Youthful Offender Designation in the Department of Corrections, Interim Report 2011–114*.

92. Ibid.

93. Rikard, R. V., & Rosenberg, E. (2007). "Aging Inmates: A Convergence of Trends in the American Criminal Justice System." *Journal of Correctional Health Care, 13*(3), 150–162.

94. Doughty, P. (1999). *A Concern in Corrections: Special Health Needs*. Oklahoma City, OK: Oklahoma Department of Corrections.

95. Sheppard, R. (2001, April 9). "Growing Old Inside." *Maclean's*, 30–33.

96. Abramsky, S., & Fellner, J. (2003). "Ill Equipped: U.S. Prisons and Offenders with Mental Illness." *Human Rights Watch*. Retrieved from http://www.hrw.org/reports/2003/usa1003/usa1003.pdf

97. Fellner, J. (2006). "A Corrections Quandary: Mental Illness and Prison Rules." *Harvard Civil Rights-Civil Liberties Law Review, 41*(2), 391–412. Retrieved from http://www.law.harvard.edu/students/orgs/crcl/vol41_2/fellner.pdf

98. Abramsky & Fellner, 2003.

99. Ibid.

100. Hammett, T. M. (2006, June). "HIV/AIDS and Other Infectious Diseases Among Correctional Inmates: Transmission, Burden, and an Appropriate Response." *American Journal of Public Health, 96*(6), 974–978.

101. Ibid.

102. Ibid.

103. Bureau of Justice Statistics. (2011). *Employment and Expenditure*. Retrieved from http://bjs.ojp.usdoj.gov/index.cfm?ty=tp&tid=5

104. InflationData.com. (2011). *Inflation Calculator*. Retrieved from http://inflationdata.com/Inflation/Inflation_Calculators/Inflation_Calculator.asp

105. Pew Center on the States. (2010, April). *Prison Count 201*. Washington, D.C.

106. Florida Department of Corrections. (2001). *Analysis of the Impact of Inmate Programs upon Recidivism*.

107. Council of State Governments Justice Center. (n.d.). "Second Chance Act." *National Reentry Resource Center*. Retrieved from http://www.nationalreentryresourcecenter.org/about/second-chance-act

108. Ibid.

109. Glaze, L. E., & Bonczar, T. P. (2010). *Probation and Parole in the United States, 2009* (NCJ 231674). Retrieved from http://bjs.ojp.usdoj.gov/content/pub/pdf/ppus09.pdf

110. "Probation." (2011). *FindLaw*. Retrieved from http://criminal.findlaw.com/crimes/criminal_stages/stages-alternative-sentences/probation.html

111. Bureau of Justice Statistics. (2011). *Community Corrections (Probation and Parole)*. Retrieved from http://bjs.ojp.usdoj.gov/index.cfm?ty=tp&tid=15

112. Ibid.

113. Ibid.

114. Ibid.

115. Federal Bureau of Prisons. (2011). *Brief History of the Bureau of Prisons*. Retrieved from http://www.bop.gov/about/history.jsp

116. Ditton & Wilson, 1999.

117. Florida Department of Corrections. (2010). *Annual Statistics for Fiscal Year 2009–2010*.

118. Scott-Hayward, C. S. (2009). "The Fiscal Crisis in Corrections: Rethinking Policies and Practices." *Center on Sentencing and Corrections*. Retrieved from http://www.pewcenteronthestates.org/uploadedFiles/Vera_state_budgets.pdf

119. Ibid.

120. Ibid.

121. Ibid.

122. Bottos, S. (2008). "An Overview of Electronic Monitoring in Corrections: The Issues and Implications." *Correctional Service Canada*. Retrieved from http://www.csc-scc.gc.ca/text/rsrch/reports/r182/r182-eng.pdf

123. DeMichele, M., & Payne, B. (2009). "Using Technology to Monitor Offenders: A Community Corrections Perspective." *American Correctional Association*. Retrieved from https://aca.org/fileupload/177/ahaidar/DeMichele_Payne.pdf

124. U.S. Department of Labor. (2011). Retrieved from http://bls.gov

125. Ibid.

126. Occupational Information Network. (n.d.). *Probation and Correctional Treatment Specialists*. Retrieved from http://www.occupationalinfo.org/onet/27305c.html

127. Ibid.

128. Ibid.

11

Special Issues in Corrections

KEY TERMS

Aftercare, Barriers to reintegration, Criminogenic needs, Discretionary release, Expungement, Fidelity to program design, Mandatory release, Offender risk, Reentry, Reentry courts, Sanctions, Second Chance Act, Therapeutic Communities (TC), Victim-offender mediation, Vocational training, Work release centers

CHAPTER OBJECTIVES

1. Understand why an increased emphasis on rehabilitation is difficult to achieve within prisons.
2. Summarize the range of rehabilitative needs of prison inmates and the degree to which these needs are met in prison.
3. Evaluate the advantages and challenges of the provision of rehabilitative programs within prisons.
4. Evaluate the degree to which inmates are prepared for their return to society.
5. Identify the needs of those released from prison and the means by which these needs can or cannot be met by the justice system.
6. Identify the factors that can influence recidivism rates and prisons' capacity to influence these factors.
7. Critique whether recidivism rates are a good gauge of the effectiveness of prisons.

Case Study: Return to Society

For the typical person released from prison and attempting to reenter society as a law-abiding citizen, there is a 50-50 chance that they will end up back in prison within a few years.[1] For those who are successful at reentry, there are many factors that support this transition, including a personal commitment to change, participation in rehabilitative programs that are designed based on scientific knowledge about human behavior, and the support of family members and community.

JB, an Illinois inmate in 2010, is one such example. The 35-year-old JB had been on probation numerous times and in and out of jail, and this time he decided he wanted to change. During his processing through the Illinois Department of Corrections, he was asked a series of questions designed to gauge the extent and nature of his substance abuse problem, and his need for treatment. JB had been through this processing system every time he went to prison, and usually only gave the answers he thought the corrections staff wanted to hear. This time, he decided to tell the truth, and described his long-term abuse of alcohol, cocaine, and marijuana. He was determined to be in need of treatment. He met the eligibility criteria to participate in a prison-based drug treatment program, and, fortunately for him, there was a slot open in the program. He was one of the lucky ones—the one out of every five inmates needing treatment who actually receives treatment.[2] During the next 12 months JB participated in daily group treatment led by certified substance abuse counselors, attended vocational training, and began to reconnect with his children. Upon release from prison, he was required to attend outpatient treatment multiple times per week, check in with his parole agent, and search for a job so he could support himself. Fortunately he was placed in a recovery home, a place where he would live in a drug-free environment, during his first four months of the transition back to the free world. After a few months he was able to find a job as a mentor for a youth violence prevention program, moved in with and married a woman he met through a church group he participated in, and was finally able to succeed in the reentry experience at which he had failed so many times before.

LB was a woman sentenced to prison in the same state, around the same time as JB. She too had been through the system multiple times, this time being convicted and sentenced to prison for retail theft. Because of time she spent in jail awaiting her conviction, and good conduct credits, her prison sentence of 18 months would ultimately keep her behind bars for just a few months. During that time she did not participate in any type of substance abuse treatment program, for two main reasons: she did not disclose her addiction to staff, and her period of incarceration was so short that she would not have moved up the waiting list in time to access treatment while in prison. Upon her release, with little support and no changes in her thinking pattern, she moved in with friends from her past. Within days of her release, she was back to using drugs, with deadly consequences. After just three days of reentry, LB died of a heroin overdose. It is likely that if she had not died, she would have ended up rearrested and back in prison, a fate so many other people released from prison experience.

It is important to realize the potential successes of the hundreds of thousands of JBs who leave prison every year, and the extreme tragedy that the LBs

Vocational training
The provision of classes and instruction designed to provide individuals with specific skills for entry into specific labor markets.

and their families experience when rehabilitation and successful reentry are not achieved. For those with a commitment to change, access to effective treatment interventions both while incarcerated and after release, and acceptance and support from family members and society as a whole, successful reentry is possible. Without these positive forces, those reentering society are often destined to continue the cycle of crime and incarceration, with expensive and potentially tragic outcomes for themselves, their families, or their victims.

Introduction

The media's portrayal of the reentry experiences of those released from prison or jail often focuses on celebrities; the experiences of the typical person trying to reenter society and lead a productive life are usually quite different. In the past two years, prominent NFL football players Michael Vick and Plaxico Burress experienced reentry from prison back to society. Similarly, Lindsay Lohan has been released from jail more than once following sentences for driving under the influence and shoplifting; in 2010, she was released from jail—where she was held in solitary confinement for her own safety—and ordered to enter a drug treatment program. For Vick and Burress, their reentry included being signed to multimillion-dollar contracts to continue playing football. In Lohan's case, she left jail to enter a private drug treatment program, and after completion, returned to her multimillion-dollar Venice Beach mansion to continue her "reentry" into society.

While these examples of celebrity reentry from incarceration capture the public's attention, they are in reality extremely uncharacteristic of what most people released from prison face. The vast majority of people released from prison in the United States do not have even minimum-wage jobs awaiting them upon release, let alone multimillion-dollar contracts, and often are shunned and ostracized by society, not celebrated and cheered.

The prison population in the United States more than doubled over the 20-year period from 1988 through 2009, increasing from 627,000[3] to more than 1.5 million.[4] Of those felons sentenced to prison in 2006 in the United States, less than 1% received a life sentence, and the average prison sentence was 59 months, with actual time served being considerably less.[5] Among those released from prison in 2009, the average time served was 29 months and the median time served was 16 months,[6] indicating that a large number of those released from prison served relatively short periods of incarceration. As a result of this dramatic increase in the number of offenders sentenced to prison, and relatively short periods of incarceration overall, an unprecedented number of inmates have been released from prison annually, with more than 725,000 inmates released during just the year of 2007[7] and nearly 820,000 offenders on some form of parole supervision at the end of 2009.[8]

One factor that has maintained these large numbers of adults in prison, and the substantial volume of admissions and exits from prison annually, has been the relatively high rate of recidivism, resulting in what some call the "revolving door" of corrections. Almost 40% of adults exiting parole return to prison within three years for a new offense or technical violation,[9] and it is has been estimated that within three years of release, more than one-half of all adults re-

FIGURE 11.1 Prison and Parole Populations 1980–2009

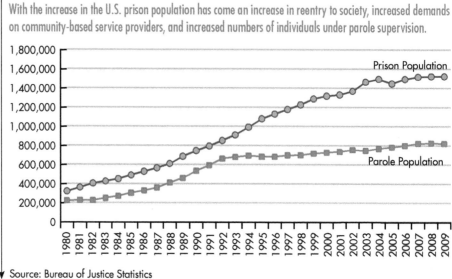

With the increase in the U.S. prison population has come an increase in reentry to society, increased demands on community-based service providers, and increased numbers of individuals under parole supervision.

Source: Bureau of Justice Statistics

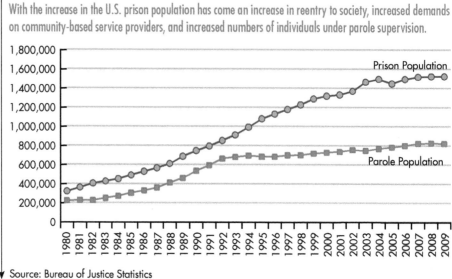

Reentry

The processes whereby the formerly incarcerated return to society, seeking to establish positive ties to the community and engage in law-abiding behaviors.

leased from prison in the United States return to prison with new sentences or due to violations of parole.[10] These high numbers of people returning to communities throughout the United States from prisons, and high rates of recidivism, have led many to call for increased rehabilitative programming in prisons and improved reentry services and support for inmates after their release.[11]

Just as those released from prison face challenges returning to society, prison administrators face challenges as they try to accomplish the multiple goals society has for prisons. There are a few indisputable facts that must be kept in mind when considering **reentry**: 1) most prison inmates have extensive, multiple criminogenic needs when they enter prison, 2) relatively few inmates have these needs met while incarcerated, 3) most people sentenced to prison are eventually released from prison, and 4) the rate at which those released from prison are rearrested and returned to prison suggests that, as a whole, much progress is needed to improve inmate reentry in the United States.

For the most part, this chapter focuses on the issues surrounding reentry from state prisons, and not local jails, since most jails serve as pretrial detention facilities and house inmates for relatively shorter periods of incarceration than prisons. However, those released from jail often experience some of the same problems and hurdles associated with reentry as do those coming out of state prisons, with unmet rehabilitative needs, returning to criminogenic environments, and the social stigma of having been incarcerated. Further, in many jurisdictions inmates under the custody of the state prison system serve their sentences in local jails due to crowding in state prisons. In fact, in 2009, more than 82,000 state and federal prison inmates—5.1% of the prison population in the United States—were being housed in local jails,[12] despite the fact that jails are primarily designed to provide short-term incarceration for sentenced misdemeanants and pretrial detainees.

IMAGE COURTESY OF THE AUTHOR.

Public policy makers are faced with choices as to how money gets spent.

Rehabilitation and Other Goals of Sentencing

In order to understand the issues and challenges facing those released from prison, it is critical to revisit and emphasize the general goals of sentencing—deterrence, punishment/retribution, incapacitation, and rehabilitation. These multiple goals of sentencing, and prison sentences in particular, create a number of challenges to institutional correctional agencies as they try to meet the expectations of citizens, taxpayers, voters, criminal justice practitioners, and policy makers. Part of what makes this a challenge is the fact that the public has mixed views as to what they expect correctional agencies to focus on, and correctional administrators must also ensure the safety of both staff and inmates.

As described earlier, when convicted offenders are sentenced, imposed sanctions may focus on deterrence, retribution, incapacitation, or rehabilitation. In some instances, only one of these goals is sought; in others, judges and prosecutors hope that all of these goals will be achieved simultaneously. Indeed, society as a whole expects multiple goals to be accomplished when someone is sentenced to prison: they want to make sure the person does not escape and therefore cannot commit other crimes while incarcerated (incapacitation), they want the specific person being sentenced to be deterred from future crime as a result of their experience of incarceration (specific deterrence) and for everyone else in society to be deterred as well (general deterrence), they seek punishment that is proportionate to the crime committed (retribution), and they also expect the person to be rehabilitated, through treatment by professionals, while incarcerated.

The public often has varying opinions of what the purpose of prisons should be. In a survey of 1,200 registered voters conducted in 2010 for the Pew Center for the States, 31% of respondents believed the primary purpose of prisons was to protect society (i.e., incapacitation), while 25% felt the primary purpose

Sanctions
Requirements imposed on those convicted of a crime that can range from financial penalties or curfew restrictions to incarceration.

was rehabilitation and 20% believed the purpose of prisons was punishment of offenders.[13] However, in a separate survey in 2006 of more than 1,000 adults for the National Council on Crime and Delinquency (NCCD), only 14% thought those coming out of prison were less likely to commit new crimes than before they were incarcerated, more than 50% thought the likelihood of new crimes was the same, and 31% believed those coming out of prison were *more likely* to commit crimes than before they went into prison.[14] These survey results indicate that if the purpose of prisons is to rehabilitate or deter offenders, the American public does not believe this is being accomplished.

Critical Thinking What aspect of incarceration do you feel is the most "punitive?" How does access to educational programming, drug treatment, and vocational training relate to punishment?

Thus, depending on the constituency, there are multiple goals correctional administrators and policy makers seek to achieve. Further, the pursuit and accomplishment of these competing goals is often viewed as contradictory and conflicting. For example, empirical evidence indicates that prison-based substance abuse treatment can reduce recidivism,[15] but there is still some political resistance to expanding the provision of treatment, because of either philosophical views (i.e., the notion of state-enforced therapy)[16] or budgetary limitations. Additionally, in some cases, the accomplishment of the rehabilitation goal may impede the accomplishment of the goals of punishment and institutional security. If an inmate is provided with vocational training or educational programming (i.e., rehabilitation), the public may not see this as adequate punishment (i.e., retribution) or may view it as inmates "getting" something law-abiding citizens cannot, or it may pose security concerns related to congregate programs and interpersonal violence between inmates in treatment together.

This conflict was illustrated by the debate over whether prison inmates should have access to college courses, and came to a head with the elimination of Pell grants—federal funding that provided support for college courses—for prison inmates in 1994. Republican Senator Kay Bailey Hutchison of Texas argued against Pell grants, claiming it was unjust for felons to receive support for college courses when up to 100,000 low-income students could not receive similar benefits.[17] This response is illustrative of what has been referred to as the principle of least eligibility, which, as described by Sparks (1996), states that "the level of prison conditions should always compare unfavorably to the material living standards of the laboring poor"[18]—in other words, prison inmates are the least eligible among the American public to receive benefits to which not all law-abiding citizens have access.

This example is also illustrative of how public backlash and political pressure can result in dramatic changes in correctional policy and practice. Before the Pell grant ban was passed, there were 350 college-degree programs for prison

Public policy makers often create new get-tough laws to appease the demands of the public to restrict perceived privileges of prison inmates.

© 2012 BY VLADEK. USED UNDER LICENSE OF SHUTTERSTOCK, INC.

inmates, but by 2005, there were only about a dozen college-degree programs in prisons.[19] Further, the timing of this Pell grant ban was part of a widespread public demand to address crime and restrict what many saw as prison inmate privileges. Around the same time as the Pell grant ban for inmates in 1994, Congress also passed the Violent Offender Incarceration/Truth-in-Sentencing (VOI/TIS) Incentive grant program (1994). This program provided states with federal funding if they implemented truth-in-sentencing policies that required those convicted of violent offenders sentenced to prison to serve 85% of the court-imposed sentence. Congress also passed the Prison Litigation Reform Act of 1996, which limited the circumstances under which inmates could file petitions in the federal courts.

However, even when correctional administrators and policy makers want to incorporate rehabilitative programming into correctional facilities, doing so can raise concerns regarding staff and inmate safety. From a prison management standpoint, allowing inmates to participate in congregate programs and allowing them movement within a facility are often seen as possible security threats, particularly given the historically limited accuracy of prison classification methods to predict prison violence.[20] In this case, the goal of rehabilitation can be seen as in conflict with the goals of incapacitation and institutional security. The number of empirical studies regarding the relationship between participation in prison-based treatment programs and prison misconduct are small, and have reached different conclusions.[21] Some assessments of the literature have found prison-based treatment programs can reduce prison misconduct,[22] while other assessments have found these have no demonstrable effect—for better or worse—on prison violence or inmate misconduct.[23,24] However, it does not take scholarly research for a prison warden to recognize that leaving inmates in their cells and not allowing them to engage in rehabilitative programs ensures that the goal of incapacitation is accomplished, even at the long-term cost and consequence that once the prisoner is released, he or she will not have received the rehabilitative support needed and will thus be more likely to return to prison.

In addition to the challenges of balancing multiple goals and institutional security and safety, there are other challenges when it comes to the provision of rehabilitative services. One major challenge is the perception by the public and policy makers that rehabilitative services are not effective. These perceptions can be shaped by media coverage, which often include selective observation—finding one person who went through treatment and concluding from that observation that treatment does not work. The media and politicians often condemn rehabilitative programs through coverage, or legislative hearings, when someone who completed a prison-based treatment program reoffends, regardless of whether the program is effective as a whole.

Similarly, research on the effectiveness of treatment can also be misused to influence public sentiment away from rehabilitation and towards retribution, deterrence, and incapacitation. One of the most significant examples of this came in the 1970s, when Robert Martinson co-authored the criminological study *Effectiveness of Correctional Treatment: A Survey of Treatment Evaluation Studies* with Lipton and Wolks, in which more than 200 studies on offender rehabilitation were examined and summarized.[25] Martinson also published an article on his own that reached the conclusion that "nothing works."[26] In fact, Jerome Miller, writing in the Washington Post in 1989, described this work as "the most politically important criminological study in the past century."[27] Others would later replicate Martinson's research. Gendreau and Ross (1979) used more sophisticated methods of analysis and more examples of programs, and reached different conclusions—treatment did work if it employed specific treatment interventions.[28] However, by then, the momentum to move away from treatment as a correctional goal and toward deterrence, retribution, and incapacitation could not easily be reversed. It would not be until the 1990s that researchers, employing meta-analyses summarizing hundreds and hundreds of evaluations and studies, were able to bring back the notion that treatment programs could be effective if they focused on criminogenic needs, were behavioral in nature and not punishment-oriented, focused on high-risk offenders, were implemented with a high degree of fidelity to the model, included aftercare, and were responsive to the learning styles of the targeted audience.[29]

What also contributed to the influence this research had on public views, and ultimately changes in state sentencing policy and practices, was the timing of the research and larger issues related to crime and crime control occurring in the 1970s. For example, from 1973 to 1979 violent crime reported to the police in the U.S. increased 40%,[30] stoking public concerns about crime and safety. Beginning in the 1970s, there were also increasing concerns that judges and parole boards were either inconsistent or error-prone in sentencing practices or decisions to release offenders. This led many states to adopt sentencing policies that reduced judicial discretion through mandatory prison sentences, and to eliminate parole boards' discretion to release or continue incarcerating inmates through the adoption of determinate sentencing structures.[31] Finally, there was the ongoing concern—continuing today—that prison inmates would feign rehabilitation and "play the game" in order to earn early release. As a result, from the early 1970s, when all states operated under indeterminate sentencing, to

2002, 17 states abandoned indeterminate sentencing structures and discretionary parole,[32] which were based on the belief that rehabilitation was possible if inmates were rewarded with earlier release for their participation. Instead, states shifted toward determinate sentencing, which did not consider or factor in an inmate's efforts at rehabilitation when it came to being released from prison. Under determinate sentencing, prisoners are released once they have served their sentences. The only criteria considered is time served, regardless of whether or not the prisoner has participated in rehabilitative programs and whether or not the prisoner is prepared for reentry into society. Indeed, when the U.S. Supreme Court upheld the federal sentencing guidelines in 1989 in *Mistretta v. United States*,[33] which focused only on the seriousness of the crime and the criminal history of the offender when determining sentence lengths and time to serve, the court had confirmed the "abandonment of rehabilitation in corrections."[34]

The other challenge to rehabilitative programs within prison is that they take time to implement and the results are not seen immediately by the public. This challenge is compounded by what Serin (2005) called prison administrators' "preoccupation with short-term operational goals (i.e., admissions, transfers, accommodation, and the daily routine of the prison) . . . [which] can easily exhaust available fiscal and human resources."[35] It is relatively quick, easy, and highly visible to pass a law that "gets tough on crime." When there is public outrage over a crime, elected officials can draft and pass a new law to increase penalties or make the crime non-probationable, the law is publicly signed, and the public is appeased. Many have pointed to the most recent war on drugs as an example of how elected officials responded to a perceived crime threat with a wide range of both substantive and symbolic legislation, without full consideration of the effectiveness or long-term consequences of these policies.[36] Similar examples of symbolic legislative responses to public crime concerns can be found in sex offender registries.[37] For the most part, sentencing enhancements can be developed, debated, and passed into law during one legislative session. On the other hand, a commitment to the provision of treatment and rehabilitation takes time, a commitment of resources for funding, time for participants to matriculate through, and then years to gauge and show the impact the program has on recidivism. To impatient voters and elected officials, this timeline is not conducive to the politics of crime control. In addition, there is a high likelihood that at least one person who goes through the program will recidivate, or commit a violent crime that may garner public and media attention, and often those individual cases are used to illustrate the ineffectiveness of treatment and justify cuts in treatment budgets in highly political environments.

Staffing patterns of prisons in the United States demonstrate that security, rather than treatment and rehabilitation, is the top priority of correctional facilities. State and federal prisons employed more than 445,000 full-time staff in 2005.[38] As would be expected, the majority—66%—of those who work in prisons are correctional officers, and their responsibilities primarily revolve around security, inmate movement within the facility, and ensuring order. Given the 1.5 million people in prison in the United States, it would appear that the ratio of

Correctional officers are trained primarily to provide security, not counseling or rehabilitative programming, and one officer is often responsible for the supervision of more than 50 inmates at a time.

© 2012 BY GALYNA ANDRUSHKO. USED UNDER LICENSE OF SHUTTERSTOCK, INC.

correctional officers to inmates—roughly 1:5—allows for close supervision of inmates by officers. However, the security aspect of prisons operates 24 hours a day, seven days a week, 365 days a year. Since staff do not work 24 hours a day, get days off, vacations, etc., and not all security staff are in direct contact with inmates (some are in towers, at entrances to the prison, etc.), often a single correctional officer can be responsible for the security and safety of more than 200 inmates at a time. Further, most correctional officers are not trained or qualified to provide inmates with clinical assessment or treatment, educational or vocational training, or counseling services. Those responsibilities fall to doctors, nurses, counselors, chaplains, psychiatrists, psychologists, social workers, classification staff, and teachers, which nationally account for less than 20% of those who work in prisons.[39] For example, there were roughly 12,000 educational staff employed in U.S. prisons in 2005, which translates to a ratio of one educator to 116 inmates nationally.[40] However, with all of these measures of prison staffing, it must be recognized that these ratios of security and treatment staff can vary dramatically from prison to prison. For example, the ratio of education staff to inmates across U.S. prisons in 2005 ranged from 1:20 to 1:1000, and varied by state, prison security classification, and other facility characteristics.[41]

As measured by these staffing patterns, it is clear that the primary emphasis of prisons relates to security and that nationally most inmates have limited access to rehabilitative services provided by educators and counselors. However, it is also clear that these staffing patterns vary dramatically from state to state and from prison to prison. It should also be noted that not included in these figures

FIGURE 11.2 Prison Staffing Numbers and Patterns 1984–2005

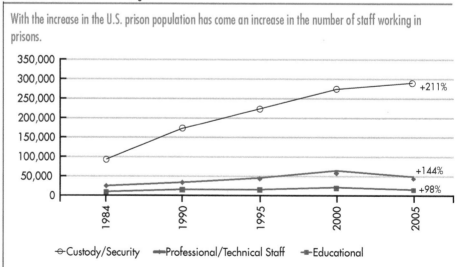

With the increase in the U.S. prison population has come an increase in the number of staff working in prisons.

Source: Bureau of Justice Statistics

are rehabilitative staff that may not be employees of the prison, but rather, are contractual service providers or volunteers.

This is not to say that prisons operate without any regard for the rehabilitative needs of those admitted to prison. Indeed, most states seek to identify offender needs during the reception and classification process, along with assessments used to make security classification decisions (i.e., **offender risk** for escape and violence towards staff and other inmates). Based on a survey of state correctional systems by the National Institute of Corrections in 2001, almost all states indicated that during the reception and classification process they gauge inmate needs related to medical needs, academic achievement, substance abuse, psychological issues, and other areas that could be the target of rehabilitation programs.[42] Given the focus of prisons on security (i.e., incapacitation and safety), facility placement and classification based on the risks relative to escape and violence within the prison system override most other rehabilitative needs the inmate may have. Additionally, given the crowding in most prison systems, and the fact that the distribution of beds across prisons is for the most part fixed, placement of inmates is often driven more by space availability than treatment needs. While maximum security prisons account for only 20% of all prisons in the United States, they house 36% of all prisoners.[43] On the other hand, minimum security prisons account for more than one-half of all prisons, but house only 21% of all prisoners.[44] These disparities are primarily driven by the fact that the maximum security prisons are extremely large and often hold thousands of inmates, such as Corcoran State Prison in California or Angola State Prison in Louisiana, both of which hold more than 5,000 inmates. In contrast, minimum security facilities usually house fewer than 500 inmates. As a result of these dynamics, inmates classified as medium security risk may be housed in maximum security facilities, since this may be where bed space is available, which limits opportunities for access to rehabilitative programming.

Offender risk
Within the context of prison security, an assessment of the likelihood that an inmate will attempt an escape or assault a staff member or other inmate. Within the context of community-based supervision, an assessment of the likelihood that a former inmate will commit a new crime.

Critical Thinking

If an inmate is considered a high security risk, he or she will likely be housed in a maximum security prison and will not have access to rehabilitative programs due to his or her dangerousness. Discuss the implications of this situation when people are eventually released because they have served their court-imposed sentences, but still remain "dangerous."

Thus, from the standpoint of public expectations and concerns by prison administrators over the immediate needs to ensure safety and security, rehabilitative treatment of prisoners may not be an emphasis. Despite this, however, it is clear that those who enter prisons in the United States bring with them a wide array of needs that, if not addressed adequately, will result in a continuation of the cycle of crime and victimization.

Before examining the extent and nature of inmate needs, practitioners and policy makers must recognize that the window to meet these needs is not limited exclusively to the time behind bars. Most of those released from prison will experience a period of supervision in the community upon release. Given this

reality, and the complexity and multiplicity of needs for many inmates, there is often more time to address the needs of those reentering society than simply the time they are behind bars. Thus, some of inmates' needs can be addressed during their incarceration, while treatment for some needs can be initiated in prison but would need to be completed or followed up on when the inmate is released. There are also some needs that are beyond the capacity of prisons to address.

For example, if an offender is admitted to prison a few credits short of completing high school, or in a position where he or she could be prepared for and pass a GED test, that is a need that could be met while the individual is incarcerated (i.e., completed in nine months) if the resources were available. Similarly, an individual who has a substance abuse disorder or a mental health issue could be provided with treatment while incarcerated (i.e., for 12 months), and in most instances, would need to continue receiving **aftercare**, or continued treatment and recovery support, after release from prison. On the other hand, an individual released from prison may have difficulty in obtaining employment or being able to find housing because of his or her felony conviction. That is not a need that a prison would be able to easily address, but rather, relates to public policy or society's views of prison releasees. Prison staff, in and of themselves, cannot address or change these realities. Thus, while prisons can have programs to assist inmates in how to conduct job searches, how to be upfront about their criminal background, and how to be effective in job interviews, prison administrators and staff cannot directly change the stigma of being a convicted felon. To accomplish this would require a change in how society views criminality, serving time in prison, or being a convicted felon.

The needs of those in prison in the United States are significant, and many of these relate directly to the likelihood of future recidivism and successful reen-

Aftercare
The process of providing continued treatment and recovery support following the conclusion of intensive or residential treatment programming.

try. As seen in Figure 11.3, the majority of those in prison were identified as being substance abusers or drug dependent, having a mental health disorder (often related to their substance abuse), and having prior arrests for violent crimes. In addition, more than one-half were parents of children under the age of 18. Further, a substantial proportion of inmates enter the prison system without a high school diploma or GED, with learning impairments, and with physical health problems. The most frequently cited health problems were arthritis (15% of all inmates), hypertension (14% of all inmates), asthma (9%), heart disease (6%), and hepatitis (5%).[45] In addition, almost 10% of inmates reported previously having tuberculosis.[46] Studies of inmate needs from individual states have highlighted other risks and needs that inmates have. For example, in a study of a drug treatment program in Illinois, Olson and Rozhon (2011) found that 45% of inmates had never held a job longer than two years, despite an average age of 36, and 70% had no valid driver's license or state-issued identification card.[47]

FIGURE 11.3 Prevalence of Needs and Risks Among State Prison Inmates in the U.S.

	Percent of U.S. State Prisoners
Mental Health Disorder[48]	56.2%
Psychotic Disorder[49]	15.3%
Substance Abuse or Dependence[50]	53.4%
Parent of a Minor Child[51]	51.9%
No High School Diploma or GED[52]	39.7%
Learning Impairment[53]	23.3%
Current Medical Problem[54]	43.8%
Prior Arrests for Violent Crime[55]	53.7%
More Than 10 Prior Arrests[56]	34.2%

Critical Thinking What criteria would you use to determine which inmates should be given priority access to treatment and rehabilitative programming?

Inmates have extensive needs that must be met in order to improve their chances of successful reentry into society and reduce the cycle of crime and incarceration. Therefore, it is important to consider the degree to which prisons offer rehabilitative programming, and the quality and form of these services. Four key factors play a role in providing prison-based rehabilitative programming: the existence of programming, the capacity of programming, to whom the programming is available, and the quality of programming.

The first factor, the existence of rehabilitative programming, is relatively easy to measure—a program either exists or it does not. In the 2005 census of prisons in the United States, 73% of all prisons had drug or alcohol programs,[57] but the availability of these programs varied considerably from state to state. For example, in five states, 90% or more of the prisons offered some type of drug or alcohol program, whereas in other states fewer than 20% of their prisons had programs.[58] As seen in Figure 11.4, some types of programs appear to be readily available in U.S. prisons, such as high school (secondary education) or GED classes, drug abuse programs, and work programs that provide facility support (i.e., inmate work that supports the operation of the prison, such as laundry, dietary, and maintenance). Other programs are not available in most prisons, such as college classes, parenting classes, or prison industry programs.

A second factor in prison-based rehabilitative programming is the capacity of these programs, which can vary dramatically from prison to prison. For example, there are numerous prisons operating across the country with small individual housing units that provide substance abuse treatment for 50 to 100 inmates. At the other extreme are prisons where all inmates participate in substance abuse treatment, including one of the nation's largest fully dedicated drug treatment prisons, the Sheridan Correctional Center in Illinois, which houses 950 inmates.[59]

A third factor is the quality or integrity of the program. If a program serving 50 inmates is operating as a Therapeutic Community (TC), with highly trained counselors, a rigorous nine-month curriculum, and an aftercare component, research has found that drug use and subsequent criminality will be reduced.[60] **Therapeutic Communities**, as defined by the National Institute on Drug Abuse, are "residential [programs] that use a hierarchical model with treatment strategies that reflect increased levels of personal and social responsibility. Peer influence, mediated through a variety of group processes, is used to help individuals learn and assimilate social norms and develop more effective social skills."[61] Therapeutic Communities are one of the most common drug treatment modalities for prison inmates,[62] and evaluations of specific programs in California,[63] Texas,[64] Delaware,[65] and Illinois[66] have documented that these TCs can substantially reduce post-release recidivism. On the other hand, a correctional boot camp that serves 500 inmates but consists only of an inmate-led self-

Therapeutic Communities (TC)
Residential programs that help individuals learn social norms and develop more effective social skills.

FIGURE 11.4 Prevalence of Selected Programs Across State and Federal Prisons in the U.S., 2005

	Percent of Prisons with Program
Educational Programs	
Secondary Education or GED	77%
Vocational Training	52%
College Classes	35%
Counseling Programs	
Drug/Alcohol Dependency	74%
Psychological or Psychiatric	58%
Parenting	48%
Inmate Work Programs	
Facility Support Services	74%
Prison Industries	31%

Source: Adapted from Table 6 in Census of State and Federal Correctional Facilities, 2005.

help group that lasts two weeks would not produce any reductions in recidivism.[67] While the latter program would make it appear that the prison is providing rehabilitation to more inmates, closer inspection might reveal that the intervention is not a substantive attempt at rehabilitation.

Critical Thinking   If you were the warden of a prison and had enough money to either provide 25 inmates with intensive, highly effective treatment or provide 200 inmates with less effective programming that occupied them for a few weeks, which would you select and why?

The current "resurgence" in prison-based treatment has been fueled by a combination of empirical evidence that treatment programs can work if implemented effectively, continued dissatisfaction with the high recidivism rates of those released from prison, and the economic pressures on states to control correctional costs. However, even with "legitimate" programs—those that are provided by trained professionals and last for several weeks—in order for them to work they must be delivered with **fidelity to program design**, or accordance with their pre-operational design, and to the appropriate clients/inmates. The consensus now is that treatment can reduce recidivism, but not all programs work for all offenders. Further, increased attention and focus on the content and treatment processes has revealed that not all programs operating within prisons have fidelity to the treatment models, and unless programs incorporate specific elements, they will not have the intended effect. For example, in his review of prison-based rehabilitative programs, Genreau (2011) concludes that cognitive-behavioral programs are most reliable in reducing recidivism, whereas programs that are punishment-oriented or focus on building character and self-esteem do not reduce recidivism.[68] Similarly, prison-based substance abuse treatment programs need to also include aftercare services for participants following their release in order to sustain and maximize the rehabilitative effects of the

Fidelity to program design
The degree to which rehabilitative programs are actually delivered in accordance with their pre-operational design.

Although small group and individual therapy with professional psychologists and counselors can be effective at reducing recidivism, most prisons do not have sufficient resources to provide these types of interventions.

© 2012 BY MARCIN BALCERZAK. USED UNDER LICENSE OF SHUTTERSTOCK, INC.

programs.[69] Thus, treatment can be effective at rehabilitation, but the public and policy makers should not expect programs to work for everyone. If funding and staffing limitations impede the ability to implement programs with a high degree of fidelity—i.e., if programs are not being delivered as they were designed—they will not have the expected effects on recidivism.

The fourth factor in providing prison-based rehabilitative programs is which inmates have access to them. Given the limited resources and capacity of this treatment, practitioners must make decisions regarding who gets access to which services and who is less of a priority. Generally, correctional treatment programs need to adhere to the principles of risk, need, and responsivity in order to have optimal outcomes.

The *risk* principle is based on the empirical evidence that the largest return on treatment investment comes from targeting the highest-risk offender.[70] By definition, offenders sentenced to prison tend to be higher-risk, at least in the minds of those involved in sentencing decisions, than offenders placed on probation. However, among those in prison, there are varying degrees of risk for subsequent recidivism, and this risk is not necessarily tied to the current conviction offense or the inmate's security classification. Because of this, practitioners need to employ risk assessment instruments when attempting to identify who is at greatest risk of future offending.

The *need* principle is also important to consider when identifying appropriate treatment interventions. Treatment programs must address **criminogenic needs**—those attributes that can be changed and that contribute directly to recidivism, such as education, substance abuse, personality and attitudes, and criminal thinking patterns. To change most of these needs requires considerable time, attention, and trained staff that can develop a strong rapport with the inmate.

The *responsivity* principle relates to the delivery of the intervention and the way it motivates the inmate to change, takes into account the inmate's cognitive abilities and skills, and is sensitive to cultural differences among the participants.[71]

When correctional practitioners make decisions regarding who will participate in treatment programming, they have to consider a number of different dimensions. First is the inmate's security classification. Does the inmate pose a high risk of escape or assault to staff and other inmates? Does allowing the inmate to leave his or her cell to participate in treatment compromise the institutional goals of security? While security classification does not necessarily indicate an inmate's likelihood of recidivating once released from prison, it does indicate the risk of an inmate attempting to escape or harm staff or other inmates.

Another consideration is whether or not the inmate's cognitive ability and mental health would allow him or her to effectively participate in the rehabilitative programming as designed. Very few prison treatment programs are delivered individually to inmates; most use group modalities. Some programs, such as Therapeutic Communities or **victim-offender mediation**, require a certain level of functioning and mental stability that some inmates may not possess.

Program administrators also have to determine if the inmate's participation would be disruptive to the overall group treatment program. One highly dis-

Criminogenic needs
The characteristics of an offender that can be changed through treatment and intervention that are directly related to continued involvement in criminal activity, including drug abuse, interpersonal skills, cognitive functioning, and vocational/employment skills.

Victim-offender mediation
A process facilitated by clinicians or trained personnel whereby crime victims are able to express to the perpetrators how the crime has impacted their lives, and the perpetrators can apologize and explain themselves to the victims.

ruptive participant can diminish the efficacy of the treatment for the entire group, and therefore prison-based treatment programs are often voluntary to ensure that participants want to be there and will not be disruptive in the hopes of being removed. Because of this, it has been suggested that providers of prison-based treatment modify their programs to address the resistance of non-voluntary participants and their potential for disrupting treatment.[72] In addition, research has also found that in custodial settings, mandated treatments were ineffective at reducing recidivism, while voluntary participation improved outcomes.[73]

Finally, administrators must ensure that inmates are exposed to an appropriate dose of the treatment. Treatment dosage—the actual number of hours or treatment sessions—and treatment duration—the days from start to finish—are separate concepts, but highly correlated in cognitive-behavioral programs for offenders.[74] Further, the higher the dose of these cognitive-behavioral programs, the lower the subsequent recidivism rates.[75] For some inmates, given the duration and intensity of their substance abuse disorders, treatment lasting nine months may be required in order to have an impact on drug use and criminal behavior. If an inmate will only be in prison for four months, should the inmate be enrolled in a prison-based treatment program when he or she really needs much more therapeutic intervention? This might work effectively if it can be guaranteed the inmate would continue his or her treatment upon release, but often access to treatment post-release cannot be ensured. Indeed, even among prison-based drug treatment programs supported through the federal Residential Substance Abuse Treatment (RSAT) initiative, which encouraged the programs it funded to include aftercare services,[76] less than one-half of programs placed inmates who received treatment in aftercare upon their release.[77] Another scenario and decision that correctional practitioners and policy makers face is whether those who will never be released or not released from prison for decades should be a treatment priority. While treatment of these individuals may not have an impact on recidivism, it could improve their behavior while incarcerated, thereby increasing staff and other inmate safety and possibly improving the prison atmosphere.

Rehabilitative programs can potentially help reduce correctional costs through two primary mechanisms: shorter lengths of incarceration if participation in and completion of these programs allow for additional sentence reductions or earlier release by parole boards, and a reduction in recidivism and therefore fewer people returning to prison with new sentences. Shorter lengths of stay can be accomplished in states with indeterminate sentencing if inmates' participation in treatment leads to early release, or in determinate sentencing states if inmates receive additional credits toward their sentences for participation in these programs. In 31 states, inmates who participate in rehabilitative programs, such as drug treatment, vocational programming, prison industry, or GED completion, are awarded additional time off their sentences above and beyond traditional day-for-day good conduct credit.[78] In Illinois, an evaluation of the Sheridan Correctional Center's Therapeutic Community found that inmates who participated in the drug treatment program and earned good conduct credits reduced the length of their incarceration by an average of 60 days per inmate. This translates to a cost savings of $2.78 million per year for the program.[79] Additional savings come in the form of lower recidivism (and lower criminal justice processing costs) and lower health care costs; two widely cited studies estimated a savings of $7 for every dollar spent on treatment.[80,81] Therefore, it is evident that in the long run, prison-based rehabilitation can reduce prison populations, crime, and victimization. However, the challenge is that policy makers often do not make decisions based on the long-term view, but rather on the short-term view of fiscal years, or at least the four-year period between election cycles.

Ultimately, the most significant factor that affects offender recidivism and successful reentry is the provision of services and treatment that address the root causes of criminality. These root causes include limited educational achievement and employment/employability, criminal thinking patterns, mental illness, and substance abuse, and are often referred to as criminogenic needs, or risk factors that can be changed through therapeutic intervention.[82] Addressing and reducing these risk factors is ultimately how offenders will reduce their involvement in criminal activity and successfully reintegrate back into society from prison. As with the availability and quality of treatment, the degree to which prisons are able to meet the rehabilitative needs of inmates varies from state to state and prison to prison. However, regardless of the quality and integrity of programming, a significant portion of inmates who have deficiencies do not participate in programming that would improve those areas of risk. For example, in 1997, of those who entered prison without a high school diploma, only 54% participated in any educational programming, and only 32% of all inmates participated in vocational training/programs while incarcerated.[83] Similarly, of those inmates in state prisons in 2004 with mental health problems, only 34% received any treatment.[84]

Substance abuse treatment and aftercare also appear to be lacking for returning inmates. Nationally, in 2004, an estimated 53% of inmates had problems with drug dependence or abuse, but it is projected that only 15% of state prison inmates meeting drug dependence or abuse criteria had participated in substance abuse treatment while in prison.[85] Additionally, despite some increases in funding for prison-based treatment through programs like the federal Residential Substance Abuse Treatment (RSAT) grants, it appears that prison-based substance abuse treatment services decreased in use among prisoners in the 1990s due to the dramatic increases in the number of offenders admitted to prison.[86]

Substance abuse treatment is often lacking for inmates returning to society.

Across the United States, the availability, capacity, and quality of prison-based programming designed to improve inmate reentry and reduce recidivism vary widely, and over time these characteristics of programming have changed. For example, a number of approaches have been used in prisons to address substance abuse treatment needs, including drug education, self-help groups such as Alcoholics Anonymous (AA) or Narcotics Anonymous (NA), group counseling within specific housing units of a prison, and prisons that operate as Therapeutic Communities (TCs). While programming such as drug education and self-help groups are inexpensive and large numbers of inmates can be served through these programs, they lack the components that make up effective interventions. On the other hand, while programs such as prison-based TCs and professional counseling are effective at reducing recidivism, they are extremely expensive and usually only serve a small number of those in need of treatment services. Thus, prison administrators and policy makers are often faced with the choice between providing limited, usually ineffective interventions to large numbers of inmates at a low cost and providing more expensive, effective interventions to a much smaller number of inmates. Often the option of providing "something" to many, even if ineffective, is more symbolic of the effort to improve the reentry process than substantive.

An examination of trends in the proportion of inmates accessing substance abuse treatment programming—distinguishing between drug education versus drug counseling—reveals this shift nationally. In 1991, when there were fewer than 800,000 adults in prison, 36% of those in need of substance abuse treatment received substantive drug treatment (professional counseling or a therapeutic community-type intervention) and about one-quarter (24%) received drug education. Inmates often receive both types of interventions, so there is double counting in the data. However, by 2004, when the prison population in the United States had reached almost 1.5 million, 34% of those in need of drug

FIGURE11.5 Percent of Prison Inmates in Need of Treatment Accessing Counseling versus Self-Help Groups, 1991–2004

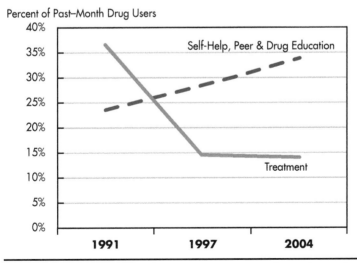

Over the past 15 years there has been a shift from drug treatment provided by counselors to drug education and self-help groups.

*Treatment defined as "residential" treatment services or professional counseling

Source: Mulola & Karberg (2006): Drug Use and Dependence, State and Federal Prisoners, 2004; Mumola (1999). Substance Abuse and Treatment, State and Federal Prisoners, 1997. U.S. Department of Justice, Bureau of Justice Statistics

treatment received drug education, compared to 14% receiving substantive drug treatment. Thus, while a larger proportion of inmates in need are receiving "some" services, most are receiving services that will do little to address their long-term, serious substance abuse problems, which will likely lead to their failing after release from prison and recidivating.

In general, most of the research on prison-based TCs and other cognitive-based rehabilitation programs has documented reductions in recidivism, which vary depending on the "dose" of treatment, the characteristics of the prison population served, and the inclusion of other components that address criminogenic needs, such as educational and vocational programming. For example, in one of the most recent reviews of prison-based treatment, it was noted that most TCs examined only served "nonviolent" offenders, and they had better outcomes than those programs that included offenders with violent and nonviolent criminal histories.[87] However, even those programs that included both violent and nonviolent offenders tended to produce lower recidivism rates than when treatment was not provided.[88] Current reviews also concluded that corrections-based TCs that served primarily white and female offenders and that required aftercare experienced better outcomes—lower recidivism rates—than did programs that primarily included minorities and males, and did not require post-release aftercare. Again, though, even these programs had better outcomes than comparison groups with no treatment.[89]

However, despite the empirical evidence that prison-based treatment and aftercare can reduce recidivism rates, there are still a number of barriers that prevent these treatment strategies from being implemented.[90] For example, many programs include restrictions on program eligibility based on the criminal backgrounds of program participants,[91] regardless of treatment need, motivation, or how long ago prohibiting offenses may have been committed. Another challenge has been the ability to attract and retain qualified staff,[92] which can be particularly problematic at prisons located far from metropolitan areas. As described earlier, the conflict within corrections between treatment and punishment also creates tension and challenges between criminal justice personnel (i.e., correctional officers) and treatment personnel (i.e., counselors).[93,94,95] Finally, from a purely financial standpoint, substantive, high-quality prison-based treatment programs, particularly TCs, are expensive to operate in the short run, regardless of the long-term benefits and cost savings.

Critical Thinking   What is it about the physical design and location of prisons that makes delivering effective correctional programming a challenge?

The capacity of prisons to meet the needs of inmates has been limited, but it is not completely absent. Efforts at rehabilitation exist, but again, in many instances the majority of resources are devoted to security and safety. Indeed, prisons do a very good job at ensuring that the goal of incapacitation is met, and they also are successful at limiting the amount of interpersonal violence between staff and inmates, as well as inmate-on-inmate violence. One indicator of prisons' degree of success at achieving the goal of incapacitation is the extremely small number of inmates that escape from prisons on an annual basis. Although the exact number of escapes from prison throughout the United States has been difficult to determine, given the multiple definitions and reporting processes, in general the rate of escapes is low—less than 0.5 per 100 inmates in 1998—and fell throughout the 1990s.[96] Based on information reported by prisons to the U.S. Department of Justice, in 2005, there were fewer than 100 escapes from prisons that were classified as medium, maximum, or supermax security facilities, which translates to approximately one escape for every 15,000 inmates housed in prisons at those security levels.[97] However, even this low number of escapes makes the prevalence seem higher, since many of these escapes were likely minimum-security inmates who were working in the facility. The majority of "escapes" from prison occur at prisons classified as minimum security, which generally do not have extensive external security perimeters; these escapes are often referred to as "walkaways" or AWOLs (inmates who are on a work-release assignment and do not return by a specified time).

Similarly, prisons' goal of ensuring that staff and inmates are not victimized appears to be met to a relatively high degree. Although there are significant limitations to accurately measuring the extent and nature of prison violence, including inmates not wanting to report victimization due to the inmate code and limited trust of staff, some measures are quite reliable. For example, the number of staff murdered by inmates—one of the most highly reliable measures of prison violence but also the most narrowly defined—totaled fewer than 10 in 2005, which translates to a rate of two murders per 100,000 staff.[98] By comparison, the murder rate in the "free world" of the United States that year was 5.6 per 100,000.[99] Similarly, the inmate-on-inmate murder rate during the period from 2001 to 2004 was four per 100,000 inmates.[100] These low murder rates have not always been the case, however. In the early 1980s, the murder rate in prisons nationally was much higher than in the free world. Through improved methods of inmate classification and an increased focus on staff and inmate safety, the rate of murder in prison has decreased, as shown by Figure 11.6.

When examining the challenges of balancing the rehabilitative needs of inmates, the goals of institutional security and safety, and the larger goal of incapacitation, it is clear that prisons do a very good job at making sure that those sentenced to prison do not escape and that prison staff and inmates are relatively safe from interpersonal violence. The degree to which these goals are accomplished can vary dramatically from prison to prison, but as a whole, the goals of security are accomplished well. On the other hand, the goals of rehabilitation and providing rehabilitative programming to inmates have been less effectively achieved. While many inmates do receive services, the majority of those in need of substance abuse treatment, mental health treatment, and improved educational and vocational skills do not receive these services while incarcerated. As a result, there is very little debate that many individuals released from prison have significant, unmet needs. However, the debate over how to meet these needs,

FIGURE 11.6 Homicide Rates in Prisons from 1980–2005

Over the past 30 years, prisons have become safer for both inmates and staff due to improved classification and security processes.

Murder Rate in Prison

Murder Rate in U.S.

Source: Bureau of Justice Statistics

how to balance offender needs with society's demands for safety, who should provide for these needs, and which needs should be addressed first is not settled among policy makers, practitioners, or the public.

Barriers to reintegration
Conditions within the community or society that impede the ability of someone released from prison to reestablish citizenship, employment, and housing.

Return to Society

From 2005 to 2009, more than 700,000 people per year in the United States were released after serving prison sentences and reentered society,[101] more than double the number of people released from prison annually during the 1980s.[102] In recent years, there has been increased emphasis on and interest in improving the reentry process of inmates, primarily driven by concerns over recidivism and increasing correctional budgets. Further, most people returning home from a period of incarceration face considerable **barriers to reintegration** that impede their ability to reestablish citizenship, employment, and housing. As a result, practitioners and policy makers are now seeking ways to improve the transition from prison back to society. Substantial federal funds to assist state and local units of government, as well as nonprofit organizations, have been made available under the federal Second Chance Act to support these efforts.

The U.S. Department of Justice defines reentry as "a research-driven process that starts when an offender is initially incarcerated, and ends when the offender has been successfully reintegrated into his or her community as a law-abiding citizen. The reentry process includes the delivery of a variety of program services in both pre- and post-release settings to ensure that the offender safely and successfully transitions from a [correctional facility] to the community."[103] The goal of restoring those in prison to full citizenship and ensuring a smooth transition back to the community has long been a focus of policy makers, but

The experience of reentry is different for each inmate, and varies based on his or her time in prison, gains made while incarcerated, and family and social support upon release.

© 2012 BY CURAPHOTOGRAPHY. USED UNDER LICENSE OF SHUTTERSTOCK, INC.

several challenges have arisen. The increased emphasis on punishment, retribution, and incapacitation during the late 1970s through the 1990s is one challenge, but another major issue is the sheer volume of individuals that prisons and agencies serving returning inmates must handle. As a result, the number of people coming out of prison getting services and assistance has grown, but this growth has not kept pace with the number of prison admissions and exits. Thus, the proportion of those receiving rehabilitative services and getting support and assistance in their reentry has decreased.

Increasingly, the process of reentry is not being viewed as something that occurs within the weeks before an inmate is released from prison, but rather, a process of preparing an offender for eventual return to society that often begins with the first contact the justice system has with an offender. Most of those who are ultimately released from prison have spent time on probation, often immediately before their current period of incarceration in prison. For example, more than 375,000 adults on probation in 2009 were negatively discharged from supervision and incarcerated either in jail or prison.[104] In addition, most of those sentenced to prison will have served a fair amount of time in a county jail awaiting trial before the convictions that result in the imposition of a prison sentence: in 2006, the median time between arrest and sentencing for felons in the United States was 265 days, or nearly nine months.[105] Finally, the majority of those released from prison are required to be supervised for a period of time following their release from prison. This perspective is important because many inmates spend relatively little time in prison, but have significant deficits and needs that must be addressed in order to improve their rates of successful reentry and reduce recidivism. Thus, while prisons may have a short period of time to prepare inmates for reentry, the criminal justice system as a whole has a significant amount of time and involvement with these offenders.

The coordination of risk assessment and service delivery would go a long way toward improving the reentry experiences and outcomes of the formerly incarcerated. Any treatment initiated while the offender is on probation or in a county jail awaiting trial should be continued when the offender is incarcerated. Similarly, any information regarding individuals' rehabilitative needs and the progress they may have made while on probation, or in jail or prison, should be shared and communicated to those who work with the individual later in the process. If treatment services are not provided or continued or planned for while an individual is incarcerated, then the prison has not done anything to rehabilitate or initiate the process of rehabilitation.

In order to understand reentry from the inmate's perspective, it is important to recognize that all inmates are unique individuals, with unique circumstances, needs, lengths of time in prison, and environments they will be returning to upon their release from prison. Among inmates released from prison in the U.S. in 2009, the median length of time served overall was 16 months, but for those who served a sentence for a violent crime, the median time served was 29 months.[106] Thus, reentry means something very different for an offender who has served a six-month sentence versus someone who has spent 20 years in prison. Both leave prison having gone through the experience of living within a controlled environment, but for one inmate the world is not much different than when he or she entered prison, whereas for the other, the use of cell phones, the Internet, ATMs, etc., may be completely foreign.

However, for many, their experiences within prison are very similar and have implications for reentry. These individuals are accustomed to living in an environment in which the prison system dictates complete control over when they wake up, when and what they eat, where they sleep, and whom they live with. Relatively little has changed for them in terms of their skills, assets, and thinking patterns. Most inmates who enter prison with a substance abuse problem receive little to no clinical treatment. Although the availability of drugs in prison is much lower than on the streets, this period of sobriety does not change the underlying reasons for the inmates' involvement in crime or use of drugs. Further, this period of sobriety is also not capitalized on through the provision of substantive treatment. Most inmates do not leave prison with markedly higher levels of educational achievement or vocational skills, and most will be going back to the same communities and environments that offered them little opportunity in the first place.

So, while most inmates sentenced to prison will eventually be released, most have not been adequately prepared for their release and reentry back into society. The mechanisms of release from prison also have implications for how effectively the reentry process can be managed and facilitated for the formerly incarcerated. Ideally, when people have been deemed dangerous enough to be incarcerated in prison, their incarceration would progress from a highly secure and structured environment to one that provides increased opportunity for rehabilitation, more interaction with society, and increasing levels of personal responsibility for their own care. This would facilitate reentry through progressive stepping down of control and increasing emphasis on independence. From a prison standpoint, this would entail moving from a high-level security status to lower levels of security. Upon release from prison, the former inmates would ideally be provided with a transitional period within a safe, structured environment that would also allow (require) them to seek employment and continue to receive rehabilitative services. These environments are often referred to as halfway houses or work-release centers. Although these types of facilities provide inmates with a more gradual transition from the highly regimented, secure setting of prison life to the free world, they also cost more and are less readily available in certain communities than simple release onto parole or post-prison supervision. Another option is for inmates to be released from prison onto electronic monitoring and home confinement. This would then be followed by a period of supervision that would be dictated by the individual risks and needs of the former inmate.

Unfortunately, the experience of most inmates is not close to this ideal. More than a third of inmates incarcerated in the United States are housed in maximum security facilities,[107] which have limited rehabilitative programming, fewer visitation privileges, and other characteristics, such as frequent cell searches, that increase the prisonization of individuals. Relatively few inmates released from prison are transitioned back to the community through **work release centers**, halfway houses, or other monitored residential settings. Instead, prison releasees shift directly from a very highly structured environment in prison where their basic needs are met to "freedom," where suddenly the individual is responsible for meeting his or her own needs. Less than one-quarter (21%) of inmates are housed in minimum security prisons, where access to services and the ability to participate in treatment would be the greatest, and less than 4% are housed in community-based correctional facilities, such as work-release centers.[108]

Extensive research has described and gauged the concerns and needs of inmates who are about to be released from prison, as well as the means by which these needs are met. The forces that shape the reentry experience of inmates can be grouped into the following categories: the individual-level risks, needs, and attitudes of the formerly incarcerated; the capacity and willingness of friends and family to provide support and assistance to the formerly incarcerated; the capacity and characteristics of the community to which the released inmate is returning; the orientation and resources available to a releasee's parole agent/officer; and finally, the degree to which society as a whole deems the released inmate to be "eligible" for restored citizenship and a second chance.

In most jurisdictions that release inmates to some form of supervision, a risk assessment is performed that often dictates levels of supervision and frequency of contact. Indeed, the assessment of offender risk is a fundamental decision-making process in community corrections.[109] The process and methods used to gauge this risk have evolved considerably over the past 30 to 40 years. Experts have generally identified three "generations" of risk assessment: subjective or clinical judgments by practitioners, actuarial or case classification approaches that employ statistical probabilities of recidivism appropriately matched to supervision levels, and criminogenic/dynamic evaluations.[110] This third approach emphasizes the need to understand offender characteristics that are related to criminal behavior that can be changed through treatment and intervention. These characteristics are dynamic, as opposed to static traits, such as gender and prior criminal behavior.

Work release centers
Correctional facilities that are designed to provide housing and secure custody of those under the jurisdiction of the prison system, but also allow for inmates to leave during specific periods of time to work or attend vocational or rehabilitative programming in the community.

Ethics & Professionalism

You are a parole agent supervising a former inmate. The inmate served two years in prison, and had a substance abuse problem before he was incarcerated, but did not access treatment while in prison due to limited availability. The requirement from the parole board is that the inmate be released onto parole, must enroll in a drug treatment program, and must be drug tested randomly while on supervision. You work to identify a program that will enroll the parolee, but he cannot enter the program for another month. You also find out that the parolee tested positive for marijuana after being out of prison for just one week. Legally, you have the ability to use your discretion to return the inmate to prison as a technical violator of parole due to his drug use, or implement graduated sanctions and require the parolee to report more frequently and undergo more frequent drug tests, or do nothing. Which would you do and why? When making this decision, are you concerned more with the costs of continued incarceration, the chances of failure on parole and therefore public safety, the possibility that you will be publicly criticized in the media for making a mistake, or the hope of rehabilitation once treatment is accessed?

Would your decision change if two weeks earlier a colleague had a similar situation, required increased reporting, and the parolee committed an armed robbery that escalated to a murder? Would your decision change if the chances of the above situation occurring are less than 1 in 100? 1 in 1,000? What would be the threshold for you to try to assist the parolee in accessing needed services?

Research shows that information beyond just the formal risk assessment is critical to improving the reentry process. With the renewed interest in and focus on the experiences and needs of those released from prison, a significant amount of research has taken place over the past decade that has been influential in the formation of criminal justice policy and practice.

In their Returning Home study, one of the largest-scale studies of inmate reentry in the United States, the Urban Institute interviewed, surveyed, and tracked thousands of inmates released from prisons across the states of Maryland,[111] Illinois,[112] Ohio,[113] and Texas.[114] The results revealed that not only do inmates leave prison with many of their rehabilitative needs unmet, but they also are forced to rely extensively on family and friends for housing and assistance in seeking employment, and usually return to the same communities they were living in before their incarceration. This is one of the paradoxes of reentry planning and transitioning inmates from prison back to the community—the places that inmates come from often have characteristics that increase the risk of their returning to crime, because they need to protect themselves from violence, need to support themselves, or lack access to mental health or substance abuse treatment. Almost all criminology theories on why offenders commit crime indicate that environmental influences such as social disorganization of neighborhoods, social cohesiveness of communities, and the social disadvantages of neighborhoods affect offenders' decisions to commit another criminal act. In a number of studies examining the characteristics of communities that inmates return to, and how these traits influence recidivism rates, it has been found that returning to a community with concentrated disadvantage increases the odds of recidivism.[115] Even soon-to-be-released inmates recognize that staying away from specific people and places will be critical to their reentry success and staying out of prison in the future.[116] However, given their limited options, most inmates return back to the same neighborhoods they came from, and often live with others involved in a pro-criminal lifestyle with antisocial attitudes. Many former inmates feel this is their only option, as most leave prison with nothing more than when they entered, in terms of risks, needs, and deficits.

Another problem that prison releasees face in their communities is that they do not have access to community rehabilitative services. Many of those released from prison are returned to communities where these types of services may be limited or difficult to access, or in more rural communities, may not exist at all because of the small number of people needing such services. In some parts of the United States, those released from prison would need to travel hundreds of miles to access specialized treatment programs or services, even assuming that treatment providers would be willing to enroll/serve someone who may have an extensive history of violence. In more urban areas, programs may be available, but access to these services may be a challenge. Research on prison-based drug treatment has reached a general consensus that post-release aftercare is critical to sustaining the benefits of in-prison treatment,[117] but the access of those released from prison to these services is often limited. The federal Residential Substance Abuse Treatment (RSAT) program encouraged states to ensure that participants in these prison-based treatment programs would receive aftercare,[118] but a number of national evaluations of these programs documented that few jurisdictions were able to provide aftercare for these program participants.[119,120] Indeed, the general conclusion is that most inmates who complete prison-based treatment do not transition back into society with thorough reentry plans or continued services in the community.[121] Some of this difficulty in providing adequate aftercare for inmates stems from the fact that the person released from prison does not always have interest in continuing treatment and often does not have adequate services in his or her community. In some jurisdictions, **reentry courts** have been implemented to ensure that those released from prison with specific requirements are monitored within a judicial setting—a local court—to ensure compliance and to modify conditions as appropriate.

Making aftercare services legally mandatory for released inmates can influence treatment compliance and completion.[122] However, aftercare cannot simply be required: it must also be available and accessible within the communities people are released to, and it requires coordination between correctional facilities, prison-based service providers, and community-based aftercare providers,

Most inmates released from prison return to the same communities where their criminal behavior evolved, with few opportunities, high rates of victimization, and high degrees of social disorganization.

Reentry courts
Courtroom working groups, including judges, prosecutors, defense attorneys, and parole agents, that monitor those released from prison to ensure compliance with conditions of release and respond to violations of these conditions through graduated sanctions and rehabilitative services.

which does not always happen.[123] Olson and Rozon (2010) found that inmates released back to more rural communities were less likely to access and complete mandatory aftercare following prison-based treatment than those released to more urban areas, other things being equal, and attributed this to lower capacity and availability of services.

Although the operations of prisons in the United States is primarily the responsibility of state government, the federal government ensures that the constitutional rights of inmates are protected, and supports and conducts research and evaluation to improve the operations of prisons and prison programming. The federal government also provides financial assistance to state governments to develop, implement, and test innovative approaches to improving inmate reentry. The most recent substantive federal act to improve offender reentry was the Second Chance Act, which was signed into law on April 9, 2008. Allowed for under this act is the provision of financial support to state, local, and tribal governments, as well as nonprofit groups, to deliver services and programs that improve the reentry of the formerly incarcerated. Congress has appropriated a substantial amount of money to assist state and local criminal justice agencies, service providers, and not-for-profit groups—close to $200 million from 2009 through 2011.[124] But when considering the number of inmates released from prison during that time period—roughly 2 million—much more needs to be done to address the significant needs and barriers inmates face.

Second Chance Act

Federal legislation that authorizes Congress to appropriate funds that support reentry programs across the country, conduct research to evaluate reentry initiatives, and develop model programs and policies to improve the reentry process.

Exhibit: Section III of the Second Chance Act of 2007: Community Safety Through Recidivism Prevention

The purposes of the Act are—

(1) to break the cycle of criminal recidivism, increase public safety, and help States, local units of government, and Indian Tribes, better address the growing population of criminal offenders who return to their communities and commit new crimes;

(2) to rebuild ties between offenders and their families, while the offenders are incarcerated and after reentry into the community, to promote stable families and communities;

(3) to encourage the development and support of, and to expand the availability of, evidence-based programs that enhance public safety and reduce recidivism, such as substance abuse treatment, alternatives to incarceration, and comprehensive reentry services;

(4) to protect the public and promote law-abiding conduct by providing necessary services to offenders, while the offenders are incarcerated and after reentry into the community, in a manner that does not confer luxuries or privileges upon such offenders;

(5) to assist offenders reentering the community from incarceration to establish a self-sustaining and law-abiding life by providing sufficient transitional services for as short of a period as practicable, not to exceed one year, unless a longer period is specifically determined to be necessary by a medical or other appropriate treatment professional; and

(6) to provide offenders in prisons, jails or juvenile facilities with educational, literacy, vocational, and job placement services to facilitate re-entry into the community.

For many of those released from prison, money is not the only, or most important, force that could improve their outcomes and success. Rather, for many inmates the biggest challenge is overcoming the social and economic stigma of their felony conviction and incarceration. In addition to the significant needs that are unmet by their incarceration—low academic achievement, limited employment history, and substance abuse and mental health disorders—having a felony conviction significantly limits their ability to find employment. Convicted felons are barred from many professions, which vary from state to state, and sometimes from even the most basic of entry-level jobs. For example, in Florida, it was estimated that 40% of public- and private-sector jobs were affected by state-established restrictions on employment of those with criminal records.[125] But even without these prohibitions from employment, many are faced with the challenge of finding employment simply because a felony conviction reported on a job application reduces the chances of being hired. In a study by Pager (2002), it was found that those with a criminal record were one-third to one-half as likely as those without a felony record to be called back for a job interview, and that blacks without a criminal record were less likely to be called back than whites with criminal records.[126] In some states, there have been efforts to address the impact that a felony conviction on a job application can have. Through the so-called "ban the box" initiative, a number of jurisdictions have sought to exclude from job applications the requirement that applicants check a box indicating if they have ever been convicted of a crime/felony. Although legislators and employers remain anxious about the potential liability and risk associated with a person they hire committing a serious crime of violence, no matter how rare the chances of that occurring, some jurisdictions have implemented this policy, at least for public employment. For example, as of early 2011, five states—Hawaii, Massachusetts, Minnesota, New Mexico, and Connecticut—have removed the box asking about felony convictions from state job applications, and at least 20 cities across the country have also implemented this practice on city job applications.[127] Another possible solution to this problem, which has been in place for a long time but is getting renewed interest, is the process of expungement of criminal records, in which the official record of an individual's criminal history is prohibited from being disclosed. However, the processes involved in expungement can take considerable time, and for those with multiple convictions, it is not always possible. Despite the increased political attention being paid to the challenges of reentry, political concerns remain about not appearing to be soft on crime.

Expungement
The legal process whereby the official record of an individual's criminal history is prohibited from being disclosed.

An even more substantial form of disenfranchisement that those released from prison face is the restriction on voting rights. The degree to which a felony conviction limits someone's right to vote varies from state to state, as does the process to restore this right. For example, in 13 states, upon release from prison, the right of convicted felons to vote is restored provided they register to vote, whereas in 23 other states, a felon can only vote once he or she has completed all aspects of his or her sentence (i.e., completion of parole).[128] In 12 states, the process to regain the right to vote is more complex, including some states where that right can only be reinstated with a pardon from the governor, while others require a certain number of years to elapse since the completion of a prison or probation sentence.[129]

Critical Thinking   If you were an employer, what incentives would you need in order to hire someone with a felony conviction?

Discretionary release

The mechanism by which those in prison are released after serving at least a minimum amount of their sentence upon the decision of a parole board.

Mandatory release

The mechanism by which those in prison must be released after having served their court-imposed sentences, minus any other sentencing credits for which they may be eligible.

Inmates sentenced to prison can be released under three primary methods: parole (**discretionary release**), **mandatory release**, and completion of sentence. As a result of these different release mechanisms, those coming out of prison have varying degrees of what can be required of them by the state. Inmates who have served their full sentences, for the most part, are released without any supervision and few requirements other than those that all law-abiding citizens must live by. They cannot be required to attend drug treatment, participate in educational or vocational programming, or attend anger management classes. On the other hand, inmates released onto parole or some form of supervision following their mandatory or discretionary release are supervised and often have conditions they are expected to abide by, such as treatment programming, urinalysis, and reporting requirements. Because of the concerns that parole boards have regarding releasing inmates before the maximum time has expired, a relatively large portion of inmates released from prison in the United States—25% in 2008—are released from prison "unconditionally," meaning they have no supervision requirements.[130]

A number of states have implemented new programs or policies to try to improve the success of inmates coming out of prison. For example, in Kansas, inmates can work in a government-private partnership program where they earn market-rate pay and are required to save money, pay for a portion of their incarceration, and make restitution.[131] Inmates who participate in this program then have the money they saved available to them when they are released. On average, during 2008 participants in the program earned an average of $13,000 per year, and collectively paid more than $1.6 million in Social Security, federal, and

FIGURE11.7 Percent of Inmates Released from State Prisons in the U.S. Under Mandatory Parole, Discretionary parole and Expiration of Sentence, 1980–2004

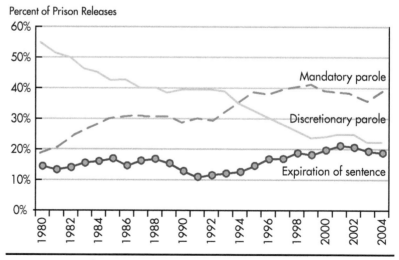

As a result of changes in sentencing policy and parole practice, more inmates are being released under mandatory parole and as a result of sentences expiring.

Percent of Prison Releases

Source: Bureau of Justice Statistics

state taxes and more than $2.6 million in "room and board" to the state of Kansas.[132] The fact that participants can save money that they can use upon release gives them some options as to where they will live, with whom they will associate, and the burden, or lack thereof, they place on those with whom they may reside upon release. In comparison, prison releasees who leave prison with the "standard" gate money of $10 to $100, depending on the state, are usually forced to rely on others for all of their needs.

Still, the prospect of inmates having significant amounts of money saved as a result of their prison labor does not always align with society's expectation that prison be punishment. Illustrative of this is a case in Illinois where an inmate had saved $11,000 over the course of his 25 years of working in a prison industry program, at a rate of about $75 per month. His intention was to provide that money to his daughter, but the state of Illinois moved to seize and use the funds to pay the state back for his incarceration because his account exceeded the threshold of $10,000.[133] Ultimately, the state backed off its effort to seize the funds.

Another factor that affects the reentry experience is the orientation of parole agencies and officers. These agencies may either enforce requirements (i.e., operate as police), refer releasees to needed rehabilitative services and support (i.e., case managers), or work directly with releasees to aid in their rehabilitation and assimilation back into society (i.e., social workers and counselors). These different approaches to the relationship between releasee and parole agent can vary from jurisdiction to jurisdiction, but also from officer to officer. As a result, part of what can influence a prison releasee's success or failure after incarceration is the orientation and emphasis placed on surveillance versus rehabilitation by parole agents.

Recidivism

In the field of criminal justice, the most frequently used measure to gauge the impact and effectiveness of interventions and rehabilitative programs is the reduction in recidivism, or reduced involvement in criminal behavior, by those who participate in the program. High rates of recidivism have led to calls for increased attention to prison-based programming and enhanced efforts at improving inmate reentry. However, accurately measuring an individual's involvement in crime is very difficult, since many crimes never come to the attention of law enforcement. Thus, for the purposes of criminal justice research, measuring subsequent involvement in crime usually involves analyses of official criminal history information, including rearrests for new crimes, new convictions, or return to prison.

Some argue that recidivism should be measured by conviction for a crime, because there would have been proof beyond a reasonable doubt that a crime was committed. The limitation with this measure, though, is that when an offender is on active parole, the prosecutor sometimes will not actually file charges or seek a conviction. This can be influenced by both the seriousness of the offense and the response to the new arrest by parole agents and a state's parole board. For example, offenders who are rearrested for drug possession while on parole can have their parole revoked and be returned to prison to serve the re-

Philosophers ask, "If a tree falls in the forest, but no one is there to hear it, does it make a sound?" Similarly, if someone commits a crime, but is not arrested or returned to prison, can he or she be considered a recidivist?

mainder of their supervision period. In this case, a prosecutor may not file charges, and therefore not seek a conviction, because the response by the parole agent and parole board achieved the goal of punishment or incarceration. On the other hand, if the crime was more serious, or the prosecutor did not view the parole board's response as sufficient, the prosecutor might choose to file charges and seek a conviction. Thus, some arrests of parolees will result in prosecution being sought, and potentially a conviction being obtained, whereas other cases will not result in additional formal processing through the courts.

Another measure of recidivism is a former inmate's return to prison. This can be influenced by rearrests or other violations of supervision/parole. As described above, inmates rearrested for a new crime while on supervision can be returned to prison because of this new arrest without being convicted, and these are usually considered "technical violations" as opposed to a return to prison for a new crime. Inmates returned to prison for violating the conditions of supervision other than a new arrest can be viewed as "purely" technical violators, and the reasons can include failure to report to their parole agent, not complying with treatment requirements, testing positive for drugs during urinalysis, etc.

Depending on which definition of recidivism is used, combined with practices and policies across the states in what threshold of behavior/violation justifies or requires being returned to prison, recidivism rates can vary dramatically.

However, the public's perception and understanding of recidivism can sometimes be skewed by what they are exposed to in the media. The media often focuses on only the most extreme examples of successes and failures of inmate reentry—those that became very successful following their release from prison or those that experienced horrific outcomes following their release from prison. In reality, most of those released from prison have experiences that fall somewhere in the middle of these two extremes. The reentry experience for most involves some successes and some failures; few experience no hurdles, and few commit horrible crimes of violence and murder. Thus, the reentry experience should be viewed on a scale or continuum, and not as a dichotomy of success or failure. Given the many needs that those coming out of prison often have, successfully addressing one or a few of these needs is often a significant accomplishment in incrementally moving someone from a lifestyle of criminality to the role of law-abiding, income-earning, responsible citizen.

Although somewhat dated, the only nationally representative recidivism rates for individuals released from prison were generated by the U.S. Department of Justice's Bureau of Justice Statistics based on a sample of inmates released from prison in 1994.[134] That study found that 67% of released inmates were rearrested for a new crime within three years and 47% were reconvicted of a new crime. More recent information collected from individual states by the Pew Center for the States found that nationally roughly 43% of inmates released from prison in 2004 were returned to prison within three years, with rates ranging from below 30% in a number of states to more than 50% in others.[135] The authors of the report concluded that comparing recidivism rates from state to state poses a number of challenges, due to differences in parole policies, lengths of supervision, and the nature of parole supervision.

Another problem with comparing rates of recidivism—as measured by official actions within the justice system, such as arrest, conviction, and return to prison—is that these data can be dramatically altered and changed as a result of changes in policies that influence arrests, convictions, and return to prison. For example, if a local police department reduces the number of police officers on patrol due to budgetary cuts or limitations, the number of police available to detect potential illegal behavior by those released from prison decreases. Similarly, if a local police department redeploys more officers to street patrol, or implements a crackdown on street-corner drug sales, the odds of illegal behavior by those released from prison (and everyone else involved in crime) being detected by the police increases. In other words, a decrease in the recidivism rate (as measured by rearrest) could be the result of improved programming and reentry planning by prisons and correctional agencies, or it could be the result of fewer police officers or a change in policing policy, or both. Similarly, if prisons become more effective at assisting inmates as they return back to society, but at the same time the police become more sophisticated at detecting illegal behavior or solving crimes, the recidivism rate based on rearrests could remain the same.

Similarly, differences in recidivism rates (as measured by return to prison) vary from state to state, often because of differences in post-prison supervision policies and practices. If one state has no post-prison supervision and another state has extensive supervision, then the latter is likely to have a higher rate of former inmates being returned to prison because technical violations by these individuals can more easily be detected. Even within individual states, these policies and practices can change over time. For example, a state may change its laws related to the duration of post-prison supervision and this may reduce the rate at which former inmates are returned to prison. Although the frequency or

Although crimes committed by those released from prison tend to be for nonviolent crimes or drug-law violations, often only the most heinous crimes committed by parolees are covered by the media and shape public perceptions.

prevalence of illegal behavior among former inmates may not change, the capacity of parole agents to detect it and return offenders to prison as technical violators does change.

An important factor to consider in recidivism is not just how *often* prison releasees reoffend, but *how* they reoffend. While some of the most shocking headlines of the past two decades have involved prison releasees committing horrendous crimes of murder and rape, which then prompted a number of changes to sentencing and prison release policy, the fact remains that these types of violent crimes are rare. Most crimes prison releasees are arrested for are property or drug crimes, indicative of releasees' limited economic opportunity and substance abuse disorders. Among the 1994 releasees the U.S. Department of Justice tracked in their national recidivism study, 33% of the rearrests involved drug-law violations and 34% involved property crimes.[136] Out of all the inmates released in 1994, only 1.4% were rearrested within three years for murder or sexual assault.[137] While these rearrest rates for the most serious forms of violence are relatively low, they still represent significant harm to victims, victims' families, and society as a whole, and often shape the perception of citizens and the electorate as to what types of behaviors those released from prison engage in once free.

Finally, another dimension of recidivism to consider is: who are the offenders, and when do they offend? For the most part, recidivists rearrested for new crimes following their release from prison tend to reoffend relatively soon after release—usually within the first six to 12 months. Nationally, of those rearrested within three years of release, almost one-half of the rearrests occurred within the first six months of release, and two-thirds of those rearrested were rearrested within one year of their release from prison.[138] Again, this is the period when the formerly incarcerated face the most significant changes to their lives—the transition from a highly regimented environment where their basic needs are met by the state to freedom and the expectation that they provide for their own needs. Released inmates who are younger, male, less educated, and have more extensive criminal histories have higher rates of recidivism, regardless of how recidivism is defined.

The degree to which inmates have access to rehabilitative programming is also related to recidivism. Still, rehabilitative programs that seek to improve specific conditions of individuals, such as their education level, substance abuse disorders, interpersonal skills, etc., are not perfect and cannot address larger societal issues and barriers that often challenge the success of those released from prison. Even if offenders' substance abuse problems have been eliminated, they still face significant barriers to employment, as described previously, and the ability to meet their basic needs of food, shelter, and safety.

Research has shown that recidivism rates have been reduced, on average, from 35% to 28% across standardized time periods.[139] These data are promising and encouraging, particularly given all of the other challenges former inmates face when released from prison. However, from a political and public policy standpoint, often these reductions in recidivism are not substantial enough. Often all it takes is for one highly sensationalized case, as rare as it might be, to bring unwarranted criticism to rehabilitative programs, which often results in the programs being eliminated and a "tough" response in terms of criminal justice policy.

Career Connections: Rehabilitative Professionals

Employment opportunities working on inmate reentry and rehabilitation include a variety of professions. These range from positions within correctional facilities or prison systems—such as teachers, counselors, psychologists, and parole agents—to positions in social service agencies that work with released inmates in the communities. Those who work in the area of child welfare will often encounter situations where the custodial parent is incarcerated or returning from prison or jail. Similarly, community-based substance abuse treatment and mental health agencies employ counselors and therapists who may work with both prison releasees and those who have not been incarcerated. Increasingly because of the emphasis on reentry, as well as the dedicated funding available through the Second Chance Act, many agencies are creating specialized units to work with those returning from a period of incarceration, including positions within employment agencies, vocational training, and job development.

The credentials needed for positions working within prisons as educators, substance abuse and mental health counselors, psychiatrists, and vocational training professionals vary from state to state as well as position to position. For most of these positions, a bachelor's degree would be the minimum requirement, but some, such as psychiatrists, would require advanced degrees. Others, such as substance abuse counselors, would require certification from state licensing boards that evaluate the credentials of clinical staff. The growing area of employment opportunities providing support for those coming out of prison—community-based treatment providers, job coaches for returning inmates, case managers—are usually within urban areas where many of the inmates are returning after their release, and often do not require college degrees. Indeed, many programs that hire mentors for those coming out of prison seek to hire formerly incarcerated individuals who know the community and can develop rapport with the clients to be served.

Chapter Summary

- Prisons face the challenge of achieving multiple goals—incapacitation, deterrence, punishment, and rehabilitation—with a diverse population of inmates who have vastly different sentences and conflicting public sentiment regarding what prisons should accomplish. While prisons attempt to balance these multiple goals, they must also seek to ensure that staff and inmates are safe from violence.

- Inmates enter prison with a wide range of needs that, if not addressed, will likely lead to continued involvement in crime. While many prisons have programs to address educational and vocational deficits, substance abuse, and mental health needs of inmates, they are generally small in scale and serve only a fraction of those needing services.

- Inmates released from prison face a variety of challenges as they reenter society, including unmet criminogenic needs, risks associated with the environments they return to, and societal attitudes that make obtaining employment and assimilating back into society a challenge.

- Increased attention to the process of inmate reentry has offered hope that inmates will receive more programming while incarcerated, and assistance and support as they transition from prison life to becoming law-abiding, contributing members of society. Both symbolically and materially, the federal Second Chance Act has changed the tone of the debate regarding inmate reentry in the United States and the need to reduce recidivism.

- Regardless of how it is measured—new arrests, convictions, or return to prison—the recidivism rate of those released from prison is at a level that has resulted in many people questioning the effectiveness of prisons at rehabilitation, although given the multiple goals of prisons, it is clear that rehabilitation has not been the focus of prisons since the 1960s.

Critical Thinking?

1. Many people point to the high costs of incarceration—roughly $25,000 per year—and the high rate of recidivism—roughly 50% of inmates return to prison within three years of release—and conclude that prisons are not effective. Do you think this is a fair statement?
2. From what you understand about how prisons operate, do you think there are ways to shift the current use of resources away from security staff toward more treatment staff without compromising the security of prisons? Are there opportunities for technology to improve the means by which prison security and/or prisoner rehabilitation is accomplished?
3. What role do you feel society as a whole should play in facilitating inmate reentry and improving the success of those released from prison? To what degree does the stigma of being a convicted felon, or a former inmate, influence successful reentry?
4. To what degree do you feel there is a disconnect between sentencing practices—sentence lengths, time served, determinate versus indeterminate sentencing—and achieving the goals of rehabilitation?

5. Explain why it is important to differentiate between the existence, scale, and quality of prison-based rehabilitative programs. Despite empirical evidence that certain types of programs do not work to reduce recidivism (i.e., drug education programs or self-help groups), why might prisons continue to operate them and offer them to large numbers of inmates?

6. Explain why, despite most prisons having drug abuse programs, most inmates in need of substantive substance abuse treatment do not receive it while incarcerated.

7. When the public considers the effectiveness of prisons, they often point to the recidivism rate and not to other measures of their effectiveness, such as incapacitation (few escapes) and ensuring safety of staff and inmates (few murders in prison). Why do you think the public fails to consider these dimensions of prison effectiveness?

8. Why do you think that, despite research showing that treatment can reduce recidivism and be cost-effective in the long run, many people still feel treatment does not work?

9. What are the different ways that recidivism has been defined or measured? Which one do you feel is the best measure of whether or not someone released from prison has engaged in illegal activity?

10. If recidivism rates of those released from prison increase (or decrease), explain how that change might have nothing to do with the success or failure of rehabilitative efforts within prisons.

Media

The Campbell Collaboration: http://www.campbellcollaboration.org/reviews_crime_justice/index.php
The Campbell Collaboration's Crime and Justice Reviews website contains objective reviews of the existing research into the effectiveness and efficacy of criminal justice programs and policies.

The Urban Institute: http://www.urban.org/projects/reentry-portfolio/index.cfm
The Urban Institute's Justice Policy Center website has an extensive collection of national and state-specific reports examining different aspects on inmate reentry, from model programs to original research documenting the experiences of those released from prison.

The National Reentry Resource Center: http://www.nationalreentryresourcecenter.org/
This website contains extensive information on reentry programs and policies across the United States, as well as webinars, announcements of upcoming meetings and training conferences, and links to other sites related to prisoner reentry.

Bureau of Justice Statistics: http://bjs.ojp.usdoj.gov/index.cfm?ty=datool&surl=/recidivism/index.cfm
The U.S. Department of Justice's Bureau of Justice Statistics website allows users to examine recidivism rates of those released from prison based on a nationally representative sample. Users can explore how various demographic, offense, and criminal history characteristics are correlated with different measures of recidivism, such as rearrest, reconviction, and return to prison.

Endnotes

1. Pew Center on the States. (2011). *State of Recidivism: The Revolving Door of America's Prisons*. Washington, D.C.: The Pew Charitable Trusts.

2. Mumola, C. J., & Karberg, J. C. (2006). *Drug Use and Dependence, State and Federal Prisoners, 2004*. Washington, D.C.: U.S. Department of Justice.

3. Beck, A. J., & Gilliard, D. K. (1995). *Prisoners in 1994*. Washington, D.C.: U.S. Department of Justice.

4. Glaze, L. E. (2010). *Correctional Populations in the United States, 2009*. Washington, D.C.: U.S. Department of Justice.

5. Rosenmerkel, S., Durose, M., & Farole, D. (2009). *Felony Sentences in State Courts, 2006: Statistical Tables*. Washington, D.C.: U.S. Department of Justice.

6. Bonczar, T. (2011). *Table 8. State Prison Releases, 2009: Time Served in Prison, by Offense and Release Type*. Washington, D.C.: U.S. Department of Justice.

7. West, H. C., & Sabol, W. J. (2008). *Prisoners in 2007*. Washington, D.C.: U.S. Department of Justice.

8. Glaze, 2010.

9. Glaze, L. E., & Bonzcar, T. P. (2006). *Probation and Parole in the United States, 2006*. Washington, D.C.: U.S. Department of Justice.

10. Langan, P. A., & Levin, D. J. (2002). *Recidivism of Prisoners Released in 1994*. Washington, D.C.: U.S. Department of Justice.

11. Travis, J. (2005). *But They All Come Back: Facing the Challenges of Prisoner Reentry*. Washington, D.C.: Urban Institute.

12. West, H. C. (2010). *Prison Inmates at Mid-Year 2009—Statistical Tables*. Washington, D.C.: U.S. Department of Justice.

13. Pew Center on the States. (2010). *National Research on Public Attitudes Towards Crime and Punishment*. Retrieved from http://www.pewcenteronthestates.org/uploadedFiles/wwwpewcenteronthestatesorg/Initiatives/PSPP/PSPP_National%20Research_web.pdf?n=6608

14. Krisberg, B., & Marchionna, S. (2006). *Attitudes of US Voters toward Prisoner Rehabilitation and Reentry Policies*. National Council on Crime and Delinquency.

15. Mitchell, O., Wilson, D. B., & MacKenzie, D. L. (2006). *The Effectiveness of Incarceration-Based Drug Treatment on Criminal Behavior*. Campbell Collaboration, Criminal Justice Review Group.

16. Cullen, F. T., & Gilbert, K. E. (1982). *Reaffirming Rehabilitation*. Cincinnati, OH: Anderson.

17. Buruma, I. (2005). "Uncaptive Minds." *The New York Times Magazine*.

18. Sparks, R. (1996). "Penal 'Austerity': The Doctrine of Least Eligibility Reborn." In R. Mathews and P. Francis (Eds.), *Prisons 2000* (pp. 74–93). New York, NY: St. Martins.

19. Buruma, 2005.

20. Byrne, J., & Hummer, D. (2007). "In Search of the 'Tossed Salad Man' (and Others Involved in Prison Violence): New Strategies for Predicting and Controlling Prison Violence." *Aggression and Violent Behavior, 12*(5), 531–541.

21. French, S. A., & Gendreau, P. (2006). "Reducing Prison Misconduct: What Works?" *Criminal Justice and Behavior, 33*, 185–218.

22. Ibid.

23. Kinlock, T. W., O'Grady, K. E., & Hanlon, T. E. (2003). "Effects of Drug Treatment on Institutional Behavior." *The Prison Journal, 83*(3), 257–276.

24. Welsh, W. N., McGrain, P., Salamatin, N., & Zajac, G. (2007). "Effects of Prison Drug Treatment on Inmate Misconduct: a Repeated Measures Analysis." *Criminal Justice and Behavior, 34*, 600–615.

25. Lipton, D., Martinson, R., & Wilks, J. (1975). *The Effectiveness of Correctional Treatment*. New York, NY: Praeger.

26. Martinson, R. (1974). "What Works? Questions and Answers about Prison Reform." *The Public Interest, 35*, 22–45.

27. Miller, J. (1989, March). "The Debate on Rehabilitating Criminals: Is It True that Nothing Works?" *Washington Post*.

28. Gendreau, P. & Ross, R.R. (1979). "Effective Correctional Treatment: Bibliotherapy for Cynics." *Crime and Delinquency, 25*, 46–489.

29. Andrews, D. A., & Bonita, J. (2010). *The Psychology of Criminal Conduct* (5th ed.). New Province, NJ: Anderson.

30. Bureau of Justice Statistics. (2011). *Key Facts at a Glance: Four Measures of Serious Violent Crime*. Retrieved from http://bjs.ojp.usdoj.gov/content/glance/tables/4meastab.cfm

31. Stemen, D., Rengifo, A. F., & Wilson, J. A. (2005). *Of Fragmentation and Ferment: the Impact of State Sentencing Policies on Incarceration Rates, 1975–2000*. New York, NY: Vera Institute of Justice.

32. Ibid.

33. *Mistretta v. United States, 488* U.S. 361 (1989).

34. Miller, 1989.

35. Serin, R. C., & Justice Institute. (2005). *Evidence-Based Practice: Principles for Enhancing Correctional Results in Prisons*. Washington, D.C.: U.S. Department of Justice, National Institute of Corrections, 4.

36. Stolz, B. A. (1992). "Congress and the War on Drugs: An Exercise in Symbolic Politics." *Journal of Crime and Justice, 15*(1), 119–136.

37. Sample, L. L., Evans, M. K., & Anderson, A. L. (2011). "Sex Offender Community Notification Laws: Are Their Effects Symbolic or Instrumental in Nature?" *Criminal Justice Policy Review, 22*(1), 27–49.

38. Stephan, J. J. (2008). *Census of State and Federal Correctional Facilities, 2005.* Washington, D.C.: U.S. Department of Justice.

39. Ibid.

40. Ibid.

41. Bureau of Justice Statistics. (2005). *Census of State and Federal Adult Correctional Facilities, 2005* [Computer file]. ICPSR24642-v2. Ann Arbor, MI: Inter-university Consortium for Political and Social Research.

42. Hardyman, P. L., Austin, J., & Peyton, J. (2004). *Prisoner Intake Systems: Assessing Needs and Classifying Prisoners.* Washington, D.C.: U.S. Department of Justice, National Institute of Corrections.

43. Stephan, 2008.

44. Ibid.

45. Maruschak, L. M. (2008). *Medical Problems of Prisoners.* Retrieved from http://bjs.ojp.usdoj.gov/index.cfm?ty=pbdetail&iid=1097

46. Ibid.

47. Olson, D., & Rozhon, J. (2011). *A Process and Impact Evaluation of the Southwestern Illinois Correctional Center Therapeutic Community Program During Fiscal Years 2007 through 2010.* Chicago, IL: Illinois Criminal Justice Information Authority.

48. James, D. J., & Glaze, L. E. (2006). *Mental Health Problems of Prison and Jail Inmates.* Washington, D.C.: U.S. Department of Justice.

49. Ibid.

50. Mumola & Karberg, 2006.

51. Glaze, L. E., & Maruschak, L. M. (2008). *Parents in Prison and Their Minor Children.* Washington, D.C.: U.S. Department of Justice.

52. Harlow, C. W. (2003). *Education and Correctional Populations.* Washington, D.C.: U.S. Department of Justice.

53. Maruschak, 2008.

54. Ibid.

55. Langan & Levin, 2002.

56. Ibid.

57. Stephan, 2008.

58. Ibid.

59. Olson & Rozhon, 2011.

60. James & Glaze, 2006.

61. National Institute on Drug Abuse. (2002). *Therapeutic Community—Research Report Series.* Washington, D.C.: Department of Health and Human Services.

62. Lurigio, A. J. (2000). "Drug Treatment Availability and Effectiveness: Studies of the General and Criminal Justice Populations." *Criminal Justice and Behavior, 27*(4), 495–528.

63. Wexler, H, Melnick, G., Lowe, L., & Peters, J. (1999). "Three Year Reincarceration Outcomes for Amity in-Prison Therapeutic Community and Aftercare in California." *The Prison Journal, 79*, 321–336.

64. Knight, K., Simpson, D., Chatham, L., & Camacho, L. (2004). "An Assessment of Prison-Based Treatment: Texas' In-Prison Therapeutic Community Program." *Journal of Offender Rehabilitation, 24*, 75–100.

65. Inciardi, J. A., Martin, S. S., Butzin, C. A., Hooper, R. M., & Harrison, L. D. (1997). "An Effective Model of Prison-Based Treatment for Drug-Involved Offenders." *Journal of Drug Issues, 27*, 261–278.

66. Olson & Rozhon, 2011.

67. Wilson, D. B., MacKenzie, D. L., & Mitchell, F. N. (2005). *Effects of Correctional Boot Camps on Offending.* Campbell Collaboration, Criminal Justice Review Group.

68. Gendreau, P. (2011). "Rehabilitation: What Works to Change Offenders." In F. T. Cullen & C. L. Jonson (Eds.), *Correctional Theory: Context and Consequences.* Los Angeles, CA: Sage.

69. Inciardi, J. A., Martin, S. S., & Butzin, C. A. (2004). "Five Year Outcomes of Therapeutic Community Treatment of Drug Involved Offenders Released from Prison." *Crime and Delinquency, 50*, 88–107.

70. Gendreau, 2011.

71. Andrews & Bonita, 2010.

72. Prendergast, M. L., Farabee, D., Cartier, J., & Henkin, S. (2002). "Involuntary Treatment Within a Prison Setting: Impact on Psychological Change During Treatment." *Criminal Justice and Behavior, 29*(1), 5–26.

73. Parhar, K. K., Wormith, J. S., Derkzen, D. M., & Beauregard, A. M. (200X). "Offender Coercion in Treatment: A Meta-Analysis of Effectiveness." *Criminal Justice and Behavior, 35*(9), 1109–1135.

74. Langenberger, N. A., & Lipsey, M. W. (2005). "The Positive Effects of Cognitive-Behavioral Programs for Offenders: A Meta-Analysis of Factors Associated with Effective Treatment." *Journal of Experimental Criminology, 1*, 451–476.

75. Ibid.

76. Bureau of Justice Assistance. (2007). *Residential Substance Abuse Treatment (RSAT) for State Prisoners Program FY 2008 Formula Grant Announcement.* Washington, D.C.: U.S. Department of Justice.

77. Lipton, D. S., Pearson, F. S., & Wexler, H. K. (2000). *Final Report: National Evaluation of the Residential Substance Abuse Treatment for State Prisoners Program from Onset to Midpoint.* Washington, D.C.: U.S. Department of Justice, National Institute of Justice.

78. Lawrence, A. (2009). *Cutting Corrections Costs: Earned Time Policies for State Prisoners.* Denver, CO: National Conference of State Legislatures.

79. Olson & Rozhon, 2011.

80. Ettner, S. L., Huang, D., Evans, E., Ash, D. R., Hardy, M., Jourabchi, M., & Hser, Y. (2006). "Benefit-Cost in the California Treatment Outcome Project: Does Substance Abuse Treatment 'Pay for Itself'?" *Health Services Research, 41*(1), 192–213.

81. Gerstein, D. R., Johnson, R. A., Harwood, H. J., Fountain, D., Suter, N., & Malloy, K. (1994). *Evaluating Recovery Services: The California Drug and Alcohol Treatment Assessment (CALDATA).* Sacramento, CA: California Department of Alcohol and Drug Programs Resource Center.

82. Gendreau, 2011.

83. Harlow, 2003.

84. James & Glaze, 2006.

85. Mumola & Karberg, 2006.

86. Mears, D. P., Winterfield, L., Hunsaker, J., Moore, G. E., & White, R. M. (2003). *Drug Treatment in the Criminal Justice System: The Current State of Knowledge.* Washington, D.C.: Urban Institute.

87. Mitchell et al., 2006.

88. Ibid.

89. Ibid.

90. Mears et al., 2003.

91. Farabee, D., Prendergast, M., Cartier, J., Wexler, J., Knight, K., & Anglin, M. D. (1999). "Barriers to Implementing Effective Correctional Drug Treatment Programs." *The Prison Journal, 79*(2), 150–162.

92. Inciardi, J. A., Martin, S. S., Lockwood, D., Hooper, R. H., & Wald, B. A. (1992). "Obstacles to the Implementation and Evaluation of Drug Treatment in Correctional Settings: Reviewing the Delaware KEY Experience." In C. G. Leukenfeld & F. M. Tims (Eds.), *National Institute on Drug Abuse Research Monograph Series #118: Drug Abuse Treatment in Prisons and Jails* (pp. 176–191). Washington, D.C.: U.S. Government Printing Office.

93. Farabee et al., 1999.

94. Morrissey, J. P., Steadman, H. J., & Kilburn, M. R. (1983). "Organizational Issues in the Delivery of Jail Mental Health Services." *Research in Community and Mental Health, 3*, 291–317.

95. Inciardi et al., 1992.

96. Culp, R. F. (2005). "Frequency and Characteristics of Prison Escapes in the United States: An Analysis of National Data." *The Prison Journal, 85*(3), 270–291.

97. Bureau of Justice Statistics, 2005.

98. Ibid.

99. Bureau of Justice Statistics. (2011). *Homicide Trends in the U.S.* Retrieved from http://www.bjs.gov/content/homicide/overview.cfm#gender

100. Mumola, C. J. (2007). *Medical Causes of Death in State Prisons, 2001–2004.* Washington, D.C.: U.S. Department of Justice.

101. West, H. C., Sabol, W. J., & Greenman, S. J. (2010). *Prisoners in 2009*. Washington, D.C.: U.S. Department of Justice.

102. Mumola, C. J., & Beck, A. J. (1997). *Prisoners in 1996*. Washington, D.C.: U.S. Department of Justice.

103. Bureau of Justice Assistance. (2011). *Second Chance Act Adult Mentoring Grants to Nonprofit Organizations FY 2011 Competitive Grant Announcement*. Washington, D.C.: U.S. Department of Justice.

104. Glaze & Bonzcar, 2010.

105. Rosenmerkel et al., 2010.

106. Bonczar, 2011.

107. Stephan, 2005.

108. Ibid.

109. Holsinger, A. M., Lurigio, A. J., & Latessa, E. J. (2001). "Practitioners' Guide to Understanding the Basis of Assessing Offender Risk." *Federal Probation, 65*, 46–50.

110. Bonta, A. (1996). "Risk-Needs Assessment and Treatment." In A. Harland (Ed.), *Choosing Corrections Options That Work: Defining the Demand and Evaluating the Supply* (pp. 4–54). Thousand Oaks, CA: Sage.

111. LaVigne, N. G., Kachnowski, V., Travis, J., Naser, R., & Visher, C. (2003). *A Portrait of Prisoner Reentry in Maryland*. Washington, D.C.: The Urban Institute.

112. LaVigne, N. G., Mamalian, C. A. Travis, J., Naser, R., & Visher, C. (2003). *A Portrait of Prisoner Reentry in Illinois*. Washington, D.C.: The Urban Institute.

113. LaVigne, N. G., & Thomson, G. L. (2003). *A Portrait of Prisoner Reentry in Ohio*. Washington, D.C.: The Urban Institute.

114. Watson, J., Solomon, A.L., LaVigne, N.G., Travis, J., Funches, M., & Parthasarathy, B. (2004). *A Portrait of Prisoner Reentry in Texas*. Washington, D.C.: The Urban Institute.

115. Hipp, J. R., Petersilia, J., & Turner, S. (2010). "Parolee Recidivism in California: The Effect of Neighborhood Context and Social Service Agency Characteristics." *Criminology, 48*(4), 947–979.

116. Visher, C., LaVigne, N. G., & Farell, J. (2003). *Illinois Prisoners' Reflections on Returning Home*. Washington, D.C.: The Urban Institute.

117. Inciardi, Martin, & Butzin, 2004.

118. Bureau of Justice Assistance, 2007.

119. Harrison, L. L., & Martin, S. S. (2000). *Residential Substance Abuse Treatment (RSAT) for State Prisoners Formula Grant: Compendium of Program Implementation and Accomplishments*. Newark, DE: Center for Drug and Alcohol Studies.

120. Lipton et al., 2000.

121. Mears et al., 2003.

122. Anglin, M. D., & Hser, Y. I. (1991). "Criminal Justice and the Drug Abusing Offender: Policy Issues of Coerced Treatment." *Behavioral Sciences and the Law, 9*(3), 243–267.

123. Mears et al., 2003.

124. Council of State Governments Justice Center. (n.d.). *Second Chance Act*. Retrieved from http://www.reentrypolicy.org/government_affairs/second_chance_act

125. Mills, L. (2008). *Inventorying and Reforming State-Created Employment Restrictions Based on Criminal Records: A Policy Brief and Guide*. The Annie E. Casey Foundation.

126. Pager, D. (2002). *The Mark of a Criminal Record*. Dissertation, Department of Sociology, University of Wisconsin, Madison.

127. Loftus, K. (2011, January 28). "More Public Job Applications Skip the Felony Conviction Box." *Capital News Service of the Michigan State University School of Journalism*.

128. ProCon.org. (2010). *State Felon Voting Laws*. Retrieved from http://felonvoting.procon.org/view.resource.php?resourceID=286

129. Ibid.

130. Sabol, W. J., West, H. C., & Cooper, M. (2010). *Prisoners in 2008*. Washington, D.C.: U.S. Department of Justice.

131. Kansas Correctional Industries. (n.d.). *Private Prison Industries: Private Companies Employing Kansas Inmates*. Retrieved from http://www.wichitamanufacturers.org/previoustours/EDCF%20Private%20Industry%20Brochure.pdf

132. Young, M. C. (2011). *Alternative Strategies for Funding Employment-Related Reentry Programs*. Northwestern University Law School.

133. Sachdev, A. (2011, March 15). "Illinois Seeks to Seize Prisoner's Wages." *Chicago Tribune*.
134. Langan & Levin, 2002.
135. Pew Center on the States, 2011.
136. Langan & Levin, 2002.
137. Ibid.
138. Ibid.
139. Mitchell et al., 2006.

Special Topics in Criminal Justice

Chapter 12: Juvenile Justice

Chapter 13: Victimology and Victims' Rights

Chapter 14: Criminal Justice in a Changing World

Chapter 15: The Future of Criminal Justice

Juvenile Justice

KEY TERMS

Adjudication hearing, Age of majority, Amenability hearing, Boot camp, Child Savers movement, Cottage reformatories, Deinstitutionalization, Diminished culpability, Disposition, Drug Abuse Resistance Education (D.A.R.E.), Houses of refuge, Juvenile delinquency, Juvenile waiver hearing, Monitoring the Future, Moral panic, National Youth Survey, *Parens patriae*, Reform schools, Scared-straight programs, Status offenses

CHAPTER OBJECTIVES

1. Describe the differences between juvenile courts and criminal courts.
2. Discuss the history of the juvenile justice system in the United States.
3. Analyze contemporary debates regarding the treatment and punishment of juvenile offenders.
4. Differentiate between types of juvenile corrections.
5. Explain theories of juvenile delinquency.
6. Examine patterns in juvenile victimization and offending.

Case Study: *Kent v. United States*

Prior to the Supreme Court's 1966 ruling in *Kent v. United States*, juveniles had few, if any, rights recognized within the legal system. This changed when the Supreme Court recognized that under the 14th Amendment to the Constitution, a juvenile had due process rights. In *Kent*, the court held that a juvenile has the right to counsel, the right to a hearing, and the right to be informed of what he or she is being charged with.

On September 2, 1961, an intruder entered a woman's apartment in Washington, D.C., stole her wallet, and raped her. Police discovered fingerprints at the scene and matched them to fingerprints taken from Morris A. Kent, a 16-year-old who had been on juvenile probation when he was 14 for housebreaking and an attempted purse-snatching. Kent was taken into custody by police on September 5, 1961. Rather than release Kent to a parent or take him to a juvenile court designee, as required by D.C. law, Kent was taken to police headquarters and interrogated for seven hours. That evening, he was taken to a local children's home, then picked up the next morning for further interrogation by the police. During his interrogations, Kent confessed to the incidents on September 2 and several other offenses. The day after his arrest, Kent's mother retained counsel for her son.

Under the D.C. Juvenile Court Act, Kent was legally a minor and therefore under the jurisdiction of the local juvenile court. The District of Columbia defines a minor as a person under the age of 18. Similar to other jurisdictions, however, Washington, D.C.'s juvenile code allowed for transfer (or waiver) of jurisdiction of a juvenile case to the adult criminal court on a case-by-case basis. To transfer a juvenile, a juvenile court judge was required to conduct a "full investigation" into the child's background and into the circumstances surrounding the offense. The court did not conduct an investigation and neither Kent, Kent's attorney, nor his mother were able to participate in a transfer decision hearing. Further, the court offered no written statement justifying Kent's transfer.

Kent was indicted on eight counts in the District Court and the case went to trial. A jury found Kent guilty on six of the eight counts and he received a total sentence of 30 to 90 years to serve.

After he was found guilty, Kent appealed his conviction and his case was eventually brought before the Supreme Court of the United States. There, the court ruled that the juvenile court's waiver of jurisdiction was procedurally invalid. The court ruled that the juvenile court, by not holding a hearing where Kent, his counsel, and his parents could have participated, violated Kent's fundamental due process rights. This violation made the waiver invalid, and the Supreme Court ordered that the case be remanded back to the juvenile court for a waiver hearing. A waiver can only be valid if the juvenile made it knowingly, intelligently, and voluntarily. The court found that Kent could not have made a knowing, intelligent, and voluntary waiver because he had been denied his due process rights.

Kent was one of the first times that the United States Supreme Court stepped in with regards to a juvenile case, and the ruling was significant. The court said that juvenile defendants were afforded rights under the 14th Amendment, including the right to counsel, the right to a hearing, and the right to know what they are being charged with.[1]

Delinquency

Delinquency can refer to many different things. Delinquency can refer to an account that has not been paid or a failure to do something that the law or duty requires. Within the context of this textbook, delinquency will refer to **juvenile delinquency**.

Juvenile delinquency can include any offense that would be a criminal offense if committed by an adult. Juvenile delinquency also includes status offenses—offenses that are criminal because of the defendant's age. Juvenile courts do not find juvenile defendants guilty or not guilty: instead, they find them either delinquent or not delinquent. In the United States in 2008, just over six out of every 100 youths from ages 10 through 17 were arrested.[2] In 1996, the juvenile arrest rate reached its highest levels in two decades, but by 2008, it had declined 33%.[3]

In order for a juvenile to be found delinquent, the burden of proof is on the state to demonstrate that the juvenile has committed a crime beyond a reasonable doubt. This occurs during the **adjudication hearing**, which is the juvenile equivalent to a trial.

A juvenile defendant can be found delinquent by committing either a crime or a status offense. Crimes are illegal acts committed by a person of any age, whereas a **status offense** is an offense that is only illegal or forbidden to a limited number of people—in this case, juveniles. A status offense describes any behavior that is illegal for children yet legal for adults.[4] Examples of status offenses include truancy, consumption of alcohol by a minor, running away from home, incorrigibility, and violating curfew ordinances. In 2004, U.S. juvenile courts processed an estimated 159,400 status offense cases, with truancy making up nearly 35% of these cases.[5] Liquor law violations, more commonly known as underage drinking, represent the second largest segment of status offenses at 19%.[6] In the late 1960s and early 1970s there was a movement, discussed later in this chapter, aimed at removing status offenses from the jurisdiction of the juvenile courts.

Like crime in general, much of juvenile crime is unreported. In order to better understand how much delinquent or criminal behavior juveniles are engaging in, academics, researchers, and politicians rely upon different methods for gathering information. The most common methods include the use of official records and self-report surveys.

One way that delinquency is measured is with the Uniform Crime Report (UCR). The UCR is an FBI compilation of information from law enforcement agencies from across the country. The UCR relies upon different agencies within each state to submit information about crimes that occur. Additionally, it compiles information from court records and police reports from across the country, and the information is further broken down by state and by major cities within each state.

Delinquency reporting is also done through self-reporting. Self-reporting allows juveniles, and others involved in criminal activity, to report their own

Juvenile delinquency
A finding of criminal behavior in the juvenile system.

Adjudication hearing
A hearing in which the juvenile offender is found to either be delinquent or not delinquent.

Status offenses
Offenses that can only be committed by a juvenile, not an adult.

criminal activity through anonymous questionnaires. Most commonly, self-reporting questionnaires are handed out at schools and local detention centers. Social scientists then use the answers to track trends. Social scientists like using self-reporting questionnaires because they think that juveniles are less likely to lie about their criminal activity when the answers are anonymous. If juveniles are required to answer out loud and in front of their friends, they may not be as truthful. They could be boasting and exaggerating to impress their friends, or they could be lying to hide their criminal activity. Without peer pressure, their answers are more likely to be truthful.

Another program that collects data on juveniles is **Monitoring the Future**, which annually surveys about **50,000** middle and high school students.[7] Monitoring the Future specifically monitors smoking, drinking, and illegal drug use among students from eighth through 12th grade. The survey asks the same questions each year and looks to see how responses to the questions change over time.

By following some of the same students year after year and by asking the same questions, Monitoring the Future is able to reflect how behaviors, attitudes, and values change across all age groups, especially as the students leave different environments and transition into new roles. The survey reflects the developmental changes that show up consistently, and shows the inherent differences within class cohorts that remain through all stages of life.

The final way that delinquency is commonly reported is through the **National Youth Survey**. The National Youth Survey is sponsored by the National Institute of Mental Health and contains a multitude of different surveys. Each survey is designed to look at specific issues ranging from gang participation to drug use to families. The questions are designed to find out participants' age, race, languages spoken, extracurricular participation, family income, family background, relationships with parents or guardians, and feelings about drugs, smoking, and alcohol. Researchers look at all of this information and try to un-

Monitoring the Future
A program that collects data on juveniles and is used by many social scientists.

National Youth Survey
A compilation of many different surveys measuring gang participation and drug use.

Monitoring the Future surveys juveniles regarding smoking, drinking, and illegal drug use.

derstand why some juveniles commit crimes and if there are any factors that would make it more likely for a juvenile to commit a crime.

The Nature and History of Juvenile Justice

Over the last few decades, the judicial system has dramatically changed the way that it treats children. Historically, in the American legal system children were treated either as property or as adults. The idea that a system should be created to deal with juveniles, and juveniles alone, did not develop until the 20th century.[8] Children under the age of five or six were considered to be the property of their parents: when they were delinquent, they were released to their parents to be dealt with as their parents saw fit. Depending upon the state, as soon as the child turned either five or six, he or she was considered to be an adult in the eyes of the law. It was assumed that a child of that age could form the requisite mens rea, or criminal intent, to be held responsible for their crimes.

Since the 1920s, the Supreme Court has continually recognized the rights of parents and guardians to raise and discipline their children. In 1923, the Supreme Court stated that it was "the natural duty of the parent to give his children education suitable to his station in life."[9] In *Prince v. Commonwealth of Massachusetts*, the Supreme Court reiterated its stance and said, "It is cardinal with us that the custody, care and nurture of the child reside first in the parents, whose primary function and freedom include preparation for obligations the state can neither supply nor hinder. . . . It is in recognition of this that these decisions have respected the private realm of family life which the state cannot enter."[10]

Dating back to the 1500s and 1600s, when children got into trouble that could not simply be disciplined by their parents or families, they could be punished in one of three ways. The first was the apprenticeship system, mostly used for middle- and upper-class children, who would serve as assistants to a skilled craftsman. A second form of punishment, used mainly for poor children, was the binding-out system, in which children could be bound out to any responsible adult for whatever purpose needed. A third form of punishment was church discipline, in which children were flogged, whipped, or branded by church officials. Punishments for children were not significantly different than those for adults.

Early social reformers pushed for changes within the judicial system. Initially, these changes took place outside the confines of the state-run legal system and were funded privately. Social reformers were the champions for change, and in 1825 the first house of refuge was founded. It later was followed by cottage reformatories and reform schools. Houses of refuge were precursors to modern-day juvenile facilities. These houses sought to help juveniles by rehabilitating them, educating them, and teaching them life skills. Cottage reformatories had goals similar to those of the houses of refuge. The main difference between the two was location: a house of refuge was located in the city and a cottage reformatory was located in the country. Juveniles housed in cottage reformatories were taught more agricultural life skills than industrial life skills. Reform schools were juvenile correctional institutes.

In 1899, Cook County in Illinois established the first American juvenile court. In doing so, Illinois was the first state to officially recognize that a child should not be treated the same way as an adult. The early juvenile court was influenced by the British legal doctrine of *parens patriae*. *Parens patriae*, Latin for "the state as parent," is the idea that the state has a duty to serve as a guardian of juveniles when parents are unable or unwilling to do so.[11] The state assumes the role of the parent and takes responsibility for punishing, guiding, teaching, and educating juveniles. Under the legal doctrine of *parens patriae*, the court is responsible for acting in the best interest of the child. By 1925, juvenile court systems had been established in 48 states.

Prior to 1904, the concept of adolescence had no distinct and formal legal meaning. In 1904, five years after the first juvenile court was established, psychologist Stanley G. Hall published *Adolescence*, an influential book in which he attempted to define adolescence. Hall described adolescence as a "turbulent period of physical, emotional, and sexual development during which youths needed to be shielded from adult duties and expectations."[12] Beginning to understand that juveniles and adults were different led to further development of the juvenile system. Psychology, a growing field at the time, helped bring attention to the differences between children and adults.

In recognizing the inherent differences between adults and children, the juvenile court sought to treat juvenile offenders differently. The juvenile court's mission was fundamentally different from that of the adult criminal court, which was designed to be punitive. Proceedings in adult courts could result in the loss of liberty, or in some cases, life. To ensure that the state does not overstep its authority in causing the loss of liberty or life, defendants within the adult system are protected by due process. In contrast, the juvenile system was designed to rehabilitate. The juvenile court's job was to fashion a **disposition**, or sentence, that would fit that particular juvenile's social and emotional needs.

Parens patriae
A legal theory, most often associated with juveniles and the mentally ill, that allows the state to step in and protect those who legally cannot protect themselves. Latin for "the state as a parent."

Disposition
The sentencing of a defendant.

Child Savers movement
A movement by a group of reformers in the early 19th century that sought to change the way juveniles were treated by the justice system.

The Child Savers Movement
Many of the changes and reforms that came about during the late 19th and early 20th centuries were the result of the **Child Savers movement**. Members of the Child Savers movement were concerned that children were being treated the same as adults. They were outraged that children could receive long prison sentences and be placed in jails with adult criminals, with no distinction between the two. Klein (1998) wrote that the Child Savers movement "believed society's role was not to ascertain whether the child was 'guilty' or 'innocent,' but 'What is he, how has he become what he is, and what had best be done in his interest and in the interest of the state to save him from a downward career.'" In their view, children should not be made to feel that they were under arrest or on trial, but rather that they were the object of the state's care.[13]

Child Savers wanted the state to step in to care for and rehabilitate wayward juveniles. They did not want to see juveniles punished as harshly as their adult counterparts, and believed that intervention and rehabilitation would "save" troubled juveniles. The Child Savers were biased in their efforts, and the majority of their efforts were directed at the poor or children of immigrants. Though middle- and upper-class white children misbehaved, they were shielded from state intervention or control.

Child Savers not only advocated for changes within the legal system, but also developed their own programs to rehabilitate juveniles, to educate them, and to teach them a craft. Many of the programs that were developed by the Child Savers, including orphan trains, houses of refuge, cottage reformatories, and reform schools, will be discussed further in the next section.

Critical Thinking   At what age should a child be considered criminally responsible?

Orphan Trains
Charles Loring Brace and other New York social reformers founded the Children's Aid Society, one of the major proponents of the orphan trains, in 1853. For the following 75 years, the Children's Aid Society helped to transport over 200,000 abandoned, orphaned, and homeless children from New York City to the Midwest.[14]

Brace's devotion to helping poor children was considered radical at the time. His goal was to transform New York's orphans into productive and contributing members of society by providing them with work opportunities, education, and a welcoming family atmosphere.[15]

Brace wanted to send New York's abandoned, orphaned, and homeless children to live with what he considered moral farm families in the Midwest. This idea was sometimes called "placing out." In placing out, a child was removed from an urban area and placed with a family in the Midwest. Brace believed the best way to help orphans improve their lives was to remove them from the poverty and debauchery of New York City streets.[16] Each orphan, upon being placed on an "orphan train," was given a small suitcase to carry his or her possessions. Often, this was just a change of clothes and nothing else.

The trains, carrying children as young as five and as old as 16, would travel from New York across the country and into Canada and Mexico. Upon arriving in each town, the children would be cleaned up, marched from the train, and taken to the meeting place. The meeting place could be anywhere—from the town square to a barn, a courthouse, or even a church. Usually, the meeting place had a platform where the children all stood. The townspeople were able to examine the children prior to agreeing to adopt them. Some were looking for children to help on the farm and would examine a child's teeth and muscles before selecting them. Still others were looking for young children, some were looking for only girls, and some were looking for boys. Once selected, children went home with their new families. If a child was not selected, he or she reboarded the train and headed to the next town.

After settling with their new families, the orphans were encouraged to forget about their old lives in New York. They were asked to forget about their parents, brothers, sisters, grandparents, aunts, uncles, and cousins—most never saw their New York families again.

Over 200,000 homeless children were transported from New York City to the Midwest on Orphan Trains.

© 2012 BY JIMMY LEE. USED UNDER LICENSE OF SHUTTERSTOCK, INC.

Orphan Trains were the precursor to state intervention in juveniles' lives and reflective of the middle- and upper-class bias of Child Savers. Poor, urban, and largely immigrant children were taken from big cities and given to farming families. It is questionable whether these children were indeed "homeless" or "abandoned." Brace's beliefs were founded in the idea of *parens patriae*. He and the others in the Children's Aid Society substituted their judgment for the judgment of the parents.

Houses of Refuge

The New York House of Refuge was the first juvenile reformatory in the country.[17] From the very beginning, the state of New York helped to organize, fund, establish daily procedures, and develop treatment programs. The New York House of Refuge officially opened in 1825 with six boys and three girls, and within a decade it had close to 1,700 inmates.[18] The New York House of Refuge did not close its doors until 1935—110 years after it first began to house inmates.

Within a few years of the New York House of Refuge opening its doors, other houses of refuge opened across the country. All followed similar models and had similar goals. Price (2009) writes: "These houses were created for juveniles who lived in an environment that produced bad habits. These habits were considered a setback for juveniles trying to escape the pressures of committing serious offenses."[19] Houses of refuge sought to rehabilitate, educate, and provide vocational training and religion to wayward youth. Children could be committed to the houses for vagrancy or because they had committed petty crimes. They could be committed indefinitely or sentenced for a period of time.

The houses were privately run, but accepted juveniles by court order. The Pennsylvania Supreme Court, in discussing a house of refuge's goal and why a house of refuge was the proper place for wayward youth, stated:

> "The House of Refuge is not a prison, but a school. . . . The object of charity is reformation by training of inmates: by imbuing their minds

Houses of refuge
Houses that sought to rehabilitate, educate, and provide vocational training and religion to juvenile offenders and vagrants.

with principles of morality and religion; by furnishing them with a means to earn a living, and above all, by separating them from the corrupting influences of improper associates. To this end, may not the natural parents when unequal to the task of education, or unworthy of it, be superseded by the *parens patriae* or common community."[20]

The concept of *parens patriae* has developed into a legal theory, most often associated with juveniles and the mentally ill, that allows the state to step in and protect those who legally cannot protect themselves. Again, the state used this theory to substitute its own decision-making abilities for those of the natural parents.

While houses of refuge fell out of favor almost 110 years after the first one opened, the doctrine of *parens patriae* is still seen today within the modern judicial system in Child In Need of Assistance (CINA) or Child In Need of Supervision cases (CHINS), as well as foster care.

CINA or CHINS cases are generally emergency cases where the state seeks to remove a child or children from the home of their natural parent or guardian. The state seeks to prove that the parent is not the proper person to have custody of the child, and that the child would be safer and better off in the care and custody of the state.

Cottage Reformatories and Reform Schools

In the mid-to-late 1880s, houses of refuge were facing harsh criticism. Critics focused on the fact that the houses were overcrowded, conditions were harsh, children were abused, and there was little rehabilitation. From these criticisms, the idea for the cottage reformatory was born. The cottage reformatory had many of the same goals as a house of refuge, but operated in a different manner.

Cottage reformatories
Reformatories that taught juveniles farm skills; designed to house 20 to 40 offenders in a cottage with cottage parents.

Cottage reformatories, unlike houses of refuge, were located in rural areas and tried to simulate family. A juvenile sent to a cottage reformatory would find himself or herself in a rural area with approximately 20 to 40 other juveniles. This process of moving a juvenile from the city to the country was commonly referred to as "placing out." The juveniles would then be broken up into smaller groups, and from there, they would go live in "cottages" with cottage parents. Cottage parents were adults that lived in the cottages with a small group of juveniles, helping simulate the family experience for the juveniles. These "parents" would teach them skills—mainly farming and manual labor—and be in charge of educating them. This was different from a house of refuge, which was located in the city and housed hundreds of juveniles in one location.

Reform schools
The first state-run schools designed to reform juvenile offenders.

Following on the heels of the houses of refuge and cottage reformatories, states began to build and fund state-run **reform schools**. In 1847, Massachusetts opened its first reform school. It was followed closely by New York in 1849, and Maine in 1853. Price writes:

"These schools were founded on strong principles: (1) Young offenders must be segregated from the corrupting influences of adult criminals, (2) Delinquents need to be removed from their environment and imprisoned for their own good and protection; reformatories should be guarded sanctuaries, (3) Delinquents should be assigned to reformatories without trial and with minimal legal requirements . . . (4) Sentences should be indeterminate, so that inmates are encouraged to cooperate in their own reform and recalcitrant delinquents are not allowed to resume their criminal careers, and (5) Reformation should not be confused with sentimentality."[21]

Reform schools remained in effect until the emergence of the modern-day juvenile justice system. Today, reform schools are referred to as juvenile detention centers. Reform schools are different from alternative schools, which will be discussed in more detail later in the chapter.

Emergence of the Juvenile Courts

In 1899, with the passage of *An Act for the Treatment and Control of Dependent, Neglected, and Delinquent Children*, Cook County, Illinois, established the first juvenile justice system. Within 25 years, 48 states had created a juvenile justice system based on the model started in Cook County.

The newly developed juvenile courts focused less on punishment and more on rehabilitation and socialization. Brink (2004) writes: "Separate juvenile correctional facilities were created that stressed educational and vocational training, sentences were often shorter, courts made greater use of probationary and other diversionary alternatives to incarceration, and the criminal records of juvenile offenders were not made a matter of public record in order to prevent stigmatization that might interfere with successful rehabilitation."[22]

For any criminal acts committed by juveniles, juvenile court holds jurisdiction.[23] In some cases, though, a juvenile court will transfer a juvenile matter to criminal court. A juvenile court may waive jurisdiction over a case, or in some instances, the legislature may mandate juveniles accused of certain crimes to be transferred to criminal court. In some jurisdictions, prosecutors have the power to choose whether to file a case in juvenile or criminal court.[24] These waiver hearings are sometimes called **amenability hearings** because the court must decide whether the juvenile will be amenable to treatment within the juvenile system or needs to be dealt with in the adult system.

Often, the prosecutor and the defense attorney are at odds over which court should have jurisdiction over a case where a juvenile defendant is involved. As discussed earlier, under *Kent v. United States*, a juvenile has the right to a juvenile waiver hearing.

Prior to a juvenile waiver hearing, a report is prepared for the judge. The report usually contains information regarding the juvenile defendant's background, including family, education, medical history, and past (if any) criminal record. The report also discusses the age of the defendant at the time the alleged crime occurred, the severity of the crime, and the defendant's amenability to treatment. The judge weighs each factor and decides whether the factor weighs in favor of the prosecution or the defense, or is neutral to both parties. Once the judge has finished weighing each factor, he or she decides whether to retain the case in the adult court or to remand the case back to the juvenile courts.

Amenability hearing
A hearing to determine how well a juvenile offender will respond to treatment within the juvenile system or if the juvenile is better suited to be in the adult system.

Juvenile waiver hearing
A hearing held before a judge to determine whether a juvenile will remain in the juvenile system or be transferred to adult criminal court.

Juvenile Court vs. Adult Criminal Court

Most people have some familiarity with the adult criminal court system through firsthand experience or television. They know that a defendant charged with a crime in the adult criminal system has certain trial rights—the right to confront witnesses; the right to a jury or bench trial; the right to remain silent; and the right to counsel. They know that a defendant can be found guilty or not guilty, and that the courtroom is open to the public.

The public's knowledge about the juvenile court system is much more limited. There are significant differences between the two systems. The first difference is the offenders themselves. The adult criminal system has exclusive jurisdiction over any defendant who committed a crime while over the age of majority (which varies depending on the state) and concurrent jurisdiction with the juvenile court system with a defendant who committed a crime while under the age of majority. Concurrent jurisdiction occurs when a defendant can be charged in the juvenile system, but, because of age, the severity of the crime, and the offender's prior criminal history, the prosecutor has charged the defendant within the adult criminal system. The defendant can only be tried in the juvenile system or the adult criminal system—not both. In *Breed v. Jones* (1975), the Supreme Court held that once a juvenile had been adjudicated in juvenile court, the juvenile could not be transferred to adult criminal court.[25] This would constitute double jeopardy.

When the adult criminal court and the juvenile court share concurrent jurisdiction over a defendant, a waiver hearing is held. In that hearing, a judge determines whether or not the defendant will be under the jurisdiction of the adult or juvenile system.

If a defendant is to be tried within the adult criminal system, all court proceedings are open to the public and the public has the right to examine the files, unless sealed by court order. If the defendant is placed under the jurisdiction of the juvenile system, the public's right to know is severely limited. Juvenile proceedings can be open or closed to the public, but juvenile records—including information about charges and sentences—are closed.

Accessibility to the public is one of the biggest differences between the juvenile and adult system. The public's accessibility to information regarding proceedings is limited because the goals of the two systems are drastically different. The adult criminal system is looking to punish those who break the law and deter them from doing it again, while the juvenile justice system is looking to rehabilitate. By limiting the public's access to juveniles' records, the juvenile jus-

Prior to a juvenile waiver hearing, the judge receives a report containing information about the crime and the juvenile defendant's background.

 **Critical Thinking** Why do you think that juvenile waiver hearings are so important in the juvenile justice system?

The juvenile justice system offers many offenders access to psychiatric and drug treatment and job training.

© 2012 BY LISA F. YOUNG. USED UNDER LICENSE OF SHUTTERSTOCK, INC.

tice system is hoping to allow juveniles to begin their adult lives without any of the baggage or limitations that attach to an adult criminal conviction.

Another major difference between the two systems is the programs that are available within the juvenile justice system. The juvenile system has many more programs available to it than the adult system, because the juvenile system is looking to rehabilitate offenders while the adult system is seeking to punish. Within the juvenile system, the offenders have access to psychiatric and drug treatment, job training, and other classes. These programs are designed to give the offenders the best chance of joining society as productive members.

With the emergence of the juvenile courts and the programs associated with them, the hope was that the juvenile system would be able to prevent juvenile offenders from re-offending once they became adults.

Critical Thinking   Assess the current differences between juvenile and adult courts. Do you believe further changes are needed to juvenile courts? What changes do you think would be appropriate?

Major U.S. Supreme Court Decisions   *Kent v. United States* was not the only major juvenile justice decision that came from the United States Supreme Court. The 1960s and 1970s saw the Supreme Court issue opinions that directly affected juvenile offenders. During this time, the Supreme Court was especially concerned because it felt that juveniles were receiving the worst of both worlds. In the juvenile system, they were being denied due process rights including the right to counsel, the right to cross-examine and confront witnesses, the right to a hearing, and so forth. *Kent*, and the cases that followed, sought to protect juveniles by guaranteeing them their due process rights.

In re Gault In 1967, the United States Supreme Court heard arguments in *In re Gault*.[26] On June 8, 1964, Gerald Francis Gault and his friend Ronald Lewis were taken into custody in Arizona because a complaint had been filed against the two by their neighbor, Mrs. Cook. Mrs. Cook alleged that the boys had telephoned her and made lewd, offensive, and sexually suggestive remarks.[27]

Gerald's parents were at work when he was taken into custody, and they did not learn that he was in custody until his older brother was sent to look for him at the Lewis home. On June 9, a hearing was held in front of a juvenile judge. No record of the hearing was made, and neither of Gerald's parents saw a notice of the hearing. A subsequent hearing was held on June 15, and again no record of the hearing was made.

Mrs. Cook, the complainant against Gerald and Ronald, was not present at the June 9 or the June 15 hearings. At the June 15 hearing, the probation officers filed a "referral report" with the juvenile judge, but the report was not given or disclosed to the Gaults. At the hearing, Gerald was committed as a juvenile delinquent to the State Industrial School until he reached the age of 21. At the time of his commitment, Gerald was 15 years old.

The Gaults appealed the case to the U.S. Supreme Court alleging that Gerald's due process rights were denied. Specifically, they alleged that Gerald, and they, had been denied notice of the charges, their right to counsel, their right to dispute evidence and to cross-examine witnesses, protection against self-incrimination, and a right to a transcript of the proceedings.

The Supreme Court reaffirmed its holding in *Kent v. United States* in *Gault* and addressed each of the Gaults' allegations. First, the court found that the Gaults did not receive adequate notice in the case. "Notice, to comply with due process requirements, must be given sufficiently in advance of scheduled court proceedings so that reasonable opportunity to prepare will be afforded, and it must set for the alleged misconduct with particularity."[28] If the juvenile offender or the offender's parents does not receive notice of a hearing, then the juvenile offender's due process rights have been violated.

Next, the court looked at the Gaults' allegation that they were denied the right to counsel. The court concluded that under the due process clause of the 14th Amendment, "the child and his parents must be notified of the child's right to be represented by counsel retained by them, or if they are unable to afford counsel, that counsel will be appointed to represent the child."[29]

The court then looked to see if Gerald's statements were lawfully obtained. The court found that neither Gerald nor his parents were informed of his right to not make a statement, and they were not informed that Gerald could be committed as a delinquent if he made an incriminating statement. The court found, after a careful examination of the language of the Fifth Amendment and looking at case law from other states, that the "constitutional privilege against self-incrimination is applicable in the case of juveniles as it is with respect to adults."[30] Because it was not made in the presence of counsel or his parents, and he was not made aware of his right to remain silent and to not make incriminating statements, Gerald's confession could not be used against him.

After the court addressed the validity of Gerald's confession, it addressed Gerald's right to confrontation and cross-examination. Mrs. Cook, the complaintant, was not present at any of the hearings, and Gerald could not confront her about her complaint or cross-examine her about anything that she said. Both were violations of his due process rights guaranteed under the 14th Amendment.

This case was important to the evolution of juvenile proceedings because the Supreme Court specifically held that juvenile defendants were to be afforded due process rights under the 14th Amendment.

Exhibit: Excerpt from *In re Gault*

"I think the Constitution requires that he be tried in accordance with the guarantees of all the provisions of the Bill of Rights made applicable to the States by the Fourteenth Amendment. Undoubtedly this would be true of an adult defendant, and it would be a plain denial of equal protection of the laws—an invidious discrimination—to hold that others subject to heavier punishments could because they are children, be denied these same constitutional safeguards. I consequently agree with the Court that the Arizona law as applied here denied to the parents and their son the right of notice, right to counsel, right against self-incrimination, and right to confront the witnesses against young Gault. Appellants are entitled to these rights, not because 'fairness, impartiality and orderliness—in short, the essentials of due process'—require them and not because they are 'the procedural rules which have been fashioned from the generality of due process,' but because they are specifically and unequivocally granted by provisions of the Fifth and Sixth Amendments which the Fourteenth Amendment makes applicable to the States."

In re Winship   Following *In re Gault*, the Supreme Court's next major decision involving juveniles was decided in 1970, in *In re Winship*.[31] In *Winship*, the court decided the question of "whether proof beyond a reasonable doubt is among the 'essentials of due process and fair treatment' required during the adjudicatory stage when a juvenile is charged with an act which would constitute a crime if committed by an adult."[32] The court decided that under the due process clause, the state was required to prove every element beyond a reasonable doubt in order to find the juvenile delinquent.

Samuel Winship, then 12 years old, was first found delinquent at a 1967 adjudicatory hearing. A judge in New York Family Court found that Winship had stolen $112 from a wallet in a locker. Winship's counsel asserted that the state needed to prove that he was guilty beyond a reasonable doubt, as required in adult criminal court. The judge disagreed and found that he only needed to find Winship delinquent by a preponderance of the evidence as required by New York statutes.

Later, at a disposition hearing, Winship was ordered to be placed in a training school for 18 months, with possible yearly extensions of his commitment until he reached the age of 18—six years later.

The case was appealed to the U.S. Supreme Court, which found that Winship was entitled to be found delinquent by the same standard, beyond a reasonable doubt, as an adult criminal charged with the same offense would.

This case further solidified the juvenile defendant's rights under the 14th Amendment and the due process clause. Most importantly, the decision held that a juvenile defendant could not be found delinquent of a crime unless the state had proved every element of the crime beyond a reasonable doubt. This changed the standard of proof in juvenile proceedings and made a juvenile proceeding more similar to an adult criminal proceeding.

Recent Changes in the Juvenile System

In 1974, Congress brought about changes within the juvenile system by enacting the Juvenile Justice and Delinquency Prevention Act (JJDPA).[33] The original act established the Office of Juvenile Justice and Delinquency Prevention to oversee programs established under the act. It was later updated in 2002.

This act provided funding for many community-based programs.[34] The JJDPA also set up requirements to assure that status offenders were not housed with delinquents in juvenile correctional facilities. In order for state juvenile justice facilities to receive federal grants, they needed to adhere to the requirements of the JJDPA.[35]

Today, the juvenile justice system does not seek to just rehabilitate and institutionalize. It seeks to rehabilitate through community-based programs to provide juveniles with the skills and tools to operate in the world.

Deinstitutionalization Movement

The deinstitutionalization movement developed in the 1970s, seeking to remove many of the nonviolent juvenile offenders and status offenders from being housed in juvenile detention centers, and to remove juvenile offenders from adult detention centers. Proponents of deinstitutionalization were fearful that status offenders and nonviolent offend-

The Supreme Court case of *In re Gault* held that juveniles were to be afforded due process rights under the 14th Amendment.

Deinstitutionalization
The process of removing status offenders from the juvenile court system and removing juvenile offenders from adult detention centers.

Exhibit: Excerpt from *In re Winship*

"We turn to the question whether juveniles, like adults, are constitutionally entitled to proof beyond a reasonable doubt when they are charged with violation of a criminal law. The same considerations that demand extreme caution in fact finding to protect the innocent adult apply as well to the innocent child. . . . In sum, the constitutional safeguard of proof beyond a reasonable doubt is as much required during the adjudicatory stage of a delinquency proceeding as are those constitutional safeguards applied in Gault—notice of charges, right to counsel, the rights of confrontation and examination, and the privilege against self-incrimination. We therefore hold, in agreement with Chief Judge Fuld in dissent in the Court of Appeals, 'that, where a 12-year-old child is charged with an act of stealing which renders him liable to confinement for as long as six years, then, as a matter of due process . . . the case against him must be proved beyond a reasonable doubt.'"

ers would learn violent behaviors while in custody. In 1980, Congress passed legislation prohibiting the United States from detaining juveniles in jails and correctional facilities, and specified that status offenders and nonviolent offenders should be removed from these institutions.[36] Juveniles who were being held for violent crimes were allowed to remain in secured juvenile detention facilities and in jails and local lockups.

Critical Thinking Should juveniles ever be housed in adult prisons? If yes, in what situations?

Contemporary Juvenile Corrections
The first goal of the juvenile justice system is to rehabilitate. The juvenile justice system hopes that rehabilitation will prevent juvenile offenders from entering the adult criminal justice system. The juvenile justice system has many tools that it employs to first try and rehabilitate and then to punish.

Juvenile Probation
As with adult offenders, juveniles can be placed on probation. Probation allows the juvenile justice system to keep tabs on offenders while at the same time keeping the offenders out of the more formal institutions like juvenile correction institutes.[37] Probation has ranges of supervision intensity. It can be highly intensive to essentially unsupervised.

Probation can follow a period of confinement, but when judges sentence juvenile offenders, they have many options when crafting a sentence. They can give the offender a straight period of confinement; a period of confinement followed by probation; a period of confinement, where either part or all has been suspended, followed by probation; or, finally, a period of straight probation.

While on probation, juvenile offenders are monitored by and have a probation agent who is specifically assigned to their case. While the duties of juvenile probation officers can vary by state or jurisdiction, these responsibilities typically include screening juvenile or family court cases, conducting a pre-sentence investigation of juveniles, and supervising juvenile offenders.[38] An offender who is on an intensive period of supervision may have to contact his or her probation agent a few times per week or every day either by phone or in person. An offender who is under less intensive supervision may only have to see the probation agent once a month.

The juvenile probation agent monitors offenders and makes sure that they are following their probation—if not, the agent will report the violations of probation to the court. Violating probation can lead to serious consequences for juvenile offenders. Periodically, probation agents will send the courts "violation of probation" reports. These reports are designed to keep the courts informed if an offender has violated any of the terms of his or her probation. Upon receiving a violation of probation report, the court will hold an evidentiary hearing in

FIGURE12.1 Juveniles in Residential Placement, 2006 Placement Status by State, 2006

State of Offense	Total	Committed	Detained	Diversion
United States	**92,721**	**64,532**	**26,238**	**1,864**
Alabama	1,752	1,251	492	6
Alaska	363	198	153	12
Arizona	1,737	1,083	636	12
Arkansas	813	660	144	12
California	15,240	8,955	6,120	159
Colorado	2,034	1,617	387	27
Connecticut	498	312	171	12
Delaware	303	165	135	0
District of Columbia	339	87	213	0
Florida	7,302	5,568	1,668	63
Georgia	2,631	1,398	465	768
Hawaii	123	96	30	0
Idaho	522	384	138	0
Illinois	2,631	1,872	747	9
Indiana	2,616	1,866	687	63
Iowa	1,062	822	198	42
Kansas	1,053	741	297	6
Kentucky	1,242	873	348	24
Louisiana	1,200	807	369	24
Maine	210	159	48	0
Maryland	1,104	525	570	6
Massachusetts	1,164	657	498	6
Michigan	2,760	2,115	630	15
Minnesota	1,623	1,221	390	12
Mississippi	444	219	174	51
Missouri	1,293	825	447	21
Montana	243	189	51	0
Nebraska	735	252	351	135
Nevada	885	561	321	3
New Hampshire	189	165	24	0
New Jersey	1,704	870	825	6
New Mexico	471	333	129	12
New York	4,197	3,432	735	30
North Carolina	1,029	804	222	3
North Dakota	240	222	18	0
Ohio	4,149	2,898	1,236	15
Oklahoma	924	624	294	6
Oregon	1,254	1,023	228	0
Pennsylvania	4,323	3,318	819	180
Rhode Island	348	330	15	3
South Carolina	1,320	816	504	0
South Dakota	597	474	117	6
Tennessee	1,419	1,035	372	15
Texas	8,247	6,396	1,809	42
Utah	864	606	252	6
Vermont	54	39	15	0
Virginia	2,310	1,455	849	6
Washington	1,455	1,011	432	6
West Virginia	579	417	162	0
Wisconsin	1,347	1,092	228	24
Wyoming	315	288	27	0
Not Reported	1,467	1,404	54	9

order to decide whether the offender is guilty or not guilty of violating his or her probation.

One of the most common and most serious ways a juvenile offender can violate his or her probation is to be found guilty of another charge. Other ways include not following a certain condition of probation. If the court finds the juvenile offender guilty of violating his or her probation, there are a number of recourses available to the judge. The judge can do one of several things: impose the balance of the offender's suspended sentence if the offender received a split sentence; impose up to the remainder of the suspended sentence if the judge suspended all of the time; continue probation; or terminate probation.

How a judge handles a violation of probation can differ from judge to judge, offender to offender, and case to case. Some judges prefer to continue offenders on probation and give them second chances, especially for minor infractions. Still others believe that by placing offenders on probation instead of strictly committing them, they have already given the offenders their second chance, and so if they violate probation, the only way to teach and reform them is to commit them.

In an effort to keep nonviolent juveniles out of juvenile detention centers as part of the deinstitutionalization movement, judges have put juvenile defendants into diversionary programs. The idea of diversionary programs was to divert a portion of the juveniles from the system. As the state created more ways to deal with offenders, it expanded the number of people it supervised, even though these programs were intended to replace or reduce more punitive options. This phenomenon is known as "net-widening," and it is an ongoing issue throughout the criminal justice system, not just the juvenile system.[39]

Career Connections: Juvenile Probation Officer

A juvenile probation officer supervises juvenile offenders who have been put on probation by a judge in the juvenile court. The juvenile probation officer's responsibilities include supervising juveniles, maintaining communications with judges and law enforcement agencies, and connecting juveniles with needed resources in the community. Juvenile probation officers prepare and maintain case records and various reports, forms, and court documents regarding the juveniles they oversee.

A juvenile probation agent may be required to make inquiries into probationers' problems, antecedents, character, family history, and environment. Further, he or she may make recommendations to the courts through written reports and oral testimony to be used during disposition. Juvenile probation officers also testify at hearings and transport clients between residential and correctional facilities.

A juvenile probation officer must have a bachelor's degree in criminal justice, social work, psychology, or a related field. The average salary for a probation agent in the United States is $47,200 per year.[40]

Community-Based Corrections

In the 1980s, the idea of community-based corrections began to take hold. Community-based correctional facilities provide nonviolent offenders with the rehabilitative programs that they need. Funding for community-based corrections was provided by the Juvenile Justice and Delinquency Prevention Act of 1974. The act defined a community-based facility to be a "small, open group home or other suitable place located near the juvenile's home or family and programs of community supervision and service which maintain community and consumer participation in the planning operation, and evaluation of their programs which may include, but are not limited to, medical, educational, vocational, social, and psychological guidance, training, special education, counseling, alcoholism treatment, drug treatment, and other rehabilitative services."[41] Examples of community-based correction centers include residential and group homes.

The goal of the community-based correction facility was to take nonviolent offenders out of the jails and prisons and place them into the community under strict scrutiny. Offenders can enter a community-based correctional program in one of two ways. The first is after they have served all or part of their sentence. Upon release, the offender is released to the custody of the community-based correction program, where that program will monitor the offender and help the offender adjust to life outside of jail or prison walls.

An offender can also enter a community-based correctional program without being incarcerated. The judge, instead of sentencing the offender to jail, can sentence the offender to report directly to the program that has been ordered.

Community-based correctional programs gained popularity for a number of reasons. One of the biggest reasons that judges began sentencing defendants to these programs was because the programs provided for greater supervision than normal probation. Defendants subject to the rules of the community-based programs are usually drug tested, or on house arrest, or living in halfway houses. The programs were designed to help juveniles better adapt to the world that they were going to be released into and to help their families cope with the problems they would soon be facing.

Additionally, community-based correctional programs are much cheaper then housing an inmate in a normal correctional facility. They also help to alleviate overcrowding issues that are prevalent in many of today's correctional facilities.

Juvenile Detention Centers

Juvenile detention centers (JDCs), sometimes called youth detention centers, house and detain juvenile offenders awaiting their hearing dates and those who have already been adjudicated. Anyone who has committed a crime while under the age of majority can be housed in a juvenile detention center.

The **age of majority** is when a person is legally recognized as an adult. This can vary from state to state. For the majority of states, an individual reaches the age of majority at 18, but in other states this age can span from 19 to 21.

Age of majority
The age at which a person reaches adulthood in the eyes of the law. This age is generally 18, but can vary from state to state.

FIGURE 12.2 Age of Majority by State and United States Possession

State	Age	State	Age
Alabama	19	Nebraska	19
Alaska	18	Nevada	18
Arizona	18	New Hampshire	18
Arkansas	18	New Jersey	18
California	18	New Mexico	18
Colorado	18	New York	18
Connecticut	18	North Carolina	18
Delaware	18	North Dakota	18
District of Columbia	18	Ohio	18
Florida	18	Oklahoma	18
Georgia	18	Oregon	18
Hawaii	18	Pennsylvania	21
Idaho	18	Puerto Rico	21
Illinois	18	Rhode Island	18
Indiana	18	South Carolina	18
Iowa	18	South Dakota	18
Kansas	18	Tennessee	18
Kentucky	18	Texas	18
Louisiana	18	Utah	18
Maine	18	Vermont	18
Maryland	18	Virginia	18
Massachusetts	18	Virgin Islands	18
Michigan	18	Washington	18
Minnesota	18	West Virginia	18
Mississippi	21	Wisconsin	18
Missouri	18	Wyoming	18
Montana	18		

Juvenile detention centers were created to separate adult inmates from juvenile offenders. The prevailing thought was that a juvenile offender was not physically or emotionally mature enough to handle the day-to-day trials that being housed in an adult facility would bring. JDCs were originally thought to be safer and easier places for juveniles to be placed.

Recent studies have shown that JDCs are facing many of the same problems that the adult facilities are facing. Juvenile delinquents are coming in with serious health problems and mental illnesses that the facilities are not capable of handling. Research has found that most juvenile delinquents quality for at least one diagnosable mental health disorder.[42] High rates of mental health issues have turned the juvenile detention centers from institutions meant to punish and hold offenders into surrogate mental health facilities.[43] Thus, juvenile detention centers need to develop more programs to help deal with the mental health needs of juveniles.

JDCs are also facing increased scrutiny as they move from being state-run centers to being run by the private sector. In 2009, two judges in Pennsylvania were accused of receiving financial kickbacks from a privately run juvenile detention center for each juvenile that was sent to them. The scheme is alleged to have run from 2004 to 2009, and involved over 5,000 juveniles. The judges are

Juvenile detention centers face many of the same problems as adult facilities.

alleged to have made over $2 million in the scheme. In August 2011, one of the judges was sentenced to 28 years in prison for his role. Many of the juveniles who appeared before the judges appeared without counsel, despite the 1976 ruling in *In re Gault* that guaranteed juvenile offenders the right to counsel. Many were first-time offenders, and many had probation agents that recommended they not be sent to detention centers.[44] Despite this, the judges sent the offenders to the privately run facilities.[45] As a result of this scandal, more attention is being paid to who is running JDCs and how many juveniles are being sent to them.

Boot Camps and Scared-Straight Programs

During the "get tough" movement, crime deterrent programs such as boot camps and scared-straight programs gained popularity with the public. These programs were designed to "scare" juvenile offenders into behaving correctly.

Boot camps are among the most well known of the alternative programs within the juvenile system. These camps follow the model of a military basic-training program and are focused on disciplining juvenile offenders.[46]

Boot camps pride themselves on their military structure. The goal is to "break" troubled juveniles and return them to their parents or guardians as obedient children. While attending boot camps, juvenile offenders are placed within small groups usually comprised of other juvenile offenders. One suggested change to the boot camp model is that the boot camp population not be selected by judges, but instead by correctional officials who would select participants based on juveniles who have been sentenced to or already confined in a facility.[47] During his or her time in the program, the juvenile offender focuses on one or two skills instead of a wide range of skills more commonly seen in other programs like community-based programs.[48]

Boot camps do not look to coddle their participants. They believe that participants will benefit from hard work. Boot camps, unlike other programs, do not provide their participants with therapy or other rehabilitative programs.

Boot camp
An alternative to juvenile correctional facilities that follows the model of a military basic-training program and is focused on disciplining juvenile offenders.

Some evidence suggests that boot camps may be doing more harm than good. According to a report by the Surgeon General's Office, "Compared to traditional forms of incarceration, boot camps produced no significant effects on recidivism in three out of four evaluations and trends toward increased recidivism in two. The fourth evaluation showed significant harmful effects on youths, with a significant increase in recidivism."[49]

Scared-straight programs involve taking juvenile delinquents, or children who may be at risk of becoming delinquent, to prison facilities. Scared-straight programs are designed to give participants a firsthand view of prison life and allow them to interact with adult inmates, in the hope that it will deter them from future offending.[50] Scared-straight programs began in the 1970s in New Jersey.[51] The first scared-straight programs featured inmates who were serving life sentences telling juveniles about life in adult prison. The prisoners spared no details, and the juveniles were told stories of rape and murder.[52] These stories aimed to scare juveniles away from a life that would lead them to prison.

Despite reports of early success rates, questions have arisen as to the effectiveness of scared-straight programs. The University of Maryland published an evaluation of over 500 crime prevention programs and found evidence that scared-straight programs were not an effective crime deterrent.[53] The study showed that juveniles' success in reentering the outside world depends more heavily upon their families, communities, and labor market. Still, these programs remain in popular use all over the country and the world, in the hope of discouraging juveniles from continuing a downward spiral that will eventually land them in adult jails or prisons.

Scared-straight programs
Programs designed to scare juveniles into behaving correctly, including boot camps and juveniles visiting inmates in prisons.

Death Penalty for Juveniles

Prior to 2005, seven states—Georgia, Louisiana, Missouri, Oklahoma, South Carolina, Texas, and Virginia—allowed for juveniles to be sentenced to death if they committed their crime prior to the age of majority. Most states did not. In 2005, the Supreme Court case of *Roper v. Simmons*[54] established a clear judgment on this issue.

The defendant, Christopher Simmons, was 17 years and three months old when he planned and committed a murder. On September 8, 1993, Simmons and one other friend entered the home of Mrs. Shirley Crook, bound her in duct tape, and drove her to a state park. Once there, Simmons and his co-defendant threw Mrs. Crook from a bridge and watched her drown.[55]

Simmons, who had begun bragging about the murder, was quickly found and taken into police custody. Upon confessing, Simmons was charged with burglary, kidnapping, stealing, and murder in the first degree. Simmons was charged as an adult, as under Missouri law a juvenile who has turned 17 must be charged as an adult.[56]

At trial, the jury found Simmons guilty of first-degree murder. At the sentencing stage, the state sought to prove three mitigating factors in order to sentence Simmons to death. First, that Simmons committed the murder for the purpose of receiving money. Next, that Simmons committed the murder to avoid or interfere with his lawful arrest. Finally, that the murder was of depraved mind and was outrageously vile, horrible, and inhuman.[57] The jury found that the state had proved its aggravating factors and recommended a sentence of death. Upon their recommendation, the trial judge sentenced Simmons to death.

After his trial concluded and he was sentenced, Simmons appealed to the Missouri Supreme Court and cited the U.S. Supreme Court's decision in *Atkins v. Virginia*,[58] which held that it was a violation of the Eighth Amendment to place a mentally retarded person to death.[59] Simmons argued that the reasoning in *Atkins* applied to his case. The Missouri Supreme Court agreed and amended Simmons' sentence to life imprisonment without eligibility for parole, probation, or release unless by an act of the governor.[60]

The modified decision was appealed to the United States Supreme Court, which affirmed the new sentence. It held that no one who committed an offense under the age of 18 shall be put to death for that offense, because it violates the Eighth Amendment that prohibits cruel and unusual punishment.[61] The court focused on three important differences between juveniles and adults. The first was that juveniles tend to lack maturity and do not have a fully developed sense of responsibility, which leads to more poor decisions than in adults. Secondly, juveniles tend to have less control over their environments because they can be easily influenced by peer pressure and other negative influences. Finally, the court recognized that the character of a juvenile is not as well developed as it is in an adult.

The Supreme Court considered all of these factors and concluded that juveniles have **diminished culpability**, or the inability to fully understand the consequences of their actions. The court considered a juvenile's limited culpability to be similar to that of a mentally handicapped defendant. Using the same reasoning as in the *Atkins* decision, the court held that it would violate the cruel and unusual punishment clause to execute a juvenile who was under the age of 18 when the crime was committed.

This ruling raises new questions for the death-penalty states. If a defendant who is found guilty of committing a murder or any other death-penalty-eligible offense was under the age of 18 at the time of the offense, what is the maximum punishment he or she should be eligible for? Many states have settled on the term of life without the possibility of parole, which means that a defendant will never have the opportunity to be eligible for a parole hearing.[62] A "life without parole" sentence, or LWOP, is different from a sentence of life with the possibility of parole. A "life with" sentence means that a defendant is eligible for parole, after serving a statutory number of years, and may petition the parole board for a parole hearing.

Diminished culpability
The inability to fully understand the consequences of an action because of age or cognitive abilities.

Critical Thinking Do you believe that life without possibility of parole is an appropriate sentence for juveniles convicted of violent crimes?

Exhibit: *Roper v. Simmons*

"Three general differences between juveniles under 18 and adults demonstrate that juvenile offenders cannot with reliability be classified among the worst offenders. First, as any parent knows and as the scientific and sociological studies respondent and his *amici* cite tend to confirm, '[a] lack of maturity and an underdeveloped sense of responsibility are found in youth more often than in adults and are more understandable among the young. These qualities often result in impetuous and ill-considered actions and decisions.' . . .

The second area of difference is that juveniles are more vulnerable or susceptible to negative influences and outside pressures, including peer pressure. . . . This is explained in part by the prevailing circumstance that juveniles have less control, or less experience with control, over their own environment. . . .

The third broad difference is that the character of a juvenile is not as well formed as that of an adult. The personality traits of juveniles are more transitory, less fixed. . . .

These differences render suspect any conclusion that a juvenile falls among the worst offenders. The susceptibility of juveniles to immature and irresponsible behavior means 'their irresponsible conduct is not as morally reprehensible as that of an adult.' Their own vulnerability and comparative lack of control over their immediate surroundings mean juveniles have a greater claim than adults to be forgiven for failing to escape negative influences in their whole environment. The reality that juveniles still struggle to define their identity means it is less supportable to conclude that even a heinous crime committed by a juvenile is evidence of irretrievably depraved character. From a moral standpoint it would be misguided to equate the failings of a minor with those of an adult, for a greater possibility exists that a minor's character deficiencies will be reformed."

Problematic Issues in Juvenile Justice

In recent years, the public has grown increasingly concerned that the juvenile justice system is not working effectively enough.[63] The media constantly covers violent juvenile crime, and the public is calling for tougher punishment for juvenile offenders. The focus on the rise of gangs and drug and alcohol abuse has contributed to the public's panic, which is sometimes referred to as a moral panic.

Moral panic
A term coined by Stanley Cohen describing the public's irrational fear and concern over a particular issue.

Stanley Cohen, a leading sociologist, coined the phrase "moral panic" in 1972 in his book *Folk Devils and Moral Panics*.[64] He focused on the media's help in causing a moral panic by portraying a group of people—in this instance, juveniles—as a threat to society's values. The media's portrayal of juvenile crime has led the public to believe that troubled youths are the downfall of society. One of the largest contributors to the moral panic is the media's coverage of extreme cases that include children killing children. Although these cases are very rare, the sensationalist way in which the media covers these crimes captures the nation's attention and often leads the public to believe that youth-on-youth violence and murder are more common than they actually are.

But while the public is calling for the juvenile justice system to crack down on violent juvenile offenders, many fail to realize or understand the complexities of the juvenile system. The juvenile system is currently experiencing many of the same problems as adult correctional facilities. Like adult correctional facilities, juvenile correctional facilities are struggling to provide mental health care so desperately needed by inmates. Juvenile correctional facilities have reported high levels of drug abuse. A survey conducted in 2000 found that nearly 56% of boys and 40% of the girls tested positive for drugs at the time of their arrest.[65] Some juvenile offenders are either a member of a gang prior to entering the juvenile system or are a member of a gang by the time they leave.[66]

Gangs The Bloods, the Crips, and the Aryan Brotherhood are three of the most well known gangs, but hundreds of others exist within jails, prisons, juvenile detention centers, and out on the street. An FBI investigation concluded, "Some 20,000 violent street gangs, motorcycle gangs, and prison gangs with nearly one million members are criminally active in the U.S. today. Many are sophisticated and well organized; all use violence to control neighborhoods and boost their illegal money-making activities, which include robbery, drug and gun trafficking, fraud, extortion, and prostitution rings."[67]

Gang members do not just commit violent crimes. Howell (1993) noted that "violent behavior is not the only behavior in which gang members partake. For the most part, gang members 'hang out' and are involved in other normal adolescent social activities, but drinking, drug use, and drug trafficking are also common."[68]

Gang presence, in addition to the streets, jails, prisons, and juvenile detention centers, is also active in schools. According to an August 2010 survey by the National Center on Addiction and Substance Abuse, 45% of high school students say that their school has gangs or students who consider themselves to be part of a gang. For middle school students, this number is 35%.[69]

As the presence of gangs in schools continues to grow, schools must adjust in order to reduce and prevent gang violence within the school. Two different approaches to preventing gangs from having a large presence in schools prevail.

One is the whole-school approach. Under the whole-school approach, schools set strict standards of behavior to assure that gang-related activity is not present in schools. Staff members are trained to identify gang trends and to closely monitor known gang members. Students also must adhere to dress-code policies that forbid gang identifiers or paraphernalia.[70]

Another approach is the individual gang intervention approach. The individual gang intervention approach has many of the same aspects of the whole-school approach, but gives extra support to particular students known to be involved in gangs. Under this approach, staff members provide gang-involved students with specific skills and support to help them pull themselves away from gang life.[71]

State legislatures have also passed legislation in hopes of reducing gangs. Many have passed "anti-loitering" laws, which are primarily targeted at juveniles. Anti-loitering laws allow for police to break up or arrest groups of people, particularly teenagers, who are hanging out in front of storefronts and on street corners. The fear is that these teenagers are members of gangs and will somehow harm businesses.

Gang crime can include robbery and trafficking as well as violent crime.

© 2012 BY LJUPCO SMOKOVSKI. USED UNDER LICENSE OF SHUTTERSTOCK, INC.

Anti-loitering laws have come under scrutiny and some, like in Chicago, have been struck down as unconstitutional because they violate citizens' rights to gather on the streets. The right to peaceably assemble is guaranteed by the Constitution under the First Amendment.

Anti-loitering laws are not the only laws that are aimed at juveniles. Both Illinois and New Mexico enacted anti-sagging laws because the public associated low-slung pants with rap music, gangs, and other parts of society it disapproved of.[72] Other states have enacted laws that ban skateboarding because there is a perception that kids on skateboards will destroy property and cause trouble.

Many of these "tough on youth" policies and laws are fueled by moral panics and by the public's perception that certain juveniles are dangerous to society. The public's perception is in some cases shaped by sensationalist media stories on juvenile crime, which do not always provide an accurate portrait of what is actually happening. As a result, many citizens and lawmakers have developed a fear of youth that overestimates the prevalence and frequency of juvenile crime.

Searches in Schools   The rights of juveniles in schools is an important issue that has been heavily debated in the criminal justice system. What rights does a student have in school that protects him or her against a Fourth Amendment search or seizure? Do schools have to follow the same standards as police when conducting a search? The U.S. Supreme Court has attempted to answer these questions through a series of rulings.

In 1985, in *N.J. v. T.L.O.*, the Supreme Court held that, "under ordinary circumstances, a search of a student by a teacher or other school official will be 'justified at its inception' when there are reasonable grounds for suspecting that the search will turn up evidence that the student has violated or is violating either the law or the rules of the school."[73] This decision affirmed that schools can conduct searches based on reasonable suspicion because of the nature of the location. This is a different standard than the one that police must abide by. Police must have probable cause in order to conduct a search or a seizure.

The Supreme Court further clarified its position on searches within the school in 1995, in *Vernonia School District 47J v. Acton*, a case that dealt with urinalysis of student-athletes.[74] The court determined that conducting urinalysis on student-athletes was reasonable and not an invasion of privacy because student-athletes had been found to be the leaders of drug culture within the schools. The court found that this was reasonable and did not declare these urinalysis tests unconstitutional. However, in 2009, the court did find that a student's rights guaranteed under the Fourth Amendment were violated when she was subjected to a strip search because there was no reasonable suspicion to believe that she was hiding drugs in her underwear.[75]

Ethics and Professionalism: Searches in Schools

Consider this scenario. A school principal hears from a student that members of the school's lacrosse team are using drugs. What should the principal do? Does the information from one student qualify as reasonable suspicion sufficient enough to conduct a search of the lacrosse players' bags? Should she gather more information before conducting a search?

Consider a scenario in which the principal decides to search the lacrosse players' bags when they return to the school after playing an away game. As the players exit the team bus, the principal pulls each student aside and asks him to open his bag so that she may search it. After the search is complete, the principal has not found any drugs, but she has discovered that several members of the team are carrying Swiss Army knives. The boys claim that they have the Swiss Army knives because they are tools they use to fix their lacrosse sticks.

Swiss Army knives are classified as weapons under the school's policy, and the policy states that the principal must report all students who have weapons in their possession on school policy. Should the principal report the boys to the police? Should she be legally compelled to do so? What would you do?

Drugs and Alcohol Drug use is an ever-present problem in today's society, and juveniles are no exception. Law enforcement agencies have increased their focus on drug crimes, launching undercover investigations to identify drug dealers who sell to minors. Legislatures have passed punitive laws against the use, possession, and sale of illegal drugs.[76]

In the 1970s, President Richard Nixon began America's "War on Drugs." The War on Drugs focuses on reducing the foreign and illegal drug trade with the hope of decreasing the use and production of drugs in America. Forty years after President Nixon began the U.S. government's War on Drugs and 50 years after the United Nations had its first conference on narcotics, the Global Commission on Drug Policy issued a report examining drug policies both nationally and internationally. In the report, the United Nations estimates that consumption of drugs from 1998 to 2008 has steadily increased and that the United States's War on Drugs has had little impact.[77] In 1998, 12.9 million people used opiates; this number grew to 17.35 million people in 2008, an increase of nearly 34.5%.[78] In that same time frame, cocaine use rose 27% and cannabis use rose 8.5%.[79]

Further, the commission compared the Dutch city of Amsterdam, famous for its cannabis cafes, to the U.S. city of San Francisco to see if different regulatory environments affected cannabis use.[80] The commission's report concluded, "Our findings do not support claims that criminalization reduces cannabis use and that decriminalization increases cannabis use . . . With the exception of higher drug use in San Francisco, we found strong similarities across both cities."[81]

Finally, the study concluded that "countries that continue to invest mostly in a law enforcement approach (despite the evidence) should focus their repressive actions on violent organized crime and drug traffickers, in order to reduce the harms associated with the illegal drug market."[82]

Los Angeles, California, started the first **Drug Abuse Resistance Education (D.A.R.E.)** program in 1983 to help keep kids off of drugs. The D.A.R.E. program consists of police-officer-led classroom lessons that teach children how to avoid drugs and violence and resist peer pressure. Shortly after the D.A.R.E. program began in 1983, First Lady Nancy Reagan released the "Just Say No" slogan. The slogan was designed to encourage juveniles to just say no to drugs and peer pressure.

Nearly 75% of schools in America have a D.A.R.E. program, but despite its popularity, D.A.R.E. has proven to be counterproductive. Many studies have shown that D.A.R.E. has little lasting impact. Some have even shown higher drug use among suburban youths who had graduated from a D.A.R.E. program. A report by the U.S. Government Accountability Office stated, "In brief, the six long-term evaluations of the D.A.R.E. elementary school curriculum that we reviewed found no significant differences in illicit drug use between students who received D.A.R.E. in the fifth or sixth grade (the intervention group) and students who did not (the control group.)"[83] The report looked at six major evaluations done on the effectiveness of D.A.R.E. Two of the evaluations showed that "D.A.R.E. students showed stronger negative attitudes about illicit drug use and improved peer pressure resistance skills and self-esteem about illicit drug use about 1 year after the intervention. These positive effects diminish over time."[84]

A 2009 National Youth Risk Behavior Survey Overview measured the drug and alcohol use of both male and female juveniles and reported that "72% of students had at least one drink of alcohol on at least 1 day during their life and 41.8% of students had at least one drink of alcohol on at least 1 day during the 30 days before the survey," and "24.2% of students had had five or more drinks of alcohol in a row (i.e., within a couple of hours) on at least 1 day during the 30 days before the survey."[85] Further, it reported that in the 30 days before the survey, 4.5% of students had drunk alcohol on school property.[86]

The same survey, in reporting on drug use, showed that more students used marijuana than any other drug, as "36.8% of students had used marijuana one or more times in their life" and "20.8% of students had used marijuana one or more times during the 30 days before the survey."[87]

Drug Abuse Resistance Education (D.A.R.E.)
A program designed to keep kids off drugs by teaching children how to resist peer pressure and avoid drugs and violence.

Still, despite these somewhat alarming numbers, drug use among juveniles has gone down. In 2009, the national Youth Risk Behavior Survey released a study entitled *Trends in the Prevalence of Marijuana, Cocaine, and Other Illegal Drug Use (1991–2009)*. The survey showed that from 1999–2009, marijuana use among high school students decreased, as did the use of cocaine and other methamphetamines.[88]

School Violence and Bullying   On April 20, 1999, in Columbine, Colorado, high school students Eric Harris and Dylan Kelbold shot and killed 12 students and one teacher and injured 24 other students before committing suicide at Columbine High School. This incident rocked the nation and made parents across the country question whether schools were really the safest place for children. In 2007, the nation was rocked again when a Virginia Tech student, Seung-Hui Cho, killed 32 people and injured 25 more.

These incidents have led to a greater focus on school violence and school bullying. It is important to note that these extreme examples of school violence are incredibly rare, and that schools in general are safe places for children to be. However, nonviolent examples of bullying can be a problem. Bullying exists at every level of life, from a kid on the playground to a boss in the workplace. One survey showed that approximately 160,000 students leave school early every day because they are afraid of being bullied.[89] Nearly 15% of all students who miss school on any given day do so because they fear being bullied.[90]

With the prominence of Facebook, text messaging, and YouTube, a new form of bullying called "cyberbullying" has emerged. Cyberbullying occurs outside of the classroom and can be done from behind closed doors and not face to face. Cyberbullying occurs when a disparaging remark about someone is spread through electronic means. It can occur through text messages, blogs, personal web pages, emails, cyberstalking, etc.

Regulation and punishment of cyberbullying can be a difficult task. For the most part, cyberbullying takes place outside of the traditional school setting, and it becomes very hard for schools to intervene.[91] Schools that attempt to discipline a student for cyberbullying actions that take place outside of school property and school hours can be sued for exceeding their authority and violating the student's right to free speech.[92] When schools are unable to address the issue, the criminal justice system can step in if the level of harassment rises to a criminal level.

For instance, in September 2010, a Rutgers University freshman, Tyler Clementi, committed suicide after his roommate and his roommate's friend secretly filmed him and a partner having sex and broadcast it on the Internet. The roommate, Dharun Ravi, and friend Molly Wei both faced criminal charges for invasion of privacy for secretly filming Clementi without his or his partner's permission. In May 2011, Wei entered into a plea deal with the prosecution. In exchange for charges against her to be dropped, she must enter into a pretrial intervention program, perform 300 hours of community service, testify at any proceeding, participate in counseling to deter cyberbullying, and cooperate with authorities.[93] In March 2012, Ravi was tried and convicted for his role. He was sentenced to 30 days in jail, 3 years probation, 300 hours of community service, a $10,000 fine and counseling on bullying and alternative lifestyles.[94]

Phoebe Prince, an Irish immigrant to the United States, committed suicide in January 2010 after enduring cyberbullying and bullying from classmates. After her death, nine students were charged with a range of felony crimes and have since pleaded to misdemeanors.[95]

Chapter Summary

- Beginning in 1966 with *Kent v. United States*, and continuing with *Roper v. Simmons*, the United States Supreme Court has issued opinions that change and mold the juvenile system and how juveniles are treated within both the juvenile and adult system. *Kent*, the first of the decisions, gave juveniles some rights under the due process clause. *In re Gault* and *In re Winship* further solidified juveniles' due process rights, while *Simmons* established that juveniles who committed death-penalty-eligible offenses while under the age of 18 could not be executed for their crimes.

- The concept of what a child is has evolved over time. Children have evolved from being treated as little adults or as the property of their parents to being treated as a distinct class that has its own understandings and limitations. The emergence of adolescence as a distinct time period within a human life helped lead to the formation of the juvenile court system.

- The juvenile court system was first implemented in 1899, in Cook County, Illinois. The juvenile court system first sought to rehabilitate juveniles, but as time went on, the emergence of a "get tough" movement and deinstitutionalization movement moved the juvenile courts away from rehabilitation and into punishment.

- Juvenile courts and adult criminal courts have some similarities and differences. Juvenile courts deal with all juveniles under the state's mandatory age, but these offenders can, after a juvenile waiver hearing, be waived into the adult criminal court. Juvenile courts do not find defendants guilty or not guilty, but rather delinquent or not delinquent. Defendants in adult criminal courts are found guilty or not guilty. In both courts, the state has the burden to prove the defendant's guilt or delinquency beyond a reasonable doubt.

- Probation is a tool used by both juvenile and adult criminal courts as a way to monitor the defendant's behavior. Juvenile defendants can be placed on probation prior to adjudication; after they have gone through the adjudication process and been given a suspended sentence; or after serving part of their sentence.

- The late 19th and early 20th century Child Savers movement can be directly linked to many of the changes that occurred to form a juvenile system. The Child Savers movement was an early form of state intervention and represented an early form of *parens patrie*. Houses of refuge and cottage reformatories were the early versions of juvenile detention facilities.

- Problematic issues still face the juvenile justice system today. The media's focus on crimes committed by juveniles has caused a moral panic in society despite the fact that juveniles commit just a small percentage of all crimes. Providing further issues for the juvenile justice system is the strong presence of gangs within schools and the community.

Critical Thinking?

1. What differences do you see between a finding of guilt and a finding of delinquency?
2. Should the juvenile court systems rid themselves of status offenses so that they can spend more time focusing on violent offenders?
3. What are some of the major differences between the juvenile courts and the adult criminal courts?
4. Do you think that placing juvenile offenders on probation is a good way to monitor defendants?
5. Do you think that community-based corrections produce results or are a waste?
6. Should there be a minimum age before the court can consider housing a juvenile defendant within an adult correctional facility? Should a juvenile ever be housed in an adult correctional facility?
7. Do you believe boot camps and scared-straight programs are effective? Why or why not?
8. Do you think that the Supreme Court was right, in *Simmons*, when it decided that anyone who committed a death-penalty-eligible offense under the age of 18 could not be subject to the death penalty?
9. What are the major problems you see facing the juvenile justice system today?
10. Should the juvenile justice system focus on rehabilitation or retribution/punishment?

Media

Office of Juvenile Justice and Delinquency Prevention: http://www.ojjdp.gov
   The Office of Juvenile Justice and Delinquency Prevention is tasked with trying to improve juvenile justice policies and practices.
U.S. Department of Education, Office of Safe and Drug-Free Schools: http://www2.ed.gov/about/offices/list/osdfs/index.html
   The Office of Safe and Drug-Free Schools helps to implement programs within the school system that relate to drug and violence prevention and promote the general well-being of students. Additionally, this organization provides the financial assistance needed for these programs.
The Coalition for Juvenile Justice: http://www.juvjustice.org
   The Coalition for Juvenile Justice is a group of volunteers devoted to helping juveniles who have been accused within the juvenile justice system. The coalition makes sure that juveniles are treated with care.
National Council on Crime and Delinquency: http://www.nccd-crc.org
   By applying research to policy and practice, the National Council on Crime and Delinquency has helped to advise and design reforms within the juvenile justice system.
Centers for Disease Control and Prevention's (CDC) Striving to Reduce Youth Violence Everywhere (STRYVE): http://www.safeyouth.gov/pages/home.aspx
   This group takes a public health approach to preventing youth violence.
Annie E. Casey Foundation: http://www.aecf.org
   This is a private organization founded by Jim Casey, the founder of UPS, to provide grants to organizations that help to meet the needs of vulnerable children and their families.

National Youth Court Center: http://www.youthcourt.net
> The National Youth Court Center is a central location for information about all youth courts. In youth courts, juveniles who are charged with minor delinquencies and status offenses are sentenced by their peers, who serve as judges, bailiffs, and attorneys.

Endnotes

1. *Kent v. United States*, 383 U.S. 541 (1966).
2. Office of Juvenile Justice and Delinquency Prevention. (2011). "Juvenile Arrest Rate Trends." *Statistical Briefing Book*. Retrieved from http://www.ojjdp.gov/ojstatbb/crime/JAR_Display.asp?ID=qa05200
3. Ibid.
4. Steinhart, D. J. (1996). "Status Offenses, The Future of Children." *The Juvenile Court*, 6(3). Retrieved from http://futureofchildren.org/futureofchildren/publications/journals/article/index.xml?journalid=55&articleid=316
5. Stahl, A. L. (2008). *Petitioned Status Offense Cases in Juvenile Courts, 2004*. U.S. Department of Justice.
6. Ibid.
7. *Monitoring the Future*. (2011). Retrieved from http://monitoringthefuture.org/
8. ABA, Division for Public Education, Part 1: The History of Juvenile Justice.
9. *Meyers v. State of Nebraska*, 262 U.S. 390 (1923).
10. *Prince v. Commonwealth of Massachusetts*, 321 U.S. 158 (1944).
11. Frontline. (2011). *Child or Adult? A Century Long View*. Retrieved from http://www.pbs.org/wgbh/pages/frontline/shows/juvenile/stats/childadult.html
12. Ehrlich, J. S. (2003). "Shifting Boundaries: Abortion, Criminal Culpability and the Indeterminate Legal Status of Adolescents." *Wisconsin Women's Law Journal*, 18, 77–116.
13. Klein, E. K. (1998). "Dennis the Menace or Billy the Kid: An Analysis of the Role of Transfer to Criminal Court in Juvenile Justice." *American Criminal Law Review*, 35, 371–410.
14. *National Orphan Train Complex*. (2011). Retrieved from http://www.orphantraindepot.com
15. The Children's Aid Society. (n.d.). *History*. Retrieved from http://www.childrensaidsociety.org/about/history
16. Ibid.
17. New York State Archives. (n.d.). *New York House of Refuge*. http://www.archives.nysed.gov/a/research/res_topics_ed_reform_history.shtml
18. Ibid.
19. Price, J. R. (2009, Spring). "Birthing Out Delinquents: Alternative Treatment Options for Juvenile Delinquents." *Criminal Law Brief*, 51–57.
20. Ibid.
21. Ibid.
22. Brink, D. O. (2004). "Immaturity, Normative Competence, and Juvenile Transfer: How (Not) to Punish Minors for Major Crimes." *Texas Law Review*, 82, 1555–1585.
23. Klein, 1998, 373.
24. Ibid., 374.
25. *Breed v. Jones*, 421 U.S. 519 (1975).
26. *In re Gault*, 387 U.S. 1 (1967).
27. Ibid., 4.
28. Ibid., 33.
29. Ibid., 41.
30. Ibid., 55.
31. *In re Winship*, 397 US 358 (1970).
32. Ibid.
33. Juvenile Justice and Delinquency Prevention Act of 1974, Pub. L. No. 93-415.
34. 42 U.S.C. 5601.

35. Weithorn, L. A. (2005, Summer). "Envisioning Second-Order Change in America's Responses to Troubled and Troublesome Youth." *Hofstra Law Review, 33*, 1305–1506.

36. Holden, G. A., & Kapler, R. A. (1995). "Deinstitutionalizing Status Offenders: A Record of Progress." *Juvenile Justice, 2*(2), 3–10.

37. *Black's Law Dictionary* (4th ed.).

38. Torbet, P. M. (1996). *Juvenile Probation: The Workhorse of the Juvenile Justice System.* Washington, D.C.: U.S. Department of Justice.

39. *Diversionary Programs: An Overview.* (1999). Retrieved from https://www.ncjrs.gov/html/ojjdp/9909-3/div.html

40. Bureau of Labor Statistics. (2011). "Occupational Employment and Wages, May 2010: 21-1092 Probation Officers and Correctional Treatment Specialists." *Occupational Employment Statistics.* Retrieved from http://www.bls.gov/oes/current/oes211092.htm#ind

41. 42 U.S.C. 5603 §103(1).

42. *Prevalence of Mental Health Disorders Among Youth: Youth With Mental Health Disorders: Issues and Emerging Responses.* (2000). Retrieved from https://www.ncjrs.gov/html/ojjdp/jjjnl_2000_4/youth_2.html

43. Ibid.

44. Associated Press. (2009). "Pa. Judges Accused of Jailing Kids for Cash." *MSNBC.* Retrieved from http://www.msnbcmsn.com/id/29142654/ns/us_news-crime_and_courts/t/pa-judges-accused-jailing-kids-cash/#.TkiWhr_gVys

45. Ibid.

46. Mental Health America. (2011). *Juvenile Boot Camps.* Retrieved from http://www.nmha.org/go/boot-camps

47. Office of Juvenile Justice and Delinquency Prevention. (1997). *Boot Camps for Juvenile Offenders*, 4.

48. Ibid., 8.

49. Surgeon General's Office. (n.d.). "Chapter 5: Ineffective Tertiary Programs and Strategies." *Youth Violence: A Report of the Surgeon General.* Retrieved from http://www.surgeongeneral.gov/library/youthviolence/chapter5/sec6.html

50. Petrosino, A., Turpin-Petrosino, C., & Buehler, J. (2003, November). "'Scared Straight' and Other Juvenile Awareness Programs for Preventing Juvenile Delinquency." In *The Campbell Collaboration Reviews of Intervention and Policy Evaluations (C2-RIPE).* Philadelphia, PA: Campbell Collaboration.

51. Ibid., 4.

52. Ibid.

53. Sherman, L. W., Gottfredson, D., MacKenzie, D. L., Eck, J., Reuter, P., & Bushway, S. (1997). *Preventing Crime: What Works, What Doesn't, What's Promising. A Report to the United States Congress.* College Park, MD: University of Maryland.

54. *Roper v. Simmons*, 543 U.S. 551 (2005).

55. Ibid.

56. *Miranda v. Arizona*, 384 U.S. 436 (1966).

57. *Roper v. Simmons*, 2005.

58. *Atkins v. Virginia*, 536 U.S. 304 (2002).

59. *Roper v. Simmons*, 2005.

60. Ibid.

61. Ibid.

62. *Death Penalty Information Center.* (2011). Retrieved from http://www.deathpenaltyinfo.org

63. McLatchey, S. F. (1999). "Media Access to Juvenile Records: In Search of a Solution." *Georgia State University Law Review, 16*(2), 337–359.

64. Cohen, S. (2002). *Folk Devils and Moral Panics: The Creation of the Mods and Rockers.* New York, NY: Routledge.

65. *Principles of Drug Abuse Treatment for Criminal Justice Populations: A Research-Based Guide*, 13.

66. Howell, J. C. (1998, August). *Youth Gangs: An Overview.* Washington, D.C.: U.S. Department of Justice.

67. Federal Bureau of Investigation. (2011). *Gangs.* Retrieved from http://www.fbi.gov/about-us/investigate/vc_majorthefts/gangs/gangs

68. Howell, 1998, 8.

69. Howell, J. C., & Moore, J. P. (2010). *National Gang Center Bulletin: History of Street Gangs.* 1–25.

70. Ibid., 4.

71. Ibid.

72. Garrison, C. (2011, July 12). "Collinsville Mayor Apologizes for City's New Anti-Sagging Law, Calls It a 'Step Backward.'" *Riverfront Times*. Retrieved from http://blogs.riverfronttimes.com/dailyrft/2011/07/collinsville_sagging_law_mayor_apology.php

73. *New Jersey v. T.L.O.*, 469 U.S. 325, 341-342 (1985).

74. *Vernonia School District 47J v. Acton, et ux., etc.*, 515 U.S. 646 (1995).

75. *Safford Unified School District #1 v. Redding*, 557 U.S. ___ (2009).

76. Belenko, S. (2000). "The Challenges of Integrating Drug Treatment into the Criminal Justice Process." *Albany Law Review*, 3(3), 833–876.

77. Global Commission on Drug Policy. (2011). *War on Drugs: Report of the Global Commission on Drug Policy*.

78. Ibid.

79. Ibid.

80. Ibid., 10.

81. Ibid.

82. Ibid., 14.

83. U.S. General Accounting Office. (2003, January 15). *Letter to Senator Richard Durbin*. Retrieved from http://www.gao.gov/new.items/d03172r.pdf

84. Ibid.

85. Centers for Disease Control and Prevention. (2011). *YRBSS in Brief*. Retrieved from http://www.cdc.gov/healthyyouth/yrbs/brief.htm

86. Ibid.

87. Ibid.

88. Centers for Disease Control and Prevention. (2010). "Alcohol & Drug Use." *Healthy Youth!* Retrieved from http://www.cdc.gov/healthyyouth/alcoholdrug/index.htm

89. Bullying Statistics. (n.d.). *Bullying Statistics 2010*. Retrieved from http://www.bullyingstatistics.org/content/bullying-statistics-2010.html

90. Ibid.

91. *Stop Cyberbullying*. (n.d.). Retrieved from http://www.stopcyberbullying.org/prevention/schools_role.html

92. Ibid.

93. Schweber, N. (2011, May 7). "In Fallout of Suicide by Student, a Plea Deal." *The New York Times*. Retrieved from http://www.nytimes.com/2011/05/07/nyregion/in-rutgers-suicide-case-ex-student-gets-plea-deal.html

94. DeMarco, M. and Friedman, A. (2012, May 21). "Dharun Ravi Sentenced to 30 Days in Jail." *The Star-Ledger*. Retrieved from http://www.nj.com/news/index.ssf/2012/05/dharun_ravi_sentenced_for_bias.html

95. Lavoie, D. (2011, April 27). "5 Teens Strike Plea Deal in Phoebe Prince Bullying Case." *The Huffington Post*. Retrieved from http://www.huffingtonpost.com/2011/04/27/phoebe-prince-bullying-case_n_854446.html

13

Victimology AND Victims' Rights

KEY TERMS

Civil lawsuit, Compassion fatigue, Compensation, Costs of victimization, Indirect victim, Just world, National Organization for Victim Assistance (NOVA), Repeat victimization, Victimology, Victim advocate, Victim impact statement (VIS), Victims of Crime Act (VOCA), Victim precipitation, Victim rights amendment, Victim services

CHAPTER OBJECTIVES

1. Describe the origins of victimology.
2. Outline the costs of criminal victimization.
3. Describe the ways to remedy the costs.
4. Describe methods used to measure victimization.
5. Discuss the victim's movement and how it increased public interest in crime victims.

Case Study: Tragedy in Tucson

On January 8, 2011, a gunman opened fire during a town hall meeting held by Democratic Rep. Gabrielle Giffords of Arizona. Rep. Giffords was shot in the head. The gunman shot and killed six people, including a nine-year-old girl and Federal Judge John McCarthy Roll. Thirteen others were wounded. The shooter, 22-year-old Jared Lee Loughner, was subdued by two bystanders at the event. Pima County Sheriff Clarence Dupnik reported that Rep. Giffords was the primary target of the shooting.

The shooting sent ripple effects throughout the community. President Obama told reporters that the events were "a tragedy for Arizona and a tragedy for our entire country. . . . but we don't yet know what provoked this unspeakable act."[1] House Speaker John Boehner, R-OH, said "I am horrified by the senseless attack on Congresswoman Gabrielle Giffords and members of her staff. An attack on one who serves is an attack on all who serve. Acts and threats of violence against public officials have no place in our society. Our prayers are with Congresswoman Giffords, her staff, all who were injured, and their families. This is a sad day for our country."[2]

The shooting affected the individuals present at the town hall meeting (direct victims), and it also affected family members, friends, community members, concerned citizens, and government officials across the nation (indirect victims). Directly or indirectly, hundreds if not thousands were victims of this heinous crime. Both direct and indirect victims of a crime may experience a wide range of reactions post-victimization, including shock, panic, fear, grief, anger, disbelief, emotional numbness, and feelings of helplessness. These repercussions can extend to vicarious victims, such as friends, family members, and social workers who deal with the aftermath of the crime.

The public is often not aware of services available to victims of crime after a criminal victimization. These services can help victims find counseling, negotiate the criminal justice system, and understand their rights.

Victimology

Criminology is the study of criminal behavior in both individuals and society. Criminologists attach great importance to the motivations of criminals: who they were, where they came from, how the justice system handled them, and what should become of them.[3] In addition, there is another important element of any crime: the victim. Crime is as an offense against an individual victim or victims as well as the state as a whole.

Victimology
The study of victimization that analyzes the role played by victims in crimes.

Rooted in criminology, **victimology** is the scientific study of victimization. It is important to note that today victimology is a broad discipline that focuses on several different types of victims, including victims of criminals, oneself, the social environment, technology, and the natural environment. For purposes of this chapter, the discussion will focus on victims of criminals. Victimology does not just focus on the crime itself, but also on addressing the needs and rights of victims once they become a part of the criminal justice system. Victimologists are interested in who is victimized, what the impact of the crime is, the experience of victims in the criminal justice system, and the role a victim may play, if any, in causing the crime. With those factors in mind, consider the case study at the beginning of this chapter. The crime consists of more than just the shooter, the details of the crime (weapon used, location, time of day, etc.), and the shooter's motivations for committing the crime. Investigators of the Representative Giffords shooting, for example, would be interested in why Representative Giffords was targeted, what made her vulnerable, and how best to attend to her needs and rights in the pursuit of justice. Investigators might ask questions about whether or not the offender knew Representative Giffords or any of the other victims, or what about the victims might have provoked a response in the offender. The welfare of the victims after the crime, in particular when they interact with the criminal justice system, would also be of interest to victimologists and other criminologists.

Victimologists are also interested in determining the full scope of what constitutes "victimhood." In the opening case study, who are the victims in the Tucson shooting? There are the direct victims that were at the town hall meeting. There are also indirect victims, such as the families of those who were shot, the community, and the state of Arizona (for being deprived of an important public official). In addition, the costs that will result from the crime—financial, emotional, and physical—affect many individuals and groups.[4]

The understanding of the meaning and purpose of victimology has evolved from an avenue of inquiry within criminology to an independent discipline. Two working definitions of victimology itself could be formulated. The first, which some will argue is outdated, defines victimology as the study of the victim's role in crime events.[5] While this definition may seem overly narrow, criminologists argue that the victim's role stretches from witnessing a crime, or perhaps even causing a crime, through the investigation and trial, and eventually through the parole process and beyond.

A more focused definition of victimology, offered by Andrew Karmen (2004), is "the scientific study of the physical, emotional, and financial harm people suffer because of criminal activities."[6] This includes the crime itself and its results, but may also include victims' experiences at the hands of the criminal justice system. These two definitions encompass the comprehensiveness of the study of victimology.

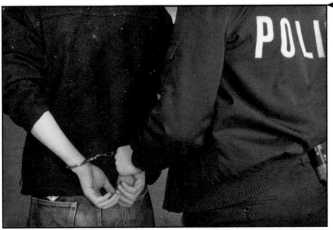

The current system for handling crime, the criminal justice system, is relatively new.

The Path from Victim Justice System to Criminal Justice System

The current system for handling crime, the criminal justice system, is relatively new. Early human societies were commonly small, tribal, and organized around a strong family unit, more properly thought of as a "clan," that served as a centering force in human social networks. There was no "state" in the sense of a locus of centralized government that would mete out impartial justice. As Doerner and Lab note, people in early societies tacitly accepted the principle that "victims were expected to fend for themselves."[7] Victims, relying on their families, had a large role in ensuring justice for themselves, as they lived in a world that depended upon personal relationships between individuals and clans. The legal codes that existed provided for either retribution or restitution, and they were enforced due to the fear of feuding and conflict between large families within the community.[8] This "victim justice system" was largely the norm in small societies.

During the Industrial Revolution, which brought rapid urbanization and the rise of the modern city-state, this system began to change. Many citizens, particularly the wealthy, believed they were entitled to restitution paid by offenders to victims.[9] With larger societies and stronger, centralized governmental power, acts of crime were seen as violations against the state instead of an individual victim.[10] State judiciaries levied fines, imposed prison sentences, and determined the outcome of court proceedings. In that way, the "victim justice system" was replaced by the "criminal justice system." The criminal justice system shifted its focus away from victims toward the offense and the rights of the offender. That said, it must be noted that today, all states' statutory codes provide extensive basic rights and protections for victims of crime. These statutes have greatly influenced the way victims of crime are treated within the criminal justice system.

Critical Thinking How do you feel about the way our system of justice understands crime? Should it be thought of as being against an individual or against society as a whole?

Early Leaders in Victimology

The academic discipline of victimology first emerged during the 1940s as an offshoot of traditional criminology.[11] The focus began to shift to look at the relationship between the victim and offender in the hope of better understanding criminal activity and identifying causes of criminal behavior.

Many individuals laid the groundwork for victimology in the early 20th century. Chief among them were Benjamin Mendelssohn, Hans von Hentig, Marvin Wolfgang, and Menachem Amir. These early pioneers spent much of their careers studying the pathology of offenders, their personal histories and backgrounds, and their relationship with society. Their focus shifted in the 1940s to examining the relationship between victim and offender. These early attempts signaled the beginning of a renewed academic interest in the victim.

Much of this early scholarly work focused on creating typologies of victims and assigning various degrees of responsibility to the victim for the criminal act. Some scholars, such as William Ryan (1976), argued that there was a preoccupation with victim blaming during this time period.[12] He asserted that such practices obscured the social inequalities that lay behind crime statistics.[13] The suggestion that victims shared responsibility for or instigated the criminal episode would lead to significant debate within this emerging field. Criticisms from scholars like Ryan were juxtaposed with others who noted that some victims are responsible for their own demise. David Luckenbill (1977), for example, draws upon the work of earlier victimologists and sees homicide as a "situated transaction," in which both the victim and offender play a part. It was already understood that victims sometimes precipitate the violence that kills them, either by throwing the first punch or firing the first shot.[14] Luckenbill, as is typical of many victimologists, was interested in how these roles develop, what patterns of interaction emerge, and what in that transaction eventuates the murder.[15] The tension between these emphases has informed much of the dialogue in contemporary victimology.

Benjamin Mendelssohn

Benjamin Mendelssohn was a Romanian lawyer and one of the founders of victimology beginning in the 1930s. He specialized in penal law, and his initial interest in victims sprang from his need, as a criminal attorney, to demonstrate to the court that the victim had a role in the criminal act.[16] In addition to his contribution of the term *victimology* itself, it was Mendelssohn who first suggested the establishment of an international society dedicated to the field.[17] This eventually was realized with the creation of institutions such as the World Society of Victimology, the American Society of Victimology, and the International Victimology Institute at Tilburg.

Mendelssohn is regarded as the "father" of victimology, not only for contributing the term, but for devising a scale that classified victims based upon what he believed was their level of blame for the crime. Based upon victim questionnaires, Mendelssohn discovered that there was frequently an interpersonal relationship between the victim and the offender.[18] Mendelssohn developed what was, in essence, a continuum of degrees of victim blame. The victim types ranged from "completely innocent victim" to "simulating or imaginary victim." On one end of the spectrum is the completely innocent victim, who in no way provokes or facilitates the offender's attack. At the other end is the imaginary victim, by which Mendelssohn meant a victim who pretended to be victimized.[19]

People who commit crime are more likely to be victimized than the general population.[20] Mendelssohn, as part of his classification system, also considered situations in which the eventual victim was initially the offender, but lost control of the situation and wound up becoming the victim. Situations in which one drug dealer attacked another, only to lose control of the situation and become injured himself, would fall under this category. This type of victim, one that Mendelssohn called "victim more guilty than offender," would become important to later work done by victimologists such as Amir and Wolfgang.[21]

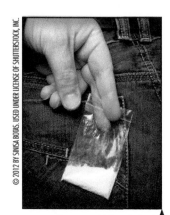

Some would-be criminal offenders instead become victims, such as drug dealers.

Hans von Hentig

Of the early victimologists, Hans von Hentig was among the more influential and controversial. Von Hentig insisted that victims were often involved, even complicit, in putting the criminal act into motion. His theory ran contrary to the prevailing ideology within criminology, which was static and one-dimensional in focusing solely upon the offender.[22] Von Hentig believed that in many cases, "we meet a victim who consents tacitly, co-operates, conspires or provokes. The victim is one of the causative elements."[23] Von Hentig saw a mutual relationship between offender and victim. He grouped his findings into a series of typologies, which are categorized observations put into logical groupings. His typologies described groups of characteristics that explained why some people are more likely to become victims than others. Von Hentig's typologies were similar to Mendelssohn's victim types, but von Hentig was less interested in assigning blame and more interested in asserting that the victim was one of several possible causes of a particular crime, possibly even a precipitating cause, as well as unlocking the relationship between the two.

Indeed, criminals often use victim status or behavior as an attempt to justify their crimes, such as rapists who claim they were perceiving signals from their victims.[24] Of particular interest to victimologists is the presence of drugs and alcohol in sexual assault cases and the role that alcohol played in the perpetrator's understanding of the crime.[25] Some perpetrators try to excuse their actions on the grounds that because the victim was under the influence of alcohol, the offender should be absolved of their crime.[26]

The point of such inquiries is to help understand the genesis of crime, the circumstances surrounding it, and the environmental cues that trigger victimization. Victimology helps researchers understand the role the victim plays in crime. This view of crime resulted in criminological theories like the Routine Activities Theory. Developed by Lawrence Cohen and Marcus Felson (1979), the theory posits that the comission of a crime requires three facilitating factors: a motivated offender, a suitable target, and an absence of capable guardians.[27] These theories enhance the understanding not only of crime, but also of how people can avoid putting themselves in the position to be victimized in the first place.

Marvin Wolfgang

Marvin Wolfgang is remembered mainly for his contributions to the development of victim precipitation, particularly in what he called the "subculture of violence theory."[28] Wolfgang was one of the first to attempt systematic research to provide empirical support for the assertion that victims contribute to the commission of a crime. As noted earlier, the typologies of Mendelssohn and von Hentig suggested that victims contributed to criminal acts, but neither presented empirical evidence to support his view. Wolfgang studied homicides in Philadelphia for the years 1948–1952. He reported that 26% of the homicides he reviewed resulted from victim precipitation. He defined victim precipitation as "those cases in which the victim was the first to show and use a deadly weapon, to strike a blow."[29]

Wolfgang was specifically interested in violent crime and victimization within Philadelphia's African-American community, as there was a dispropor-

Wolfgang found that many victims of homicide had a preexisting relationship with their attacker.

tionate level of violence in this community compared to the general population.[30] Wolfgang came to the controversial conclusion that the high rates of homicide among blacks were due to the subculture within the African-American community that emphasized and even valued violence. Wolfgang's studies attempted to analyze the context in which crimes occur, and to illuminate social inequalities that may be the root of the problem. Wolfgang identified several factors typical of what he called victim-precipitated homicides. He found that a great many victims of homicide had a preexisting relationship with their attacker, the homicides were often a product of small disagreements that escalated, and alcohol had often been consumed by the victim. Wolfgang's research suggested that some homicide victims were not completely passive individuals who were preyed upon by aggressive predators.[31]

Menachem Amir　Menachem Amir, a student of Marvin Wolfgang, attempted to present an empirical analysis of rape incidents in Philadelphia. He reviewed police reports of rape between 1958 and 1960 and asserted that 19% of all the forcible rapes reported during that time period were victim-precipitated.[32]

Amir's application of the concept of victim precipitation deviated substantially from Wolfgang's initial conception. Wolfgang argued that victim precipitation occurred when a victim first initiated the violence (e.g., the victim was the first to commit or attempt to commit a crime). In contrast, Amir suggested that victim precipitation occurred when factors such as alcohol consumption, flirtatious behavior, revealing clothing, risqué language, being at the wrong place at the wrong time, and personal reputation were present on the part of the victim.[33] Therefore, Amir argued that a woman who drank alcohol or engaged in flirtatious behavior caused her own rape. Not surprisingly, Amir's claims were perceived as misogynistic and incendiary. His research was heavily criticized by victim advocates and women's groups as using rape myths to blame victims and giving scientific legitimacy to this practice. Amir's research articulated a view of victim precipitation that remains contentious today.

Critical Thinking Do you think that studying the role rape victims play in their own victimization is inherently problematic? Does inquiring about whether or not they "precipitated" the event imply that they are at fault?

Victim precipitation
Actions by the victim, either passive or active, that help to trigger the offense.

Victim Precipitation Early pioneers in the field of victimology were concerned with the way victims contributed to the criminal act. They suggested that the victim's role could be conscious or unconscious, and could come through carelessness, recklessness, or imprudence.[34] Von Hentig, Mendelssohn, Amir, and others asserted that victims could have a motivational role, which could take the form of attracting, arousing, enticing, inducing, or inciting. They also believed that victims could have a functional role, whether through provoking, precipitating, triggering, facilitating, or actively participating.[35] These varying degrees of victim involvement in the criminal act fall under the heading of victim precipitation.

Victim precipitation can be defined as actions on the part of victims that cause, partly or completely, their own victimization.[36] Victim precipitation can be either passive or active. Different victimologists had different interpretations and points of emphasis when discussing victim precipitation. For example, Von Hentig focused more on passive victim precipitation, while Mendelssohn focused on a more active characterization of victim precipitation.

The understanding of victim precipitation has evolved over time. Although not emphasized as much as it was in the past, contemporary interpreters still integrate it into their work. For example, David Luckenbill's theory of situated transaction sees crime as a contest of character between victim and offender. Luckenbill accepted that victims could precipitate their own victimization, but felt victimology had not gone far enough in understanding how the relationship developed and the roles played by victims and offenders.[37]

The Assumptions of Victim Precipitation As a result of the reactions to Amir's work, victimologists began to challenge the precipitation argument as it had developed to that point. Many suggested that it was important to critically examine the assumptions that provided the foundation for the victim precipitation argument. Franklin and Franklin[38] suggested that there were four main assumptions to consider and critically evaluate. First, victim precipitation assumes that the behavior of the victim can explain the criminal act. Second, victim precipitation assumes that the offender is provoked by signals from the victim. Third, victim precipitation assumes that a victim's behavior is in and of itself enough to instigate a criminal act. Finally, victim precipitation assumes that the victim's intent can be measured by the victimization incident itself, without taking the offender into account.

Critical evaluation of these assumptions reveals several problems. First, certain types of precipitous behavior can occur without leading to any victimization (e.g., dressing provocatively or consuming alcohol to excess does not always lead to rape). Second, offenders often plan their crimes in advance, and are not simply acting in response to stimuli from the victim. Third, offenders may either respond to or ignore the actions of the victim and commit the crime anyway.[39]

Critics argue that studies of victim precipitation only focus on the behavior of the victim, diverting attention away from perpetrators and their responsibility for the crime.[40] Many critics view victim precipitation as "victim blaming." For example, Courtney Ahrens (2006) found that rape victims who were perceived as having instigated their own attack were the target of negative reactions from the people who were supposed to help them.[41] Rape victims who disclosed details of their assault often met with suspicion and suggestions that they were at fault.

Critical Thinking
Is the concept of victim precipitation the same as blaming the victim? Is the difference purely semantic? Justify your response with arguments.

The "Just World" Concept and the "Legitimate" Victim

The concept of a "just world," or one in which people get the consequences they deserve for their actions during their lives, also contributes to our understanding of victimhood and deviance. People who adhere to the idea of a just world do not want to believe that innocent people could be victims of random acts of violence and evil. Instead, they believe that the victims must have transgressed or misbehaved in some way to deserve what happened to them. Under this philosophy, the idea that victims are in some way responsible or partially complicit in their own victimizations is reassuring. Because of this, victims are often unfairly stigmatized and are not able to receive the support they need after their victimization. This "just world" belief creates an environment where victims are seen as different from nonvictims and as deficient in some way. The idea of a "culturally legitimate" victim[42] is that the victim is in some sense deserving, or "fair game." For example, criminals are often victims of violence themselves,[43] and, as their own involvement in criminal activity makes them less likely to seek help from authorities, they are seen as legitimate targets.[44] This process of creating culturally legitimate victims, though problematic and overly generalized, in some ways makes society believe it is "acceptable" for certain people to be victimized.

Just world
A worldview in which everyone gets the consequences they deserve for their actions.

Critical Thinking What are some examples of culturally legitimate victims? How have these victims been constructed as different and/or deficient from nonvictims?

Contemporary Approaches to Victimology Contemporary victimology tends to approach victimization as largely subjective.[45] This approach emphasizes looking at the specifics of an individual situation, and attending to the perspectives of all involved.[46] For example, the concept of "bystander blaming" has been reintroduced. The "bystander," as Cohen argues, is the third part of a triad of victim, offender, and bystander.[47] In the case of a victim of sexual harassment, the innocent bystander's perspective is considered to give a more complete account of the perspectives and roles in the criminal act.

Another contemporary trend in dealing with victims, as well as criminals, is restorative justice. Restorative justice differs from the traditional model in that it places less emphasis on an adversarial system, such as is found in traditional criminal or civil proceedings. It seeks to repair the damage to all parties involved by facilitating dialogue between victim and offender, and making the offender realize the consequences of his or her actions. The theory acknowledges that three parties are damaged by crime: the victim, the offender, and society. By doing so, it shifts away from the idea of offending as being against the state and toward a notion of offending as being against an individual and the community.[48] Restorative justice also seeks to address the underlying causes that led to the crime in the first place.[49] Restorative justice can be practiced through methods such as victim-offender mediation, family group conferencing, and restorative conferencing, among others. These approaches typically include mediated conferencing between victims, offenders, family members, and friends. They address issues of restitution and consequences.[50]

The costs of victimization go beyond just the tangible costs.

Victims' Rights Movement   Victims often feel marginalized and alienated from the criminal justice system. Joanne Wemmers (2008) found that crime victims desire increased recognition and involvement with the criminal justice system.[51] This has led to several initiatives over the past couple of decades that have extended additional rights to crime victims. This victims' rights movement has strived to address the needs of crime victims and help them deal with the trauma of victimization.

Costs of Victimization   Victimization imposes tremendous psychological, physical, emotional, and financial costs on the victim, the victim's family, and society as a whole. The costs of victimization refer to the costs associated with crime. These costs include not only the direct cost from the criminal event, but the losses that victims and witnesses incur when they enter the criminal justice system. The chart below breaks down the costs of victimization for the major types of crime into tangible and intangible costs. It should be noted that the costs below reflect only *victim*-related costs; the chart does not address the costs incurred by the criminal justice system.

Costs of victimization
The costs incurred by a victim as a result of victimization. These include financial, emotional, psychological, and social costs.

FIGURE 13.1 Total Cost of Victimization: 1987–1990.

Crime	Tangible Costs	Intangible Costs	Total Costs
Murder	$1,030,000	$1,910,000	$2,940,000
Rape/Sexual Assault	5,100	81,400	86,500
Robbery/Attempt with Injury	5,200	13,800	19,000
Assault or Attempt	1,550	7,800	9,350
Burglary or Attempt	1,100	300	1,400

Source: http://www.ncjrs.gov/pdffiles/costcrim.pdf

As is evident in the table above, the intangible costs of crime are nearly always greater than the tangible ones, indicating that the true cost of victimization goes far beyond the mere value of property. Tangible costs include medical expenses, damaged or lost property, and time missed from work. Intangible costs refer to pain, trauma, and lost quality of life for victims.[52] There is also the cost to society as a whole, not just in terms of the amount of money it costs to prosecute a criminal case, but also the cost to the economy that results from a victimized worker who can no longer work.

First Victimization   The trauma of the victim at the hands of the offender is often called the "first victimization." At this stage, victims suffer physical injury, property loss, missed time from work, and disruption of their normal lives. Other costs, though more difficult to quantify, include emotional distress and anguish, as well as strained relations with their friends and family due to the trauma of victimization.[53]

In 1996, T.R. Miller studied victimization data, including the NCVS, to try to get a clear picture of what criminal victimization costs Americans. His study did not include white-collar crime, such as tax evasion and corporate crime, and

Damaged or lost property at the hands of a criminal offender is part of the first victimization.

instead consisted mostly of data on street crime. The results were, nonetheless, staggering. He concluded that 3% of medical spending and 14% of injury-related medical spending were the results of violent crime. Violent crime also caused a loss of earnings that equated to 1% of all American earnings. Finally, violent crime was responsible for roughly 10–20% of mental health spending in the United States, due mostly to the treatment victims required as a result of their victimization.[54] This statistic does not cover emotional trauma and grief, which is incalculable.

Second Victimization   Entering the criminal justice system can present its own set of challenges to victims. Victims may be subjected to insensitive questioning by detectives and, later, defense attorneys, an unavoidable reality of the criminal justice process. They may discover, after the fact, that their victimizer has been acquitted, with no warning from the state. Similarly, in some cases, victims are not told if the offender makes bail or is paroled after serving only part of the original sentence.[55] While many jurisdictions have attempted to address such problems through policy changes, these issues can sometimes still occur. This leads to what victimologists call the "second victimization."[56]

A victim's testimony in a criminal case is often crucial, but as witnesses, victims may endure challenges. When they take the stand, they are frequently cross-examined in an aggressive or hostile manner by defense attorneys. Their personal lives are frequently put on trial and their credibility attacked.[57] Defendants have a constitutional right to confront their accusers, so these situations are often unavoidable and simply part of the process of a robust criminal justice system. Still, these experiences can sometimes cause victims to feel marginalized.

The marginalization of victims was researched by Frank Cannavale in 1976. Cannavale determined that the single greatest impediment to successfully prosecuting a case was that victims were less and less cooperative. They did not want to help the system, as they thought it did not care about their needs.[58] Victims and witnesses often fail to appear in court, despite it being a required civic duty, because they believe it is not worth the high cost and aggravation to do so.

In acknowledging the problem, the justice system has done a great deal to secure cooperation from victims. To prosecute offenders more effectively, the justice system must have witnesses who are willing and happy to help. Witnesses who are confident and informed and benefit from assistance programs are better equipped to deal with the emotionally draining experience of testifying. This leads to lower dismissal rates and higher conviction rates, as well as a restoration of the public's confidence and trust.[59]

Critical Thinking   What do you think is the best way to address victims' rights issues? Does providing federal- or state-funded legal support conflict with the rights of the accused? Explain.

Women's rights leaders fought for changes in the criminal justice system to better respond to victims of rape and sexual assault.

Victims' Rights Dissatisfaction with the treatment of crime victims by the criminal justice system has been an important force in mobilizing the victims' rights movement. Thirty years ago, victims of crime had few legal rights within the criminal justice system. Over the past several decades, advocates and activists have campaigned for an expansion of victims' rights. Victims often report frustration from participating in the criminal justice system.[60] Early victims' rights advocates equated their struggle with other movements for social justice, including the movements for civil rights, gay rights, women's rights, workers' rights, students' rights, children's rights, patients' rights, and prisoners' rights.[61]

Special Interest Groups Numerous special interest groups and advocates for social justice have been linked with the development of victims' rights. The women's rights movement in the 1960s and 1970s fought for changes in a criminal justice system that did not adequately respond to victims of rape and sexual assault. In particular, the criminal justice system did not always attend to the emotional and psychological needs of victims. The women's rights movement helped establish rape crisis centers and domestic violence shelters to better address these needs.[62]

Although possibly the most prominent, women's groups and rape/sexual assault advocates were not the only special interest groups that championed victims' causes. In 1974, Families and Friends of Missing Persons was founded to provide support for the loved ones of missing individuals. Mothers Against Drunk Driving (MADD) followed in 1980, after Candy Lightner's daughter was killed by a drunk driver who was a repeat offender. These organizations usually began as support groups that evolved into a political advocacy role.[63]

National Organization for Victim Assistance (NOVA)

A conglomerate of victims' rights groups that advocate on behalf of victims and victims' issues.

Many of these organization have been instrumental in shaping federal legislation. See Figure 13.2 for a listing of federal legislation passed.

Several of these groups joined forces to form the **National Organization for Victim Assistance (NOVA)**. Since 1975, NOVA has helped to raise awareness of victims' issues and provided training for those who work with victims.[64] There are many other government and private organizations that exist today to provide assistance and advocacy for victims. For example, the Victim Rights Law Center (VRLC) provides representation for victims of rape and sexual assault, the Identity Theft Resource Center provides information and assistance for victims of identity theft, the National Center on Elder Abuse advocates for the rights of elder Americans, and so forth.

Career Connections: Guardian ad Litem

A guardian ad litem is, as described by the Children's Guardian Fund, "a volunteer appointed by the court to protect the rights and advocate the best interests of a child involved in a court proceeding primarily as a result of alleged abuse or neglect."[65] He or she must act as the spokesperson for the child. Such guardians are frequently attorneys, social workers, or simply volunteers. Some states (e.g., Florida) utilize trained volunteers from the community. A guardian ad litem differs from the more commonly known "legal guardian" because they do not control the property of the child and do not furnish the child with a home. Their sole purpose is to act in the best interests of the child.

Such positions are temporary and last only for the duration of the legal proceedings. Guardians come from diverse backgrounds, and the requirements vary by state. Applicants must complete an application, a background check, and an interview, and successfully complete a training course. Guardians spend most of their time (60%) visiting their charges at home or formal meetings.[66] The funding for these programs generally comes from the court's budget.

Guardians are expected to gather information about the conditions and needs of the child. They make recommendations to judges about what they deem to be in the child's best interest in terms of treatment plans and permanent homes in the case of abuse. They also monitor the progress of the child, the case, and the parents (if applicable).

Victims of Crime Act (VOCA)

An act that allowed federal money to subsidize state compensation programs for victims.

Federal Initiatives   In 1982, President Reagan established a Presidential Task Force on Victims of Crime. This task force argued for a greater role of crime victims in court and led to the creation of federal legislation establishing a federal Office for Victims of Crime in the U.S. DOJ. In addition, the task force recommended that an amendment to the U.S. Constitution be created giving victims the right to be present and to be heard at all critical stages of judicial proceedings. In 1984, the **Victims of Crime Act (VOCA)** was passed. This allowed the federal government to provide compensation to victims of federal offenses, as well as funds for state governments to use in their own compensation programs. VOCA not only provides funds, but has helped to systematize compensation programs so that there is greater consistency among states.[67]

Advocates have attempted to add a victim rights amendment to the U.S. Constitution.

Victim Rights Amendment (VRA)   Since the 1982 Presidential Task Force, there have been a number of attempts over the years to incorporate language that would address the rights of victims into the U.S. Constitution. The text of a (recent) version of one **Victim Rights Amendment** is contained below. It was a Proposed Federal VRA for the 108th Congress. The purpose of the amendment was to provide victims with guaranteed rights when they enter the justice system.

> **Victim Rights Amendment**
> A proposed constitutional amendment that would provide victims with guaranteed rights similar to those given to offenders under the Sixth Amendment.

To date, efforts to pass such an amendment have been unsuccessful. Critics have noted that the Seventh Amendment allows victims to sue offenders for restitution, and that this is sufficient.[68] Others felt that the idea was inherently misguided because the purpose of the Bill of Rights is to protect citizens from the government, specifically as it relates to personal freedom and liberty. Victims' issues have nothing to do with freedom, and are therefore outside the scope of the Bill of Rights.[69]

Federal Constitutional Reform Efforts   There have also been attempts to amend the existing Bill of Rights, specifically the Sixth Amendment, instead of adding an entirely new amendment. Victims' advocates wanted to add the following sentence: "Likewise, the victim, in every criminal prosecution shall have the right to be present and to be heard at all critical stages of judicial proceedings."[71] This, too, met with resistance. Critics argued that the language of the revised amendment did not address property crimes, which was highly problematic because theft is far more prevalent than rape, assault, and murder.[72]

State Constitutional Reform Efforts   Advocacy groups for victims have had success at the state level. Since 1980, nearly every state has enacted statutes that address basic rights for victims of crime. These typically include the rights to attend court proceedings, to have stolen property returned, to be protected from reprisals by the accused, and to restitution.[73] By the year 2000, 33 states had amended their constitutional charters to address the needs of victims.[74] Advocacy groups hope that these changes to state law will eventually lead to changes to the U.S. Constitution.

Exhibit: Text of the Proposed Amendment (108th Congress)

The following article is proposed as an amendment to the Constitution of the United States, which shall be valid to all intents and purposes as part of the Constitution when ratified by the legislatures of three-fourths of the several States, and which shall take effect on the 180th day after ratification of this article:

1. Article–SECTION 1. The rights of victims of violent crime, being capable of protection without denying the constitutional rights of those accused of victimizing them, are hereby established and shall not be denied by any State or the United States and may be restricted only as provided in this article.

2. SECTION 2. A victim of violent crime shall have the right to reasonable and timely notice of any public proceeding involving the crime and of any release or escape of the accused; the rights not to be excluded from such public proceeding and reasonably to be heard at public release, plea, sentencing, reprieve, and pardon proceedings; and the right to adjudicative decisions that duly consider the victim's safety, interest in avoiding unreasonable delay, and just and timely claims to restitution from the offender. These rights shall not be restricted except when and to the degree dictated by a substantial interest in public safety or the administration of criminal justice, or by compelling necessity.

3. SECTION 3. Nothing in this article shall be construed to provide grounds for a new trial or to authorize any claim for damages. Only the victim or the victim's lawful representative may assert the rights established by this article, and no person accused of the crime may obtain any form of relief hereunder.

4. SECTION 4. The Congress shall have the power to enforce by appropriate legislation this article. Nothing in this article shall affect the President's authority to grant reprieves or pardons.

5. SECTION 5. This article shall be inoperative unless it shall have been ratified as an amendment to the Constitution by the legislatures of three-fourths of the several States within seven years from the date of its submission to the States by the Congress. This article shall take effect on the 180th day after the date of its ratification.[70]

Federal Victims' Rights Legislation in the U.S. The federal government has taken an active role in addressing the plight of victims in the United States. Figure 13.2 summarizes key victims' rights legislation passed in the United States since 1974. The biggest piece of federal legislation was the 2004

Crime Victims' Bill of Rights. It incorporates standard rights for victims such as the right to be notified, the right to be included in court proceedings, the right to be heard at plea and parole hearings, the right to confer with the prosecutor, the right to restitution, the right to be protected from reprisals, and the right to fairness and privacy.

FIGURE 13.2 Key Federal Victims' Rights Legislation

1974 Child Abuse Prevention and Treatment Act

1980 Parental Kidnapping Prevention Act

1982 Victim and Witness Protection Act

1982 Missing Children's Act

1984 Victims of Crime Act

1984 Justice Assistance Act

1984 Missing Children's Assistance Act

1984 Family Violence Prevention and Services Act

1985 Children's Justice Act

1988 Drunk Driving Prevention Act

1990 Hate Crime Statistics Act

1990 Victims of Child Abuse Act

1990 Victims' Rights and Restitution Act

1990 National Child Search Assistance Act

1992 Battered Women's Testimony Act

1993 Child Sexual Abuse Registry Act

1994 Violent Crime Control and Law Enforcement Act

1994 Violence Against Women Act

1996 Community Notification Act ("Megan's Law")

1996 Antiterrorism and Effective Death Penalty Act

1996 Mandatory Victims' Restitution Act

1997 Victims' Rights Clarification Act

1998 Crime Victims with Disabilities Act

1998 Identity Theft and Deterrence Act

2000 Trafficking Victims Protection Act

2001 Air Transportation Safety and System Stabilization Act (established September 11th Victim Compensation Fund)

2003 PROTECT Act ("Amber Alert" law)

2003 Prison Rape Elimination Act

2003 Fair and Accurate Credit Transactions Act

2004 Justice for All Act, including Title I The Scott Campbell, Stephanie Roper, Wendy Preston, Louarna Gillis, and Nila Lynn Crime Victims' Rights Act

2006 Adam Walsh Child Protection and Safety Act

2010 Tribal Law and Order Act

Source: http://ovc.ncjrs.gov/ncvrw2011/pdf/landmarks.pdf

Victim impact statements allow victims to participate in the trial of the offender.

Victim impact statement (VIS)
A statement from the victim to the judge during the sentencing phase of the offender's trial.

Victim Impact Statements (VIS)

One key advancement for victims' rights is the use of victim impact statements. A **victim impact statement (VIS)** allows the victim to actively participate in the sentencing hearing of the offender: it is a statement given at sentencing in which the victim can tell the court exactly how the victimization has affected his or her life. These statements can be delivered in person (known as allocution) or submitted in writing as part of a pre-sentence investigation report (PIR).[75]

Victim impact statements have drawn enough controversy to merit appeals that have gone all the way to the U.S. Supreme Court. In *Booth v. Maryland*, the court reversed a capital sentence because the jury had heard an especially emotional VIS. The impact statement detailed how the slaying of an elderly couple had destroyed the lives of three generations of a family. The court ruled that the use of such a statement was inflammatory and unconstitutional because of its arbitrary nature. The court felt it was wrong to determine the penalty based upon perceptions of a victim's perceived "worth."[76] This ruling was later overturned, however, in *Payne v. Tennessee* in 1991. The case involved the murder of a mother and child; during sentencing the prosecution wanted to enter a VIS detailing the emotional duress of a three-year-old survivor of the attack. The court ruled that a VIS was permissible in a capital case. The grounds for this ruling was that if prosecutors are allowed to present evidence as to the repercussions of the crime on victims, then there is nothing to preclude a jury from hearing it.[77]

Balancing the rights of victims with the rights of the accused is not easy. Victim impact statements in particular are controversial. Critics charge that victim impact statements tarnish the objectivity of the judicial process.[78] The emotionally charged testimony of a suffering victim has the potential to be highly prejudicial, especially if their testimony simply talks about what a great person the victim was. Critics assert that judges may be overcome with emotion and accede to pleas from victims who would use a VIS vindictively to exact revenge or unfairly influence sentencing. The claim is not without merit. A particular fear is that the emphasis will shift from offender to victim, leading to unjustly stiff sentences for offenders who commit crimes against especially sympathetic victims.[79]

While victim impact statements remain the subject of controversy, they undeniably give victims a greater voice in the justice system, and the Supreme Court ultimately upheld them. The Supreme Court decided in *Payne v. Tennessee*[80] that such statements are admissible as testimony during the sentencing phase of the trial. They ruled that such statements were not unconstitutional, and that the punishment should fit the crime.[81] Additionally, advocates for VIS have noted that proper statements help judges and prosecutors to understand in a visceral way the emotional devastation caused by crime, and therefore hand down more appropriate sentences.[82] A study conducted in Australia determined that there was no discernible change in sentencing patterns following the newly implemented use of VIS.[83]

Remedying the Costs of Crime Victimization

Remedying the costs of victimization can take several forms. The legislative reforms discussed earlier aim to help victims who enter the criminal justice system. However, returning the victim to their pre-victimization state often requires financial restitution. This can take the form of compensation from the state, restitution from the offender, or civil lawsuits. The criminal justice system needs witness testimony to get convictions. A victim may refrain from contact with the criminal justice system because they feel that, financially, they will be better off not participating.[84] Compensation, restitution, and civil lawsuits are all common ways to ease the financial burdens of victims and witnesses.

Compensation

Victim **compensation** involves monetary reimbursement paid by the state to the victim for losses sustained as a result of crime. The primary sources of funds for state compensation are financial assessments imposed on convicted businesses and individuals, bond forfeitures, and fines. Victim compensation is based on the idea that the government has an obligation to care for the safety and well-being of its citizens and to provide a minimum standard of living for citizens. Some advocates and social scientists argue that crime can be attributed to economic and social inequalities such as racism, poverty, and so on. In this way, they argue, the state is in some sense liable for crime.[85] Compensation is one method to recover monetary losses for victims. One of the challenges with compensation is that many states require victims to exhaust all other options (e.g., private insurance) before applying for compensation from the state. As a result, victim compensation is often viewed as a source of last resort.

Compensation
A financial reward for a wrong incurred at the hands of an offender.

Restitution

Restitution, which involves compensation paid to victims by offenders who cause harm through action or negligence, is one of the oldest forms of redress available to victims. The idea is related to the ancient custom of *wergild*, in which compensation was paid to either the victim or the victim's family.[86] The practice also has parallels in the legal codes of Hammurabi and Justinian, as well as the Mosaic Law. Restitution is appealing for a number of reasons. It is an intuitive solution: crimes are committed by individuals against individuals, not just society, and therefore victims should be compensated by their victimizers. Even if the offense is against society, offenders can pay symbolic restitution in the form of money or service to the community. This is important in making the victim(s) whole again.[87]

Restitution has the additional advantage of enticing victims to assist the justice system. If victims and witnesses are reluctant to help the state prosecute offenders because of the financial consequences, then ensuring restitution from offenders may go a long way towards solving the problem. This provides a tangible reward for citizens' cooperation.

There are several drawbacks of offender restitution. Offenders, particularly those who commit theft, frequently do not have enough money to provide immediate restitution, as they are unemployed or incarcerated. In addition, the criminal justice system—in keeping with its idea of crime as committed against the state rather than the victim—is often more concerned with penal fines than compensating victims.[88]

Critical Thinking

How do you feel about exacting compensation from the state? Is it fair to make taxpayers pay for the actions of offenders?

Civil lawsuit
A case in which a plaintiff sues the defendant to recover money damages for negligence or harm.

Civil Suits   A final method of aiding victims, and one provided for by the Bill of Rights, is civil lawsuits. **Civil lawsuits** have the benefit, much like victim impact statements, of empowering victims and letting them participate in the court process, instead of leaving everything to the discretion of a state prosecutor. Victims who seek financial restitution can sue for punitive or compensatory damages. Punitive damages are meant to punish and deter the offender, while compensatory damages are meant to compensate victims for specific costs that they incur.[89]

Civil lawsuits have a number of advantages, aside from empowering the victim. Successful prosecution in a criminal case is difficult. As discussed earlier, the criminal justice system is constitutionally slanted toward the rights of offenders. To get a conviction, the level of proof must be "beyond a reasonable doubt," whereas in civil suits, all that is required is a "preponderance of evidence."[90]

Civil court is not without its problems. Victims are often unaware of this remedy, or have no idea of how to secure an attorney's services. A greater problem is that many victims are unable to afford an attorney, and, therefore, lower-class victims are often unable to pursue civil suits as a method of recourse.[91] Also, many offenders possess few assets, so victims will likely receive very little from the offender even if they win the case.

Victimization Surveys   The final section of this chapter will focus on the development and use of victimization surveys. As discussed earlier in the chapter, early victimologists recognized that they needed a better way to measure the effects and causes of victimization. As early victimologists suspected, there was

a great deal to be learned about criminal acts by collecting data about the victims. Victimization surveys have revealed that crime and victimization both occur in clusters in certain groups and in certain areas.[92] This allows criminologists and victimologists to track trends in crime and victimization, and to assess the risk certain populations have of becoming either victims or victimizers.

Measuring the Extent of Crime   There are three main sources that victimologists use to statistically assess crime and victimization rates.[93] The first, and oldest, of the major sources of crime data is the Uniform Crime Report. The UCR is a collection of official records from police departments, published annually by the FBI, that allows police departments to share information. This allows officials to track the magnitude of crime over time.[94]

The UCR tracks index crimes, which group crimes by the nature of the incident. It also provides geographic data, as it groups offenses by reports that come from the police forces of towns, states, cities, etc.[95] Other tables feature data about the people arrested for these crimes, including sex, age, race, resident status, and past arrest record. This demonstrates that the attention is primarily focused upon the offenders, rather than the victims. Indeed, one shortcoming of the UCR is that it contains limited information about victims. In addition, many crimes go unreported to law enforcement and are not reflected in the UCR. Individuals will not report an act to law enforcement unless they clearly label the act as criminal in their own minds. As a result of these limitations, victimologists look for other sources of data.

Another source is self-report surveys, in which respondents are asked—with the promise of confidentiality—to disclose information about themselves and any crimes they have committed. Even with the inherent risk of exposure, the respondents' replies are eye-opening. It is apparent that much more crime is committed than the official UCR indicates.[96] Self-report surveys also include the demographic and personal information about respondents that the UCR lacks.

Building on this, the next logical step for researchers was to ask people not about offenses they had committed, but about any experiences of victimization in their lives. Victimization surveys went through several iterations before arriving at the National Crime Survey (NCS). The NCS was first administered in 1973 to 100,000 households. Each household was contacted twice a year for three years. The survey was redesigned in 1979, and officially renamed the National Crime Victimization Survey (NCVS) in 1992. Questions were updated for increased accuracy, and to capture as much information as possible about the victim and the circumstances surrounding the criminal event.[97] The survey is more than 20 pages long, and includes questions such as "Have you been robbed in the past six months?" If the response is affirmative, the survey proceeds to ask detailed questions about the experience and the subsequent consequences. Data are categorized into property and personal victimizations. Personal crimes include rape and sexual assault, aggravated and simple assault, robbery, and purse-snatching or pocket-picking. Property crimes include theft, motor vehicle theft, burglary, and vandalism.[98]

FIGURE 13.3 Crime in the United States by Volume and Rate per 100,000 Inhabitants, 1990–2009

Year	Population[1]	Violent crime	Violent crime rate	Murder and nonnegligent manslaughter	Murder and nonnegligent manslaughter rate	Forcible rape	Forcible rape rate	Robbery	Robbery rate
1990	249,464,396	1,820,127	729.6	23,438	9.4	102,555	41.1	639,271	256.3
1991	252,153,092	1,911,767	758.2	24,703	9.8	106,593	42.3	687,732	272.7
1992	255,029,699	1,932,274	757.7	23,760	9.3	109,062	42.8	672,478	263.7
1993	257,782,608	1,926,017	747.1	24,526	9.5	106,014	41.1	659,870	256.0
1994	260,327,021	1,857,670	713.6	23,326	9.0	102,216	39.3	618,949	237.8
1995	262,803,276	1,798,792	684.5	21,606	8.2	97,470	37.1	580,509	220.9
1996	265,228,572	1,688,540	636.6	19,645	7.4	96,252	36.3	535,594	201.9
1997	267,783,607	1,636,096	611.0	18,208	6.8	96,153	35.9	498,534	186.2
1998	270,248,003	1,533,887	567.6	16,974	6.3	93,144	34.5	447,186	165.5
1999	272,690,813	1,426,044	523.0	15,522	5.7	89,411	32.8	409,371	150.1
2000	281,421,906	1,425,486	506.5	15,586	5.5	90,178	32.0	408,016	145.0
2001[2]	285,317,559	1,439,480	504.5	16,037	5.6	90,863	31.8	423,557	148.5
2002	287,973,924	1,423,677	494.4	16,229	5.6	95,235	33.1	420,806	146.1
2003	290,788,976	1,383,676	475.8	16,528	5.7	93,883	32.3	414,235	142.5
2004	293,656,842	1,360,088	463.2	16,148	5.5	95,089	32.4	401,470	136.7
2005	296,507,061	1,390,745	469.0	16,740	5.6	94,347	31.8	417,438	140.8
2006[3]	298,754,819	1,435,951	480.6	17,318	5.8	94,782	31.7	449,803	150.6
2007[3]	301,290,332	1,421,990	472.0	17,157	5.7	91,874	30.5	447,155	148.4
2008[3]	304,374,846	1,392,629	457.5	16,442	5.4	90,479	29.7	443,574	145.7
2009	307,006,550	1,318,398	429.4	15,241	5.0	88,097	28.7	408,217	133.0

[1] Populations are U.S. Census Bureau provisional estimates as of July 1 for each year except 1990 and 2000, which are decennial census counts.

[2] The murder and nonnegligent homicides that occurred as a result of the events of September 11, 2001, are not included in this table.

[3] The crime figures have been adjusted.

NOTE: Although arson data are included in the trend and clearance tables, sufficient data are not available to estimate totals for this offense. Therefore, no arson data are published in this table.

Although the survey focuses on fewer types of crime than the UCR (it does not address kidnapping, extortion, or blackmail, for example), it does provide far more information about the victims and any previous relationship between victims and offenders.[99] The NCVS records information about the number of victimizations, the relationship between the victim and offender (if any), and the losses and consequences incurred by the victimization, among other data.[100]

Of the three major sources of crime data, the NCVS holds the most promise for victimologists.[101] The NCVS is the primary source for the extent and nature of victimization. It provides important details about victims, which may help track patterns in victimizations. The UCR is limited in that it only accounts for crimes that are reported to the police. The NCVS depends upon the victim's perception of events, as opposed to that of a third-party observer. One limitation of the NCVS is that it is a survey, and therefore depends upon honest an-

Aggravated assault	Aggravated assault rate	Property crime	Property crime Rate	Burglary	Burglary rate	Larceny-theft	Larceny theft rate	Motor vehicle theft	Motor vehicle theft rate
1,054,863	422.9	12,655,486	5,073.1	3,073,909	1,232.2	7,945,670	3,185.1	1,635,907	655.8
1,092,739	433.4	12,961,116	5,140.2	3,157,150	1,252.1	8,142,228	3,229.1	1,661,738	659.0
1,126,974	441.9	12,505,917	4,903.7	2,979,884	1,168.4	7,915,199	3,103.6	1,610,834	631.6
1,135,607	440.5	12,218,777	4,740.0	2,834,808	1,099.7	7,820,909	3,033.9	1,563,060	606.3
1,113,179	427.6	12,131,873	4,660.2	2,712,774	1,042.1	7,879,812	3,026.9	1,539,287	591.3
1,099,207	418.3	12,063,935	4,590.5	2,593,784	987.0	7,997,710	3,043.2	1,472,441	560.3
1,037,049	391.0	11,805,323	4,451.0	2,506,400	945.0	7,904,685	2,980.3	1,394,238	525.7
1,023,201	382.1	11,558,475	4,316.3	2,460,526	918.8	7,743,760	2,891.8	1,354,189	505.7
976,583	361.4	10,951,827	4,052.5	2,332,735	863.2	7,376,311	2,729.5	1,242,781	459.9
911,740	334.3	10,208,334	3,743.6	2,100,739	770.4	6,955,520	2,550.7	1,152,075	422.5
911,706	324.0	10,182,584	3,618.3	2,050,992	728.8	6,971,590	2,477.3	1,160,002	412.2
909,023	318.6	10,437,189	3,658.1	2,116,531	741.8	7,092,267	2,485.7	1,228,391	430.5
891,407	309.5	10,455,277	3,630.6	2,151,252	747.0	7,057,379	2,450.7	1,246,646	432.9
859,030	295.4	10,442,862	3,591.2	2,154,834	741.0	7,026,802	2,416.5	1,261,226	433.7
847,381	288.6	10,319,386	3,514.1	2,144,446	730.3	6,937,089	2,362.3	1,237,851	421.5
862,220	290.8	10,174,754	3,431.5	2,155,448	726.9	6,783,447	2,287.8	1,235,859	416.8
874,048	292.6	10,031,359	3,357.7	2,196,304	735.2	6,636,615	2,221.4	1,198,440	401.1
865,804	287.4	9,872,815	3,276.8	2,187,277	726.0	6,587,040	2,186.3	1,098,498	364.6
842,134	276.7	9,775,149	3,211.5	2,228,474	732.1	6,588,046	2,164.5	958,629	315.0
806,843	262.8	9,320,971	3,036.1	2,199,125	716.3	6,327,230	2,060.9	794,616	258.8

swers. For that reason there may be underreporting, as people are unlikely to report crimes committed by members of their own family. An additional limitation is that individuals are not asked about crimes that they themselves have committed.[102]

Victimization surveys are the most important tool victimologists have for studying victimization. They provide researchers with the number and types of victims, as well as the biographical information needed to compare trends from one geographical area to another. Additionally, surveys ask questions about feelings and experiences, which help therapists develop treatments to assist in victim recovery programs.[103] Researchers use surveys, in conjunction with the UCR, to try to map trends in crime and victimization. For example, victimologists can compare dates from the UCR and NCVS to determine whether more robberies are leading to homicides. They can determine this by cross-referencing victim-

FIGURE 13.4 Crime Victimization

Criminal victimization, numbers, rates, and percent change, by type of crime, 2007 and 2008

Types of crime	Number of Victimizations		Rates[a]		Percent change 2007–2008[b]
	2007	2008	2007	2008	
All crimes	22,879,720	21,312,400	~	~	
Violent crimes[c]	5,177,130	4,856,510	20.7	19.3	–6.9%
Rape/sexual assault	248,280	203,830	1.0	0.8	–18.5
Robbery	597,320	551,830	2.4	2.2	–8.3
Assault	4,331,530	4,100,850	17.3	16.3	–6.0
Aggravated	858,940	839,940	3.4	3.3	–2.9
Simple	3,472,590	3,260,920	13.9	12.9	–6.8
Personal theft[d]	194,060	136,710	0.8	0.5	–30.1%
Property crimes	17,508,530	16,319,180	146.5	134.7	–8.1%*
Household burglary	3,215,090	3,188,620	26.9	26.3	–2.2
Motor vehicle theft	979,640	795,160	8.2	6.6	–19.9*
Theft	13,313,800	12,335,400	111.4	101.8	–8.6*

Note: Detail may not add to total because of rounding. Total population age 12 or older was 250,344,870 in 2007 and 252,242,520 in 2008. Total number of households was 119,503,530 in 2007 and 121,141,060 in 2008.

~Not applicable

*Difference is significant at the 95%-confidence level.

[a]Victimization rates are per 1,000 persons age 12 or older for violent crime or per 1,000 households for property crime.
[b]Percent change calculated based on unrounded estimates.
[c]Excludes murder because the NCVS is based on interviews with victims and therefore cannot measure murder.
[d]Includes pocket picking, completed purse snatching, and attempted purse snatching.

ization reports of robberies with homicide data from the UCR.[104] The results have concluded that murders during robbery are rare, and usually are not the result of premeditation; the robber's goal is almost always to steal and run.

According to the data available from 2008, the most recent NCVS, both violent and property crime rates are at their lowest levels in 30 years.[105] Figure 13.4 represents NCVS data on victimization from 2007–2008.

Notice that the NCVS tracks many of the same crimes as the UCR, but the numbers differ significantly from the UCR numbers in Figure 13.3. This suggests that there is a substantial amount of crime that goes unreported to law enforcement. For this reason, the FBI and other authorities regard the reports as complementary to one another.

Figure 13.5 breaks down the demographic information of victims. This gives social scientists a clearer picture of how crime disproportionately affects certain populations.

Because the NCVS tracks victims over a period of time, it allows researchers to study repeat victimization. Typically, **repeat victimization** is defined as the recurrence of a crime either in the same place or with the same victim. Some crimes are more likely to be repeated than others. For example, women who are

Repeat victimization
The recurrence of a crime either in the same place or with the same victim.

FIGURE 13.5 Rates of Crime Victimization in 2008 by Age, Race, and Gender.

Demographic characteristic of victim	Population	All	Rape/sexual assault	Robbery	All assault	Aggravated assault	Simple assault
Gender							
Male	123,071,020	21.3	0.3†	2.7	18.3	3.9	14.5
Female	129,171,510	17.3	1.3	1.7	14.3	2.8	11.5
Race							
White	204,683,500	18.1	0.6	1.6	15.9	3.0	12.8
Black	30,709,860	25.9	1.9†	5.5	18.5	5.2	13.3
Other race*	13,952,240	15.2	0.9†	3.0†	11.3	2.8	8.5
Two or more races	2,896,930	51.6	1.9†	6.8	42.9	6.8	36.1
Hispanic origin							
Hispanic	34,506,680	16.4	0.6†	3.4	12.4	3.5	8.9
Non-Hispanic	217,351,750	19.7	0.8	2.0	16.9	3.3	13.6
Age							
12–15	16,414,550	42.2	1.6†	5.5	35.2	6.1	29.0
16–19	17,280,270	37.0	2.2	4.8	30.0	5.6	24.5
20–24	20,547,620	37.8	2.1	5.4	30.3	8.7	21.5
25–34	40,649,500	23.4	0.7	2.3	20.5	4.0	16.5
35–49	65,123,030	16.7	0.8	1.9	14.1	2.7	11.4
50–64	55,116,320	10.7	0.2†	0.8	9.7	2.0	7.7
65 or older	37,111,240	3.1	0.2†	0.2†	2.7	0.4†	2.3

Violent victimizations per 1,000 persons age 12 or older

Note: Violent crimes measured by the National Crime Victimization Survey include rape, sexual assault, robbery, and aggravated and simple assault. Because the NCVS interviews persons about their victimizations, murder and manslaughter cannot be included.

†Based upon 10 or fewer sample cases.

*Includes American Indians, Alaska Natives, Native Hawaiians, and other Pacific Islanders.

victims of intimate partner violence are rarely only victimized by one type of assault and are assaulted repeatedly over time. Analysis also reveals that certain crimes are likely to be repeated within a certain period of time. Fifteen percent of the time, domestic offenders will repeat within 24 hours. The chances increase to 25% over the course of five weeks. Property crime at school is among the most recurring; there is a 70% chance of repeat victimization within one month.[106]

Direct and Indirect Victimization

Victimization is not limited merely to those directly victimized. In addition to the particular victim, or victims, of a criminal act, there are secondary victims who are victimized indirectly. Indirect victims, or derivative victims, are those affected by traumatic events even though they are not direct victims of crime, as shown in the Gabrielle Giffords case at the beginning of the chapter.[107] These victims include not just friends and family members of direct victims, but all those who are affected by the "ripple effect" of victimization.

Indirect victim
A person who suffers vicarious trauma as a result of crime even though he or she is not a direct victim.

Compassion fatigue
Emotional exhaustion as a result of treating traumatized victims.

Victim advocate
A person who works in victim services to attend to the needs and rights of victims.

Ripple Effect   Indirect victimization is best illustrated by the "ripple effect." The term, coined by Remer and Ferguson, refers to the effects of victimization, which "spread out like waves from victims to all those with whom they have intimate contact."[108] Furthermore, the trauma felt by victims can negatively affect the social workers and victims' advocates who handle their case. This transference of emotion is called **compassion fatigue** and results in case workers being so emotionally invested in their clients that they are unable to attend to the emotional needs of their own lives.[109] **Victim advocates**, or people trained to help victims handle traumatic events, are particularly susceptible to compassion fatigue. Victim advocates were initially volunteers. As a result of the development of victimology, victim advocacy has become an established profession.[110]

Underreporting   Underreporting is a problem that affects all three of the main sources of statistics. The UCR overlooks what is termed the "dark figure of crime," which refers to any crime that the police are unaware of.[111] The NCVS is a self-report survey of victimization, and thus relies on the honesty of respondents and does not ask about respondents' criminal behavior. The NCVS also does not interview anyone under the age of 12, and includes no questions about arson or crimes against businesses. If such crimes go unreported, they will not appear in the UCR either, leading to significant underreporting.

Fear of Crime   Social scientists have long known that fear of crime is a powerful social force in American society. Crime is frequently a centerpiece of political campaigns and evening newscasts, and ranks highly in polls measuring the importance of certain domestic issues to Americans. This fear has very real consequences. Citizens may feel the need for locks, car alarms, and security systems. Fear of crime has spurred the federal government to spend massive amounts of money on countermeasures. Major public events, such as parades, holidays, and sports games, must have extensive security.

Victimization can have a "ripple effect" that spreads to many people.

Ethics and Professionalism: Child Services

You are a case worker with Child Protective Services. One of your clients, Marie, has been successfully working on her case plan for a neglect charge for the past 11 months. Marie has secured employment, gone to treatment, attended all mandatory meetings, attended school, and been to every scheduled visit with her children. On your most recent visit to Marie's home, you saw an empty bottle of alcohol in her garbage can. Alcohol use is in violation of her case plan.

Should you report Marie's violation? Or should you not report her and give her a second chance? If she is found to have violated her case plan, Marie would have to start her case plan from the beginning, resulting in her children remaining out of her custody until she successfully finishes. Her children have been in foster placement for the past 11 months.

That fear, though, is misdirected in many cases. People typically imagine a scenario in which a masked hoodlum breaks into their home, bent on inflicting bodily harm upon them. Statistics show, however, that in the case of violent crimes, people are more likely to be victimized by an acquaintance or relative.[112] In 2003, for example, 68% of female victims were victimized by someone who was not a complete stranger. This is particularly true in the case of violent offenses such as rape or assault.[113]

There is something of a paradox among crime victims: Those who are least likely to be victims are the most likely to be afraid. Statistics show that the fear of crime has not diminished over the past 20 years, despite the fact that crime itself has dropped. Over the last two decades, the rate of violent crime in the U.S. has been reduced by half, while property crime has dropped by 60%.[114] Results of a recent Gallup poll suggest that fear of crime is increasing even though crime is decreasing. In 2010, two-thirds of those surveyed said they thought that nationwide crime was on the rise.[115] Ironically, those who self-identified as being the most fearful—women and the elderly—are statistically at a lower risk than the general population.[116]

The Role of Media   Modern mass media have a profound effect on fear of crime. The media coverage that surrounds the most heinous crimes—which are the most aggressively pursued by journalists—subjects victims to public exposure that can be traumatizing. Female victims in rape cases are particularly vulnerable, as defense attorneys may put their personal lives and past sexual history on trial despite shield laws that should protect this information from being released.

However, the media's influence can be positive as well, particularly when it comes to raising awareness of certain types of victimization. The media's coverage of a high-profile case can help the public become aware of legislation that addresses a particular type of crime or victimization. This can incite the public to clamor for legislative action. For example, the compulsory notification of the community prior to the release of a sex offender, known as "Megan's Law," was

The media coverage that surrounds the most heinous crimes can subject victims to traumatic public exposure.

© 2012 BY LOREN RODGERS. UNDER LICENSE FROM SHUTTERSTOCK, INC.

the result of the murder of a seven-year-old girl named Megan Kanka. Megan was sexually assaulted and strangled by her neighbor, a two-time convicted sex offender who had recently been released from prison. Nobody in the neighborhood, including Megan's parents, was notified about the background of this man. The media coverage of this case, and the resulting public outcry, led to the creation of Megan's Law.

It should be acknowledged that the public discourse that surrounds victimization and victims' rights is highly politicized. Politicians are fully aware they will never lose votes by espousing their support for victims. Their support for victims' rights is often calculated to score political points. For example, a bill recently passed in New Mexico to eliminate the death penalty required that savings from not performing executions be transferred to programs for victims.[117] The inclusion of language that supported victims made it politically unpopular to oppose the legislation, and allowed conservative legislators, normally supportive of capital punishment, to back the bill.[118] While this may seem cynical, it is important to remember the politically charged nature of the debate about victimization.

What Statistics Suggest about Crime

A comprehensive review of statistics from both the UCR and the NCVS reveals some surprising conclusions about crime in the U.S. Firstly, crime is not rising sharply, despite the claims of some politicians. Victimization has actually been declining since 1981, per the NCVS, and violent crime in particular has decreased since 1993.[119] Over the course of the 1990s, the murder rate per 100,000 dropped from 9.8 to 5.6.[120]

Statistics also tell us that offenders and victims often inhabit the same environment, and usually share certain characteristics. Both are disproportionately male, young, urban residents, unemployed, unmarried, not in school, and—in the United States—African-American.[121]

Limitations of the Criminal Justice System   It is, of course, impossible for the criminal justice system to solve all problems related to crime. Many of the causes of crime, both violent crime and property crime, are systemic, due to social inequalities, and cannot be immediately fixed by the actions of the court. Prosecutors and courts are often overworked, and lack the support necessary to effectively attend to every case.

Attempts to Address the Needs of Victims   The criminal justice system and the government have made progress in their attempts to address the needs of crime victims. States have implemented policies designed to ease the plight of victims during their involvement with the criminal justice system. Some have designed educational programs on sensitive topics such as rape and sexual assault to better equip officials to treat victims properly. Often, states are required to keep the victim informed of the case's progress. Additionally, prosecutors and the police are trained to help victims find the support they need, in the form of rape crisis centers, domestic violence shelters, or victim assistance centers. State compensation programs help victims with medical costs, and judges are encouraged to order offenders to pay restitution to offset the lost value of stolen or destroyed property.[122]

Future Directions   The past 30 years have shown significant progress in securing rights for crime victims. Today, there are several programs in the United States that offer degrees in victimology and **victim services**. It is important to reiterate that the field of "general victimology" is very broad and focuses on many different types of victims. In this chapter, we have focused on issues and concerns for victims of criminals.

Victim services
Programs and support systems for victims of crime.

Victimology faces several challenges. First, there is a need to continue dialogue between researchers, legislatures, criminal justice officials, and victims' groups to ensure that the appropriate policies and initiatives are put in place to help crime victims. Second, there is a need for constant monitoring and evaluation of these initiatives to ensure that they are truly effective for victims of crime and to suggest new initiatives that may be needed. For example, mandatory arrest policies for domestic violence swept the nation in the 1990s. In spite of widespread adoption of these policies, research now suggests that these policies may actually cause further harm to victims.[123] Third, there is a need to continue to raise awareness about the challenges that victims of crime face and the role of the criminal justice system in alleviating (or exacerbating) these challenges. This increased awareness can provide a foundation for additional research and the development of programs and policies that address this population's specific needs.

Chapter Summary

- Victimology is the scientific study of victims and victimization. It grew out of recognition that in order to understand the motivations of criminals, it is necessary to understand the role of the victim in the crime. Understanding the dynamic that exists between offender and victim is key to understanding the genesis of the criminal act.

- Early leaders in victimology included Benjamin Mendelssohn, who classified victims based upon what he believed was their level of blame for the crime; Hans von Hentig, who devised typologies that explained why some people are more likely to become victims than others; and Marvin Wolfgang, whose studies attempted to analyze the context in which crimes occur, and to illuminate social inequalities that may be the root of the problem.

- The costs of victimization are the psychological, physical, emotional, and financial costs to the victim, the victim's family, and society as a whole. This includes the first victimization—the crime at the hands of the offender—and the second victimization, the challenges the victims may face from the criminal justice system.

- The movement to add a Victims' Bill of Rights (VRA) to the U.S. Constitution is ongoing. Laws have been passed in most states to ensure victims have a right to be present at the trial, to be protected from harassment, and to make a statement at sentencing.

- Criminologists and victimologists now study a more statistically comprehensive picture of crime using the UCR, self-report surveys, and victimization surveys. Victimization surveys (such as the National Crime Victimization Survey) help reveal the substantial extent to which crime goes unreported.

- Victimization is not limited merely to those directly victimized. In addition to the direct victims of a criminal act, there are secondary victims who are victimized indirectly. Victimization spreads like a "ripple effect" to all those with whom the direct victims have intimate contact.

Critical Thinking ?

1. How are victims portrayed in the media?
2. Do you think there is ever a situation where it would be appropriate to have crime victims pay for evidence collection? Explain.
3. Compare and contrast the UCR and NCVS. What are the advantages and disadvantages of each?
4. Can both victims' rights and the rights of the accused be fairly protected? Would the Constitution have to be amended in order to do so? Explain your reasoning.
5. Critically evaluate the fairness of civil suits and restitution as recourse methods. Specifically address whether or not the Eighth Amendment protects impoverished victims who may be unable to afford an attorney to pursue a civil suit.
6. Do you think that victim impact statements could be subjective and cause the jury and judge to overlook the objective facts in a case?
7. Explain the difference between restitution and compensation.
8. Should offenders have the right to profit from selling accounts of their crimes to the media? Why or why not?

9. Why do you think certain segments of the population (e.g., the elderly) are highly fearful of victimization when their lifestyle places them at statistically low risk?

10. Explain the effects, both positive and negative, that the media has on public perceptions of crime rates and victims.

Media

Office for Victims of Crime: http://www.ojp.usdoj.gov/ovc
The Department of Justice's page for crime victims provides updates and news on victims' rights as well as contact information for victim support programs.

National Victim Assistance Academy: https://www.ovcttac.gov/nvaa/
This website for programs coordinated through the Office of Justice includes resources for training victim advocates and social workers in the United States.

National Center for Victims of Crime: http://www.ncvc.org
The NCVC, a research and advocacy group for victims of crime, lobbies for legislation aimed at furthering the cause of victims' rights.

National Coalition Against Domestic Violence: http://www.ncadv.org
This organization is dedicated to providing support and raising awareness for victims of domestic violence, especially women and children, and provides support for shelters for battered women.

Rape Abuse and Incest National Network: http://www.rainn.org
RAINN, the largest anti-sexual-abuse network in the United States, provides confidential services for victims via rape treatment hotlines and educates the public about sexual assault.

International Victimology Institute Tillburg: http://www.victimology.nl
The International Victimology Institute based at Tillburg University in the Netherlands specializes in interdisciplinary research aimed at empowering and supporting victims of crime.

Endnotes

1. "Remarks by the President on the Shootings in Tucson, Arizona." (2011). *The White House*. Retrieved from http://www.whitehouse.gov/the-press-office/2011/01/08/remarks-president-shootings-tucson-arizona

2. "Boehner Condemns Attack on Congresswoman Gabrielle Giffords." (2011). *Speaker of the House John Boehner*. Retrieved from http://www.speaker.gov/News/DocumentSingle.aspx?DocumentID=219343

3. Karmen, A. (2004). *Crime Victims: An Introduction to Victimology*. Toronto, Canada: Wadsworth.

4. Cole, G., & Smith, C. (2007). *The American System of Criminal Justice*. Belmont, CA: Wadsworth, 38.

5. Siegel, L. J. (2005). *Criminology* (9th ed.). Belmont, CA: Wadsworth, 14.

6. Karmen, 2004, 9.

7. Doerner, W. G., & Lab, S. P. (2008). *Victimology*. Newark, NJ: LexisNexis, 1.

8. Karmen, 2004, 2.

9. Schafer, S. (1968). *The Victim and His Criminal*. New York, NY: Random House.

10. Doerner & Lab, 2008, 2–3.

11. Cole & Smith, 2007, 39.

12. Ryan, W. (1976). *Blaming the Victim*. Vintage.

13. Ibid.

14. Schafer, 1968, 79–83.

15. Luckenbill, D. F. (1977). "Criminal Homicide as a Situated Transaction." *Social Problems, 25*(2), 176–186.

16. Hoffman, H. (1992). "What Did Mendelsohn Really Say?" In S. Ben David & G. F. Kirchhoff (Eds.), *International Faces of Criminology*. Monchengladbach: WSV Publishing.

17. Mendelssohn, B. (1956, July). "The Victimology." *Etudes Internationale de Psycho-sociologie Criminelle*.
18. Ibid., 23–26.
19. Doerner & Lab, 2008, 6–7.
20. Singer, S. (1981). "Homogenous Victim-Offender Populations: A Review and Some Research Implications." *Journal of Criminal Law and Criminology*, 779–788.
21. Doerner & Lab, 2008, 13.
22. Fattah, E. A. (2000). "Victimology: Past, Present and Future." *Criminologie*, 17–46.
23. Hentig, H.V. (1948). *The Criminal and His Victim*. New Haven, CT: Yale University Press, 436.
24. Scully, D., & Marolla, J. (1984). "Convicted Rapists' Vocabulary of Motive: Excuses and Justifications." *Social Problems, 31*(5), 530–544.
25. Groth, N. A. (1979). *Men Who Rape*. New York, NY: Plenum Press.
26. McCaghy, C. (1968). "Drinking and Deviance Disavowal: The Case of Child Molesters." *Social Problems, 16*(1), 43–44.
27. Cohen, L. E., & Felson, M. (1979). "Social Change and Crime Rate Trends: A Routine Activity Approach." *American Sociological Review, 44*(4), 588.
28. Wolfgang, M. E., & Ferracuti, F. (1967). *The Subculture of Violence: Towards an Integrated Theory in Criminology*. London, UK: Tavistock Publications.
29. Ibid.
30. Ibid.
31. Ibid.
32. Amir, M. (1971). *Patterns in Forcible Rape*. Chicago, IL: University of Chicago Press.
33. Doerner & Lab, 2008, 11.
34. Fattah, 2000.
35. Fattah, E. A. (1991). *Understanding Criminal Victimization*. Scarborough: Prentice Hall Canada.
36. Dussich, 120.
37. Luckenbill, 1977.
38. Franklin, C. W., & Franklin, A. P. (1976). "Victimology Revisited: A Critique and Suggestions for Future Direction." *Criminology*, 177–214.
39. Doerner & Lab, 2008, 12.
40. Van Ness, D. W. (1986). *Crime and Its Victims: What We Can Do*. Downers Grove, IL: InterVarsity Press, 29.
41. Ahrens, C. (2006). "Being Silenced: The Impact of Negative Social Reactions on the Disclosure of Rape." *American Journal of Community Psychology, 38*, 263–274.
42. Fattah, 1991.
43. Siegel, 2005.
44. Fattah, 1991.
45. Cole, A. M. (2007). *The Cult of True Victimhood: From the War on Welfare to the War on Terror*. Stanford, CA: Stanford University Press.
46. Ronel, N., Jaishankar, K., & Bensimon, M. (2008). *Trends and Issues in Victimology*. Cambridge, UK: Cambridge Scholars Publishing.
47. Cohen, S. (1993). "Human Rights and Crimes of the State: The Culture of Denial." *Australia and New Zealand Journal of Criminology, 26*, 97–115.
48. Marty Price, J. D. (2001, Fall). "Personalizing Crime." *Dispute Resolution Magazine*.
49. Braithwaite, J. (2002). *Restorative Justice and Responsive Regulation*. New York, NY: Oxford University Press, 249.
50. O'Connell, T., Wachtel, B., & Wachtel, T. (1999). *Conferencing Handbook: The New Real Justice Training Manual*. Pipersville, PA: The Piper's Press.
51. Wemmers, J. (2008). "Victim Participation and Therapeutic Jurisprudence." *Victims and Offenders, 3*(2&3), 165–191.
52. Cole & Smith, 2007, 45.
53. Doerner & Lab, 2008, 58.
54. Miller, T., Cohen, R., & Wiersema, B. (1996). *Victim Costs and Consequences: A New Look*. Washington, D.C.: National Institute of Justice.
55. Cole & Smith, 2007, 48.

56. Campbell, R., & Raja, S. (1999). "Secondary Victimization of Rape Victims: Insights from Mental Health Professionals Who Treat Survivors of Violence." *Violence and Victims, 14*(3), 261–75.

57. Karmen, 2004, 168–169.

58. Cannavale, F. J. (1976). *Witness Cooperation*. Lexington, MA: Institute for Law and Social Research.

59. Rootsaert, D. (1987). *A Prosecutor's Guide to Victim/Witness Assistance*. Alexandria, VA: National District Attorneys Association.

60. President's Task Force on Victims of Crime. (1982). *Final Report*. Washington, D.C.: U.S. Government Printing Office.

61. Viano, E. (1987). "Victim's Rights and the Constitution: Reflections on a Bicentennial." *Crime and Delinquency*, 438–451.

62. Young, M. A. (2009). "History of the Victims Movement in the United States." *International Organization for Victim Assistance*. Retrieved from http://www.iovahelp.org/About/MarleneAYoung/USHistory.pdf

63. Ibid., 72.

64. Doerner & Lab, 2008, 391.

65. Children's Guardian Fund. (n.d.). *Frequently Asked Questions*. Retrieved from http://www.childrensguardianfund.org/faq.html#D

66. Minnesota Judicial Branch, 4th District. (2005). *Guardian Ad Litem Frequently Asked Questions*. Retrieved from http://www.mncourts.gov/Documents/4/Public/Guardian_Ad_Litem/GAL_FAQ.pdf

67. Derene, S. (2005). *Crime Victims Fund Report: Past, Present, and Future*. Washington, D.C.: National Association of VOCA Assistance Administrators.

68. Gahr, E. (1997, March). "Advocates Raise Wide Support for Victims Rights Amendment." *Insight on the News*, 42.

69. Dolliver, J. M. (1987). "Victims' Rights Constitutional Amendment: A Bad Idea Whose Time Should Not Come." *The Wayne Law Review*, 87–93.

70. Doyle, C. (2004). "Victims' Right Amendment: A Proposal to Amend the United States Constitution in the 108th Congress." *CRS Web*. Retrieved from http://royce.house.gov/UploadedFiles/RL31750.pdf

71. President's Task Force on Victims of Crime, 1982.

72. Gahr, 1997.

73. Fattah, 2000, 32.

74. Young, 79.

75. Doerner & Lab, 2008, 408–409.

76. Triebwasser, J. (1987, September 29). "Victims' Non-Impact on Sentence." *Law Enforcement News*, 5.

77. *Payne v. Tennessee*, 501 U.S. 808 (1991).

78. Fattah, 2000, 33.

79. Dugger, A. (1996). "Victim Impact Evidence in Capital Sentencing: A History of Incompatibility." *American Journal of Criminal Law, 23*, 375–404.

80. *Payne v. Tennessee*, 1991.

81. Ibid.

82. Mulholland, C. (1995). "Sentencing Criminals: The Constitutionality of Victim Impact Statements." *Missouri Law Review, 60*, 731–748.

83. Hinton, M. (1995). "Expectations Dashed: Victim Impact Statements and the Common Law Approach to Sentencing in South Australia." *University of Tasmania Law Review*, 81–99.

84. Doerner & Lab, 2008, 83.

85. Childres, R. (1964). "Compensation for Criminally Inflicted Personal Injury." *New York University Law Review*, 455–471.

86. Fattah, 2000, 35.

87. Abel, C., & Marsh, F. (1984). *Punishment and Restitution: A Restitutionary Approach to Crime and the Criminal*. Westport, CT: Greenwood Press.

88. Fattah, 2000, 35.

89. Karmen, 2004, 302–303.

90. *The 1996 Victims' Rights Sourcebook: A Compilation and Comparison of Victims' Rights Laws*. (1996). Retrieved from http://www.ncvc.org/law/sbooks/toc.htm

91. Barbieri, M. (1989). "Civil Suits for Sexual Assault Victims: The Downside." *Journal of Interpersonal Violence, 4*(1), 110–113.

92. Fattah, 2000, 28.

93. O'Brien, R. M. (1985). *Crime and Victimization*. Beverly Hills, CA: Sage.

94. FBI. (1954–2003). *Uniform Crime Report: Crime in the United States (Selected Years 1953–2001)*. Washington D.C.: U.S. Government Printing Office.

95. Karmen, 2004, 54.

96. Karmen, 2004, 51.

97. Skogan, W. G. (1990). "The National Crime Survey Redesign." *Public Opinion Quarterly*, 256–272.

98. National Archive of Criminal Justice Data (NACJD). (2011). *National Crime Victimization Survey Resource Guide*, 1.

99. Karmen, 2004, 52.

100. NACJD, 2011.

101. Doerner & Lab, 2008, 27.

102. Cole & Smith, 2007, 29–30.

103. Young, 2009, 120.

104. Cook, P. (1985). "Is Robbery Becoming More Violent? An Analysis of Robbery Murder Trends Since 1968." *Journal of Criminal Law and Criminology*, 480–490.

105. Rand, M. R. (2009). *National Crime Victimization Survey: Crime Victimization, 2008* (NCJ 227777). Retrieved from http://bjs.ojp.usdoj.gov/content/pub/pdf/cv08.pdf

106. Weisel, D. L. (2005). *Analyzing Repeat Victimization*. Washington, D.C.: Department of Justice, Office of Community Oriented Policing Services.

107. Tomz, J. E., & McGillis, D. (1997). *Serving Crime Victims and Witnesses*. Washington, D.C.: U.S. Department of Justice.

108. Remer, R., & Ferguson, R. (1995). "Becoming a Secondary Survivor of Sexual Abuse." *Journal of Counseling and Development*.

109. Boscarino, J. A., Figley, C. R., & Adams, R. E. (2004). "Evidence of Compassion Fatigue Following the September 11 Terrorist Attacks: A Study of Secondary Trauma among Social Workers in New York." *International Journal of Emergency Mental Health*, 98–108.

110. Weigend, T. (1983). "Problems of Victim/Witness Assistance Programs." *Victimology*, 91–101.

111. Coleman, C., & Moynihan, J. (1996). *Understanding Crime Data: Haunted by the Dark Figure*. Open University Press.

112. Cole & Smith, 2007, 43.

113. Bureau of Justice Statistics. (2003). *Criminal Victimization in the United States—Statistical Tables, 2002*. Retrieved from http://bjs.ojp.usdoj.gov/index.cfm?ty=pbdetail&iid=1154

114. Beam, C. (2011). "Head Case: Crime Rates Have Plummeted over the Last 20 Years. Why Aren't We Less Scared?" *Slate*. Retrieved from http://www.slate.com/id/2284662/

115. Jones, J. M. (2010, November 18). "Americans Still Perceive Crime on the Rise." *Gallup*. Retrieved from http://www.gallup.com/poll/144827/americans-perceive-crime-rise.aspx

116. Cole & Smith, 2007, 46.

117. New Mexico Coalition to Repeal the Death Penalty. (n.d.). *Victims' Families First*. Retrieved from http://www.nmrepeal.org/issues/victims_families_first

118. Death Penalty Focus. (2009). *New Mexico Becomes the 15th State to Eliminate the Death Penalty; Other States Consider Taking Similar Action to Ease Budget Concerns*. Retrieved from http://www.deathpenalty.org/article.php?id=333

119. Cole & Smith, 2007, 30.

120. Karmen, 2004, 44.

121. Gottfredson, M. R. (1984). *Victims of Crime: The Dimensions of Risk*. London, UK: Home Office Research and Planning Unit.

122. Cole & Smith, 2007, 49–50.

123. Iyengar, R. (2006). *Does the Certainty of Arrest Reduce Domestic Violence? Evidence from Mandatory and Recommended Arrest Laws*. Retrieved from http://www.utdt.edu.ar/download.php?fname=_119522597271880400.pdf Iyengar, R. (2007, August 7). "The Protection Battered Spouses Don't Need." *New York Times*, late ed., 19.

14

Criminal Justice IN A Changing World

KEY TERMS

Biometrics, Black hat hacker, Business continuity plan, Cybercrime, Cyberterrorism, Department of Homeland Security, Emergency Management Assistance Compact, Extradition, Federal Emergency Management Agency (FEMA), Government cybercrime, Homeland security, Identity theft, International Court of Justice, INTERPOL, Malware, National Incident Management System (NIMS), National Response Framework, Patriot Act, Personal cybercrime, Property cybercrime, Stafford Act, Tabletop exercise, Terrorism, Tribunal, United Nations, White hat hacker

CHAPTER OBJECTIVES

1. Demonstrate the ability to discuss digital evidence and computer forensics.
2. Identify the range of employment possibilities in homeland security, continuity, cybercrime, and information assurance.
3. Identify the primary goals of homeland security initiatives in the United States.
4. Compare and contrast the major types of threats to homeland security the U.S. faces.
5. Analyze international collaboration efforts related to the investigation and prosecution of terrorism.
6. Discuss the International Court of Justice.

Case Study: The BTK Killer   The serial murderer known as the BTK ("Bind, Torture, Kill") killer first emerged in 1971 when he murdered four members of a Wichita, Kansas family. The BTK killer continued his crimes through the 1980s and '90s. During this time, the killer sent detailed letters to news outlets and law enforcement detailing the murder scenes. He continued this behavior until 1991 when the last known murder was reported. All letters and communication ceased and so did the murders.

In 2004, the BTK killer sent a letter to law enforcement admitting other killings previously not accounted for. From these killings, police were able to retrieve DNA evidence from under the victims' nails and conducted DNA testing on 1,100 men, but had no luck in discovering the BTK killer's identity. From 2004 through 2005, the killer communicated with police and other law enforcement 11 times.

In 2005, the BTK killer sent a floppy disk containing his final letter to a news station, which led to a breakthrough in the case. The disk contained a deleted Microsoft Word document belonging to an author with the first name Dennis. Furthermore, the Word license in question belonged to Christ Lutheran Church in Wichita. During further investigations, investigators discovered the BTK killer was a deacon at the church named Dennis Rader. With the help of Rader's daughter, police ran a DNA test and were able to positively identify Rader as the BTK killer. Without the use of computer forensics tools, Dennis Rader would more than likely never have been convicted.[1]

The investigation of the BTK killer is considered one of the best-known cases utilizing computer forensics investigators. As technology has advanced in the 20th and 21st centuries, the criminal justice system has progressed with it. In 2007, the Department of Homeland Security and Alabama state officials unveiled the National Computer Forensics Institute in Hoover, Alabama. Its purpose is to assist in the computer forensics field analyzing digital evidence.[2]

Advanced technology is just one of the ways in which the U.S. government is striving to protect the homeland from both internal and external threats. Since the beginning of the 21st century, the government has introduced a variety of measures to secure the United States not only from terrorism, but also from cyber warfare and natural disasters. This chapter will explore these 21st century criminal justice issues.

Homeland security
The preparedness measures taken to protect and ensure the security and safety of the homeland and its citizens.

Homeland Security   Homeland security is a widely used term, and one that has garnered increased attention in recent history following the attacks against the United States on September 11, 2001. Today, the term is used in reference to preparedness, response, and recovery measures taken at national, regional, state, and local levels. Homeland security addresses issues related to terrorism, natural disasters, and anything else that threatens the safety and security of the nation and its people. The growing impact of homeland security in the United States and throughout the world has a far-reaching effect on the criminal justice system, civil liberties, and life safety.

History and Goals of Homeland Security in the United States

Broadly speaking, terrorism can be defined as the use or threat of violence toward civilians in order to attain political, religious, or ideological goals. However, it is important to note that although this definition is used for our purposes, it is not a universal one. There are many other ways to define the term. For example, the Oxford English Dictionary defines it as "a system of terror" or "a policy intended to strike with terror those against whom it is adopted; the employment of methods of intimidations; the fact of terrorizing or condition of being terrorized."[3] Or, perhaps more helpful in getting to the meaning of the term, the United States Code defines it as "premeditated, politically motivated violence perpetrated against noncombatant targets by subnational groups or clandestine agents."[4]

The threat of terrorism has long been a part of history in the United States and around the world. Terrorist incidents have taken place at international venues, U.S. embassies, and on American soil. Perpetrators of these events have been foreign terrorist organizations or individuals and Americans themselves. For example, the first time a U.S. aircraft was hijacked, on May 1, 1961, a Puerto Rican national forced the pilot of a National Airlines flight to land in Cuba, where he was granted asylum.[5] In 1968, the U.S. Ambassador to Guatemala was assassinated by a rebel faction in Guatemala City, and in 1969 the U.S. Ambassador to Brazil was kidnapped by a Marxist revolutionary group.[6] On July 31, 1970, an advisor for the U.S. Agency for International Development was kidnapped in Uruguay; his body was found 10 days later.[7] These unfortunate events are representative of a long series of terrorist incidents, but gave no indication of what was to come later on American soil in Oklahoma City in 1995 and New York City in 2001.

One of the deadliest terrorist acts committed in the United States was the 1995 Oklahoma City bombing. The bombing, perpetrated by two Americans, targeted a federal building in downtown Oklahoma City, killing 168 people and injuring about 850.[8] However, the deadliest terrorist act committed on American soil took place on September 11, 2001, when attacks on the World Trade Center and the Pentagon killed approximately 3,000 people and gave rise to the most comprehensive reorganization ever taken by the federal government: the establishment of the **Department of Homeland Security (DHS)**.

DHS was officially established with the passage of the Homeland Security Act of 2002. The act defines the mission of DHS generally, including protecting the homeland by preventing and reducing the country's vulnerability to terrorist attacks, as well as minimizing damage, assisting in recovery, and acting as the coordinating body for crises and emergency planning at a national level.[9] Because of the wide spectrum of responsibilities housed within DHS, it is comprised of many federal agencies and offices, such as the Transportation Security Administration (TSA), U.S. Immigration and Customs Enforcement (ICE), U.S. Coast Guard, **Federal Emergency Management Agency (FEMA)**, U.S. Secret Service (USSS), and U.S. Customs and Border Protection (CBP).

It is important to note that, based on its mission, DHS is not solely focused on terrorism: it is also responsible for coordinating national response to natural

Terrorism
The use or threat of violence toward civilians in order to attain political, religious, or ideological goals.

Department of Homeland Security (DHS)
An agency created by the Homeland Security Act of 2002 whose mission is to protect the homeland by preventing and reducing the country's vulnerability to terrorist attacks, as well as minimizing damage, assisting in recovery, and acting as a focal point for crises and emergency planning.

Federal Emergency Management Agency (FEMA)
An agency within the Department of Homeland Security whose mission is to build, sustain, and strengthen the nation's capability to address all hazards through preparation, response, and recovery measures.

Hundreds of thousands of families and individuals requested temporary housing from FEMA following the destruction of Hurricane Katrina.

disasters and crises. The agency primarily responsible for this function within DHS is **FEMA**. FEMA's mission is to build, sustain, and strengthen the nation's capability to address all hazards through preparation, response, and recovery measures. This mission was put to the test as FEMA took center stage following Hurricane Katrina, which struck the Gulf coast in August 2005 and was the costliest natural disaster in U.S. history.[10] It killed nearly 2,000 people and displaced hundreds of thousands of families and individuals. FEMA played a major role in coordinating and responding to the disaster, but among its most visible tasks were the deployment of search and rescue teams and providing housing assistance for victims of the storm. Unfortunately, it became apparent that despite its efforts, the agency was suffering from insufficient manpower and lacked a clear understanding of roles and responsibilities in responding to the event. In turn, the government was largely criticized for its delayed and ineffective response.

Much like the events of September 11, the devastation of Hurricane Katrina was dramatic and has had a lasting impact on the country. These events exemplify the threats to homeland security faced by the U.S. in the 21st century. Although a manmade event (terrorist attack) is fundamentally different than a natural disaster, both types of threats require preparedness, response, and recovery efforts in order to protect the life and safety of potential victims. These three concepts provide the basis for homeland security and emergency management at all levels of government.

Preparedness Federal, state, and local governments place a heavy emphasis on preparedness, and in general, focus on two issues: (1) preparing the government, and its partners, for a coordinated response to a disaster, and (2) encouraging individuals to prepare themselves and their families for a disaster. One of the centerpieces of the federal focus on preparedness is the **National Response Framework (NRF)**, which is a comprehensive national guide for incident management and response to domestic incidents. The NRF takes an all-hazards ap-

National Response Framework (NRF)

A framework that forms the basis for coordination between all levels of government and the private sector in responding to a disaster. It establishes a comprehensive structure, method, and standard terminology for management of incidents.

FIGURE 14.1 Top 10 Most Costly Catastrophes in the United States.[11]

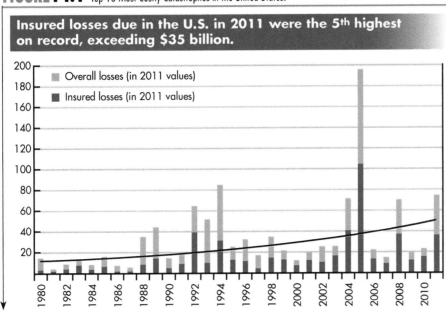

Insured losses due in the U.S. in 2011 were the 5th highest on record, exceeding $35 billion.

- Overall losses (in 2011 values)
- Insured losses (in 2011 values)

proach to dealing with incidents: it does not differentiate between a hurricane, a tornado, and a terrorist act, and it accounts for incidents ranging in size from small to catastrophic. Further, the NRF organizes national response by describing the roles of the federal government, states, private sector, and nongovernmental organizations during and after a disaster in an effort to make all response players more prepared in advance of an event.

The NRF works hand in hand with the **National Incident Management System (NIMS)**. NIMS provides an overall template for shared management of incidents and can be applied at all levels of government, including state, local, and tribal. A focal point of NIMS is a concept called the Incident Command System (ICS). ICS helps ensure a clear order of command in the management of an incident by assigning planners and responders to defined roles that work with one another and report to a single incident commander. Through the employment of ICS, NIMS streamlines how an incident can and should be managed, and provides a backbone for the specifics of the NRF at a national level. Used in conjunction with one another, NIMS and the NRF aim to integrate emergency management practices at all levels of government into a cohesive national framework.

Although the NRF and NIMS provide a valuable tool for the nation's policy-makers and responders, the government also emphasizes the importance of individuals' participation in preparedness efforts. For example, in 2002, President Bush launched Citizen Corps, a program designed to integrate citizens into protecting the nation and supporting first responders in their communities after a disaster.[12] Although the program was launched by the president and FEMA is responsible for its national coordination, it is an excellent example of state and local preparedness efforts as well. Citizen Corps volunteers work to

National Incident Management System (NIMS)
A national system that provides a consistent nationwide approach for government, the private sector, and nongovernmental organizations to work together in preparation, response, and recovery from domestic incidents.

strengthen community preparedness through state, local, and tribal Citizen Corps Councils.[13] The councils are formed in states and localities throughout the United States and create local strategies to encourage preparedness. They often work directly with state and local emergency management agencies.

Also related to individual preparedness is FEMA's Ready program, which highlights preparedness for individuals and their families, businesses, and kids.[14] The program encourages individuals and businesses to have a plan and be informed, because when an incident occurs—whether it is an act of terrorism, an accident, or a natural disaster—it may be several hours, or days, before relief workers can provide assistance. For individuals and families, this means thinking about food, water, first aid, and a plan for staying or evacuating depending on the circumstances. For businesses, this means focusing on continuity, and more specifically, creating a **business continuity plan**.

Business continuity plan

A plan that helps a business continue its essential functions in order to operate during and after a disaster or other disruptive event.

A business continuity plan helps a business continue its essential functions in order to operate during and after a disaster or other disruptive event. It is largely the same as a continuity of operations plan, which is implemented in the public sector. Both of these plans are fundamental to the preparedness of an agency, institution, or business and help the organization streamline its operations so that it can continue to function even with the constraints caused by an event. Most often these constraints relate to the physical structure of an organization—the personnel, equipment, or other tools and materials the organization normally relies on in accomplishing its day-to-day activities. For example, during a snowstorm or following a hurricane, employees may be unable to access the building to report for work. Alternatively, during a pandemic flu it may be unsafe for employees to gather at their normal place of work. Although these events are fundamentally different, they each require plans for allowing business to continue at an alternate location or with alternate staff. A continuity plan allows an organization to prioritize the essentials of its business so that a minimal amount of disruption takes place. Obviously a plan does not prevent disruption from occurring, but it better positions an organization to deal with an event if and when one does occur. And, as with all preparedness initiatives, it is imperative that continuity plans are exercised and tested.

There is a national standard for homeland security exercises called the Homeland Security Exercise and Evaluation Program (HSEEP). According to DHS, HSEEP "provides a standardized methodology and terminology for exercise design, development, conduct, evaluation, and improvement planning."[15] In particular, HSEEP notes seven types of exercises that range in complexity, goals, and outcomes. The least complex, a seminar, simply orients participants to the plan, concept, or idea. The most complex, a full-scale exercise, involves multiple agencies and jurisdictions, and tests many aspects of emergency response and recovery as if an event were actually happening. Though there are several types of exercises that fall somewhere between a seminar and a full-scale exercise, one commonly used option is a **tabletop exercise**. This is a discussion-based exercise related to a hypothetical situation. It allows participants to talk through a given scenario and discuss how plans or policies would be used to prevent, respond to, or recover from the scenario.

Tabletop exercise

An exercise presenting a hypothetical situation for discussion, used to assess preparedness by allowing participants to discuss how specific plans or policies would be implemented to prevent, respond to, or recover from the scenario.

Japan was devastated by a 9.0 earthquake and tsunami on March 11, 2011.

Response and Recovery   No matter how prepared a nation is, it cannot always prevent a crisis from occurring. Therefore it is equally important for a homeland security program to place emphasis on response and recovery efforts. A real-world example that brings this point to light occurred on March 11, 2011, when one of the most powerful earthquakes in recorded history hit Japan. It was followed by a devastating tsunami. The numbers of dead and missing were estimated to be over 28,000.[16] Prior to the catastrophe, Japan was well prepared in terms of its warning systems, mitigation efforts, and overall individual citizen preparedness to deal with natural disasters, and in particular, earthquakes and tsunamis. However, no amount of preparedness can prevent such a catastrophe, and in the aftermath of the events, the country immediately shifted gears to focus on response and recovery. For Japan, this meant relying on itself and its international partners to respond to the needs of the many survivors, including providing shelter, food, and health services.

In the United States, response and recovery from a disaster almost always begin at a local level, and depending on the severity of the event, can shift to the state and eventually federal levels. As such, all of these players must work together to provide timely and effective responses to an event and continue to play a role in the recovery process. Response and recovery efforts begin nearly immediately during an emergency, and often go hand in hand with a formal disaster or emergency declaration. The federal government has the power to issue a federal disaster declaration, but states have similar, parallel powers. The process of declaring a disaster varies by state, but in general, a governor may declare a state of emergency after consulting with local officials, thus triggering the state's emergency plan. In addition, it is generally true that a state's emergency plan allows for a change in the powers of government to deal most effectively with the emergency at hand. For example, if the disaster includes a threat to public health, many state emergency plans allow the governor, or another appropriate state official, to issue quarantine and isolation orders, which they would not be able to do otherwise.[17]

Stafford Act
A congressional act passed in 2009 that provides a method for states to request federal assistance to respond to a disaster. Short for The Robert T. Stafford Disaster Relief and Emergency Assistance Act.

However, if a governor determines that recovery is beyond the state's and localities' capabilities, he or she may request federal assistance under the Robert T. Stafford Disaster Relief and Emergency Assistance Act (**Stafford Act**).[18] In accordance with Stafford Act procedures, the governor must certify that federal assistance is necessary because the magnitude of the disaster exceeds what the state is capable of handling. The governor must also certify that the state executed its emergency plan, and that the state will share costs as needed.[19] In response to this request, FEMA completes a preliminary damage assessment, where personnel from FEMA work with the state's emergency management agency, other county and local officials, and the U.S. Small Business Administration to review damage, costs, and impacts of the disaster in affected areas.[20] Based on this assessment and recommended course of action, the president may issue a formal disaster declaration, thereby bringing the federal government's resources to the aid of the state in need.[21]

Legal Framework of U.S. Homeland Security and Emergency Management

Ensuring the nation's homeland security requires cooperation from all levels of government, along with nongovernmental organizations, private-sector businesses, and citizens. Because of the complicated nature of providing security and safety to the country, there is an equally comprehensive legal framework that delineates the authorities, powers, and roles of these players.

Patriot Act
A congressional act passed shortly after the September 11, 2001 terrorist attacks in the U.S., focusing primarily on providing law enforcement with legal authority to support efforts to fight terrorism. Short for The Uniting and Strengthening America by Providing Appropriate Tools Required to Intercept and Obstruct Terrorism (USA Patriot) Act.

Federal Bases of Authority

Arguably the cornerstone of legal authority for modern homeland security in the United States is the Uniting and Strengthening America by Providing Appropriate Tools Required to Intercept and Obstruct Terrorism (USA PATRIOT) Act of 2001. Commonly referred to as the **Patriot Act**, its focus is primarily on providing law enforcement agencies with legal authority to support efforts to fight terrorism. In particular, it addresses law enforcement's authority related to collecting information on and detaining suspected terrorists in an effort to deter terrorists from entering and operating within the U.S.[22] The legislation is quite lengthy, but a few key provisions include:[23]

- Loosening the restrictions between U.S. law enforcement and intelligence officers when sharing information.
- Making it illegal to knowingly harbor terrorists.
- Authorizing "roving wiretaps," allowing law enforcement officials to tap any phone a suspected terrorist might use rather than one specific phone or device.
- Increasing subpoena power for email records of terrorist suspects.
- Greatly expanding the number of border patrol personnel, and other customs and immigration inspectors on U.S. borders.
- Expanding measures against money laundering by requiring identification of certain account holders and additional record keeping and reports for some transactions.
- Eliminating statutes of limitation for prosecuting especially egregious terrorist acts.

The Patriot Act sparked controversy because of the content of some of these provisions, but also because of the haste in which it was passed. President Bush announced that he would be seeking passage of the act on September 24, 2001, barely two weeks after the September 11 attacks, and it was signed into law just one month later on October 26, 2001. Many critics of the Patriot Act have questioned the constitutionality of several of its provisions and the methods by which law enforcement agencies would use their new authorities. In particular, critics pointed to the lack of specificity in many of the provisions, which they claimed would allow the government to gather information about and related to citizens not involved in any terrorist activity. For example, the act provides that the FBI can monitor the use of a public computer—at an Internet café or library, for example—if it is being used by a suspected terrorist. Therefore, if an ordinary person used that same computer, the FBI would be permitted to monitor all of that person's Internet usage as part of their investigation and monitoring of the computer.

One of the leading proponents of the Patriot Act, and the U.S. Attorney General at the time, John Ashcroft, argued that these authorities were necessary to effectively fight terrorism. Further, proponents pointed to the fact that the act included several provisions that were to expire on December 31, 2005. However, since that time, Congress and the president have reauthorized the act twice and extended the provisions, thereby continuing to extend the authorities granted to law enforcement agencies.

Critical Thinking   The Patriot Act sparked much debate in the country regarding the appropriate role of government and limitations, or lack thereof, on its powers. Did Congress act too impulsively in passing this legislation, or was the action appropriate given the mood of the country at the time?

Not long after passing the Patriot Act, Congress passed the Homeland Security Act of 2002, which had sweeping effects on the federal framework relative to homeland security. This legislation officially established the Department of Homeland Security and provided it with a structure and mission. Much like the Patriot Act, this legislation was passed primarily in response to the September 11 attacks and the perceived government inefficiencies that allowed for such an event to occur. Also in response to this perception, and on the heels of the Homeland Security Act of 2002, the White House released Homeland Security Presidential Directive No. 5 (HSPD-5).[24] HSPD-5 tasked DHS with developing a single, comprehensive National Incident Management System, and thus became the underlying authority for the establishment of NIMS and the NRF.[25]

The federal homeland security framework continued to evolve, but did not undergo another major change until Congress passed the Post-Katrina Emer-

Exhibit: Patriot Act of 2001

Title I, Section 102: SENSE OF CONGRESS CONDEMNING DISCRIMINATION AGAINST ARAB AND MUSLIM AMERICANS

(a) FINDINGS.—Congress makes the following findings:

(1) Arab Americans, Muslim Americans, and Americans from South Asia play a vital role in our Nation and are entitled to nothing less than the full rights of every American.

(2) The acts of violence that have been taken against Arab and Muslim Americans since the September 11, 2001, attacks against the United States should be and are condemned by all Americans who value freedom.

(3) The concept of individual responsibility for wrongdoing is sacrosanct in American society, and applies equally to all religious, racial, and ethnic groups.

(4) When American citizens commit acts of violence against those who are, or are perceived to be, of Arab or Muslim descent, they should be punished to the full extent of the law.

(5) Muslim Americans have become so fearful of harassment that many Muslim women are changing the way they dress to avoid becoming targets.

(6) Many Arab Americans and Muslim Americans have acted heroically during the attacks on the United States, including Mohammed Salman Hamdani, a 23-year-old New Yorker of Pakistani descent, who is believed to have gone to the World Trade Center to offer rescue assistance and is now missing.

(b) SENSE OF CONGRESS.—It is the sense of Congress that—

(1) the civil rights and civil liberties of all Americans, including Arab Americans, Muslim Americans, and Americans from South Asia, must be protected, and that every effort must be taken to preserve their safety;

(2) any acts of violence or discrimination against any Americans be condemned; and

(3) the Nation is called upon to recognize the patriotism of fellow citizens from all ethnic, racial, and religious backgrounds.

gency Management Reform Act of 2006 (Post-Katrina Act).[26] In the aftermath of Hurricane Katrina, many people criticized the government's slow and ineffective response to the disaster. For example, pre-staged resources, such as food and water, were drastically inadequate at shelters, including at the Superdome in Louisiana. These limited resources were quickly depleted, and people with special needs were not adequately addressed, which led to civil unrest in some cases.[27] Critics blamed FEMA's bureaucracy and the fact that many of its preparedness functions had been reassigned to other DHS divisions as part of a department-wide reorganization plan implemented by DHS Secretary Michael Chertoff in 2005. As such, the Post-Katrina Act transferred most of the preparedness functions back to FEMA and elevated the agency's status in the Department by establishing it as a "distinct entity" within DHS.[28] This distinction gave the FEMA administrator direct access to the president and Congress.[29] Specifically, the FEMA administrator is the principal advisor to the president, the secretary of DHS, and the Homeland Security Council on all emergency management matters, and the president is authorized to assign the administrator to serve as a member of the cabinet during disasters.[30]

State and Regional Authorities   State and regional homeland security powers and sources of authority vary across the country, as each state has the power to enact its own laws and regulations. However, it is important to note that in addition to working together with the federal government to respond to a disaster, states often work with one another to respond regionally to a threat or event. The primary vehicle for doing so is the **Emergency Management Assistance Compact (EMAC)**. EMAC is an interstate compact, ratified by Congress, that provides a framework for mutual cooperation.[31] The process of obtaining interstate resources is actually quite simple: once a governor declares a state of emergency, the state may place a request for resources through EMAC, and if assisting states have the resources available, they mobilize and deploy them to the state in need. This mutual cooperation is extremely valuable to states because, while some emergency situations may require additional response and recovery assistance, they may not warrant full federal involvement. At the same time, even for those emergencies that do require federal aid, EMAC can be invoked to supplement federal efforts.

Emergency Management Assistance Compact (EMAC)
An interstate mutual aid agreement, ratified by Congress, that allows states to assist one another in responding to disasters.

Impact of Homeland Security Measures in the United States
The increased focus on homeland security in the 21st century has left an indelible mark on the United States. Almost immediately after the September 11 attacks, there was a rise in hate crimes against Muslim-Americans and other targeted groups, as well as a dramatic increase in security measures at airports and other public places. As such, there has been a visible impact on the criminal justice system and the debate regarding civil liberties across the country.

Following the September 11 attacks, there was a rise in hate crimes against Muslims, Sikhs, and people of Arab and south Asian descent. In the first nine weeks after the attacks, more than 700 violent incidents were reported that targeted Arab Americans or those perceived to be Arab Americans, Arabs, and Muslims.[32] In the year following the attacks, from September 11, 2001 to October 11, 2002, there were 80 cases of aircraft passengers being illegally and discriminatorily removed, 800 cases of employment discrimination, and many other instances of discrimination in service and housing, as well as denial of service.[33] In response, the Civil Rights Division of the Department of Justice prioritized the prosecution of perpetrators of these crimes and reached out to the affected communities to educate them about their rights. To date, the Civil Rights Division, the FBI, and the offices of the U.S. Attorneys have investigated more than 800 such incidents and have brought federal charges against 48 defendants, resulting in 44 convictions.[34]

In one 2006 case, a defendant pleaded guilty to threatening the director of the Arab American Institute and other staff members through email and voice mail at their office in Washington, D.C. The defendant received a 12-month

Screening of baggage and passengers at airports has dramatically increased since 9/11.

prison sentence followed by three years of supervised release. He also received a $10,000 fine and was ordered to complete 100 hours of community service.[35] In another case, four defendants pleaded guilty to plotting to destroy an Islamic education center. The defendants received substantial prison sentences for conspiracy to violate civil rights, firearms violations, attempted destruction of religious property, and conspiracy to detonate explosive devices.[36] In a third case, a defendant pleaded guilty to assaulting a Sikh postal carrier with a pellet rifle. The victim suffered a severe neck injury, requiring surgery that caused him to miss work for several months. The defendant was sentenced to a prison term of 70 months and was ordered to pay over $25,000 in restitution.[37] These cases help illustrate the effect that threats to homeland security, and specifically the terrorist events of September 11, have had on the U.S. criminal justice system.

The aftermath of the September 11 attacks also sparked great controversy over civil liberties in the country. As the government increased security measures at airports and surveillance measures in general in an effort to prevent terrorist activities, critics of these measures argued that they had gone too far in curtailing individual rights guaranteed by the U.S. Constitution. Specifically, one issue that has arisen from these concerns is what some perceive to be violations of due process rights. Most often, this issue has come up regarding government scanning and searching procedures at airports. For example, following a passenger's attempt to blow up a plane on Christmas Day in 2010, the United States introduced tougher screening rules for passengers arriving at airports from 14 countries considered high-risk and linked to terrorism. Critics of this policy argued that the screening of individuals based on country of origin was essentially racial profiling and a threat to civil liberties. Similarly, when the government began introducing full-body scanners for all airline passengers, debate arose over not only their effectiveness, but their threat to personal privacy. The United States places a high value on privacy and individual rights, and finding the right balance between keeping the country secure from terrorist threats and respecting those rights has proven to be a complicated task.

Critical Thinking

Is a trade-off between civil liberties and security measures necessary to identify and deal with threats to homeland security? Or can threats be dealt with effectively without affecting individual rights?

International Justice

International criminal justice is a movement in the international community to establish appropriate venues, such as criminal courts and tribunals, to respond to violations of international law. Most often, these violations relate to humanitarian law and other gross violations of human rights around the world. Prosecuting such crimes presents a difficult challenge for the international community because each country operates within its own legal structure and bounds. Enforcing international law is an evolving process, and one that requires a unique form of collaboration among many partners.

United Nations (UN)
An international organization formed by 51 member states in 1945 in an effort to promote international peace and security following World War II. The organization has grown to include 192 member states and is best known for its peacekeeping efforts and humanitarian assistance around the world.

The International Court of Justice

Any discussion regarding international justice must include the United Nations and the International Court of Justice. The United Nations (UN) is an international organization formed in 1945 by 51 original member states in an effort to promote international peace and

Countries around the world work together in pursuing international justice.

International Court of Justice (ICJ)

The primary judicial organ of the UN, established in June 1945.

security following World War II. It has grown to include 192 member states and is best known for its peacekeeping efforts and humanitarian assistance around the world. The **International Court of Justice (ICJ)**, also established in June 1945 by the charter of the UN, is one of the oldest and most respected institutions in the international community and plays a significant role in enforcing international law.[38] It is the principal judicial organ of the UN and is located at the Peace Palace in The Hague, Netherlands.[39] The ICJ serves two primary roles with respect to international law: settling legal disputes submitted to it by states/countries, and issuing advisory opinions on legal questions referred to it by the UN and other agencies.[40] The court consists of 15 judges, elected to nine-year terms by the United Nations General Assembly and the Security Council.[41] The panel of judges may not include more than one national from the same country at a time, and as a whole it must represent all of the major civilizations and principal legal systems of the world. This makes the ICJ a truly international organization.

The ICJ's impact on the international community is vast. As of March of 2011, 151 cases had been presented to the court since the first case was submitted on May 22, 1947.[42] The first case, *Corfu Channel Case (United Kingdom v. Albania)*, dealt with a dispute arising from incidents in the Corfu Strait of Albania on October 22, 1946. Two British ships suffered damages and deaths after striking mines in the Albanian waters.[43] The United Kingdom submitted an application to the ICJ to hear the matter,[44] and after the proceedings, in accordance with international law, Albania was ordered to pay compensation to the United Kingdom.[45] The court's decision in that case has been cited numerous times and remains relevant to central questions of international law in the 21st century, such as due diligence, maritime operations, navigation in international

The International Court of Justice acts as a world court on matters of international law.

waters, and humanitarian concerns. Since its first case, the ICJ has addressed a variety of other matters, including issues such as diplomatic relations, immunities of the state, use of force, and territorial disputes.[46]

International Collaboration: Investigating and Prosecuting Terrorism

Although international justice covers a wide range of topics, one of the primary issues it must address in the 21st century is the investigation and prosecution of terrorism. Sometimes terrorism originates within and affects only one country, but acts of terrorism are increasingly crossing international boundaries. As such, international collaboration to prevent and fight terrorism is of the utmost importance. The following section discusses a variety of tools, including organizations, methods, and venues, that are currently in place to facilitate this collaboration.

International Policing

The International Criminal Police Organization (INTERPOL) is charged with facilitating cross-border police cooperation and providing assistance in preventing or combating international crime. INTERPOL, created in 1923, is the world's largest international police organization, comprised of 188 member countries.[47] The organization addresses the threat of terrorism by:[48]

International Criminal Police Organization (INTERPOL)
The world's largest international police organization, which consists of 188 member countries and facilitates cross-border police cooperation.

1. supporting member countries in combating terrorism, specifically through resources focused on bioterrorism, weapons of mass destruction, firearms and explosives, maritime piracy, and attacks against civil aviation;
2. collecting and exchanging information among member countries about suspected groups and individuals, and coordinating alerts and warnings related to terrorists, criminals, and weapons threats to member countries; and
3. creating the Fusion Task Force. The task force's primary objectives are to "identify active terrorist groups and their members, solicit, collect and share information and intelligence, provide analytical support, and enhance the capacity of member countries to address the threats of terrorism and organized crime."[49]

Similar to INTERPOL, the European Union Law Enforcement Agency (EUROPOL) aims to improve cooperation of authorities in member countries to prevent and combat terrorism as well as organized crime and drug trafficking.[50] The agency works closely with non-European Union (EU) partners such as Australia, Canada, the United States, and Norway.[51] Headquartered at The Hague, the organization disseminates information to law enforcement partners who use it to prevent, detect, and investigate suspected terrorists. In particular, EUROPOL produces regular assessments of crime and terrorism in the EU; these Organized Crime Threat Assessments (OCTA) identify and analyze emerging threats. In addition, the agency publishes the EU Terrorism Situation and Trend Report (TE-STAT) annually to provide a detailed account of terrorism in the EU.[52]

FIGURE14.2 There were 272 convictions of terrorists in EU member states in 2008 according to the TE-STAT published in 2009.

Member State	Convicted	Acquitted	Total Verdicts	Acquitted %
Belgium	7	5	12	42
Denmark	11	6	17	35
France	74	1	75	1
Germany	10	0	10	0
Ireland (Republic of)	7	2	9	22
Italy	23	2	25	8
Spain	87	75	162	47
Sweden	1	0	1	0
The Netherlands	7	6	13	46
UK	45	15	60	25
Total	272	112	384	23

Extradition

The formal surrender of a person by a country to another country for the purpose of prosecution or punishment.

Extradition Treaties Extradition treaties can be effective tools to prevent the spread of terrorism because they allow countries to work together to bring criminals to justice despite traditional jurisdictional boundaries. **Extradition** is the formal surrender of a person by one country to another country for the purpose of prosecution or punishment. The United States has over 100 extradition treaties in place with countries around the world.[53] Extradition treaties are bilateral agreements that require one nation to send a person in custody to another country if there is evidence to suggest that the person committed a serious crime that is subject to imprisonment in both countries. However, the content of individual treaties may vary, so it is important that the request for extradition be made in accordance with the applicable terms. For example, treaties provide explicit lists of crimes or offenses for which extradition is appropriate and those for which it may, or even must, be denied.[54] In addition, the terms of most extradition treaties include an exemption for political offenses, thus placing terrorists out of reach for traditional extradition in many cases. The United States has tried to limit this exemption for terrorists by requiring a fugitive to demonstrate that the crime was committed during a violent political disturbance (war, rebellion, etc.) in order to avoid extradition.[55] Other treaties limit the exemption more directly by explicitly excluding terrorist acts from the definition of political crimes. Because of these terms and exemptions, the role of extradition treaties in the context of terrorism is not always clear-cut.

Critical Thinking The United States had an extradition treaty with the former Yugoslavia, which is now comprised of several individual nations. Fugitives seeking refuge in these successor governments have claimed that the U.S. has no extradition power over them. How should the United States deal with this issue?

United Nations Counter-Terrorism Implementation Task Force (CTITF)

The UN is uniquely positioned to encourage international collaboration because of its international membership. In 2005, the secretary-general of the UN capitalized on this fact and established the Counter-Terrorism Implementation Task Force (CTITF). This task force coordinates counterterrorism efforts and assists member states in implementing the UN Global Counter-Terrorism Strategy (Global Strategy).[56] Specifically, CTITF works with member states to implement the four pillars of the Global Strategy, which are:[57]

1. "Measures to address conditions conducive to the spread of terrorism;
2. Measures to prevent and combat terrorism;
3. Measures to build states' capacity to prevent and combat terrorism and to strengthen the role of the UN in this regard; and
4. Measures to enact respect for human rights and the rule of law as the fundamental basis of the fight against terrorism."

CTITF operates through working groups devoted to supporting victims of terrorism, responding to terrorist attacks, disrupting terrorists' financing and Internet use, and protecting vulnerable targets and human rights.[58] These working groups assess threats, run exercises, develop partnerships, make recommendations, and bring stakeholders together to fight terrorism more effectively around the world. For example, based on a series of roundtable discussions with banking, intelligence, law enforcement, and criminal justice experts, the Working Group on Tackling the Financing of Terrorism published a report in 2009 covering five specific areas of combating terrorist financing: "(a) the criminalization of terrorist financing; (b) the enhancement of domestic and international cooperation; (c) value transfer systems; (d) non-profit organizations; and (e) the freezing of assets." These recommendations provide best practices for how to effectively reduce terrorists' access to finances in an effort to reduce their ability to commit terrorist acts.[59]

Tribunal
A specialized venue for enforcing international law. International tribunals can be formed by United Nations charter, Security Council resolution, or international treaty.

International Courts and Tribunals International courts and tribunals are the primary means for prosecuting terrorism and ensuring the legitimacy of counterterrorism policies and actions. These special venues may be formed by UN Security Council resolution, UN charter, or international treaty.

The International Court of Justice (ICJ) is a prime example of an international court. As discussed previously in this section, the ICJ is the primary judicial organ of the UN. Formed by UN charter, it deals with all matters related to international law, including protecting human rights.

Another international court is the International Criminal Court (ICC), which was the first permanent, treaty-based criminal court established within the international community. It is governed by the Rome Statute and, like the International Court of Justice, its seat is at The Hague, in the Netherlands.[60] The Rome Stat-

Special courts and tribunals are established to enforce international law.

© 2012 BY ZIMMYTWS, UNDER LICENSE FROM SHUTTERSTOCK, INC.

ute provides that the ICC "shall have the power to exercise its jurisdiction over persons for the most serious crimes of international concern . . . "[61]

The International Criminal Tribunal for Rwanda (ICTR) is an example of a tribunal. It was created by UN Security Council Resolution 955 on November 8, 1994.[62] Its purpose was to facilitate national reconciliation and maintain peace in Rwanda in response to genocide and other international law violations that were committed in the country over several months in 1994.[63] Resolutions like this one outline the tribunal's purpose, powers, jurisdiction, structure, composition, and procedural rules. Tribunals like the ICTR are generally established to try crimes related to a specific conflict and committed during a specific time frame.

Exhibit: A Closer Look: The International Criminal Tribunal for Rwanda

Formation: Created by UN Security Council Resolution 955 on November 8, 1994.

Powers: ICTR has power to prosecute individuals for violations of international law in Rwanda between January 1 and December 31 of 1994. It also has the power to prosecute citizens of Rwanda who committed such crimes in neighboring countries during the designated timeframe.

Structure: There are three trial chambers and one appeals chamber consisting of 16 independent judges, and no two judges may be nationals of the same country. The Office of the Prosecution is in charge of investigation and prosecution for both the trial and appellate level. The Registry administers and manages the Tribunal and provides judicial and legal support for the trial chambers and prosecution. The Tribunal includes a Witness & Victims Support Section, responsible for protecting witness security and assuring their availability for court procedures. The Tribunal also includes a Defence Counsel & Detention Management Section, which assures that suspects are provided with competent counsel and that detention of suspects conforms with international standards. Two other sections of the Tribunal include the Court Management Section, which provides support to the three trial chambers and appellate chamber to ensure smooth proceedings, and the Procurement Section, which procures any goods or services required to support the operations of the ICTR.

Governing Documents: The governing documents of the ICTR include the ICTR Statute, annexed to Security Council Resolution 955, other Security Council Resolutions, Bilateral Agreements, and Directives.

For more information: Official ICTR Website http://www.unictr.org/Home/tabid/36/Default.aspx

Regardless of how an international court or tribunal is formed—whether it is by a UN Security Council resolution, UN charter, or international treaty—it is based on the notion that there is an international presence behind the proceedings. Such entities are excellent examples of international collaboration in the context of investigating and prosecuting terrorism as well as other matters of international law.

Ethics and Professionalism: Prosecuting International Terrorism

On December 21, 1988, Pan Am Flight 103 exploded over Lockerbie, Scotland. The explosion killed all 243 passengers and 16 crew members as well as 11 Lockerbie residents, resulting in a total of 270 deaths.[64] Following the crash, a massive investigation took place in which the United States and United Kingdom joined forces for three years collecting evidence and interviewing witnesses. The investigation uncovered evidence indicating that explosives were placed in a suitcase originally dispatched from Malta and eventually loaded onto Flight 103 at Heathrow Airport in London. That suitcase contained clothing sold by a shopkeeper in Malta to a man he described as having a Libyan appearance, and whom he later identified as Abdel Baset al-Megrahi, a Libyan intelligence officer and head of security for Libyan Arab Airlines (LAA). The trigger for the explosion was a specific timer of which a substantial quantity had been supplied to Libya.[65]

As a result of this evidence, taken in context with the rest of the case, the court determined that the attacks were perpetrated by Libyan agents. Charges were brought against al-Megrahi and Lamin Khalifah Fhimah, an LAA station manager in Malta. Both al-Megrahi and Fhimah faced a Scottish trial, beginning in May 2000.[66] Fhimah was found not guilty, but Megrahi was convicted of 270 counts of murder and received a life sentence in 2001.[67]

Although Libya's leader, Moammar Gadhafi, claimed no personal involvement in the act, the country admitted responsibility in 2003 and the Gadhafi government agreed to pay the victims' families compensation.[68] Despite his government's admission of responsibility, Gadhafi lobbied for al-Megrahi's release from Scotland. Finally, in 2009 al-Megrahi was released from Scottish prison after he was diagnosed with terminal prostate cancer and given only months to live.[69] He was welcomed as a hero in Libya, where many claimed he was wrongly convicted based on a false identification by the Maltese shopkeeper. Despite his diagnosis, which influenced Scottish officials to grant his release, al-Megrahi survived much longer than the mere months predicted by doctors. In fact, although a London news source reported his death in May 2011, al-Megrahi's lawyer confirmed that he was still alive as of June 2011.

As civil unrest exploded in Libya against the Gadhafi regime in 2011, some former Libyan officials admitted publicly that the Lockerbie bombing was ordered by Gadhafi himself and that he lobbied on behalf of al-Megrahi to cover his own involvement. Some even alleged that al-Megrahi blackmailed Gadhafi into securing his release so that he would not divulge Gadhafi's hand in the event.[70] If the recent allegations concerning Gadhafi's involvement are true, who would prosecute him and in what venue? How should the prior trial and prosecution of al-Megrahi be dealt with? Further, regardless of Gadhafi's alleged involvement, was it appropriate for Scotland to grant al-Megrahi's 2009 release on humanitarian grounds, especially in light of the fact that he remains alive years after he was said to have only months to live?

Computer Crime   With the many technological breakthroughs and advancements over the past few decades, the criminal justice system has taken on an increased focus on cybercrime. *Cybercrime* is a relatively new term used frequently in both the news media and in scholarly articles as these crimes become more prevalent: it refers to crime committed utilizing computers and the Internet. Generally, it involves acquiring a person's or organization's sensitive information. The media has given much attention to issues surrounding cybercrime,

Cybercrime
Crime committed utilizing a computer and the Internet.

Cybercrime is crime committed utilizing computers and the Internet.

White hat hacker

An ethical computer hacker who hacks for beneficial reasons, such as solving complex problems.

Black hat hacker

An unethical computer hacker who hacks with malicious intent to commit a crime.

Identity theft

The crime of stealing someone's identity and using it for malicious purposes.

particularly cases involving child pornography, unethical hacking, and copyright infringements.[71]

History of Cybercrime

Cybercrime came into existence even before the establishment of companies such as Microsoft or Apple Computer. In the 1960s and 1970s, a group of students from the Massachusetts Institute of Technology (MIT) created an organization called Tech Model Railroad Club (TMRC) that built sophisticated railroad models. The members of this club created advanced control systems for railroads using computer programming. They were considered the very first **white hat hackers**. Early hackers were considered white hat hackers or ethical hackers because they solved complex computer problems. If either software or hardware were not available, these hackers would develop them and solve the issue at hand. Today we have two types of hackers: white hat hackers and **black hat hackers**. The difference between the two types of hackers is that a white hat hacker places ethics highly and expects this to be honored by others. A black hat hacker, on the other hand, hacks with malicious intent.[72]

In 1970, the computer became commercial with the development of the Altair 8800, which is considered the first personal computer (PC). In those days the computer did not come assembled, but rather the user had to build it—and the software—himself or herself. This process allowed early hackers to learn programming.

Hacking became more prevalent with the development of the Internet in the late 1980s. Using Internet access provided by early companies such as AOL, Prodigy, and CompuServe, online criminals and hackers could gain access to other people's personal information.

During the early 1990s, people became increasingly concerned with Internet privacy, or methods of keeping sensitive information safe. Based on these concerns the first encryption software was created, called PGP (Pretty Good Privacy), designed to hide sensitive information for online users. PGP, however, was also utilized by criminals to hide evidence of their crimes.

When the first online bank opened in 1994, the scope of cybercrime shifted and expanded, opening even more doors for cybercriminals. Phishing, cracking of passwords, and stealing people's information have become major threats, not just to the consumer, but to organizations and governments across the world.[73]

Identity Theft

The Federal Trade Commission (FTC) is an independent organization that was created in 1914 to protect consumers. On a daily basis, the FTC polices crimes related to false advertising, credit card fraud, and any matter dealing with consumer protection. In recent years the FTC has also been tasked with investigating crimes relating to identity theft, and has created an entire division dealing only with identity theft.[74] **Identity theft** is the criminal act of stealing someone's identity with malicious intent. These identity thefts most often involve misuse of credit cards.

Identity theft could be considered the crime of the 21st century because so many Americans are affected by it each year. According to the FTC, 2010 marked the 11th year in a row in which identify theft topped the list of FTC complaints.[75] In 2009, 11.2 million Americans were victims of identity theft, and the cost of these crimes was estimated to be around $54 million. The average cost per record (one person's information) is estimated to be around $200. When an organization is involved in data breaches, the average cost to the organization is $6.6 million. When you consider the fact that thousands of records get stolen at the same time, the amount adds up. For example, in 2008 more than 285 million records were breached, which is more than the combined total from 2001 through 2007. The FTC reported that 83% of these cases could have been avoided through simple and intermediate controls such as software updates, antivirus systems, and compliance with organizational policies and procedures.[76]

There is no "silver bullet" for information protection; there is no single technology or method that can be implemented to make information and assets 100% safe from internal and external threats. However, individuals and organizations can take steps to protect themselves. The National Security Agency (NSA) has outlined a method for best practices relating to information protection that involves a three-dimensional layered defense approach called Defense-in-Depth (DiD). This method integrates people, process, and technology for better protection for the organization's critical information. One example of a layered defense approach that an organization could use is requiring computer logs (such as log-on times) and auditing those requirements. This process incorporates both technological safeguards (computer logs) and human supervision (auditing) to ensure safety of the organization's information.[77]

Categories of Computer Crimes

Computer crime can generally be categorized as one of three types: **personal cybercrime**, which includes identity theft and harassment; **property cybercrime**, which includes damage to computer technology caused by malware; and **government cybercrime**, which covers cyberterrorism.[78]

Personal and Property Cybercrime

Personal cybercrime is the category that most people are probably most familiar with. In addition to identity theft, personal cybercrimes include digital harassment such as cyberstalking (using social networking sites, search engines, forums, and discussion boards to pursue a victim), inappropriate email communication, etc.

Property cybercrime is also fairly common. This type of crime involves purposely infecting equipment with some type of malware. *Malware* is short for *malicious software* and is generally designed to disrupt or prevent further use of a system. There are two main groups of malware: viruses and worms, or Trojan horses. Viruses infect executable files on machines; when the executable is run, the virus spreads to other executable files on the system. Worms are considered a little more complex, as they do not need an executable to spread. A worm simply attaches to a file such as a Microsoft Word or Excel document, which is why it can spread so quickly when a user is attaching these files to an email. In

Personal cybercrime
Cybercrimes that involve a direct attack on a person, including identity theft and cyber harassment.

Property cybercrime
Cybercrimes that involve a criminal purposely installing malware on computer equipment.

Government cybercrime
Cybercrimes that involve attacks on government information systems, including cyberterrorism.

Malware
Malicious software designed to disrupt or prevent further use of a system.

essence, a worm will scan a computer network for vulnerabilities and will replicate through the vulnerability. Worms need no human interaction to spread and can therefore spread at an incredible speed.

A Trojan horse works a bit differently than a worm or a virus. In general terms, a Trojan horse is attached to a desirable piece of software to "tempt" a user to download and install it using the Internet. Spyware is a common way for a Trojan horse to be distributed. Spyware is self-installing software that gathers information such as Internet searches, shopping preferences, and passwords, and submits this information to a third party for commercial profit.

Government Cybercrime: Cyberterrorism

Cyberterrorism
An unlawful method of attacking and threatening government computer systems and networks, and the information stored on these systems, to further political or social objectives.

Cyberterrorism is an unlawful method of attacking and threatening government computer systems and networks, and the information stored on these systems, to further the cyberterrorist's political or social objectives. To fully qualify as cyberterrorism, an incident must result in violence against a person or property. Examples include water contamination, explosions, plane crashes, or other attacks that lead to physical injury, death, or severe economic loss.[79] Cyberspace is constantly under attack, and cyberterrorism is becoming increasingly well known in every country across the world. Counterterrorism organizations in the United States have reported that close to 140 foreign intelligence organizations attempt to hack into official U.S. government agencies on a regular basis.[80]

Cyberterrorism has become more organized, especially by terror organizations such as Hamas, the Islamic Jihad Group, and Al-Qaeda. The terrorist attacks of 9/11 have raised the general public's and government's awareness of the implications of cyberterrorism and terror in general. The U.S. government has created 11 critical infrastructures in an effort to determine where likely terror attacks will occur and how these infrastructures should be protected in the event that cyberterrorism occurs. The 11 infrastructures are electricity distribution, gas production, oil and oil products production, telecommunication, water supply, agriculture, heating, public health, transportation, financial services, and security services.[81] The DHS states that the protection of these critical infrastructures requires cooperation between the public and private sector.

Because people often associate cyberterrorism with terrorist attacks, it is important to discuss whether cyberterrorism is having an impact on the terror rate. Little evidence exists that it is. However, links between the two can be found when discussing money laundering, computer resources, and transit lines. For example, Osama bin Laden, the mastermind behind the 9/11 attacks, was able to use computer resources to communicate through the use of public Internet access.[82]

Obviously, a cyberterrorist's weapon of choice is the computer. The use of the Internet makes it easier for terrorists to meet people with similar thought processes and ideals. Therefore, groups and organizations can actually be entirely created utilizing technology.[83]

Cyberterrorism is appealing to terrorist organizations because it can reach a global audience and can potentially make a bigger impact than committing a violent act in a single location. The Internet is very important both for personal

Cyberterrorism is appealing to terrorist organizations because it can reach a global audience and can potentially make a bigger impact than committing a violent act in a single location.

and business use, and it is virtually impossible to close it down completely, so governments must carefully consider how to protect their countries and information from this type of terror.[84] With the use of technology such as honeypots, it is possible for governments and organizations to deter cyberterrorist attacks before they even occur.[85] Honeypots are traps that are designed to detect unauthorized access to information systems. Usually a honeypot is designed to look like a system on a network, but is in fact isolated from the rest of the organization's network and is monitored for attacks.[86] Honeypots can prevent unauthorized access of information technology.[87]

Cybercrime Statistics The FBI publishes data on cybercrimes in the annual Internet Crime Report, created by the Internet Crime Complaint Center (IC3). In 2010, this report claimed that the FBI receives 25,000 complaints of cybercrime each month, a number that keeps increasing every year. Since its beginnings, the Internet Crime Report has shown a steady increase of annual reports of cybercrimes. In 2000, when IC3 was created, it received almost 17,000 complaints. In 2010 the IC3 had an incident report of 303,000, with an average of 25,000 complaints per month. Figure 14.3 lists the report's findings on the most frequent types of cybercrime.

FIGURE 14.3 Types of Cybercrime

Type	Percentage
Non-Delivery Payment of Merchandise	14.4%
FBI-Related Scams	13.2%
Identity Theft	9.8%
Computer Crime	9.1%
Miscellaneous Fraud	8.6%
Advance Fee Fraud	7.6%
Spam	6.9%
Auction Fraud	5.9%
Credit Card Fraud	5.3%
Overpayment Fraud	5.3%

The IC3 also performs demographic statistics on its reported cases. On top of that list is the state of California, with 15.6% of all cases. Florida and New York follow. For a detailed report on this data or updated data, refer to the IC3 website.[88]

Cybercrime Investigations and International Cybercrime The Internet is considered relatively new, and over the past 25 years this space has changed drastically. Since its creation, the Internet has become affordable and available to nearly everyone. Because of this, several laws and statutes have been created on the state and federal levels that are intended to protect innocent users from crimes committed online.

Enforcing cybercrime laws, however, has proven challenging. There are several reasons for this, the main one being jurisdiction. Because not all state laws are the same, cybercriminals may have to be tried on a federal level instead of at the state level. The area gets even more complex when considering the fact that cybercrime cases often originate outside the United States. Though there are some international regulatory bodies such as the United Nations (UN) and the European Union that set regulatory requirements for its members, other nations have few or no requirements. When crimes originate from a different region or from a less regulated country, it becomes extremely difficult to prosecute a criminal.

Another issue with cybercrimes is anonymity and identity. Before we can even consider jurisdiction, it is necessary to discover where and who the criminal is. Obviously this is a difficult problem with online crimes because there are so many technologies one can use to hide one's identity. There are services that are able to mask an IP address by routing traffic through various servers. This type of technology makes it difficult to track down the criminal.

Finally, the nature of the evidence in cybercrime cases can also make them difficult to investigate and prosecute. The first step in a cybercrime case is to image the evidence (make a duplicate), which is why it is critical to create a hash value before and after the image has been created. A hash value is a numerical representation that represents a piece of data. No two hash values are the same; in other words, if someone changes any of the data on the evidence item, such as adding or deleting a file, the hash value will change, and therefore, the evidence has been tampered with. This is why protecting the evidence and chain of custody becomes so extremely critical. An investigator can easily contaminate the evidence during the investigation unless precautions are taken.[89]

Critical Thinking   The Internet is relatively new and, while there are some regulations and laws regarding this technology, no common laws have been introduced worldwide to make it easier to control and convict these types of crimes. How do you suggest the United States should cooperate with most of the world regarding this issue? Is the creation of a worldwide court an option to keep these crimes under control?

New Technologies in Crime Fighting   Thirty years ago, few people thought that technology and computers would be such a big part of everyday life. Because most people have a computer or at the very least have access to one, by nature, computer crimes have increased. When a cybercrime is committed, it generally involves a computer. This computer and its storage and activities become a place where evidence is stored or recorded. By the early 1990s, computer tools were available to assist in digital investigations; however, these tools were not yet commercially available. As computers continued to evolve, software companies started producing software that was available to individuals and organizations, not just governments. Today there are several computer forensics tools available.

Computer Forensics Tools   The most common and widely accepted tools in the market today are the Forensics Toolkit (FTK) by AccessData and EnCase by Guidance Software. Both of these software suites are considered premier forensics tools and are acceptable tools for presenting evidence in the court system.

The FTK and EnCase suites include functions and features allowing investigators to acquire and create images. These include registry investigations that contain information regarding browser history, when users log on and off, what devices have been connected to the computer and what documents have been edited or created, as well as password recovery tools. Another critical component in computer forensic investigations is data carving, which allows investigators to reconstruct files that are fragmented (deleted or embedded). Data carving may be very time-consuming, but it may be well worth it if the files are critical to the case.

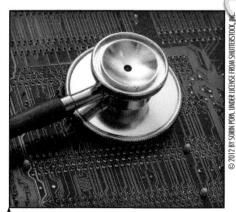

Computer forensics tools such as FTK and EnCase allow investigators to obtain information on a suspect's browser history, files, and more.

Several cases in the 21st century have been investigated utilizing EnCase and FTK. One of the most famous was the case of the BTK Killer, discussed in the opening case study, where investigators were able to identify Rader based on files recovered from a floppy disk. Another famous case in which computer forensics tools were utilized was the 2005 murder trial of Scott Peterson, who was sentenced to death after being found guilty of murdering his wife and unborn child. During the investigation, investigators utilized the FTK software and GPS data from Peterson's car and cell phone as well as Internet history from his personal and business computers. The data revealed that Peterson had been viewing classified ads for a fishing boat, as well as maps, fishing reports, and charts of currents in the San Francisco Bay area. Peterson also zoomed in on a map close to Brooks Island, near where the remains of his wife and unborn child were later discovered.

The key to an investigation is to collect evidence, and it is important to follow generally acceptable methods when handling evidence. To ensure that the evidence can be accepted by the court system, a forensic investigator must ensure that documentation is kept, and at the very least clearly document where the evidence was stored, who had access to it, and what was done to the evidence during the investigation process. Ensuring proper documentation will ensure that the evidence is not tampered with and is kept in its original state should the case go to court.

The initial step to any investigation is to seize the evidence. Once the evidence is secured, an image of the digital evidence must be created so that the investigator does not work with a live evidence item. Once the image has been created, the investigator can start the digital forensics investigation utilizing FTK or another forensic tool.

As the world moves ahead with new technologies, it is also important that these software suites keep up-to-date to ensure compatibility. FTK has a tool called Mobile Phone Examiner that allows for investigation of cellular devices.

Another upcoming technology that will pose a challenge to computer forensics and businesses as a whole is cloud computing, which is a type of technology that allows for remote storage and other services designed to help an organization. Essentially, it will allow organizations to increase the capacity of their systems quickly with far less resources than acquiring their own technology. Another benefit of cloud computing is savings, as this type of technology does not require additional training, new employees, or acquisition of new software licenses. Cloud computing is designed to extend existing capabilities and is considered a subscription-based service.

Cloud computing is still at an early stage, and research has shown many security threats to this type of service.[90] Most notably, there are so many cloud computing services that it is safe to conclude not all of them reside in the United States. Hence forensic investigators are likely to face challenges related to control of the evidence, including the collection, preservation, and validation.[91]

Cameras   In the 21st century, criminal justice has changed in more ways than just digital forensics. Today, after 9/11, we live in a world where we are on camera in some form or another for much of our day. Surveillance cameras are located at malls, airports, subways, and many other public buildings.

With surveillance cameras at malls, airports, subways, and many other public buildings, people are on camera in some form for much of their day.

The Department of Homeland Security has given millions of dollars to states and local law enforcement agencies to purchase high-tech surveillance technologies. In recent years, several cities have received grants and financing from the DHS. St. Paul, Minnesota, received a grant of $1.2 million for the installation of 60 cameras downtown. Pittsburgh, Pennsylvania, received a similar grant allowing them to install 83 cameras downtown.[92] Smaller towns have also received funding from the DHS to install surveillance equipment in parks and other public places.

Cameras also have a big impact on police officers and their investigations. For example, car thefts have long been a major problem; in 2006, statistics indicated that a car got stolen in the United States every 26.4 seconds, and only 12.6% of cases were cleared by arrest. New technologies in cameras have allowed police to develop automated license plate recognition systems that can be used by patrol cars or helicopters to track auto thefts. The cameras can scan license plates at a distance and compare them to a database of registered car thefts.[93]

Biometrics
A method of authenticating a person's identity through behavioral or physiological characteristics such as iris scanners and fingerprinting.

Biometrics   Another relatively new technology utilized today for identification is biometrics, which is an automated method of recognizing a person based on behavioral or physiological characteristics. Biometric tools can authenticate a person's identity in a variety of ways, such as fingerprints, hand geometry, and handwriting, or by iris, retinal, vein, or voice scanning. Biometrics has become a very popular method of authentication for highly secure areas as identity theft becomes more common and passwords are becoming less secure. Biometrics is used in federal, state, and local governments, as well as in military and commercial applications. Law enforcement and the health care sector have significantly benefited from this technology.[94]

Biometric tools can authenticate a person's identity through fingerprints, hand geometry, and other methods.

3D Imaging Software

Technology is becoming an increasingly larger part of law enforcement as a tool to solve crimes. One of the newer technologies that allows investigators to reconstruct a crime scene is 3D imaging software. This 3D technology is so sophisticated that it is actually possible to recreate a scene where a bullet has been fired and compare that to previous cases involving bullets fired. The Forensic Science Institute in Connecticut, for example, uses the DeltaSphere-3000 3D Scene Digitizer to recreate crime scenes.

3D imaging software can also be used to investigate terrorism. Japan has employed facial-recognition technology to help prevent foreign nationals from committing crimes. Law enforcement organizations in Germany and the United Kingdom are using 3D software to reconstruct three-dimensional images of public places and structures, which assist law enforcement in averting future terrorist attempts.[95]

Critical Thinking

Surveillance is a controversial subject because it breaches the Fourth Amendment to the U.S. Constitution. How would you propose finding a compromise to allow certain forms of surveillance?

Mobile Devices

With the introduction of a plethora of new mobile devices and operating systems, it is important to consider a few important issues. While these mobile devices (such as the iPad, iPhone, BlackBerry, etc.) have become an integral part of society and how people do business, it does pose a challenge to the computer forensics field as these devices become more complex with features, Internet connectivity, and greater storage capabilities. These devices, similar to PCs, collect information regarding the user and the user's habits such as Internet searches, text messages, and even emails. These may be extremely valuable to investigators, law enforcement, and the court system. Therefore, it is important that investigators strictly adhere to the chain of evidence when performing forensics investigations on mobile devices.[96]

Career Connections: Computer Forensics

Computer forensics is a relatively new field, but the job outlook is very strong. Because of increased usage of digital technology everywhere in our society, and the fact that computer crimes have become a part of everyday life, the need for computer forensics investigators is increasing every year.

Computer forensics experts serve a variety of roles during the criminal investigation. First, these experts uncover and analyze data from digital devices and preserve the data to be used as evidence in court. Uncovering data may entail examining digital evidence on hard drives, storage devices (USB drives, iPods, etc.), cell phones, PDAs, or other electronic devices that may be used in a court setting. Their tasks may include retrieving deleted data in many forms, such as emails, documents, Internet history, and formatted hard disks. During the investigation, a computer forensics expert analyzes and determines the availability and reliability of digital evidence and helps prepare this evidence for trial. A computer forensics expert may work on a variety of cases involving crimes such as hackings, embezzlement, identity theft, and security breaches. The complexity of an investigation can range from a personal computer to an entire network server and its traffic.

An individual who wishes to start in the computer forensics field will need a degree in computer forensics or a related degree such as criminal justice, computer science, information security, or engineering. The individual will likely also need additional computer forensics training. As with any rapidly changing field, it is critical that professionals stay current with training and certifications even after entering the job market.

This type of work requires a person to be very analytical and to have a good foundation in technology, both hardware and operating systems as well as individual software packages such as Microsoft Office. A computer forensics expert is generally tech-savvy and enjoys investigations of digital cases. Computer forensics experts must also be able to communicate effectively, in both non-technical and technical language, and this type of work may require presenting evidence in court to a judge and jury. In addition, computer forensics experts should constantly keep themselves updated on new technological advancements and techniques and current events in the field.[97]

Freedom vs. Security

With the development of new technologies to combat crime, privacy in society has rapidly decreased. Citizens are constantly the subjects of camera surveillance and other digital monitoring issues that some say interfere with their basic rights, including those granted by the Fourth Amendment.

One study completed by the British government, which has utilized cameras throughout the country, has determined that surveillance has no overall impact on crimes. Studies have also been done in Los Angeles with similar results. However, not all studies agree. Research studies in Chicago, Baltimore, and Washington, D.C. have concluded that in certain areas surveillance has been able to decrease the monthly crime numbers.[98]

Since the events of 9/11, there have been no terrorist attacks on the United States. Many people claim that it is because of the new policies introduced in the months and years following 9/11, including the Patriot Act, discussed earlier in the chapter. While some argue that the Patriot Act is the reason we have not had further attacks, other groups, including the American Civil Liberties Union

(ACLU), have taken issue with the Patriot Act. They claim it has taken away some of the privacy rights provided to Americans in the Fourth Amendment.

As the U.S. government continues to establish new policies and utilize new technologies to combat terrorism, cybercrime, and other 21st century criminal justice issues, it is perpetually walking a fine line. Government officials must find the right balance between doing what is necessary to protect the homeland from outside attacks and, at the same time, refraining from infringing on American citizens' rights. This balance of security and freedom remains a controversial issue, and the debate continues to this day.

Chapter Summary

- The focus on homeland security in the United States has grown since September 11, 2001. It encompasses preparedness, response, and recovery efforts at all levels of government in an effort to protect the safety and security of U.S. citizens. Furthermore, it addresses all threats to the security of the country, including natural disasters such as a hurricane or tornado as well as manmade events such as a terrorist attack.

- The Department of Homeland Security (DHS) was established in 2002 and acts as the coordinating body for response to national incidents. The department is made up of many federal offices and agencies, including the Federal Emergency Management Agency (FEMA). The legal framework, including sources of power and authority, of homeland security in the United States is complex and still evolving. The major pieces of the federal framework are the Patriot Act of 2001 and the Homeland Security Act of 2002. States also have varying sources of authorities in this framework, but one unifying document is the Emergency Management Assistance Compact (EMAC), an agreement that allows states to share resources to respond regionally to an event.

- The impact of 21st-century homeland security in the United States may be seen in many facets of society. Following the terrorist attacks on September 11, 2001, there was a rise in hate crimes in the United States against specific groups of people. In response, the government placed a priority on prosecuting perpetrators of these hate crimes. At the same time, in an effort to prevent future terrorist attacks, the government increased surveillance and screening measures at airports. Critics of these measures argue that the government is curtailing civil liberties guaranteed by the U.S. Constitution by threatening privacy rights and due process.

- International criminal justice represents a movement in the international community to enforce international law, including investigating and prosecuting terrorism. Because terrorism is a global threat in the 21st century that crosses international boundaries, it is vital that countries collaborate with one another to identify and deal with terrorists. Special venues such as the International Court of Justice (ICJ), the International Criminal Court (ICC), and specific criminal courts and tribunals exist to enforce violations of international law, including terrorism. These venues are established and run with international support, lending legitimacy to their proceedings. In addition, the international community works together through international policing, extradition treaties, and United Nations efforts to prevent and respond to the threat of terrorism.

• Cybercrime is a new type of crime facing the criminal justice system in the 21st century. Cybercrimes are crimes committed using a computer and Internet resources; they can be classified as personal cybercrime (identity theft, cyberstalking), property cybercrime (malicious software), or government cybercrime (government systems and networks). A common type of cybercrime is identity theft, which is extremely costly and time-consuming for both organizations and victims.

• Cybercrimes can be investigated utilizing computer forensics software. Several types of this software exist in the market today. Both EnCase and the FTK Toolkit are law-enforcement-endorsed for investigating cybercrimes.

• Surveillance is increasingly becoming an important issue to the public. Research has shown mixed results as to whether increased surveillance is effective in reducing crimes. Other technologies introduced and designed to deter crimes and make investigations more accurate and less time-consuming are biometrics and 3D imaging software for reconstruction of crime scenes.

Critical Thinking?

1. Homeland Security deals with both natural and manmade threats. What are issues common to both and what sets them apart from one another?
2. Is the legal framework that supports current homeland security measures sufficient? Are the roles of federal, state, and local players clearly defined?
3. There has been an increased focus on homeland security in the U.S. since the attacks of September 11, 2001. Is the country better prepared to prevent or respond to such an event today?
4. How can international response to terrorism be improved? Is there sufficient coordination and collaboration to deal with the international threat?
5. The International Court of Justice and the International Criminal Court act as world courts to prosecute violations of international law. With these institutions already in place, is the formation of other specialized international courts and tribunals necessary?
6. What are some of the positives and negatives regarding camera surveillance in today's society?
7. What are some of the challenges a computer forensics investigator faces regarding new technologies?
8. Identify theft is among the most common cybercrimes. What should you do to prevent identity theft, and how can you protect yourself?
9. Why is it important for a computer forensics investigator to be a great communicator? Consider the different venues in which such an investigator may have to communicate.
10. As cybercrime and security breaches become more common, will technology gradually become a less integral part of society? Why or why not?

Media

FEMA: http://www.fema.gov/

> FEMA's website offers a wide variety of information regarding the agency's planning, preparedness, response, and recovery efforts, and provides information on what citizens can do to better prepare themselves for an emergency.

National Response Framework Resource Center: http://www.fema.gov/emergency/nrf/

> The National Response Framework Resource Center provides the most up-to-date information about the federal government's framework for dealing with an emergency on a national level. It acts as a library for documents related to the NRF, including annexes and reference materials.

The International Criminal Police Organization (INTERPOL): http://www.interpol.int/

> INTERPOL's website has a wealth of information about the organization's structure and initiatives as well as relevant current events. The website is updated frequently with news stories and materials in multiple languages.

Department of Homeland Security: http://www.dhs.gov/files/cybersecurity.shtm

> This website offers important information regarding homeland protection and cybersecurity.

Federal Trade Commission: http://www.ftc.gov/bcp/edu/microsites/idtheft/

> The FTC website provides information about identity theft and how to report such crimes.

Computer Forensics World: http://www.computerforensicsworld.com/

> This website is a great resource for publications, research tools, and other computer forensics questions.

Endnotes

1. Criminal Justice Schools. (2010). *10 Famous Criminal Cases Cracked by Forensics*. Retrieved from http://www.criminaljusticeschools.org/blog/10-famous-cases-cracked-by-forensics

2. Department of Homeland Security. (2007). *National Computer Forensic Institute Unveiled*. Retrieved from http://www.dhs.gov/xnews/releases/pr_1173477460607.shtm

3. *Oxford English Dictionary*. (n.d.). Retrieved from http://www.oed.com/view/Entry/199608?redirectedFrom=terrorism#eid

4. 22 U.S.C.§ 2656f(d)

5. U.S. Army Timeline of Terrorism.

6. Ibid.

7. Ibid.

8. Oklahoma City National Memorial & Museum. (2011). *A Look at the Numbers*. Retrieved from http://www.oklahomacitynationalmemorial.org/secondary.php?section=5&catid=145

9. Homeland Security Act of 2002, 6 U.S.C. §§101-557 (2002).

10. Insurance Information Institute. (2011). *Catastrophes: U.S.* Retrieved from http://www.iii.org/facts_statistics/catastrophes-us.html

11. Ibid.

12. Citizen Corps. (n.d.). *About Citizen Corps*. Retrieved from http://www.citizencorps.gov/about/

13. Ibid.

14. Federal Emergency Management Agency (FEMA). (n.d.). *Ready: Prepare. Plan. Stay Informed*. Retrieved from http://www.ready.gov/

15. Ibid.

16. United Nations Office for the Coordination of Humanitarian Affairs (OCHA). (2011). "Japan Earthquake & Tsunami." *Situation Report No. 16*. Retrieved from http://reliefweb.int/updates?sl=environment-report_listing%252Ctaxonomy_index_tid_content_format-10%252Ctaxonomy_index_tid_source-1503%252Ctaxonomy_index_tid_country-128

17. Catastrophic Health Emergencies Act of Maryland, Md. Health-Gen. Code Ann. § 18-905 (2002).

18. Robert T. Stafford Disaster Relief and Emergency Assistance Act, 42 U.S.C. §§ 5121-5206 (2009).

19. Ibid.

20. Ibid.

21. Ibid.

22. Uniting and Strengthening America by Providing Appropriate Tools Required to Intercept and Obstruct Terrorism Act of 2001 ("Patriot Act"), Pub. L. No. 07–156, 116 Stat. 272 (2001).

23. Bullock, J. A., et al. (2006). *Introduction to Homeland Security*. New York, NY: Elsevier, 41–42.

24. Department of Homeland Security (DHS). (2003, February 28). *Homeland Security Presidential Directive 5: Management of Domestic Incidents*. Retrieved from http://www.dhs.gov/xabout/laws/gc_1214592333605.shtm#1

25. Ibid.

26. Post-Katrina Emergency Management Reform Act of 2006, Pub. L. No. 109–295, 120 Stat. 1355 (2006).

27. Department of Homeland Security Office of Inspector General, Office of Inspections and Special Reviews. (2006, March). *A Performance Review of FEMA's Disaster Management Activities in Response to Hurricane Katrina*. Retrieved from http://www.dhs.gov/xoig/assets/mgmtrpts/OIG_06-32_Mar06.pdf

28. Ibid.

29. Ibid.

30. Ibid.

31. Emergency Management Assistance Compact, Pub. L. No. 104-321, 110 Stat. 3877 (1996).

32. American-Arab Anti-Discrimination Committee. (2003). *Report on Hate Crimes and Discrimination Against Arab Americans: The Post-September 11 Backlash September 11, 2001–October 11, 2002*. Retrieved from http://www.adc.org/PDF/hcr02.pdf

33. Ibid.

34. U.S. Department of Justice. (n.d.). *Initiative to Combat Post-9/11 Discriminatory Backlash*. Retrieved from http://www.justice.gov/crt/legalinfo/discrimupdate.php

35. *United States v. Syring*, 522 F. Supp. 2d 125 (D.D.C. 2007).

36. U.S. Department of Justice, n.d.

37. Ibid.

38. International Court of Justice. (n.d.). *The Court*. Retrieved from http://www.icj-cij.org/court/index.php?p1=1&PHPSESSID=7a3b31f1d2a92d51efc5cb98b1612b96

39. Ibid.

40. Ibid.

41. International Court of Justice (ICJ). (n.d.). *Statute of the International Court of Justice: Chapter 1: Organization of the Court*. Retrieved from http://www.icj-cij.org/documents/index.php?p1=4&p2=2&p3=0#CHAPTER_I

42. International Court of Justice. (2011). *List of Contentious Cases by Date of Introduction*. Retrieved from http://www.icj-cij.org/docket/index.php?p1=3&p2=3

43. Corfu Channel case (*United Kingdom v. Albania*), 1949 I.C.J. Rep. 244. Retrieved from http://www.icj-cij.org/docket/files/1/1663.pdf

44. Corfu Channel case (*United Kingdom v. Albania*), Preliminary Objection, 1948 I.C.J. Rep. 15. Retrieved from http://www.icj-cij.org/docket/files/1/1569.pdf

45. Corfu Channel case (*United Kingdom v. Albania*), 1949 I.C.J. Rep. 244.

46. ICJ, 2011.

47. INTERPOL. (2011a). *About INTERPOL: Overview*. Retrieved from http://www.interpol.int/About-INTERPOL/Overview

48. INTERPOL. (2011b). *Terrorism*. Retrieved from http://www.interpol.int/Crime-areas/Terrorism/Terrorism

49. Ibid.

50. Europol. (2011). *Frequently Asked Questions: What Is Europol's Mission?* Retrieved from https://www.europol.europa.eu/faq

51. Europol. (2010). *Europol Profile*. Retrieved from https://www.europol.europa.eu/sites/default/files/publications/edoc-465620-v1-europol_profile_-_en.pdf

52. Ibid.

53. Garcia, M. J., & Doyle, C. (2010). *Extradition To and From the United States: Overview of the Law and Recent Treaties.* Retrieved from http://www.fas.org/sgp/crs/misc/98-958.pdf

54. Ibid.

55. *Kostotas v. Roche*, 931 F.2d 169, 171 (1st Cir. 1991), citing *Eain v. Wilkes*, 641 F.2d 504, 512 (7th Cir. 1981).

56. United Nations. (2011). *Counter-Terrorism Implementation Task Force.* Retrieved from http://www.un.org/en/terrorism/ctitf/index.shtml

57. Ibid.

58. United Nations. (n.d.). *Working Groups.* Retrieved from http://www.un.org/terrorism/workinggroups.shtml

59. United Nations. (n.d.). *Working Group on Tackling the Financing of Terrorism.* Retrieved from http://www.un.org/terrorism/financing.shtml

60. International Criminal Court. (n.d.). *About the Court.* Retrieved from http://www.icc-cpi.int/Menus/ICC/About+the+Court/

61. International Criminal Court. (2002). *Rome Statute of the International Criminal Court* (I.C.J. Doc. A/CONF.183/9). Retrieved from http://untreaty.un.org/cod/icc/statute/english/rome_statute(e).pdf

62. UN Security Council. (1994). *Resolution 955* (UN Doc. S/RES/955). Retrieved from http://www.unictr.org/Portals/0/English/Legal/Resolutions/English/955e.pdf

63. International Criminal Tribunal for Rwanda. (n.d.). *About ICTR.* Retrieved from http://www.unictr.org/About ICTR/GeneralInformation/tabid/101/Default.aspx

64. Federal Bureau of Investigation (FBI). (2003). *A Byte Out of History: Solving a Complex Case of International Terrorism.* Retrieved from http://www.fbi.gov/news/stories/2003/december/panam121903

65. BBC News. (2009a). *Megrahi: "A Convenient Scapegoat?"* Retrieved from http://news.bbc.co.uk/2/hi/uk_news/scotland/8211596.stm

66. Scottish Criminal Cases Review Commission. (2007). *News Release: Abdelbaset Ali Mohmed Al Megrahi.* Retrieved from http://www.sccrc.org.uk/ViewFile.aspx?id=293

67. Ibid.

68. FBI, 2003.

69. BBC News. (2009b). *Megrahi: Profile of a Bomber.* Retrieved from http://news.bbc.co.uk/2/hi/uk_news/scotland/7728434.stm

70. Associated Press. (2011). "Report: Gadhafi Ordered Lockerbie Bombing." *MSNBC News.* Retrieved from http://www.msnbc.msn.com/id/41734924/ns/world_news-europe/

71. Babu, M. (2004). "What Is Cybercrime?" *Computer Crime Research Center.* Retrieved from http://www.crime-research.org/analytics/702/

72. Schell, B. H., & Martin, C. (2004). *Cybercrime: A Reference Handbook.* Santa Barbara, CA: ABC-CLIO.

73. Thomas, J. (2006). *Cybercrime: A Revolution in Terrorism and Criminal Behavior Creates Change in the Criminal Justice System.* Retrieved from http://voices.yahoo.com/cybercrime-revolution-terrorism-criminal-53862.html

74. Creditor Web. (2011). *Federal Trade Commission.* Retrieved from http://www.creditorweb.com/definition/federal-trade-commission.html

75. Federal Trade Commission. (2011). *2010 Consumer Complaints.* Retrieved from http://www.ftc.gov/opa/2011/03/topcomplaints.shtm

76. Godwin, G. (2010). "2010 FTC Identity Theft Statistics." *Examiner.com.* Retrieved from http://www.examiner.com/pop-culture-in-detroit/2010-ftc-identity-theft-statistics

77. Lovaas, P. (2010). *A Holistic IT Audit Program.*

78. Babu, 2004.

79. Denning, D. (2000). *Cyberterrorism.* Retrieved from http://www.cs.georgetown.edu/~denning/infosec/cyberterror.html

80. Stanton, T. H. (2008). *Defending Cyberspace.* Retrieved from http://advanced.jhu.edu/bin/g/z/Defending_Cyberspace.pdf

81. DHS. (2003). *Homeland Security Presidential Directive 7: Critical Infrastructure Identification, Prioritization and Protection.* Retrieved from http://www.dhs.gov/xabout/laws/gc_1214597989952.shtm

82. Nagre, D., & Warade, P. (2008a). *Cyber Terrorism.* Retrieved from www.contrib.andrew.cmu.edu/~dnagre/Final_Report_dnagre_pwarade.pdf

83. Gordon, S. (2010). *Cyberterrorism.* Retrieved from www.symantec.com/avcenter/reference/cyberterrorism.pdf

84. Tucher, D. (2000). *The Future of Armed Resistance: Cyberterror? Mass Destruction.* Retrieved from http://www.nps.edu/Academics/Centers/CTIW/files/substate_conflict_dynamics.pdf

85. Science Daily. (2011). *How Do We Fight the War Against Cyber Terrorism?* Retrieved from http://www.sciencedaily.com/releases/2011/04/110411103717.htm

86. Honeynet Project. (2005). *Know Your Enemy: GenII Honeynets.* Retrieved from http://old.honeynet.org/papers/gen2/

87. Science Daily, 2011.

88. FBI. (2010). *2010 IC3 Annual Report.* Retrieved from http://www.ic3.gov/media/annualreports.aspx

89. Nagre, D., & Warade, P. (2008b). *Cyberterrorism: Vulnerabilities and Policy Issues.* Retrieved from http://www.andrew.cmu.edu/user/dnagre/

90. Lawton, G. (2011). "Cloud Computing Poses New Forensic Challenges." *SearchCloudComputing.* Retrieved from http://searchcloudcomputing.techtarget.com/feature/Cloud-computing-crime-poses-unique-forensics-challenges

91. Ibid.

92. Head, T. (n.d.). "Big Brother Is Watching: A History of Government Surveillance Programs." *About.com Civil Liberties.* Retrieved from http://civilliberty.about.com/od/waronterror/tp/Surveillance-History.htm

93. Ibid.

94. Biometric Consortium. (2011). *An Introduction to Biometrics.* Retrieved from http://www.biometrics.org/html/introduction.html

95. Family Home Security. (2011). *The Latest in Crime Fighting Technologies.* Retrieved from http://www.familyhomesecurity.com/the-latest-in-crime-fighting-technology/

96. NIST. (2009). *Mobile Forensics and Security.* Retrieved from http://csrc.nist.gov/groups/SNS/mobile_security/index.html

97. Criminal Justice Careers & Education. (2011). *Computer Forensics Job Description.* Retrieved from http://www.criminaljusticeschoolinfo.com/computer-forensics-job-description.html

98. Homeland Security News Wire. (2011). *Do Security Cameras Deter Crime?* Retrieved from http://www.homelandsecuritynewswire.com/do-security-cameras-deter-crime

15

The Future of Criminal Justice

KEY TERMS

Anti-Terrorism Assistance Program (ATAP), Customs and Border Protection (CBP), Evidence-based models, Federal Wiretap Act, Fusion center, Global Positioning System (GPS), I-24/7, I-Link, Israeli Model, Joint Terrorism Task Forces, Legalization, Michigan Prisoner Reentry Initiative (MPRI), Social networking, Visa

CHAPTER OBJECTIVES

1. Compare various models of intervention including evidence-based models.

2. Evaluate perceptions of the death penalty both in the United States and across the globe and their implications for its existence in the future.

3. Explain trends in drug laws and the difference between decriminalization and legalization.

4. Analyze the implications of technology and social networking in relation to enhancing security and protecting individual liberties and privacy rights.

5. Describe the growing reliance on global coordination and information sharing between law enforcement agencies and correctional institutions.

6. Identify the new policies and technologies that are being developed and implemented in the United States and abroad in order to provide for more secure borders and travel.

Case Study: Harrison Bergeron

In "Harrison Bergeron," author Kurt Vonnegut, Jr. presents the reader with a frightening vision of a dystopian society in which the state has assumed near-absolute control over the lives of its citizens. The government has just passed the 211th, 212th, and 213th Amendments to the Constitution, which are designed to create absolute equality among all citizens. The government has imposed a series of severe social engineering mechanisms intended to suppress any exceptional qualities in members of society, thereby restricting people from reaching their full potential. These social engineering mechanisms include blaring noises into the ears of those who are intelligent, making them unable to focus their thoughts or concentrate for any given period of time. Those who are muscular or graceful are forced to wear heavy weights to impair their movement and those who are beautiful are forced to don hideous masks to conceal their faces.

The story is told from the perspective of George and Hazel Bergeron, parents of the titular character. George is extremely intelligent and is forced to endure the piercing noise roughly every twenty seconds; Hazel is much less intelligent and because she is unable to think very long about anything, she is not required to wear any equipment to impair her abilities. The couple watches a ballet on television; most of the ballerinas are carrying multiple handicapping devices to impair their ability to dance, as well as their beauty. The accompanying musicians are also forced to wear devices that impair their abilities, and the music they produce is uninspired and drab.

Hazel hates the discomfort that the restraints cause her husband and encourages him to remove some of them. George refuses to do so; first arguing that if he were caught he would face strict punishment, but later taking the position that he has to obey the law because if everyone cheated the law then society would crumble. George's view of these controls raises issues concerning the nature of liberty and security; in this case George has become convinced that the only way security can be attained is by sacrificing much of his, and every other person's, personal freedoms. George posits that if everyone were permitted more liberties, society would descend into chaos.

As the story proceeds, the ballet performance is interrupted by a news bulletin reporting that George and Hazel's son, 14-year-old Harrison, has escaped from jail. Harrison is a genius, a tremendous athlete, handsome, and enormous in stature. His restraints are the most repressive ever designed. During the broadcast, Harrison enters the television studio, declares himself emperor, and then easily destroys his restraints. Harrison frees a ballerina and the musicians from their handicapping devices. As Harrison and the ballerina began dancing to the music, soaring above the room, the Handicapper General enters the studio and shoots both of them dead.

At home, Hazel cries as she watches the scene end, but when asked by her husband what is upsetting her, she is unable to remember what had triggered these emotions. He teases her playfully, suggesting that he too has forgotten that it was his son on the screen.

Trends in the Criminal Justice System
The issues that Kurt Vonnegut, Jr. raises in *Harrison Bergeron* are very pertinent to present-day society. First, what are the implications for a society that places too much emphasis on any one quality like security or equality? What happens to its other values? The criminal justice system is largely concerned with maintaining order, but how invasive should these measures be? As the United States has given increased emphasis to security since the events of September 11th, these discussions are more pertinent than ever before. Extensions of security often impact other core values such as liberty, values that must be considered when any new policy or technology is developed and implemented. Future criminal justice professionals are faced with interesting questions as new policies and technologies allow law enforcement to gather information, generate intelligence, monitor citizens, and pursue offenders in new and innovative ways. Some of these new approaches present concerns regarding the manner in which they implicate individual rights and liberties.

Furthermore, Vonnegut's treatment of the effect that these impositions have on members of society must also be considered. George is one of the most severely impacted by these restraints, and yet, he is extremely committed to them and refuses to remove them to have a moment of respite. In this way Vonnegut forces the reader to consider the impact that these types of controls eventually have on their recipients. George has fallen into such absolute compliance with the impositions placed upon him that he is unable to recognize the gravity that his son's actions and ultimate sacrifice carry with them. The threat of severe punishment clearly motivates some of George's decisions; in this way, Vonnegut forces the reader to confront the issue of the effect of deterrence. The reader must think about the types of restrictions we accept in our own lives. What restraints have we accepted in order to feel safe? Are we safer? Finding an appropriate balance between security and personal freedom is something that all societies, and criminal justice professionals, must deal with.

As society looks toward the future of the criminal justice system, there are some issues, rooted in the past and present, that will require particular attention. These issues, or trends, set the stage for the future of criminal justice in terms of how society views criminal activity, intervention, and punishment. Trends within these topics may shed light on the next phase of criminal justice and what is on the horizon for those that work in and study this field.

The criminal justice system faces many challenges in the future.

Models of Intervention
As with most facets of the public sector, the criminal justice system must continue to evolve as society and the world changes over time. Part of that evolution requires taking a step back and assessing what the system looks like today, including its successes and failures. If lawmakers know what "works" and what doesn't, they can shape the criminal justice system of the future to be a more effective

framework for administering justice and yielding the results that society seeks. This notion of "what works" is most clearly linked to models of intervention and their relative effectiveness.

What Works for Juvenile Offenders

As discussed in Chapter 12, following an arrest, juvenile offenders can be officially processed through the courts, released without referral or services, or diverted into a community-based service. Research shows that depending on what track the juvenile follows, rates of recidivism, and in turn, threats to the community, vary widely. For example, studies show that the following interventions have little success in reducing recidivism, and in some cases, actually tend to increase criminal behavior:[1]

- Transfer to adult criminal court: Transferring juveniles to adult criminal court for trial and sentencing can be accomplished through various means, including prosecutor discretion, statutory exclusion, and judicial waiver laws. Studies have shown that transferred juveniles are associated with higher recidivism rates than their counterparts who are adjudicated in juvenile court.[2]

- Shock incarceration programs: The most well known shock program is *Scared Straight*—it exposes juveniles to adult prisons and attempts to "scare" them into non-criminal activity through threats, bullying, and intimidation by inmates. Numerous studies have shown that the program does not deter criminal activity, and some studies have demonstrated that such interventions actually increase criminal behavior of juveniles.[3]

- Residential placement: Residential placements include group homes, detention centers, treatment centers, boot camps, and wilderness camps. These facilities attempt to rehabilitate offenders and to protect the community by removing juvenile offenders from the general population. Studies have shown that such facilities often fail on both accounts.

- Interventions such as these that are ineffective at reducing criminal activity expose a need for change in the criminal justice system. Although juvenile justice systems vary from state to state, they should all be focused on effective interventions—for the good of the juveniles in the system as well as the communities in which they live and take part.

- In contrast to the interventions discussed above, there are several models of intervention for juvenile offenders that have yielded positive results and that studies have shown to be effective. A few of these **evidence-based models**, as described by Hengfeler and Sohoenwald (2011), include:

- Functional family therapy (FFT): FFT is an evidence-based therapy rooted in family or community. It integrates behavioral and cognitive interventions into treatment and places emphasis on engagement with family members.[4]

- Multisystemic therapy (MST): MST is also a family or community-based treatment program that focuses on offenders in the context of their homes, families, schools, community, and social network. It is one of the most extensively validated treatment programs.[5]

Evidence-based models
Models of intervention proven effective through social scientific research and study.

- Multidimensional treatment foster care (MTFC): MTFC is a community-based foster care system, and is an alternative to state detention and group care facilities. MTFC emphasizes social learning, including behavioral principles.[6]

The commonalties of these effective programs form the bases of successful interventions for juvenile offenders. In particular, effective programs specifically address key risk factors; are rehabilitative in nature; and are well specified in scope.[7]

Intervention programs may be more effective in handling juvenile offenders programs than incarceration.

What Works for Adult Offenders

Juvenile offenders are a particular and special population, but these same principles apply to adults as well. According to an April 2011 study by the Pew Center on the States and the Association of State Correctional Administrators, 45.4% of prisoners released in 1999 and 43.3% of prisoners released in 2004 were re-incarcerated within a three-year window for committing another new crime or violating conditions of their release.[8] The survey gathered information from approximately three dozen states and organized data by state in order to examine variation among the states and the causes for variation. The survey examined successful use of policies and practices in helping reduce recidivism rates among the states and found that the employment of evidence-based strategies, such as the use of advanced risk assessments, strategic re-entry planning, and post-release supervision designed uniquely for each offender, helped states increase the likelihood that released persons would not be re-incarcerated.[9]

There are several examples of states putting evidence-based programs into practice, and they should serve as models for other states in the future. For example, Oregon has one of the lowest recidivism rates in the country and had the largest decline of recidivism in the Pew survey.[10] Among other factors, Oregon has adopted effective practices that include: requiring any state-funded correctional program to use evidence-based design and execution; conducting a risk and needs assessment at intake for all inmates, providing offenders with targeted case management during their incarceration, and providing inmates with transition planning beginning six months before their release.[11] Similar to Oregon's policies, Michigan created the **Michigan Prisoner Reentry Initiative (MPRI)** with a mission of equipping released offenders with the tools they need to succeed in the community.[12] Under MPRI each prisoner receives individualized programming based on risk, needs, and strengths determined by intake evaluations. Then the prisoner is transferred to a reentry facility prior to parole where he or she receives a transition plan dealing with housing, employment, transportation, as well as rehabilitative needs including counseling, mentoring, and treatment. Following the implementation of MPRI in 2003, Michigan's inmate population has shrunk by 12% over a 10-year period. Further, parolees released through the MPRI program were re-incarcerated 33% less frequently than offenders who did not take part in the program.[13]

Moreover, research has highlighted some key policy differences that help explain the different recidivism rates among states. One such example is the dif-

Michigan Prisoner Reentry Initiative (MPRI)
A state imitative implemented in 2003 with a mission of equipping released offenders with the tools they need to succeed in the community.

ference between states' sentencing policies. If a state focuses on sentencing high-risk offenders to prison and puts low-risk offenders on probation or in alternative programs, then that state is likely to have a higher rate of recidivism than a state that habitually sends low-risk offenders to prison. This is because low-risk offenders are, by definition, at less risk of being re-incarcerated, and so, a state with more high-risk offenders in prison is likely to see a comparatively higher rate of recidivism.[14] The comparative recidivism rate of a state is also affected by how the state handles parole violations. Simply put, the fewer parolees a state has, the fewer technical violations it will have. Therefore, states like Arizona, which has an extremely strict truth in sentencing policy (in which offenders serve 85% or more of their prison term),[15] wind up with significantly lower rate of re-incarceration for a technical violation; according to the Pew survey, Arizona's rate in 2004 was 11.5%, one of the lowest rates in the survey.[16]

It is clear that while juveniles and adults can present different challenges, applying evidence-based interventions works for both populations. Thus, the challenge for the future of the criminal justice system is how to implement these practices in a meaningful way. One way of dealing with this issue is to bring stakeholders and components of the justice system together to collaborate and work toward the common goal of identifying and implementing new policies and programs. Ideally, the collaborators would include criminal justice agencies, community organizations, court personnel, attorneys' groups, victim advocates, and elected officials so as to capitalize on a myriad of perspectives. A second challenge is that after new policies and programs are developed, the system will have to take major steps to remodel its infrastructure and retrain personnel to implement the changes. For example, the physical infrastructure in our current prisons may need to be altered to meet the structural requirements of effective therapies. Moreover, personnel would need to be educated in the models of therapy or care being implemented. An extreme example might be retraining staff who are accustomed to facilitating *Scared Straight* programs to instead focus on community or family based therapies. The California Correctional Peace Officers Association highlighted some of these challenges in a January 2010 report focused on reducing costs and rehabilitating inmates. Specifically, the report found that the state must reassess the "design, mission and staffing of existing prisons, as most do not provide sufficient staff or space for successful rehabilitation programs."[17] Further, the report conceded that the process would be a lengthy one considering the number of stakeholders and the amount of change necessary.[18]

Capital Punishment

One of the most contentious issues regarding criminal justice is the death penalty. Determining when, if ever, it should be applied is an ever-present debate. Capital punishment jurisprudence in the United States was defined in the 1970s in a series of landmark decisions by the Supreme Court. In 1972, the court ruled in *Furman v. Georgia*[19] that a statute giving juries complete discretion could lead to arbitrary sentencing and thereby violated the Eighth Amendment, which protects against cruel and unusual punishment. In response, some states passed laws that mandated the sentence for capital crimes. The

Supreme Court also found this practice unconstitutional in *Woodson v. North Carolina*.[20]

States began providing sentencing guidelines that allowed judges and juries to consider various aggravating and mitigating factors. In 1976, the Supreme Court stated that these types of guidelines were constitutional in three cases referred to as the Gregg decision (*Gregg v. Georgia*,[21] *Jurek v. Texas*,[22] and *Proffitt v. Florida*[23]). The Court also found that the death penalty was constitutional under the Eighth Amendment.

In the United States, as of 2011, there were 34 states that have the death penalty.[24] In spite of this, the use of the death penalty has been declining since 2000. Furthermore, there were fewer capital sentences from 2007–2010 than in any period since its reinstatement in 1976.[25] In 2010 there were 114 death sentences issued and 112 in 2009, representing a 50% decline from the 1990s.[26] Public attitudes towards the death penalty are one of the oldest trends that Gallup has followed; there has been little change in this perception. In 1936, 59% supported the sentence and that number stood at 64% in 2010.[27] Interestingly, support for the death penalty drops to approximately half of the population when individuals are presented with the opportunity to sentence offenders to a life sentence without the possibility of parole.[28]

A key distinction lies in the difference between the issuance of a capital sentence and the actual execution phase. Interestingly, there has also been a decline in the number of sentences carried out. In 1999, 98 people were executed, which was the greatest number ever; however, by 2008 that number had fallen to 37 (this number rebounded slightly with 52 executions in 2009 and 38 in 2010).[29] One explanation for the falling numbers is an extreme shortage of sodium thiopental, one of the three key drugs used in the lethal injection cocktail.[30] Some have advocated using a substitute drug; however, because this would be different from protocols already established by various states, this could serve as grounds for appeal for defendants who have been sentenced.

The tremendous administrative costs associated with carrying out the death penalty have also caused it to be used with less frequency. It was originally thought that the death penalty reduced such costs as opposed to sentencing prisoners to life sentences.[31] However, according to Radelet and Borg (2000), the various legal protocols, prison and security costs, and actual amounts needed to carry out such a sentence require tremendous amounts of money and can actually end up being more expensive than a life sentence.[32]

Finally it should be remembered that there are few issues in criminal justice that incite the emotions of people like the death penalty. The gravity and finality of the sentence often cause people to base their views of the death penalty on opinion and emotion, rather than facts and evidence. Moreover, within the United States support for the death penalty is split between other personal distinctions such as political ideology, race, and gender.[33] The death penalty is an issue that has become increasingly polarized along these ideological lines. However, use of the death penalty in the United States will most likely decline, though not disappear completely, over the next several years due to the increased costs of carrying out the sentence.

The United Nations has been one of the strongest global advocates calling for abolition of the death penalty.

The International Community and the Death Penalty   Because each country is autonomous within its own borders, capital punishment at the international level is controlled through suggestive guidelines and voluntary compliance. From an international perspective, capital punishment is disfavored. The modern international movement to end the death penalty was formalized with the United Nations adoption of the Universal Declaration of Human Rights, specifically Article 3, which states, "Everyone has the right to life, liberty and security of person" and Article 5, which states, "No one shall be subjected to torture or to cruel, inhuman or degrading treatment or punishment[.]"[34] Sixteen countries had abolished the death penalty entirely by 1977, and 35 countries had done so by 1988, while 18 others retained it only for exceptional crimes such as treason.[35]

In 1989, the United Nations General Assembly adopted the "Second Optional Protocol to the International Covenant on Civil and Political Rights, aiming at the abolition of the death penalty[.]"[36] In this agreement, member nations agreed to abolish the death penalty within their borders, with an allowance to pass a reservation allowing execution for grave crimes in times of war. As of September 2011, 73 states had joined the Optional Protocol.[37]

At the global level, the use of the death penalty has fallen dramatically. During the 1990s an average of 40 different countries carried out executions, but by the end of the first decade of the 21st century that number had fallen into the mid-20s.[38] In 2010, a total of 23 countries executed a convict and at least 67 imposed death sentences.[39]

The number of countries with an outright ban on the death penalty increased from 108 in 2001 to 139 in 2010.[40] By the close of the year, 96 countries had abolished the death penalty for all crimes and 139 countries abolished capital punishment in law or practice.[41] Additionally, Gabon removed the sentence from its laws in 2010 and Lebanon, Mali, Mongolia, and South Korea had all proposed legislation that would do the same.[42] It is also important to note that abolition of the death penalty is required for membership in the European Union.[43]

Finally, the United Nations General Assembly passed a third moratorium on the use of the death penalty. In fact, more UN member countries supported the measure in 2010 than in 2008.[44] The trend is clear; worldwide support of the death penalty continues to decrease. There are some exceptions, such as: China, Iran, Pakistan, and the United States, to name a few, but research indicates that support for the death penalty will continue to decline.

Critical Thinking   With such widespread condemnation of the death penalty, the United States is in a small group of countries that still impose it. Do you believe the United States will eliminate the death penalty in the near future? Why or why not?

Drug Laws   One recurring debate in criminal justice questions whether the prohibition on drug use should be reconsidered. There are arguments to be made on either side of this issue. One key factor is the costs involved with enforcement, investigations, and detention of offenders. Legalization would free up these funds to be used for other initiatives. In addition to these savings, drug sales could be taxed, resulting in enormous amounts of revenue for governments at all levels. However, critics argue that these fiscal benefits will be offset by the costs incurred due to increased addiction rates across society.[45] Some simply view it as a normative issue; they believe drug use is wrong and that it leads to disorderly behavior for society, and thus society should not condone or tolerate its use. Their opponents take the position that these same types of arguments apply with equal force to tobacco and alcohol use, and yet, these products are clearly legal.

Economist Jeffrey Miron (2010) estimates that if the United States were to legalize drugs, it would result in a savings of $48.7 billion a year. Most of these savings would be enjoyed by state and local governments, but the federal government would save roughly $15.6 billion of this total.[46] These are staggering amounts and only contemplate savings; if there were complete **legalization** and these drugs were taxed at rates comparable to alcohol and tobacco, they would generate an additional $34.3 billion in annual revenues.[47] Such an approach could also reduce the strain on the corrections system by reducing the number of people incarcerated for drug offenses.

There would naturally be increased costs related to regulation; however, these would still be significantly lower than enforcement costs, writes Jeffrey Miron (2010).[48] For these amounts to be realized, the drug market would have to be regulated, but there would not be enforcement against possession or trafficking in any way that resembles the current regime.

Legalization
Removing legal barriers to drug possession and use in an effort to make it a regulated and taxable portion of the economy.

In some states, medical marijuana can be found at your local pharmacy.

There has been some support for this position. A coalition of leaders from Central and South America have suggested that the U.S. policy on drugs is untenable, especially in light of the large number of consumers. These leaders argue that this demand is fueling the drug trade and the transit countries end up paying the price in terms of violence and suffering.[49]

Several European countries have relaxed their drug laws over the past decade, most notably the Netherlands with regard to possession of marijuana.[50] In spite of this, the decriminalization of drug possession in the United States has yet to gain much momentum. In 2010, California, long held as a state with less restrictive drug laws, introduced Proposition 19, a referendum that sought to decriminalize possession of small amounts of marijuana for recreational use.[51] The measure was defeated by a double-digit margin at the ballots.[52]

However, this is a trend that must be followed by criminal justice professionals going forward. Recent polls demonstrate that the percentage of Americans who favor the legalization of marijuana use has steadily increased over the last decade, with a new high of 50% reported in 2011.[53] Additionally, several states, including California,[54] Washington,[55] and Missouri,[56] have added propositions to their ballots to legalize marijuana in some form.

Perhaps the most important trend to follow is the way that drug laws interact with public health considerations in the future. The use of marijuana for medical purposes is now supported by 70% of Americans.[57] Sixteen states, as well as the District of Columbia, have laws allowing the use of medical marijuana, even though use of any marijuana is still technically illegal under federal law.[58] This has led to direct conflicts between state and federal officials. The Treasury Department has compelled banks to close accounts of dispensaries operating legally under state law; the IRS has required medical marijuana dispensaries to pay taxes not required of any other business; and the Bureau of Alcohol, Tobacco, Firearms and Explosives declared that medical marijuana patients are not permitted to purchase firearms.[59] In California, several operators of medical marijuana dispensaries have received orders for eviction.[60] The recent crackdown on these facilities is based on allegations of widespread criminal activity within the medical marijuana industry.[61] There have also been complaints regarding the proximity of dispensaries to schools.[62] The decision by the federal government to aggressively attempt to close these centers is also driven by persistent questions concerning violations of federal drug and money-laundering laws.[63] The conflict between recent federal policy and state laws has led to a great deal of confusion regarding the legality of medical marijuana dispensaries and, as such, has led to such confusion that individuals have filed lawsuits to have the issue resolved.[64]

The United States may examine other countries' attempts to reach a compromise regarding drug laws. Portugal, overwhelmed by the rising costs of enforcement and rampant use, has adopted an approach that focuses on the public health component of addiction. Drug possession is still not legal; however, an offender is not placed into the criminal system. Instead the offender is directed to counseling and other intervention programs aimed at combating addition.[65] This approach has some appeal because it seeks to address the causes of the behavior. Critics argue that this is unacceptable because it makes drug use and addiction appear more acceptable.[66] While it is too early to determine whether this has been a successful endeavor, future criminal justice professionals should continue to monitor the effectiveness of Portugal's approach to determine if any of these aspects can be incorporated in the United States.

Privacy and Civil Liberties

It is impossible to predict exactly what the criminal justice system will look like or what it will face in the future, but there are some emerging issues that certainly seem to be on the forefront. Chief among these issues is the balance between civil liberties and effective law enforcement. Though this issue is not a new concern, it has taken a new form against the backdrop of innovative technologies used by law enforcement, social networking, and the public's right to know. As the world changes and society's expectations of privacy and civil liberties change, it is vital to revisit these important issues that form the cornerstone of our criminal justice system.

Technological Advances in Law Enforcement

Chapter 14 provided an overview of many of the new technologies employed by law enforcement agencies in the 21st century. These technologies include computer forensics tools, cameras, biometrics, 3D imaging software, and mobile devices. Although these tools allow law enforcement greater access to information in a more timely and accurate way than previously available, they simultaneously raise concerns related to the civil liberties and privacy of individuals under investigation, and sometimes individuals who are merely caught up in the investigation.

The use of **Global Positioning System (GPS)** technology presents a similar problem when law enforcement uses it in the course of an investigation. GPS is increasingly used by law enforcement agencies in monitoring and gathering evidence.[67] In one case in Virginia, after 11 women were attacked, police installed a GPS device on a van owned by a suspect who was a convicted rapist and lived near the crime scenes. Police tracked his movements and eventually intercepted him while he was dragging a woman to a remote location.[68] In another case, Wisconsin police attached a GPS device to a suspect's car based on a tip about a methamphetamine manufacturer. The device led police to a large tract of land, and a search of the property yielded paraphernalia used to manufacture methamphetamines.[69] In a

Global Positioning System (GPS)
A system of satellites that orbit the earth and transmit signals to allow receivers to display accurate location, speed, and time information.

An automated fingerprint authentication system analyzes arches, swoops, and whorls.

third case, New York police officers used evidence from a GPS device placed on a suspect's car to confirm a witness's report that the suspect had been observing a store that was later burglarized. The evidence showed that the suspect had driven past the store multiple times, thus corroborating the witness testimony.[70] Each of these cases demonstrates a different use of GPS in gathering evidence, but all three raise concerns about how far law enforcement can go during the course of an investigation to obtain evidence without infringing upon an individual's rights or expectations of privacy as outlined in the Constitution.

Although imaging software, biometrics, GPS, and other technologies are used by law enforcement to prevent and investigate criminal activity, a parallel issue arises when non-law enforcement agencies use the same or similar tools. For example, class action lawsuits were filed in 2011 against a software company called CarrierIQ and phone manufacturers HTC and Samsung in response to a "keystroke-sniffing" software embedded in millions of HTC and Samsung Android devices.[71] The lawsuits allege that CarrierIQ's software captures every keystroke on a device in addition to location and other data, thereby allowing those with access to the information to see the content of text messages, emails, and any other data entered into a phone. Further, the lawsuits allege that the software makes such data available to CarrierIQ's customers.[72] CarrierIQ responded that the software was "not recording keystrokes or providing tracking tools . . . and [that] CarrierIQ does not sell personal subscriber information to 3rd parties."[73] Although the outcome of the lawsuit is pending, it brings to light the issue of individual privacy expectations.

Expectations of Privacy   In an ever more technological world in which law enforcement and private companies use highly technical devices to interact with, track, and monitor individuals, the question becomes: What is a reasonable expectation of privacy and what expectations or rights are protected by the Constitution? The Fourth Amendment of the U.S. Constitution protects individuals "against unreasonable searches and seizures" by the government. Over time, the language of the Amendment has been debated, but its meaning, in part, has been interpreted by the Supreme Court to protect an individual from warrantless searches or seizures if the individual has a justifiable expectation of privacy. The seminal case that led to this understanding of the Amendment and how it relates to privacy was *Katz v. United States.*[74]

Charles Katz was convicted in U.S. District Court in California for violating a law prohibiting interstate transmission of bets or wagers by wire communication. Katz used a telephone in a public phone booth to transmit wagers from Los Angeles to Miami and Boston. As part of their investigation, the FBI attached a recording device to the booth. Using this device, the FBI agents were able to obtain the audio evidence necessary to convict Mr. Katz in the District Court. On appeal, the Court of Appeals affirmed the decision, and Katz petitioned the U.S. Supreme Court to hear the case. Katz argued that the FBI's actions, electronically listening to and recording his words in a public telephone booth, violated his privacy and constituted an unreasonable search and seizure in violation of the Fourth Amendment.[75]

The Future of Criminal Justice **529**

The Supreme Court held that despite the fact that the telephone booth was in the public domain, Katz sought to preserve his privacy and that he had a justifiable expectation that his conversations were private. As such, the Court reversed the lower courts' decision and ruled that the recorded evidence amounted to an unreasonable search and seizure.[76]

Based on this understanding of a justifiable expectation of privacy, law enforcement and courts must determine how to appropriately use technology like GPS during an investigation. This is by no means a straightforward analysis and it presents opportunity for a serious debate about how the criminal justice system will operate in the future.

Limiting the Use of Technology   It stands to reason that if some uses of technology by law enforcement violate an individual's justifiable expectation of privacy, limits should be in place to protect those rights and mitigate that threat. Because reliance on technology in law enforcement is continually growing, the response in how to deal with this threat and protection of civil liberties is also evolving, and is sometimes unclear. For example, regarding GPS devices, some states have enacted statutes that impose penalties for improper use of tracking devices or automatically exclude evidence from an electronic device unless police acted with use of a warrant.[78] Yet, in other states, courts have ruled that using a GPS device to track a vehicle on public streets is not considered a search or seizure at all.[79]

The Supreme Court did not weigh in on police use of GPS until their January 2012 decision in *United States v. Jones*. In that case, the government obtained a search warrant allowing police to install a GPS device on a vehicle belonging to a suspect's wife.[80] The suspect, Antoine Jones, was being investigated on suspicion of narcotics trafficking by the FBI and District of Columbia police. The warrant authorized the installation of the GPS device in the District of Co-

Katz was in a public phone booth, but his conversation was protected by the Fourth Amendment.

© 2012 BY JAMIE WILSON. UNDER LICENSE FROM SHUTTERSTOCK, INC.

Exhibit: Excerpt from *Katz v. United States* (1967)[77]

"The Government stresses the fact that the telephone booth from which the petitioner made his calls was constructed partly of glass, so that he was as visible after he entered it as he would have been if he had remained outside. But what he sought to exclude when he entered the booth was not the intruding eye—it was the uninvited ear. He did not shed his right to do so simply because he made his calls from a place where he might be seen. No less than an individual in a business office, in a friend's apartment, or in a taxicab, a person in a telephone booth may rely upon the protection of the Fourth Amendment. One who occupies it, shuts the door behind him, and pays the toll that permits him to place a call is surely entitled to assume that the words he utters into the mouthpiece will not be broadcast to the world. To read the Constitution more narrowly is to ignore the vital role that the public telephone has come to play in private communication."

lumbia within ten days. Despite those requirements, law enforcement agents installed the device on the eleventh day in Maryland while the vehicle was parked in a public parking lot.[81] Police monitored the vehicle's movements for the next 28 days and later used data gathered from the device during that time to obtain an indictment against Jones. The same data was used at trial, where a jury ultimately found Jones guilty and the court sentenced him to a life sentence in prison.[82] Jones appealed and the D.C. Circuit Court reversed the trial court's decision, concluding that admission of evidence admitted by warrantless use of the GPS violated Jones' Fourth Amendment rights. The Supreme Court affirmed this decision. The Court held that placement of the GPS device on the vehicle constituted a "search" of Jones' private property under the Fourth Amendment, and that doing so outside of the warrant's requirements amounted to an unlawful act by the government.[83]

Although limitations related to the use of GPS devices are still being decided in the courts, there are some other well-established limitations placed on law enforcement's use of technology. A primary example is the Electronic Communications Privacy Act of 1986, also called the **Federal Wiretap Act**, which forbids acquiring the contents of communications without the users' consent. The Act provides specific provisions for prohibited activities, government access, and consequences of a violation. Within these provisions are guidelines for law enforcement, which provide exemptions from the prohibitions on intercepting wire, oral, and electronic communications under three circumstances:[84]

1. Pursuant to or in anticipation of a court order;
2. With the consent of one of the parties to the communication; and
3. With respect to the communications of an intruder within an electronic communications system.

Moreover, the Act provides procedures for law enforcement officials to secure an interception order based on probable cause that the wiretap or electronic eavesdropping will produce evidence of a federal crime or the whereabouts of a fugitive fleeing prosecution of a federal offense.[85]

Federal Wiretap Act
An act, also called the Electronic Communications Privacy Act of 1986, that forbids acquiring the contents of electronic communications without users' consent and includes provisions for prohibited activities, government access, and consequences of a violation.

Critical Thinking Are CarrierIQ's alleged actions substantially different than law enforcement's use of GPS to monitor and track individuals' movements? What are the implications of each in terms of privacy rights considering one is a private entity and one is a government actor?

Social networking
A web-based service that allows users to construct personal profiles and connect and communicate with other users.

Social Networking An integral part of the discussion of privacy and the criminal justice system of the future relates to **social networking** or social media. The pervasiveness of social media in the United States and the international community at large cannot be overstated. Worldwide, 72% of Internet users are part of a social network.[86] The top three ways that people share information online are Facebook, e-mail, and Twitter.[87] Facebook has over 600 million users; Twitter has over 200 million users producing an astounding 110 million tweets (140-character messages) per day.[88]

More and more people are accessing the Internet from a mobile device instead of a traditional computer.[89] Smartphones outsold personal computers worldwide in the last three months of 2010; surprisingly, 48 million people in the world have a mobile phone, but do not have electricity.[90] As of 2011, 60% of U.S. mobile Internet use was for social networking purposes and consequently, mobile data traffic was expected to rise 40-fold by 2015.[91]

Social networking, through various platforms, has allowed individuals to share massive amounts of information in real time with an almost unlimited number of users. As such, it has sparked debate about privacy expectations of its users, its link to collective action and social unrest, and limitations on its usage in certain settings and circumstances.

People are increasingly interconnected through a variety of electronic networks.

Social Networking and Privacy Expectations

Social networking services feature personal information of users through personal profiles, pictures, status updates, tweets, and e-mail or instant messages to other users. These services give users the ability to share information more easily than ever with family, friends, and co-workers. Users are allowed to make privacy choices so as to control who can access the information they share on a social networking site, and through these choices they are arguably making decisions about their expectations of privacy. Much like the case of Mr. Katz in the telephone booth, it can be argued that if a user marks something as private in a social networking service they have a justifiable expectation of privacy with respect to the Fourth Amendment. On the other hand, many users do not use the privacy controls and therefore do not express any expectation of privacy. Still, the expectation of privacy based on privacy controls is not necessarily conclusive. Some users may expect privacy but simply do not understand the policies and options of the social networking service and thus do not utilize privacy controls.

Due to the increasing use of social networking systems, privacy expectations related to social networking are beginning to work their way through the justice system. In one recent case, the social networking giant Facebook was investigated at the behest of consumer groups and the Electronic Privacy Information Center. The Federal Trade Commission (FTC) charged that Facebook deceived its consumers "by telling them they could keep their information on Facebook private, and then repeatedly allowing it to be shared and made public."[92] Facebook did not admit wrongdoing and was not fined, but agreed to a proposed settlement in which it was barred from misrepresenting the privacy of users' personal information and was prohibited from changing any user's privacy preferences without his or her express consent. Facebook was also required to establish a privacy program to protect the confidentiality of users' information.[93]

Why do privacy settings and controls in social networking matter? For one thing, information posted on social networking systems does not just go away.

The social networking site Twitter announced that its 20 billionth tweet was posted on July 31, 2011.

When a user enters information, personal or otherwise, it remains accessible, sometimes even after users think they have deleted it and long after they have accessed the information themselves. For example, Twitter and the Library of Congress signed an agreement in 2011 that allows for an archive of every public tweet ever sent to be stored at the Library.[94] The agreement with Twitter means that there will be billions of tweets stored for the public to peruse at any time in the future. Though the archive will not include specifically protected tweets (messages that users choose to keep private) it does mean that data shared on social networking systems can be stored and accessed for much longer than a user may intend. Moreover, the agreement comes during a time when the National Archives and Records Administration for federal agencies is pushing to better archive government social media postings and emails as government records. If this trend continues, the issue of privacy expectations with respect to social networking will only grow.

Relationship with Collective Action and Social Unrest   Though social networking has many applications, one particularly relevant point is its relationship to collective action, including mobs, rioting, and social uprisings. Because social networking offers instant communication and the capability to organize like-minded individuals, it presents an avenue for those seeking to organize collective action. There has been much debate about whether the relationship between social networking and collective action is causation or merely correlation, but the fact remains that there is some relationship between the two.

This relationship made headlines in recent years against the backdrop of social unrest in various settings around the world. For example, following a police shooting of a man in London, peaceful protests quickly turned to large-scale riots that spread across London and into other parts of the country in August 2011. Some blamed Twitter, Facebook, and other social networking systems for contributing to the mass chaos and criminal activity that ensued, while some have argued instead that social networking was a positive force in helping organize clean-up operations. One thing is certain—social networking systems were incredibly busy, and for many, they were the most responsive and timely sources of information.[95]

Similarly, there were protests in Moldova, Iran, Tunisia, and Egypt, among others, in which social networking played a preeminent role. Election protests in Moldova and Iran in 2009 and 2010 relied on social networks to publicize and promote action.[96] Tunisia and Egypt were the first in a series of Middle Eastern and North African countries to engage in pro-democracy protests, also known as the Arab Spring, beginning in December 2010 and continuing through the fall and winter of 2011.[97] The Tunisian and Egyptian protests used social networking as a means of instant communication and rallying support. President Obama described this technology as a key variable that both enabled and encouraged citizens of these countries to unite and demand accountability from their governments.[98]

Egyptian citizens used Facebook to organize and plan meetings and protests, and this was one of the primary mechanisms responsible for gathering nearly 100,000 people for the January 28th protest.[99] Twitter also played a critical role in the information sharing process. It provided a medium for a perpetual stream of information, including pictures and video, posted by people on the ground in Egypt and elsewhere to reach the larger world. Twitter contained information on everything from warnings of tear gas usage to notifications of locations where free food was being distributed.[100] Because social networking systems are adaptable enough to be used on any device, Egyptians could tell the world what was going on using nothing more than a mobile phone.

Criminals can take advantage of social networking sites to access victims' personal information.

As the recent events in Egypt and elsewhere have demonstrated, technological advances have helped shape a world that relies on social networking systems for instant communication and information sharing of all types. However, just as social networking can be used to spur positive collective action, it can similarly be used by criminals for nefarious purposes, such as conspiring with other criminals or accessing other people's private information for their own personal gain. As such, the prevalence of social networking systems present a variety of challenges to the criminal justice system.

Future Implications of Social Networking   Because of the nature of social networking, lawmakers have sought to impose limitations on some users and the type of information they share. Two primary categories of such limits are law enforcement (e.g., stopping the flow of information between would-be criminals) and protecting classified information (e.g., preventing a leak of classified military information). These limitations must be evaluated in the context of both individual users and society as a whole; the government must address the core issue of balancing individual users' rights versus public safety and security of the community at large.

Apart from the important ethical and policy discussions concerning limiting the use of or access to social media, there are practical questions too. Is it even possible for governments to prevent access to these platforms? During the events surrounding the revolution in Egypt, the government shut down internet and cell phone service across the country, endeavoring to halt all use of social networking sites in an attempt to quell the protests.[107] However, it did not take long for users to discover and implement ways in which to gain access. Users who were more technologically savvy circumvented these restrictions by using dial-modems to access phone lines in other countries, allowing the information to be shared in a variety of ways, including sending faxes.[108] Various applications such as Speak2Tweet, which converts spoken phone messages into posts on Twitter, were also effectively employed by those involved.

For law enforcement purposes it would seem to be a dangerous assumption that the government can control social media. It is better to accept the premise that the public will find a way to spread information no matter what governments do to stop them. If those involved in criminal justice accept this as the re-

Ethics and Professionalism: Occupy Boston Twitter Account Subpoenaed

On December 10, 2011, Boston police swept through the Occupy Boston encampment, evicting and arresting demonstrators.[101] The Occupy Boston demonstration was one of the country's largest continuous demonstrations, lasting 10 weeks, and was inspired by New York City's Occupy Wall Street Movement that protested inequality, unemployment, corruption, and undue influence of large corporations, particularly in the financial sector.[102] The eviction came two days after a Boston judge lifted a temporary restraining order that had previously prevented police from evicting demonstrators. City officials, including the Mayor, said that the eviction was in the interest of public safety.[103]

Less than a week later, on December 14, 2011, the District Attorney's office of Suffolk County, Massachusetts, subpoenaed Twitter. Twitter was asked to provide subscriber information for accounts associated with a user named Guido Fawkes, including information linked to his Twitter user name, and hashtags (keywords used to categorize tweets) related to the Occupy Boston movement.[104] Twitter, in accordance with its policy, notified the user of the request despite the fact that the subpoena asked that they not do so "in order to protect the confidentiality and integrity of the ongoing criminal investigation. . . ."[105] In turn, the user, Guido Fawkes, posted a link to the subpoena, making it widely publicly available.

The issuance of the subpoena, as well as its brief contents, raises several concerns related to law enforcement's use of social media and how the two can and should interact. The subpoena stated that it was seeking information as part of an ongoing criminal investigation, yet some critics claimed it was in response to tweets criticizing and mocking law enforcement during the Occupy Boston protest. Further, in what Guido Fawkes described as his "official statement to the Boston DA in regards to their subpoena," he declared, "You cannot arrest an idea. You cannot subpoena a hashtag."[106] This notion seemingly puts law enforcement and social media users at odds. Are there situations in which law enforcement should or should not be monitoring social media? What factors should be considered before police respond to such messages? Does law enforcement have any obligation to alert a user, such as Guido Fawkes, of their interest in his account or activity either before or after issuing a subpoena?

ality of the situation, then they will not be blindsided in the manner that the Egyptian government was and they might instead think of creative ways to use social media. Because the information provided on these platforms is fresh, it can provide law enforcement officials with access to instant, real-time situational awareness.

There are a few basic characteristics of social media platforms that criminal justice officials must consider for the future. First, it should be noted that information travels in both directions; reports come from those who are on the scene and spread outward leading to various outcomes. Conversely, external information will flow back down to those who are directly involved with a situation and affect how they respond to it. Each informs the other. Law enforcement officials should also remember that these mechanisms can be used to gather information for situational awareness and disseminate it to reassure the public or provide critical information. Social media platforms have been in the past, and will continue to be used in the future, to ask for help during a crisis, as well as to respond to such requests.

Balancing the government's ability to enforce the law with the public's right to know is not an easy task. Recognizing the careful balance that must be reached, the Code of Federal Regulations (CFR) outlines provisions for the release of information by Department of Justice personnel related to criminal and civil proceedings. The CFR highlights the balance that must be reached in sharing versus protecting information. Further, it recognizes that while each case is unique, there must be some uniformity to how and when certain information is shared. These provisions are used by federal agencies to establish specific guidelines for the dissemination of information to the public. Inevitably, as technology continues to shape our world, it will simultaneously affect the criminal justice system, and these provisions will continue to evolve and reflect those changes.

Critical Thinking
Are there situations in which law enforcement should exercise control over social media systems?

Moving into the future, lawmakers will continue to attempt to strike a balance between liberty and security. The U.S. Department of Defense (DoD) issued a policy in 2010 that allows military personnel to access social networking sites from its non-classified computer network; however, it places limits on the information a user can share.[109] Though military personnel have expectations of privacy, like other social networking users, the policy points out that "because these interactions take place in a public venue, personnel acting in their official capacity shall maintain liaison with public affairs and operations security staff to ensure organizational awareness."[110] As such, military users must comply with public affairs, ethics, and other disclosure policies and procedures even when using social networking systems such as Twitter and Facebook. The policy is aimed at striking a balance between appropriate security measures and individual interests and, much like its civilian parallel, it presents an opportunity for the military justice system to address the issue of privacy and technology.

Global Partnerships
Advances in technology, especially in the information, communication, and transportation sectors, have truly made the world a global community. This has led to an unprecedented sharing of information and culture; people are able to see and speak with others on the other side of the planet by simply going online. Although this has enriched the lives of countless people by exposing them to new ideas and experiences, it has also been accompanied by problems, too. Criminal activity and organizations do not adhere to geographic or political bounds. In an increasingly connected world it is clear that concerted action is required; new partnerships must be established and cooperation encouraged in order to provide for a safe and secure future.

Global partnerships play a vital role in our criminal justice system.

I-24/7

An information sharing network designed to enable law enforcement officers in every member country to share sensitive police data.

I-Link

An operating system that has the ability to identify common aspects of ongoing investigations that are seemingly unrelated.

The Importance of Information Sharing

The international community is founded upon the notion that each country is autonomous within its own borders. There is no international police force that has jurisdiction in every country at any given time. Consequently, the only way to combat these expanding criminal threats is to build partnerships between law enforcement officials in different countries. By developing better systems and protocols to acquire and process data, develop and share intelligence, and implement appropriate responses, it will be possible for future law enforcement officials to apprehend wrongdoers and protect the innocent, while ensuring that the autonomy of individual states is upheld.

Sharing Law Enforcement Data

Because each country acts as an autonomous state, creating an international police force would be difficult, if not impossible, as it would require member states to sacrifice some of their autonomy. It was the realization of these facts that led to the creation of INTERPOL (International Criminal Police Organization).[111] INTERPOL is the primary agency facilitating international police cooperation, providing communications and database assistance for law-enforcement agencies of its member countries.[112] To facilitate this coordination, INTERPOL sends out color coded notices to member countries with information about arrest warrants, extradition, wanted criminals, missing persons, unidentified victims, and possible threats.[113] INTERPOL had nearly 25,000 active notices as of February 2009.[114]

Recently, INTERPOL implemented a series of powerful intelligence tools designed to help combat criminal activity by increased law enforcement officers' access to data. The first of these initiatives is known as I-24/7, which is an information sharing network designed to enable law enforcement officers in every member country to share sensitive police data.[115] Those officials who have been authorized to use the system have access to an array of INTERPOL databases, which include information on such issues as suspected criminals, fingerprints, DNA profiles, and stolen travel documents, administrative documents, motor vehicles, and art.[116] Another of these systems is known as I-link, an operating system that centralizes and enhances database features.[117] One of the most important features of this system is its ability to identify common aspects of ongoing investigations that are seemingly unrelated.[118]

While INTERPOL is the largest and most similar to traditional law enforcement and intelligence-building organizations, it is not the only institution whose aim is to share information that is relevant to law enforcement officials. The International Association of Chiefs of Police[119] is an organization aimed at improving the police profession across the globe by gathering and sharing best practices concerning administrative, technical, and operational facets of law enforcement. It also promotes cooperation and information sharing between officials all over the world.[120] A similar but independent organization is the International Police Association.[121] This group seeks to advance the principles described in the Universal Declaration of Human Rights by sharing professional experience to broaden their members' general knowledge and cultural awareness.[122]

The Vera Institute of Justice, a nonprofit national research and policy organization based in the United States, works with local, state, and national officials to plan, implement and evaluate various initiatives in the fields of law enforcement, courts, and social services.[123] The Open Society Justice Initiative, founded in 1984 by investor and philanthropist George Soros, is an organization established to help countries make the transition from communism.[124] The initiative seeks to protect human rights by solving international crimes, ending racial discrimination, supporting freedom of expression, and protecting natural resources, as some of its aims.[125]

Criminal justice professionals of the future must recognize that these types of entities and partnerships will only increase in importance. Because there is no world police force with jurisdiction to cross all political boundaries and apprehend perpetrators across international borders, these associations realize that the only way for justice to prevail is to build global partnerships. These partnerships connect those who are actually responsible for enforcing the law in their own countries and those at the international level who have access to intelligence that law enforcement officials need. By further developing these partnerships, it is possible to bring to justice criminals who cross international boundaries, while still respecting the autonomy of individual states. It is unlikely that countries will be willing to sacrifice enough of their autonomy to create a world police force; therefore, entities like INTERPOL will become more and more important to coordinate and inform law enforcement efforts across the planet.

Critical Thinking
What logistical or substantive issues might arise when countries share law enforcement data with one another?

Sharing Corrections Data   The corrections system has developed new international data-sharing initiatives and programs. These organizations address issues including the purposes of confinement, best practices for corrections professionals, technological advancements in the facilities, maintaining the health of the prison population, and reentry of offenders into society. These associations serve as clearinghouses of information that can be used to develop more effective correction systems.

The Global Detention Project[126] is a program whose aim is to chart both the growth and the effectiveness of various detention facilities. Researchers are creating a database that allows researchers and professionals to gain detailed information about facilities around the world, including security, facility type, command structure, spatial segregation, and size.[127] Looking into the future, this database will provide crucial data for professionals aiming to evaluate the

Bory Prison in Pilsen, Czech Republic, is one of the world's most recognizable correctional facilities.

current status of various corrections facilities and will enable them to design and build more effective institutions.

Several other interesting entities have emerged in the field of corrections to help coordinate and share corrections data for future use. Chief among them is the Asian and Pacific Conference of Correctional Administrators.[128] This group holds an annual conference and uses it to generate a report that documents myriad factors, including prison statistics, emerging concerns for corrections professionals, assessing the performance of corrections programs, increasing public awareness, and managing the health of inmates.[129] In Europe, the Health in Prisons Project seeks to evaluate prisons and develop reports on the condition of various facilities throughout the continent.[130]

The International Centre for Prison Studies is one of the leading initiatives established to review and develop policies for prisons, providing information concerning the appropriate uses of detention and working as a consultant for both government and non-governmental entities.[131] Two organizations that provide similar information are the International Community Corrections Association (ICCA)[132] and the International Corrections and Prisons Association.[133]

One of the most persistent challenges for criminal justice professionals—and one that will continue into the future—is how to handle former inmates once they have completed their sentence. A great deal of debate has been generated concerning the efficacy of these programs, and there seem to be no simple solutions. However, organizations like the Conférence Permanente Européenne de la Probation attempt to leverage multiple approaches to try and use the best of each. The Conférence Permanente Européenne de la Probation is intended to reintegrate offenders back into society through programs including probation, community service, mediation, and conciliation, as a means to improve the end of the correctional process.[134]

In this way, corrections data sharing initiatives provide valuable insight and guidance for lawmakers and the criminal justice system moving into the future. Criminal justice professionals are getting increasingly descriptive information about the characteristics of prisoners and prison facilities around the world. They have a better understanding of who inmates are and how they can be most effectively treated. Policy makers can evaluate and change current programs and facilities to make future corrections systems all the more effective.

Border Protection   As transportation systems lead to a more interconnected planet, the crossing of international borders presents a wide array of challenges. Such challenges include normative issues concerning profiling and protecting the rights of the individual. There are also political considerations, including how different countries should work with one another, what policies need to be adopted, and how much autonomy countries should sacrifice. Finally, there are practical issues regarding sufficient staffing levels, the level of training and information needed by officials, and the types of technologies in which countries should invest. All of these issues demonstrate that border protection will remain a dynamic area of concern for the criminal justice system.

The U.S. Border   In recent years, the question of what policy to pursue concerning the shared United States and Mexico border has been a hotly debated issue. Traditionally, concerns regarding illegal entry into the United States have been centered on issues of drug smuggling, human trafficking, and undocumented persons seeking work opportunities in the United States.

These issues have received heightened scrutiny due to the rise in violent crime and narcotics smuggling attributed to the increased power of drug cartels. These issues alone are cause for concern, but additionally, individuals with known ties to terrorism have been arrested or detained at the border in recent

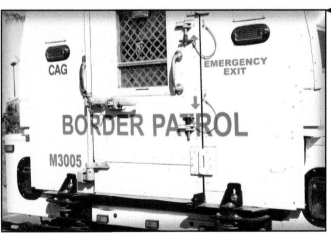

The patrol and protection of borders has a significant impact on the criminal justice system.

years, making the situation increasingly dire. This suggests that law enforcement must pursue new policies and technologies in order to prevent future acts of terrorism, in addition to combating traditional crime.

Many of those arrested do not come from Mexico, Central America, or South America, but instead originate from countries that have ties to terrorism, such as Yemen, Iran, Sudan, Somalia, and Afghanistan.[135] For instance, Ahmed Muhammad Dhakane was indicted for smuggling hundreds of people from Brazil to Mexico and then bringing them into the United States. Among those he brought across the border were Somalis from the terrorist group Al-Shabaab.[136] In another example, Anthony Joseph Tracey, an individual with admitted ties to Al-Shababb, was prosecuted for illegally bringing more than two hundred Somalis across the Mexican border after he fraudulently obtained Cuban travel documents.[137]

These incursions into the United States are not limited to crossings of the southwestern border. While there are certainly fewer people crossing from the north, it is important to remember that the northern border between the United States and Canada spans 4,000 miles, making it twice as long as the southern border between the United States and Mexico. Additionally, significantly more agents are deployed per mile over the southern border as opposed to the northern one (one agent for every two miles of the northern border as compared to eight agents deployed for every mile of the southwestern border).[138] In 1999, Ahmed Rassam, also known as the Millennium Bomber, attempted to gain entry into the United States to carry out an attack on Los Angeles International Airport. Rassam used a car ferry from Victoria, British Columbia, to Port Angeles, Washington and was actually to able clear U.S. immigration services and board the ferry.[139] When the ferry docked, Rassam was the last to exit the ship. A U.S. Customs inspector found his behavior suspicious and ordered a second search, finding the materials needed to detonate a major explosion.[140]

Future Challenges in Border Security As border concerns have become more prevalent, a variety of problems must be effectively addressed in order to secure international borders. While there are many reasons that border security is not as strong as it could be, a great number of these relate to how information is gathered, processed, and shared, both within a given country and the international community at large. One of the largest issues that needs to be addressed is how the laws of various jurisdictions impact the privacy interests of those who are not residents of their region. The laws that impact privacy interests in the United States are very different than those that impact European countries. These differences are rooted in fundamental concerns about how individual liberties should be protected and balanced against the government's need for information. Resolving these differences is a complicated task. Changing policies, laws, and even countries' constitutions presents a host of procedural difficulties. Beyond that, these approaches are often based on a particular nation's deep-rooted beliefs and mores. Therefore, careful consideration must be given when considering a change to these laws.

A recurring problem involved in the policy debate concerns the issuance of visas, or authorization of a foreign citizen's entry into a country. Many coun-

Visa
An official authorization permitting a foreign citizen entry into the United States for either a temporary stay or permanent residence.

tries use expedited procedures, and in certain cases, an entire waiver of visa requirements, with less strict requirements for entering the country. While this certainly makes for a more efficient bureaucracy, there are obvious concerns that this relaxed approach could have serious consequences.

Technical issues, too, pose problems for border security. In many countries there are simply no databases that officials can access to check the legitimacy of those who are seeking to travel across the border.[141] Furthermore, approximately 50% of countries use passports that contain no biometric information such as fingerprints, photographs, and signatures stored electronically inside the passport.[142] It is also somewhat surprising that 18 countries still use passports that cannot be read by machine.[143]

There are problems with the human aspect of border protection as well. A great deal of corruption exists in some passport issuance offices and immigration agencies. In addition, immigration officials may be undertrained, receiving minimal training about how to identify suspicious behavior and recognize fraudulent travel documentation.

Domestic Border Security Moving forward, the United States must continue to improve its information sharing capabilities, both within its own borders and internationally. Clearly, the need for inter-governmental coordination will only grow more important as the global community becomes more integrated. Therefore, it is unlikely that the United States will be able to combat criminal activity and terrorism if it attempts to act in isolation or only in concert with its traditional partners. Policies and relationships must be developed that permit relevant intelligence to be shared across political boundaries; this requires the development of mechanisms to process foreign intelligence and also share appropriate data with other governments.

Several advancements in domestic information sharing suggest the manner in which these capabilities will be advanced. The Terrorist Screening Center represents a new type of entity that will see increased use in the future to track and provide information to law enforcement. This center coordinates terrorist screening data.[144] It conducts numerous operations including a consolidated 24/7 call center for identification assistance, a mechanism to coordinate law enforcement response at the federal, state, and local level, a formal process for tracking encounters, and a system for ensuring feedback is supplied to the appropriate entities.[145]

Additionally, **Joint Terrorism Task Forces** now exist in 103 cities throughout the United States. These entities are comprised of representatives from various federal agencies, as well as state and local law enforcement, and serve as clearinghouses of information for a given region.[146] In this way information that is gathered on various individuals and activities can be shared between all those who are responsible for protecting a specific region.

Efforts to improve information sharing also proceed at the regional and local level. The National Capital Region's Strategic Plan is a document that describes the capabilities that Washington, D.C. and the surrounding areas of Maryland and Virginia intend to focus on establishing and sustaining over the a three to five year period.[147] The plan is built around four goals, one of which is

Joint Terrorism Task Forces
Entities that serve as a clearinghouse of terrorism-related information for a specified region. Task forces are comprised of federal, state, and local law enforcement representatives.

Barbed wire fences are one example of physical border protection.

Fusion center

An information sharing center that allows a state to assess threats and implement corrective action, while at the same time increasing state and local law enforcement agencies' awareness of terrorist-related activity within their borders.

improving information sharing within the region, indicating that this will be one of the principal focus areas for protecting the nation's capital.[148] Virginia itself has taken a lead in enhancing information sharing at the local level through the use of its **fusion center**. The Virginia Fusion Center's Virginia Terrorism Threat Assessment allows the state to assess relative threats within the state and then implement corrective action as appropriate.[149] This increases the state and local law enforcement agencies' awareness of terrorist-related activity within their borders.

In future years it is likely that the use of fusion centers will continue to increase in jurisdictions across the country. These entities are not only repositories for data, but rely on analysts to create intelligence products that can be exported and acted upon. In this way, their resources are likely to be leveraged to track and apprehend individuals who illegally cross borders into the United States. Another action that is likely to be pursued in the coming years is improved coordination and information sharing between U.S. agencies responsible for tracking watch-listed individuals.

International Border Security   Improving domestic information sharing is only part of the challenge facing officials responsible for border protection; improved coordination with foreign countries is essential as well, and will remain so for the foreseeable future. Numerous initiatives are already underway that attempt to bridge this gap. One of these programs is the International Criminal Investigative Training Assistance Program (ICITAP), which allocates funds to the Department of Justice to provide database systems to countries currently lacking them.[155] This allows countries to screen for potential terrorists and other individuals attempting to illegally cross borders. A similar program also intended to augment the identification and detection process is the State Department's Terrorist Interdiction Program. This program provides participating countries with hardware and software to develop, maintain, and act on information acquired during the screening process.[156]

Career Connections: Border Patrol Agent

The United States Customs and Border Protection (CBP), which operates within the Department of Homeland Security, is an agency whose responsibility is to prevent terrorists and weapons from entering the country by protecting borders and ports of entry.[150] Presently, CBP has almost 60,000 employees in the United States and abroad acting as border patrol agents, air and marine interdiction agents, agricultural specialists, and revenue collectors.[151] In recent years, as interest in protecting U.S. borders has increased, so too has the need for CBP employees, and specifically the need for border patrol agents.

In the United States, border patrol agents protect 4,000 miles of the northern border and 1,900 miles of the southern border. CBP looks for candidates to help detect, prevent, and apprehend people crossing those borders in violation of immigration laws. The agency lists requirements for interested candidates, including an age limit (under 40 unless you meet specific exceptions), a citizenship requirement, the ability to speak or learn Spanish, possession of a valid driver's license, and the ability to pass a background investigation, medical examination, fitness and drug tests.[152] Candidates hired by CBP must complete basic training at the U.S. Border Patrol Academy in New Mexico before they are sent on assignment. Basic training covers a variety of subject areas, including immigration laws, physical fitness, marksmanship, and language skills.

Once placed on assignment, border patrol agents have many duties, but one of their primary tasks is "line watch." "Line watch" involves detecting, preventing, and apprehending terrorists and undocumented aliens at the border through covert surveillance.[153] In addition, agents engage in farm and ranch checks, traffic observations, city patrol, transportation checks, and other intelligence and anti-smuggling activities.[154]

Customs and Border Protection (CBP)
The largest law enforcement agency within the U.S. Department of Homeland Security. Its primary mission is to detect, prevent, and apprehend terrorists and terrorist weapons from entering the country through land borders or ports of entry.

The State Department also runs the Anti-Terrorism Assistance Program (ATAP), which offers myriad training programs to combat terrorism in at-risk countries.[157] One of these trainings is aimed at assisting immigration officials in identifying fraudulent travel documentation recognition.[158] If more officials were able to identify these faulty documents, then more criminals could be prevented from illegally crossing international borders.

Many different approaches could be pursued to improve international collaboration. Moving forward, there are several areas that law enforcement professionals should consider. First, there should be universal reporting to INTERPOL of lost or stolen passports. This will reduce the likelihood that unauthorized persons will be able to cross into other countries on a stolen but otherwise valid passport. The second reform that should be vigorously pursued is providing assistance, both in terms of finances and training, to assist foreign governments in detecting corruption in issuing travel documentation. By placing additional emphasis on stolen passports and forged documents, border officials will remove the two primary sources of false identification that criminals use to cross international boundaries, thereby increasing the overall security of these boundaries.

Anti-Terrorism Assistance Program (ATAP)
A State Department program that offers myriad training programs to combat terrorism in at-risk countries.

Other considerations must be addressed as well. In general, there have already been and will continue to be more stringent and attentive visa and passport application evaluations. Despite some improvements, though, the system still has several weaknesses that must be addressed. One possible fix is to require more frequent renewal for passports. This would improve verification of the carrier's identity and reduce the use of stolen and forged documents by travelers. Furthermore, countries that currently do not issue machine-readable passports must be convinced to do so. Non-machine-readable passports impose too many risks and inefficiencies into the system and every effort must be made to end this practice. Within the United States it is crucial to develop a more comprehensive document fraud prevention curriculum to train federal, state, and local document issuers and reviewers on establishing document fraud prevention. These officials must also be instructed on risk management programs and intelligence methods used to identify fraudulent travel documents.

Major challenges loom regarding the protection of the physical borders of the United States. From 2000–2010, the U.S. Border Patrol's manpower and budget has more than tripled, but 85% of that manpower has been allocated to the southwestern border.[159] Given the constraints imposed by the recent global economic downturn, it is unlikely there will be sufficient funding to increase the number of agents at the northern border to a level that is commensurate with that of the southwestern, relative to its risk. Exploring technological solutions is the most promising approach to securing this border. In order to compensate for the disproportionate number of agents at the northern border compared to the southwest, further use of cameras and sensors along the northern border, as well as the use of patrol aircraft could deter terrorists from using the border as an entry point.[160]

Anti-Terrorism Measures   Since 2001, security for air travel has been at the forefront of debate. The efficacy of using various approaches, including TSA pat-downs, the backscatter imaging technology scan, and the active millimeter wave technology scan, to detect potential terrorists has repeatedly been called into question. Security must be improved by identifying and targeting suspects who display suspicious behavior, independent of race, ethnicity, or religion. Certain behaviors tend to indicate that an individual may have criminal intentions. This piece of information alone is hardly sufficient to reach such conclusions, but integrated with other pieces of intelligence it can enable those responsible for security to identify these perpetrators.

To augment this intelligence, many experts advocate the use of some aspects of the Israeli Model. One of the hallmarks of this approach is the use of screeners who look intently into the face of the subject as a series of probing personal questions are asked.[161] The interviewer looks for the miniscule signs and tics that indicate deception. This approach is coupled with meticulous searches of every item an individual is carrying, from socks to cosmetics to books and magazines.[162] There is heightened attention given to all passengers, and searches occur in both a random and targeted manner. In all cases the presence of security is much more obvious and all passengers undergo a higher level of scrutiny while traveling by air. This model, while invasive, has the potential to

Israeli Model
A method of interrogation in which the interrogator looks intently into the face of the subject and asks a series of probing personal questions.

increase security at airports across the planet. However, it would be difficult to adopt wholesale in the United States, where the sheer number of passengers, flights, and destinations dwarfs those in Israel.

Emerging technologies referred to as "mind readers" are also being developed. These novel systems flash symbols related to terrorism or other illicit activity, which generally only those involved in would recognize, throughout the airport. The machines then track any changes in heart rate and body temperature, and can even look for any suspicious movements.[163] The individual exhibiting these changes could then be pulled aside for further screening. New polygraph devices, like the Future Attribute Screening Technology, are also being developed for use.[164] These machines scan the human face for any signs of deception during questioning and would be primarily used for individuals targeted for additional screening.

These and other anti-terrorism measures remain a hotly controversial subject in modern-day society, and these debates will only grow stronger in the future. How can government achieve a balance between securing its borders from terrorists or other criminals, while at the same time upholding the basic rights and freedoms afforded to all citizens under the U.S. Constitution? With many new technological advancements changing the face of crime and criminal justice, the line between liberty and security is becoming increasingly blurred. Looking into the future, lawmakers and criminal justice professionals must make critically important decisions that will have dramatic effects on the criminal justice system and society as a whole.

Critical Thinking   Are there concerns related to an increased reliance on technology in fighting terrorism, specifically in terms of screening and interrogating individuals?

Chapter Summary

- Trends in the justice system provide evidence of issues that will be addressed in the criminal justice system of the future. Some of these trends include an increased focus on evidence-based models of intervention, a decrease in the use of the capital punishment both in the United States and internationally, and increased debate over the legalization or decriminalization of drugs.

- Finding the balance between civil liberties and effective law enforcement has taken new form in light of technological advances. Technology, such as GPS, allows law enforcement to monitor and gather evidence in innovative ways, but can present challenges with respect to privacy expectations and the Fourth Amendment. As such, the question of what constitutes a justifiable expectation of privacy in a world of GPS, biometrics, and imaging software takes on great importance.

- Social networking systems have had and will continue to have a profound effect on the criminal justice system. Users of social networks have the ability to share massive amounts of information with a nearly countless number of individuals, which presents questions about a user's expectations of privacy. Moreover, because of the ease with which information can be shared, there is an undeniable link between social networking collective action and social unrest. Some governments have considered controlling social networking for purposes of law enforcement, and the military has placed restrictions on social networking for protection of classified information.

- Because of advances in technology, especially related to information, communication, and transportation, criminal activity is no longer confined by geographic boundaries. Thus, there is an increased reliance on international information sharing between countries to combat criminal activity. In particular, partnerships and organizations that focus on sharing law enforcement and corrections data have flourished, including policing, policy, and corrections entities and associations.

- Border security is poised to remain a major topic facing the criminal justice system. It raises normative issues of profiling and individual rights, political considerations including how countries should interact with one another, and practical issues regarding personnel and training. The U.S.'s northern and southern borders each present unique challenges for security and combating terrorism. In order to combat these challenges, the United States has engaged in domestic and international initiatives focused on the border itself and those seeking to cross it.

Critical Thinking?

1. If there are evidence-based models of intervention that have been proven effective, why do we still engage in other forms of intervention?
2. Describe the controversies related to legalizing or decriminalizing drug use in the United States. Where do you stand on the issue?
3. What are some of the primary advances in technology that are used by law enforcement officers?
4. What are some concerns related to the potential misuse of new technologies by law enforcement?
5. What legitimate privacy interests can an individual assert if he or she is willing to share personal information through various social media platforms?
6. Discuss the link between social networking systems, collective action, and social unrest.
7. Does the ease with which information can be shared through social networking alter the public's perception or law enforcement's obligation to share information related to ongoing investigations, trials, etc.?
8. How do countries interact with one another in combating criminal activity?
9. What are the implications for United States' sovereignty over its criminal justice system when working with global partners?
10. How does the United States protect its physical borders? What are the challenges in protecting the southern and northern borders of the country?

Media

Library of Congress Digital Preservation: http://www.digitalpreservation.gov/

The Library of Congress hosts a Digital Preservation website that houses the National Digital Stewardship Alliance, Digital Preservation Outreach and Education and the National Digital Information Infrastructure Program. These initiatives aim to preserve digital communications and media.

U.S. Department of Defense Social Media: http://www.defense.gov/home/features/2009/0709_socialmedia/

The Department of Defense highlights its relationship with social media, including its social media policy. The site provides information about the way in which the military uses various social media and social networking systems.

U.S. Customs and Border Protection: http://www.cbp.gov/

The United States Customs and Border Protection website highlights the agency's mission, its organizational structure, history, statistics and job postings. It also provides contacts and resources for further research.

Travel.State.Gov: http://travel.state.gov/visa/

The Bureau of Consular Affairs of the U.S. Department of State provides information regarding visas for foreign citizens traveling to the United States. In addition, it provides information for Americans traveling abroad, including information about U.S. embassies and consulates.

Endnotes

1. Hengfeler, Scott W. and Sohoenwald, Sonja K., *Social Policy Report Evidence-Based Interventions for Juvenile Offenders and Juvenile Justice Policies that Support Them*, Society for Research in Child Development vol. 25, no. 1, page 4 (2011).

2. Redding, R. E. (June, 2010). Juvenile Justice Bulletin: Juvenile transfer laws: An effective deterrent to delinquency? Washington, DC: U.S. Department of Justice, Office of Justice Programs, Office of Juvenile Justice and Delinquency Prevention.

3. Finckenauer, James O. (1982). Scared Straight and the Panacea Phenomenon. Englewood Cliffs, New Jersey: PrenticeHall.; *See also* Buckner, J.C., and M. Chesney-Lind (1983). "Dramatic Cures for Juvenile Crime: An Evaluation of a Prison-Run Delinquency Prevention Program." Criminal Justice and Behavior 10:227–247; *See also* Lewis, R.V. (1983). "Scared Straight—California Style: Evaluation of the San Quentin Squire Program." Criminal Justice and Behavior 10:209–226.

4. Hengfeler, Scott W. and Sohoenwald, Sonja K., *Social Policy Report Evidence-Based Interventions for Juvenile Offenders and Juvenile Justice Policies that Support Them*, Society for Research in Child Development vol. 25, no. 1, page 5–6 (2011); *See also* Alexander, J. F., & Parsons, B. V. (1982). Functional family therapy: Principles and procedures. Carmel, CA: Brooks/Cole.

5. What Is Multisystemic Therapy?, Multisystemic Therapy Services (2010), available at: http://mstservices.com/; see also Hengfeler, Scott W. and Sohoenwald, Sonja K., *Social Policy Report Evidence-Based Interventions for Juvenile Offenders and Juvenile Justice Policies that Support Them*, Society for Research in Child Development vol. 25, no. 1, page 5–6 (2011).

6. Hengfeler, Scott W. and Sohoenwald, Sonja K., *Social Policy Report Evidence-Based Interventions for Juvenile Offenders and Juvenile Justice Policies that Support Them*, Society for Research in Child Development vol. 25, no. 1, page 5–6 (2011); *See also* Chamberlain, P. (2003). Treating chronic juvenile offenders: Advances made through the Oregon multidimensional treatment foster care model. Washington, DC: American Psychological Association.

7. Hengfeler, Scott W. and Sohoenwald, Sonja K., *Social Policy Report Evidence-Based Interventions for Juvenile Offenders and Juvenile Justice Policies that Support Them*, Society for Research in Child Development vol. 25, no. 1, page 6–7 (2011).

8. Pew Center on the States, State of Recidivism: *The Revolving Door of America's Prisons*, page 2 (Washington, DC: The Pew Charitable Trusts, April 2011).

9. Ibid.

10. Ibid.

11. Ibid.

12. Ibid.

13. MPRI 2010 Progress Report, available at: http://www.michigan.gov/documents/corrections/MPRI_2010_Progress_Report_343664_7.pdf. (Accessed Feb. 1, 2012)

14. Pew Center on the States, State of Recidivism: *The Revolving Door of America's Prisons*, page 17 (Washington, DC: The Pew Charitable Trusts, April 2011).

15. Bureau of Justice Statistics Special Report: "Truth in Sentencing in State Prisons"(Jan. 1999), available at http://bjs.ojp.usdoj.gov/content/pub/pdf/tssp.pdf (Accessed Feb. 1, 2012).

16. Pew Center on the States, State of Recidivism: *The Revolving Door of America's Prisons*, page 19 (Washington, DC: The Pew Charitable Trusts, April 2011).

17. California Correctional Peace Officers Association, CCPOA on Prison Reform, New Directions (Jan. 2010), available at: http://www.ccpoa.org/issues/ccpoa_on_prison_reform#infrastructure, accessed on Feb. 1, 2012.

18. Ibid.

19. *Furman v. Georgia*, 408 U.S. 238 (1972).

20. *Gregg v. Georgia, Proffitt v. Florida, Jurek v. Texas, Woodson v. North Carolina,* and *Roberts v. Louisiana*, 428 U.S. 153 (1976).

21. Ibid.

22. Ibid.

23. Ibid.

24. Facts About the Death Penalty, Death Penalty Information Center, December 13, 2011 *available at* http://www.deathpenaltyinfo.org/documents/FactSheet.pdf.

25. Death Penalty Trends, Amnesty International (2011) *available at* http://www.amnestyusa.org/our-work/issues/death-penalty/us-death-penalty-facts/death-penalty-trends.

26. Facts About the Death Penalty, Death Penalty Information Center, December 13, 2011 *available at* http://www.deathpenaltyinfo.org/documents/FactSheet.pdf.

27. Frank Newport, "In U.S., 64% Support Death Penalty in Cases of Murder," November 8, 2010, *available at* http://www.gallup.com/poll/144284/support-death-penalty-cases-murder.aspx.

28. Ibid.

29. Death Penalty Trends, Amnesty International (2011) *available at* http://www.amnestyusa.org/our-work/issues/death-penalty/us-death-penalty-facts/death-penalty-trends.

30. Emma Marris, Death-Row Drug Dilemma, Lack of anaesthetic used in lethal injection exposes ethics gaps in the supply chain, Scientific American, January 27, 2011 *available at* http://www.scientificamerican.com/article.cfm?id=death-row-drug-dilemma.

31. Michael L. Radelet and Marian J. Borg, The Changing Nature of Death Penalty Debates, Annual Review of Sociology 49–50 (2000).

32. Ibid.

33. Joseph Carroll, "Who Supports the Death Penalty?" The Gallup Organization (2004) *available at* http://www.deathpenaltyinfo.org/gallup-poll-who-supports-death-penalty.

34. The Universal Declaration of Human Rights, Article 3 and Article 5, United Nations *available at* http://www.un.org/en/documents/udhr/.

35. Death Penalty Trends, Amnesty International (2011) *available at* http://www.amnestyusa.org/our-work/issues/death-penalty/us-death-penalty-facts/death-penalty-trends.

36. Second Optional Protocol to the International Covenant on Civil and Political Rights, aiming at the abolition of the death penalty, United Nations *available at* http://treaties.un.org/Pages/ViewDetails.aspx?src=TREATY&mtdsg_no=IV-12&chapter=4&lang=en.

37. Ibid.

38. Death Sentences and Executions 2010, Amnesty International 6(2010) *available at* http://www.amnesty.org/en/library/asset/ACT50/001/2011/en/ea1b6b25-a62a-4074-927d-ba51e88df2e9/act500012011en.pdf.

39. Ibid.

40. Death Penalty Trends, Amnesty International (2011) *available at* http://www.amnestyusa.org/our-work/issues/death-penalty/us-death-penalty-facts/death-penalty-trends.

41. Death Sentences and Executions 2010, Amnesty International 6(2010) *available at* http://www.amnesty.org/en/library/asset/ACT50/001/2011/en/ea1b6b25-a62a-4074-927d-ba51e88df2e9/act500012011en.pdf.

42. Ibid.

43. EU Memorandum on the Death Penalty, European Union *available at* http://www.eurunion.org/legislat/deathpenalty/eumemorandum.htm.

44. Death Sentences and Executions 2010, Amnesty International 3(2010) *available at* http://www.amnesty.org/en/library/asset/ACT50/001/2011/en/ea1b6b25-a62a-4074-927d-ba51e88df2e9/act500012011en.pdf.

45. Speaking Out Against Drug Legalization, Drug Enforcement Agency 39–45 (2010).

46. Jeffrey A. Miron, The Budgetary Implications of Drug Prohibition 2 (2010).

47. Ibid.

48. Ibid.

49. William Booth, Latin leaders fault U.S. drug users, Washington Post (December 19, 2011) *available at* http://www.washingtonpost.com/world/latin-american-leaders-assail-us-drug-market/2011/12/16/gIQAjyy63O_story.html.

50. Speaking Out Against Drug Legalization, Drug Enforcement Agency 57 (2010).

51. Ray Sanchez, California's Proposition 19 Rejected by Voters, November 3, 2010 *available at* http://abcnews.go.com/Politics/proposition-19-results-california-votes-reject-marijuana-measure/story?id=12037727#.TvC_uNTOy5I.

52. Ibid.

53. Frank Newport, "Record-High 50% of Americans Favor Legalizing Marijuana Use" Gallup (2011) *available at* http://www.gallup.com/poll/150149/record-high-americans-favor-legalizing-marijuana.aspx .

54. Don Thompson, "California Marijuana Supporters Get Approval For Ballot Petitions" Huff Post San Francisco (2011) *available at* http://www.huffingtonpost.com/2011/07/25/california-marijuana-supporters-ballot-petitions_n_909226.html.

55. Rachel La Corte, "WA Pot Legalization Signatures Submitted to State," Seattle PI (2011) *available at* http://www.seattlepi.com/news/article/WA-pot-legalization-signatures-submitted-to-state-2431453.php.

56. Deborah Morgan, "Missouri voters may vote on legal marijuana industry in November 2012" Examiner.com (January 16, 2012) *available at* http://www.examiner.com/political-buzz-in-kansas-city/missouri-voters-may-vote-on-legal-marijuana-industry-november-2012.

57. Ethan Nadelmann, Reefer Madness, New York Times (November 6, 2011) *available at* http://www.nytimes.com/2011/11/07/opinion/reefer-madness.html.

58. Ibid.

59. Ibid.

60. Zusha Elinson, Medical Marijuana Dispensary in Oakland Is Focus of Federal Government, New York Times (October 29, 2011) *available at* http://www.nytimes.com/2011/10/30/us/richard-lees-medical-marijuana-dispensary-in-oakland-is-shut-down-and-quickly-reopens.html.

61. Ibid.

62. Ibid.

63. Feds Order California Pot Dispensaries to Shut Down, (Oct. 6, 2011), http://sanfrancisco.cbslocal.com/2011/10/06/feds-order-california-pot-dispensaries-to-shut-down/.

64. Marc Lacey, Legal Marijuana in Arizona, but Not for the Sellers, New York Times (July 22, 2011) *available at* http://www.nytimes.com/2011/07/23/us/23pot.html?pagewanted=all.

65. Michael Specter, Portugal decriminalized drugs a decade ago. What have we learned?, The New Yorker (October 17, 2011); Speaking Out Against Drug Legalization, Drug Enforcement Agency 57 (2010).

66. Ibid.

67. CRS Report, Law Enforcement Use of Global Positioning (GPS) Devices to Monitor Motor Vehicles: Fourth Amendment Considerations (February 28, 2011), page 2, available at: http://assets.opencrs.com/rpts/R41663_20110228.pdf

68. CRS Report, Law Enforcement Use of Global Positioning (GPS) Devices to Monitor Motor Vehicles: Fourth Amendment Considerations (February 28, 2011), page 2, available at: http://assets.opencrs.com/rpts/R41663_20110228.pdf, citing Ben Hubbard, *Police Turn to Secret Weapon: GPS Device*, Wash. Post, A1 (August 13, 2008), *available at* http://www.washingtonpost.com/wpdyn/content/article/2008/08/12/AR2008081203275.html?nav=rss_metro/va; *see also* Ramya Shah, *From Beepers to GPS: Can the Fourth Amendment Keep Up with Electronic Tracking Technology?*, 2009 U. Ill. J.L. Tech. & Pol'y 281, 281 (Spring 2009)

69. CRS Report, Law Enforcement Use of Global Positioning (GPS) Devices to Monitor Motor Vehicles: Fourth Amendment Considerations (February 28, 2011), page 2, available at: http://assets.opencrs.com/rpts/R41663_20110228.pdf, citing *United States v. Garcia*, 474 F.3d 994, 995 (7th Cir. 2007).

70. CRS Report, Law Enforcement Use of Global Positioning (GPS) Devices to Monitor Motor Vehicles: Fourth Amendment Considerations (February 28, 2011), page 2, available at: http://assets.opencrs.com/rpts/R41663_20110228.pdf, citing *People v. Weaver*, 909 N.E.2d 1195, 1195-96 (N.Y. 2009).

71. Phone 'Rootkit' Maker Carrier IQ May Have Violated Wiretap Law in Millions of Cases, November 30, 2011, available at http://www.forbes.com/sites/andygreenberg/2011/11/30/phone-rootkit-carrier-iq-may-have-violated-wiretap-law-in-millions-of-cases/.

72. Ibid.

73. Ibid

74. *Katz v. United States*, 389 U.S. 347 (1967).

75. Ibid.

76. Ibid.

77. *Katz v. United States*, 389 U.S. 347, 352 (1967).

78. CRS Report, Law Enforcement Use of Global Positioning (GPS) Devices to Monitor Motor Vehicles: Fourth Amendment Considerations (February 28, 2011), page 7, available at: http://assets.opencrs.com/rpts/R41663_20110228.pdf, citing *United States v. Maynard*, 615 F.3d 544, 564 (D.C. Cir. 2010)(listing several states and the relevant legislation in each). See, e.g., Utah Code Ann. §§ 77-23a-4, 77-23a-7, 77-23a 15.5; Minn. Stat. §§ 626A.37, 626A.35; Fla. Stat. §§ 934.06, 934.42; S.C.Code Ann. § 17-30-140; Okla. Stat., tit. 13, §§ 176.6, 177.6; Haw. Rev. Stat. §§ 803-42, 803-44.7;18 Pa. Cons.Stat. § 5761.

79. CRS Report, Law Enforcement Use of Global Positioning (GPS) Devices to Monitor Motor Vehicles: Fourth Amendment Considerations (February 28, 2011), page 7, available at: http://assets.opencrs.com/rpts/R41663_20110228.pdf, citing *See Osburn v. State*, 44 P.3d 523 (Nev. 2002); *Folt v. Commonwealth*, 698 S.E.2d 281 (Va. Ct. App. 2010), *reh'g en banc granted and mandate stayed by* 699 S.E. 2d 522 (Va. Ct. App. 2010).

80. *United States v. Jones*, No. 10-1259 (S. Ct. Jan. 23, 2012).

81. Ibid.

82. Ibid.

83. Ibid.

84. CRS Report, Privacy: An Overview of the Electronic Communications Privacy Act (March 30, 2011), page 23, available at: http://assets.opencrs.com/rpts/R41733_20110330.pdf, citing 18 U.S.C. 2516–2518, 18 U.S.C. 2511(2)(c), and 18 U.S.C. 2511(2)(i).

85. CRS Report, Privacy: An Overview of the Electronic Communications Privacy Act (March 30, 2011), page 23–24, available at: http://assets.opencrs.com/rpts/R41733_20110330.pdf.

86. Mike Sachof, Nearly Three-Quarters Of Internet Users Visit Social Networks, WebProNews, March 29, 2010 *available at* http://www.webpronews.com/nearly-three-quarters-of-internet-users-visit-social-networks-2010-03.

87. What Americans Do Online: Social Media And Games Dominate Activity, NielsenWire, August 2, 2010 a*vailable at* http://blog.nielsen.com/nielsenwire/online_mobile/what-americans-do-online-social-media-and-games-dominate-activity/.

88. Twitter's Biz Stone On Starting A Revolution, NPR (February 16, 2011) *available at* http://www.npr.org/2011/02/16/133775340/twitters-biz-stone-on-starting-a-revolution.

89. Smartphones have conquered PCs, CNNMoney, February 9, 2011 *available at* http://money.cnn.com/2011/02/09/technology/smartphones_eclipse_pcs/index.htm.

90. Ibid.

91. Erick Schonfeld, Mobile Data Traffic Expected To Rise 40-Fold Over Next Five Years, Tech Crunch, March 30, 2011 *available at* http://techcrunch.com/2010/03/30/mobile-data-traffic-rise-40-fold/.

92. Facebook Settles FTC Charges That It Deceived Consumers By Failing To Keep Privacy Promises, (November 29, 2011) Federal Trade Commission, Available at: http://ftc.gov/opa/2011/11/privacysettlement.shtm.

93. Ibid.

94. Library of Congress to Receive Entire Twitter Archive, Federal News Radio (December 6, 2011), available at: http://www.federalnewsradio.com/?nid=247&sid=2658996.

95. How the London Riots Showed Us Two Sides of Social Networking (August 10, 2011), available at: http://arstechnica.com/tech-policy/news/2011/08/the-two-sides-of-social-networking-on-display-in-the-london-riots.ars.

96. Ibid.

97. Arab Spring: An Interactive Timeline of Middle East Protests, The Guardian (November 29, 2011), available at: http://www.guardian.co.uk/world/interactive/2011/mar/22/middle-east-protest-interactive-timeline

98. Digital Media and the Arab Spring, The Great Debate (February 16, 2011), available at http://blogs.reuters.com/great-debate/2011/02/16/digital-media-and-the-arab-spring/.

99. Fatma Naib, Online activism fuels Egypt protest, January 28, 2011, *available at* http://www.aljazeera.com/news/middleeast/2011/01/2011128102253848730.html.

100. Erick Schonfeld, The Egyptian Behind #Jan25: "Twitter Is A Very Important Tool For Protesters", TechCrunch, February 16, 2011 *available at* http://techcrunch.com/2011/02/16/jan25-twitter-egypt/.

101. Bidgood, Jess, Police Evict Protestors From Occupy Boston Site, New York Times (December 10, 2011), available at: http://www.nytimes.com/2011/12/11/us/police-evict-protesters-from-occupy-boston-site.html

102. OccupyWallStreet.Org, About, available at: http://occupywallst.org/about/.

103. Bidgood, Jess, Police Evict Protestors From Occupy Boston Site, New York Times (December 10, 2011), available at: http://www.nytimes.com/2011/12/11/us/police-evict-protesters-from-occupy-boston-site.html

104. Sheets, Connor Adams, Twitter Subpoena Reveals Law Enforcement Monitoring OWS Via Social Media, International Business Times (December 27, 2011) available at: http://www.ibtimes.com/articles/273273/20111227/twitter-subpoena-reveals-law-enforcement-monitoring-ows.htm

105. Ibid

106. Ibid

107. Christopher Rhoads and Geoffrey A. Fowler, Egypt Shuts Down Internet, Cellphone Services, The Wall Street Journal, January 29, 2011 *available at* http://online.wsj.com/article/SB10001424052748703956604576110453371369740.html.

108. Ibid.

109. Memorandum for See Distribution: Directive-Type Memorandum (DTM) 09-026 – Responsible and Effective Use of Internet-based Capabilities (February 25, 2010), available at: http://www.defense.gov/NEWS/DTM%2009-026.pdf

110. Ibid.

111. INTERPOL, Homepage *available at* www.interpol.int.

112. INTERPOL, Overview *available at* http://www.interpol.int/About-INTERPOL/Overview.

113. INTERPOL, Notices *available at* http://www.interpol.int/INTERPOL-expertise/Notices.

114. Audit Report 09-35, Office of the Inspector General, Audit Division, The United States National Central bureau of INTERPOL, U.S. Departmnet of Justice (September 2009) *available at* http://www.justice.gov/oig/reports/plus/a0935/final.pdf.

115. INTERPOL, Data Exchange *available at* http://www.interpol.int/INTERPOL-expertise/Data-exchange/I-24-7.

116. Ibid.

117. Ibid.

118. Ibid.

119. International Association of Chiefs of Police, Homepage *available at* www.theiacp.org/.

120. Administration of Justice, World Criminal Justice LibraryElectronic Library *available at* http://andromeda.rutgers.edu/~wcjlen/WCJ/links/international.html.

121. International Police Association, homepage, *available at* www.ipa-iac.org/.

122. Administration of Justice, World Criminal Justice LibraryElectronic Library *available at* http://andromeda.rutgers.edu/~wcjlen/WCJ/links/international.html.

123. Vera Institute of Justice, Services and Programs *available at* http://www.vera.org/programs/centers.

124. Open Society Justice Initiative, Open Society Foundations *available at* http://www.soros.org/initiatives/justice/about

125. Ibid.

126. Global Detention Project, About *available at* www.globaldetentionproject.org/.

127. Ibid.

128. Asian and Pacific Conference of Correctional Administrators, About *available at* http://www.apcca.org/introduction.html.

129. Asian and Pacific Conference of Correctional Administrators 2010 Report, Agenda Topics 2, 4, and 7 (2010) *available at* http://www.apcca.org/pubs/30th/APCCA_30_Report.pdf.

130. Prisons and Health, Regional Office for Europe, World Health Organization *available at* www.euro.who.int/prisons.

131. International Centre for Prison Studies *available at* www.kcl.ac.uk/schools/law/research/icps.

132. International Community Corrections Association a*vailable at* www.iccaweb.org/.

133. International Corrections and Prisons Association *available at* www.icpa.ca.

134. The European Organisation for Probation *available at* www.cep-probation.org

135. Jana Winter, Feds Issue Terror Watch for the Texas/Mexico Border, Fox News (May 26, 2010), http://www.foxnews.com/us/2010/05/26/terror-alert-mexican-border/.

136. Ibid.

137. Jana Winter, Feds Issue Terror Watch for the Texas/Mexico Border, Fox News (May 26, 2010), http://www.foxnews.com/us/2010/05/26/terror-alert-mexican-border/; Alex Sundby, Feds Worried About 300 Missing Somalis, CBS News (April 13, 2011) *available at* http://www.cbsnews.com/8300-503543_162-503543.html?keyword=Anthony+Joseph+Tracy.

138. Jana Winter, Feds Issue Terror Watch for the Texas/Mexico Border, Fox News (May 26, 2010), http://www.foxnews.com/us/2010/05/26/terror-alert-mexican-border/.

139. *United States v. Ressam*, 553 U.S. 272, 273 (2008).

140. Ibid.

141. U.S. Gov't Accountability Office, GAO-11-637, Combating Terrorism: Additional Steps Needed to Enhance Foreign Partners' Capacity to Prevent Terrorist Travel 6 (2011).

142. U.S. Gov't Accountability Office, GAO-11-637, Combating Terrorism: Additional Steps Needed to Enhance Foreign Partners' Capacity to Prevent Terrorist Travel 8 (2011).

143. Ibid.

144. National Strategy to Combat Terrorist Travel, National Counterterrorism Center 11 (May 2, 2006), http://www.nctc.gov/docs/u_terrorist_travel_book_may2_2006.pdf.

145. Ibid.

146. Ten Years After 9/11: Preventing Terrorist Travel: Hearing Before the S. Comm. on Homeland Sec. & Governmental Affairs, 112th Cong. 1 (2011) (statement of Sen. Susan M. Collins).

147. National Capital Region, Homeland Security Strategic Plan, 3, 6 (2010), *available at* http://www.mwcog.org/uploads/pub-documents/pF5fXFg20101001065843.pdf.

148. Ibid.

149. Commonwealth of Va. Dep't of State Police Virginia Fusion Center, 2009 Virginia Terrorism Threat Assessment, (Mar. 2009).

150. U.S. Customs and Border Protection, We Are CBP! (2010) available at: http://www.cbp.gov/xp/cgov/careers/customs_careers/we_are_cbp.xml

151. Ibid.

152. U.S. Customs and Border Protection, Your Career as a Border Patrol Agent (2010) available at: http://www.cbp.gov/xp/cgov/careers/customs_careers/border_careers/bp_agent/

153. U.S. Customs and Border Protection, FAQs—Working for Border Patrol (2010) available at: http://www.cbp.gov/xp/cgov/careers/customs_careers/border_careers/bp_agent/faqs_working_for_the_usbp.xml

154. Ibid.

155. United States Department of Justice, International Criminal Investigative Training Assistance Program, "Forensic Services" (2011) *available at* http://www.justice.gov/criminal/icitap/programs/forensics.html.

156. United States Government Accountability Office, "Combating Terrorism: Additional Steps Needed to Enhance Foreign Partners' Capacity to Prevent Terrorist Travel 10 (2011) *available at* http://www.gao.gov/new.items/d11637.pdf.

157. Office of Antiterrorism Assistance, Fiscal Year 2010 Year in Review 3 (2010) *available at* http://www.state.gov/documents/organization/177500.pdf.

158. Ibid.

159. Chad C. Haddal, Border Security: The Role of the U.S. Border Patrol, Summary and 11 (2010) *available at* http://books.google.com/books?id=9OQ2Z2sOXOsC&printsec=frontcover&source=gbs_ge_summary_r&cad=0#v=onepage&q&f=false.

160. Chad C. Haddal, Border Security: The Role of the U.S. Border Patrol, 7–8 (2010) *available at* http://books.google.com/books?id=9OQ2Z2sOXOsC&printsec=frontcover&source=gbs_ge_summary_r&cad=0#v=onepage&q&f=false.

161. Michael Tarm, Mind-Reading Systems Could Change Air Security, Huffington Post, January 8, 2010 *available at* http://www.huffingtonpost.com/2010/01/08/wecu-mindreading-systems-_n_416123.html.

162. Ibid.

163. Ibid.

164. Ibid.

Glossary

Absconder One who leaves without authorization. This term is usually used in reference to walk-offs from work crews, work release centers, halfway houses, and other inmate areas not inside the main secure facility.

Actus reus The act that is committed in a crime.

Adjudication hearing A hearing in which the juvenile offender is found to either be delinquent or not delinquent.

Administrative law The area of law that controls, creates, and/or governs the administrative and regulatory agencies of the government.

Aftercare The process of providing continued treatment and recovery support following the conclusion of intensive or residential treatment programming.

Age of criminal responsibility The general age at which a juvenile can be found criminally responsible; varies from state to state.

Age of majority The age at which a person reaches adulthood in the eyes of the law. This age is generally 18, but can vary from state to state.

Aggravating circumstances Circumstances that go above and beyond the basic requirements for a crime to be considered serious; the facts or situations that increase the seriousness of a criminal act.

Aggressive patrol Patrolling the community by making frequent and numerous traffic stops and field interrogations of suspicious persons.

Alibi A defense to a criminal charge stating that the accused was somewhere other than at the scene of the alleged crime.

Alter ego rule A criminal defense where one person defends another person who cannot defend themselves.

Amenability hearing A hearing to determine how well a juvenile offender will respond to treatment within the juvenile system or if the juvenile is better suited to be in the adult system.

Anti-Terrorism Assistance Program (ATAP) A State Department program that offers myriad training programs to combat terrorism in at-risk countries.

Appellate brief A written memorandum filed by the prosecution or defense attorney to explain why the decision of a lower court was erroneous.

Approach the witness An action that occurs when an attorney moves closer to a witness, who is currently on the witness stand, in order to question the witness further or show him or her an exhibit or document. In most jurisdictions, the attorney must request permission from the judge to approach the witness.

Atavistic man An identification of individuals participating in criminal activity as throwbacks from a primitive time.

Attorney-client privilege The privilege that any information shared between a defense attorney and his or her client is kept confidential and does not need to be shared with other members of the court or the public.

Auburn System A prison system, also known as the New York System, in which silence is enforced at all times. Inmates work during the day and spend nights in solitary confinement.

Bail A sum of money that the court receives if a defendant flees from court proceedings.

Bailiff A law enforcement officer, such as a sheriff's deputy, assigned to a particular courtroom to assist the judge and courtroom staff and keep the peace.

Barriers to reintegration Conditions within the community or society that impede the ability of someone released from prison to reestablish citizenship, employment, and housing.

Bias-based profiling Selection of individuals based solely on a common trait of a group such as race, ethnicity, gender, sexual orientation, or economic status.

Bifurcated trial A criminal trial that has two separate phases: the first phase determines the defendant's guilt or innocence, and the second phase determines the defendant's potential punishment.

Biological theories Theoretical propositions that look to the body to identify individuals who are predisposed to criminal offending.

Biometrics A method of authenticating a person's identity through behavioral or physiological characteristics such as iris scanners and fingerprinting.

Black codes Laws created after the end of slavery designed to regulate the activities of African American citizens.

Black hat hacker An unethical computer hacker who hacks with malicious intent to commit a crime.

Blue code of silence The unwritten code of protection among police officers.

Boot camp An alternative to juvenile correctional facilities that follows the model of a military basic-training program and is focused on disciplining juvenile offenders.

Bridewells   Jails and police stations in England and Ireland in the 16th century that typically housed petty criminals.

Broken windows theory   A theory involving crime and disorder that states that if a community is allowed to physically deteriorate, an impression will be given that no one cares, causing crime to occur.

Business continuity plan   A plan that helps a business continue its essential functions in order to operate during and after a disaster or other disruptive event.

Case law   The entire collection of published legal documents and decisions of the courts; comprises a large portion of the legal rules that apply to modern society.

Case-in-chief   The portion of a criminal case presented by the prosecution.

Causation   A definitive link between the offender's criminal act and the victim's suffering.

Challenge for cause   A specific legal reason to exclude a potential juror.

Chicago School   A specialized body of work in urban sociology that made use of the city of Chicago to study alcoholism, homelessness, suicide, psychoses, and poverty.

Child Savers movement   A movement by a group of reformers in the early 19th century that sought to change the way juveniles were treated by the justice system.

Civil law   A body of laws that regulate non-criminal disputes, derived from Roman law. In civil law, laws are written and codified.

Civil lawsuit   A case in which a plaintiff sues the defendant to recover money damages for negligence or harm.

Classical school   A philosophy of crime that placed the responsibility for behavior on the offender.

Classification officer   The officer assigned to determine individual inmate needs and assign them to appropriate custody levels, institutions, and programs.

Closing argument   The final legal argument of a case presented separately by the prosecution and the defense before the case is given to the jury for deliberation.

Common law   Law that is based on customs and legal precedents developed in Britain over hundreds of years.

Community corrections   A halfway house, rehab facility, or home detention that helps an individual move from a correctional facility to complete freedom.

Community policing   A method of policing that emphasizes community participation in police decision-making and police officer participation in community activities.

Community service Unpaid labor or service to the community as an intermediate sanction ordered by the court.

Compassion fatigue Emotional exhaustion as a result of treating traumatized victims.

Compensation A financial reward for a wrong incurred at the hands of an offender.

Complaint A document listing the criminal charges brought against a defendant.

COMPSTAT A managerial system that uses criminal intelligence to identify crime problems and determine a crime reduction strategy.

Compurgation A method of handling offenses during the pre-classical time period, in which individuals who could find a reputable person in their community to speak on their behalf would be found innocent.

Concurrence The combination of actus reus (the commission of the crime) and mens rea (the intent to commit the crime).

Conditional release The release of a defendant under specific conditions such as an order to enter a treatment program.

Conflict model The idea that when a group comes together to form a society there will be differences within the group—i.e., age, race, and socioeconomic differences—that will make it difficult to come to an agreement about what is criminal. The group in power will set the standards.

Conflict theory A theory concerned with how power is maintained in a society rather than how individuals function within that continuum. Conflict theory holds that those with the most wealth in society are more likely to create the laws, maintain control, and have power over the lower classes.

Consensus model The idea that when a group comes together to form a society, they will have mutually shared values and norms and will come to a consensus about what is a crime.

Constable A local law enforcement officer who was responsible for collecting taxes and enforcing ordinances in the colonial and post-colonial United States, similar to a sheriff; today, constables are typically law enforcement officers in small towns.

Constitutional law A judicial interpretation of the U.S. Constitution for court cases.

Corpus delicti The body of evidence; proof that a crime has been committed.

Correctional institution A jail or a prison where offenders are confined.

Correctional officer An officer, also called a prison guard, jail guard, or corrections officer, who oversees and supervises all inmate activity.

Corruption   Abuse of police authority for personal gain.

Costs of victimization   The costs incurred by a victim as a result of victimization. These include financial, emotional, psychological, and social costs.

Cottage reformatories   Reformatories that taught juveniles farm skills; designed to house 20 to 40 offenders in a cottage with cottage parents.

Counsel   A title for an attorney presenting a case in court.

Court of last resort   The highest court of appeal in a state court system: typically, a state supreme court.

Court record   The official written record of everything that occurs in a court case.

Court reporter   A person who uses a shorthand typewriter to record everything that occurs or is said during a court hearing.

Court-appointed attorney   An attorney typically selected from a list of all criminal attorneys in private practice near the jurisdiction who are willing to accept appointed cases.

Courtroom workgroup   The judge, courtroom staff, prosecutor, and defense attorney.

Crime   A legally prohibited action that injures the public welfare or morals or the interests of the state.

Crime analysis   A systematic collection and analysis of crime data used to support police efforts in crime and disorder reduction and crime prevention.

Crime control model   A model of the criminal justice system that focuses on controlling crime and protecting the public in the most efficient way.

Crime index   An index reported by the Uniform Crime Reports. Crimes are divided into Part I and Part II index offenses. The Part I index includes a total of eight offenses divided by violent crime index and the property crime index. The Part II index includes a total of 21 categories of crimes.

Crime mapping   A process of using geographic information systems to conduct spatial analysis and investigation of crime.

Criminal behavior   Behavior defined by legislation, statutes, and codes.

Criminal investigation   A lawful investigation to reconstruct the circumstances of an illegal act, determine or apprehend the guilty party, and assist with the state's prosecution.

Criminal justice system   The police, courts, and correctional departments.

Criminal law   A set of rules and statutes that defines conduct prohibited by the government and establishes punishment for committing prohibited acts.

Criminogenic needs   The characteristics of an offender that can be changed through treatment and intervention that are directly related to continued involvement in criminal activity, including drug abuse, interpersonal skills, cognitive functioning, and vocational/employment skills.

Cross-examination The act of challenging a witness's testimony by asking more questions. Cross-examination is conducted by the other side of the case; the prosecution will cross-examine a defense witness, and the defense will cross-examine a witness for the state.

Custodial interrogation The questioning of a witness by law enforcement while he or she is under arrest.

Customs and Border Protection (CBP) The largest law enforcement agency within the U.S. Department of Homeland Security. Its primary mission is to detect, prevent, and apprehend terrorists and terrorist weapons from entering the country through land borders or ports of entry.

Cybercrime Crime committed utilizing a computer and the Internet.

Cyberterrorism An unlawful method of attacking and threatening government computer systems and networks, and the information stored on these systems, to further political or social objectives.

Damages Monetary compensation awarded by the court when someone has wronged another person or their property.

Dark figure of crime Offenses that go unreported to the police.

Day fine A fine based on a person's daily income; the amount of the fine is progressive in relation to the money the offender earns.

Day reporting center A location for offenders to receive services such as counseling, life skills education, drug abuse treatment, and substance abuse testing. The offender only reports according to a specified schedule and does not live there.

Decriminalize To legalize something that used to be a crime.

Deep cover Undercover police operations for a lengthy period of time.

Defendant A person charged with a crime.

Defense attorney The attorney who represents the defendant in a criminal case.

Deferred adjudication A type of probation in which the court's decision of the case disposition is delayed while the defendant completes certain requirements of probation.

Degradation ceremony The tactic of presenting someone in a negative light so that others may look unfavorably upon that individual. A prosecutor may do this to a defendant, or a defense attorney may do this to a witness for the prosecution.

Deinstitutionalization The process of removing status offenders from the juvenile court system and removing juvenile offenders from adult detention centers.

Department of Homeland Security (DHS) An agency created by the Homeland Security Act of 2002 whose mission is to protect the homeland by preventing and reducing the country's vulnerability to terrorist attacks, as well as minimizing damage, assisting in recovery, and acting as a focal point for crises and emergency planning.

Department of Justice (DOJ) A department within the executive branch of the federal government designed to enforce the laws of the United States.

Deprivation Described in Sykes's "pains of imprisonment" as loss of freedom, a scarcity of goods and services, and the loss of domestic relationships for inmates.

Determinate sentence A sentence for a specific criminal act that is determined by the state legislature; a sentence that requires a specific amount of time, as ordered by the trial judge, for a person to serve in prison.

Deterrence The threat of punishment that will result from criminal activity. Deterrence is further categorized into general deterrence, which threatens everyone with criminal sanctions, and specific deterrence, which is a threat to a specific individual who may offend or reoffend.

Deterrence theory A theory of punishment based upon the premise that in order for any punishment to be effective it must be swift, severe, and certain. There are two forms of deterrence: general and specific.

Developmental pathways A description of the various paths a youth may take into delinquent or criminal offending. These pathways include the authority conflict pathway, covert pathway, and overt pathway.

Deviance Behaviors considered outside of or inconsistent with normal behavior for a community or group.

Differential association theory A sociological theory positing that crime is a product of the social environment whereby values are gained from those around individuals.

Diminished culpability The inability to fully understand the consequences of an action because of age or cognitive abilities.

Direct examination The act of a witness being first called to the stand to testify.

Directed patrol Spending an allotted amount of time patrolling a specific area of the community that is considered to be a high-crime area.

Disciplinary report A written report describing the inappropriate behavior or the breaking of institutional rules by an inmate.

Discovery The court-ordered process by which attorneys learn about their opponents' cases to prepare for trial.

Discretion The autonomy a police officer has to choose from a variety of courses of action in various situations.

Discretionary release   The mechanism by which those in prison are released after serving at least a minimum amount of their sentence upon the decision of a parole board.

Disposition   The sentencing of a defendant.

Doing time   Jargon used by inmates to describe their good behavior.

Double jeopardy   A provision of the U.S. Constitution that prohibits state and federal governments from prosecuting individuals for the same crime more than once, or imposing multiple punishments for a single offense.

Drug Abuse Resistance Education (D.A.R.E.)   A program designed to keep kids off drugs by teaching children how to resist peer pressure and avoid drugs and violence.

Due process   The requirement that an accused person receive notice of the charges made against him or her and the right to respond to those charges before being deprived of life, liberty, or property.

Due process model   A model of the criminal justice system that focuses on protecting the rights of the accused.

Early release   Release from a correctional institution prior to the expiration of an offender's sentence.

Early Warning Systems   A means used by police leadership to identify a potentially problematic officer before his or her behavior becomes very serious; sometimes called Early Intervention Systems.

Electronic monitoring   A form of technology used with house arrests to track and limit an offender's movement outside the home with telephone or radio signals.

Emergency Management Assistance Compact (EMAC)   An interstate mutual aid agreement, ratified by Congress, that allows states to assist one another in responding to disasters.

En banc   A French term indicating that all the judges of an appellate court will together consider an appeal.

Escape   The illegal departure of an offender from legal custody.

Evidence-based models   Models of intervention proven effective through social scientific research and study.

Ex post facto   A law dictating that a person cannot be charged or punished for a crime that occurred before the rule, law, or procedure was created.

Excessive force   An amount of physical force beyond that which is necessary to control a suspect.

Exclusionary rule   A legal mandate applied when a piece of evidence has been obtained in a manner that violates the rights of the defendant under due process.

Expert witness A person considered to be an expert in his or her profession or field of study who applies that expertise to the facts or circumstances of a case.

Expungement The legal process whereby the official record of an individual's criminal history is prohibited from being disclosed.

Extradition The formal surrender of a person by a country to another country for the purpose of prosecution or punishment.

Extralegal policing Policing that is not regulated or sanctioned by law.

Federal Emergency Management Agency (FEMA) An agency within the Department of Homeland Security whose mission is to build, sustain, and strengthen the nation's capability to address all hazards through preparation, response, and recovery measures.

Federal Wiretap Act An act, also called the Electronic Communications Privacy Act of 1986, that forbids acquiring the contents of electronic communications without users' consent and includes provisions for prohibited activities, government access, and consequences of a violation.

Felony A crime that is punishable by imprisonment in excess of a year or by death.

Feminist theories Theoretical explanations of crime, justice, and the entire criminal justice system from an androgynous perspective.

Fidelity to program design The degree to which rehabilitative programs are actually delivered in accordance with their pre-operational design.

Field interrogation A temporary detention of an individual in order to question the individual about a suspicious circumstance.

Follow-up investigation Continuation of the preliminary investigation in an attempt to reconstruct the circumstances of a crime.

Forensic science The application of physical and social sciences to legal and criminal issues.

Fruit of the poisonous tree Evidence obtained by law enforcement as a result of an illegal search or seizure.

Fusion center An information sharing center that allows a state to assess threats and implement corrective action, while at the same time increasing state and local law enforcement agencies' awareness of terrorist-related activity within their borders.

General deterrence A form of deterrence used to deter the populace from committing future criminal acts by ensuring that the principles of punishment are focused on potential criminals as opposed to the individual.

General strain theory An expansion of strain theory stating that the more strain individuals are exposed to, the more likely they are to participate in delinquent or criminal activity. Types of strain include the failure to achieve positive goals, the removal of positive stimuli, and the presentation of negative stimuli.

General theory of crime   A theoretical proposition that crime is not controlled by bonds to society, but rather by an individual's ability to demonstrate self-control. Under this theory, crime in general is not a planned event; rather, offenders act on impulse as a mechanism for gratifying their needs.

Global Positioning System (GPS)   A system of satellites that orbit the earth and transmit signals to allow receivers to display accurate location, speed, and time information.

Good time credit   The amount of time that a state penitentiary gives the offender for maintaining good behavior while incarcerated; time that is taken off the sentence.

Government cybercrime   Cybercrimes that involve attacks on government information systems, including cyberterrorism.

Grand jury   A group of 16–23 people that hears evidence and decides if probable cause exists to believe a person has committed a crime.

Grass eaters   Those police officers who engage in relatively passive forms of inappropriate behavior by accepting small favors or money for looking the other way when illegal activities are taking place.

Gross negligence   Lack of care or obvious disregard for another that results in damage or injury to another.

Halfway house   A group home often used by newly released offenders who have nowhere else to go. Many halfway houses are specifically designed for sex offenders, providing a supervised residence and resources specifically designed for this population.

Homeland security   The preparedness measures taken to protect and ensure the security and safety of the homeland and its citizens.

House arrest   A method of punishment in which the defendant is kept under close supervision in his or her own home rather than in prison.

Houses of refuge   Houses that sought to rehabilitate, educate, and provide vocational training and religion to juvenile offenders and vagrants.

I-24/7   An information sharing network designed to enable law enforcement officers in every member country to share sensitive police data.

I-Link   An operating system that has the ability to identify common aspects of ongoing investigations that are seemingly unrelated.

Identity theft   The crime of stealing someone's identity and using it for malicious purposes.

Importation   The tendency for inmates to bring into the prison the criminal culture they participated in outside of prison.

Incapacitation   A theory of punishment that imprisons offenders to prevent them from committing other crimes while incarcerated.

Incarceration   The act of confining a person in a jail or prison facility.

Indeterminate sentence   A sentence of incarceration without a specific term or ending date. Parole boards or other professionals generally determine when the offender will be released.

Indictment   A written document issued by a grand jury to indicate that there is probable cause to believe a person has committed a crime.

Indigenous model   A model that refers to the scarcity of all that was previously known socially and materially to the inmate. This model evolves from the isolation, constant monitoring, loss of possessions, and loss of freedom an inmate will experience.

Indirect victim   A person who suffers vicarious trauma as a result of crime even though he or she is not a direct victim.

Infraction   A lesser crime that is usually punishable by a fine.

Initial appearance   The court hearing at which a defendant hears the formal charges levied against him or her.

Inmate   An offender or an arrestee in a correctional institution.

Inmate code   Rules and roles that inmates adopt while incarcerated.

Institutional capacity   The maximum number of inmates an institution can hold.

Integrated theories   Theories that identify the most powerful elements of other theories and combine two or more of them into one explanation.

Intelligence-led policing   A business model in which data analysis and criminal intelligence are used to facilitate crime reduction, crime prevention, and enforcement strategies that target the most serious offenders.

Intensive supervision probation   A type of probation with a higher level of offender supervision, plus a stricter regimen of other services, including such stipulations as treatment programs and community service.

Intermediate appellate court   The lower level of state appellate courts.

International Court of Justice (ICJ)   The primary judicial organ of the UN, established in June 1945.

International Criminal Police Organization (INTERPOL)   The world's largest international police organization, which consists of 188 member countries and facilitates cross-border police cooperation.

Israeli Model   A method of interrogation in which the interrogator looks intently into the face of the subject and asks a series of probing personal questions.

Jail   A correctional facility that holds people accused of or convicted of crimes.

Joint Terrorism Task Forces   Entities that serve as a clearinghouse of terrorism-related information for a specified region. Task forces are comprised of federal, state, and local law enforcement representatives.

Judge   A public officer elected or appointed to administer justice and hear cases in a court of law.

Judicial review   The power of the federal judiciary to overturn any legislation or other governmental action ruled inconsistent with the Constitution, Bill of Rights, or federal law.

Jurisdiction   The power of a court to adjudicate a case, issue orders, and render a decision.

Jurisprudence   The philosophy of law.

Jury nullification   A process that occurs when a jury uses information not provided during a court case to determine the guilt or innocence of a defendant.

Just deserts   A philosophy of punishment that states that a person who commits a crime should suffer for that crime; the amount of time or type of punishment for a particular offender is generally proportionate to the type of offense that was committed.

Just world   A worldview in which everyone gets the consequences they deserve for their actions.

Juvenile   A young person, usually a minor.

Juvenile delinquency   A finding of criminal behavior in the juvenile system.

Juvenile waiver hearing   A hearing held before a judge to determine whether a juvenile will remain in the juvenile system or be transferred to adult criminal court.

Labeling theory   A theoretical tradition in which criminals become set in their roles as criminals as a result of their stigmatized status.

Law Enforcement Assistance Administration   A body created by the 1968 Omnibus Crime Control and Safe Streets Act to serve as a federal resource for local law enforcement agencies.

Law Enforcement Bulletin   A publication of the Federal Bureau of Investigation that includes articles on law enforcement issues as well as information on wanted federal suspects.

Law violation   A new criminal charge against an offender on probation.

Lay witness   An everyday citizen who has some personal knowledge about the facts of a case.

Left realism   A philosophical approach advocating for more minimal responses or sanctions for street-level crimes and less serious offenses, and more stringent responses and social control for white-collar crimes and crimes against society.

Legal cause   In tort law, the behavior or action that causes harm or proximate cause.

Legalization   Removing legal barriers to drug possession and use in an effort to make it a regulated and taxable portion of the economy.

Life course theories   The contention that criminal offending is influenced by an individual's previous experiences as well as traits or characteristics that are not changeable, such as impulsivity, age, etc.

Light cover   Undercover police operations for a short period of time.

Limited admissibility   Evidence that may be used for one specific purpose but cannot be applied in other ways.

Lynch mob   A group of individuals seeking to punish someone suspected of having committed a social transgression.

Malware   Malicious software designed to disrupt or prevent further use of a system.

Mandatory minimum   A sentence that is imposed by the state legislature with no discretion given by the trial judge. The defendant is required by law to serve a certain amount of time in the state penitentiary.

Mandatory release   The mechanism by which those in prison must be released after having served their court-imposed sentences, minus any other sentencing credits for which they may be eligible.

Meat eaters   Police officers who are more aggressive in their illegal behavior and actively search for ways to make money illegally while on duty.

Mens rea   The intent to commit a criminal act.

Michigan Prisoner Reentry Initiative (MPRI)   A state imitative implemented in 2003 with a mission of equipping released offenders with the tools they need to succeed in the community.

Miranda rights   The obligation of police officers to inform suspects of their right to remain silent and their right to an attorney.

Misdemeanor   A lesser crime that is punishable by jail time for up to one year and/or a fine.

Mitigating circumstances   Circumstances that do not justify a criminal act, but make the crime less reprehensible and may be used to reduce the sentence in a criminal trial.

Mitigation specialist   A person educated in the social sciences who assists the defendant in obtaining evidence to minimize the impact of punishment. Mitigation specialists are generally social workers or criminologists who compile past history of the defendant's life to assist with the defense.

Monitoring the Future A program that collects data on juveniles and is used by many social scientists.

Moral panic A term coined by Stanley Cohen describing the public's irrational fear and concern over a particular issue.

Motive In a criminal investigation, a probable reason that a person committed a crime.

National Crime Victimization Survey (NCVS) A survey conducted on households in the United States that includes detailed descriptions of criminal events, including the victim, potential precipitation, consequences of the event, and the offender.

National Incident Management System (NIMS) A national system that provides a consistent nationwide approach for government, the private sector, and nongovernmental organizations to work together in preparation, response, and recovery from domestic incidents.

National Incident-Based Reporting System (NIBRS) A national crime data collection program created and implemented during the 1980s in an effort to enhance the methodology for collecting, analyzing, and publishing crime data.

National Organization for Victim Assistance (NOVA) A conglomerate of victims' rights groups that advocate on behalf of victims and victims' issues.

National Response Framework (NRF) A framework that forms the basis for coordination between all levels of government and the private sector in responding to a disaster. It establishes a comprehensive structure, method, and standard terminology for management of incidents.

National Youth Survey A compilation of many different surveys measuring gang participation and drug use.

Net-widening A phenomenon in which the number of offenders within the court system increases as the criminal justice system expands the number of offenders it must supervise.

Night watches Groups of local, unpaid citizens who would patrol the community at night to deter crime and alert residents of the time, weather, and hazards.

Nolo contendere A plea in which the defendant does not admit the charges, but will not contest them.

Norms Social expectations for appropriate behavior.

Offender One who breaks a rule or commits a crime.

Offender risk Within the context of prison security, an assessment of the likelihood that an inmate will attempt an escape or assault a staff member or other inmate. Within the context of community-based supervision, an assessment of the likelihood that a former inmate will commit a new crime.

Opening statement The initial statement of a trial that an attorney makes to the jury, which outlines the argument that will be made during the trial.

Operational styles The approaches police officers use to perform their duties.

Order maintenance A method of policing whereby officers interpret the law and decide a course of action based on each individual situation when assigning blame and choosing whether or not to arrest.

Outlaw motorcycle gangs Organized criminal networks with a motorcycle lifestyle.

Pains of imprisonment Described by Gresham Sykes as the pains that develop from the deprivations and frustrations of those who are incarcerated.

Panopticon A circular prison designed with a central observation area so that officers can view all parts of the facility, originally designed by Jeremy Bentham. Variations of this concept are still used in modern correctional facilities so that correctional officers have an unobstructed view of most inmate areas.

Pardon To forgive, release, or exempt a person from a penalty.

Parens patriae A legal theory, most often associated with juveniles and the mentally ill, that allows the state to step in and protect those who legally cannot protect themselves. Latin for "the state as a parent."

Parole A supervised release from incarceration in lieu of serving a full sentence.

Parole board The governmental board that will determine if an offender receives parole and under what conditions.

Patriot Act A congressional act passed shortly after the September 11, 2001 terrorist attacks in the U.S., focusing primarily on providing law enforcement with legal authority to support efforts to fight terrorism. Short for The Uniting and Strengthening America by Providing Appropriate Tools Required to Intercept and Obstruct Terrorism (USA Patriot) Act.

Peacemaking criminology A theory proposing the use of mediation, love, respect, and forgiveness to resolve societal conflicts and reduce recidivism and crime.

Penal code A set of codified laws in a legal system that describe a crime and its punishment at the state level.

Pennsylvania System A penal system advocated by Quakers that used solitary confinement and penitence to reform offenders. Eventually, work such as shoemaking and weaving was allowed to be done in the cells.

Peremptory challenge An attorney's objection to the jury service of a potential juror without a particular argument against the juror.

Personal cybercrime Cybercrimes that involve a direct attack on a person, including identity theft and cyber harassment.

Personality theories   Theories of crime that look to explain criminal behavior as an expression of impulsiveness, aggression, or sensation-seeking.

Pinkertons   A private investigation and security company formed in the 1880s that assisted in protecting goods, tracking down suspects, and breaking strikes.

Plain view   A method by which police observe physical evidence that is plainly visible to the human eye, without the need for an intrusive search.

Plea   A defendant's in-court statement that he or she is guilty, is not guilty, or will not contest criminal charges.

Plea bargain   An agreement between the state and defense on a plea and sentence.

Policing   Enforcing the law by monitoring suspected criminal activity and apprehending violators of law.

Positivist school   A school of thought on crime arguing that some behavior occurs as a result of factors outside the control of individuals.

Posse   A group of residents temporarily enlisted by law enforcement agencies to assist in law enforcement functions.

Pre-classical school   A school of thought that held that crime was caused by supernatural forces as opposed to natural forces.

Pre-sentence investigation   A report to the court which outlines the defendant's prior alcohol and drug history, medical history, criminal history, education, and other factors that is given to the judge to assist with determination of sentence. Pre-sentence investigations are generally written by local probation departments.

Precedent   A prior opinion from a court of appeals establishing the legal rule or authority for future questions on the same legal matter.

Preliminary investigation   Evidence-gathering activities performed at the scene of a crime immediately after the crime was reported to or discovered by the police.

Pretrial diversion   An informal arrangement that involves referring the defendant to rehabilitative programs prior to arraignment in an attempt to address the offense reasonably while offering the defendant the opportunity to keep the offense off his or her criminal record.

Preventive patrol   Patrolling the community on an unpredictable and routine or random basis.

Principle of least eligibility   The view that those who commit crimes, particularly those in prison, are the least deserving members of society to benefit from government-provided assistance and support, such as education, vocational training, and other forms of support.

Prison A correctional facility that confines those convicted of felonies; may hold both misdemeanants and felons convicted of federal crimes.

Prison gangs Organized criminal networks within the federal and state prison systems.

Prisonization The taking on in greater or lesser degree of the customs and general culture of the penitentiary.

Probable cause Reasonable belief that the accused committed the crime with which he or she is charged.

Probation A supervised release from incarceration in lieu of serving any time or a full term in jail.

Probative value Value that is useful in a case.

Problem-oriented policing An approach to policing in which the underlying causes of crime are identified and addressed.

Procedural law A set of laws that describe the formal steps to be taken in the legal process to protect the rights of all parties.

Property cybercrime Cybercrimes that involve a criminal purposely installing malware on computer equipment.

Prosecutor The attorney, representing the state, who argues the criminal case against the defendant.

Public defender An attorney elected in a local jurisdiction to represent indigent defendants in criminal trials.

Racial profiling The use of race or ethnicity as the primary or the only indicator that an individual may be participating in criminal activity.

Reasonable doubt The standard of guilt that the state must meet to convict a criminal defendant; if reasonable doubt exists, the defendant must be acquitted.

Recidivism The rate of repeat crime by offenders; the rate of relapse back into criminal activity or behavior.

Recusal The decision by a judge to remove himself or herself from a case if there is a conflict of interest.

Reentry The processes whereby the formerly incarcerated return to society, seeking to establish positive ties to the community and engage in law-abiding behaviors.

Reentry courts Courtroom working groups, including judges, prosecutors, defense attorneys, and parole agents, that monitor those released from prison to ensure compliance with conditions of release and respond to violations of these conditions through graduated sanctions and rehabilitative services.

Reform schools The first state-run schools designed to reform juvenile offenders.

Rehabilitation   A philosophy of punishment that is based on the idea that the offender's behavior can and will change through treatment programs by professionals. Rehabilitation can involve treating offenders for drug and alcohol issues, anger problems, mental health counseling, and other services.

Reintegrative shaming   A process whereby offenders are punished, therefore repaying their debt to society, and then forgiven for their transgressions and reintegrated back into society.

Remand   An appellate court's process of returning a case to a lower court for further proceedings.

Repeat victimization   The recurrence of a crime either in the same place or with the same victim.

Restitution   Punishment that requires the offender to repay the victim for the harm that was caused, generally through monetary remuneration or community service.

Retribution   The idea that a criminal should be punished in a manner that is commensurate, or as equal as possible, to the crime committed.

Role   The position one holds within a social structure.

Role conflict   The conflict between what a person may prefer to do and what the person is expected to do.

Role expectation   The behaviors and activities that people expect from a person in a particular role.

Routine activities theory   A theory of criminal offending positing that crime is a function of opportunity—the convergence of a motivated offender, a suitable target, and a lack of guardianship.

Rule of law   A doctrine that no branch of government or public official may act arbitrarily outside the law. The rule of law dictates that any law enforced by the government must be fair, moral, and just.

Sanctions   Requirements imposed on those convicted of a crime that can range from financial penalties or curfew restrictions to incarceration.

Sanctuary   A sacred place of worship where one can take refuge.

Scared-straight programs   Programs designed to scare juveniles into behaving correctly, including boot camps and juveniles visiting inmates in prisons.

Second Chance Act   Federal legislation that authorizes Congress to appropriate funds that support reentry programs across the country, conduct research to evaluate reentry initiatives, and develop model programs and policies to improve the reentry process.

Selective enforcement   The decision made by police as to which laws they wish to enforce and when they choose to enforce them.

Self-defense   The use of force to protect oneself or one's family from bodily harm from an attacker.

Self-report survey   A data collection effort asking participants to report the number of criminal offenses or activities they have committed.

Sentence   A punishment imposed by a judicial body on an offender who has committed a crime.

Sequester   To remove the jury, and any alternate jurors, from all possible influences that may affect their abilities to fairly judge the accused.

Sheriff   A local law enforcement officer responsible for collecting taxes and enforcing ordinances in the colonial and post-colonial United States, similar to a constable; today, sheriffs serves as law enforcement officers at the county level.

Shock probation   A type of probation in which the court sends offenders to prison for a short period of time to "shock" them by exposing them to the limits of prison life, then returns them to the original jurisdiction to be placed on probation.

Sidebar   A discussion conducted during a court hearing between the judge and attorneys outside the hearing of the jury.

Slave patrols   Regulatory groups in the South in the colonial era focused on regulating the activities of slaves.

Social contract   An agreement between the public and government in which the public allows the government to provide safety and security.

Social control theory   A theoretical proposition that contends that the more strongly individuals are bonded to their community, the less likely they are to participate in delinquent activity.

Social disorganization theory   A theoretical proposition stating that communities with higher rates of social ills, such as breakdown in family composition, dilapidated buildings, unsupervised teenagers, high rates of poverty, high rates of residential mobility, and ethnic heterogeneity, are most likely to experience high rates of crime and delinquency.

Social networking   A web-based service that allows users to construct personal profiles and connect and communicate with other users.

Special Housing Unit (SHU)   Usually an area of confinement within a correctional facility designed to hold the more dangerous or violent inmates, those who are discipline problems, or those who need supervised protection from others.

Specific deterrence   A form of deterrence used to deter an individual from committing future criminal acts by focusing the punishment on that individual.

Speedy Trial Act   A federal law requiring district courts to ensure that a criminal defendant is brought to trial no later than 100 days after his or her arrest, with some exceptions.

Stafford Act   A congressional act passed in 2009 that provides a method for states to request federal assistance to respond to a disaster. Short for The Robert T. Stafford Disaster Relief and Emergency Assistance Act.

Stare decisis   The doctrine that a trial court must adhere to appellate decisions or precedents raised in a lower court.

Status offenses   Offenses that can only be committed by a juvenile, not an adult.

Statutory law   A written law explicitly describing actions that are prohibited.

Strain theory   A theoretical proposition contending that crime rates are produced by an individual's inability to conform to cultural values or achieve monetary success through accepted norms.

Street gangs   Organized criminal networks that originate at the street level.

Subpoena   A written document that officially notifies someone that he or she must appear in court.

Supervised release   Court-ordered supervision of someone who is awaiting trial or serving probation or parole.

Suppression hearing   A pretrial hearing where a defendant asks the court to suppress, or disallow, evidence that the police obtained illegally.

SWAT (Special Weapons and Tactics) team   A paramilitary policing unit originally formed to deal with dangerous confrontations, but increasingly being used in everyday policing.

Symbolic assailant   An individual whose dress, behavior, and gestures indicate suspicion and possible danger to a police officer.

Tabletop exercise   An exercise presenting a hypothetical situation for discussion, used to assess preparedness by allowing participants to discuss how specific plans or policies would be implemented to prevent, respond to, or recover from the scenario.

Technical violation   A parole violation that is less serious than a law violation and could include failure to report to the probation officer, failure to make child support payments, or failure to complete other stipulations of probation such as community service hours.

Terrorism   The use or threat of violence toward civilians in order to attain political, religious, or ideological goals.

Testimony   The statement of a witness, given under oath, typically in court.

Texas Rangers   One of the earliest law enforcement agencies in the American West.

Therapeutic Communities (TC)   Residential programs that help individuals learn social norms and develop more effective social skills.

Thin blue line   The line between the lawful and the lawless and between social order and chaos on the streets.

Third degree   The infliction of pain by police officers in order to solicit evidence about a crime.

Three-strikes law A specific legislative mandate that requires offenders, after their third conviction for any offense, to serve a minimum amount of time in incarceration.

Tort A breach of a civil duty or wrongful act that results in an injury to another or damage to their property.

Total institution An institution that provides everything a person needs for survival, usually at a lower level than what is enjoyed in an open society.

Transport officer A law enforcement officer who transports inmates to and from court and jail.

Trial by battle A mechanism for privately resolving disputes during the pre-classical time period, in which the victim or a chosen member of the victim's family would battle with the offender or a chosen member of the offender's family to determine guilt.

Trial by ordeal A method of handling conflict privately during the pre-classical time period, in which proving innocence involved the use of extremely painful or life-threatening methods of punishment.

Trial court A court of original jurisdiction that tries a case and renders a judgment.

Tribunal A specialized venue for enforcing international law. International tribunals can be formed by United Nations charter, Security Council resolution, or international treaty.

Uniform Crime Reports (UCR) An official data-reporting tool created in 1930 to provide uniform definitions for crime data so that results could be compared by month, year, state, and jurisdiction.

United Nations (UN) An international organization formed by 51 member states in 1945 in an effort to promote international peace and security following World War II. The organization has grown to include 192 member states and is best known for its peacekeeping efforts and humanitarian assistance around the world.

Vengeance The idea, based on the biblical philosophy of "an eye for an eye," of seeing that a criminal is punished, and that some satisfaction is taken from the fact that the criminal is punished.

Verdict Finding of guilt or innocence by a judge or jury.

Victim advocate A person who works in victim services to attend to the needs and rights of victims.

Victim impact statement (VIS) A statement from the victim to the judge during the sentencing phase of the offender's trial.

Victim precipitation Actions by the victim, either passive or active, that help to trigger the offense.

Victim rights amendment A proposed constitutional amendment that would provide victims with guaranteed rights similar to those given to offenders under the Sixth Amendment.

Victim services Programs and support systems for victims of crime.

Victim-offender mediation A process facilitated by clinicians or trained personnel whereby crime victims are able to express to the perpetrators how the crime has impacted their lives, and the perpetrators can apologize and explain themselves to the victims.

Victimology The study of victimization that analyzes the role played by victims in crimes.

Victims of Crime Act (VOCA) An act that allowed federal money to subsidize state compensation programs for victims.

Vigilantism The taking on of law enforcement responsibilities and the dispensing of punishment by private citizens.

Visa An official authorization permitting a foreign citizen entry into the United States for either a temporary stay or permanent residence.

Vocational training The provision of classes and instruction design to provide individuals with specific skills for entry into specific labor markets.

Warrant Legal authorization from a judge to make an arrest, conduct a search or seize evidence.

Wedding cake model of justice A four-layer model in which the top layer is celebrated trials, the second layer is major felonies, the third layer is less major felonies, and the fourth layer is misdemeanors.

White hat hacker An ethical computer hacker who hacks for beneficial reasons, such as solving complex problems.

White-collar crime Crimes against businesses by people in high-profile positions.

Wickersham Commission (National Commission on Law Observance and Enforcement) A commission that published a comprehensive report on the state of the American criminal justice system the 1930s.

Witness An individual who gives testimony in court because he or she has information that is pertinent to the case.

Work release centers Correctional facilities that are designed to provide housing and secure custody of those under the jurisdiction of the prison system, but also allow for inmates to leave during specific periods of time to work or attend vocational or rehabilitative programming in the community.

Writ of certiorari A document issued by the U.S. Supreme Court to confirm that it will review the decision of a federal circuit court of appeals or a state supreme court.

Youthful offender Typically, an offender under 18 years old, though the age requirements may be different among the several states.

Index

A

Actus reus, 91
Adam Walsh Child Protection and Safety Act, 465
Adjudication hearing, 417
Administrative law, 88
Administrative Office of U.S. Courts, 136, 142
Adolescence, 420
Advance fee fraud, 505
Aftercare, 382
Age of majority, 433–434
Aggravating circumstances, 281
Aggressive patrol, 163
Agricultural law, 86
Air Transportation Safety and System Stabilization Act, 465
Al-Qaeda, 85
Alcatraz, 314–315
Alcohol, 441–443
Alibis, 93
Alter ego rule, 94
Alternatives to prison, 359–360
"Amber Alert" law, 465
Amenability hearing, 424
American Revolution, 196–197
Amir, Menachem, 455–456
Amount of process due, 214–215
Anti-terrorism assistance program, 543
Anti-terrorism measures, 544–545
Antiterrorism and Effective Death Penalty Act, 465
Apodaca v. Oregon, 254
Appellate brief, 215
Approaching witness, 247
Arraignment, 20
Arrest, 217–218
Arson, NIBRS offense category, 41
Articles of Confederation, 198
Ashe w. Swenson, 99
Assault, 41, 48
ATAP. *See* Anti-terrorism assistance program

Atavistic man, 53
Atkins v. Virginia, 283, 437
Attica Correctional Facility, 327
Attorney-client privilege, 247
Auburn system, 314
Auction fraud, 505
Automated fingerprint identification system, 170–171

B

Babylonian Code, 304
Bail, 221
Bail hearing, 20
Bailiff, 243
Ballistics identification system, 171
Barker v. Wingo, 250
Barriers to reintegration, 392
Battered Women's Testimony Act, 465
Bearden v. Georgia, 270–271
Beccaria, Cesare, 13, 265, 269, 308–309
Bentham, Jeremy, 309
Bergeron, Harrison, 518
Bias-based profiling, 153
Bifurcated trial, 255
Bill of Rights, 212–213, 318
Biological theories of crime, 52–55
Biometrics, 508–509
Black codes, 117
Black hat hacker, 502
Blackmail, 41
Block v. Rutherford, 341
Blue code of silence, 178
Boot camps, 435
Booth v. Maryland, 466
Border, U.S., 539–540
Border patrol agents, 543
Border protection, 539–545
    anti-terrorism measures, 544–545
    challenges, 540–541
    domestic border security, 541–542

international border security, 542–544
U.S. border, 539–540
Bounds v. Smith, 317
Brady v. United States, 290
Branch v. Texas, 280–281
Breaking and entering, 41
Bribery, NIBRS offense category, 41
Bridewells, 311–312
Broken windows theory, 173
BTK killer, 484
Bullying, 443–444
Bureau of Alcohol, Tobacco, Firearms and Explosives, 136, 142
Bureau of Diplomatic Security, Diplomatic Security Service, 136, 142
Burglary, NIBRS offense category, 41
Business continuity plan, 488
Business law, 86

C

CALEA. *See* Commission on Accreditation for Law Enforcement
Cameras, 508
Capital punishment, 278–284, 522–525
Capitol Police, U.S., 142
Case-in-chief, 233
Case law, 80, 89–90
Categories, 503–505
Causation, 92–93
CBP. *See* Customs and border protection
Challenge for cause, 252
"The Challenges of Crime in a Free Society," 127
Changes in juvenile system, 429
Chapman v. California, 214
Checks, bad, 41
Chicago school, 56

Child Abuse Prevention and Treatment Act, 465
Child In Need of Assistance, 423
Child In Need of Supervision cases, 423
Child Savers movement, 420–421
Child services, 475
Child Sexual Abuse Registry Act, 465
Children's Aid Society, 421–422
Children's Justice Act, 465
CHINS. *See* Child In Need of Supervision cases
Chronically ill inmates, 357
CINA. *See* Child In Need of Assistance
Circuit courts of appeals, 208
Civil courts, 198
Civil law, 86–88
Civil lawsuit, 468
Civil liberties, 527–535
Civil War, 116, 118
Classical school, 51–52
Classification officer, 323
Closing arguments, 236–237
Code of Draco, 304
Code of Hammurabi, 267, 304
Code of Justinian, 304
Codex Justinianus, 304
CODIS. *See* Combined DNA Index System
Cohen, Stanley, 438
Coker v. Georgia, 283
Collateral estoppel, 99
Collective action, 532–533
Colonial judiciary, 196–197
Combined DNA Index System, 168
Commission on Accreditation for Law Enforcement, 131
Commission on Law Enforcement and Administration of Justice, 127
Common law, 80, 195
Community-based corrections, 433
Community Notification Act, 465
Community Oriented Policing Services, 174
Community policing, 133, 173–175
Community service, 273–274
Compassion fatigue, 474
Compensation, 467
Complaint, 219
COMPSTAT, 175
Compurgation, 50

Computer crime, 501–506
  categories, 503–505
  cybercrime, 503–504
    investigations, 505–506
    statistics, 505
  cyberterrorism, 504–505
  history of cybercrime, 502
  identity theft, 502–503
  international cybercrime, 505–506
Computer forensics, 510
  tools, 507–508
Computer worms, 503
Concurrence, 92
Conditional release, 322
Conflict model, 17
Conflict theory, 62
Consensus model, 17
Consent, 95
Constable, 115
Constitution, U.S., 198–200
Constitutional basis for due process, 214
Constitutional guarantees, 212–216
  amount of process due, 214–215
  constitutional basis for due process, 214
  defendants' rights, 214–215
  remedies for violations, 215–216
Constitutional law, 77–79
Consumer law, 86
Contemporary juvenile corrections, 430–438
  boot camps, 435
  community-based corrections, 433
  death penalty for juveniles, 436–438
  juvenile detention centers, 433–435
  juvenile probation, 430–432
  scared-straight programs, 435
Contemporary prisons, 314–316
Control of police corruption, 183–184
Controversial police roles, 152–154
COPS. *See* Community Oriented Policing Services
Corfu Channel Case (United Kingdom v. Albania), 496
Corporate law, 86
Corporations, prison, 329–320
Corpus delicti, 92
Correctional institution, 308

Correctional officers, 323, 330–332
  subcultures, 351–353
Correctional treatment specialist, 362
Corrections, 299–412
  correctional officers, 330–332
  correctional treatment specialist, 362
  culture of prisons, 340–353
  growth of, 353–362
  history of, 303–316
  history of prisons, 303–316
  jails, 301–338
  prison life, 339–369
  prisons, 301–338
    role, 317–318
  privatization, 328–330
  recidivism, 401–405
  rehabilitation, 375–392
  return to society, 372–373, 392–401
  sentencing goals, 375–392
  structure of, 317–318
Corrections data, sharing, 537–539
Correlates of crime, 49
  age, 49
  previous exposure to violence, 49
  race, 49
  socioeconomic/education status, 49
Corruption, 117
  police, 183–184
Cottage reformatories, 423–424
Counsel, 240
Counterfeiting, NIBRS offense category, 41
County courts, 204–205
Court-appointed attorney, 248
Court clerk, 241
Court process server, 243
Court record, 242
Court reporter, 241–242
Court structure, 202–210
  county courts, 204–205
  district courts, 204–205
  structure of state courts, 203–206
Court system, 191–298
  accused, 255–257
  arrest, 217–218
  articles of confederation, 198
  circuit courts of appeals, 208
  civil courts, 198
  constitutional guarantees, 212–216

amount of process due,
214–215
constitutional basis for due
process, 214
defendants' rights, 214–215
remedies for violations, 215–
216
court structure, 202–210
county courts, 204–205
district courts, 204–205
structure of state courts,
203–206
courtroom, 229–261
courtroom staff, 237–243
courtroom workgroup, 230–231
courts of last resort, 205
criminal procedure, 210–222
custodial interrogation, 218
defense, 243–249
due process, 210–222
federal courts, 198–202
history, 194–202
colonial judiciary, 196–197
state courts, 196–198
identification, 217
intermediate appellate courts, 205
judge, 237–243
judgment, 263–297
jury, 249–255
law enforcement investigations,
216–218
Marbury v. Madison, 198,
201–202
municipal courts, 204–205
presumption of innocence, 194
pretrial proceedings, 219–222
bail, 221
discovery, 221
grand jury, 219–220
indictment, 219–220
initial appearance, 219
pleas, 222
speedy trials, 222
suppression hearing, 221–222
prosecution, 243–249
road to judicial review, 200–201
search, 217–218
seizure, 217–218
sentence types, 270–284
sentencing, 263–297
goals of, 264–270
specialized federal courts, 210
specialized state courts, 205–206
state court systems formalization,
197–198

structure of federal courts,
206–210
trial, 231–237
U.S., background history,
194–202
U.S. Constitution, 198–200
U.S. district courts, 207–208
U.S. Supreme Court, 208–210
warrant exceptions, 217
warrant requirement, 217
Courtroom, 229–261
accused, 255–257
bailiff, 243
court clerk, 241
court process server, 243
court reporter, 241–242
courtroom staff, 237–243
defense, 243–249
deliberations, 253–255
judge, 237–241
duties, 240–241
qualifications, 239–240
selection, 238–239
jury, 249–255
selection of, 251–253
jury trials, Supreme Court
justification, 249–251
probation officer, 242–243
prosecution, 243–249
trial, 231–237
closing arguments, 236–237
jury instructions, 236–237
verdict, 237
witness testimony, 233–235
workgroup, 230–231
Courtroom staff, 237–243
Courtroom workgroup, 23, 230–231
Courts Administrative Office, U.S.,
142
Courts of last resort, 205
Crawford v. Washington, 235
Credit card fraud, 505
Crime analysis, 169
mapping, 169
Crime control model, criminal justice
system, 7
Crime index, 36
Crime labs, 106
Crime mapping, 169
Crime statistics, 46–48
Crime Victims with Disabilities Act,
465
Crimes and Punishment, 308
Criminal behavior, 33–73
correlates of crime, 49

age, 49
previous exposure to violence,
49
race, 49
socioeconomic/education
status, 49
crime statistics, 46–48
criminal victimization, 48
drop in crime rates, 48
measuring crime, 35–46
National Crime Victimization
Survey, 41–46
National Incident-Based
Reporting System, 39–41
property crime trends, 46
self-report measures, 45
theories of crime, 50–66
biological theories of crime,
52–55
classical school of thought,
51–52
positivist school, 52–66
pre-classical school, 50–51
psychological theories of
crime, 55–56
social control, elements of,
60–66
sociological theories of crime,
56–60
Uniform Crime Reports, 36–39
violent crime trends, 47
Criminal investigation, 166
Criminal justice, 318
process steps, 87
Criminal justice system, 1–110
challenges, 25–27
constitutional law, 77–79
criminal law, 75–110
defenses, criminal, 93–102
elements of crime, 90–93
features of crime, 90–93
formal criminal justice process,
18–23
history, 13–18
idealogy, 104–107
informal criminal justice system,
23–24
models, 6–12
policy choices, 104–107
politics, 104–107
punishments, 102–104
purpose of law, 79–80
rule of law, 80–82
types of law, 82–90
wedding cake model, 24

Criminal law, 75–110
  constitutional law, 77–79
  defenses for crimes, 93–102
    abuse defense, 102
    accident, 95–96
    age, 96–97
    alibis, 93
    collateral estoppel, 99
    consent, 95
    defense of home, property, 94
    defense of others, 94
    denial of speedy trial, 99–100
    diminished capacity, 98–99
    double jeopardy, 99
    duress, 96
    entrapment, 100
    excuses, 93–99
    insanity, 98
    involuntary intoxication, 97
    justifications, 93–99
    lack of probable cause, 102
    mistake, 97
    mistaken identity, 102
    necessity, 94–95
    police fraud, 100–101
    police misconduct, 101
    procedural defenses, 99–102
    prosecutorial misconduct, 100
    provocation, 97–98
    qualified immunity defense,
      102
    resisting of unlawful arrest, 95
    selective prosecution, 100
    self-defense, 93–94
    unconsciousness, 97
  elements of crime, 90–93
    actus reus, 91
    causation, 92–93
    concurrence, 92
    guilty mind, 91
    mens rea, 91
  penal code
    federal crimes, 84–85
    felonies, 83
    infractions, 83–85
    misdemeanors, 83–85
    special crimes, 84–85
  purpose of law, 79–80
  rule of law, 80–82
  types of law, 82–90
    case law, 89–90
    civil law, 86–88
    criminal law, 82
    penal code, 82–85
    procedural law, 88–89

Criminal Law Act of 1967, 93
Criminal procedure, 210–222
Criminal trial, 231–237
Criminogenic needs, 386
Cross-examination, 234
Cruel and unusual punishment, 306
Cruz v. Beto, 341
Culture, prison, 340–353
Curfew, NIBRS offense category, 41
Custodial interrogation, 218
Custody levels, 324–326
Customs, 543
Customs and Border Protection,
  U.S., 142
Cybercrime, 501, 503–505
  history of, 502
  investigations, 505–506
  statistics, 505
Cyberterrorism, 504–505

D

Damages, 86
DARE. *See* Drug abuse resistance
  education
*Daubert v. Merrill Dow
  Pharmaceuticals,* 234
Davis, Troy, 27
Day fine, 362
Day reporting center, 362
de Tocqueville, Alexis, 309–310
Deadly force, 150
Death penalty, 278–284, 524–525
  for juveniles, 436–438
  limits to, 282
  rulings, Supreme Court, 283
Decriminalize, 18
Deep cover, 167
Defendants, 231
  rights, 214–215
Defense, 243–249
Defense attorneys, 14–15, 234, 248
Defense of home, property, 94
Defense of others, 94
Defenses for crimes, 93–102
  accident, 95–96
  age, 96–97
  alibis, 93
  consent, 95
  defense of home, property, 94
  defense of others, 94
  diminished capacity, 98–99
  duress, 96
  excuses, 93–99
  insanity, 98

involuntary intoxication, 97
  justifications, 93–99
  mistake, 97
  necessity, 94–95
  procedural defenses, 99–102
    abuse defense, 102
    collateral estoppel, 99
    denial of speedy trial, 99–100
    double jeopardy, 99
    entrapment, 100
    lack of probable cause, 102
    mistaken identity, 102
    police fraud, 100–101
    police misconduct, 101
    prosecutorial misconduct, 100
    qualified immunity defense,
      102
    selective prosecution, 100
  provocation, 97–98
  resisting of unlawful arrest, 95
  self-defense, 93–94
  unconsciousness, 97
Deferred adjudication, 272
  probation, 272–273
Degradation ceremony, 257
Deinstitutionalization, 429–430
Deliberations, 253–255
Delinquency, 417–419
Democracy in America, 310
Denial of speedy trial, 99–100
Department of Homeland Security,
  137, 485
Department of Justice, 13
Deprivation, 342
Determinate sentence, 285
Deterrence, 51, 265–266, 316
Developmental pathways, 65
Deviance, 35
DHS. *See* Department of Homeland
  Security
Differential association theory, 58
Diminished capacity, 98–99
Diminished culpability, 437
Direct examination, 234
Directed patrol, 162
Disciplinary report, 326
Discovery, 221
Discretion, 178
Discretionary release, 400
Disorderly conduct, NIBRS offense
  category, 41
Disposition, 420
District courts, 204–205
  U.S., 207–208

The Division of Labor in Society, 104
Dixon v. United States, 96
DNA profiling, 168
DNA registry, 25
Doing time, 346
DOJ. *See* Department of Justice
Domestic border security, 541–542
Double jeopardy, 99
Draco Code, 304
Driving under influence, 41, 274
Drop in crime rates, 48
Drug abuse resistance education, 442
Drug Enforcement Administration, 136, 142
Drug laws, 525–527
Drug offenses, NIBRS offense category, 41
Drugs, 441–443
Drunk Driving Prevention Act, 465
Drunkenness, NIBRS offense category, 41
Due process, 210–222
Due process model, criminal justice system, 7
DUI. *See* Driving Under Influence
Duress, 96
Duties of police officers, 154–158
    crime prevention, 157
    law enforcement, 155–156
    order maintenance, 156–157

E

Early intervention systems, 129
Early punishments, 304–307
Early release, 316
Early warning systems, 129
Eberheart v. Georgia, 283
Economic realities, 357–359
Edward III of England, King, 85
Effects of police stress, 181–182
    management of police stress, 182
Elderly inmates, 356
Electronic monitoring, 276–278
Electronic surveillance, 169–170
Elements of crime, 90–93
    actus reus, 91
    causation, 92–93
    concurrence, 92
    mens rea, 91
EMAC. *See* Emergency Management Assistance Compact
Embezzlement, NIBRS offense category, 41

Emergency Management Assistance Compact, 493
Employment law, 86
En banc, 205
English Bill of Rights, 196
English Penal Code, 278
Entertainment law, 86
Entrapment, 100
Escape, 322
Escobedo v. Illinois, 90, 130
Estelle v. Gamble, 341–342
Ethics, 27, 106, 129, 216, 248, 273, 333, 353, 396, 441, 475, 501, 534
Ethnic minority federal law enforcement officers, 142
Ethnicity, full time personnel, local police departments, 142
European Union, 497
European Union Law Enforcement Agency, 497
EUROPOL. *See* European Union Law Enforcement Agency
Evidence-based models, 520
Ex post facto, 81
Excessive force, 177
Exclusionary rule, 11
Excuses, 93–99
Execution, 282–284
Execution methods, 281–282
Expert witness, 233
Expert witness, 234
Expungement, 399
Extortion, NIBRS offense category, 41
Extradition, 498
Extradition treaties, 498
Extralegal policing, 118

F

Fair and Accurate Credit Transactions Act, 465
Family law, 86
Family offenses, nonviolent, NIBRS offense category, 41
Family Violence Prevention and Services Act, 465
FBI special agent, 105
Fear of crime, 474–476
Federal Bureau of Investigation, 136, 142
Federal Bureau of Prisons, 136, 142
Federal courts, 198–202
Federal crimes, 84–85

Federal Emergency Management Agency, 485
Federal judge, 206–207
Federal law enforcement, 135–138
Federal law enforcement agencies, 136
Federal sentencing guidelines, 287–289
Federal victims' rights legislation, 465
Federal Wiretap Act, 530
Federalism, 194
Felonies, 13, 83
FEMA. *See* Federal Emergency Management Agency
Female inmates, 355
Feminist theories, 62
Fidelity to program design, 385
Field interrogation, 163
Fines, 270–271
Fingerprint identification system, 170–171
Fish and Wildlife Service, U.S., 142
Florida State Correctional Officers' Code of Conduct, 351
Flowchart, criminal justice system, 19
Folk Devils and Moral Panics, 438
Follow-up investigation, 166
Foot patrol, 162–163
Ford v. Wainwright, 283
Forensics Toolkit, 507
Forgery, 41
Formal criminal justice process, 18–23
Forms of police corruption, 183
Fortresses, 311–312
Fraud, 41, 505
Fruit of poisonous tree, 215
FTK. *See* Forensics Toolkit
Functions of police, 160
Furman v. Georgia, 280–281, 294, 522
Fusion center, 542

G

Gambling offenses, NIBRS offense category, 41
Gangs, 34, 348–351, 439–440
Gender, sentencing, 291
General deterrence, 51
General strain theory, 58
General theory of crime, 60
Gideon v. Wainwright, 230, 248, 258

Gideon's Trumpet, 230
Global partnership, 535–545
Global positioning system, 527
Goals of sentencing, 375–392
Good time credit, 287
Government cybercrime, 503
GPS. *See* Global positioning system
Grand jury, 20, 219–220
Grass eaters, 127
Gregg v. Georgia, 281, 294, 523
Gross negligence, 87
Growth of corrections, 353–362
Guantánamo Bay Naval Base, 302–303
Guardian ad litem, 462
Guillotine, Joseph-Ignace, 305
Guilt implies, 231
Guilty mind, 91

H

Halfway house, 362
Hall, Stanley G., 420
Hammurabi Code, 267, 304
Hate Crime Statistics Act, 465
Hells Angels Motorcycle Club, 350
History of criminal justice system, 13–18
History of U.S. court system, 194–202
 colonial judiciary, 196–197
 state courts, 196–198
Homeland Security, 26, 484–495
 impact of, 493–495
Homeland Security Act, 138
Homeland Security and Emergency Management, U.S., legal framework, 490–493
Honest reporting, 45
House arrest, 276–278
Household burglary, 48
Houses of refuge, 422–423
Howard, John, 308
Hudson v. Palmer, 341
Hulks, 311–312

I

IBIS, 171
ICJ. *See* International Court of Justice
Idealogy, 104–107
Identification, 217
Identity theft, 502–503, 505
Identity Theft and Deterrence Act, 465
Ideology, role in law, 105

Imaging software, 509
Immigration and Customs Enforcement, U.S., 142
Importation, 347
In re Gault, 427–428, 444
In re Oliver, 250
In re Winship, 428–429, 444
Incapacitation, 268–269
Incarceration, 268
Indeterminate sentence, 284
Indictment, 219–220
Indigenous model, 347
Indirect victim, 473
Informal criminal justice system, 23–24
Information sharing, 536–539
Infraction, 84
Infractions, 83–85
Initial appearance, 219
Initial contact, 18
Inmate, 309
Inmate code, 346
Inmate subcultures, 346–347
Inquisition, 304
Insanity, 98
Institutional capacity, 316
Integrated ballistics identification system, 171
Integrated theories, 63
Intelligence-led policing, 175–176
Intensive supervision probation, 275
Intermediate appellate courts, 205
Internal Revenue Service, Criminal Investigation, 136, 142
International border security, 542–544
International collaborations, 497–501
International community, 524–525
International Court of Justice, 495–497
International courts, 499–501
International criminal police organization, 497
International Criminal Tribunal for Rwanda, 500
International justice, 495–501
International law, 86
International policing, 497–498
International terrorism, 501
INTERPOL. *See* International criminal police organization
Intervention models, 519–522
 adult offenders, 521–522
 juvenile offenders, 520–521

Investigations, 165–166
Investigator tools, 167–171
Involuntary intoxication, 97
Israeli model, 544

J

Jackson v. Georgia, 280–281
Jail, 301–338
J.E.B. v. Alabama ex rel. T.B., 252
JJDPA. *See* Juvenile Justice and Delinquency Prevention Act
Job stress, 180–182
Johnson v. Louisiana, 254
Joint terrorism task forces, 541
Judge, 237–241
 duties, 240–241
 qualifications, 239–240
 selection, 238–239
Judgment, 263–297
Judicial review, 201
Jurek v. Texas, 281, 523
Jurisdiction, 203
Jurisprudence, 79
Jury, 249–255
 instructions, 236–237
 nullification, 254
 selection, 251–253
 trials, Supreme Court justification for, 249–251
Just deserts, 267
Just world, 457
Justice Assistance Act, 465
Justice for All Act, 465
Justifications, 93–99
Justinian Code, 304
Juvenile corrections, 430–438
 boot camps, 435
 community-based corrections, 433
 death penalty for juveniles, 436–438
 detention centers, 433–435
 probation, 430–432
 scared-straight programs, 435
Juvenile court *vs.* adult criminal court, 425–426
Juvenile courts, 424–430
Juvenile delinquency, 417
Juvenile detention centers, 433–435
Juvenile justice, 415–448
 alcohol, 441–443
 bullying, 443–444
 changes in juvenile system, 429
 Child Savers movement, 420–421

contemporary juvenile
corrections, 430–438
boot camps, 435
community-based corrections,
433
death penalty for juveniles,
436–438
juvenile detention centers,
433–435
juvenile probation, 430–432
scared-straight programs, 435
cottage reformatories, 423–424
deinstitutionalization movement,
429–430
delinquency, 417–419
drugs, 441–443
gangs, 439–440
history of, 419–424
houses of refuge, 422–423
juvenile court *vs.* adult criminal
court, 425–426
juvenile courts, 424–430
orphan trains, 421–422
reform schools, 423–424
school violence, 443–444
schools, searches in, 440–441
Supreme Court decisions,
426–429
Juvenile Justice and Delinquency
Prevention Act, 429
Juvenile probation officer, 432
Juvenile waiver hearing, 424

K

Katz v. United States, 528–529
Kennedy v. Louisiana, 283
Kent v. United States, 416–417, 424,
426–427, 444
Kerner Report, 126
Kidnapping, NIBRS offense
category, 41
King, Rodney, 76–77
Klopfer v. North Carolina, 249
Kyllo v. United States, 169

L

Labeling theory, 61
Lack of probable cause, 102
Larceny, NIBRS offense category, 41
Law Enforcement Assistance
Administration, 127
Law enforcement bulletin, 122
Law Enforcement Code of Ethics
from International Chiefs of
Police, 184

Law enforcement data, sharing,
536–537
Law enforcement investigations,
216–218
Law Enforcement Management and
Administrative Statistics, 132
Law enforcement officers, 138
Law violation, 272
Lay witness, 233
Left realism, 62
Legal cause, 86
Legalistic style, 159
Legalization, 525
LEMAS. *See* Law Enforcement
Management and Administrative
Statistics
Lewis v. Casey, 317
Life course theories, 64
Life in prison, 339–369
Light cover, 167
Limited admissibility, 240
The Limits of Criminal Sanction, 6
Liquor law violations, NIBRS offense
category, 41
Local policing, 131–135
Loitering, 41
Lynch mob, 118

M

MADD. *See* Mothers Against Drunk
Driving
Magna Carta, 251
Majority, age of, 434
Malicious software, 503
Malware, 503
Mamertine prison, 311
Mandatory minimums, 286
Mandatory release, 400
Mandatory Victims' Restitution Act,
465
Mapp v. Ohio, 78, 129, 152
Marbury v. Madison, 198, 201–202
Marshals Service, U.S., 142
McClesky v. Kemp, 283
Measuring crime, 35–46
Meat eaters, 128
Media, role of, 475–476
Medical malpractice, 86
"Megan's Law," 465
Mendelsshon, Benjamin, 453
Mens rea, 91
Mentally ill inmates, 356–357
Michigan Prisoner Reentry Initiative,
521
Mincey v. Arizona, 90

Minority federal law enforcement
officers, 142
Miranda rights, 130, 218
Miranda v. Arizona, 14, 78,
217–218
Misdemeanors, 13, 83–85
Missing Children's Assistance Act,
465
Mistake, 97
Mistaken identity, 102
Mitigating circumstances, 281
M'Naghten test, 98
Mobile devices, 509–510
Models of criminal justice system,
6–12
crime control model, 8–9
crime control *vs.* due process
model in courts, 10–11
due process model, 9–10
public perspective, 11–12
Monitoring future, 418
Montesquieu, Charles Louis, 307–
308
Moral panic, 438
Mothers Against Drunk Driving, 461
Motive, 83
Motor vehicle theft, 48
NIBRS offense category, 41
MPRI. *See* Michigan Prisoner
Reentry Initiative
Municipal courts, 204–205

N

Narcotic offenses, 41
National Advisory Commission on
Civil Disorders, 126
National Child Search Assistance Act,
465
National Commission on Law
Observance and Enforcement,
123
National Crime Survey, 469
National Crime Victimization Survey,
41–46, 469–472
National Incident-Based Reporting
System, 39–41
National incident management
system, 487
National Institute on Drug Abuse,
384
National Organization for Victim
Assistance, 462
National Park Service, 136
Ranger Division, 142
U.S. Park Police, 142

National response framework, 486
National Youth Risk Behavior Survey Overview, 442
National youth survey, 418
NCS. *See* National Crime Survey
NCVS. *See* National Crime Victimization Survey
Necessity, 94–95
Negligence law, 86
Net-widening, 16
NIBRS. *See* National Incident-Based Reporting System
Night watches, 115
NIMS. *See* National Incident Management System
N.J. v. T.L.O., 440
Nolo contendere, 222, 245
Norms, 17
North Carolina v. Alford, 290–291
NOVA. *See* National Organization for Victim Assistance
NRF. *See* National response framework

O

Obscene material, 41
OCTA. *See* Organized Crime Threat Assessments
Offender risk, 381
Ohio v. Roberts, 234
Omnibus Crime Control and Safe Streets Act of 1968, 128
On Crime and Punishments, 13
Opening statement, 232
Operational styles of policing, 158–172
   Broderick's styles of policing, 159
   functions of police, 160
   Muir's styles of policing, 159–160
   patrol, 160–166
      preventive patrol, 160–162
   Wilson's styles of policing, 159
Organized Crime Threat Assessments, 497
Orphan trains, 421–422
Outlaw motorcycle gang, 350–351
Outlaws Motorcycle Club, 350
Overpayment fraud, 505

P

Packer, Herbert, 6
Pains of imprisonment, 342
Panopticon, 309
Pardon, 318

Parens patriae, 420, 422–423
Parental Kidnapping Prevention Act, 465
Park Police, U.S., 142
Parole, 104, 360–361
Parole board, 284
Passing bad checks, NIBRS offense category, 41
Patriot Act, 490, 492
Payne v. Tennessee, 466
Peacemaking criminology, 62
Peel, Sir Robert, 117
Peeping Tom, NIBRS offense category, 41
Pell v. Procunier, 341
Penal code, 82–85
   federal crimes, 84–85
   felonies, 83
   misdemeanors, 83–85
Pennsylvania system, 313–314
Peremptory challenge, 252
Personal theft, 48
Personality theories, 56
Philosophy of policing, 172–176
Pillory, 305
Pinkertons, 120
PLAA. *See* Poor Law Amendment Act
Plain view, 221
Plea bargaining, 20, 289–291
Pleas, 222
Plummer v. State, 95
The Police and Modern Society, 123
Police discretion, 178–180
Police dispatcher, 143
Police ethics, 182–184
Police fraud, 100–101
Police job stress, 180–182
Police misconduct, 101
Police officer roles, 150–158
   controversial police roles, 152–154
   duties of police officers, 154–158
      crime prevention, 157
      law enforcement, 155–156
      order maintenance, 156–157
   service provider, 157–158
Police stress
   effects of, 181–182
   management of, 182
   sources of, 181
Police subculture, 176–178
   authoritarianism, 176–177
   cynicism, 177–178
   solidarity, 178

Police system, 113–147
   contemporary law enforcement, 131
   diversity, 139–143
   federal law enforcement, 120–122, 135–138
   history of, 115–120
      changes, 129–131
      in northeast, 115–117
      in south, 117–118
      in "wild west," 118–120
   law enforcement officers, 138
   local policing, 131–135
   state-level policing, 131–135
   structure of, 114–131
Policing, 18, 111–190
   challenges, 176–184
   contemporary law enforcement, 131
   of crime, 113–147
   force, amount of, 150
   functions, 149–189
   history of police systems, 114–131
   law enforcement officer, becoming, 138
   operational styles, 158–172
   philosophy, 172–176
   roles of police officer, 150–158
   systems structure, 114–131
   Wickersham Commission, 114
Policing of crime, 111–190
Policy choices, 104–107
Politics, 104–107
Poor Law Amendment Act of 1834, 340–341
Pope v. Illinois, 236
Pornography, NIBRS offense category, 41
Positivist school, 52–66
Posse, 118
Posse comitatus, 120
Postal Inspection Service, U.S., 142
Pre-sentence investigator, 270
Precedent, 80
Preliminary hearing, 20
Preliminary investigation, 166
Presumption of innocence, 194
Pretrial diversion, 278
Pretrial proceedings, 219–222
   bail, 221
   discovery, 221
   grand jury, 219–220
   indictment, 219–220
   initial appearance, 219
   pleas, 222

speedy trials, 222
suppression hearing, 221–222
Prima facie evidence, 219
Prince v. Commonwealth of Massachusetts, 419
Principle of least eligibility, 341
Prison, 301–338
  culture, 340–353
    adjusting to prison life, 342–346
    gangs, 349–350
    life, 339–369
    privatization, 328–330
Prison Rape Elimination Act, 465
Prisonization, 346
Privacy, 527–535
  expectations of, 528–529
Privy Council in England, 197
Probable cause, 207
Probation, 103, 271–272, 360–361
Probation officer, 242–243
Probative value, 240
Problem-oriented policing, 174
Procedural defenses, 99–102
  abuse defense, 102
  collateral estoppel, 99
  denial of speedy trial, 99–100
  double jeopardy, 99
  entrapment, 100
  lack of probable cause, 102
  mistaken identity, 102
  police fraud, 100–101
  police misconduct, 101
  prosecutorial misconduct, 100
  qualified immunity defense, 102
  selective prosecution, 100
Procedural due process, 211
Procedural law, 88–89
Professionalism, 27, 45, 106, 129, 216, 248, 273, 333, 353, 396, 441, 475, 501, 534
Professions
  border patrol agent, 543
  computer forensics, 510
  correctional officer, 331
  defense attorney, 14–15
  FBI special agent, 105
  federal judge, 206–207
  guardian ad litem, 462
  juvenile probation officer, 432
  police dispatcher, 143
  pre-sentence investigator, 270
  prosecutor, 246
  rehabilitative professionals, 405
  uniformed police officer, 164

Proffitt v. Florida, 281, 523
Property crime, 48
  trends, 46
Prosecution, 243–249
Prosecutor, 234, 246
Prosecutorial misconduct, 100
Prostitution offenses, NIBRS offense category, 41
PROTECT Act, 465
Provocation, 97–98
Psychological profiling, 170
Psychological theories of crime, 55–56
Public defender, 248
Punishments for crimes, 102–104
Purpose of law, 79–80

Q

Qualified immunity defense, 102
The Queen v. Dudley and Stephens, 94

R

R. v. Doughty, 98
Race
  full time personnel, local police departments, 142
  sentencing, 291
Racial minority federal law enforcement officers, 142
Racial profiling, 132
Rape, 48
Reasonable doubt, 215
Rebuttal evidence, 235
Recidivism, 303, 401–405
Recusal, 207
Reentry, 374
Reentry courts, 397
Reform schools, 423–424
Rehabilitation, 268, 375–392
Rehabilitative professionals, 405
Reintegration shaming, 61
Remand, 208
Remedies for violations, 215–216
Repeat victimization, 472
Report on Lawlessness in Law Enforcement, 13
Reporting, honest, 45
Residential Substance Abuse Treatment, 388
Resisting of unlawful arrest, 95
Restitution, 276, 467–468
Restorative justice, 269–270
Retribution, 266–268
Return to society, 372–373, 392–401

Right to counsel, 230
Road to judicial review, 200–201
Robbery, 41, 48
Roe v. Wade, 17
Role conflict, 151
Role expectation, 151
Roper v. Simmons, 97, 283, 436, 438, 444
Routine activities theory, 52
RSAT. *See* Residential Substance Abuse Treatment
Rule of law, 80–82
Runaway, NIBRS offense category, 41

S

San Quentin Prison, 327
Sanctions, 375
Sanctuaries, 311–312
Saturation patrol, 163–164
Scared-straight programs, 435–436
School searches, 441
School violence, 443–444
Schools, searches in, 440–441
Search, 217–218
Searches in schools, 440–441
Second Chance Act, 398
Second Chance Act of 2007: Community Safety Through Recidivism Prevention, 398–399
Secret Service, U.S., 142
Seizure, 217–218
Selective enforcement, 155
Selective prosecution, 100
Self-defense, 93–94
Self-report measures, 45
Sentence types, 270–284
  capital punishment, 278–284
  community service, 273–274
  deferred adjudication probation, 272–273
  electronic monitoring, 276–278
  fines, 270–271
  house arrest, 276–278
  intensive supervision probation, 275
  pretrial diversion, 278
  probation, 272
  restitution, 276
  shock probation, 274–275
Sentencing, 263–297
Sentencing goals, 264–270
  deterrence, 265–266
  incapacitation, 268–269
  rehabilitation, 268
  restorative justice, 269–270

Sequester, 253
Serious violent crime, 48
Service provider, 157–158
Sex offenses, NIBRS offense
    category, 41
Sexual assault, 48
Sheriff, 115
Shock probation, 274–275
SHU. *See* Special housing unit
Sidebar, 240
Simpson, O.J., 4–8
Sing Sing Prison, 327
Size of justice system, 15–16
Slave patrols, 117
Social contract, 151
Social control
    elements of, 60–66
    theory, 59
Social disorganization theory, 57
Social networking, 530–535
    privacy, 531–532
The Society of Captives, 342
Sociological theories of crime, 56–60
Sources of police stress, 181
Spam, 505
Special housing unit, 326
Special police functions, 171–172
Special populations, 355–357
Special weapons, tactics team, 135
Specialized federal courts, 210
Specialized state courts, 205–206
Specific deterrence, 51
Speck, Richard, 340
Speed indicates, 231
Speedy trial, 99–100, 222
Speedy Trial Act, 222
The Spirit of Laws, 307
Sports law, 86
Stafford Act, 490
Stanford v. Kentucky, 283
Stare decisis, 90
State court systems formalization,
    197–198
State courts, 196–198
State-level policing, 131–135
*The State of Prisons of England and
    Wales,* 308
State of Texas v. Robert Coulson, 264
Status offenses, 417
Statutory law, 80
Stolen property offenses, NIBRS
    offense category, 41
Strain theory, 58
Street gangs, 349

Stress, 181–182
    police, 180–182
        effects of, 181–182
        management of, 182
        sources of, 181
Structure of federal courts, 206–210
Structure of state courts, 203–206
Strunk v. United States, 250
Styles of policing, 158–172
    automated fingerprint
        identification system, 170–171
    Broderick's styles of policing, 159
    case investigations, 167
        terrorism investigations, 167
        undercover investigations, 167
    community policing, 173–175
    crime analysis, mapping, 169
    DNA profiling, 168
    electronic surveillance, 169–170
    functions of police, 160
    integrated ballistics identification
        system, 171
    intelligence-led policing, 175–176
    investigator tools, 167–171
    Muir's styles of policing, 159–160
    patrol, 160–166
        aggressive patrol, 163
        criminal investigation defined,
            166
        directed patrol, 162
        foot patrol, 162–163
        investigations, 165–166
        preventive patrol, 160–162
        saturation patrol, 163–164
        traffic, 164–165
    philosophy of policing, 172–176
    police subculture, 176–178
        authoritarianism, 176–177
    psychological profiling, 170
    special police functions, 171–172
    stress, 181
    Wilson's styles of policing, 159
Subpoena, 243
Sumerian Code, 304
Supermax, 326
Supervised release, 322
Suppression hearing, 221–222
Supreme Court, 208–210, 426–429
    death penalty rulings, 283
Survey researcher, 44
Swain v. Alabama, 252
Sykes, Gresham, 342
Symbolic assailant, 177

T
Tabletop exercise, 488
Tax law, 86
TC. *See* Therapeutic communities
TE-STAT. *See* Terrorism Situation
    and Trend Report
Technical violation, 272
Technological advances, 527–530
Technologies, 506–519
Technology, limiting use of, 529
Tent city, Maricopa County,
    315–316
Terrorism, 485, 501
Terrorism investigations, 167
Terrorism Situation and Trend
    Report, 497
Testimony, 233
Texas rangers, 118
Theft, 41, 48
Theft of identity, 505
Theories of crime, 50–66
    biological theories of crime,
        52–55
    classical school of thought, 51–52
    positivist school, 52–66
    pre-classical school, 50–51
    psychological theories of crime,
        55–56
    social control, elements of, 60–66
    sociological theories of crime,
        56–60
Therapeutic communities, 384
Thin blue line, 151
Third degree, 123
Thompson v. Oklahoma, 283
Three-strikes law, 286–287
Tibet's Drapchi Prison, 327
Tort, 86
Total institution, 342
Traffic, 164–165
Trafficking Victims Protection Act,
    465
Transport officer, 256
Treaties, extradition, 498
Trespass of real property, NIBRS
    offense category, 41
Trial
    by battle, 50
    closing arguments, 236–237
    criminal, 231–237
    jury instructions, 236–237
    by ordeal, 50
    verdict, 237
    witness testimony, 233–235

Trial court, 203
Tribal Law and Order Act, 465
Tribunal, 499
Trojan horse, 503
Truth in sentencing, 287
Types of civil law, 86
Types of law, 82–90
  case law, 89–90
  civil law, 86–88
  criminal law, 82
  penal code, 82–85
    federal crimes, 84–85
    felonies, 83
    infractions, 83–85
    misdemeanors, 83–85
    special crimes, 84–85
  procedural law, 88–89

U

UN. *See* United Nations
Unconsciousness, 97
Undercover investigations, 167
Uniform Crime Report, 36–39, 417, 469–472
Uniformed police officer, 164
United Kingdom v. Albania, 496
United Nations, 495
  Counter-Terrorism Implementation Task Force, 499
United States of America v. Walton Dawson, 97
United States v. Booker, 287
United States v. Jones, 529
United States v. Lovasco, 250
United States v. Moylan, 255
Unreported offenses, 38
U.S. border, 539–540
U.S. Capitol Police, 136, 142
U.S. Constitution, 198–200
U.S. court system, background history, 194–202
U.S. Courts Administrative Office, 142
U.S. Customs and Border Protection, 136, 142
U.S. district courts, 207–208
U.S. Fish and Wildlife Service, 136, 142
U.S. Homeland Security and Emergency Management authority, 490–493
  legal framework, 490–493
U.S. Immigration and Customs Enforcement, 136, 142

U.S. law enforcement agencies, 136
U.S. Marshals Service, 136, 142
U.S. Park Police, 142
U.S. Postal Inspection Service, 136, 142
U.S. Secret Service, 136, 142
U.S. Supreme Court, 208–210, 426–429
U.S. victims' rights legislation, 464–466
USDA Forest Service, 142
  Law Enforcement and Investigations, 136

V

Vagrancy violation, 41
Vandalism, NIBRS offense category, 41
Vengeance, 267
Venire, or *venire facias,* 252
Verdict, 222, 237
Vernonia School District 47J v. Acton, 441
Veterans Health Administration, 136, 142
Victim advocate, 474
Victim and Witness Protection Act, 465
Victim characteristics, 289
Victim impact statements, 466–467
Victim-offender mediation, 386
Victim precipitation, 456–457
Victim Rights Amendment, 463–464
  federal constitutional reform, 463
  state constitutional reform, 463–464
Victim services, 477
Victimization, costs of, 459–461
  first victimization, 459–460
  second victimization, 460–461
Victimization surveys, 468–477
Victimology, 449–482
  victims' rights, 449–482
Victims of Child Abuse Act, 465
Victims of Crime Act, 462, 465
Victims' rights, 449–482
  federal initiatives, 462–463
  special interest groups, 461–462
Victims' Rights and Restitution Act, 465
Victims' Rights Clarification Act, 465
Victims' rights legislation, 464–466
Victims' rights movement, 459–468
Vigilantism, 117

Violence Against Women Act, 465
Violent crime, 48
Violent Crime Control and Law Enforcement Act, 465
Violent crime trends, 47
Violent Offender Incarceration/ Truth-in-Sentencing Incentive grant program, 209, 377
Viruses, 503
VIS. *See* Victim impact statements
Visa, 540
VOCA. *See* Victims of Crime Act
Vocational training, 372
VOI/TIS. *See* Violent Offender Incarceration/Truth-in-Sentencing Incentive grant program
Voir dire, 252–253
Vollmer, August, 123
von Hentig, Hans, 454
VRA. *See* Victim Rights Amendment

W

Walnut Street jail, 312–313
Warrant exceptions, 217
Warrant requirement, 217
Warrants, 217
Weapon law violations, NIBRS offense category, 41
Wedding cake model of justice, 24
Weems v. United States, 280
Wergild custom, 467
White-collar crime, 25
White hat hacker, 502
Whren v. United States, 10
Wickersham Commission, 114, 123
Williams v. Florida, 251
Williams v. Illinois, 270
Willingham, Cameron Todd, 4–5
Witherspoon v. Illinois, 280
Witness testimony, 233–235
Wolff v. McDonnell, 320–321, 341
Wolfgang, Marvin, 454–455
Woodson v. North Carolina, 523
Work release centers, 395
Worms, computer, 503
Wright v. State of Delaware, 95–96
Writ of certiorari, 209

Y

Younger v. Gilmore, 317
Youthful inmates, 355–356
Youthful offender, 322